Books under Suspicion

geimma lucis et virtutis·

...ans ⁊ deus senectutis·

Elorati gloria·

Presul via veritatis·

Imitator paupitatis

Sancte ricard

BOOKS

under Suspicion

Censorship and Tolerance of Revelatory
Writing in Late Medieval England

KATHRYN KERBY-FULTON

University of Notre Dame Press

Notre Dame, Indiana

7104415-7

Manufactured in the United States of America

All royalties from the sale of this book will be donated to Amnesty International.

Library of Congress Cataloging-in-Publication Data

Kerby-Fulton, Kathryn.

Books under suspicion : censorship and tolerance of revelatory writing in late medieval

England / Kathryn Kerby-Fulton.

p. cm.

Includes bibliographical references and index.

ISBN-13: 978-0-268-03312-5 (cloth : alk. paper)

ISBN-10: 0-268-03312-9 (cloth : alk. paper)

1. Private revelations. 2. Visions in literature. 3. Censorship. 4. Christian literature,

English (Middle) 5. Christian literature—History and criticism. 6. England—

1066–1485. 7. Church history—Middle Ages, 600–1500. I. Title.

BV5091.R4K47   2006

820.9'001—dc22

2006024196

∞ *The paper in this book meets the guidelines for permanence and durability of the Committee on Production Guidelines for Book Longevity of the Council on Library Resources.*

For John

Sanctorum siquidem revelationes autenticas novimus, apocriphas non curamus.

—John Pecham

Perhaps we might say that only when intelligent and educated men ceased to take prophecy seriously were the Middle Ages truly at an end. The contention here is that this change hinges on a change in our whole attitude to history and to our participation in it.

—Marjorie Reeves

What þis metels bymeneþ, ye men þat ben murye,
Deuyne ye, for I ne dar, by deere god in heuene.

—*Piers Plowman* B. Prol.209–210

We must recreate that modicum of justice left to us.

—Simon Wiesenthal

Contents

CHAPTER FOUR

CHAPTER FIVE

Illustrations

Acknowledgements

A project of this scope does not come into the world without the kindness of both academic friends and strangers. When I first started to track the history of controversial revelation, I had no idea how many foreign fields I would have to visit, and how many expert guides would be there to help.

The mammoth task of reading this entire book fell to five people: in the revising stage, Steven Justice, Linda Olson, John van Engen, and an anonymous reader for the press all bravely took on the job. Their extraordinary care, erudition, and generosity saved me from many mishaps, and will, I trust, allow them to "passen thorgh purgatorie penaunceles." Heather Reid, whose own current doctorial research is gratefully cited here, also helped us check minute details with cheering enthusiasm and created the indexes. For help with individual chapters or sections, I would like to thank the following people: Mark Vessey, for expert advice during the adolescence of chapter 1, "Silencing Optimism," originally given as a plenary address at the History, Apocalypse and Augustine's *City of God* conference at University of British Columbia in 1999. Similarly, "Dangerous Reading" (Case Study 1) began life as the Morton Bloomfield Memorial lecture at Harvard University, for which I gratefully acknowledge invaluable leads from Robert Lerner and Marjorie Reeves, and the kind invitation of Derek Pearsall. "Through the Hiding of Books" was blessed with aid from John Fleming, E. Randolph Daniel, and Marjorie Reeves, and was originally written for the session in Marjorie's honour at the Medieval Academy Conference, Stanford, in 1998 (a session for which Marjorie, then 93, made the pilgrimage from England). Her steady engagement with all the Joachite-related sections of this book was unfailing, and ended only with her recent death. David Burr and Kevin Madigan also willingly helped answer my queries about Olivi on various occasions (chapter 2), and Curt Bostick has been invaluable on the

Opus arduum, trusting me with pre-publication materials (see also Appendix B). I would like to thank Giles Constable and the members of the 1999 Medieval Seminar at the Institute of Advanced Study, Princeton, for constructive engagement with "Two Condemned Books" (chapter 3) during its genesis, and, on some specific points, Penn Szittya, Kenna Olsen, Magda Hayton, and Fiona Somerset. Fiona also engaged with an earlier version of the "A Woman's Right to Teach" portion of chapter 8, a chapter which has benefited from communications with Maidie Hilmo and Laura Pringle. Nicholas Watson and Felicity Riddy offered lively critique of "Urban Devotion and Female Preaching" (chapter 6) in its early form at the New Chaucer Society conference, London, in 2000. I would like to thank Anne Hudson for crucial advice on an earlier version of "Extra Fidem Scripture" (chapter 4), and for pre-publication news of her discovery of John Bale's extracts from Peter Pateshull (Case Study 2). Richard Emmerson, in his capacity as editor of *Speculum*, kindly gave permission to republish a revised version of "Prophecy and Suspicion: Closet Radicalism, Reformist Politics and the Vogue for Hildegardiana in Ricardian England" from volume 75 (2000): 318–41. That chapter first benefited from the support of the Centre for the Study of Religion and Society at the University of Victoria and the stimulating commentary of David Wallace and the University of Pennsylvania Medieval Seminar when it was presented there. Jonathan Juilfs has been an invaluable reader of "The M. N. Glosses" (chapter 7), the "Heresy of the Free Spirit" portion of chapter 6, and of the Chronology. "Visions from Prison" (chapter 5) was enhanced by discussions with Annabel Patterson, Lee Patterson, Margot Fassler, and Paul Freedman on the occasion of its first being read at the Yale Medieval and Renaissance seminar. Also at Yale, Tom Barton's research and enthusiasm helped me answer many questions about Ockham (chapter 9). I would also like to thank Andrew Cole for sharing pre-publication copies of two of his essays with me, John Van Engen for help with beatific vision questions, and Aaron Thom for allowing me to cite his unpublished work on Uthred—all invaluable for helping me sort out the complexities of chapter 10. One of the greatest friends to this book must be the University of Victoria, which supported me in every imaginable way through most of its writing—with leave time, funding, and genial working conditions. The secretaries in the English Department at the University of Victoria all deserve special mention for their dedicated technical assistance and their unfailing moral support: Darlene Hollingsworth, Diana Rutherford, Colleen Donnelly, Jenny Jessa, and Puri Pazzo-Tores. I also gratefully acknowledge the Social Sciences and Humanities Research Council of

Canada for generous financial support over many years, and, more recently, the University of Notre Dame for aid with funding the reproduction of images.

The kindness of strangers is nowhere more evident than in the many libraries to which I have made pilgrimages and at University of Notre Dame Press. I would like to thank the staff of Duke Humphrey's Library in the Bodleian at Oxford, the British Library Manuscripts Reading Room, the Cambridge University Library Manuscripts Room, Corpus Christi College Oxford, Corpus Christi College Cambridge, and York Minster Library. The Institute for Advanced Study at Princeton took me in for three separate terms, and the librarian there, Marica Tucker, was invaluable. For technical assistance at the Press, I would like to thank Rebecca DeBoer, Marge Gloster, and Wendy McMillen, and finally, the Press's editor, Barbara Hanrahan, for bearing with the publication of a book that grew so fat. My sincere hope is that it will do justice to the cornucopia of kindness I have tried, however inadequately, to describe here.

There are also debts that cannot ever be described or specified. The late Robert Brentano, whose academic and personal generosity to me I will never forget, taught us all to let our *sources* "ask the questions." In some small way, I hope I have lived up to that here. On the thorniest of those questions the sources posed with regard to the history of revelatory theology, my greatest mentor was, and remains, the late Marjorie Reeves, who wrote that "only when intelligent and educated men ceased to take prophecy seriously were the Middle Ages truly at an end." (In this book, and only in that sense, we will see the "morning star of the Reformation.") Most importantly, Marjorie's example taught me to study the sources I loved, regardless of what the rest of the world might consider worth studying at any given moment. Finally, John Van Engen, whose scholarship I knew before I knew him, has taught me how very *literary*— that is, how intuitively and closely read—all good historical interpretation must be. Most profoundly, he has taught me how to honour the dead we study—not just the historically dead, but, what is harder, the *culturally* dead. I know no scholar so gifted at letting medieval voices speak for themselves, and no scholar so liberal with "archival footage" not usually seen. This book is dedicated, in joy and admiration, to him—as exemplary in his own scholarship as in his life and his love of life.

Chronology of Non-Wycliffite Cases
of Heresy and Related Events in
Post-Conquest England and Ireland,
with Other Relevant Dates

This chronology does not include most cases involving sorcery, unless they involve unusual doctrinal views. Sorcery was not technically part of heresy proceedings ever since a bull of Alexander IV in 1258 instructing inquisitors not to interfere in cases of divination "unless they manifestly savor of heresy" (*Lib. Sext.* De heret. 5.2.c. 6; see Bacher, *Prosecution*, 24). The chronology also does not contain reference to most cases of apostate Judaism, unless, again, they involve unusual theological positions.[1] Only "pluralist" cases of Wycliffite heresy are recorded or cases that touch upon those we are examining. All literary dates that are not otherwise noted come from the chronology in the appendix of Wallace, *Cambridge History.*

1161–66 The coming of the "Patarini" or "Cathari," the first recorded case of heresy in post-Conquest England.[2]

---

1. For both of these types of prosecutions, see Bacher, *Prosecution*; other studies dealing with heresy before Wyclif include Richardson, "Heresy and Lay Power," 1–25; Arnold, "Lollard Trials," 81–94; and Larsen, "Are All Lollards Lollards?" 59–72. Broader studies include Lea, *History of the Inquisition*; Leff, *Heresy*; Kelly, *Inquisitions*; McNiven, *Heresy and Politics.*
2. Principal source is William of Newburgh, *Historia Rerum Anglicarum*, 131 ff., although many other chroniclers notice the arrival; see Biller, "William of Newburgh," 11–30. The case was handled just as a Continental case would have been, although the arrests were made by the king's officers.

1179   Death of Hildegard of Bingen, to whom the earliest known papal approval for a book is attributed via a blessing (benedictionem) from Pope Eugenius III in 1147.[3]

1200   Testamentary letter of Joachim of Fiore, the second known case of seeking papal approval for books, listing a letter from Clement III in 1188 and orders from Lucius III (d. 1185) and Urban III (d. 1187).[4]

1204   Peter of Blois writes to the archbishop of York complaining of heretic preachers in the diocese.[5]

1210   One (or more) Cathars burned in London.[6]

1215   Fourth Lateran Council condemns Joachim's views on the Trinity.[7]

1219   Beatrice de Munfichet and her adherents (fautores) excommunicated for sacrilege by the bishop of Lincoln.[8]

1222   Council of Oxford promulgates decisions of Fourth Lateran Council (including Joachim's condemnation) and examines the case of an apostate deacon, having converted to Judaism, who is relaxed to the secular arm and burned.

———   Also at the council a separate case of a young man who refused the sacraments, gathered followers, and caused himself to be crucified. Among his followers was an older woman who claimed Marian status and who boasted that she could celebrate mass, for which she had made a chalice and patten of wax. They were condemned to be immured, also a Continental practice for heretics.[9]

---

3. Grundmann, "Zur Vita s. Gerlaci," 1.187–94; Kerby-Fulton, "Hildegard of Bingen," but see also Silvestris, *Cosmographia*, 2, for rumour of a near contemporary case.

4. Crocco, *Gioacchino da Fiore*, 67–68; discussed in Reeves, *Influence*, 28–29.

5. *PL* 207, Ep. 113; Bacher, *Prosecution*, 6.

6. *De antiquis legibus*, 3, states one was burned; Higden notes that "Albigensian heretics came to England, some of whom were burned" (*Polychronicon*, 8.190–92); Bacher, *Prosecution*, 6.

7. See ch. 1 below.

8. *Curia Regis Rolls*, 8.66; Arnold, "Lollard Trials," 84.

9. *Annals of Dunstable* in *Annales Monastici*, 3; Ralph of Coggeshale, *Chronicon*; *Memoriale of Walter Coventry*; for both cases, see Maitland, *Roman Canon Law*, 158 ff.; Bacher, *Prosecution*, 10. Immuration could involve either "murus largus" or "murus strictus" (Maycock, *The Inquisition*, 181–91).

1230	Prosecution of heretics at Strasbourg leads to information that there are Cathari in England.[10]
1233	Sheriff of Northampton ordered to send John of Hanslope to Newgate on heresy charges; in the same year Pope Gregory IX published bulls against the Cathars.[11]
1236	A York Dominican pursuing (apparently wealthy) heretics in Yorkshire is reined in by the king and his officers, who regard the arresting of heretics as their jurisdiction.[12]
———	Ernald of Périgueux charged with heresy and his goods confiscated by the king; later acquitted.[13]
1240	Matthew Paris records the case of a Carthusian held by Dominicans of Cambridge for refusing to enter any church and for claiming that Pope Gregory IX was a heretic.[14]
1241	Stephen Plecier of Agen arrested by bailiffs of Bristol on charges of heresy and his goods confiscated; later acquitted.[15]
1251	Matthew Paris reports that a leader of the "Pastoureaux" came to England, attracted followers, and was captured and cut to pieces.[16]
1252	*Ad extirpanda* authorizes the use of torture in inquisition for heresy.
1254	Scandal of Gerard's *Evangelium eternum,* for which Matthew Paris is the earliest extant source in Europe.[17]

10. Trithemius, *Annales Hirsaugienses,* 1.543. Trithemius died in 1516, but his source (he writes) is the *Chronicon* of the Abbey of Hirschau (Bacher, *Prosecution,* 7).

11. *Calendar of Liberate Rolls,* 1226–40, p. 107; Richardson, "Heresy and Lay Power," 1–2, who also notes that 1233 is a significant year in the history of Cathar prosecution, given Gregory IX's bulls of April that year.

12. *Calendar of Close Rolls,* 1234–37, p. 358; Bacher, *Prosecution,* 11; Richardson, "Heresy and Lay Power," 2; wealthy heretics were a tantalizing prize because their goods were forfeit.

13. *Calendar of Close Rolls,* 1234–37, pp. 293, 359, 485; on the acquittal, see Richardson, "Heresy and Lay Power," 2.

14. Paris, *Chronica Majora,* 3.32 ff.; Bacher, *Prosecution,* 11; Richardson, "Heresy and Lay Power," 2.

15. *Calendar of Close Rolls,* 1237–42, p. 368; Richardson, "Heresy and Lay Power," 2.

16. Paris, *Chronica Majora,* 253; Bacher, *Prosecution,* 7.

17. See ch. 1 below for discussion; and Paris, *Chronica Majora, Additamenta,* 335–39. We do not know Matthew's source, but his early knowledge fits the pattern of his engagement with apocalyptic problems and his interest in other instances of heresy. See Reeves, *Influence,* 62.

——— Honorius VI issues a denunciation of a book he calls *Perifisis* or the *De divisione nature* of John Scotus Erigena, noting that Erigena is especially revered in England as a martyr, according to William of Malmesbury. Honorius orders all copies to be burned because of its tendency to foster Albigensian doctrines. The book, which treats Neoplatonic mysticism, emanationism, pantheism (allegedly), Christian creationism, and theism, had been condemned at councils in Valencia (855) and Langres (859), mainly for predestination opinions. It may have influenced thirteenth-century mystics, Eckhart among others, and contains ideas perhaps paralleled in Walter Brut's thought.[18]

1255 Condemnation of Gerard's *Liber introductorius* by Alexander IV based on the Anagni commission report (Protocol of Anagni) that also examines Joachim's genuine works.[19]

——— William of St. Amour publishes his *De periculis novissimorum temporum*.[20]

1256 Condemnation and exile of William of St. Amour for extreme antifraternal opinions that led him to deny the *plenitudo potestatis* of the papacy.[21]

——— First recorded case of heresy in Ireland and apparent attempt to establish a regional inquisition there when the bishop of Raphoe complained to Rome of laymen in his diocese disputing articles of faith and papal authority as well as committing idolatry and incest.[22]

18. *Calendar of Papal Letters*, 101, Jan. 23, 1225; Bacher, *Prosecution*, 21, for the description of Erigena's *De divisione nature*.

19. Verardi, *Gioacchino da Fiore, Il Protocollo*, for the text, and see the discussion of the Protocol of Anagni in ch. 3 below.

20. *Magistri Guilielmi de Sancto Amore Opera Omnia* (Constanciae, 1632); this edition was suppressed, and therefore not easily accessible. The version best known in England was edited by E. Brown in 1690; see E. Brown, *Appendix ad Fasciculum*. The text was partially edited in Bierbaum, *Bettelordern*, 1–36.

21. *Chartularium*, 1.331; William's condemnation was more severe than Gerard's a year earlier. Pecham's *Tractatus Pauperis* refers to the condemnation: "Some, whose heresies the apostolic see condemned, were accused by the friars before, . . . and caused some of them to be banished from the kingdom of France: but they were treated mercifully, since the same fire did not devour them and their heresies" (ed. and this passage trans. Little, in Pecham, *Fratris Johannis Pecham*, 18). Pecham was clearly aware that burning was standard sentence for heresy.

22. The pope directed the vicar of the provincial prior of the Dominicans to appoint two friars to aid the bishop; Theiner, *Vetera Monumenta Hibernorum*, p. 71, no. 184 (see *Calendar of Papal Letters*, 1.329) and 185; Bacher, *Prosecution*, 12.

1257–68 Sometime during this period Roger Bacon is put under certain restrictions with respect to his writing, likely as part of a general policy in the Franciscan order in the wake of the scandal of the Eternal Gospel (1254) forbidding publication without prior approval.[23]

1259 Alexander IV issues a bull denouncing certain "rismos et cantilenas de novo ut dicitur indecenter compositas,"[24] apparently referring to the series of satires against the friars written by Rutebeuf (fl. c. 1250–80) about twenty years before Jean de Meun poeticized the key arguments of William of St. Amour.[25]

1260 First appearance of the *Flagellanti* sect, and the year widely forecast in Joachite prophecy for the coming of Antichrist and the tribulations that would usher in the Third Status.[26]

1263 Condemnation of Joachim's own works at the Council of Arles.

1274–79 Hieronymus de Ascoli, minister general of the Franciscan order, condemns the teachings of Roger Bacon because they contain "aliquas nouitates suspectas." Bacon is imprisoned, although the minister general's attempt to gain papal condemnation apparently fails. Bacon is apparently freed during the generalship of Raymond Gaufridi (1289–95).[27]

1277 March 7, Bishop Stephen Tempier condemns 219 errors related to Aristotelian teachings at Paris (some drawn from the works of Thomas Aquinas); March 18, Archbishop Robert Kilwardby condemns thirty similar teachings at Oxford.[28]

23. Daniel, *Franciscan Concept of Mission*, 57.

24. *Chartularium*, 1.351.

25. See Rutebeuf, *Poèmes concernant L'Université de Paris*; for Jean de Meun's *Roman de la Rose*, see ch. 3 below.

26. Leff, *Heresy*, 1.485. See 1351 below.

27. Daniel, *Franciscan Concept of Mission*, 65, citing the *Chronica XXIV generalium*.

28. *Chartularium*, 1.432, 473, 474; see "Contra Kilwardby," ed. Tocco in Pecham, *Fratris Johannis Pecham*, 116–20; many of these condemned articles turned on the nature and form of the soul. Thirteen errors had been condemned in 1270, but had been ably defended by Aquinas; however Aquinas died in 1277, leaving Tempier a clear path. For further analysis, see Leff, *Paris and Oxford*; Douie, *Archbishop Pecham*, 37–38. The bishop was "acting in excess of his instructions," as Douie explains, and met with a storm from younger faculty, having been only asked to *investigate* the Paris teachings and report back to John XXI.

1278   John Pecham succeeds Kilwardby as archbishop and continues to prevent the rehabilitation of Aristotelian and Thomist teachings.[29]

1279   Unnamed woman attacks John Kenneslaw for making the sign of the cross and is burned "per iudicium tocius cleri."[30]

——   (approx.) Jean de Meun's continuation of *Romance of the Rose*, including an account of the condemned books of Gerard of Borgo San Donnino and William of St. Amour, supporting the latter, as had Rutebeuf (1259).

1282   The minister general turns the works of Pecham's former student Peter Olivi over to a committee of Paris theologians which condemns thirty-four of his propositions (his treatise on the Virgin Mary had already been burned, apparently for his opposition to the Immaculate Conception). Throughout his career many of his opinions would come under fire, including those on marriage, grace, baptism, the divine essence, the nature of the soul, Franciscan poverty (usus pauper), and, after his death, apocalypticism.[31]

1283   Censure of Olivi carried out by a Paris council of the Franciscan order and recorded both in an official *rotulus* and in the "Letter of the Seven Seals," signed and sealed by the seven key examiners. The *rotulus*, along with the letter, was to be read out publicly in all the convents (per omnes conventus nostrae provinciae coram fratribus omnibus publice legere-

29. The Dominican order had mounted a massive defence of Aquinas at the Curia, while the Franciscan order moved in the opposite direction: the general chapter at Assisi of 1279 had forbidden, on pain of suspension of office, the defence of any of the opinions condemned by Tempier. Three years later a general *inquisitio* into the orthodoxy of members of the order and the prosecutions of Bacon and Olivi (both to different degrees Joachite in outlook) reflect a growing nervousness in the order (Douie, *Archbishop Pecham*, 38). It is at this point that copies of the *Summa theologiae* began to travel under correction with William de la Mare's *declarationes*, or criticisms, copied into their margins; eventually these were expanded into the *Correctorium fratris Thomae*, detailed criticism of 123 passages from the *Summa* and other works by Aquinas (Douie, op. cit., 39; Pelster, "Das Ur-Correctorium," 220–35).

30. Richardson, "Heresy and Lay Power," 4 n. 3.

31. Olivi was born 1248, joined the Franciscans at Béziers at twelve, studied at Paris under Bonaventure and Pecham, and became a lector in his home province, where he attracted attention as a charismatic preacher in the tradition of Hugh of Digne (d. 1257). Olivi was a trained scholastic philosopher, who nonetheless regarded current Aristotelianism as a harbinger of Antichrist. See Lee et al., *Western Mediterranean Prophecy*, 17–26, on Olivi's life; Burr, *Olivi's Peaceable Kingdom* on his apocalypticism; Burr, *Persecution*, 35–40 especially, on the other issues mentioned here.

tur), and Olivi's writings confiscated. Of the opinions condemned in the *rotulus*, Olivi himself wrote: "Some were judged false [falsa], some heretical [haeretica], some doubtful in the context of the faith [fide dubia], some dangerous [periculosa] to our order, some ignorant, some presumptuously [praesumptuose] stated, and some crucified as it were or marked with the sign of the cross [crucifigenda seu crucis signo signanda]."[32]

1284   Archbishop Pecham insists on an ecclesiastical tribunal for heretics held as king's prisoners on charges of apostasy (infidelity).[33]

1285   Olivi successfully refutes charges made against him.

1286   Pecham investigates heretical teaching at Oxford.[34]

——   Pecham cites Richard Knapwell, a Dominican, to appear for publicly teaching condemned Thomist doctrine (on unity of form); a provincial council condemns eight controverted articles, excommunicating Richard and anyone who aids him. The provincial prior of the Dominicans appeals the case to the pope.

1288   Knapwell silenced at Rome, preaches heresy in Bologna, and, according to the *Annals of Dunstable*, suffers horrible punishment and death.[35]

1290   Expulsion of Jews from England.

1294   December 13, abdication of Celestine V (elected July 5, 1294), dashing Franciscan Joachite hopes for a papacy committed to the ideal of poverty.

1298   Death of Peter Olivi.

1300   Condemnation of Arnold of Villanova, learned Joachite-influenced layman, by theologians at Paris and Oxford, in 1313 especially by Oxford chancellor Henry of Harclay, for Arnold's pro-Jewish tendencies, notably in making precise calculations of the End using rabbinic principles.[36]

1302   Deans of Worcester and Gloucester instructed to keep "certain heretical clerks convicted of [unstipulated] crimes before the Justices of the King."[37]

32. The passage is translated in Burr, *Persecution*, 41, with my Latin insertions from Olivi's 1385 *Responsio quam fecit*, 132.

33. Richardson, "Heresy and Lay Power," 3; Pecham, *Registrum*, 2.705; Bacher, *Prosecution*, 13.

34. Pecham, *Registrum*, 3.xxxv–xxxvii, 921–23; Little, *Grey Friars in Oxford*, 73–74.

35. "Incidit in desipientiam et miseriam magnam valde; ita ut evulsis oculis, vitam cum angustia terminet" (*Annals of Dunstable* in *Annales Monastici*, 341; Bacher, *Prosecution*, 22–23).

36. See Pelster, "Die Quaestio Heinrichs von Harclay," 51–82; Reeves, *Influence*, 314–17; and Lerner, *Feast of St. Abraham*, 27 and n. 21.

37. *Sede Vacante Register*, 6; Bacher, *Prosecution*, 13.

1305   Avignon papacy begins with Clement V, under whom the Clementine decrees are drafted (see 1311–12).

1307   Accession of Edward II.

1308   Templars arrested by the king's officers in England, tried for heresy by bishops in London, Lincoln, and York, trials in which evidence was gathered by appointed inquisitors (both native and foreign) in a procedure of papal inquisition. Foreign and native inquisitors clashed over English unwillingness to use torture, an issue never resolved. After convictions and abjurations were completed, victims were confined to monasteries for life, and the order's property confiscated by the king and lords of whom the Templars had held their lands.[38]

1309–77 "Babylonian Captivity" of the papacy in Avignon.

1310   Thirty Templars tried by inquisitors (some locally appointed friars) in Ireland, some charges include eucharistic irregularity.[39]

———   Execution of Marguerite Porete for continuing to publish her *Le Mirouer des Simples Ames* (*Mirror of Simple Souls*) and arrest of Guiard de Cressonessart, an adherent (fautor) with Franciscan Spiritual leanings.[40]

1311–12 The drafting of the *Clementines,* containing legislation against Beguines, Beghards, and the heresy of the Free Spirit, at the Council of Vienne.[41]

38. Later appropriated by the pope in Council of Vienne and given to the Hospitallers (see Bacher, *Prosecution,* 7–8). The unpublished portion of Bacher's "Prosecution," his University of Pennsylvania dissertation of the same title, contains detailed analysis of the many sources for the English inquisition of the Templars, pp. 66 ff. On the relationship between the prosecution of the Templars and the Beguine, Marguerite Porete, as well as associations with Franciscan Spirituals, see Lerner, *Heresy of the Free Spirit,* 68–78.

39. Cotter, *Friars Minor in Ireland,* 126.

40. Porete, *Mirourer,* ed. Guarnieri and Verdeyen. For the later Middle English translation, see Porete, "Margaret Porete: *The Mirror,*" ed. Doiron, 241–355. For the trial documents, see Verdeyen, "Le procès d'inquisition," 47–94.

41. Although some of the decrees that came to be known as the *Clementines* (after Pope Clement V) might not have been discussed at the Council of Vienne, *Ad nostrum* was, the crucial one for understanding the heresy of the Free Spirit and Marguerite Porete. See Friedberg, *Corpus iuris canonici,* 2.1183–84; Lerner, *Heresy of the Free Spirit,* 81 and n. 53. The final version of the *Clementines* was delayed by the death of Clement in 1314 and not published until 1317 under John XXII (Lerner, op. cit., 46). The other crucial decree, *Cum de quibusdam mulieribus,* cast suspicion upon the popular women's groups known as Beguines; see Friedberg, op. cit., 1.1169. For detailed discussion of the *Beguini/ae* and related groups, see Appendix C below.

1312   Legislation of Council of Vienne, developed under Clement V, but not promulgated until 1317.

1315   Masters of Theology at Oxford condemn eight articles taught by Nicholas Trivet, all concerning the role of Persons of the Trinity in creation and issues of *potentia absoluta*. Trivet retracts the articles.[42]

1316   English Franciscans in the Province of Ireland complain to Michael of Cesena, minister general, of sedition among the Irish Franciscans.

1317   John XXII issues the *Clementines*. *Ad nostrum* and *Cum de quibusdam mulieribus* were issued at this time.[43]

——   Ledrede appointed bishop of Ossory.

1318   First Franciscan Spirituals burned on Continent (Marseilles).[44]

——   Eight-man commission appointed to examine Olivi's works, reporting in 1319.

1319   General chapter of Franciscan order censures Olivi's works and persecutes his followers.[45]

——   Margaret Syward of Milton Keynes, Buckinghamshire, examined for heretical opinions about the Incarnation and eucharist (having "hidden her face" so as not to see the elevation of the host) by Archbishop Reynolds on visitation to the diocese of Lincoln, excommunicated, but later reconciled.[46]

1322   John XXII undertakes to censure Olivi's Apocalypse commentary himself.[47]

c. 1323   William of Pagula's *Summa summarum* (a practical and internationally consulted manual used by English clergy), Book 5 of which concerns

---

42. *Munimenta Academica*, 101–2. Trivet's mode of thought resembles Ockham's in certain respects.

43. See n. 41 above.

44. The Franciscan Spirituals were those who clung most fiercely to the strictest interpretation of the Rule of St. Francis on poverty and tended to view themselves as the *viri spirituales* predicted by Joachim of Fiore, as religious with a special mission in the imminent Third Status.

45. Douie, "Olivi's Postilla," 68.

46. Richardson, "Heresy and Lay Power," 3; Churchill, *Canterbury Administration*, 1.313–14; "Margareta Syward distulit per biennium peccata sua confiteri, ipsaque incarnacionem Domini non credens abscondit faciem suam ad eleuacionem corporis Christi in missa vt illam non videat, aliud, vt dicitur, senciendo de incarnacione quam ecclesia sancta docet et tenet."

47. See n. 51 below.

"de accuscionibus et inquisicionibus," setting out procedures for heresy prosecutions.[48]

1323   Bernard Gui writes his *Practica inquisitionis*.[49]

——   The provincial chapter at Cambridge examines certain articles allegedly drawn from Ockham's works and requires he explain himself.[50]

——   November, John XXII issues *Cum inter nonnullos*, in practice overturning Nicholas III's *Exiit qui seminat*'s (1279) ruling on Franciscan poverty and its basis in Christ's poverty, partly with a view to the censure of Olivi.[51]

1324   The English bishop, Richard Ledrede, appointed to Ossory in 1317, prosecutes (using standard Continental inquisitional practices) Alice Kyteler, William Outlaw, Petronilla of Meath, and nine others. The charges are heresy and sorcery, otherwise vague; Petronilla and others burned (Alice's case alluded to in poetry of the "Kildare" MS).[52]

——   Marsilius of Padua, *Defensor pacis*.

——   July, Ockham travels from Oxford to Avignon, remaining in the Franciscan convent there for four years while his case was being investigated.[53]

---

48. See Arnold, "Lollard Trials," 90–92, describing in particular the copy in British Library, MS Royal 10. D.X, which was owned by the monks of Reading and heavily annotated for inquisitional use; it also contains the conclusions ascribed to Brut's trial (1391). On the *Summa*'s popularity and distribution in England and elsewhere, see Boyle, "Oculus Sacerdotis," 81–110.

49. See Guidonis, *Practica inquisitionis*, 1.115–116, especially on *Beguini/ae* followers of Olivi. See Appendix C below for further details.

50. The articles are edited (with some errors) and translated by Etzkorn, "Ockham at a Provincial Chapter," 557, and 566–67 for Latin text.

51. On *Cum inter nonnullos*, see Burr's helpful summary: "John wanted [Olivi's] Revelation commentary condemned because he saw the use to which it was being put by the spirituals. By the time the commission of eight had finished its work, he saw that a thoroughgoing censure of the commentary and its message could be carried out only if he could rid himself of the doctrine of Franciscan poverty as accepted by the order as a whole and even apparently by Nicholas III in *Exiit qui seminat*, particularly the notion that the Franciscans, in owning nothing, were restoring the life-style of Christ and the apostles. He attacked both ends of this proposition in 1322 and 1323, dispensing first with the Franciscans' absolute poverty and then with Christ's" (*Persecution*, 87). Burr is building on the work of Koch, especially, "Der Prozess," 302–15.

52. Wright, *Proceedings*; Bacher, *Prosecution*, 13–14; Colledge, *Latin Poems of Ledrede*, xx. Ledrede had been an inquisitor on the Continent. The charges against Alice and her adherents also included denial of the faith and demonology. On the so-called "Kildare" manuscript, British Library, Harley 913, see Hatfield-Moore, "Paying the Minstrel."

53. There is some controversy among scholars as to the interpretation of the evidence; it looks as if John XXII regarded the period in 1327 as the most important stage of Ockham's for-

——— John Lutterell's commission is appointed to examine William Ockham's works.

1327 Accession of Edward III, whose consort Phillipa comes from Hainault, home of Marguerite Porete.

——— (or 1328) Adam Duff burned in Dublin for denying the Incarnation, the Trinity, and the resurrection of the dead, the purity of the Virgin Mary (whom he called a harlot), the veracity of the scriptures ("fabulas"), and the apostolic sanctity of the bishops.[54]

1328 May 26, flight of Ockham and Michael of Cesena from Avignon,[55] eventually finding refuge with Louis of Bavaria, who had been excommunicated by John XXII for refusing to submit his election as Roman emperor for papal examination. (Louis had responded by invading Italy.)[56]

——— June 6, Ockham excommunicated by John XXII; implicitly condemned as a heretic in John's bull, *Quia quorundam* (1324), which condemns those who reject his earlier bull on evangelical poverty, *Cum inter nonnullos.*

——— Magnates Arnold le Poer and Roger Outlaw accused of heresy for protecting William Outlaw; le Poer (who supposedly scorned a consecrated

mal inquisition, but Ockham traveled to Avignon, most likely because of the charges, in 1324. See Courtenay, *Schools and Scholars*, 194–95, for lucid discussion of sources.

54. "Quod negaverat incarnationem Cristi, affirmavitque non posse tres personas et unum deum, asseruit Mariam matrem domini esse meretricem, negavit mortuorum resurrectionem, asseruitque sacras scripturas fabulas esse et sacrosanctae apostolicae sedis falsitatem, qua propter per decretum civile die lunae post octavas paschae combustus est" (Butler, *Jacobi Grace*, 106–8; Colledge, *Latin Poems of Ledrede*, xxi). Ledrede's own extensive body of religious poetry shows him to be, as Colledge mentions, "truly Franciscan" in that he believes in and teaches the still much controverted doctrine of the Immaculate Conception (op. cit., xlv). Given that Franciscans seem to be leading the inquisitional initiatives in Ireland during the pontificate of John XXII and during mid-century, this recurrence of "contumacy" on Marian questions seems worth remarking. See also the case of burnings prosecuted by Roger Cradock, O. F. M., bishop of Waterford, in 1353 below.

55. By May 26, Ockham had fled and no formal condemnation was ever issued. For these and other items relating to Ockham here, see Ockham, *Letter to the Friars Minors*, xxxv–xxxvii. Michael Cesena, who had hitherto supported John XXII's persecution of the Spirituals (*fraticelli de paupera vita*) now led the Michaelists (so-called *fraticelli de opinione*). Together with William Ockham, he launched devastating legal arguments against John's position; see Leff, *Heresy*; Dupuy, "Unwilling Prophet," 239 n. 14; Tierney, *Origins of Papal Infallibility.*

56. *Calendar of Papal Letters*, 2.485; Sbaralea, *Bullarium Franciscanum*, 5: no. 711; Bacher, *Prosecution*, 8.

host carried by Ledrede) died in prison in 1329 and is alluded to in several "Kildare" poems.[57]

1329   Bishop Grandisson of Exeter pursues a necromancy case that he believes constituted heresy; the victim, a married clerk, Master Peter Beare, eventually took his case to the secular courts, where hostility is shown to Grandisson.[58]

1329–30   A papal nuncio arrests four Franciscan friars, Henry de Costesy (or Cossey), Peter of Saxlingham, John of Hacklington, Thomas Helmeden, all Cambridge lectors, on charges of preaching openly against John XXII; the prisoners are in the custody of the Franciscan convent at Cambridge. Edward III is notified, and all four are ordered to Avignon; a further letter suggests that transportation of Henry and Thomas might not be necessary, depending on their guilt.[59]

c. 1330   The production of British Library, MS Harley 2253.

1330   English Franciscan Spirituals (perhaps including women) burned "in a certain wood."[60]

---

57. When confronted by the theatrical Bishop Ledrede and a procession of friars, le Poer called Ledrede "ille vilis rusticus trutannus de Anglia cum suo hordys quem portat in manibus" (cited in Colledge, *Latin Poems of Ledrede*, xxi, from Wright, *Proceedings*, 14). Arnold le Poer is connected with several poetic texts in British Library, MS Harley 913, including those given modern names, "Foolish Is the Man Who Puts His Trust in Brute Force," "The Proverbs of Count Desmond" (fol. 14v), and "Young Men of Waterford" (now fragmentary and extant only in British Library, MS Lansdowne 418, fol. 92r); on these connections, see Hatfield-Moore, "Paying the Minstrel." For editions, see Heuser, *Die Kildare-Gedichte*, and Lucas, *Anglo-Irish Poems*.

58. *Register of Grandisson*, 1.278; see Bacher, *Prosecution*, 33, for a more detailed account.

59. *Calendar of Papal Letters* 1305–42, 2.492, 493; Sbaralea, *Bullarium Franciscanum*, 5: nos. 806 and 807, p. 401. There seems to be some concern in the latter that the king will not release them. See Douie, *Nature and Effect*, 207. For detailed discussion, see below, ch. 2. According to Bale (*Index*, 160), Henry of Costesy died at Babwell, near Bury St. Edmunds. (Babwell was the source of prophetic texts for Kirkestede.) For the English Franciscan response to John's draconian measures, see Douie, op. cit., ch. 2. Douie makes the point that the provincial William of Nottingham played an important role in early opposition to John and discusses three treatises by English Franciscans during this period against John's *Ad conditorem*. English Franciscans seem to have agreed, like the majority of their counterparts abroad, that the ideal of poverty as embodied in the Rule and in Nicholas III's *Exiit qui seminat* (1279) represented the highest form of perfection on earth (Douie, op. cit., 203). See also Douie, "Three Treatises," 341–54.

60. Thomas Burton (writing c. 1395), *Chronicon*, 2.323: "Et in anno Domini 1330, in Narbona, in Carcasona, in Tholosa, in Gerunda, in Bononia, in Thauro, in Neapoli, in confinibus Alemanniae et Burgundiae, et in Anglia in quadam sylva, combusta sunt viri 55 et mulieres 8

1331–32 English Dominican theologian, Thomas of Waleys hunted, arrested, and imprisoned at Avignon until the pontificate of Clement VI, despite protests of theologians at Paris and Oxford, for disagreeing with John XXII on the beatific vision.[61]

1332 Bishop Ledrede accuses Robert de Couton (or Coulton) and others of heresy.

—— Archbishop Alexander Bicknor accuses Ledrede of heresy, himself incurring investigation by a papal legate, still unresolved in 1349 at Bicknor's death.[62]

1332–34 Ockham writes the *Opus nonaginta dierum*, presenting the Michaelist position on John XXII's views of Franciscan poverty.

1334 Ockham writes his *Epistola ad Fratres Minores*, listing John's errors on evangelical perfection. (Ockham would continue writing works against John, including his *Dialogus* and his *Octo quaestiones de potestate papae*, until his death.)[63]

—— Bishop Grandisson tries a certain hermit, William, for "sacrilegious and perverse doctrines," and the bishop begins collecting legal materials for prosecution of heresy (see 1355 below), especially of Franciscan Spirituals.[64] (These included, from the south of France, a 1334 sentence and formula of degradation for a "pertinacious" Franciscan Spiritual of clerical status and an undated sentence for a relapsed Franciscan Spiritual lay brother.)

eiusdem ordinis et erroris." It is not possible to determine whether any of the eight women were included in the English case, but the geographical spread is accurate in highlighting the other well-known hotspots of Olivian Beguine activity, and the comment "eiusdem ordinis et erroris" is also accurate, that is, both Franciscans (including tertiaries) and others of the same errors. See ch. 2 below for discussion. Bacher, *Prosecution*, 9, makes the point that Thomas's tally just prior to this regarding the burning of heretics in 1318 is entirely accurate. The event is recorded in the same way in the Beguin Martyrology; see Burnham, "So Great a Light," 315–20; and Larsen, "Are All Lollards Lollards?" 61.

61. Kaeppeli, *Le procès contre Waleys*; Smalley, "Thomas Waleys," 50–57; Courtenay, *Schools and Scholars*, 282–83.

62. See *Calendar of Papal Letters*, 1342–62, 3.227, 231–32, 432; Richardson, "Heresy and Lay Power," 4 n. 2; and Colledge, *Latin Poems of Ledrede*, xxvii–xxxi, for other sources.

63. See Offler, *Guillelmi de Ockham Opera Politica*, and McGrade, *Political Thought of Ockham*.

64. Bacher, *Prosecution*, 15–17, from *Register of Grandisson*, 2.751 ff. See Arnold, "Lollard Trials," 88–89, for the evidence that Grandisson gained access to more inquisitorial apparatus.

—————   Henry de Staunton, hermit tried for heresy under William Melton, archbishop of York, accused of giving rise to "a certain sect" (quaedam secta) that caused "schism" (schisma) between clergy and people.[65]

1336   London imprisonment of an apostate English Franciscan for heretical views on the sacraments and faith, examined by theologians and by Stephen Gravesend, bishop of London, but died in prison.[66]

—————   Benedict XII condemns John XXII's views on the beatific vision.[67]

—————   Benedict attempts a revision of the statutes of the Franciscan order to make them like the Benedictines (that is, able to accept endowments in their own right). At the time of Benedict's death these statutes were repealed at the urgent petition of the Franciscan order.[68]

1337–40   During this period Ockham writes *An princeps*, directed to Edward III and arguing that the king may appropriate clerical wealth for his needs in time of war.[69]

1338–44   Archbishop Bradwardine working on his *De causa Dei*, attacking both Ockham's and Joachim of Fiore's Pelagianism.[70]

1339–40   Statutes at the University of Paris forbidding the reading of Ockham.[71]

1340s   Major writings of mystic Richard Rolle, hermit of Hampole.

1341   Uthred de Boldon becomes a monk at Durham Priory.[72]

---

65. Arnold, "Lollard Trials," 85; *Register of Melton*, 3.131.

66. Bacher, *Prosecution*, 15; Richardson, "Heresy and Lay Power," 3; *Chronicles of Edward II*, 1.365.

67. Douie, *Nature and Effect*, 206. It is important to remember that John XXII's views were personally held and not pronounced *ex cathedra*.

68. Ibid., citing *Redemptor noster*, Sbaralea, *Bullarium Franciscanum*, 6: no. 51, pp. 25–42 (Avignon, Nov. 28). This is exactly what Langland prophesies for the friars in C.V.

69. Offler, *Guillelmi de Ockham Opera Politica*, 1.220 ff.

70. See especially Bradwardine, *De causa Dei*, lib. I, cap. 47, p. 436; and Reeves, *Influence*, 84. Bradwardine followed Augustinian views of God's foreknowledge and predestination, believing that human beings could not earn their own salvation. His opponents, the "moderni," sometimes labeled Pelagians, emphasized instead the capacity for human beings to save themselves *ex puris naturalibus*. They also stressed a human's capacity "to do what is in him" (facere quod in se est) to earn salvation. For the phrase *ex puris naturalibus* as used by Ockham and nominalists, see Oberman, *Harvest of Medieval Theology*, 47–56; for both phrases, Oberman's appendix, "A Nominalistic Glossary." For a literary perspective, see Rhodes, *Poetry Does Theology*, 27.

71. Thijssen, *Censure*, 62–63.

72. For this and other details of Uthred's life given below, see Emden, *Biographical Register*, vol. 3.

1344   John of Rupescissa first placed under house arrest by the Franciscan provincial of Aquitaine.

1346   A recluse Maude de Algekirk examined for suspect beliefs.[73]

1348   Grandisson brings charges of heresy and sorcery against Margery Ryval, whose practices he believed caused her to deviate from the true faith.[74]

1348–49   Black Death sweeps Europe.

1349   Death of Richard Rolle.

——   Death of Bradwardine.

——   *Flagellanti* reach London (Feast of St. Michael's). Pope Clement warns English and Irish bishops of the *Flagellanti* threat, accuses friars of stirring up trouble, and later has all Franciscans examined.[75]

——   Death of Ockham in exile.

——   John of Rupescissa moved to the papal prison at Avignon and allowed, as a papal ward, to write down his prophecies and visions; judged not *hereticus,* but *fantasticus* by inquisitors later this year, but retained in prison until his death (see 1366).[76]

1350s   Ledrede writes his Latin poetry.

——   Richard Kilvington, dean of St. Paul's, acquires *Excerptiones librorum . . . Ioachim,* with a copy of the Protocol of Anagni (British Library, MS Royal 8. F.XVI).

73. *Victoria History of Huntingdon,* 1.46 n. 2; Larsen, "Are All Lollards Lollards?" 61.

74. *Register of Grandisson,* 2.1044.

75. See the account by Robert of Avesbury, in Fredericq, *Corpus,* 2.121. On August 18, Clement VI sent instructions to a number of bishops, including the archbishops of Armagh, Dublin, Cashel, Tuam, Canterbury, York, and the Scottish bishops (*Calendar of Papal Letters,* 311; Walsh, *Fourteenth-Century Scholar,* 340–41). Clement claimed that some of the friars were responsible for encouraging this resurgence of the *Flagellanti* as fomentors of hysteria. Shortly afterward Clement had the entire position on apocalypticism of the Franciscans (especially the Spirituals) subjected to examination.

76. John's four main works are: *Commentum in oraculum beati Cyrilli* (c. 1345–49), *Liber secretorum eventuum* (1349), *Liber Ostensor* (1356), *Vade mecum in tribulatione* (1356). See Bignami-Odier, *Etudes;* Dupuy, "Unwilling Prophet," 229–50. Throughout this study I quote the *Vade mecum* from Brown's *Appendix ad Fasciculum* (for the deficiencies in this text, our only printed edition, see Dupuy, op. cit.). See also *Liber secretorum eventuum,* ed. Morerod-Fattebert, with introduction by Robert Lerner. Dupuy (239 n. 14), points out that John carefully distinguished himself from the Michaelists.

1350   Archbishop Richard FitzRalph begins to steer a doctrinally dangerous course by arguing that the friars' privileges were a violation of the ideals of the founders (thereby indirectly attacking the popes who had granted them and aligning himself with condemned Franciscan Spiritual opinions).[77]

—   Uthred de Boldon already warden of Durham College.

1351   Clement VI bans the *Flagellanti* in his *Inter solicitudines*, for "denying the [Church] the power of the keys [claves]," taking up an unapproved habit, and gathering in illegal conventicles (conventicula).[78]

1353   Two heretics in the Franciscan province of Ireland convicted before Roger Cradock, bishop of Waterford, and burned for opinions (perhaps Olivian?) against either the Immaculate Conception or the life-long purity of Mary.[79]

1354   Two Franciscan Spirituals burned at Avignon and their confessions recorded in a Bedfordshire document, perhaps later to be Knighton's source for the story.[80]

1355   Pope Innocent VI notifies John Thoresby, archbishop of York, of heresy in his diocese on issues of the role of grace and works in salvation and of original sin.[81]

---

77. Walsh, *Fourteenth-Century Scholar*, 435–36.

78. Fredericq, *Corpus*, 1.200–1; Leff, *Heresy*, 485.

79. "[D]e heresi, videlicet de contumelia in beatam virginem per modum humani coytus commissa" (Fitzmaurice and Little, *Materials for the History*, 144, from British Library, Cotton Vespasian B.XI, fols. 127B and 133 [two versions appear in the same manuscript]); see Colledge, *Latin Poems of Ledrede*, xxii, and Gleeson, "Fourteenth-Century Clare Heresy Trial," 37–42. The case was not even in Cradock's jurisdiction.

80. Whitfield, "A Bedford Fragment," 1–11; Knighton, *Knighton's Chronicle*, lxii–lxiii, 132–34. The confession of one of the heretics names four papal bulls issued by John XXII as heretical (*Ad conditorem, Cum inter nonnullos, Quia quorundam, Quia uir reprobus*), and names all the popes who succeeded John XXII as heretical, as well as all bishops and ordained clergy. Knighton comments that "quidam fratres de ordine Minorum" hold this to be true. Asked whether the pope had the right to grant them dispensations to have *granaria* and *cellaria* in which to keep food supplies, they said no. The issues, of course, were evangelical poverty in the rigorist Franciscan sense.

81. The views represent a mixed bag of positions, many echoing those under debate in the schools at the time: that it is impossible to merit eternal life by good works, even when informed by or proceeding from grace; that original sin does not deserve damnation; that heaven is not the due of baptized infants, that sin was not the cause of Adam's death, and that original sin is no fault (Bacher, *Prosecution*, 16, summarizing *Calendar of Papal Letters*, 3.565, Aug. 18, 1355). On issues of grace and good works, see the discussions of Ockham and Bradwardine in ch. 9 below; on issues of infant salvation, see discussion of Uthred and Olivi in ch. 10 below.

—— Bishop Grandisson of Exeter accuses Ralph of Tremur, former rector and Oxford M.A., of preaching against the doctrine of transubstantiation, creating doubt about the witness of St. Peter and St. John (a common motif in Joachite thought), and of gaining adherents, both in the diocese and in London. Ralph escapes custody.[82] Grandisson's determination to inflict the death penalty is made clear by his collecting the Avignon sentences (see 1334 above) and his commentary.[83]

—— FitzRalph preaches at Kells and warns his congregation of the practices of the *Flagellanti.*[84]

1356 Date of *The Last Age of the Church,* a Middle English reformist tract copied into a Wycliffite anthology but containing no Wycliffism, although many references to Franciscan Joachite sources.[85]

1357 FitzRalph preaches at St. Paul's Cross and publicly complains that the friars are taking steps to have him silenced (a royal order had already been secured to prevent Richard Kilvington from preaching).[86]

—— FitzRalph writes *Defensio curatorum.*

—— March 25, FitzRalph's last recorded London sermon (from the less prestigious pulpit of St. Mary's Newchurch).

—— March 31, Edward III issues a mandate forbidding FitzRalph to leave the country to take his case to Avignon.[87]

—— April 7, Edward III issues further orders to prevent FitzRalph and any other religious, especially "any Augustinian" from leaving the country's ports without royal license (both FitzRalph and his opponent, Austin John of Arderne, slip out of the country and reach Avignon later in the year).[88]

---

82. *Register of Grandisson,* 1147–49; Bacher, *Prosecution,* 16; Arnold, "Lollard Trials," 85. The exact nature of Ralph's heresy is unclear.

83. Issuing a warning not to abet the escaped heretic he writes, "that by the Apostolic rod, if his contumacy shall make it necessary, with a rod of iron, the unprofitable vessel may be broken, and he may be brought to the destruction of the flesh in order that his spirit may be saved" (trans. Bacher, *Prosecution,* from *Register of Grandisson,* 151 ff). This is an unusual insight into the prosecuting mentality.

84. Walsh, *Fourteenth-Century Scholar,* 340 n. 71, for manuscript sources in FitzRalph's sermon diaries.

85. Kerby-Fulton, *Reformist Apocalypticism,* 184–86, for references, quotation, and discussion.

86. Walsh, *Fourteenth-Century Scholar,* 420–21, for this and the next two items.

87. *Foedera,* III, I.353.

88. *Calendar of Close Rolls* 1354–60, 399; *Calendar of Papal Letters* 1342–62, 583.

1357–58 Tribunal hears FitzRalph's case at the curia, including the inquisitor of Franciscan Spiritual heretics, Guillaume Court.[89]

1358 Friar John condemned at Oxford for views on disendowment, tithing, and clerical corruption deemed heretical; forced to publicly recant and barred from teaching.[90]

———— FitzRalph's opponents charge him with committing the heresy for which Jean de Pouilly was condemned, and the charges are taken seriously.[91]

———— Edward III quietly supports FitzRalph's opponent, William Jordan, Dominican prior of York; FitzRalph begins losing ground at the curia.[92]

1359–60 Normandy campaign and Treaty of Bretigny (1360), mentioned in Langland's A text (which Langland likely begins to compose during this decade).

1360s Chaucer translates at least a considerable part of *The Romance of the Rose* before abandoning it at an unknown date.

1360 Death of FitzRalph.

1361 Dates of the first events mentioned in the Franciscan-sympatheic *Continuatio* of the *Eulogium historiarum*, which runs to 1413, carrying the full text of John of Rupescissa's *Vade mecum* embedded within it, and other Joachite material (see 1349 and 1374).

1362 John Erghome, Austin friar, composes a commentary on the Bridlington prophecies, dedicating it to Humphrey de Bohun, earl of Hereford. Erghome's extraordinary collection of prophetic texts forms part of the library of the York Austins.[93]

1364 John Ball preaching "articles contrary to the faith" around the country.[94]

1366? Death of John of Rupescissa.

---

89. Walsh, *Fourteenth-Century Scholar*, 427.

90. *Munimenta Academica*, 1.208–211, and for further discussion, see ch. 3 below. Note also Steven Justice's suggestion that Wyclif may have known this incident (*De veritate*, 1.336) (*Writing and Rebellion*, 236 n. 135).

91. Walsh, *Fourteenth-Century Scholar*, 441–45.

92. Ibid., 447, and *Calendar of Patent Rolls* 1358–61, 27, 101.

93. The so-called "Prophecies of John of Bridlington" are edited in Wright, *Political Poems and Songs*, 1.123–215. For discussion of the prophecies, commentary, and the extensive library of the York Austins, see Reeves, *Influence*, 254–56, and ch. 2 below.

94. See Larsen, "Are All Lollards Lollards?" citing *The Patent Rolls of Edward III*, 12.476.

1366   John Ball cited to appear before Archbishop Langham for subversive preaching.[95]

——   Statutes of Kilkenny, forbidding Anglo-Irish to associate with Irish minstrels and other performers and attempting to legislate all language and cultural activities in order to stem the tide of Anglo-Irish assimilation to native culture.

1367–68?   *Terminus a quo* for first copying of Langland's A text of *Piers Plowman*.[96]

1368   Condemnation of Uthred of Boldon's opinions on salvation, which include parallels with Ockham, Olivi, and Nicholas of Autrecourt.[97]

1369   Bishop Wykeham of Winchester examines Marion (or Margery) Rye, nun of Romsey, for attempted apostasy and denial of the eucharist, and commands severe disciplinary measures ("in so far as she can support them without danger to her life").[98]

——   Renewal of war with France.

1370   Nicholas Drayton, formerly warden of King's Hall Cambridge and possibly later baron of the Exchequer, charged with unstated heresy and

95. See Wilkins, *Concilia*, 3.64–65; for an account of Ball's early career, see Justice, *Writing and Rebellion*, 102–3, and 149 for discussion of the connection with Bocking (Langham's order went to the dean of Bocking).

96. For the dating of this text and the B and C texts below, see Kerby-Fulton, "Piers Plowman"; see also Alford, *Companion to Piers Plowman*, especially Kane, "The Text," 184–86, who notes that the *terminus a quo* for the first copying of A in the form we now have it must be 1367–68 (although topical allusions in the poem go back to the Bretigny campaign of 1359–62, which may indicate that Langland was at work earlier in the 1360s). Kane believes the *terminus a quo* for B is 1377, although other scholars have seen an allusion in B.Prol.100–11 to the schism issues of 1378, and in B.13.173–6 and B.19.428–46 to the warfare of rival popes in 1379. Kane places the most important C revisions in the period between 1381 (on the basis that the poet is clearly reacting to the events of the Rising in C.Prol.112–13 and elsewhere) and 1386, as trouble developed for Richard II (cf. C.3.208–10; 4.189–94). The issues of the Rising and their further textual impact are discussed in Kerby-Fulton, "Langland and the Bibliographic Ego," and the possibility of extending the date of C to 1388 or later (on the basis of the vagrancy legislation put forward by the Cambridge Parliament in that year) is discussed in Middleton, "Acts of Vagrancy." For a recent survey of dating issues, see Hudson, "Langland and Lollardy?"

97. On Uthred of Boldon (or Bohdon), see Knowles, "Censured Opinions," 305–42; and see below, ch 10. For his adoption of modernist views associated with Nicholas of Autrecourt, see Emden, *Biographical Register*; see also Trapp, "Augustinian Theology," 201–39.

98. Trans. Bacher, *Prosecution*, 18, from *Register of Wykeham*, 2.77–78; Arnold, "Lollard Trials," 85.

sought by the bishop of London, apparently having powerful lay protectors.[99]

1370?–1400?   Poems of the *Pearl* manuscript.

1370s–80s   *Cloud of Unknowing* (followed shortly after by *Book of Privy Counsel*).[100]

1371–78   Wyclif associated with John of Gaunt and Black Prince.

1371   Commons challenge clergy to reciprocal taxation commitment, and two
Augustinian friars lay pro-disendowment articles before Parliament.[101]

———   Collapse of Wykeham's ministry of king's clerks, replaced by lay clerks.

99. There are three separate references to Nicholas Drayton in *Foedera*: the first mentioning his position at Cambridge (3.716), the second regarding the charge of unspecified heresy
(3.889), the third referring to him as baron of the Exchequer. All three are accepted by Bacher,
Prosecution, 23–24, as referring to the same Nicholas Drayton. Richardson, "Heresy and Lay
Power," 4 n. 1, however suggests that the baron of the Exchequer might be someone else. We
have no information about the nature of his heresy. Richardson infers powerful protectors because the bishop applied to the king for permission to imprison him until he should be reconciled
with the church. Nicholas was tried before the bishop "et certis magistris in theologia et aliis viris
literatis propter hoc congregatis" (cited in Richardson, op. cit., 4). Possibly he was preaching to
the (powerful) laity on pro-disendowment issues. The intensifying of war with France in 1369
had brought renewed interest in disendowment. The case is also interesting for its assertion that
heretics are kept in prison as a matter of policy so as to prevent the "spread of poison."

100. *Cloud*, ed. Hodgson, a work on the contemplative life, explicitly and cautiously addressing itself to a specialized audience and drawing on the intellectually difficult Pseudo-Dionysian
Neoplatonist theology (apophatic or "negative" mysticism). This tradition could be considered
dangerous when made available in the vernacular (see Wogan-Browne et al., *Idea of the Vernacular*, no. 3.3 and ch. 8 below on Porete and Julian transmission). The text mainly circulated within
Carthusian communities. *The Cloud* shares with Porete a disdain for professional intellectuals, all
the while demanding the most intellectual effort on the part of their audiences.

101. Wyclif writes in *De civilio domino*, 2.7, that he heard a speech "of a certain peer" made
in this parliament using the exemplum of a plucked owl who borrowed feathers from other birds,
but found itself again denuded when a hawk appeared and the birds were forced to flee. The application, of course, was to the property of the monasteries rightfully belonging to the kingdom
in times of war. Workman notes that the story appears as well in John of Rupescissa's *Vade
mecum*, in Froissart, and elsewhere (see Bignami-Odier, *Etudes*, 215). Fear of invasion was running high, the king in debt, and yet the representatives of the monasteries still claimed exemption
from taxes; this was the setting in which the two friars, John Bankyn and probably Thomas Ashbourne, presented their articles supporting disendowment (without, however, success). They
cited traditional sources, especially Augustine and Bernard, for their claim that "all possessions
both of the clergy and of others should be held in common in all cases of necessity," an idea, as
Workman points out, founded on the *Decretum* of Gratian (though with a push from some more
radical direction). An Austin friar in this period had just been associated with another instance of
advocating disendowment (see 1358 above) and John Erghome, also an Austin, was collecting

1372   The temporalities of sixteen bishops seized for alleged detention of part of their subsidy.[102]

1373   Death of Bridget of Sweden; her spiritual director and editor Alphonse of Jaén composes *Epistola solitarii ad reges* shortly thereafter, a defence of her visionary and prophetic career that demonstrates her adherence to the guidelines of *discretio spirituum*.[103] The Latin text of her *Revelaciones* (at least the first seven books) already in circulation.

——   Julian's first visionary experience, giving rise to the earliest version of her *Revelation of Love* (the Short Text), likely completed by 1388.[104]

——   Likely date of birth for Margery Kempe.[105]

——   Bishop of Emly condemned William Lyn, vicar of Any, and David Browery on an unknown charge of heresy; their goods are confiscated by the king *secundum jura ecclesiastica;* an appeal is made to the pope.[106]

——   Pope Gregory XI demands a subsidy for his Italian wars from English clergy, already providing a subsidy to King Edward for the French wars, and the clergy complain in Parliament.[107]

Joachimism (see 1362). See Workman, *John Wyclif*, 1.221, citing from Galbraith, "Articles Laid," 579–82, for the bill and Gratian, *Decretum*, D.8c.1, where it is argued that private property exists merely "jure constitutionis et jure consuetudinis," both subordinate to "jus naturale." Langland's character "Need" makes a similar argument, probably also indebted to fraternal sources. In the same parliament the problem of "king's clerks" was addressed, and prelates in the key offices were forced to surrender to laymen (including the chancellor, Wykeham).

    102. Workman, *John Wyclif*, 1.212, from *Register of Wykeham*, 2.577–79. These temporalities were later restored, but the act alone is significant as an indication of the mood of the day.

    103. The *Epistola* was intended to serve as a preface to the eighth book of *Sancta Birgitta Revelaciones*, that is, the *Liber celestis imperatoris ad reges*. For an edition of the Latin text with facing Middle English, see Voaden and Jönsson, "Recommended Reading." For the Middle English translation, with helpful notes outlining the differences with the Latin, see Voaden, *God's Words*. See ch. 8 below for quotations from both the versions.

    104. Nicholas Watson has suggested that because the 1388 vision does not appear in the Short Text, it was likely completed by then. The original exemplar of the now single manuscript in which the Short Text occurs was dated 1413 by the scribe writing c. 1450. (See Colledge and Walsh's description in Julian, *Book of Showings*, 1.1 ff. and see Riddy, "Julian and Self-Textualization," 106.) Watson has also suggested that the vision of 1393 triggered Julian's desire to rewrite and produce the Long Text; see Watson "Composition," 637–83.

    105. For this and other dates, see the full chronology in Kempe, *The Book*, ed. Windeatt. All citations refer to *The Book*, ed. Meech and Allen.

    106. Richardson, "Heresy and Lay Power," 4 n. 2.

    107. *Register of Wykeham*, 2.245; Wilkins, *Concilia*, 3.95; Workman, *John Wyclif*, 1.226–27.

———   Uthred de Boldon sent as an envoy from King Edward to the curia at Avignon to discuss papal provisions and subsidies; Uthred captured in France and returns to England in 1374.[108]

1374   Great Council on papal exactions and disendowment issues, Franciscan and Austin representatives triumph over "possessioner" representatives, including Uthred.[109]

1374–80   Chaucer writes *House of Fame*; Ralph Strode (the "philosophical Strode" to whom, along with "moral Gower," Chaucer would shortly dedicate the *Troilus*) leases a house in Aldgate at about the same time as Chaucer (1374–86).[110]

1376   Royal letter patent instructing two Colchester rectors and others to hand John Ball over to the sheriff of Essex for offences against the church.[111]

———   Alice Perrers accused of sorcery among other charges of influencing King Edward III, along with an unnamed Dominican accomplice alleged to have performed the spells; he is brought before the duke and magnates for trial, where a sentence of burning was discussed until the intervention of the archbishop of Canterbury (also a Dominican) persuaded the judges to allow the accused to be kept for life in strict custody within the order.[112]

———   Good Parliament.

———   End of Avignon papacy and return of the papacy to Rome, a cause famously championed by Bridget of Sweden's prophecies and activism.

---

108. Emden, *Biographical Register*.

109. Edward demanded (in March 1374) an exact accounting of the list of benefices held by aliens, especially cardinals (this would have been a long list), as a way of intimidating Gregory (see 1373) and in preparation for the Great Council, presided over by the Black Prince, in order to come up with an answer to the pope. For the council, see *Eulogium*, 3.337 ff., and for discussion, Catto, "Alleged Great Council."

110. *Troilus*, V, 857–59; Ralph Strode, London lawyer (1374–86), now generally identified with the Oxford Thomist philosopher of international reputation in the 1360s who contended with Wyclif and possibly the author of an elegaic poem entitled "Phantasma Radulphi" recorded in the *Merton Vetus Catalogus* (of 1442). See Crow and Olson, *Chaucer Life Records*, 146 and 282–84; Workman, *John Wyclif*, Appendix Q, 2.412.

111. *Calendar of Patent Rolls* 1374–77, 415; Justice, *Writing and Rebellion*, 103.

112. *Chronicon Angliae*, 98 ff.; *Gesta Abbatum S. Albani*, 230 ff.; Bacher, *Prosecution*, 34.

1377   Gregory XI condemns Wyclif's writings.[113]

———   Accession of Richard II.

1377–79? Langland's B text of *Piers Plowman*.

1378   Great Schism begins.

c. 1380–96 Walter Hilton, *Scale of Perfection*.

c. 1380–92 Wycliffite Bible, associated with Nicholas Hereford and John Purvey.

1380   Deed of release by Cecily Champain to Geoffrey Chaucer from all
        further actions in relation to her *raptus* (the word in legal Latin mean-
        ing either 'rape' or 'abduction'), witnessed by "W. Beauchamp, W. de
        Neyville, and J. de Clanvowe," on Chaucer's behalf[114] (for Neville and
        Clanvowe, see 1387 and 1386 respectively).

———   Dominican friar, Richard Helmyslay, accused of heresy in Newcastle
        with charges ranging from preaching the transfer of tithes and endow-
        ments to the friars to Joachite claims for the superiority of the friars' or-
        ders in the coming age.[115]

1381   Rising, during which rebel leader John Ball preaches against tithing on
        grounds similar to Friar John's (see 1358).[116]

———   Wyclif condemned at Oxford.

113. See Hudson, *Premature Reformation*, 177 and n. 18, and 337 and n. 125 for sources.

114. Crow and Olson, *Chaucer Life Records*, 434. Clanvowe is author of the "Cuckoo and the Nightingale," explicitly framed as a "phantasma" in Macrobius' terminology (cf. the title of the lost piece by Strode, n. 110 above). Clanvowe's poem obliquely registers concern about rising heresy, and in his "The Two Ways," a sense of persecution of those called "lollars." See Hudson, "Langland and Lollardy," 99; Havens, "Shading." On Chaucer's relations with the so-called "Lollard Knights" and the difficulties of this term, see Strohm, *Theory and the Premodern Text*, 174–75, and ch. 9. n. 95 below.

115. Documents appear in an antimendicant collection, Oxford, Bodleian Library, MS Bodley 158, 142b–145a, beginning "Libellus datus coram domino cardinali [Petro] Corsiensi contra fratrem Ricardum Helmyslay de ordine Predicatorum pro parte cleri Dunelmensis diocesis . . ." with the articles and judgement delivered and a letter from Henricus Hedelham. The case concerned the parish of St. Nicholas in Newcastle on Tyne c. 1380 (described in Hunt, Madan, and Craster, *Summary Catalogue*, no. 1997). Hedelham is listed as dean of Chester in 1382, as vicar of Newcastle in 1384, and prebend of Darlington in 1384. The episode is mentioned briefly in Bloomfield, *Piers Plowman as Apocalypse*, 204; Lerner, *Powers of Prophecy*, 108 n. 56; and now edited from the Durham muniments by Spencer, "Richard," 13–39 (not mentioning the Joachite dimensions of the case).

116. For these details and sources, see Justice, *Writing and Rebellion*, 102 and n. 1.

——— Adam Easton made cardinal, with title of St. Cecilia, for services to the papacy of Urban VI, including his *Defensorium ecclesiasticae potestatis* directed primarily against Ockham and Marsilius of Padua.[117]

c. 1381–c. 88? C text of *Piers Plowman*.

c. 1381–85 Chaucer's *Boece (Consolation of Philosophy), Troilus and Criseyde*, and early version of the "Knight's Tale."

1382 May 15, Nicholas Hereford's sermon for Ascension Day, followed by Oxford Chancellor Rygge's stand against Archbishop Courtney in defence of university liberties.

——— May 17, Blackfriars Council begins, later formally condemns twenty-four Wycliffite conclusions.[118]

——— *Heu quanta desolacio* published in broadside.

——— June 15, Henry Crumpe is suspended from activities at Oxford apparently for publicly, in St. Mary's, the university church, calling the followers of Wyclif "Lollardos" (in accordance with Continental traditions for heretical or overly pious groups).[119]

——— Hereford excommunicated and disappears to the Continent to appeal his case to Urban VI and is imprisoned for life.[120]

——— Jacobus de Theramo's *Belial*, and therefore earliest possible date for "Kingdom" prophecy in Cambridge University Library, MS Dd.i.17.

——— Death of pro-Urbanist canon lawyer, John of Legnano.

---

117. For the information here and below on Easton, see Knowles, *Religious Orders*, 57–58, and Pantin, "*Defensorium* of Easton," 675–80.

118. Both in Hereford's sermon and in several places in Wyclif's writings concern about martyrdom for their beliefs occurs. For Hereford, see ch. 5 below; for Wyclif, see Workman, *John Wyclif*, 2.100 and 308, referring to *Polemical Works*, 2.466; *Sermones*, 3.520, 4.49; *Opera minora*, 10. Workman links these fears to Hereford's and Wyclif's knowledge of the executions of Franciscan Spirituals and cites Walsingham, *Historia Anglicana*, 1.278 and other sources.

119. "Suspenditur Henricus Crumpe . . . quia vocavit haereticos 'Lollardos'," *Fasciculi Zizanorum*, 311–12. For a recent account of this episode, see Hudson, "Langland and Lollardy," 95. This episode is an indication of the international vocabulary in use at an early stage in the movement. At this time the name was also being used against followers of Gerhard Grote, the founder of the *Devotio Moderna* movement (see Van Engen, "Devout Communities"); and it had been in use for Beghards since at least 1309 (see Lerner, *Heresy of the Free Spirit*, 40). See Scase, *Piers Plowman and Anticlericalism*, 152–55, for the derivation of the word; and for more recent studies, see Appendix C, n. 1 below.

120. See Emden, *Biographical Register*, 2:914. He escapes in 1385 (see that date below).

1384   Death of Wyclif.

——   *Speculum Vitae* allegedly investigated for heresy, according to a colophon in three manuscripts.[121]

1385   Imprisonment of Cardinal Adam Easton for criticism of Urban.

——   Hereford escapes papal prison during a popular rising and returns to England, where his excommunication is renewed by Courtney. Reportedly takes refuge with Sir John Montague, one of the "Lollard knights" (according to Walsingham).[122]

——   Heresy trial before the bishop of Meath,[123] who condemns the Irish Cistercian, Henry Crumpe, on seven conclusions against confession to friars and one conclusion regarding the eucharist;[124] the documents concerning this trial were discovered too late for use in the 1392 trial (see 1392).

1385–86?   Thomas Usk's *Testament of Love*.

1386–91?   Clanvowe's "The Cuckoo and the Nightingale."[125]

1386   Council of the Regency.

c. 1387–1400   Chaucer's *Canterbury Tales*.

1387   Parliamentary mandate issued against the books ("quosdam libros, libellos, schedulas, et quaternos") of Wyclif and Hereford.[126] Hereford is placed in the Nottingham town jail in January; by February 1, orders are given for his transfer to more amenable custody in Nottingham Castle at the request of Sir William Neville, warden of the castle, because of

---

121. Hudson suggests the colophon was backdated; see *Premature Reformation*, 416.

122. Emden, *Biographical Register*, 2.914; Walsingham, *Historia Anglicana*, 2.159–60; for discussion regarding the credibility of the story, see Hudson, *Lollards and Their Books*, 59.

123. *Fasciculi Ziʒanorum*, 349–56; "Calendar of Sweteman," 29.234; *Calendar of Ormond Deeds*, 2.168–82; Richardson, "Heresy and Lay Power," n. 4.

124. For these conclusions and accompanying documentation, a copy of which the bishop sent to Oxford, see *Fasciculi Ziʒanorum*, 349–56. The conclusions, mostly aimed at denying the validity of confession to friars, were primarily FitzRalphian in tone; see Emden, *Biographical Register*, 1.524–25. On the special role of Anglo-Irish polemicists in this decades-long campaign, see Walsh, *Fourteenth-Century Scholar*, 360. See also, Cotter, *Friars Minor in Ireland*, 148, who notes that Crump was an Oxford-educated Cistercian who preached this doctrine to congregations in the diocese of Meath and claimed to be following in the footsteps of FitzRalph.

125. Scattergood, *Works of Clanvowe*. For a recent account of Clanvowe and Lollardy, see Havens, "Shading," 342–43, and Hudson, "Langland and Lollardy," 99.

126. Wilkins, *Concilia*, 3.204.

"the honesty of his person" and with the promise that he would not be allowed to "walk abroad nor preach errors."[127]

———— Hereford inhibited from preaching August 10 by the bishop of Worcester in his diocese.

———— Adam Easton escapes death at hands of Urban, attributing his delivery to the spiritual intervention of Bridget of Sweden, of whom he writes a defence, urging her canonization.

c. 1388? The "John But" passus added to 'complete' Langland's A text.

1388 Execution of Thomas Usk.

———— Merciless Parliament.

———— Cambridge Parliament enacts draconian labour laws, perhaps alluded to in passus V of Langland's C text.[128]

———— Thomas Wimbledon's sermon, quoting Joachim and Hildegard.[129]

c. 1389?–1401? *The Chastising of God's Children*, containing chapters on visionary *discretio* and heresy of Free Spirit.[130]

1389 An anchoress named Matilda is examined by Archbishop Courtney in Northampton for heretical beliefs associated by Knighton with Lollardy (although no details are recorded).[131]

———— William Ramsbury tried before Bishop Waltham of Salisbury, for a mixture of Wycliffite and heresy of Free Spirit doctrines and for having performed an unorthodox version of the mass (one accommodating aspects of both heresies).[132]

———— Widespread orders issued in several parts of England for the surrender of books and tractates by Nicholas Hereford.[133]

127. *Calendar of Close Rolls* 1385–89 (1921); and see Logan, *Excommunication*, 193; McFarlane, *Lancastrian Kings*, 198–99; and Hudson, *Lollards and Their Books*, 59.

128. See Middleton, "Acts of Vagrancy."

129. For a recent account of the manuscript transmission, see Havens, "Shading," 341–42.

130. *Chastising*; for a recent account of the dating, see Sutherland, "Chastising: Neglected Text," 356–57.

131. Knighton, *Knighton's Chronicle*, 532–34.

132. The sources for this case come from the Waltham register, fols. 222–23v, and from Walsingham, *Historia Anglicana*, 2.188, extensively discussed in Hudson, *Lollards and Their Books*, 111–23. For the Free Spirit aspects, see ch. 6 below. Waltham, like other bishops mentioned here (Grandisson above, 1329, 1334, 1355, and Grey below, 1457), had a strong interest in Roman civil law and canon law.

133. *Calendar of Patent Rolls* 1385–89, 427, 430, 448, 468, 536, and 1388–92, 172.

—— Richard restored to power.

—— Adam Easton restored to the cardinalate of St. Cecilia by Boniface IX after the death of Urban VI.

1389–90 *Opus arduum* (commentary on the Apocalypse by imprisoned Wycliffite) complains of the confiscations of books by Olivi, Rupescissa, Ockham, and William of St. Amour.

1390–1410 Between these dates an anonymous Carthusian attacked the genuineness of Richard Rolle's claims to fervor ("ardor divini amoris") and "spiritualia sentimenta," an attack that is well versed in visionary validation issues.[134]

1390?–91 Clanvowe's *The Two Ways* (see 1386–91).

1391 Bridget canonized, among the many defences are three written by Englishmen.[135]

—— Recantation of Hereford, and by December 12 he must be granted the king's protection because of "his zeal in preaching privately and openly in opposition to false teachers who subverted the Catholic faith."[136]

1391–93 Bishop of Hereford, John Trefnant, investigates Walter Brut and prosecutes the case in October 1393. (Nicholas Hereford is one of the assessors at Brut's trial.)[137]

1392 Henry Crumpe charged before a distinguished panel of theologians at the Council of Stamford with having held ten condemned conclusions and is compelled to abjure them. The conclusions (as in 1385) are again entirely obsessed with antimendicant doctrine, but now show more

134. The episode is known only, as Nicholas Watson explains, from the *Defensorium contra oblectratores* by a hermit, Thomas Bassett. The Carthusian regards as dangerous Rolle's experience of "burning" in love, which, his attacker insists, can only be experienced (safely!) in metaphorical terms. This is exactly the kind of concern raised by the Carthusian annotator in the margins of *The Book of Margery Kempe* (see Parsons, "Red Ink Annotator"). Bassett's reply cites from Bridget of Sweden, indicating that he, too, is aware of the *discretio* issues swirling around the turn of the century. See Watson, *Richard Rolle*, 263–64, and 333 n. 12. The *Defensorium* (which is dated to 1405) survives only in Uppsala, University Library MS c. 621, an indication, as Watson suggests, that either Syon or Sheen was circulating Rolle within the international order (which was the nature of the monastic grapevine).

135. See Ellis, "Text and Controversy," 305–6.

136. Emden, *Biographical Register*, 2.915.

137. For the proceedings, see *Registrum Johannis Trefnant*; on Hereford's role, Emden, *Biographical Register*, 2.915.

historical sophistication, referring to specific papal bulls, to John XXII's condemnation of Jean de Pouilly, and, most interestingly, denying the validity of Pope Innocent's dream about the Franciscan order upholding the church (well known in Joachite circles).[138]

1393   Papal condemnation of Beguines, Lollards, and "Sisters" prompting defences of women's houses.[139]

1393–c. 1415   Julian of Norwich experiences a new vision apparently prompting the rewriting of her *Revelation of Love* to create the Long Text, a text in which all reference to her gender disappears. This version is likely not finished before 1413.[140]

1395   Thomas Burton records the burning of Franciscan Spirituals for 1330.

———   *Twelve Conclusions of the Lollards.*[141]

138. The 1392 conclusions, along with Crumpe's replies, are documented in *Fasciculi Ziʒanorum*, 341–48. See, for instance, Conclusion I: "Papa Johannes XXII male damnavit tres conclusiones Johannis de Poliaco contentas in isto statuto *Vas electionis.*" Some make reference to the *Decretals* (e.g., III and IX) and challenge the power of the pope on issues of doctrine (e.g., II). Most have to do with the FitzRalphian fetish about confession to friars, in ever increasingly ingenious ways. Conclusion X has to do with undercutting one of the great founding myths of the friars, the pope's famous dream: "Item dixit quod fratres de quatuor ordinibus mendicantium non sunt nec fuerunt domino inspirante instituti, sed contra concilium generale Lateranense sub Innocentio tercio celebratum, ac per ficta et falsa somnia papa Honorius suasus a fratribus eos confirmavit." The dream was actually Innocent's and was followed immediately by the pope confirming the rule. For the famous iconography as painted by Giotto, see Lunghi, *Basilica of St. Francis*, 70–74. Crumpe's motivation may be anti-Joachite since Innocent had condemned Joachim at the Lateran Council and Honorius had defended him. Honorius confirmed the Franciscan order officially in 1219; Innocent only orally in 1210.

139. See ch. 6 below for discussion.

140. Watson, "Composition," 641, and Riddy, "Julian and Self-Textualization." Watson ("Censorship," 850 n. 80) argues that one can trace Julian's reaction in the Long Text against Arundel's Constitutions as evidence for a final composition date of later than 1409. He feels that the prominent way in which the Long Text places the date of the original version is similar to contemporary Wycliffite tracts which backdate themselves in order to avoid coming under the Constitutions. For somewhat different views of Julian's process of composition, see Riddy, op. cit., 101–24; and Aers, "Julian and the Crisis of Authority," esp. 138–39 on the problem of rolling revision such as scholars see in Langland's texts.

141. For the Latin text, see *Fasciculi Ziʒanorum*, 360–69; for the Middle English text, Hudson, *Selections*, 24–29. This is an accomplished piece of satirical writing, and contains one of the scarce positive references to post-biblical revelation in Wycliffite writings. The tenth conclusion is against war and capital punishment as being "expresse contraria Novo Testamento" if it is carried out "sine spirituali revelatione." My impression is that revelation could once in a while be invoked as a loophole of convenience. Here it is designed to appeal to a parliamentary audience

after 1395   Hereford retires to the Carthusian house in Coventry.[142]

c. 1396   Death of Walter Hilton.

1397   Richard II punishes Lords Appellant.

———   Death of Uthred de Boldon.

1399   Richard II prohibits the entry of the *Flagellanti* (described as a sect dressed in white and committed to extreme penitence; see 1260 and 1349).[143]

———   Deposition of Richard II and accession of Henry IV.

c. 1400   The *Liber celestis,* translation of Bridget of Sweden's *Revelaciones* into Middle English.[144]

1400   Chaucer's "Complaint to His Purse," and in same year, the death of Chaucer (latest possible date for "Retraction").

———   Walsingham suppresses the "Scandalous Chronicle" from British Library, Royal MS 13. E.IX (also containing a letter by Rupescissa).

———   The papal decree *Vas electionis* reissued for Ireland, probably because John Whitehead, Anglo-Irish cleric from Armagh, was preaching against the validity of friars to hear confessions and other sacraments.[145]

1401   *De heretico comburendo,* execution of first Wycliffites begins.

———   William Sawtry is first to be burned; he had been Margery Kempe's parish priest before 1399.[146]

1402   Parliamentary legislation against prophecies (variously described as "divinationes, messonges & excitations") spread about by poets, musicians,

(perhaps modeled on biblical instances in which God orders certain deaths; Langland invokes one of these in his David and Saul exemplum, which is also invoked in the highly political Bridlington prophecies).

142. Emden, *Biographical Register,* 2.215.

143. *Rotuli Parliamentorum,* 3.428, no. 82, condemning "une novele Secte des certains gentz vestuz de Blanche Vesture et soi pretendantz de grande seintetee," further, that "Proclamation soit fait du chescun Counte & Port du meer deins son Roialme d'Engleterre, Q[u]e nul tiele Secte soit soeffert aucunement d'entrer le dit Roialme." This was the *Flagellanti* with masked faces, who scourged themselves severely via slit-backed garments. For discussion of this phenomenon in relation to Margery Kempe, see Kempe, *The Book,* ed. Meech and Allen, 314–15 n. to 124.13.

144. For versions and excerpts, widely disseminated, see Ellis, *"Ad Flores Fabricandum,"* 163–86.

145. See Emden, *Biographical Register,* 3:2037; Cotter, *Friars Minors in Ireland,* 148. See 1409 below.

146. Hudson, *Premature Reformation,* 435.

and vagabonds (Rymours, Mynstrales, ou Vacabundes) provoking political insurrection and rebellion (in Wales especially).[147]

—— Jean Gerson begins lecturing on mysticism with a view to promoting university reform in Paris.[148]

1404–5 Christine de Pisan, *Cité de Dames*.

—— Various Franciscans executed on charges of sedition and/or propagating prophecies.[149]

—— Trial of Richard Wyche before Walter Skirlawe, bishop of Durham.[150]

1405 Archbishop Richard Scrope leads York rebellion against Henry IV (many clerics, including Franciscans, join his army) and is executed when it fails.

—— December 3, the archbishop of Canterbury and the chancellor of England issue the first of repeated bans on the publication of miracles at the tomb of Scrope.

1406 April 5, York Minster clergy ordered to embark on a campaign of visionary *probatio* interrogation, likely larger than any previously undertaken in England.[151]

—— Legislation against disendowment prophecies.[152]

1407 Interrogation of William Thorpe by Archbishop Arundel.[153]

1407–9 Archbishop of Canterbury Thomas Arundel's Constitutions, requiring a license for any vernacular preaching and forbidding the translation of the scriptures into English without approval.[154]

1409 A Franciscan John Cuock and an Austin Adam Payn, both from Ireland, journey to the Council of Pisa to have the antimendicant writings

147. *Rotuli Parliamentorum*, 3.508, and see 1406 below.

148. See especially Gerson, *De theologia mystica*, 3:250–92; and Glorieux, "Le Chancelier Gerson," 285–98.

149. See ch. 5 below; Catto, "Alleged Great Council"; and Strohm, *England's Empty Throne*, ch. 1.

150. Copeland, "William Thorpe," 201–2; *EHR* 5 (1890): 531–44.

151. See Case Study 3 below.

152. *Rotuli Parliamentorum*, 3.583–84. See ch. 4 below, esp. nn. 45 and 63 for details. For the view that this legislation severely hampered the transmission of popular political prophecy, see Coote and Thornton, "Merlin, Erceldoune, Nixon," 135.

153. Thorpe's account of his trial is edited by Hudson, *Two Wycliffite Texts*.

154. The Constitutions are edited in Wilkins, *Concilia*, 3:314–19. See Appendix A below for discussion of the issues raised by the Constitutions.

of John Whitehead condemned. Alexander V complies in *Regnans in excelsis*.[155]

by 1410   John Walton's translation of Boethius's *Consolation*, apparently seeking to "correct" Chaucer's penchant for pagan classicism.[156]

c. 1410   Nicholas Love, prior of Mt. Grace, Yorkshire, *Mirrour of the Blessed Life of Jesu Christ*.

1410   Trial of John Badby.[157]

after 1410   Mechthild of Hackeborn's visions translated into English as *The Book of Ghostly Grace*.[158]

1410–12   Lydgate's *Troy Book*, apparently published as a "corrective imitation" of Chaucer's *Troilus and Criseyde*; the poem attacks fictional versions of the Troy story and claims the serious ethical purpose of history for its own.[159]

c. 1413   Alan of Lynn offers to write Margery's revelations and she is warned by revelation that it is too soon.

1413   Margery Kempe interviewed by Philip Repingdon and Arundel.[160]

———   Henry V founds Sheen.

after 1413?   The original exemplar of the earliest extant Julian manuscript (British Library, MS Additional 37790, of Carthusian provenance) containing (Porete's) *Mirror of Simple Souls* as translated and revised by "M. N.," which appears with the only extant medieval copy of Julian of Norwich's Short Text.

1414   Sir John Oldcastle (Lord Cobham) leads Rising.

---

155. Cotter, *Friars Minor in Ireland*, 236 nn. 140–141, especially the sources he lists indicating the unity of the Irish friars' orders against the attack, which he connects to the satirical poems in British Library, MS Cotton Cleopatra B.II. See Case Study 2 below. Whitehead's conclusions were officially condemned by Arundel in 1410; see Wilkins, *Concilia*, 3.234.

156. Boethius, "De Consolacione," and discussed by Ian Johnson in Wogan-Browne et al., *Idea of the Vernacular*, no. 1.5.

157. For these and the Wycliffite trials listed below, see Hudson, *Premature Reformation*, 50.

158. For the text, see the edition by Halligan, published on microfiche; and see also Barratt, *Women's Writing*, 50–59. That the translator was in certain (not always predictable) ways concerned about orthodoxy issues is discussed below in ch. 9.

159. Commentary on Lydgate's Prologue, and Prologue itself, to the *Troy Book* in Wogan-Browne et al., *Idea of the Vernacular*, no. 1.7. See especially Watson, "Outdoing Chaucer." For the concept of "corrective imitation," see the entries by Ian Johnson in Wogan-Browne et al., op. cit., discussed below ch. 9.

160. Kempe, *The Book*, ch. 16.

——— Thomas Netter compiles *Fasciculi Zizaniorum*.

——— October 7, Margery visits chapel of St. Bridget in Rome.[161]

——— John Talbot, governor of Ireland, attempts to stem exodus of Anglo-Irish.

1414–18 Council of Constance, at which the execution of Jan Hus takes place. The council was attended by an English delegation including the Carmelite Thomas Netter; the Great Schism is formally ended (see 1417 below).

1415 Margery returns from Rome.

——— John Claydon charged with possession of a Wycliffite text, *The Lantern of Lizt*, and burned with his books at Smithfield.

——— Henry V founds the Bridgettine convent of Syon (supposedly to atone for his father's sins).

c. 1415–17 Sometime during this period, Netter's prohibition to Alan of Lynn (and general prohibition to members of his order) regarding laywomen claiming spiritual gifts and publicity (see 1421).

c. 1415–25 *Speculum devotorum* written by an anonymous Carthusian of Sheen.[162]

1417 End of Great Schism, when the Council of Constance (1414–18) forces three rival popes to resign and elects Pope Martin V (1417–31) as universally acceptable.

——— Margery Kempe summoned to appear before Thomas Peverel, bishop of Worcester, followed by her detention and trial at Leicester[163] and examination at York before Henry Bowet, archbishop of York.[164]

161. Ibid., ch. 39.

162. No full published edition exists, but one is currently in preparation by Paul Patterson; for a partial edition, see Hogg, *Analecta cartusiana*. The anonymous Carthusian is writing for his "gostly syster" soon after Henry V founded Sheen. Most striking is that the Carthusian is writing after Arundel's *Constitutions*, and after the publication (c. 1410) with Arundel's blessing of Nicholas Love's *Mirrour of the Blessed Life of Jesu Christ*, a very well-known translation of the *Meditationes vitae Christi* attributed to Bonaventure. In a "prefacyon" to the book, the writer confesses to being both awed by Love's text and disturbed by its use of "ymagynacyons," which the writer twice equates with the "carnal." His preference, instead, for the revelatory ("revelacyons") is an important counter-witness to the modern sense of the pervasiveness of Arundel's project and Love's *Mirrour*. See Ian Johnson's discussion and an extract from the preface in Wogan-Browne et al., *Idea of the Vernacular*, no 1.12; and see ch. 5 below.

163. Kempe, *The Book*, chs. 45–49.

164. Ibid., chs. 51–52.

———— Execution of Sir John Oldcastle.

1418 Irish civil servant arrested carrying a copy of *Modus tenendi parliamentum*.[165]

c. 1420 Margery Kempe begins to compose *The Book*.

1420–40 Catherine of Siena's *Dialogo della divina providenzza* translated into English as *The Orcherd of Syon* from the Latin translation by Cristafono Guidini.[166]

1421–27 Netter writes his *Doctrinale fidei catholicae contra Wiclevistas et Hussitas* at the request of Henry V, denouncing publicity of women with spiritual gifts, especially preaching,[167] and connecting Wyclif with Olivi and William of St. Amour.

after 1420 John Whethamstede, abbot of St. Albans (1420–40 and 1452–65), commissions a copy of Olivi's Matthew commentary for Gloucester College, Oxford.

c. 1423 James Yonge translates *Secreta secretorum*, embellishing it with Irish material and material from *Piers Plowman*.

1423 Trial of William Taylor.

1424 Friar John Russell is made to revoke opinions regarding sexual freedom reminiscent of Free Spirit beliefs.[168]

1428–31 Heresy trials in the diocese of Norwich (including the trial of Margery Baxter); several held negative views on marriage and celibacy, and one on sexual freedom, such as might be associated with Free Spiritism.[169]

1429 Oxford, Bodleian Library, MS Douce 104, an illustrated copy of *Piers Plowman*, made in Dublin Pale.

1430 Joan of Arc captured and delivered to the English.

1431 Joan of Arc burned.

---

165. See Kerby-Fulton and Justice, "Reformist Intellectual Culture."
166. *Orcherd of Syon*, ed. Hodgson and Liegey.
167. Netter, *Doctrinale*. For detailed discussion, see ch. 6 below.
168. *Register of Chichele*, 3.98–100.
169. Anne Hudson remarks, "Rejection of ecclesiastical ceremony in matrimony is a regular feature of the Norwich diocese group, together with opposition to celibacy, but only one (Westminster Cathedral MS, p. 294) seems to have favoured promiscuity" (*Lollards and Their Books*, 114 n. 6). On Margery Baxter and the records of the Norwich group, see Justice, "Inquisition, Speech, and Writing."

———   A case of mixed Free Spirit and Wycliffite beliefs tried before Bishop Langdon (Rochester).[170]

1434   Margery visits Syon Abbey.[171]

1436   *Book of Margery Kempe* 1 (Proem).

1437   Priest begins to write *Book* 2.[172]

1440   Dean of St. Patrick's, Philip Norreys's teachings against the friars are condemned by Eugene IV in *Ad perpetuam*.[173]

1443   A case of mixed Free Spirit and Wycliffite beliefs tried before Bishop Aiscough (Salisbury).[174]

1443–47   Osbern Bokenham's *Legendys of Hooly Wummen*, apparently "correcting" Chaucer's narratives of pagan seduction.[175]

1448   Nicholas V excommunicates Philip Norreys for his antifraternal opinions.[176]

1457   Condemnation of Reginald Pecock and burning of his books.[177]

———   A case of mixed Free Spirit and Wycliffite beliefs tried before Bishop Grey (Ely).[178]

170. Fol. 94 of the Langdon *Register*, cited in Hudson, *Lollards and Their Books*, 114 n. 6.

171. Kempe, *The Book*, 2, ch. 10.

172. Ibid., 2, ch. 1.

173. Emden, *Biographical Register*, 2.1365–66.

174. Vol. II, fol. 53v, of Aiscough *Register*, cited in Hudson, *Lollards and Their Books*, 114 n. 6.

175. For this argument, see Ian Johnson, no. 1.11 in Wogan-Browne et al., *Idea of the Vernacular; Legendys* is edited by Serjantson.

176. Sbaralea, *Bullarium Franciscanum*, n.s., 1.621–22, and Walsh, *Fourteenth-Century Scholar*, 360. See 1440 above.

177. Hudson, *Premature Reformation*, 55–58, on his opposition to the Lollards.

178. Fol. 131, Grey *Register*, cited in Hudson, *Lollards and Their Books*, 114 n. 6. Bishop Grey was an avid collector of prophetic materials from the Continent; see Kerby-Fulton, "English Joachimism." Recognition of Free Spirit doctrine depended on knowledge of Continental materials (see the case of Ramsbury, 1389), and this may account for why it was not recorded in England as often as it might have been.

A Word about Intellectual Freedom and Intolerable Tolerances in Schism England

I often try to imagine what Abbot John Whethamstede (former prior of students and generous donor to Gloucester College, Oxford) said if ever he noticed the mutilation of a large parchment volume he himself had specially commissioned for the college. The flyleaves of the volume, a copy of Peter Olivi's brilliant commentary on the Gospel of Matthew, had been excised, no mark of its identity remained, and the only evidence of his patronage left was the small "lamb and flag" symbols on the first page.[1] Worse, an anonymous hand had written this note on the lower margin of the last folio:

> Erat quidam Petrus Iohannis hereticus, unus ex complicibus Ioachimi abbatis heresiarche. Cum ergo non constat cuius Petri Iohannis hoc opus sit, non alienum putavi ab offitio meo imprudentem lectorem admonere. (Oxford, New College MS 49, fol. 159v, col. b)[2]

> There was a heretic named Peter, the son of John, an accomplice of the heresiarch, Abbot Joachim. Since it is uncertain which Peter, son of John, wrote this work, I have thought it my duty to warn the imprudent reader.

What would this great Benedictine, now abbot of St. Albans, think of the sacrilege to his book, the insult to his personal choice and to the intelligence of the Benedictine faculty students of Oxford? We do not know, but we do know that someone had found his tolerance intolerable, and acted.

1

This book explores censorship and tolerance of controversial revelatory theology in England from 1329 to 1437. The two dates, just over a century apart, denote the arrest of Henry of Costesy (or Cossey) on heresy charges (see Chronology, 1329–30), the first arrest for revelatory authorship in late medieval England, and the writing of Part II of Margery Kempe's *Book* in 1437.³ These two authors also "meet" again in history when Margery's Carmelite mentor, Alan of Lynn, chose to compose an annotated index to Henry's Apocalypse commentary. Starting from one end of the broad spectrum of audience response to controversial writing we have, next to official censorship itself, suspicion, and in the middle, grudging tolerance, followed by tacit tolerance, then, even further along, enthusiastic tolerance, and, finally, "intolerable tolerance." When someone's tolerance becomes intolerable to someone else, the spectrum can become a cycle. The historical record we are about to witness shows every one of these attitudes toward revelatory theologies. And the genres vary as widely as the attitudes: prophecy, inspired exegesis, visions from prison, mysticism, dream vision, miracles, inquisitional testimonies. All have one thing, and sometimes *just* one thing, in common: a claim, implicit or otherwise, to divine inspiration. With the exception of magic and astrology (both mercifully beyond the scope of this already bulging study), the book records more than a century's worth of visionary pluralism and its uneven reception.

The study of religious censorship in medieval England has been, from the Reformation to the present day, the study of Wycliffism.⁴ The narrative that has developed runs something like this (and here I quote myself):

> Wyclif was first brought to trial in 1377, but English political and anti-papal sentiment favoured him, and his ideas were not seriously or authoritatively challenged until the Blackfriars Council of 1382. The Council condemned 33 opinions, virtually Wyclif's entire reformist programme, as heretical and latently seditious. Many clerics who had flirted with Wycliffism, either publicly or privately, now either recanted or made stealthy revisions to their works; by 1389, English translations of the Bible and English interpretive works were being systematically confiscated and burned, and those who wrote them imprisoned; by 1401, the Statute *De heretico comburendo* was in effect, and now not only suspicious books, but authors, could be consigned to the flames; by 1407 it was an offence to preach the faults of the clergy before the laity; by 1409, virtually any religious literature written in English could be suspect, unless issued with episcopal approval.⁵

It is not that this narrative, in itself, is wrong, although in fact very, very little *non*-Wycliffite vernacular literature did incur any official suspicion under this legislation.[6] The problem is that the narrative is too lonely and always has been. A broader historiography was doomed from the start: it suited Protestant Reformation historians, understandably, to valorize Wyclif, England's most obvious proto-Luther, above any other dissenting voice. Equally, it suited Catholic Reformation historians, also understandably, to see Wycliffism as the *only* threat to an otherwise pristine record of Insular orthodoxy.[7] More recently, literary scholars, also understandably, have hailed Wycliffism as a driving force behind the period's upsurge in vernacular writing, and even as the vanguard of a new proletariat fighting chronic gender or social injustices.[8]

Wycliffism by itself, however, as has become increasingly apparent, cannot sustain such a massive burden of literary, social, and political agency. It was many things, many important things, but it was not omnipresent, it was not unique (it was not even wholly original), and it was not alone in being suspect. This book proposes that we open some doors and windows in a room that has needed airing since the Reformation. Let us take, as a small start, one key episode of early Wycliffism, and see what the view from an open window or two might show.

In 1382 Nicholas Hereford, one of Wyclif's most flamboyant young followers, was audaciously chosen to give the official Oxford University Ascension Day sermon, an honour normally reserved for someone of higher faculty rank.[9] Hereford preached emotionally in English, calling the friars a name recorded in Latin as "luridici," pressing the urgent need for confiscation of the wealth of the clergy, deploring that the king had no justiciars to carry this out, and urging the faithful ("O fideles Cristiani") to take matters into their own hands.[10] In the wake of the 1381 Rising it would have taken even less than this to provoke the inevitable charge that he was "excitans populum at insurrectionem" (inciting the people to insurrection).[11]

He was also inciting the authorities. An anti-Wycliffite faculty member, Peter Stokes, had secretly commissioned a notary to do a *reportatio* of the sermon's most inflammatory points, prompting Archbishop Courtney to send a letter banning all further disputation of Wycliffite topics.[12] When Stokes delivered the prohibition to the university chancellor, Robert Rygge, Rygge responded by accusing Stokes of infringing the privileges and liberty of the university "libertatum et privilegiorum universitatis Oxoniensis."[13] Although Rygge's was hardly a disinterested defence of an ideal of intellectual freedom in the modern sense (an empathizer with Wyclif,[14] he is alleged to have gathered a hundred armed men to intimidate Stokes!), he was nevertheless availing himself of a medieval concept of intellectual freedom in the university.[15] In open defiance of the archbishop's condemnations, Rygge allowed yet another outspoken Wycliffite, Philip Repingdon, to preach the Corpus Christi Day sermon. For weeks Rygge ignored or equivocated or made excuses about every order to publish the condemnations, even under questioning before the Blackfriars Council in London.[16] It was only, in the end, a mandate from the royal council that brought him to heel — and instantly.

This episode is usually treated, of course, as a chapter in the history of Oxford Wycliffism. But that is not all it is. This is a story, like Wycliffism itself, with many histories. It represents the confluence of several different, indeed larger, kinds of struggle and dissent, all of which also deserve fair hearing. For contemporaries, the episode looked not like the beginning of a movement, but sadly, even wearyingly, familiar. It raised yet again topics of controversy and condemnation that had long pre-dated Wyclif: intellectual freedom, antimendicantism, church and state confrontation over disendowment and taxation issues, and the growing *international* problem of "lollardi," that is, self-appointed semi-religious reformers or fanatics.[17]

So, for instance, we only have the text of Hereford's sermon because Bury librarian Henry of Kirkestede[18] (the creator of the first known union catalogue in England) had overseen the gathering of an extraordinary archive containing pre-Wycliffite disendowment documents and prophecies. For Benedictines like Henry and his younger assistants, Hereford's sermon was but a skirmish in the century-long war over disendowment, a struggle that in England went back in popular memory at least to the fall of the Templars, the poverty controversies of the Spiritual Franciscans, and Ockham's polemic.[19] More recently, they would remember the petition that friars laid before the Parliament of 1371, urging the appropriation of ecclesiastical finances (Bury had made what is today the sole surviving copy). And most likely they knew of the climactic Great Council of 1374 presided over by the Black Prince, in which Uthred (or Uhtred) de Boldon, the Benedictine representative, was forced to the humiliating admission that the church had only spiritual, not temporal dominion.[20] For someone like Langland, writing his B text c. 1377–79, all this — not newfangled Wycliffism — is what disendowment represented. And just as Langland associated the topic directly with apocalyptic thought, so did England's foremost librarian, whose archive of disendowment documents included a world-class collection of Continental prophecy on the subject.[21] For Henry, too, Wycliffites were just Johnny-come-latelys on a scene he had watched anxiously for decades, and disendowment was as much a prophetic, exegetical topic as a polemical one. This Oxford episode then was for contemporaries a chapter in a much older and more international book than Wycliffism was, or, in fact, was ever to be.

Rygge's stand on behalf of Hereford and against the archbishop is also a little noticed chapter in the history of medieval intellectual freedom. As J. M. M. H. Thijssen has pointed out in his recent study of academic freedom and teaching authority at Paris, the only area in which we can talk without anachronism about academic freedom in the medieval university is with regard to the university's right to manage its own affairs.[22] This, however, is still a considerable right, and accounts for quite a range of opinions that were allowed to surface in university disputations (such as we will examine in relation to Ockham, Uthred, and academic responses to Brut, opinions that startle even modern scholars). The university's autonomy, I will suggest, also accounts for a *collective* language of heretical accusation that arises, for instance, in a censured friar's charge that Oxford was a "gymnasium haereticorum" (1358), or in Courtney's retort to Rygge after Hereford's sermon that the university was a "fautrix haeresum" (facilitor of heresies) (1382).[23] Wycliffism, then, in 1381, would have looked like part of a long-standing tradition of academic enquiry and interclerical controversy that periodically exploded into public struggle, as here, with external authorities.

The Ascension Day episode is just one such case, and informative because it tells us that in a doctrinal struggle between academic and archiepiscopal powers, the university had a fighting chance. At least in 1382, an Oxford chancellor was willing to go on equivocating indefinitely as long as it was only the archbishop of Canterbury he was wrestling with—merely, that is, the highest church authority in England. But no one who valued his skin wanted to wrestle with the *secular* arm of the law, most especially the king. Adam Usk was eloquent on this aspect of contemporary censorship. Having been indicted as the chief instigator among the Welsh students of the Oxford riots in 1389, and only "scarcely . . . liberated" (vix . . . liberari) by a jury in the presence of one of the king's justices, he wrote, "Before this I had lived in ignorance of the power of the king, but henceforth I feared him and his laws, and I placed a bit between my jaws [maxillis meis frenum imponendo]."[24]

The story of those heady days of university *libertas* in 1382 is a gripping one as well for what it tells us of recourse to violence and intimidation in academic settings. We read of scholars appearing with daggers thinly disguised under their cloaks,[25] the laity attending university sermons in droves, the faculty split down factional lines,[26] and the informant for the archbishop of Canterbury, Peter Stokes, going in fear of his life.[27] Although all this sounds too much like rough justice today, the university was nonetheless flexing its intellectual muscle in a largely legal way. While the medieval concept of academic freedom was much more narrow than ours (which is primarily a nineteenth-century German invention), the freedom of the *universitas,* as Peter Classen has shown, rested upon formal privileges of *libertas scholastica* which were granted by papal or royal authorities.[28] Officially, in canon law, the *magisterium* (teaching authority) of the university fell within the larger *magisterium* of the bishops and ecclesiastical hierarchy. There the great canon lawyer, Gratian, had distinguished the two keys Christ gave Peter as the key of knowledge (clavis scientiae) and a key of power (clavis potestatis), acknowledging that theologians held the key of knowledge to a greater degree than even the pope.[29] But the episcopal hierarchy held the key of *power,* and church lawyers attributed to the pope at the pinnacle of that hierarchy a special authority in supervising doctrine.

Two things, however, in my reading of the problem appear to have somewhat destabilized this hierarchy of power in the Ricardian period. The first was the impact of the Great Schism (when Pope Urban VI was challenged by the anti-pope, Clement VII), causing a crisis of doctrinal authority at the top of the hierarchy.[30] Universities were affected even in the most practical matters: the University of Paris, for instance, was split into factions over which pope should be appealed to for an authoritative statement on doctrine when a faculty member came under censure.[31] The crisis was reflected at all levels in confronting urgent new questions regarding authority as popes, chancellors, and theologians turned, sometimes desperately, to alternative sources of authority—among them new revelation—for answers.[32] The good news in all this—and here I want to avoid a methodological penchant in current historicism emphasizing what has aptly been called "Foucauldian gloom"—is that this kind of crisis opened the door to certain impulses toward intellectual autonomy as academics played a role in reformulating doctrinal authority.[33] In this context even the early Wycliffite attempt at reformulation of the role of the papacy does not look quite so shocking, nor even original.[34] The second, dating from the famous Paris condemnations of 1277 and escalating during John XXII's pontificate, was the culmination of a long-standing intellectual tradition within the universities of disputations probing the *one* problem which, it was agreed, could override any episcopal censure: the question of *what was necessary to salvation.*[35]

In 1277 Bishop Stephen Tempier's condemnations of Paris academics (paralleled at Oxford in the same year) rocked the international university world as an episcopacy tried to rein in Aristotelian theology, a process that would make even Thomas Aquinas a suspect author for a generation. The fallout from these condemnations aroused in university authors a new sense of concern for intellectual freedom, if not strictly in our modern sense, a concern nonetheless. This indignation would be even further heightened in the early fourteenth century by Clementine legislation against academics who aided speculative beguine mysticism and by Pope John XXII's often brutal persecutions of dissenting academics. Without these events, or the tradition of academic defences accompanying them, not only would Oxford's Wycliffism have been unthinkable, but, more broadly, so would much of the intellectual engagement that impacted Marguerite Porete, William Langland, Julian of Norwich, and Geoffrey Chaucer.[36]

One of the most important contributions was made by Godfrey of Fontaines, regent master in the Paris theology faculty from 1285–98. Godfrey is probably best known to literary scholars for his remarkable letter of support (*approbatio*) for Porete's *Mirror* before she was burned at the stake in 1310.[37] In the early 1290s in his *Quodlibet VII* he had raised the issue of whether a master of theology may contradict an article condemned by a bishop (question 18: "Utrum magister in theologia debet dicere contra articulum episcopi si credat oppositum esse verum").[38] His answer makes the distinction between "truths that are necessary to salvation and truths that are neutral to faith." Strikingly, he decided that on truths necessary to salvation a theologian should *not* comply with a condemnation he felt to be wrong, even if others are scandalized by his disobedience.[39] On matters neutral to faith, however, he should be more compliant, at least if he remains within the bishop's jurisdiction, since it is better not to break obedience to a bishop.

No scholar of Langland (or the *Pearl* poet, or Porete, or Julian, or even Chaucer's "Retraction") can read the history of quodlibetal writings on this subject without being moved. They were vernacular writers, not academics, of course, but in our search to understand what gave Ricardian writers and translators the courage to defy or enhance authority and convention, official theological positions on intellectual freedom cannot be wholly ignored. And if we look closely, there is plenty of evidence that they were not ignored. The issue for medieval scholars like Godfrey was not so much *personal* academic freedom (in our modern sense), as "enquiry into and knowledge of the truth" (inquisitio et notitia veritatis). Thus, Godfrey suggested, even when complying with a bishop on non-critical points one should insist on the right to discuss a topic, because the honing of the intellectual faculties through being able to discuss freely (libere tractare) was itself a duty.[40] A distinction like Godfrey's, then, with its insistence on disobeying a bishop "si credat oppositum esse verum"[41] reminds us that there *were* spaces for tolerance—or intolerance of authority. Somewhere in that space ambitious vernacular texts would also take on just such a duty to freely discuss (libere tractare) and seek out knowledge of truth (notitia veritatis). Nor was Godfrey just a voice crying in the wilderness.[42] In 1325, restoring topics related to Thomas Aquinas that had been suppressed by Tempier, Bishop Stephen of Bourret uses the same language of freedom for scholastic discussion: "eosdem discussioni scolastice libere relinquendo."[43] Moreover, various controversial episcopal and papal condemnations against university theologians (especially Olivi, Ockham, and Thomas of Waleys) gave rise to overt confrontations on the topic by the end of John XXII's pontificate.[44] These writers were carefully read in England (indeed, Waleys and Ockham were English, and Olivi had been a student of John Pecham). Ockham had been especially lucid on the subject and wrote that it was absurd to have inquisitors "who are not very learned persons" deciding on complex academic matters.[45] He drew a distinction between explicit and implicit heresy, between heretics (who represented the former) and mere opinions (which might or might not represent the latter). Admittedly Ockham had quite a personal stake in the subject, but he was not alone in trying to safeguard a space for speculative academic thought.[46]

What texts inhabited that space for elbow room in episcopal authority—an authority that modern scholars too easily assume to be the monolithic power structure of the medieval church? In fact, a plurality of texts can be found there—and were contested there, in universities, in convents, in literary circles, and elsewhere. Nor were all the contests lost, as some of the cases discussed in this book demonstrate.[47] In late medieval English studies, our perceptions are heavily influenced by Wycliffism and our hindsight of 1401's death penalty legislation. But there was genuine debate and even toleration in that space both before and after that terrible date, as scholarship is just beginning to show.[48]

This book is about what happened to texts written in *revelatory* genres (or espousing revelatory theology) when they entered that contested space, a question I am not sure has ever been asked, at least in this form. There is a surprising degree of tolerance toward such texts, alongside a serious degree of suspicion—a mingling of ambivalence, fear, respect, contempt, mystery, and awe. In the academic sphere, for instance, there were revelatory texts condemned by the episcopal authorities which nonetheless earned academic approval — a famous case being Porete's ill-fated book. On the other hand, there were visionary texts approved by the episcopal and even papal authorities, but condemned by academics — a famous case would be Jean Gerson's attack on the canonization of Bridget of Sweden.[49] These paradoxical examples highlight three contested areas of freedom of discussion in medieval thought: *visionary experience, mystical theology,* and *apocalyptic theology,* and the unpredictable relations each had with the official theological authorities.[50] These were sources both of theological freedom and of theological danger, and all the writers discussed in this book opened themselves to both possibilities.

Among Oxford condemnations or book confiscations of non-Wycliffite writers in the fourteenth century, we will look at a case involving Richard Fitz-Ralph and a certain Friar John in 1358, whose ideas on disendowment of the clergy were apparently considered too close to those of Franciscan Joachites. We will also look at the case of Oxford professor Uthred de Boldon in 1368, whose innovative revelatory theology of salvation threatened established doctrines of grace, baptism, and church mediation. Uthred's links to the beatific vision controversies recall the earlier case of theologian Thomas of Waleys, imprisoned by John XXII for dissent on this doctrine in 1331. These earlier cases bear parallels to the 1389 confiscations of books by four suspect Continental authors ordered in Oxford and Salisbury: William of St. Amour, Peter Olivi, William Ockham, John of Rupescissa. To this list, which is already heavy in visionary and eschatological writers, we can add another: Joachim of Fiore, also under renewed suspicion in the 1380s, as the anonymous Wycliffite academic author of the *Opus arduum* indicates. Joachimism was a serious threat to Wycliffism (because many of its critiques were so similar), and was in plenteous, though often surreptitious, circulation in learned circles. By the fifteenth century, Olivi's work is marked by censorship even in the Benedictine college library at Oxford. This gives us eight non-Wycliffite writers under suspicion to examine, and in connection with Oxford alone.

Cambridge comes into the picture as the home of Henry of Costesy (cited to Avignon for radical Franciscan apocalypticism in 1330, but avidly read by Cambridge theologians well into the fifteenth century). A former warden of King's College is in trouble for heresy in 1370, perhaps for preaching disendowment, although we know too little of the case.[51] Cambridge was also a centre for concern about the heresy of the Free Spirit in the 1390s, which, together with the presence of prominent Cambridge scholars at Walter Brut's trial, suggests special expertise in a range of non-Wycliffite concerns, as I will suggest. Moreover, the East Anglian and Carthusian connections in the transmission of Marguerite Porete's text betray some evidence of non-Wycliffite suspicions.[52] In this decade of the 1390s academics were also debating—and from sources Continental in origin—the question of women assuming clerical roles *on the basis of revelatory authority* (never a question in Lollardy). These are not the only instances in the period, but these ten in total are the main ones that will claim our attention here.

Introduction

The Dead under Inquisition

I once wrote that the best way to write was to do so as if one were already dead: afraid of no one's reactions, answerable to no one for one's views. I still think that is the way to write. . . . In the society in which I live and work—apartheid South Africa—the legal frame work of censorship affects the work even of dead writers; so there is no freedom to be gained there, in my dictum of writing as if from beyond the grave. A banned work remains banned, even if the writer is no longer living, just as it does in the case of the exiled writer, who is alive but civically 'dead' in his own country.[1] (Nadine Gordimer)

There was to be no freedom beyond the grave for several banned Continental writers whose works found their hapless way to England in the fourteenth century. Most surprising, perhaps, is the English vendetta against the works of three dead friars, Olivi, Rupescissa, and Ockham, which appears in 1389.[2] Since Wycliffites had by then bitterly renounced the friars, the confiscations suggest that the authorities had other concerns.[3]

What those concerns might have been we can see, for instance, in the enigmatic case of Friar Richard Helmyslay, who was accused of heresy in 1380 while preaching Olivian-Joachite style claims for the superiority of the four friars' orders, over not only the secular clergy, but even the four Gospels in the present age.[4] Indeed, many officials and many writers of the period register concerns about dissent other than Lollardy. The author of *The Chastising of God's Children*, probably written for the nuns of Barking sometime between 1389 and 1402, filled two chapters with warnings against the heresy of the Free Spirit. Claiming that these heretics posed *more* of a threat than Wycliffites (whom he dismisses in a sentence),[5] he stresses instead the dangers that can affect "goostli lyuers" who desire "reuelacions": "Now longe I haue taried ȝou to shew ȝou . . . hou sum wiþ her errours bien taken wiþ wikked spirtis, and *hou sum in [disseit] after her desire han reuelacions*" (145, my emphasis). Not long after this, about 1415, Thomas Netter, the eminent Carmelite provincial, issued a general prohibition to stop members of his order from encouraging lay women who publicly proclaimed revelations, an injunction that for a time prevented Margery Kempe from speaking with her beloved Alan of Lynn.[6] Since Wyclif had had no truck with revelations—Wyclif, indeed, had scorned them as "extra fidem scripture" (outside the faith of scripture)—and no Lollard woman is ever known to have claimed any revelation, we must assume that Netter was casting a wider net.[7]

These instances could be, and will be, multiplied, but they are enough for now, I hope, to indicate a broader range of concern about and interest in non-Wycliffite radical thought in England.[8] In this book I will speak mainly of non-Wycliffite suspect doctrine, and here is why. We know a great deal about what upset the English authorities generally about Wycliffism—we have hundreds of pages of trial records, condemned articles, chronicle accounts, treatises, and anti-heterodox legislation. These reveal a deceptively (as I will suggest) homogenous set of doctrines—homogenous enough to have lulled modern scholars into feeling that intellectual radicalism in the period can be subsumed under the heading of Wyclif's influence *simpliciter* just because it dominates the official records.[9] Undeniably, no other suspect doctrine of the period managed to draw upon the same potent configuration of political and ecclesiastical forces and fears. Aristocratic and lay support for Wycliffism was impressive, and so was, in the early days, academic support, all of which pushed church authorities to move on it decisively. But that does not mean that other suspicions were not in evidence, other types of radicalism influential—whether blended with Wycliffism or, more often, not.

Arguably, the major literary writers of the period show *at least* as much, if not more interest in kinds of radicalism other than Lollardy. Langland, for instance, shows massive interest in radical views on salvation (like those censured as "Pelagian" in the university cases of both Ockham and Uthred de Boldon).[10] He also displays detailed knowledge of antimendicant views condemned by the papacy in William of St. Amour and Jean de Pouilly, views for which FitzRalph himself only narrowly escaped censure, and some of which had to be recanted by the Irish Cistercian, Henry Crumpe, in 1392.[11] These views were especially alive while Langland was young: by the 1350s, England and Ireland had become the settings for the biggest campaign against the friars that Europe had seen since William of St. Amour approached the papacy in the 1250s. Langland also airs views on apocalypticism not unlike some condemned in Olivi and Rupescissa.[12] How much radical mysticism he knew is unknown to us, but his poem bears some significant methodological parallels to Marguerite Porete's use of allegory.[13] Chaucer, albeit more playfully, shows interest in controversies over predestination (including Ockhamist fideism), classical humanism, and, of course, antimendicantism as well.[14] The *Pearl* poet is certainly moved to air or challenge conservative doctrines of salvation (especially if he also authored *St. Erkenwald*), using unnoticed Franciscan Spiritual exegesis of the *Pearl* Parable of the Vineyard.[15] Julian of Norwich shows profound interest in the kind of speculative mystical theology that would cause her work to be copied alongside Marguerite Porete's in our only extant medieval manuscript of her *Revelation of Love*.[16] She lived and revised through the period when Bridget of Sweden's revelations were under attack, when defences of them were being translated into Middle English, and also when a rash of contemporary texts written in eastern England warned of Free Spiritism.[17] Even Margery Kempe, who belongs to the next generation and who, alone among all our major writers, came in explicitly for suspicion of Lollardy, was questioned for Free Spirit heresy and was most certainly under suspicion for false revelations.[18] And it is much more this latter concern (which amounts to an obsession with Margery herself) that the Carthusian annotator of our single Margery Kempe manuscript reflects. In addition to his constant attention to issues of visionary *discretio*, he sporadically censures or deletes mystical doctrines smacking of Spiritist sexual libertarianism and "enthusiasm."[19] But at *no* point does suspicion about any doctrine she might accidentally share with Lollardy disturb him.

I have put those introductory points with nearly reckless brevity here (and all will be developed at later stages in the book), but with enough clarity, I hope, to indicate that we need to reexamine two currently dominant narratives. First, we have become accustomed to the idea that either Lollardy or its suppression accounts for much literary and cultural decision making in Ricardian and early Lancastrian England. Indeed, in the last fifteen years the study of Lollardy has transformed how we look at issues as diverse as the Rising of 1381, the Wife of Bath's habit of preaching, or the consolidation of Henry IV's reign. This brings us to the second dominant narrative we now have, the view that the new Lancastrian dynasty sought to shore up its credibility by promoting safe, conservative, politically reconstituted Ricardians (among whom Gower held pride of place). This narrative is also deeply indebted to observations about the role of anti-Lollard ideology.[20]

My goal here, however, is by no means to deny the importance of these paradigms, or the cogent body of scholarship that gave rise to them. It is rather a gentle reminder that these views need to be seen as part of a larger and less insular world of intellectual history. These two narratives have become so dominant that we are missing other trends, concerns, and influences, and most notably this: that Ricardian and Lancastrian radicalisms were both more pluralist and more adventurous (and Wycliffism often more conservative) than we have so far imagined. Moreover, other constraints on intellectual freedom both predated and outran those on Lollard thought and impacted importantly on clerical thought and on the writers we most love. Even a book, however, is not a large enough space to do all that needs doing. So I will look at only revelatory evidence here, to suggest: (1) that during the entire period there were types of heresy or controversial thinking that were still considered *more* dangerous than Wycliffism; (2) that even Wycliffites were working to dissociate themselves from these radicalisms (and thereby prove themselves mainstream); (3) that the insularity of English spiritual thought (from the Latin and the Continental traditions) is a construct which creates a rather monolithic ideology of the "vernacular";[21] (4) that an area at least as controversial as Lollardy for the medieval English church was *revelatory theology*—which is, as I define it, novel theological perspectives arrived at via a claim to visionary or mystical experience.[22]

The charge of holding "new" or "novel" views was a serious one. The word "new" is used, for instance, in the canonical definition of a heretic as one "who discovers a new opinion" (qui *nouam* opinionem inuenit).[23] It is also used in a 1406 parliamentary petition, which also recognizes Lollards as only one of many who seek to subvert and delude via des *Novelx* ("les Lollardes, & *autres* parlours & controvours des *Novelx* & des Mensonges"), in this case regarding disendowment or false (faux) prophecies.[24] Poets, prophetic exegetes, and contemplatives from certain orders (Franciscan, Bridgettine, and Carthusian especially) are among those who participated in or borrowed from what Robert Lerner has broadly called "ecstatic dissent."[25] Women in particular were considered to be both successful at revelatory theology and high risk for meddling with it.

The history of visionary writing changes sharply with the Great Schism, which provoked a whole new interest in revelatory theology. As Marjorie Reeves memorably wrote, "Above all, it was the fact of the Great Schism itself that set the seal of truth on the prophets from Joachim to St. Francis to Jean [of Rupe-scissa]."[26] Turn of the century moves to incorporate mysticism, humanism, and prophetic literature into university curricula are apparent in intellectuals on both sides of the Channel. In England we have the instance of John Whetham-stede and his patronage of Oxford, in which he encouraged and commissioned the copying of writings of all three kinds.[27] If the Schism, as Reeves says, was a boon to male visionaries, it was an absolute godsend to female ones. Their writings fed a Carthusian and Bridgettine readership that radically foregrounded the position of women in the church. But Wyclif, who had approved of neither humanism nor modern revelation, inspired a movement that pushed back hard against these very energies, and this is, I will suggest, one of the untold stories of the "Premature Reformation." What may surprise the reader most in this study is to see Wycliffism come up time and again as a force for certain kinds of "conservatism" (ultimately not a very helpful word) and constraint of its own.

The Failure of Censorship in a Manuscript Culture and Questions of Constraint on Authorship in Ricardian Literature

When I first started researching this book I came to it looking for evidence of constraint on freedom of expression—or to put that in the language of a generation trained up in the shadow of New Historicism, a master narrative of containment and subversion.[28] Instead, I have been continually struck by the diversity of medieval intellectual and spiritual experience and the tolerance ac-corded it by a host of authorities: ecclesiastical, secular, authorial, scribal, per-sonal. I realize that tolerance is not always a universally accepted value, es-pecially in the present era of what some call "censorship of enlightenment," in which "tolerationism" can be as readily the sin without forgiveness as the ac-colade without question. But—to lay my cards on the table—I regard reli-gious tolerance as a good thing, and I rejoice when I find it in medieval culture, which is too rarely mistaken for enlightenment of any sort to be at much risk of charges of "tolerationism."[29] What Archbishop Thomas Arundel would have made of Marcuse's dictum that anything that has to be censored is "not real art" we already know.[30] In Article 7 of the Constitutions, Arundel legislates against statements of any unorthodox or immoral nature, even if they "might be defended by a certain curiosity [or subtlety] of words or terminology" (etiam si quadam verborum aut terminorum curiositate defendi possint), because "often what is well said is not well understood" (saepius quod bene dicitur, non bene intelligitur). As we will see shortly, an author like Gerson would also have dismissed Marcuse's dictum, and so would the Wycliffite author of the *Opus* (chapter 5), both capable of draconian attitudes toward artistic writing. The cases in this book, then, so many of which fall in neither camp, are a welcome change.

The present study uses, I hope, every possible tool at hand, including intellectual history, reception history, codicology, and medieval literary theory, to shed light on corners and angles that are not usually seen and to break out of some of the binaries that plague us.[31] And it makes no apologies for straying freely beyond the vernacular canon: vernacularity was (sadly, for those who were monolingual) a boundary to very few of the writers and thinkers who shaped this period. Studies of vernacularity itself are valid and important in their own right and have been revealing in their own way, but they have come to monopolize what we do and artificially fence off bodies of literature in a way that would have puzzled literate Ricardians.

Determining the extent of constraint in the period, in either Latin or the vernacular, is difficult, but as many of the cases in this book show, this was an age of *failed* censorship. Arundel's Constitutions, as other scholars have begun to establish, were as censorship tools largely "abortive."[32] This is true even in the area where they were most potent (the suppression of vernacular Bibles and the arrest of their owners). Throughout the fifteenth and sixteenth centuries, many respectable laity owned family Wycliffite Bibles, and—judging by their widespread use as autograph books for important visitors—apparently without fear. In this, as in many cases of censorship right down to the Victorian era, legislation restricting accessibility to books is at least partly a class issue.[33] Moreover, commercial bookshops continued to produce these Bibles, often with expensive decoration, throughout the century that followed 1409. If this was backdoor trade, it was nonetheless carriage trade.

In this book we will also look at what I have called Arundel's anti-revelatory Constitutions, an attempt in 1406 to stop the literary and material productions of the country's biggest new cult, that of Archbishop Richard Scrope—also an abortive act of censorship.[34] Moreover, this was the age of a dramatically increased revelatory vernacularity generally. It was the age in which the writings of some of the most controversial women mystics of Europe were flooding into English translation. And these English works were not, as we now know, simply translations; they were creative and editorial reshapings—at times and for certain audiences, suppressive, but at times and for others, not at all so. As

such, they do and must count in any catalogue of exciting new vernacular theology produced in Arundel's England.[35] In another act of failed censorship, secular legislation in 1402 and 1406 singled out prophecy in particular, in part because political predictions of Richard *redivivus* were troubling Henry IV, as were
Franciscan agitators.[36] But manuscripts of the period are a riot of prophecy and
vision. Moreover, this was an age of widespread transmission, in which women,
laymen, and many of lesser means increasingly read challenging revelatory authors like Langland, an author considered "too hot to handle" in the prestigious
London bookshops busy turning out Gowers, Hoccleves, and Lydgates, but
avidly copied elsewhere.[37] It was also an age in which nunnery libraries kept current (more current than their male colleagues did) with the most recent vernacular writing.[38] These are just some of the areas in which the impact of Arundel's
anti-Wycliffite Constitutions needs rethinking.

The truth is that effective "censorship," as we understand it, was ultimately
impossible, indeed, in any absolute sense an impractical task in the age before
print. Manuscript culture, as it has come to be called, was not much amenable
even to *authorial* control, let alone authoritarian control. Imposing modern notions of publication on medieval authors has resulted in all kinds of misunderstanding about what book censorship, or even self-censorship, is or could be in
late medieval England. In the period before print, and therefore before the attempts to control book production through licensing that prevailed during the
Renaissance and Reformation, we cannot assume the kind of state- or church-
centred power structures that made New Historicism so enticing for the study
of later periods.[39] Contrary to what those models have taught us, manuscript
culture was, in fact, an enormously empowering mode of publication for the adventurous author. Because reproduction time was slower, texts could be more
easily kept, at least early on, within reading circles, where oral delivery to a select group allowed yet more freedom. Some of the revelatory texts we will examine here make overt pleas—whether we take these at face value or not—to
the reader to keep the circulation "secrete."[40] The vast majority of medieval
manuscripts contain little or no or inaccurate authorial attribution, and little
concrete evidence of ownership.[41]

Publication itself was an entirely different process: it could be handled through
a patron, whose political clout might well promote and protect an author from injury, but who might prove skittish or Philistine or simply bored and noncommit-
tal. One could write over the head of one's patron (which Chaucer parodies
in Prologue to *The Legend of Good Women*).[42] Or one could write to one's coterie

(which *looks* like what is happening at the end of *Troilus,* especially in relation to Strode and Gower: as Paul Strohm has said, "a text with an unconscious will most certainly have a conscious, too").[43] Or one could challenge the concerns of one's coterie (which Chaucer seems mischievously to be doing in the Introduction to the "Man of Law's Tale," and, as I will suggest, in its suppressed Endlink). Or one could pretend to (as Hoccleve does in "Complaint and Dialogue").[44] Audiences were stratified, and the adept writers exploited that. Certain kinds of reading circles are identifiable for circulating texts that pushed the limits; some of the ones we will notice in this book are monastic (Benedictine and Carthusian, especially), fraternal (Franciscan and Austin almost exclusively), university audiences, certain audiences of women (especially Bridgettine), and the civil service. For sophisticated vernacular writers a civil service setting provided one of the ideal places from which to write, a place where political and ecclesiastical reformist or *avant garde* thought could be tested within intelligent, politically discreet reading circles. Such was Chaucer's and Hoccleve's situation, and recent scholarship is beginning to reach a consensus that it was in some way Langland's.[45] Even here, however, techniques of indirection and constraint abound, and some wrote anonymously or, as is likely the case with Langland and his disciple John But, under a pen name (see chapter 10).

How, then, do we trace a sense of constraint or fear of censorship in a complex age of ad hoc transmission, anonymity, and hazard-prone patronage, and how do we distinguish constraint from all the other kinds of motivation for revision, silence, or allegory? First, there is history of official censorship or confiscation or disapproval, where we have that. Second, audience response is helpful: annotation, manuscript context, and ownership or early provenance can tell us a great deal about who was reading possibly suspect materials and what other works they associated them with. A third great source of information is imitation: to take an example of which scholars have long been aware, why exactly does *Piers Plowman* inspire a work like *Mum and Sothsegger,* a work explicitly about the political astuteness of keeping silence in situations where truth telling is too dangerous? What, that is, does this tell us about *Piers* itself or its early readers? Finally, there are stylistic clues (rhetoric of constraint, textual evidence of self-censorship, implied attitudes toward vision and intellectual freedom), and ideological clues (infiltration of Continental ideas, intraclerical controversy, destabilizing polemic). Widespread and concrete evidence of self-censorship (both gestured and actual) in Ricardian writers is available to modern scrutiny largely, it should be noted, because the fluidity of the text in a manuscript culture allows us to compare revisions with earlier versions in all our major authors. All these things need to be looked at before we can say whether something is written under constraint or not. If the reader will be patient I will start, archaeologically, piece by piece, dragging out shards. This is the only way that a past literary culture (rather than its extant chief monuments in free-floating modern isolation) can be historically understood. In much of the first part of the book I am trying, with the help of unnoticed codicological evidence, to tell an intellectual history that has been largely untold for England. The literary history will emerge gradually in relation to it, but never, I hope, as one-for-one cause and effect scenarios.

In the three Case Studies, and most heavily in the second half of the book, five major vernacular writers will be examined: Langland, Chaucer, Julian, Porete (in M. N.'s translation), and Kempe — each to the relative degree that issues of constraint, or censorship, or (more happily) intellectual freedom may apply. Langland and Porete are the most obvious cases reflecting these issues, but my primary concern throughout is not to force intellectual historical issues upon literary texts, but rather to explore how literary texts are also the children of that history. And in doing so, I have no wish to downplay other factors (aesthetics, genre popularity, literary models, and other equally critical influences on authors) in the production of literary texts. Unlike official censorship or imprisonment or the more dramatic types of evidence, a sense of constraint is much harder for the modern scholar to excavate.[46] Rhetorical strategies for writing under constraint, however, are widespread in the literature. As Annabel Patterson says, "It is to censorship that we in part owe our very concept of literature, as a discourse with rules of its own."[47] This book is as much about constraint as about censorship, in the formal sense of the word. The constraint appears not only in textual and manuscript evidence (everything from authorial revision or deletion to scribal caveats or erasures). There is also the use of or allusion to material known to be officially condemned, often in the form of what Patterson calls "functional ambiguity"—that is, ambiguous reference and phrasing used deliberately by a writer in self-defence. In her own words:

> Functional ambiguity frees us somewhat from more radically skeptical conclusions about indeterminacy in language and its consequences for the reader or critic; unlike other theories, it does not privilege either writer or reader, or eliminate either. It is hospitable to, and indeed dependent upon, a belief in authorial intention; yet it is incapable of reduction . . . [to] meanings that authors can fix.[48]

Functional ambiguity, then, exploits the indeterminate nature of language for its own ends. And when we look at censorship history both before and after Wyclif, we suddenly see why many of these measures like manuscript mutilation, editorial intervention, literary ambiguity, or even a claim to divine inspiration might have been a comfort.

A Word about Visionary Genres:
Writing under Constraint and Recipes for Tolerance

One of the single, most distinctive features of late medieval English culture is the amount of writing in revelatory genres it boasts. These range from the classicized genres that so influenced Chaucer,[49] to the popular romance dream-forms,[50] the ubiquitous Otherworld vision,[51] the prophetic (religious and political), the mystical, and even the intellectual vision.[52] Clearly some of these forms are "literary" in a way that others are not; some contain daring topics and some do not. Just as clearly, audience expectations of controversy, narrative authenticity, and autobiographical experience (nearly all visions are narrated in the first person) differ widely with each genre, a problem that is still being unraveled by scholars.[53] But reception study shows that for medieval readers genre distinctions did not always function as we might assume today. An extensive body of evidence in manuscripts of Dante and other widely disseminated visionary writers, for instance, points toward the fact that "literariness" was not necessarily a mark of fictionalization for medieval readers.[54] This suggests an instability of reception that, I believe, added to the demands made upon poets, and also added to their opportunities for the creation of ambiguity.

Scholarship has given us many, many studies of medieval visionary writing, tracing down a host of sources and models in biblical, classical, and contemporary Latin, French, or Italian literary texts.[55] I will allude gratefully to many of these throughout this book, the more so since this is *not* a study of visionary literature itself. It is rather a study of the circumstances in which this literature comes under suspicion.

It will be helpful here, nonetheless, to briefly review some key points. Among the important reasons for writing dream vision, authors seem to have been influenced by the following:

1. the popularity of the form, both in secular (romance, political, polemical), and religious writing;
2. its inherent provision of an excuse or reason to write, especially in an age of obligatory humility, having a figure of otherworldly authority commission the writing was liberating;
3. the literary freedom of the dream or vision form, allowing for sudden shifts in plot, or plot movement by symbolic association rather than by the determinacy of realism;
4. the possibility for allegorical complexity, as, for example, when dramatic allegorical personifications can act independently or can be mixed with "real" people in the narrative;
5. the potential for freer treatment of symbolism, especially as everything in visionary landscape becomes potentially symbolic, it is easier to use symbolism than in a strictly realist setting;
6. the political, polemical, or intellectual freedom and safety the form seems to guarantee.

One can see from a list like this that freedom of thought is only one among many attractions of the form (and my purpose here is by no means to slight the other five); *any* of them can play supporting roles to a polemical agenda.

Medieval attitudes toward vision were importantly shaped by patristic writers, among whom Augustine and Gregory were crucial. In an often quoted passage from Augustine's *Literal Commentary on Genesis* (*De Genesi ad litteram*), Augustine had defined three levels of vision, using the example of reading the commandment "Love thy neighbour as thyself," in which the letters are seen "corporeally," the neighbour is seen "spiritually," and the love is beheld "intellectually."[56] These three levels were widely used in both Latin and vernacular English texts. *The Chastising of God's Children*, for instance, explains the "þre principal kyndes of visions," as, first, "corporal vision . . . when any bodili þyng bi þe ʒift of god is shewid . . . whiche oþer men seen nat," as when Balthasar saw the handwriting on the wall. The second kind is "spiritual vision or imaginatif" which takes place when "a man is in his sleepe, or . . . rauysshed fulli in spirit in tyme of preier, or in oþer time seeþ ymages and figures of diuerse þinges, but no bodies, bi shewyng or reuelacion of god," as St. John did "as we rede in þe apocalips." The third kind is "intellectual vision" "whanne no bodi ne image ne figure is seen," but when "in suche a rauysshyng þe insiʒt of þe soule bi a wonderful miȝt of god is clierli fastned in vnbodili substaunce wiþ a sooþfast knowyng," such as when St. Paul was "rauysshed."[57] This third kind is "most excelent" and "more worþi" than the other kinds. As we will see, there are interesting gender differences among visionaries in their use of these levels. Julian of Norwich perhaps cited all three types most overtly, but the distinctions among them were both understood and exploited (sometimes even parodied) by a full range of writers discussed here.

Thus Augustine recalled Macrobius' three established categories of authentic vision (the *visio,* the *somnium,* and the *oraculum*)[58] in discussing St. Paul's ecstatic experience in Book 12 of *De Genesi ad litteram,*

> I might compare these visions to those experienced in dreams. Some are false, some true; some unsettled, some serene. Some offer images of the future, sometimes plainly (aperte) announced, while at other times the prophecies are given through enigmatic (obscuris) meanings or figurative pronouncements (figuratis locutionibus).[59]

Gregory was even more unhelpful:

> Dreams are generated either by a full stomach or by an empty one, or by illusions, or by our thoughts combined with illusions, or by revelations, or by our thoughts combined with revelations.[60]

The statement, as J. S. Russell says, "seems intentionally confused, featuring the kind of manic randomness we associate with the Prologue to Book One of the *House of Fame.*" Here, in a passage that does duty for generations of medieval literary texts on the *topos* of ambivalence about dreams, Chaucer wrote:[61]

> God turne us every drem to goode!
> For hyt is wonder, be the roode,
> To my wyt, what causeth swevenes . . .
> And why th' effect folweth of somme,
> And of somme hit shal never come;
> Why that is an *avision,*
> And this a *revelacion,*
> Why this a drem, why that a sweven,
> And noght to every man lyche even;

Why this a *fantome,* why these *oracles,*
I not; but whoso of these miracles
The causes knoweth bet then I
Devyne he . . . .
(*House of Fame,* 1–14, with omissions)

Ranging through four of Macrobius' dream types (emphasized above), both valid and invalid, the narrator, Geoffrey, admits defeat, but not until he has offered a reprise. This takes the form of a dizzying list, running for about forty lines more, of possible causes of dreams ranging from the divine to the physical to the ephemeral. Dreams, for example, can be the effect for some of

. . . to gret feblenesse of her brayn,
By abstinence, or by seknesse,
Prison-stewe or greet distresse.
(24–27)

Finally, shunning all scholarly opinion, he takes refuge at last in the Cross (a momentary example of an experimental Christian humanism he would largely abandon later, as we will see in chapter 9):

For I of noon opinion
Nyl as now make mensyon,
But oonly that the holy roode
Turne us every drem to goode!
(56–58)

The tone is comic, but the exasperation, if we can judge by the abundance of parallels in contemporary poets, entirely genuine—and ultimately poetically useful. What all modern scholars agree on is that the ambiguity in visionary literary genres is deliberate.

Ambiguity, meanwhile, was the last thing the medieval church wanted when confronted with claims to visionary experience. As John Pecham, who was no friend to contemporary visions, mused, "If only we know the authentic revelations of the holy, we do not care about the apocryphal ones" (Sanctorum siquidem revelationes autenticas novimus, apocriphas non curamus).[62] This suggests that even a scholastic thinker like Pecham had to and did allow for the possibility of real contemporary revelation. Even one of the greatest scholastic thinkers, Aquinas, offered this among his definitions of prophecy, "truths exceeding the present reach of the prophet's mind," thereby affirming the expectation of interpretive confusion.[63] Where confusion became most troublesome was where the theology implied in the vision deviated from biblical or established church doctrine—and here we have the problem most encountered in this book.

In order to weed out ambiguity, a genre of professional manuals on how to tell true visions from false visions arose.[64] These treatises on testing, *probatio*, or discretion of spirits, *discretio spirituum*, drew on the rich commentary available in the early church fathers, and, increasingly, in late medieval writers. This is especially the case at the end of the Avignon papacy and with the onset of the Great Schism, the latter a crisis that required urgent *discretio spirituum* amidst new prophetic propaganda. Among the popular Latin treatises of the Schism period known in England was Alphonse of Pecha's defence of Bridget of Sweden (written just after her death in 1373), and Jean Gerson's *De probatione spirituum*, *De distinctione verarum visionum a falsis*, and *De examinatione doctrinarum* written in the first decades of the fifteenth century.[65] Throughout this period these texts traveled internationally in manuscripts with mysticism, defences of lay and women's movements (like the *Devotio Moderna*), inquisitorial texts, and women's visions in particular.[66] Alphonse's was partially translated twice into Middle English, once in *The Chastising*, and once in a freestanding translation, heavily "abridged" (in certain passages virtually eviscerated) for lay readers and, apparently, a female audience.[67] Langland, Julian, the M. N. translator of Porete's *Mirror*, and all the major Middle English mystics knew such treatises or their key doctrines in some form and exploited their audience's knowledge of them. Even Chaucer knows the "rules" of *discretio* and applies them seriously in his saint's legends, and elsewhere in parody or semi-parody.

Claims to vision made in accordance with the "rules" of *discretio spirituum* could acquire for writers the right to treat freely (*libere tractare*, to borrow the academic phrase) new or contentious material. This we will see especially in relation to Langland, the women's writings of Bridgettine Carthusian transmission, and, most exceptionally, the two orphan "prison" visionaries of the early Wycliffite movement. Throughout the thirteenth and fourteenth centuries, at least up to the Schism period, it was hard to gain respect for contemporary visions in the academic world. This may have been, I would suggest, at least in part because academic life had its own "free space" for theological speculation and its own preferred mode. But in the world of Latin writers at least two top-ics, it seems, regularly provoked claims to visionary inspiration (claims suit-ably modified as "spiritual intellection"): alternative salvations and alternative salvation histories. The early and final chapters of this book discuss these twin themes and their massive importance, not only in medieval exegesis contain-ing "novel thought," but in contributing to the extraordinary rise of visionary genres as a defence for thought that dared to be novel.

Barbara Newman has recently made a thoughtful contribution to this whole problem of the intersection of theology and literary art, and the censorship questions it raises.[68] The question of heresy, she says with justice, is too freely used by modern literary critics, who imagine "texts, ideas, or even metaphors designated 'heretical' because they impress a modern reader as subversive or in violation of some preconceived theological norm." She reminds us that me-dieval heresy was a juridical concept, and that books or beliefs only became heretical when authoritative churchmen bothered to pronounce upon them. But "medieval bishops were busy men," as she succinctly puts it, and, nor-mally, "potential heretics came to their attention only if their activities were sufficiently public and widespread to cause anxiety, or else if they were de-nounced by their enemies." This is precisely why the anti-Wycliffite Constitu-tions were so ineffectual as *literary* censorship (if, indeed, they were ever even intended as such, which is itself a debatable interpretation).[69] As I have just suggested, the technologies of medieval book production—in which anyone with pen and parchment could produce a text, and anyone with a pen could alter one—defied large-scale authoritative control for the same reasons that they defied authorial control. Thus only heresies that had some larger, visible, and active political implication, or which threatened to supersede present priestly roles or power structures (like the Lollard devaluation of the sacraments or the Joachite "Age" of the Holy Spirit) provoked prosecutions. Literary works, and especially visionary ones, written in often demanding and even obscure genres were not ripe for inquisitional picking—Hildegard's visions being a great case in point. Newman's book, which deals extensively with visionary-allegorical genres, shows clearly "how a nonscholastic literary form might protect even the most audacious theological writings." Authors, too, were often, for this rea-son, physically relatively safe. Newman points out that the four writers whose works "arguably made the greatest impact on later heretics (Joachim of Fiore, Peter John Olivi, Meister Eckhart, and John Wycliffe) were all permitted to die in peace." She also points out "that we don't hear of Langland being personally persecuted, despite the role of *Piers Plowman* in the Rising of 1381," and that "even Porete, had she deigned to defend herself by showing how her ideas could be interpreted as orthodox, might have escaped the flames."

All this is true in many ways, and, more importantly, it redresses a balance. There is none of the Foucaldian paranoia or hysteria that has now coloured a whole generation's mental world in the hermeneutics of suspicion. What it is important to say, however, is that although many of these writers died in their beds, many of their followers did *not*. Many paid the ultimate price, and paid it excruciatingly. And these authors themselves must have had many anguished nights in their beds: Olivi was repeatedly censured, even at one point denied access to his own writings; Wyclif worried incessantly from early on about martyrdom, and was forced to withdraw from his job at Oxford.[70] Eckhart spent the last months of his life under examination. Joachim sought protection in the form of *approbationes* from three popes, but underwent posthumous censure anyway. And Langland—who wrote under a pen name from all we can tell— likely withdrew from London (as the distribution of C manuscripts strongly suggests) and apparently engaged in a large-scale campaign of protective and polemical revision. No matter what his precise politics, he must have lived the rest of his life feeling anxious that something he had written caused men to die. At the very, very least, Langland single-handedly disproved Auden's great claim in his elegy for Yeats that "poetry makes nothing happen."[71]

Porete is unusual in dying for the text she wrote, but this book discusses some others whose penalties for writing were also severe. Among visionary or eschatological exegetes, John of Rupescissa and the anonymous author of the *Opus arduum* suffered torture or duress in prison (the former's horrible); Gerard of Borgo San Donnino died excommunicate in prison; William of St. Amour ended his life condemned and in exile; Uthred de Boldon was quietly transferred out of his position at Oxford. Ockham, Thomas of Waleys, Friar John, like other non-visionary Englishmen, suffered similar fates (exile, imprisonment, and debarment from teaching, respectively). Their works, especially the autobiographical ones, form part of the canon of "representations of dissent," too, in Rita Copeland's words and need to be read with literary as well as historical awareness. There is "a kind of hegemonic power in writing as the victim," as Copeland rightly says.[72] There is also a kind of hegemonic power in writing *for* the victim. We as modern scholars must be alert to all these complexities. Still, no amount of literary critical construction changes shattered bones, lives, or spirits.

Among overtly "literary" writers there were fewer penalties, but they did occur. In addition to Porete's terrible case, and the trail of censure the text left behind, and Langland's likely acts of self-editing and self-exile, we have glimpses of other evidence. Rutebeuf's poetry, for instance, taking up William of St. Amour's banned cause, was implicated in general papal censure (see Chronology, 1259). Awareness of this is evident in Jean de Meun's continuation of the *Roman,* which again took up William's cause and was the subject of controversy well into the fifteenth century. In Anglo-Ireland the Statutes of Kilkenny attempt to legislate against mixed-race culture, including minstrelsy in 1361, reflecting the ethnic tensions we will see in the Anglo-Irish poetry dealing with heresy, and more broadly in relation to Ledrede and FitzRalph. Chaucer apparently felt insecure enough theologically to offer his harsh "Retraction," which, although overtly moral in thrust, has the effect of cutting out everything philosophically experimental, and must also have cost him sleepless nights. Julian of Norwich submerged her gender in her final version of the *Showings.* English legislation attempts to control prophetic dissemination in 1402, 1405, and 1406. And Margery Kempe was accused of heresy and hauled in for examination on more than one occasion.

This raises, of course, the issue of what constitutes a "literary" work, a problem that in visionary literature often presents itself as a more specialized question: which writings are literary or fictional constructs, and which are, or claim to be, "experienced" visions? Peter Dinzelbacher's distinction between "literarische Visionen" and "erlebte Visionen" (that is, "lived visions") captures the question succinctly, the various characteristics of which I have set out elsewhere, especially in relation to Langland, Hildegard of Bingen, and other apocalyptic thinkers.[73] Many medieval visionary works behave themselves and slide neatly into one of the two categories. But many types of visions do not: apocalyptic works, for instance, are not cooperative on this front, nor are mystical works always cooperative either, or works of what Newman calls "imaginative theology" in *God and the Goddesses.* What is most surprising to find is that even intellectuals (depending on how scholastic their orientation is) can invoke subtle visionary claims and the literary conventions that accompany those claims. This means that we need to make room in our literary taxonomy for works like the *Opus arduum,* an Apocalypse commentary with its rich authorial intrusions of "bibliographic ego," or Olivi's Matthew commentary with its oblique appeals to visionary authority, stunning mysticism, and allegorical exegesis. It also means that, going back to Newman's list again, Joachim, Olivi, and Eckhart all have claims in fact as *literary* writers.

Some recent scholarship has also helped to complicate our nice boundaries between the "literarische" and the "erlebte" in relation to other texts. So, for instance, Lynn Staley has sought to shift Margery Kempe's book away from the transparently "experienced" category, and toward the "literary," by questioning the representation of the scribe in the text.[74] Rita Copeland has similarly unburdened William Thorpe of some of the "erlebte" in relation to his prison writings, exploring his representation of subjectivity and helpfully opening up the world of intellectual discourse to expose its hermeneutic art.[75] Barbara Newman gives us a nuanced reading of the difficulties of the two categories in relation to allegorical visions containing deified female figures.[76] She, too, is interested in texts that upset the categories, such as "literary" works like *Piers Plowman* and Christine de Pizan's *City of Ladies* that draw seriously on the conventions of "experienced" vision.

There is, in fact, no neat dividing line between the literary and the intellectual or authoritative in the Middle Ages—although not all academics were good literary readers. Wyclif, for instance, was a ham-fisted reader of Hildegard's *style*, but an acute reader of genre. And Jean Gerson, chancellor of the University of Paris, although an innovative man of letters in the fully humanist sense of the phrase, nonetheless was an equally ham-fisted reader of the style of Jean de Meun.[77] Gerson's attack on the *Roman de la Rose* takes the form not of a treatise, but an allegorical dream poem. As David Hult points out,

> not only does Gerson's thereby attempt to undermine the allegory by means of its own discursive strategy, but he then, somewhat disingenuously, condemns this strategy, declaring that it does not make any difference who is speaking. Heretical doctrines, he tells us, must be proscribed in any context: "Lequel est pis: ou d'ung crestien clerc preschier en la persone d'ung Sarrasin contre la foy, ou qu'il amenast le Sarrazin qui parlast ou escripst? / What is worse: for a Christian clerk to assume the character of a Saracen preaching against the Faith, or for him to introduce a real Saracen speaking or writing against the Faith?"[78]

As Hult goes on to point out, Gerson's frustration arises from the fact that the text never speaks its own voice in favour of, or against, a particular doctrine. Rather,

"Tout semble estre dit en sa persone: tout semble estre vray come Eu-vangille . . . et, de quoy je me dueil plus — tout enflamme a luxure, meis-mement quant il la semble reprouver / Everything seems to be said in his own person; everything seems as true as the Gospel. . . . And I regret to say, he incites the more quickly to lechery even when he seems to re-proach it."[79]

This is not the kind of reader to whom any literary writer would want to trust his or her fate, and we can bet that Ricardian poets and mystics felt similarly.

Literary writers poised their pens, then, amidst a spectrum of consequences and attitudes: Late Antique scepticism about dreams, early Christian dream typology, biblical revelation, and, increasingly, injunctions to *discretio*. These arose from medieval theologians wrestling with a whole new set of issues (in-cluding academic caution, influential women visionaries, Schism propaganda, and a legacy of prophets under suspicion and condemnation). The great vi-sionary models like Joseph, Scipio, St. Paul, St. John, St. Perpetua, Macrobius, Boethius, Alan of Lille, the *Roman de la Rose* authors, and Dante rub shoul-ders, even at times in the same manuscripts, with the apocalyptic, mystical, or reformist visionaries like Hildegard, Joachim, Olivi, Porete, Rupescissa, Brid-get, Catherine of Siena, or Mechthild of Hackeborn. It was a rich, rich inheri-tance of writers, many of whom had written from prison, exile, under condem-nation, or at great risk of censure.

Non-Wycliffite Heresy in Late Medieval England

Post-Reformation emphasis on Wycliffism has perhaps somewhat obscured our sense of what the theological world actually looked like at the time that Ri-cardian writers began their careers. Classic historical overviews setting out the landmark issues debated long prior to Wyclif include lists of topics such as: evan-gelical poverty, antimendicantism, Ockhamism, disendowment, supremacy of church or state, predestination and grace, monastic perfection, salvation history, the Immaculate Conception, anti-intellectualism, the beatific vision.[80] Many of these, of course, Wycliffism would exploit, but not before the formative years of Ricardian writers were well under way.

To get a sense of how heresy was defined before the rise of Wyclif, we can turn to the *Omne bonum*, an encyclopedia made up most prominently of canon law sources and created by James le Palmer, a civil servant in Westminster between 1359 and 1375.[81] During these years Langland composed his A text; Chaucer was translating *The Romance of the Rose*, and writing some of his early visionary poems (*House of Fame* any time from 1374); Julian had had her first vision (1373). The *Omne bonum*, known mainly to Middle English scholars for the light its virulent and learned antimendicantism sheds on Langland and Chaucer, also has a long article on the topic of "Hereticus." This gives several definitions or aspects of "the Heretic," including: one who is doubtful in faith (dubius est in fide); one who is *symoniacus;* one who badly interprets scripture (male interpretatur Scripturam Sacram); one who discovers a new opinion (nouam opinionem inuenit); one who takes away *priuilegium romane ecclesie;* or, lastly, one who transgresses the precepts of the Roman church (transgreditur precepia romane ecclesie), including Jews and non-believers (iudeos & gentilis).[82] By these definitions, much that is interesting in any of our major vernacular writers could come into question—at least theoretically. The illuminated initial of James's "Hereticus" article (figure 1) shows two opposing groups of men, one of which is marked by long noses (an iconography also used, in flagrant contradiction of Langland's text, for the portrayal of Trajan in the Douce *Piers Plowman*[83]). But even in the 1360s and early 1370s, when Langland, Chaucer, Julian, and likely the *St. Erkenwald* poet were all beginning their careers, one would not have to look so far afield as the exotic pagan to find heresy. As the other definitions indicate, *anyone* who created doubt about faith (the very charge leveled at Ockham in 1339–40)[84] or anyone who threatened the clergy with disendowment (as Friar John did in 1358), or anyone who discovered a new theological opinion (as Uthred de Boldon did in 1368), or anyone who interpreted the scriptures "badly," as four Franciscan Joachite lectors were charged with doing at Cambridge in 1329–30, was *hereticus.*[85] This is the kind of information that can shed light on uneasiness that might have led to various kinds of concern in any of our major writers.

The picture we are always given of England, however, is of an intellectual history beset by controversy, sometimes sensational, but never by theological danger, *until Wyclif,* and then only *from Wyclif.* But this ignores a different history, a history still less documented, the history of dissent *before* Wycliffism, and even parallel to it. And in this prior history we can find recorded cases of censure, heresy, and inquisition, including ritual humiliation,[86] recantation,[87] interrupted academic careers,[88] self-censorship of theological writings,[89] shattered

1. London, British Library, MS Royal 6. E.VII, fol. 200, from James le Palmer's *Omne bonum*, showing the image for the article entitled "Hereticus." Reproduced by permission of the British Library.

lives, enforced penance,[90] public branding,[91] flogging,[92] imprisonment,[93] life-confinement in convents,[94] exile, prevention of travel, confiscation of property, and even death[95]—even by burning.[96] The Chronology at the front of this book outlines many of these cases (footnoted with detailed explanation or indications of where in this book or elsewhere further discussion can be found).

Several things must be said about this history: first, that many cases were never recorded, and those that were often lie buried in unedited bishop's registers, manuscripts, and other archival materials. These will doubtless eventually tell us more.[97] Second, glimpses of Continental heresies, both popular and academic, active in English domains appear from the twelfth century onward.[98] What is really illuminating about a chronology like this is that it reveals a pattern of small clusters of related persecutions in England and Ireland, at *each* historical point where an emergent heresy is being most pursued on the Continent. Take, for instance, the first upsurge in persecutions beginning c. 1162, involving the "Patarini" (Cathari); or the second tragic cluster c. 1222 at the Council of Oxford (the main mandate of which was to promulgate the reforms of the Fourth Lateran Council); or the third upsurge c. 1250s, with appearances of the Pastoureaux, the Neoplatonists, the censures of Joachimism and St. Amour, and the *Flagellanti*. Some of these groups reached England physically (and suffered there), others known only by report, still others through short, anonymous prophecies (which are abundant in English manuscripts for 1260).[99] But these clusters reflect in microcosm exactly the patterns one finds reported in the hysteria of Europe as the terrifying year of 1260 approached. Matthew Paris, acting as chief watchdog not only for England, but Europe on some of these events, reflects events at home and abroad with accuracy.[100] The next cluster surrounds the condemnations of Aristotelianism beginning in 1277, and unease about radical Joachimism, both exemplified in Archbishop Pecham's work. England is quiet again until 1308, which ushered in the terrible years of the Templars' prosecutions (and Porete's abroad), the Clementine ban on the Beguines, and the Johannine censures of Franciscan Spirituals affecting English clerics like Ockham (1328), Henry of Costesy (1329–30), and Thomas of Waleys (1331–32). In this period we have a flurry of Insular activity, with early prosecutions like Bishop John de Grandisson's (1329, 1334) and Bishop Richard Ledrede's (1324), the latter fresh from Avignon, hunting for Continental heresy in the Irish countryside.[101] Through these years, and coming right up to the next cluster of activity in the 1350s and 1360s, the mendicant controversies spawn charges of heresy involving Archbishop FitzRalph (1350–60) and his opponents and culminating suspiciously in the condemnation of Uthred (1368). During this period both Bishop Grandisson and Archbishop John Thoresby are active in matters of heresy (see Chronology, 1355). In some cases we can make direct links with papal campaigns or prominent Continental inquisitors.[102]

These are the main "bulges" of heresy-related history before Wyclif that I have been able to reconstruct. They reveal a pattern I do not believe has been much noticed before: there are an unexpected number of these clusters, all of which have clear relations to heresies in the international world. The fact that this surprises us, as scholars of England, asks us to rethink our historiography. The punishments meted out were also real and severe. As John Bacher put it, "It is clear that the death penalty [prior to 1401] for unrepentant heretics in England was no mere theory of the legal writers, but an actual practice, though not one to which recourse was often necessary."[103] John Arnold, in a recent article comparing heresy prosecution in England and France, has asked why, "with few exceptions, the historiography of heresy in England has been resistant to the idea that *inquisitio heretice pravitatis*—inquisition into heretical depravity—was ever used in that realm?"[104] Arnold shows the presence of certain kinds of vocabulary in pre-Wycliffite records, although fragmentary, indicates "the hitherto unrecognized presence of inquisition in England." While no one could pretend that the numbers of victims are as high as on the Continent or as during the worst years of Wycliffite persecution, it would nonetheless be misleading, faced with this data, to assume that writers working before Wyclif began his public campaign could have felt utterly unconstrained in expressing theological opinion. The corollary also applies: that the coming of Wycliffite persecution was not so utterly altering of the mental landscape as recent scholars often suggest.

Harsh penalties, then, and even death for deviant opinions, were possible in the centuries before *De heretico comburendo* and Arundel's Constitutions.[105] What determined the harshness of the penalty was what canon law called "pertinacity" in holding unacceptable opinions. The fact that many in England, over the centuries prior to Wyclif, chose to submit to the church rather than be named pertinacious and risk more severe treatment does not mean that pre-Arundel England was necessarily a "friendlier" place to write radical theology.

What is true is that England and Ireland did not have a *papally* appointed regional inquisition. But, in fact, no country did in the sense of a *continuous* office during the Middle Ages, although many witnessed much more steady activity than England. The first problem here is one of terminology. Edward Peters helpfully distinguishes among "inquisition" (meaning the *officium inquisitionis*, or inquisitorial *function* of any single inquisitor); "Inquisition" (in the sense of a regionally appointed institutional base, which in the Middle Ages would most often be the rooms of a local friary set aside for the purpose);[106] and "The Inquisition" (in the notorious and largely later sense of, for instance, the Spanish Inquisition). Richard Kieckhefer, building on Peters's work, has summarized the whole problem this way: "If reference to a monolithic 'Inquisition' in the medieval West seems absolutely out of place, and reference to local and regional Inquisitions requires cautious attention to local specificities, this is not because there was no institutional development underway."[107] Finally, Arnold, echoing all responsible scholars on this subject, suggests we forego "imagining 'the Inquisition' as a kind of permanent tribunal of hard-faced Dominicans . . . mercilessly torturing or burning" large numbers of helpless victims. We should, rather, think of "'inquisition into heretical depravity' as a set of legal processes, drawn from an accumulation of papal bulls, local conciliar statutes, and latterly inquisitorial manuals."[108] Of course by the time we are speaking of, fourteenth-century England, even early fourteenth-century England, these manuals and other tools are well established (see Chronology, c. 1323). We can also think of inquisition as a "discourse," as Arnold puts it, "a 'discourse' in the Foucauldian sense of a set of language and practices that claims to produce and police a field of knowledge (namely heresy)."[109]

In both these senses, then, we *do* find inquisition in both England and Ireland. Certainly the cases of the Templars, for instance, and Bishop Ledrede's terrible proceedings, and some of Grandisson's qualify under these terms.[110] We are severely hampered in some of the cases listed in the Chronology by lack of extant or sufficient or indexed records. But as Bacher shows, the lack of evidence for England does not arise because inquisition would not have found anything to do there; rather, the opposite: that "the absence of Inquisition from England goes a long way to account for the small number of cases of heresy recorded there."[111] While one can argue the question of circular reasoning, one cannot argue with the many recorded statements of Insular churchmen between the twelfth and fourteenth century calling for attention to the spread of heresy.[112] As historians have observed, the absence of inquisition was no doubt in part because of the rapid development of the royal courts and of English common law, both of which took a strong hold early. These were perhaps both less equipped and less interested in prosecuting heresy.[113] The role of sheriffs in heresy inquisition remains largely unstudied. And, as the pre-Wycliffite cases in the Chronology attest, there was often a tension between church and state when heresy reared its head.[114] Most shocking to modern sensibilities is the fact that heretics had to be wealthy to make the process really worthwhile, especially for secular authorities. As Nicolas Eymeric laments in his *Directorium inquisitorum,* "In our days there are no more rich heretics; so that princes, not seeing much money in prospect, will not put themselves to any expense; it is a pity that so salutary an institution as ours should be so uncertain of its future."[115] Words fail us. But, sadly, this was one of the reasons that the Templars case—which held out the prospect of confiscating the endowments of a whole order in England— exerted an early, if slightly guilt-ridden, appeal for King Edward (see Chronology, 1308).[116]

Another reason scholars believe that there were fewer prosecutions in England is because the English bishops took the Fourth Lateran Council of 1215 so seriously. We will see a great deal of evidence, for instance, of concerted attempts in England to suppress Joachim's writings, simply on the basis of a relatively small technical point in his trinitarian theology for which he was— unluckily—condemned at that highly influential council. The strange outbreak of heresy prosecutions at the Council of Oxford (1222) is doubtless evidence of Fourth Lateran zeal. The church, it cannot be stressed enough, was an *international* institution with a common language (Latin), a common legal system (canon law), and as many cross-border grapevines as there were bishoprics and religious orders. Since inquisition was an *office,* not in a physical sense, but in the sense of "officium" (a function), its legal processes were applied in pre-Wycliffite England both when Continental heresies appeared and when someone had the time, motivation, or erudition to pursue anything that contravened canon law definitions. These factors are the real ones, and the real limitations on inquisition of any sort. Indeed, in a legal system that prosecuted heresy largely by the lights of precedent, there was less scope for escaping the Continental assumptions, labels, and forms of sentencing. In addition to recent, late medieval heresies, another aspect of precedent was the conjuring (sometimes out of desperation) of Late Antique heresies. These loomed large in theological accusations, as we will see, for instance, in the charges of Pelagianism directed against Ockham, and even against Joachim, by Thomas Bradwardine. Some of these charges were likely an outgrowth of academic disputation gone sour (as we see in John Lutterell's attack on Ockham, or William Jordan's on Uthred, neither of which resulted in harm to life or limb). Others were much more serious, especially any in which genuine inquisitional process was in place.

Walter Ullman has explained papal inquisition in a passage worth quoting at length:

> Specially commissioned inquisitors taken mainly and understandably from the ranks of the mobile itinerant [fraternal] Orders, were sent to regions to 'enquire' into any matters which might constitute a charge of heresy. Everyone was compelled to bring to the inquisitor's notice any manifestation or suspicion of heresy. The proceedings were secret, the suspected or accused individual did not know who the informants were, there was no means of cross-questioning witnesses who might have been convicted perjurors. . . . The accused knew no details of the charge and no appeal to a higher court was allowed, because the inquisitors themselves functioned 'by apostolic authority' and their verdict was in reality a papal verdict. . . . Torture was not employed to obtain the truth, but a confession, the only restriction being that it could not be repeated against the same accused. This was easily circumvented. . . . There never was an acquittal; all that occurred juristically was that no further proceedings took place.[117]

Now here is grist a plenty to the Foucauldian mill. And mercifully Insular evidence of such full judicial procedures, guided by mendicant appointees, is, as we have just seen, rarer than it was on the Continent. The role of English secular law, and by the mid-fourteenth century, English anti-papalism and anti-mendicantism, all combined to mitigate these practices in England and Ireland. But we are fooling ourselves if we believe them to have been entirely absent. In fact, the only element of inquisitional process we do *not* find in England—and this is good news of a kind history too rarely affords—is the official use of torture to gain confessions from heretics. In an incident made famous during the Templar trials, the inquisitors had difficulty obtaining permission for the use of torture from the king and an official had to be brought in from Agen to supervise it. Three Templars did make partial confessions, but the foreign inquisitors had left England by this time, complaining of the barriers to the use of torture the English persisted in putting in their way.[118] Lest even here, however, we claim too much for Insular sensibilities, we should note that England was not the only place that torture was repugnant. Robert Brentano's sensitive study, *A New World in a Small Place*, found the same repugnance in Italy, and even during the terrible years of John XXII's papacy. In Rieti, Giacomo Leoparducci is recorded as having said in 1334, "For the sake of the good reputation of the people of Rieti and the honour of the city the man should not be tortured."[119] We need to be very careful, then, not to overestimate the insularity, or the innocence, or the even uniqueness, of Insular theological culture.

The Wycliffite movement suffered from a great many of these events, used others for its own ends, and fled, like Blake's Thel, from just as many more. The jury is still out on the degree of impact it had on many of them. But there is no historical evidence that Wycliffism *dominated* the minds of all those who led or lived through these events in the way we sometimes assume today. Less studied have been the other radical and controversial positions, some of which were harshly punished. How or whether these things impacted on Ricardian and early Lancastrian writers is very difficult to assess, and much of what I hope to do here is to simply open up new possibilities to allow others to explore and judge for themselves. But, at the very least, this history was part of the backdrop against which our authors wrote, and against which they repeatedly elected to use visionary genres themselves.

The history of book condemnations and suspicions in late medieval England will be examined at more leisure, as we proceed in discovering how revelatory theology—whether primarily *intellectual, apocalyptic,* or *mystical* in nature— shaped and challenged fourteenth-century literary culture. These three types are the primary ones discussed in this book: apocalypticism and its antimendicant and often Wycliffite enemies in chapters 1 through 5, mysticism in 6 through 8, and intellectualism in 9 and 10. One of the main earlier sources of radical information on issues we think of as Wycliffite was reformist apocalypticism, and that is where we will begin. Apocalypticism had been one of the most prominent sources of radical thought throughout the fourteenth century, long before Wycliffism was a suspect body of texts. Visionary apocalyptic texts were the first revelatory texts to seek papal protection, the first to engender an ironclad defence of revelatory intellection (*intellectus spiritualis*). This book begins, then, with apocalypticism because without it the work of many radical non-apocalyptic writers like Porete, Ockham, Uthred, Julian, even Wyclif (an eschatological but not an apocalyptic thinker) would have been very different.

Chapter One

SILENCING OPTIMISM

The Criminalizing of Alternative Salvation Histories

Revelatory Theology and the Persecution of the Dead:
Four Confiscated Non-Lollard Authors in Late Medieval England

Long before Lollardy emerged, revelatory theology had been in use as a discourse of radical reform, and it, too, had a history of official censorship.[1] Even Lollards regarded it as rather suspect. Wyclif, for instance, distrusted the orthodoxy of Hildegard of Bingen's revelations because they were unbiblical, "extra fidem scripture," as he said, giving voice to a doubt that had dogged the reception of visionary thought since the formation of the biblical canon.[2]

Although England is usually thought not to have had much heresy before Lollardy, a surprising array of non-Wycliffite tracts, books, and opinions came under suspicion throughout the fourteenth and early fifteenth centuries. Not all suspicions, of course, become official condemnations; not all official condemnations were equally significant.[3] But four areas of suspicion turn up amidst pre- or non-Lollard records of investigations for suspected heresies:

(1) suspicions about the writings of Joachim, and/or later Franciscan Joachites who contravened John XXII's decrees on evangelical poverty;[4]

(2) antimendicantism, especially since the condemnation of William of St. Amour's eschatology, which "evoked the same sense of crisis as the Joachites he attacked";[5]

(3) suspicions about the Continental heresy of the Free Spirit, enigmatically related to sporadic evidence of concern about the rise of radical mysticism, including Marguerite Porete's anonymously transmitted *The Mirror of Simple Souls*;[6]

(4) suspicions about teaching speculative doctrines in the universities, as indicated by the inquisition of Ockham at Avignon, or the condemnation of disendowment theology in Oxford in 1358, or the censuring of Uthred de Boldon's radical salvational theory of *clara visio* in 1368.[7]

What is most striking is that revelatory theologies were implicated in all these areas.

These radical non-Wycliffite writings posed a wholly separate strand of difficulty for the church—a tangled strand of revelatory, speculative, and apocalyptic theologies. The church had been actively suppressing many of these texts, especially the Joachite ones, throughout the thirteenth and fourteenth centuries. That this revelatory material was also being quietly confiscated by English ecclesiastical authorities even during the years of Wycliffite repression has almost entirely escaped modern notice. Thus the *Opus arduum* author, an imprisoned Wycliffite writing in 1389, complains that not only are the bishops burning all the new vernacular religious works, the friars, their "procurators," have taken to confiscating and locking up of the works of William of St. Amour, whose books are enclosed behind locks and doorbars (multis seris et vectibus clauduntur) at Oxford and Salisbury. And also, he continues, they operate through the confiscation and hiding of books (per absconsionem librorum), like those William Ockham wrote *contra papam Romanam*, those of John of Rupescissa, and Peter of John [Olivi]'s *super Apokalipsim*, and such (et talium).[8] These four authors make for very strange bedfellows, and their conjunction here is a mystery which this book will attempt to solve by tracing the complex historical evidence and cross-relations of this fourfold inquisition and its branches, which reached even to women's mysticism.[9]

Olivi and Rupescissa, of course, were Continental Franciscan Joachite apocalyptic writers who had urged the reform of the friars from within and suffered severe persecution (Rupescissa, decades of imprisonment) for doing so. William of St. Amour had been officially condemned in Paris in 1256 for doing the opposite, attacking the friars and Joachimism from without, and for creating a school of eschatological antifraternal thought which was to prove remarkably enduring. Enjoying a huge revival in mid-fourteenth-century England,[10] this "school," for reasons we will explore in chapter 4, was intimately connected with the dissemination of Hildegard of Bingen's writings, as originally poached by William of St. Amour and his circle. It is difficult to know which of Ockham's writings "contra papam" the author means: likely those on the limitations of papal power and (in Ockham's view) the pope's erroneous ideas on Franciscan poverty and the beatific vision, all produced from exile abroad. But aspects of his salvational theology also came under inquisition, and what perhaps most interested the *Opus* author was Ockham's politics. This would include his polemical works like *An princeps*, written home to England, arguing that King Edward ought to be able to avail himself of clerical property during time of war, and that the secular powers had the right to confiscate goods from corrupt clergy ("faith should not be kept with a faithless enemy" was his pungent comment). Similar sentiments appear in a work translated by John Trevisa and falsely attributed to Ockham, which may also account for some official alarm.[11]

Why did the English authorities care about these particular authors in 1389? What all four confiscated writers had in common was that they had come into conflict with the papacy in some way; moreover, three of them had advocated disendowment or voluntary poverty (prophetically or otherwise), and three had written alternative eschatology of some kind. Only one of the writers (Ockham) had ever lived in England. Most puzzling, in view of the complaint raised in 1389, is that another thing the four writers had in common was that they were dead—by this time, well and truly dead (John of Rupescissa, the youngest, had died about 1365, some twenty-five years earlier; the two oldest, William of St. Amour and Peter John Olivi, both died before the thirteenth century was out). This was truly an inquisition of the dead and, for us today, a surprising one. It is too often assumed that Joachite writers (which would include Olivi and Rupescissa) exerted no influence whatsoever in late fourteenth-century England,[12] but apparently the contemporary authorities knew better than modern scholars—no one bothers to lock up material they do not consider influential. Nor can we explain these confiscations simply by saying that the English church was so rattled by mounting Wycliffism that paranoia had set in, because Wycliffites were by this time "uniformly and shrilly hostile" to the friars.[13] Wyclif had himself made no explicit reference to two of them (Olivi and Rupescissa) and little reference to the others. However much he might have agreed with some selective aspects of their reformist polemical positions, he firmly denounced the prophetic genres in which three of the four wrote. These genres were entirely antithetical to his manner of thought and to many of his disciples. In one scathing comment, for instance, Wyclif dismissed Joachim ("vanam abbas Joachym") and all other deluded "calculatores" who try to predict the End.[14] Ockham, presumably a more congenial figure for Wyclif in intellectual terms, is cited very rarely in his works. Even William of St. Amour, a writer one would think virtually a kindred spirit for the later Wyclif, appears rarely enough in his works that his modern cataloguer, W. R. Thomson, exclaims over a citation.[15]

Even a generation later, when Thomas Netter was writing his comprehensive *Doctrinale* against the Wycliffites and names three of these writers, none of them is given more than passing notice.[16] What, then, were these early confiscators looking for? Apparently they were looking for the already established heretical writers whose impact on the fourteenth century, by 1389, was a known quantity and whose presence or precedent they darkly suspected. Judging from their list they were especially interested in Joachite writers of Franciscan Spiritual persuasion. But Joachim in particular was, at best, alien to Wycliffites, at worst, even overtly cursed.[17] Thus, the very author of the *Opus arduum* who protests the confiscations of Rupescissa and Olivi elsewhere condemns (attributing it directly to Joachim of Fiore himself) the radical pseudo-Joachite view that the time for "the gospel law" (lege ewangelica apostolica) is passing and that it has been superseded by the "new law of the Holy Spirit" (nova lex quam spiritus sancti appellavit [fol. 143v, col. a]), an opinion, he says, that is condemned as the most impious of doctrinal abominations (tamquam nephandissimum abominationibus catholicis improbatur [col. a–b]). As we will see in a later chapter, the *Opus* author's own relation to the confiscated Franciscan writers was a complex one, but he leaves no doubt about where he stood on Joachim himself.[18] Even Wycliffite writers, then, were nervous or contemptuous about the orthodoxy of Joachimism. Non-biblical revelatory genres made them very uncomfortable, and those few who did borrow from them usually did so on the sly—and sometimes under cover of avowed condemnation, as here, or by altering what they borrowed.[19] What they were looking for was antimendicantism, antipapalism, and pro-disendowment propaganda, topics in plentiful supply in late Joachimism and Hildegardiana. But the combination of the revelatory genres in each writer and the history of brutal persecution that Franciscan Joachimism carried throughout the fourteenth century kept Wycliffites away—and in droves.[20]

The revelatory literature kept intruding itself, however, into their domain, most often in works not Wycliffite in content, but easily mistaken for Wycliffism by the causal scribe or reader. So, for instance, in 1388, a year before the *Opus* was written, Thomas Wimbledon gave "the most famous sermon ever delivered at Paul's Cross" in London. In it, Wimbledon was doing something which was expressly forbidden and which we have just seen Wyclif condemn in Joachim: calculating the time of the coming of Antichrist and the End. Others had done it recently, too, but usually in the privacy of a Benedictine scriptorium, or in an unsigned prophetic collection, or, more rarely, a university lecture, but not normally from the pulpit, and not in the vernacular.[21] Thus Wyclif's contemporary, the celebrated Oxford astronomer John Ashenden, had denounced a colleague (socius) for a lecture in which he proved "the same unacceptable conclusion as the Abbot Joachim . . . who tried to determine exactly [determinare certum] the date of the end of the world."[22] This denunciation would have been in Latin, yet Wimbledon's vernacular sermon, with its prominent and respectful Hildegard and Joachim quotations, was one of a number of such texts being circulated alongside Wycliffite material and swelling the ranks of originally non-aligned books now under vague suspicion.[23]

Not many years after Wyclif died, some of his enemies and academic disciples noticed the dangerous alliance of Wycliffite and prophetic texts. Hildegard's presence in reformist territory had been mostly an annoyance for Wyclif personally, of the same ilk, he said, as Merlin, and just as easily dismissed. Joachim's works were different: they were officially unorthodox, and Wycliffites had enough of their own problems in that department. More worryingly still, Joachimism, which had long ago infiltrated the Franciscan Spiritual movement, had contributed to the deaths of many in the very recent past for tenets similar to Wycliffism, and Wycliffites were concerned about martyrdom, at least by 1382. Even an earlier work like *Piers Plowman*, since 1381 publicly associated with the executed John Ball and already being enmeshed in a tangle of reception and imitation issues with Wycliffism, was laced with just this kind of prophecy (as compilers of *Piers* manuscripts were well aware).[24] As we will see, the *Opus* author was not alone in his desperate attempt to salvage reformist ideology and dissociate the movement from Joachim.[25]

The problem for Wycliffites of dangerous associations was broader still, as the *Opus* author's list intimates. Joachite, Olivian, Ockhamist, and Amourian thought had already prompted arrests, suspicions, inquisitions, or official action of various sorts in England prior to the rise of Wycliffism. Free Spiritism, a phenomenon the papacy had investigated since the time of the Council of Vienne alongside Olivian *Beguini* or *Beguin(a)e,* was also implicated in certain Wycliffite trials.[26] Although all the evidence is still not in, there is enough to indicate that the struggle for orthodox ground in England in the 1380s was no longer—if, indeed it had ever been—simply a binary one.[27]

To understand any of the confiscations and condemnations mentioned above, we must first understand the history of two massive controverted topics, both, in late medieval England, associated with revelatory theology: alternative salvation histories and (more closely related than scholars have realized) alternative salvation theology. The first five chapters address alternative salvation *histories* and some of the ways they impacted on Chaucer and especially Langland. The last two examine Chaucer and Langland in relation to alternative salvation *theology.* The three intervening chapters look at radical Continental influence in English female mysticism. To do any of this, however, we must start briefly with the two twelfth-century figures who tried most prominently to create a safe space in orthodoxy for revelatory theology. Or so they hoped.

Two Twelfth-Century Visionaries under Papal Protection

The story of revelatory books under suspicion in late medieval England begins where we might least expect it: with books under papal protection, that is, books thought at the point of their inception, during the reformist controversies of the twelfth century, to be so controversial that their authors claimed the special protection of the papacy. Hildegard of Bingen and Joachim of Fiore— the inseparable twins of all late medieval discussion of reformist revelation— are also the starting point in the later Middle Ages for censorship issues in revelatory thought of all kinds. This is because Hildegard's *Scivias* was virtually the first medieval work *of any genre* to lay claim to papal approval.[28] And Joachim of Fiore's prophetic writings were the second such case.[29] What this tells us is that revelatory writing, and especially writing that offered controversial reformist thought, was felt from very early on in the twelfth century, indeed, during the authors' active careers, to need special protection.[30]

Both writers also laid claim to something even more powerful: divine inspiration. This was visionary, for Hildegard, largely in Augustine's second sense; for Joachim, it was intellectual vision, largely in Augustine's third sense,[31] or, as Joachim chose to call the experience, *intellectus spiritualis.* Utterly independently of each other, they set a massive new precedent for authorization of radical political and theological thought, repeatedly acknowledged throughout the remainder of the Middle Ages.

Hildegard's reputation for both gifts, divine and papal, was international, long-lived, and influential during the powerful vogue her writings enjoyed in fourteenth-century England.[32] A full survey of the nature, scope, and creativity of Hildegard's visionary works and the question of their approval by Pope Eugenius and his mentor, Bernard of Clairvaux, are topics that would take us far beyond, or better, *before* the scope of this study.[33] However, we can get a flavour of the awe she inspired from a remark by one of her contemporaries, who wrote that Hildegard was learned only as the Psalmist David was, that is, taught through the Holy Spirit (Spiritum sanctum edocta). Yet concerning her revelations ("de divinis oraculis et sacramentis sibi revelatis"), he writes, not only were they approved (canonizata) by Pope Eugenius, but caused to be numbered, remarkably, "inter sacras scripturas."[34] This would make her not only the first "approved woman" (in the sense that Bridget of Sweden, Catherine of Siena, and Mechthild of Hackeborn were believed to be later on), but nearly the first approved writer *of either gender* in the Middle Ages.[35]

As we will see in chapter 4, even this remarkable and widely publicized claim did not prevent her works from encountering suspicions, and especially with later scholastics — those, that is, trained in an entirely different mode of thought from the Cistercian one that dominated the papacies under which Hildegard and Joachim flourished.

Testimony to Joachim's claims to papal approval survives in two manuscripts containing his genuine works, stating that Pope Lucius III "approved and confirmed [them] in perpetuity" (canonizavit ac in perpetuum confirmavit).[36] Luke of Cosenza's memoir of Joachim tells us that "in the presence of the Lord Pope and his consistory, he began to reveal understanding of the scriptures" (revelare intelligentiam Scripturarum).[37] It was this pope, as Luke goes on to say, "from whom he received license for writing, and he began to write" (a quo et licentiam scribendi obtinuit, et scribere coepit). Furthermore, Joachim lists the *approbationes* he had received from three popes, Lucius, Urban, and Clement, in his testamentary letter of 1200, while urging the future leadership of his order to also submit themselves to the Holy See:

> Let them receive correction from that same Seat in my place and *explain my faith and devotion to it*. I have always been prepared to hold what it

commanded or will command. I would defend no view of mine against its holy faith . . . firmly believing that the gates of hell will not prevail against it.[38]

Joachim, a true prophet on this point at least, saw that his followers would have some explaining to do. Although often accepted as orthodox, not much more than a decade after his death, Joachim would come under posthumous censure, and his name would become a flashpoint for controversy and sometimes even anathema for centuries to come.

The fates of these two visionaries, and their massive reputations, would be very different. Hildegard would remain an approved voice for most medieval readers, but at times suspect among scholastic readers, mainly because of her visionary method. Joachim would go down in history as a highly contested voice, overshadowed by condemnation. And their reception in late medieval England would be no different than anywhere else, excepting the fact that Joachim was even more suspect there, and Hildegard even more popular.

The Early History of Alternative Eschatology and Salvation Theologies: Pre-existing Rivals to Wycliffite Thought

For at least a millennium after his death, Augustine was the single most influential eschatological thinker known to Western Christendom. As Bernard McGinn puts it simply, "Augustine is the fountainhead of all anti-apocalyptic eschatology in the Middle Ages."[39] His ideas had so powerful a hold on both the institutional church and the doctrinal literature which earned its approval that Augustinian eschatology became the default position, so to speak, of medieval orthodoxy. Heavily endorsed by the schoolmen from about the mid-thirteenth century onward,[40] Augustinian eschatology reigned throughout the later Middle Ages untoppled, but not unchallenged. We will look here at the significant few who dared to differ with Augustine, and so with the medieval church, on the course and consummation of salvation history and which groups would live eternally to enjoy it.

Even though they likely never knew each other in any way, the most important late medieval challenges to Augustinian eschatology were initially posed by our two earliest writers under papal protection—Hildegard, who lived and preached in the Rhine region, and her slightly younger contemporary, Joachim of Fiore, who wrote and prophesied far to the south, in Calabria. They independently founded the two great revelatory apocalyptic traditions which came closest (if and when anything did) to challenging the Augustinian eschatological monopoly of the later Middle Ages. It is no accident that both Hildegard and Joachim were monastic thinkers, both products of what Giles Constable calls the "Reformation of the Twelfth Century."[41] Each developed a unique reformist apocalypticism, by which I mean an apocalypticism that prophesied both major church reform and unparalleled spiritual renewal *here on earth*, before, not after the end of history.[42]

In *City of God*, 22.30, Augustine had placed the Sabbath of his World Week, the last of his Seven Ages, *after* the Second Coming and the Last Judgement. In doing so, he effectively closed the door on the possibility of universal spiritual renewal on this earth.[43] Hildegard, by contrast, predicted two future periods of massive renewal, not counting the period of bliss immediately following the demise of Antichrist (this period, of the so-called "refreshment of the saints," brief in most medieval exegesis, is in Hildegard of undetermined length).[44] Joachim's apocalyptic exegesis was even bolder; he placed the largest period of renewal immediately *after* the greatest of the Antichrists (whom he believed to be imminent).[45] This period was Joachim's glorious Third Age, or, more accurately "Status" (that is, *state* or *condition*) of world history—the word seems to imply for Joachim, a spiritual state more than a literal utopian condition. In chapter 4 of the *Liber concordia*, Joachim explains these three periods, initially using the word "tempus," and then consciously shifting to "status": "Thus the harvest or the particular property of the first *tempus*—or as we ought better say of the first *status*—lasted from Abraham to Zachary, the father of John the Baptist."[46]

Neither Hildegard nor Joachim was a millennialist in the strict sense of the term,[47] but both believed that the best of history was still to come—and that made them unusual among medieval theologians. It also made them potentially doctrinally dangerous. Hildegard's reformist apocalypticism was never directly condemned, but she became, in the thirteenth and fourteenth centuries, the pet of closet radicals and of various and variously censured groups across northern Europe (including the antimendicants, certain Franciscan Spirituals, the Flagellants, certain Wycliffites, and eventually the Protestant reformers).[48] Some of these groups were repressed by brutal measures, even though Hildegard's work itself was not. But even more overtly dangerous to the church was Joachim's reformist apocalypticism, which, especially in the clumsier hands of his more radical thirteenth-century disciples, spawned a spectacular and bloody series of church condemnations, particularly among *Beguini/ae* and Franciscan Spirituals. It is these condemnations — the Joachite ones — and their legacy that would deeply affect reformist revelatory spirituality in the fourteenth century.

Why so much fuss — indeed, so much bloodshed — over what, after all, no one could prove? Among the many beliefs human beings have persecuted each other for, opinion about the course of the future seems particularly gratuitous.[49] But the polemical thrust of reformist apocalypticism was by its very nature anti-institutional. As Curt Bostick writes, the traditional Augustinian eschatology was very pro-institutional: "Its appeal lay in its promise that although Antichrist will wreak havoc across the globe, one may find safe harbor in the confines of the church."[50] Augustinian eschatology was, then, doctrinally and politically a great boon to the official church, but that was where its psychological comforts ended. Not only was there to be no coming *renovatio* (spiritual or otherwise) here on earth, there was also no way to measure history or chart its course, because Augustine had no patience with historicization: "Now this age is the sixth, to be measured by no number [Sexta nunc agitur nullo generationum numero metienda], because of that which is spoken: 'It is not for you to know the seasons, which the Father has placed in His own power (Acts 1:7)'" (*City of God*, 22.30). So in the Augustinian model — at least, as the late medieval church came to perpetuate it — aside from attending to one's own interior reformation and good works, one could only watch and pray, but for what? A collectively dismal earthly end. Alternative apocalypticism, however, usually called for social activity: it urged reform (institutional as well as personal), predicted hope, enunciated signs. From this perspective, contemporary political and ecclesiastical leaders were either part of the problem or part of the solution, so to speak, but either way, they mattered. Although not necessarily heretical, reformist apocalypticism was rife with predictions disturbing to current church governments: such as the Joachite view that the papacy, representing the active life of the church, would decline in importance during the Third Status, and that this would be heralded by violent reform or even annihilation of corrupt church institutions; or that new orders of "spiritual men" would arise, who, rejecting temporal ecclesiastical possessions, would lead the church triumphantly into a full religious *renovatio*, fully realized here on earth.[51]

These factors, as any student of late medieval England immediately realizes, would make Joachimism a direct threat to — that is, a dangerous competitor with — the new Wycliffite project. One reason for this is that reformist apocalyptic thinkers unlike their Wycliffite counterparts have, in certain specific senses, "secular imaginations," in the phrase of Robert Markus.[52] These late medieval apocalyptic thinkers are much more preoccupied with the mixed "secular" realm, invoking a model of an earthly Jerusalem or blessed state *prior to the eschaton* and resisting what might be thought of as the classically apocalyptic impetus to escape it. There are two key areas in which they depart from Augustine's pervasive vision as it is articulated in *City of God*.[53] In *City of God*, of course, he not only refuses to historicize his interpretation of the biblical apocalyptic texts (that is, to read current events into them), he also demolishes apocalyptic systems of reckoning. So, for instance, he scotches the counting up of the ten persecutions (by analogy with the Old Testament's plagues of Egypt), and this though he is not elsewhere shy of numerological interpretation. He also dismisses others' claims to possess the spirit of prophecy. Here he is in *City of God*, 18.52:

> But I think that that is not to be rashly affirmed, which some do think, namely, that the Church will suffer no more persecutions until Antichrist's time than the ten already passed, and that his shall be the eleventh and last. . . . For some hold the plagues of Egypt being ten in number before Israel's freedom to have reference to these . . . but I take not those events in Egypt to be in any way pertinent unto these, either as prophecies or figures, although they that hold otherwise have made a very ingenious [ingeniose] adaptation of the one to the other, but not by the spirit of prophecy [non prophetico spiritu], but only by human conjecture [coniectura mentis humanae], which sometimes may err, as well as not.

What is striking about this passage—reading it backward, so to speak, from a late medieval perspective—is that in it Augustine deconstructs, with a mixture of common sense and earthly pessimism, three of the premises upon which later medieval alternative apocalypticisms were also based:

(1) that progressive persecutions or periods of Antichrist's activity could be counted and measured;
(2) that biblical concordances (here, the pre-Christian plagues of Egypt) could be used to forecast, by extrapolation, what would happen during the Christian history;
(3) that human conjecture, so difficult to tell from the spirit of prophecy, can add anything to the sum of received Christian revelation.

The medieval church would later share, or at least aspire to share, Augustine's confidence in distinguishing the difference between conjecture and prophecy, and so would Wyclif.[54] In this Wyclif was not only utterly orthodox, but on the conservative side of orthodox. What is especially noticeable about Augustine's position is how bleak it is: his main argument against the ten persecutions is that ten is not nearly a big enough number, and the rest of the argument spirals into a litany of uncounted persecutions, such as the stoning of Stephen, the imprisoning of Peter, and his trump card, "But what will they that hold this affirm of the persecution wherein Christ was killed?"[55]

Most of this is very persuasive (Augustine is always persuasive; persuasion was his profession), but it is extremely pessimistic in earthly terms. So, too, is his reading of the Thessalonians passage on the unnamed "withholder" of the mystery of iniquity, that is, the force described enigmatically by St. Paul in 2 Thessalonians 2:7 which would hold back the tide of Antichrist: "St. Paul's words to the Thessalonians about the manifestations of Antichrist, whose times shall *immediately forerun* the day of the Lord," as a rubric to *City of God*, 20.19 runs. It is no wonder, then, that some visionaries of the later Middle Ages wearied of the Augustinian vision of a world merely worsening toward an end worse yet.

But such visionaries were not, as one might assume, just starry-eyed idealists. Hildegard's decisive break with Augustinian tradition was provoked by her disillusionment with the institutional church, currently torn by schism and imperial politics. Theologically she was inspired by the symbolist method of reading biblical concordances, which led her to assert, for instance, that since there had been peace prior to the First Coming of Christ, so too, there would be an era of peace before the Second.[56] During this time Hildegard also foresaw the conversion of the Jews, which was to be an increasingly important theme for late medieval apocalyptic thinkers. The unnamed "withholder" was, for Hildegard, not the church (as it was for more conservative theologians of her day). Nor was it, for her, the Roman Empire—even Augustine was willing to pay Rome, and historicizing theology, this compliment in *City of God*, 20.19. The mysterious "withholder" for Hildegard (as for Langland, two centuries later) represented the faithful remnant, the beleaguered heirs of the Gregorian reformers, struggling against not only evil outside the church, but evil within it. She placed no real faith in the church as an international institution, nor any in the empire—*neither*, she believed, would stand the test of time.[57] And now we are coming to see something of why she sought papal protection.[58] And why her writings posed such a problem for Wyclif's project. Her authority was extra-biblical, and therefore, for him, dubious however attractive her reformist ideas. Joachim's prophecies were worse, he thought, because they actually deluded. Wyclif's largely harsh reaction against Hildegard and modern prophets generally, I would suggest, was in part a recognition that to take such revelatory reformist thinkers into the fold was perilous.

Joachim and the Foundations of the Joachite Tradition

Joachim and the Joachite tradition he inspired also represented a rival to the Wycliffite movement, and a much more dangerous one than Hildegard. It, too, offered a programme of serious church reform, also eschatological in conception, like Wyclif's own. But the Joachite materials were an attractive alternative because of their renewalism (not normally found in Wycliffite eschatology) and their much more humane salvation theology (the opposite of Wycliffite predestination). By the late fourteenth century, however, Joachite history was in part a history of martyrdom. This is a history of bloody repression for which nothing, certainly not the history of Hildegard's reception, prepares us. As we will see, Wyclif, Hereford, and others in the Lollard movement were well aware from the earliest days of the risks Joachimism posed. And the confiscation and mutilation of Joachite materials in England during this period tends to confirm the realism of their concerns.

As in Hildegard, the conversion of the Jews and the fate of the institutional church were radical themes in Joachim's thought, but with some dramatic consequences. His optimistic salvation history foresaw not only an austere reform of the church and universal spiritual blessedness to come, but also the salvation of the non-Christian peoples. This was based on an unusual exegetical privileging of the Jews, even Old Testament women, and of anticipated evangelical orders of *viri spirituali* "spiritual men."[59] The result, especially when it was gripped with missionary zeal by the newly formed mendicant movements, was an explosive reception history no one, least of all Joachim, could have predicted.

Joachim himself had departed decisively from Augustine's anti-millenarianism to show, as McGinn says of his *Liber concordia* (Book of Concordances), "the gradual transition of slavery to freedom in the course of the history of salvation."[60] For Joachim the concordances between Old and New Testaments revealed not just an internal historical logic, but provided clues to the coming

Third Status of history. His trinitarian theology of history was perhaps Joachim's most misunderstood—certainly his most abused—concept. What less subtle disciples and opportunists never understood was that the three *status* are not simply progressive, but overlapping, and organic (Joachim, always a visual thinker, diagrammed this as three overlapping circles, figure 2a).[61] Joachim's theory, known to Middle English scholars since the nineteenth century because of its suggestiveness for Langland's portrayal of salvation history, ran as follows: the First Status, associated with the Father, began with Adam and lasted until Christ; its most fruitful period was during the Old Testament Patriarchs' time, its mode of religious perfection, marriage. The Second Status, associated with Christ, ran from Josiah to the present; its most fruitful period began with the life of Christ, its characteristic mode of perfection, clerical or pastoral service. The Third, associated with the Holy Spirit, began with monasticism and will run to the end of time; its most fruitful period would represent the zenith of contemplative life, still to come.[62] This broad, threefold movement across salvation history, from marriage to active ministry to the building of contemplative community, has had resonance for scholars in relation to the fluid temporal shifts in *Piers Plowman* and changes in Langland's hero, Piers.

If for Shakespeare all the world's a stage, for Joachim, it is a monastery. In his *Liber figurarum,* the most famous copy of which has been in Corpus Christi College, Oxford (MS 255A), since the sixteenth century (if not earlier), he diagrammed the Third Status as seven oratories, in which each group, including the married, would live in peaceable, humanely regulated contentment. These regulations are given in some detail. In the seventh oratory the married, for instance, will hold food and clothing in common, will fast on Fridays, and wear simple, undyed clothing. This clothing will be woven by approved women who will also teach doctrine to the young girls—a passage that may have sown some of the seeds of the southern beguine movement, strands of which eventually came under church censorship.[63]

Also misunderstood, and dangerously so, was his view of the Second Status as the glory of Peter, who epitomized the active ministry of the church, and the pope himself, while the Third was to be the glory of John, who epitomized the contemplative life. His ideas were based on intricate biblical exegesis: e.g., in the Gospel account, Peter had entered Christ's sepulchre first, though John was the first to arrive and the last to enter; similarly, Christ had foretold Peter's death, but had told John to tarry until his Coming.[64] As Joachim wrote in his *Expositio in Apocalypsim,* reflecting on the vision of the church as Mt. Sion in

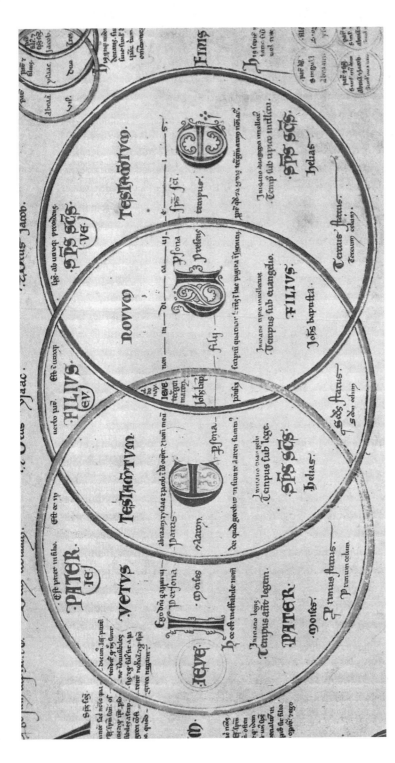

2a. Oxford, Corpus Christi College, MS 255A, fol. 7v, showing Joachim's own trinitarian diagram of the three *status* of history: the first circle represents God the Father and the Old Testament period, the second circle represents Christ, and interlocks both with the first and third circle, which represents the Holy Spirit. The fact that the third circle interlocks with both the first and second indicates Joachim's belief in the "double procession" of the Holy Spirit from both the Father and the Son; the fact that the two words "novvm testamentvm" link the second and third circle indicates that the New Testament is not ever to be superceded by Joachim, a subtely lost on later followers. The heresy that the New Testament would be superceded was condemned in the Protocol of Anagni. Reproduced by permission of the President and Fellows of Corpus Christi College, Oxford.

St. John's Revelation: "Great Peter, Prince of the apostles and of all the prelates of the Church: but oh how happy is John. . . . This one [Peter] greater in glory, that one [John] happier in love."[65] One can see how quickly this precision instrument of creative exegesis could become a blunt tool—in fact, an antipapal bludgeon. And after his death, it did—and so notoriously a feature of Joachite thought as to be very precisely satirized in *The Romance of the Rose*.[66] More potentially dangerous still, the monastic life of the Third Status was characterized not only by prayer, peace, and contemplation, but by *intellectus spiritualis*—a kind of direct, *unmediated* spiritual understanding.[67] Any kind of claim to unmediated knowledge or privilege could be a real stumbling block for medieval church authorities and inquisitors. These ideas would form part of the basis for the condemnation of his most brilliant follower, Peter Olivi, and, ultimately, for Franciscan and lay bloodshed that would have been unimaginable to Joachim himself. Even though the traditional roles of the institutional church seem less and less important in Joachim's thought, anti-institutionalism was never his intention, and, as we have seen, he submitted all his works to the church for correction.

But his trinitarian theology, from which all his apocalypticism sprung, was the first thing to get him into hot water with the authorities, and was formally condemned in 1215, thirteen years after his death. This was merely an academic condemnation, unfortunately for Joachim occurring at one of the most influential councils of the later Middle Ages, the Fourth Lateran Council. The condemnation turned on his conception that two persons of the Trinity, the Son and Holy Spirit, proceed from the Father; and that one proceeds from two, that is, the Holy Spirit from the Father and Son, as shown in his famous and often reproduced trinitarian diagram of the three overlapping spheres (figure 2a).[68] The condemnation was particularly disastrous for Joachim in English reception because the English took the teachings of the Fourth Lateran Council so seriously. English attitudes toward Joachimism are the subject of our next chapter, but Wyclif's attitude toward Joachim's condemnation will suffice for the moment as very typical of those of his countrymen. In his *De universalibus* he twice breaks off his commentary to insist that Joachim's heresy arose through ignorance of the nature of universals (ex ignorancia universalium dixit [i.e., Joachim] falsissimum et summe hereticum). Citing the original famous decretals from the Fourth Lateran Council, he repeats the harsh incipit of the condemnation of Joachim's "little book" (*Dampnamus et reprobamus* libellum abbatis Ioachim), written against Peter Lombard on the unity or essence of the Trinity (contra magistrum Petrum

Lumbardum de unitate seu essencia trinitatis).[69] Wyclif's comments are illuminating, technically scholastic though they are, because they show Wyclif *defending orthodoxy* with all the righteous indignation imaginable:

> Thus it was by the eternal ordinance of the Holy Spirit that the faithful doctors of the church, gathered together to treat the dispute between Abbot Joachim and master Peter Lombard, were so instructed in the truths of universals that they saw that a personal action within the divinity was not to be attributed to the divine nature, just as a universal nature cannot be predicated in this way, since acts are acts of persons.

Joachim himself had some premonition of the problem: "I do not say this in order that one should believe that the kingdom or the work of one person [of the Trinity] should be divided from the kingdom or work of the two other persons—that would be abhorrent to the hearts of believers."[70] But, sadly, his theological distinctions proved too subtle for most of his later readers. This was a relatively abstract theological problem and, in the end, this was not what caused him his largest posthumous difficulty; it was another aspect of his trinitarian theology, his unusually optimistic apocalypticism. As McGinn says, "Joachim was adamant" that the Third Status would reach a level of perfection "unimaginable to those still trapped in the trials of the present. Thus there is no reason to hesitate over calling Joachim's a theology of progress, as long as we remember that this advance [for him] is not man's doing but the work of the Holy Spirit."[71] Still, theology of progress was a problem for the medieval church, especially one that hinted that Peter's primacy would fall away.

The evolution of further diagrams in this trinitarian form by later pseudo-Joachite writers added greatly to this problem. Take, for example, the one at the opening of the popular little figure collection known as the *Praemissiones,* here reproduced from the fourteenth-century manuscript, British Library, Cotton Tiberius B.V., Part II (figure 2b). One can instantly see the way the three status, although shown as overlapping and equally balanced, emphasize the importance of the two new *orders* (ordines) in the Third Status, not the papacy. Entirely missing now is the central inner lobe of figure 2a, with its space for the pope (pontifex). The progression moves from the leadership of figures like Moses and Aaron in the First Status, through Paul and Barnabas in the Second, to the two orders as the witnesses (testes) in the Third. Peter now figures nowhere in the scene, for reasons we are about to see.

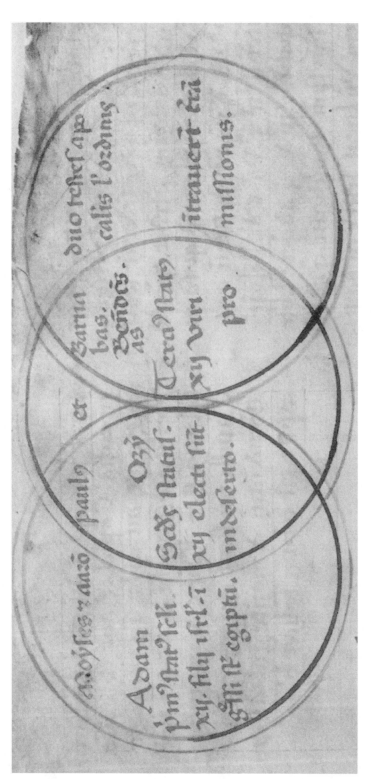

2b. London, British Library, MS Cotton Tiberius B.V, Part II, fol. 1 (fol. 89, old foliation), showing the opening of the *Praemissiones*, a small Joachite figure collection which precedes *Super Esaiam*. The image shows the overlapping of the Second and Third Status, and the prominent role of the two orders in the Third ("duos ordines futuros" represented by the "duos testes" of the Apocalypse), but loses the precision and centrality of Joachim's treatment of the New Testament. Most significantly, it also drops the innermost chamber of the overlapping circles, which in Joachim's original (see 2a) carried the name "of the Son" ([persona] filii), and the name of the pope ([summus] pontifex). Reproduced by permission of the British Library.

Criminalization and Official Suppression of Joachite Thought

Cumque legisset Iudi tres pagellas vel quattuor, scidit illud scalpello scribae et proiecit in igni qui erat super arulam, donec consumeretur omne volumen igni. (Jer. 36:23)

———

And when he had read three or four pages to the King of Judah, he [the king] cut it with a penknife; and he cast it into the fire that was upon the hearth, till all the volume was consumed.

The history of the censorship of Joachim's thought was signified for his thirteenth-century disciples in the stark image from Jeremiah of the king of Judah wielding his penknife.[72] It is an image that would grow more and more apt with each passing generation, and finally horribly apt as Franciscan Joachites went to the flames themselves in the early fourteenth century. How did it happen?

As his testamentary letter indicates, Joachim had died at peace with the church, and during the early years of the thirteenth century, it was only the odd reference to the condemnation of his trinitarian view that troubled his reputation. For a brief period, rather utopian in itself, Joachite views gained official approval when early ministers general of both the Franciscan and Dominican orders overtly supported his prophecies of coming *viri spirituales*—they, of course, believed that their own fledgling religious orders were the realization of the prophecy. All that changed in 1254 with the scandal of the Eternal Evangel.[73] And here we come, at last, to the history of how the optimistic apocalyptic eschatologies were officially silenced.

In 1254 Paris university theologians condemned an introduction to Joachim's works, *Liber introductorius*, written by an injudicious Franciscan adulator, Gerard of Borgo San Donnino. Gerard made headline news by predicting the coming of the Third Status for 1260—a mere six years away—and the triumph of the Franciscan order over all the institutions of the current church. To crown all, he identified Joachim's writings with the "Eternal Evangel (or Gospel)" (the *evangelium aeternum* of Revelation 14:6), declaring them to be about to supersede the *Evangelium Christi*.[74] This "Eternal Gospel," now newly and conveniently published in Gerard's own anthology—one can imagine the booksellers' ads[75]—created one of the immortal scandals of medieval intellectual history, still sizzling nearly a decade or so later when Jean de Meun was writing *The Romance of the Rose*. It was a scandal from which Joachimism never really recovered respectability in official circles. Heads rolled: the saintly Joachite minister general of the Franciscan order, John of Parma, was forced to resign, and another of the great Joachites (*maximi Johacite*),[76] Hugh of Digne, personally known to leading English scholars, retreated into obscurity.

Now alerted to potential doctrinal perils in Joachim's works, condemnations followed thick and fast: the papal commission condemned Gerard's *Liber introductorius* at Anagni in 1255 and raised concerns about Joachim's own writings. The document produced is known as the Protocol of Anagni, and was to become, as we will see, a prize possession of the antimendicant lobby in mid-fourteenth-century England. When William of St. Amour presented the case for the secular clergy against the mendicants to Rome that year, he also took with him a copy of thirty-two excerpts from Gerard's *Liber introductorius*.[77] Innocent IV, too, condemned it, and began to issue bulls curtailing the mendicant's privileges. Finally, one of Gerard's original inquisitors convened an inquisition of Joachim's own works at Arles in 1263.[78] Reading these condemnations today, one has to be struck by how the inquisitors seek refuge in Augustinianism, and also in pessimism, which seems to have been the fashionably orthodox position.[79]

Among condemnatory treatises written at the time by Paris masters, the *Liber de Antichristo* is the fullest anti-Joachite polemic. It is usually attributed to William of St. Amour, or at the very least to one of his camp of antimendicant polemicists. Based on impeccable authorities like Augustine and Gregory the Great, the author forecasts the loss of miraculous power that the church will suffer through corruption as the End approaches, an emphasis intended to counter Joachim's predictions of a coming glorious age of the Spirit.[80] He denies, moreover, that there will be any period at all after Antichrist's defeat. Any outpouring of the Holy Spirit the world was going to have, he insists, was had at the Pentecost (this would become a standard official refutation). He dashes any hope of a coming new order of spiritual men to renew the church—in fact, anything at all that had a melioristic ring to it. Since William and all the likeliest candidates for the authorship of the *Liber* were engaged in a pitched battle with the mendicants over papal privilege and the lucrative business of cure of souls, we may wish to discount it as an objective indication of orthodoxy's anti-Joachimism. Indeed, William of St. Amour's known attacks on the friars were so virulent that they were very shortly condemned themselves by the papacy.[81]

But it is harder to discount Thomas Aquinas, and he sports precisely the same fashion for eschatological cynicism.

Aquinas, in fact, agrees with the antimendicant author of the *Liber de Antichristo* on Joachim and Joachites — a testimony to the credibility of the *Liber*'s position if ever there was one, because Aquinas certainly had no reason to love antimendicant propagandists, whatever sibling rivalry existed between Dominicans and Franciscans. His attacks on Joachim (more measured and respectful than the *Liber*'s) contain, as McGinn points out, a long critique of apocalyptic theologies of history based on Augustine and attacks on Joachim's system of *concordiae* and his Third Status. For Aquinas, too, the Holy Spirit has already divulged all that will be divulged, again, at the time of the Pentecost. Aquinas states that looking for exact correspondences between Old and New Testaments is erroneous, explicitly citing the passage from *City of God* that we noticed above (that is, comparing the ten plagues of Exodus with the ten persecutions of the church, *De Civitate Dei*, 18.52). There is something here not only of Augustine's eschatology, but of his distrust of non-biblical conjecture and contemporary (that is, post-biblical) revelation.[82] Thomas then says, "And the same seems true about the sayings of the Abbot Joachim who predicted some truths about future events through such conjectures [per tales conjecturas], and was deceived in others [et in aliquibus deceptus fuit]."[83] We might note how similar the negative half of this is to the wording in Wyclif's denunciation of Joachim.[84]

Even though Aquinas himself was still considered dangerous reading in the Franciscan order (where the *Summa* circulated only under official correction), it was nonetheless Aquinas's opponent, Peter Olivi, who was to suffer severe official censure when the dust of the pamphlet wars settled.[85] Olivi himself had undergone questioning, formal censorship (in 1283 and before), and the confiscation and burning of his works, but fortunately he never lived to see the brutal persecution of his followers, which began not long after his death in 1299.[86]

Meanwhile, the group of radical Franciscans, who came to be called the Franciscan Spirituals after Joachim's prophecy of "spiritual men," began to encounter condemnation and persecution. These were men who, often also holding Joachite opinions, chose to adhere tenaciously to a strict interpretation of St. Francis's guidelines on personal poverty. From about 1280 to about 1330 there was a protracted struggle between the Spiritual and the Conventual parties within the Franciscan order. Even by the pontificates of Clement V (1309–14) and John XXII (1316–34), a long line of papal bulls had failed to solve the key points at issue — especially the question of how absolute a vow of poverty followers of St. Francis were called upon to uphold. The Conventuals, the majority, believed that accommodations to modern institutional needs of a large order were necessary; the Spirituals, a minority, opposed any but the most stringent denial of ownership.[87] Members of this group would famously carry Joachim's apocalyptic ideas with charisma and fearlessness for decades to come.

By 1316, Michael of Cesena, the minister general of the Franciscan order, had begun an even fiercer campaign against the Spirituals under the newly elected John XXII—a strategy which would eventually backfire, but which caused significant bloodshed before it did. Franciscan Spirituals were rooted out, brought to inquisition, and by 1318 the first of those who refused to recant were burned at Marseilles.[88] The order ruthlessly sought out followers of Olivi, punishing them in convent prisons with a degree of physical cruelty such as modern readers associate with the case histories of Amnesty International. Just one such example will suffice to illustrate how dangerous adhering to an Olivian interpretation of Franciscan poverty could be. The great Franciscan Spiritualist mystic, Ubertino da Casale, pleading on behalf of the wretched prisoners of conscience languishing in convent prisons, tells of the sort of treatment meted out to rank and file Spirituals. A certain Brother Pounce was imprisoned for saying that even though he owned no copies of Olivi's works, if he had them he would "surrender them for correction only to the pope" (that is, he would not surrender them merely to the Franciscan authorities). As if determined to show him how authoritative the order could be, he was thrown in prison and left so tightly fettered that he became ill from sitting in his own excrement. Having finally died, those who buried him found that his body "was eaten away by worms from the loins downwards."[89]

Under such persecution the apocalyptic ideology and rhetoric of the Franciscan Joachites became more and more sensational; and as so often in the history of medieval heresy, some members of what began as an orthodox reformist movement were thrust by circumstance into spiraling heresy. The Spirituals "became a resistance movement, complete with an underground railroad."[90] Ubertino da Casale, saintly and distinguished enough to be untouchable, was allowed to retire as a Benedictine; Angelo of Clareno (the closest to a political leader of the Spirituals) retired as a Celestinian.[91] Lesser men were not as lucky. Ostensibly, of course, these men were suffering for their belief in the radical poverty of Christ (a belief made officially heretical under John XXII).[92] But the inquisitors also looked for radical apocalyptic ideas as a sure marker of the heresy, at least by 1283, especially by 1318.[93] In a strange turn of events, Michael of Cesena eventually fled Avignon, along with William Ockham, when John XXII's policies became more extreme than even Michael's own.[94] Once mixed with the potent scholastic and polemical "heresies" of Ockham, also a Franciscan who opposed John XXII on poverty, this became a heady brew of ideologies.

Conditions were not much better during the decades from about 1340 to about 1365, when Olivi's most famous disciple, John of Rupescissa, was writing from Franciscan and papal prisons.[95] Speaking of the Apocalypse prediction that Satan would be bound for 1,000 years, he says that Augustine "did not interpret this well" and that Joachim, who prophesied that *after* Antichrist the world would enjoy an unprecedented spiritual *renovatio*, was closer to the true interpretation.[96] John's projections of coming tribulation for the clergy included mass uprisings of the laity which he saw as *iusticia popularis*, a papacy reduced to barefoot poverty, and a schism (all, by the way, later to be read with great interest in fourteenth-century England amidst rising Wycliffism, anti-papalism, the Great Schism, and the revolt of 1381).[97] Rupescissa's pronouncements were couched as exegetical insight and would hardly seem to have deserved terrible persecution.[98] But the conditions of his imprisonment were appalling: he writes poignantly of being fettered so closely and inhumanely for weeks that he suffered many of the same horrors as Brother Pounce did, his clothing gradually disintegrating from his body.[99] Harshnesss seems to have been standard treatment for Spirituals over the decades they were persecuted—John, in fact, more famous than some and protected in part by his claim to see by *visione intellectuali*,[100] perhaps fared better. That a religious order would take such measures against its own members is staggering, but it reminds us how deeply threatened the authorities actually were by the Joachite and especially the Olivian dimension of the poverty controversies. Olivi was, by Rupescissa's time, such a dangerous author that Rupescissa draws upon his work extensively but only silently,[101] as would the author of the English *Opus arduum* as late as 1389–90. Rupescissa, less cautious and more sensational in every way, had repeatedly prophesied violent clerical chastisement and stripping away of ecclesiastical temporalities, most pithily in his popular *libellus*, the *Vade mecum in tribulatione*. The English had extensive access to Rupescissa's works, extant in over a dozen English copies,[102] and even during the days of his imprisonment in the mid-fourteenth century, manuscripts began to cross the Channel.[103]

It is difficult to summarize in a few words exactly what it was about Olivi's Joachite apocalypticism that so threatened the authorities (both the Franciscan order and, later, the papacy). Olivi had prophesied that ecclesiastical possessions would no longer be necessary in the Third Status,[104] and had deplored the fact, as David Burr writes, that "[c]arnal elements outside the [Franciscan] order insist that evangelical perfection is achieved, not by renouncing all possessions, but by having them in common, while carnal elements within it argue that it is not an essential element in the highest poverty."[105] Central to Olivi's thought is the seven period divisions of history (in Joachim's system the seven *tempora,* most often, we will see, highlighted and annotated in English manuscripts of Joachim's thought).[106] For Olivi the fifth *tempus* would be a period of corruption in the church, while the sixth would be a period of Antichrist's persecution and of evangelical renewal (that is, the persecution of those trying to bring about the renewal, especially through adherence to apostolic poverty). The seventh would be a period of spiritual peace and contemplation. For him, too, the attack of the Paris masters spearheaded by William of St. Amour was a sign that Joachim's generational calculations for the coming of Antichrist were accurate: "Thus in Paris in the forty-second generation there was the persecution by those masters who condemned evangelical mendicancy."[107] Also important in Olivi's thought is the expectation of a "Mystical Antichrist," who would gain political control and set up a pseudopope "who will contrive something against the Evangelical Rule."[108]

But most famous, perhaps, was the series of measures against Olivi's teachings undertaken by John XXII. An eight-man committee began working in 1318 to examine Olivi's commentary on the Book of Revelations.[109] In 1319 the general chapter meeting of the Franciscan order at Marseilles was also culling errors from Olivi's works, and strenuous measures were being taken against followers of his cult (in 1318 Olivi's body was removed from his tomb, the site of miracles, and the tomb destroyed), not unlike strategies for suppressing the revelatory we will see in England in 1405.[110] In 1322 the pope asked a panel of judges to examine the Revelation commentary. The result was a condemnation of four of Olivi's irenic views:[111]

1. that the papacy had originally been given to Peter without temporal possessions, and that although temporal possessions were *justly* held in the current age, in the next (the "contemplative age of John") they would be unnecessary;
2. that a coming Third Status would see a fuller revelation of wisdom from the Holy Spirit (against which view the commission asserts the Pentecost argument, associating Olivi with Gerard's heresy);

3. that the conversion of the Moslems, Jews, and other pagans would come during the Third Status (which the panel sees as an attack on the doctrine of predestination, not unlike later English censorship of Uthred);[112]

4. that pontifical authority will be transferred to an order observing evangelical poverty at some future date.

These condemned views had a charisma and nearly an innocence that made them instantly empathetic, often among lay followers.

In 1322 John XXII himself went through Olivi's Apocalypse commentary, posing theological questions for the panel about the four articles. He was struck by Olivi's belief that during the Third Status knowledge of the Incarnate Word would be so profound as to be available not only by simple *intelligentia*, but also by taste and touch (gustativa et palpativa experientia).[113] This last, I would suggest, was one of the aspects of his thought that may have attracted the empathy of certain Free Spirit devotees, some of whom were enigmatically connected with radical Franciscan Spiritualism, including (or so her interrogators seem to have thought), Marguerite Porete.[114] Shortly after Porete was executed in 1310, the Council of Vienne had been charged to examine the problem of whether the Franciscan Spirituals had been infected with the heresy of *spiritus libertatis*, at the same time as they were examining Olivi's orthodoxy. Olivi's theology upset John XXII so much that he preached a sermon c. 1325–26 saying that Olivi's predictions of greater human knowledge in the final age would make men "not *viatores* but *comprehensores*, needing no mediator."[115] This same fear that the church's mediation would become irrelevant also underlay the censure of Uthred de Boldon[116] (there was, as we will see, a strong connection between the persecutions of this papacy against Ockham, Olivi, Joachim, Thomas of Waleys, and Uthred's later condemnation). In fact, the idea of needing no mediator was often the unstated threat to ecclesiastical authorities confronted with the spectre of revelatory theology. In the years that followed, any Franciscan caught teaching such things as Olivi had dared to write was to be sent to the papacy for questioning, and worse.

Joachim and Wyclif (or: Workman's Shot in the Dark)

And this is precisely what happened to four English Franciscan lectors at Cambridge in 1330—the first episode in a series of Insular persecutions and suspicions of Joachite-related thought we will examine shortly. This brings us to the key question: how did all this repression affect the transmission of alternative salvation theologies in later medieval England—a country traditionally thought to have been untouched by the radical Continental apocalypticism I have been discussing so far? Our next chapter is devoted to answering this question, but first I want to look briefly at the historiography of a preconception that has largely prevented this subject from being studied in the past. That is the widespread myth (comparable in academic circles to urban folklore) that there is no Joachimism in England.[117] Influential books like Herbert Workman's were key to divorcing Wycliffite studies and Joachite studies. Workman, like many older scholars, was extremely well informed about Continental theology, though limited by the state of research at the time. So, for instance, Workman asserted in his biography of Wyclif that the scandal of the Eternal Evangel "had little or no influence in England," and that "the only MS of Joachim in England is at Balliol, Cod. 296 *Contra Lombardum.*"[118] In fact, unknown to Workman, Oxford, Balliol College, MS 296 is the *only* manuscript of the *Contra Lombardum* extant today *anywhere in the world*—its preservation in England is part of an immense, virtually unnoticed, and very serious Insular preoccupation with Joachite materials.[119] That heritage also includes one of only two extant copies—again, *anywhere in the world*—of the Anagni commission's condemnation of Gerard's book.[120] These two items alone, not to mention over sixty others that contain some form of Joachite thought, however popularized, make England a highly important site for the abbot's legacy, both for contemporaries and modern scholars.[121] Yet Workman, knowing none of this, struggles valiantly and repeatedly to explain sporadic Franciscan Joachite "intrusions" into the fourteenth-century world of Wyclif. What is impressive about Workman is that he *recognized* many of them when he bumped into them. He just had no idea how they came to be there.

Of course, Workman was writing in 1926, but in many respects the myth has survived to the present day and has profoundly affected the shape of Wycliffite studies.[122] Not without good reason, however. Not only is English Joachite material still largely uncatalogued, but the few Wycliffites themselves who borrowed directly from it usually did all they could to cover their tracks. Yet Franciscan Spiritualism (which, as we have seen, is not necessarily the same thing as Joachite Franciscan Spiritualism) has long been known to be a factor of some sort in the evolution of Wyclif's thought.[123] The complexity of allegiances can be measured in the fact that many established Franciscan scholars stayed away from Blackfriars in 1382—still reluctant to condemn their ally of old on poverty and disendowment issues.[124] Wyclif himself sometimes expressed admiration for some Franciscan rigorist and polemical ideals, or ideals parallel to them, such as apostolic poverty, mentioning Bonaventure in particular.[125] Of course, to admire Bonaventure is not necessarily to be empathetic with radical Franciscanism, but—after the legislation of John XXII—to insist that Christ owned no possessions *is*.[126] Thus, even though Wyclif's views were mixed, and even though they changed to hostility after he felt the friars let him down, still there was just enough overlap that Wyclif, Hereford, and other well-informed members of the movement must have felt some vulnerability in the face of Franciscan history. English chronicles, as Workman showed, were full of accounts of the burnings of hundreds of Spirituals abroad, and the English on tour of duty in southern France in the fourteenth century were intimate with events and culture there.[127] English clergy used many of the same manuals as their Continental counterparts, and they all used the same canon law.[128] It is no wonder then perhaps, as Workman points out, that "frequent but misleading references in Wyclif's works to possible death for his opinions" appear.[129] And even *before* Blackfriars itself, Nicholas Hereford feared martyrdom more than anything else. For Englishmen in their generation the most recent and current knowledge of such a fate suffered for similar principles to theirs was Franciscan Spiritual martyrdom. And they knew, as learned men, that that was exactly where prospective inquisitors would turn in a system of heresy law based upon precedent.

What kept Wyclif from more overt identification with the Spirituals, then, was first of all danger. As Michael Wilks has astutely written, "radical Franciscan theory" was the pretext "for which he might have been condemned far more successfully than he ever was."[130] And the second reason Wyclif kept his distance was, I would suggest, his utter distrust of the revelatory mode in which writers like Rupescissa and (to a lesser extent) Olivi operated. With Joachim, however, whose works were not as polemically useful, Wyclif had not a shred of empathy or patience. We have seen that Wyclif alludes to Joachim's condemnation in 1215 (knowledge Workman believed he gleaned from Higden's *Chronicle*), and to his being a deluded prophetic "calculator."[131] His other references to Joachim show ignorance and contempt.[132]

This, then, is the broader picture. A full study of Wycliffite relations with Franciscan Spiritualism is beyond the scope of this book, but we will look at several specific cases. For the moment we will take one important example and trace it down to its source in a way that Workman apparently could not. So, for instance, Workman rightly noted what he sensed to be striking parallels between one of the condemned Blackfriars articles (no. 24) and Franciscan Joachimism, the kind of parallel usually unnoticed in more recent scholarship. He connected it to Gerard's *Evangelium eternum,* which he thought the likeliest source of the article.[133] But knowing nothing about its transmission in England, he had to content himself with the assertion that "When Wyclif was a student these ideas *were in the air,* if only by the tradition of Ockham's teaching."[134] We can be a good deal more precise.

The article in question is the opinion that after Urban VI there is not to be another pope, but that national churches should be independent of the papacy, and governed "in the manner of the Greeks, each under its own law" (24. Item quod post Urbanum sextum non est aliquis recipiendus in Papam, sed vivendum est, more Grecorum, sub legibus propriis). It is indeed a curious article, because in the form it appears here it smacks much more of Joachite prophecy than of straight ecclesiastical polemic, and this makes it stand out rather oddly among the Wycliffite opinions. Workman relates the article to a comment by Wyclif "that the Greeks had kept more perfectly the faith of Christ,"[135] which, however, is at best a generalized basis for a much more specific and radical proposition. Recognizing this, Workman adds in the same note "this belief in the Greeks was a mark both of the Spiritual Franciscans and the Waldensians." He gives no specifics, though earlier in the study, as we have seen, Workman associated this condemned article vaguely with Gerard's Eternal Evangel and, again, with Franciscan Spiritual thought. He leaves his reader to do the footwork— and the footnotes.

Indeed, the germ of the idea does appear in Olivi, where it derives from his analysis of the three languages on Christ's cross, and his projection of missions to the Jews and Greeks. For Olivi, the Latin church's rejection of evangelical poverty would soon drive the true apostles of the sixth age to the Greeks: "In the coming days, however, the message will not be heard so readily in the carnal church of the Latins as among the Greeks, Saracens and Jews."[136] And, in fact, in the period immediately after Olivi's death, the Greek church did become "a handy refuge," in David Burr's words, for Spirituals escaping persecution.[137] Moreover, John of Rupescissa, in the Twelfth Conclusion of his *Vade mecum,* predicts the coming of a reforming pope (an "Elijah") who will command that the cardinals will henceforth, to the end of time, be drawn from the Greek church.[138] Furthermore, some of Olivi's *sectatores,* under brutal persecution in the early decades of the fourteenth century, expected a reformation of the church to occur in Constantinople.[139] In short, Workman is right: the source is Franciscan Joachite.

Even more specific to the article condemned, however, is the case of the popular pseudo-Joachite *Vaticinia de summis pontificibus*, where Urban VI is associated with the final pope in some glosses. The *Vaticinia* had a distinguished early transmission history in England (in fact Robert Lerner once argued for its having been composed there), and was well enough known by the mid-fourteenth century to be cited in Middle English.[140] The *Vaticinia* traveled as pictorial prophecies of popes to come, trailing cryptic captions, and these had been on the loose in England from the early fourteenth century. There had originally been two separate sets of these prophecies, but, as Marjorie Reeves has shown, in the second half of the fourteenth century they begin to be joined in transmission to create exactly the kind of Joachite optimism modern scholars too often assume England did not see. This "meant that the figure of Antichrist became less menacing in the middle of the sequence and that it culminated [that is, at the End of Time] in the clear angelic portraits of the first series." This genuinely Joachite sensibility was organized so that "by the time the number fifteen (that is Antichrist) was reached in actuality it could be interpreted as Urban VI and associated with the Schism."[141] This, indeed, is the case in the Benedictine, Henry Kirkestede's own copy, Cambridge, Corpus Christi College MS 404, where it occurs along with Hildegard's prophecies and her own prediction of the decline of the papacy.[142] There, Urban VI is the final pope, and there is no second set of angelic popes to come to redeem the gloomy picture. Henry, a gifted librarian and vigilant polemical eschatologist of the Abbey of Bury St. Edmunds, was also a devout collector and reader of Joachimism. Upset with Urban over the Schism and other local matters, Henry identified the beast on fol. 95r of Corpus Christi 404 as Urban VI (figure 3).[143] The *Vaticinia* prophesies that the fourth pope after Clement VI (1342–52) will be the final one, equal in bestiality to the dragon of the Apocalypse who would pull down the stars. Kirkestede must have made this identification after 1378 (when he recorded the death of Gregory XI). This suggests something we will see repeatedly in this study: the free reign that Benedictines in particular had to collect and study suspect materials, and interpret or annotate them in almost any way they pleased.[144]

The presence of this prophecy as a *condemned* opinion in the Blackfriars' list of 1382 is revealing on several scores. It suggests that Joachite writings in England were infiltrating either anthologies of Wycliffite literature *or* its inquisitorial process. The latter is entirely plausible since inquisition worked by precedent and Franciscan Spirituals were both the most recent and the most doctrinally similar to Wycliffism among heretical groups known in 1382. The former is also plausible given, for instance, the fact that the *Vaticinia* is cited as Joachim's in a reformist Middle English work, *The Last Age of the Church*, dated 1356, but often mistaken for a Wycliffite tract (apparently even by its medieval copyist).[145] This work, as its Victorian editor, J. Todd, showed, was associated with the wildly popular Joachite prophecy, "Gallorum levitas," which in one Insular version contains extra lines referring directly to the persecution of Olivi's *sectatores*.[146] Todd mistakenly attributed *The Last Age* to Wyclif himself and saw it as a sign that Wyclif was reading Olivian literature. The mistake, however, is not unintelligent, and suggests the kind of alertness Workman also had to international influences. The manuscript in which *The Last Age* survives is the Wycliffite anthology of Dublin, Trinity College, 244, which also contains a copy of the Rule of St. Francis. We have a similar case in the presence of Wimbledon's sermon in Oxford, University College MS 97 (which contains Clanvowe's *Two Ways*, the earliest Lollard work by an identifiable author). The sermon has its Hildegard and Joachim references noted prominently in marginal annotations, and MS 97 also has an unnoticed excerpt translated into Middle English from a pseudo-Joachite work embedded in a common Becket prophecy.[147] British Library, Cotton Titus D.XIX has a Wycliffite item added to a little group of prophecies, two of which are usually associated with Joachite materials.[148] And, as a final example, the popular little Joachite poem, "Cum fuerint," is copied at the end of an article on Antichrist in the Wycliffite compilation, the *Floretum*.[149] As these instances suggest, there is *just* enough overlap in the manuscript traditions (much of it apparently inadvertent) to give anyone who disapproves of either Joachim or Wyclif some pause.[150]

Prophetic materials, then, were in broad competition with Wycliffite ones for the hearts and minds of non-aligned readers interested in reformist policy. Langland, for instance, drew on the former and was exploited by the latter; as this book will suggest, his poetry is an important buffer zone between the clash of these two cultures. If it seems odd to think of prophecy as *policy*, we should remember that even the highest authorities of the day like Richard II and Urban VI are on record as acting on visions.[151] We will see a further case of this in the Appellant magnate, Thomas of Woodstock, who—no matter what his actual leanings—had representative works from both prophetic and Wycliffite sources at his seat in Pleshy. Reformist prophecy, moreover, was heavily collected by certain groups of friars, and they had been Wyclif's allies at a very

3. Cambridge, Corpus Christi College, MS 404, fols. 94v–95r, showing Henry Kirkestede's identification of Pope Urban VI as the last pope and beast of Revelation 12:4, written in his copy of the popular pseudo-Joachite *Vaticinia de summis pontificibus*. Urban is preceded by Gregory XI (d. 1378) on 94v. Reproduced by permission of the Master and Fellows of Corpus Christi College, Cambridge.

early stage and had themselves been advocating poverty and disendowment since before Wyclif was born. On the rare occasions when Wycliffites borrow from genuinely revelatory sources like these, they tend (with two exceptions we will discuss in chapter 5) to suppress the revelatory dimension—and their indebtedness.[152] The reason is not far to seek: Joachite texts had been under official condemnation throughout fourteenth-century Europe, including England and Ireland, and—together with certain specific banned antimendicant writings—account for the highest number of Insular condemnations and even burnings before Wyclif. No wonder Wyclif and his confreres were gun shy.[153]

The corollary of this for us as modern scholars is that to explain reformist elements in Middle English writers, we need no longer turn simply to Wycliffism. When we look at the way it interfaces with Wycliffism, then, the history of Franciscan Spiritual persecution and Joachite manuscript transmission in England takes on a new significance. In the next chapter we will look at aspects of this transmission, some of the recorded persecutions, and evidence of manuscript mutilation and suppression of authorship. What we will begin to see is that the Wycliffite project to use biblical revelation to drive out contemporary revelation was an aspect of its ultimate failure, or, if one prefers, "prematurity." What we will learn—and from sources largely unstudied in England—about the attitudes toward revelation is how very capacious they were.

Chapter Two

"THROUGH THE HIDING OF BOOKS"

The Codicological Evidence for Joachite Franciscanism and
Censorship in England before and after Wyclif

"Abbatis Joachim dampnamus scripta": England and the Suppression of Joachimism

In þis tyme was Abbot Joachim in Calabir, þat wrote many þingis vpon
þe Apocalypise, but he erred in many þingis, first in a mater concernyng
þe holy Tryntye, for þe Cherch hath determined his opinion fals in þe beginning of þe *Decretales, capitulo, Dampnamus.* . . . This same abbot mad
also a oþir book, *De Seminibus Literarum,* where be gret craft he droue
oute þe ȝere in whech þe Day of Dome schuld falle; but he failed foule,
and erred in his counting. (John Capgrave)

Given the dramatic Continental history we have just seen, it will come as no
surprise to learn that the *official* English history of contact with Joachimism is a
repressive one, and those willing to sign their names to full-fledged Joachite interpretations or admit to manuscript ownership were few. (And outside of a convent, precious few.) However, official or named items in a manuscript culture

represent at best the tip of the iceberg. The story of Joachite and Franciscan Joachite impact in England is virtually untold, and it is one that has taken me many years to begin to understand. By sifting through the shards left behind in manuscript libraries, citations, and often-fragmentary official records, the early sketches of a history can be made. However, a detailed history of medieval English reception of Joachite thought from the twelfth century onward (starting with the Anglo-Normans on crusade who gave Joachim his first non-Italian audience) is too complex to undertake here. What we can do is briefly mention some of the key points for England,[1] beginning with the widely publicized 1215 condemnation of Joachim in the decrees of the Fourth Lateran Council, for which an English chronicle source is the earliest in Europe, and the most influential.[2] Moreover, the earliest surviving reference to it is an English monastic poem of c. 1220, which versifies the condemnation of Joachim's writings ("Abbatis Joachim dampnamus scripta . . ."), and sets him in opposition to the Creed itself.[3]

In spite of these, English Franciscan interest in Joachim emerged strongly in mid-century, spearheaded in part by the brilliant Franciscan scientist and philosopher, Roger Bacon, who was likely the first in Europe to predict a holy, world-reforming pope. This pope would purify canon law and inspire mass conversions of the non-Christian peoples, a project for which he advocated the learning of Hebrew, Arabic, Greek, and the exploration of shared philosophies. But sometime between 1257 and 1268, when he returned to Oxford from Paris, Bacon was apparently placed under censorship. These years, of course, fall in the wake of the scandal of Eternal Evangel, during which no member of the Franciscan order could publish without the order's approval. But Bacon's difficulties were more specific, and in the last two decades of his life he was condemned and imprisoned (sometime between 1274 and 1292), although the exact details are unclear. The minister general of the order from 1274–79 is said to have reprobated Bacon's teachings on the grounds that they contained "aliquas nouitates suspectas."[4] As we saw in the previous chapter, Olivi's famous assertion that "in the coming days . . . the [gospel] message will not be heard so readily in the carnal church of the Latins as among the Greeks, Saracens and Jews"[5] is a reflection of this Franciscan mission impetus. Joachite liberalism helped create the popular Franciscan alternative to crusading that by the next century would turn up in vernacular literature like *Mandeville's Travels* and *Piers Plowman*.[6]

But the 1254 scandal created by Gerard's "Eternal Gospel" made suspect Joachimism a Franciscan problem, and an English source, Matthew Paris, was, again, the earliest in Europe to break the news.[7] An English manuscript (British Library, Royal 8.F.XVI) of the Protocol of Anagni, the 1255 condemnation of Gerard's book, is one of two extant copies known anywhere today. It implicated Joachim's prophecies of the coming Third Status, roundly condemned by the Council of Arles in 1263 because "it was now realized . . . they constituted an incitement to subversive thought and action that was dangerously infectious."[8] Not long afterward in the 1270s John Pecham attacked Joachim and Hildegard as unreliable visionaries, even as Pecham's former student Olivi was beginning to come under official suspicion in the order. In 1300 and again in 1313, the Joachite works of Arnold of Villanova came under attack at Oxford. By the time of the vicious English heresy-hunter Richard Ledrede's appointment as bishop of Ossory in 1317, the Insular impact of John XXII's persecutions had begun both in Ireland and in the 1330 witch hunts at Cambridge (where the papacy searched for disciples of Ockham and Olivi).

This is where the fourteenth-century history we are about to examine begins, but what even this much tells us is that in England Joachite history is both impressive and by European standards, intellectually *repressive*. English chroniclers were unusually critical and Insular history includes everything from papal inquisition to book mutilation. According to the chronicler John Capgrave, by the mid-fifteenth century Joachim was known in England first and foremost by the 1215 condemnation: "for þe Cherch hath determined his opinion fals in þe beginning of þe *Decretales, capitulo, Dampnamus*. And Maystir Pers þe Lumbard, þat mad þe iiii Bokes of Sentens, aftir bischop of Paris, mad mech þing ageyn þis Abbot Joachim."[9] Joachim was also known, thanks largely to the popular pseudonymous literature, as someone who had dared and failed to do the forbidden, that is, calculate Doomsday. Here Capgrave shares the widespread assumption that Joachim wrote *De seminibus*, which predicts the future based on the letters of the alphabet. He writes wryly, "This same abbot mad also a oþir book, *De Seminibus Literarum*, where be gret craft he droue oute þe ȝere in whech þe Day of Dome schuld falle; but he failed foule, and erred in his counting." Most interestingly, as Capgrave's modern editor Peter Lucas points out, the "but he erred . . ." portion is an addition of Capgrave's own to his source, Martinus Polonus. This was the cautious man's gesture, and we see it often repeated throughout the entire English reception. But as Lucas also points out, "Of the theological additions [that is, throughout the chronicle], the most numerous are in the accounts of the various heretical beliefs held by a section of the Church from time to time."[10] In this Capgrave reflects a more general interest and concern about Continental heresy in England. There is also positive English chronicle response to Joachim, but it often emanates from specific groups as the last section of this chapter shows.

The reference to operating "through the hiding of books" (per absconsionem librorum) at the head of this chapter comes, of course, from the *Opus arduum*'s description of the confiscating of Continental books in 1389 (see Appendix B). However "hiding" worked both ways. Scribes, editors, and owners could "hide" suspect material simply by changing the author's name but leaving the text intact, or by cutting out the rubric or colophon, or by cataloguing the work under "Supersticiosa," or any of several ruses. No one has ever before surveyed the manuscript evidence of Joachite and Franciscan Joachite reception in England; having done so, I can testify that it is a mess of suppression, haphazard survival, and secretive hoarding. One could suppress suspect material in multiple ways, and with multiple motives. Serious Joachimism, however, was disseminated, loads of it, and continued to come across the Channel, often from and into convent libraries where the authorities rarely went looking for problematic books. It also went into privately owned prophetic collections on international church politics, especially during the period of the Avignon papacy and the Schism, although mostly anonymously transmitted. Perhaps even more remarkable is the fact that serious Joachimism was *composed* in England, too.

A Brief History of English Condemnations of Franciscan and Related Doctrines from Pope John XXII to Netter's *Doctrinale*

John Pecham had expressed fears about Joachimism and its infiltration of his Franciscan order in an anti-prophetic diatribe addressed to Robert Kilwardby, whom he succeeded as archbishop of Canterbury in 1278.[11] His fears were indeed realized in England, but decades after his death, in the arrests at Cambridge of four named English Franciscan lectors in 1329–30. This is the first evidence, so far as we know, of the actual *persecution* of Joachite writers in England (Ireland may be a little earlier), lending weight to independent evidence that Franciscan Spirituals were actually burned in England in 1330. The Avignon authorities were looking to Cambridge to arrest one of Olivi's most talented students, Henry of Costesy, whose case we will examine in detail below. They were also, judging from the context of the surviving papal correspondence, looking for the fugitive Ockham, whose relations with this group are shadowy to us, but (rightly or wrongly) must have been beyond question to John XXII's advisors and to many other contemporaries.[12]

Just as in other countries, the pontificate of John XXII brought the first evidence of serious persecution to England. For 1330, the same year that the Cambridge Franciscan lectors were arrested, the Cistercian Thomas Burton recorded in his chronicle an international listing of Franciscans burned at the stake, and in England specifically, "in a certain wood."[13] Earlier historians, like William Stubbs, had no idea what to make of this account, but as John Bacher points out, the English statistics appear in a highly reliable list (as we know from Continental sources) of Franciscans who died in other countries. One of the most convincing aspects of this account, I would add, is the presence of *women* among those burned. It is unclear from the way the account is worded whether any of those burned in England were women,[14] but the wording certainly opens this possibility. If that were the case, it would mean that a fully Olivian contingent of *Beguini* and *Beguinae* had reached England. Either way, the victims were in significant enough numbers to be noticed—and in numbers apparently too large for execution in a civic place. On the Continent, women were among the significant leaders of this group and protectors of Franciscan Spirituals, involved even in the "underground railroad."[15]

Bishop Ledrede's inquisitions of the same period also targeted women. Ledrede had set off from John XXII's Avignon at exactly the right moment to have been affected by the hysteria surrounding Porete's execution, followed by those of Olivian *sectatores*.[16] The Cambridge arrests and the burnings of the Spirituals may be among the events that prompted Bishop Grandisson of Exeter to actively investigate heretics in his diocese in 1334 and collect legal material for sentencing them, including "an undated sentence against a relapsed and impenitent Franciscan."[17] The fact that he would want a model for the sentencing of both ordained and *lay* Franciscan heretics, I would suggest, also points to Insular suspicions about Olivian *sectatores*, many of whom were Franciscan tertiaries or layfolk on the Continent. (The inquisitor Bernard Gui complained that the heretics pose as Franciscan tertiaries, gathering in conventicles.)[18] In the same year, 1334, as learned English Franciscans and others would have known, the excommunicated Ockham wrote his famous *Epistle to the Friars Minor* from indignant exile, accusing John XXII of many heresies.[19] And c. 1337 he also wrote *An princeps* to King Edward III of his native land, setting out the limitations of the papacy and arguing the king's right to a share in clerical finances, even against the will of the pope.[20] Though Ockham was not Joachite in any way known to modern scholars, medieval contemporaries repeatedly associate him with the Franciscan Spirituals on issues like clerical poverty; in fact, he was routinely seen as the enemy by pro-papal, and later anti-Wycliffite, forces like Netter.

Grandisson's action against heresy was a straw in the wind because it heralded a series of smaller English inquisitions and condemnations of Franciscans or Austins (the friars next most likely to carry Joachimism) in 1336, 1353, and 1358.[21] In colonial Ireland some serious cases emerge at just this time, prosecuted by Franciscan authorities.[22] Antimendicantism (the sometimes unhelpful broadbrush label we use to describe both attacks against the friars, but also those of friars against each other) played a massive role in many English heresy cases. Grandisson, for instance, issued a terrible letter to his diocese in 1358, full of apocalypticism in the tradition of William of St. Amour.[23] It was aimed directly against the friars and unlicensed preachers, a group he specially targeted as heretics throughout his tenure, urging: "Videte ne quis vos seducat" (Watch that no one leads you astray [Matt. 24:4]). Persecutions for "errant" views on the Immaculate Conception (a topic for which Olivi was also condemned),[24] the miraculous conception, and the beatific vision (another of John XXII's obsessions) interweave themselves with the antimendicant-related cases throughout these decades. As mentioned above, it was daring to disagree with John's position on the beatific vision that landed Thomas of Waleys in prison,[25] an event that further demonstrated the limitations of intellectual freedom during this papacy and evoked more attacks on the pope by Ockham. It is also in the 1340s that Joachim is prominently and learnedly cited as guilty of the heresy of Pelagianism in archbishop of Canterbury, Thomas Bradwardine's groundbreaking *De causa Dei contra Pelagianum*, which so influenced Wyclif's generation in favour of predestinarian theology.[26] This represents yet another area in which Wycliffite thought opposed Joachimism. The issue in *De causa Dei* is explicitly Joachim's salvational liberalism, and as we will see in chapter 10, Bradwardine's source is a genuine treatise by Joachim.

At this time there is also Insular concern about the arrival of the *Flagellanti*, a movement involving bands of self-flagellating pilgrims who moved from city to city in the wake of the Black Death in 1349, an event that had aroused apocalyptic expectation across Europe. One account describes the arrival in London of a large group ("plus quam xxvj"), mostly from the Low Countries ("de Selond et Houland"), in that year. They went to St. Paul's and performed their public ritual flagellation, using their trademark "trinitarian" scourges ("flagellum cum tribus cordulis") and wearing a special garment which allowed them to strip from the waist up.[27] This renewal of the Flagellant movement (which had originated in the Joachite-provoked hysteria surrounding 1260) evoked warnings to a number of English and Irish archbishops from Pope Clement VI about the spread of this quasi-Joachite phenomenon.[28] Clement was concerned enough to order a complete examination of the question of Franciscan incitement of the *Flagellanti*—a clear indication that it was the Joachite element that worried him. By 1351 Clement had issued *Inter solicitudines*, banning the movement from holding conventicles and denouncing its unorthodox uniform and its denial that the church held "the power of the keys." That the group used non-ecclesiastical methods to atone for the plague clearly made an impression on spectators as they traveled from city to city (their own rules allowed them to stay no longer than one night in any place). This is suggested most reliably by Robert of Avesbury's 1349 account, and perhaps also by the existence of a misericord in New College, Oxford, showing what may be a later fourteenth-century memory of the *Flagellanti*. The figure is dressed in a linen cloth (panno lineo cooperti), as Robert's account says, and stripped to the waist (toto residuo corporis denudato).[29] (See figure 4.) While misericord specialists disagree about its iconography, what no one disputes is that the artist makes no bones about which method of attacking the plague is most effective, the church's, which is parodied as a demon tugs on the hood of the priest exorcising the Hydra-like evil shown in the centre, or the flagellant's.[30]

One of the archbishops who preached Clement's ban most strenuously was Richard FitzRalph, whose obsessive antimendicantism was creating a resurgence of Insular interest in the now century-old scandal of the Eternal Evangel and the apocalyptic writings of William of St. Amour. Antimendicantism, although we do not always notice this aspect of it, was a major source of dissemination of Joachimism (albeit a hostile one), and perhaps a sign that it was alive and well in the mendicant orders. This is especially the case in Anglo-Irish sources.[31] FitzRalph and his partner Richard de Kilvington were extraordinarily well informed about Joachimism from their Continental connections. Particularly important and complex is the 1358 case of a Friar John who, with FitzRalph's help, was condemned at Oxford for publicly advocating disendowment (discussed in our next chapter). The number of surviving manuscripts containing Joachimism, some of Irish provenance as well as English, is sufficient testimony to Insular interests, as was England's Europe-wide reputation for love of prophecy. A case very similar to Friar John's appears in Durham in 1380, in

4. Late fourteenth-century misericord in New College Chapel, Oxford, depicting the threat of evil, likely the plague, as a multi-headed beast (centre), and two methods of countering it: a flagellant, stripped to the waist (right supporter), and a priest performing an exorcism (left supporter). Reproduced by permission of New College, Oxford, and photography by permission of Juanita Wood, from *Wooden Images: Misericords and Medieval England* (London: Associated University Presses, 1989). Photo credit: Charles A. Curry.

which a friar (Richard Helmyslay) is also charged with heresy, also for urging that the laity withdraw tithes from their secular clergy, and for holding eccentric Joachite-like views on the friars' mission and the gospels. This last aspect of his doctrine is so alarming that it is likely the factor which drew papal attention to the case, landing him in Rome and in prison.[32]

Between 1368 (when Uthred de Boldon is censured for liberal salvation opinions, some of which have Joachite associations) and 1380 (when Richard Helmyslay is charged), there is a remarkable, and, I will argue, *purposeful* lull in official antagonism toward Franciscan Joachimism. In fact, it becomes, dare one say, almost fashionable in an avant-garde sort of way (the Schism, with its many seriously heard international prophets, being one factor, and renewed war with France in 1369 being another). From 1380 onward, however, and in parallel with the rise of persecution of Wycliffism, evidence of a crackdown comes once again. This little window, as will be immediately evident to students of Ricardian literature, is not insignificant: Langland was writing the B text, which, unlike A, includes for the first time extensive religious and disendowment prophecy. Moreover, a fact that may or may not be significant, Chaucer is also working on his translation of *The Romance of the Rose* — which, however, he may have abandoned for reasons unknown before he reaches Jean de Meun's infamous, pro-Amourian account of the scandal of the Eternal Gospel (discussed later in chapter 3).

In 1388 Wimbledon positively invoked Joachim at Paul's Cross in London, preaching the infamous Joachite prediction of Antichrist's arrival in the thirteenth century: "Also Abot Joachym in exposicion of Jeremye seyþ: Fro þe ʒeer of oure Lord a þousand *and* two hundred, all tymes beþ suspecte to me, *and* we be passid on þis suspect tyme neiʒ two hundrid ʒeer."[33] The very next year the confiscations of Franciscan Joachite writers are reported in the *Opus,* and two or three years later Walter Brut is writing Joachite-style prophecy in his affidavits (discussed in chapter 5). As Schism issues provoked conciliarism abroad, the English church became more international in its efforts to fight heresy. At the turn of the century we see more English evidence of concern about Free Spiritism, already linked to Joachimism and Hussitism on the Continent. At this point Netter, especially in the wake of the Council of Constance, shows awareness of all three and begins to overtly connect Wyclif with Joachimism (most especially Olivi) — clear, important, but rather late evidence for official thinking. The impact of Constance on England's response to heresy, potentially as critical as Arundel's Constitutions, remains to be fully assessed.

In the *Doctrinale*, written between 1421 and 1427, Netter lists "Abbas Joachim & post eum Petrus Joannis [i.e., Olivi]" as among those heretics to whom "noster Wicleffus" made himself a disciple.[34] Of Joachim he says nothing specific, but concerning Olivi he has a good deal more to say, quoting as his authority fellow Carmelite Guido de Perpiniano's "libellus de haeresibus." He charges Olivi with holding that "the Roman Church is the carnal Synagogue of Satan" (Ecclesia Romana est carnalis Synagoga Sathanae) and that "the Roman Church is to be destroyed in the Third Status, just as the Synagogue was destroyed in the Second Status" (quod Ecclesia Romana destructa est in statu tertio, sicut synagoga destruebatur in statu secundo). This is, of course, an absurdly bald reduction of Olivi's delicate sense of the biblical historical concords between the Second and Third Status, but it gives us a helpful glimpse of the two doctrines by which Olivi was best known in England: the supposed equation of the Roman Church with the "carnal" as opposed to the "spiritual" church (his famous *ecclesia carnalis* and *ecclesia spiritualis*), and the belief in Third Status decline of the institutional church. Netter then insists that Wyclif relied on Olivi for his interpretation *de abominatione desolationis* (traditionally a great crux in apocalyptic exegesis), although he gives no further bibliographic details for either writer. Netter may be referring to Wyclif's assertion that the "abomination" signifies the blasphemous claim of equality with Christ, which Wyclif levels "de pseudopapa, qui est potissimus Antichristus."[35] He finishes by charging that another "pestiferous" *sector* of Wyclif's was "Gerardus Segarellus de Parma." Segarelli was a Franciscan Spiritual with sketchy links to Free Spiritism, whom Netter charges with the belief that the whole power of the church was "emptied on account of the wickedness of prelates" (evacuata propter malitiam Praelatorum), and that the Roman church is the "whore of Babylon" (meretrix Babylon), fallen from faithfulness to her spouse, Christ.

Elsewhere in the *Doctrinale*, Netter has cause to mention, though only in passing, Ockham (whose ideas on papal power he aligns with Wyclif's), and elsewhere again, William of St. Amour (whom he places, oddly, at the end of a list of the Late Antique heretics as being one of those who believe that "he alone has the spirit of God" [se solum Spiritum Dei habere]).[36] What is especially interesting about Netter's reductive invocation of all these writers, but especially the Franciscan Spirituals, is that one might expect it to reflect official Carmelite thinking. Yet even within Netter's own order, his contemporary, Alan of Lynn, was creating an index for England's most popular native Joachite writer, Henry of Costesy, even as Netter wrote. In a later section we will get a sense of what different worlds these two learned clerics, although within the same order, could occupy. Also at this historical moment we have seen the Benedictine abbot of St. Albans, John Whethamstede, commissioning a full and lavish copy of Olivi's commentary on Matthew for the Benedictine college at Oxford, which someone would later supply with a grim warning about heresy. These cases open a window for us on tensions over intellectual freedom that existed both among and within certain clerical groups and orders. They underline the fact that the early fifteenth century was not a monolithic world of censorship — that tolerance existed even as Netter fumed and as Arundel legislated.

Marked by Suspicion: A Sampler of Mutilated Books, Hidden Authors, and Tolerant Patrons from the Edwardian to the Lancastrian Periods

We will examine here four authors (Joachim, Olivi, Henry of Costesy, and Rupescissa), whose books are physically marked, mutilated, or hidden in extraordinary ways in fourteenth- or early fifteenth-century England, and those known book-owners or patrons who managed publicly to defy the trend toward suppression. This codicological evidence reveals a surprisingly wide range of opinion on revelatory Joachimism, Franciscan or otherwise, and even glimpses of the mainstream tolerance of the Lancastrian period. It should be noted at the outset, however, that codicology has never before been used to study English Joachimism; much remains to be done and this is only a sampler. There are, moreover, limitations. It is sometimes difficult to assess whether leaves were lost through ordinary stress on an unbound volume (common when the leaf is an initial or final one in its quire) or whether through censorship. In the cases here, however, *both* quire structure and evidence of deliberate violence support the motives for textual excision. Authorship, moreover, is much more often absent or suppressed in these texts than is normative even in medieval book production.

Henry of Costesy's Brush with Inquisition and the Fate of His Manuscripts

The first of these, chronologically, is Henry of Costesy, arrested at Cambridge along with three other Franciscan lectors (Peter of Saxlingham, John of Hacklington, and Thomas Helmeden), on charges of preaching publicly against

Pope John XXII.[37] The prisoners were ordered to be confined in the Franciscan convent at Cambridge until they could be sent to Avignon for trial, but further correspondence shows that Henry and Thomas may have been able to clear themselves of the charges. The case was high profile, and there seems to have been some concern in the correspondence that the king would not allow the four men to be sent abroad (another piece of evidence of the relative independence of English secular powers in matters of heresy). Some English Franciscans, like many elsewhere, opposed John XXII's bull on Franciscan poverty, *Ad conditorem,* an opposition that could prove dangerous. Henry was likely one of these. But Henry had extra cause to fear for his safety. He was a learned scholar of Joachim and Olivi, both writers under serious suspicion in the curia of John XXII.[38]

Henry of Costesy (or Cossey, as it is pronounced) was a native of East Anglia. Costesy is four miles from Norwich, the part of England most open to Continental influences coming across the English Channel, as we know from the writings of Julian and Margery Kempe later in the century, and from expatriots like Adam Easton and William Flete. But nothing quite prepares us for Henry, because we tend to think of English Joachimism—if we think of it at all—as likely to be watered down. In fact, David Burr says, "Henry [of Costesy] is, next to Olivi, the *most* Joachite Franciscan commentator whose works have survived"—*anywhere,* that is.[39] This in itself has to change how we view English Joachimism, especially since Henry's commentary was quite influential in England: five manuscripts survive, and nine attestations in English medieval library catalogues, showing broad distribution across different orders and regions.[40] It was still of so much interest in the era of print that John Bale records seeing it in Richard Grafton's printing shop in the sixteenth century.[41] Most significantly for us, in the early fifteenth century it was popular enough to warrant indexing by Alan of Lynn, the Cambridge Carmelite who acted as a mentor to Margery Kempe, another native of East Anglia.

Henry's commentary shows that, like all serious Joachites, he was fascinated by the concords between the Old and New Testament, and what they could betray about the mysteries of history, past and future. He also appears to have been fascinated by, though frightened to be explicit about, the expectation of a period of rest and spiritual renewal *after* Antichrist, whom Joachites believed, of course, to be imminent.[42] He is able to show more overt interest (like the anonymous English editors and readers of other Joachite manuscripts discussed below) in the patterns of sevens (the seven *bella* or battles of the Old Testament, the seven *etates* of the world, and the seven orders of preachers), a much safer topic than Joachim's trinitarian patterns. Copies of Henry's texts contain numerous handwritten diagrams (part of the Joachite habit of mind) that exploit visual ambiguities to clarify such historical and theological complexities, rather like figure 2a above.[43] But one of the areas in which Henry feels able to betray a *little* of his more dangerous Joachite passion is on the topic of the apocalyptic conversion of the non-Christian peoples, especially by a new evangelical order. In the present sixth age, he writes, this order will excel in understanding the biblical *concordia*, and through the divinely inspired gift of *spiritualis intelligentia* will "in the end convert the Jews and other unfaithful through preaching" (in fine convertit iudeos et alios infideles per predicacionem [fol. 71r]).[44] This is a genuine Joachite expectation, and it suggests that missions to the non-Christian peoples were critical for Henry. He was clearly drawn to that charismatic blend of Franciscan missionary fervour and Joachimism that we see in Olivi's idealism. He follows Joachim and Olivi minutely except for his maintaining a stark silence on two dangerous key topics: identification of false Christians with the "carnal" or institutional church of the present, and the glories of the coming Third Status.[45] This was an act, no doubt, of self-censorship, since these are highly censurable topics, and the commentary was written *after* (no more than three years after) he managed to extricate himself from inquisition in Avignon. At least two of his fellow friars did not.[46] Their status as Cambridge intellectuals would have done relatively little to protect them, since in other cases, like that of Thomas of Waleys, John XXII did not hesitate to imprison an academic who dissented with his views.

It is perhaps no surprise, then, that there is a dramatic change, as A. G. Little noticed, between Henry's earlier and later commentaries. Of the Apocalypse commentary, Little wrote: "There are no allusions to St. Francis or to Franciscan doctrines, no allusions to contemporary writers, . . . no comparison with modern conditions. . . . I cannot think the attribution to Costesy is true."[47] But it is true. Judging from the extreme caution of Henry's *Commentarius super Apocalypsim*, it looks as if the arrests were traumatic for him. Henry died at Babwell, a convent that must have been rife with serious *Joachitia*, likely including Olivi, because we know it was an important source of such materials for Edwardian England's first union cataloguer, Kirkestede.[48]

Still, for all of Henry's care, his interpretations and/or his name must have made some Insular readers and owners nervous. Most of the extant manuscripts of his works display a remarkable codicological pattern, that is, they are either somehow mutilated or show suppressed or absent authorship attribution.[49] And here we come to the phenomenon that we will see repeated throughout this century: physical evidence that English owners of Joachite material were nervous about overtly possessing it, especially if they were not highly and impeccably positioned clerics. In the case of Henry's commentary, three of the five extant manuscripts have been mutilated, and Henry's identity is absent or suppressed in three. Not only, for instance, was the opening rubric carefully cut away in Oxford, Bodleian Library, MS Laud Misc. 85 (which would remove any identification of the text and authorship attribution), but an important part of Henry's discussion of the mystery of the name of the beast has been torn out (figure 5).[50] This is the section in any Apocalypse commentary that attempts current historical interpretation, and perhaps the most sensitive part. What was Henry discussing in the torn leaf? As David Burr has very kindly confirmed for me, Henry's commentary does not seem "all that radical."[51] I would suggest, however, that in an *English* context—if not from a European one (the usual context in which Henry has been studied)—Henry is indeed radical. More important, his immediate historical and personal situation made *anything* he would write about chapter 13 of the Apocalypse (a chapter highly likely to contain criticism of the papacy in Joachite exegesis) susceptible to dangerous reading. Henry appears here and throughout to have flirted with coded writing, a concept well understood by Apocalypse commentators: *Si quis aurem audiat* ("if one has an ear, let him hear" Apoc. 13:9). In fact, this was precisely the verse Henry was interpreting just before the leaf was torn in the Laud manuscript. For anyone "with an ear" to hear, St. John went on to promise in verse 10 that those who live by violence will die by it, and that "this is the patience and faith of the saints" (hic est patientia et fides sanctorum [13:10]). This was surely comforting to a man who had just been under papal persecution a couple of years before, but no Franciscan Joachite writing under his own name in the period of John XXII could afford to be as bold as Olivi, especially with the verses that follow. Olivi, as Burr shows, had read the passage after 13:9–10 this way: John's second beast, coming up from the land (*vidi aliam bestiam ascendentem de terra* [13:11]), was the mystical antichrist or the pseudopope who would make all the inhabitants of the earth adore the first beast (adorare bestiam primam), the beast whose mortal wound had been healed (cuius curata est plaga mortis). This wound, Olivi suggested, had been dealt against the carnal church by St. Francis's and his disciples' commitment to evangelical poverty. (As we will see later, radical Franciscan exegesis like this was probably the source of Langland's

5. Oxford, Bodleian Library, MS Laud Misc. 85, fol. 122v, and torn stub of the next page in which Henry of Cossey had treated the exegetical crux of the mysterious identity or "number" of the Beast in St. John's Revelation. Reproduced by permission of the Bodleian Library, University of Oxford.

prophecy that the monasteries would be disendowed "and *incurable* þe wounde" [C.V.177].)

For Olivi, however, the mortal wound was even now healing as revived carnality gripped the church, demanding the *patientia* of the suffering faithful. Henry could not and did not suggest anything as dramatic as this, at least judging from the version I have compared it with in Oxford, Bodleian Library, Rawlinson C.16, fols. 200v–206v. Of course, we do not know for certain what was on the leaf torn from Laud, but we do know that the next biblical verses, with or *without* exegesis, could appear to Franciscans as a reproach to John XXII: this beast would cause fire (ignem) to come down from heaven (13:13), and he would cause any who did not adore the image of the beast to be killed (13:15). Given a contemporary papacy that was burning Franciscan Spirituals, it would be difficult to finesse *any* interpretation of these verses in a Franciscan commentary that could appear uncontroversial. Is it any surprise, then, that Henry's treatment of *all* these verses was torn out in the Laud copy? What is missing runs from Apocalypse 13:9, *si quis aurem audiat* (bottom of fol. 122v) to the discussion of the number of the beast "qui habet intellectum conputet numerum bestiae numerus enim hominus est" (let anyone who has understanding compute the number of the beast, for it is the number of a person [top of fol. 123]). The torn portion runs, then, from John's own covert appeal to the reader to "decode" into another such appeal. (Discussion of the number of the beast is already well under way at the top of fol. 123, where the first rubricated verse appears as: "Iohannis dicens quod numerus eius est numerus hominis.") Whoever tore this section out was knowledgeable enough about Franciscan Joachite exegesis to know it could be trouble.

What survives is Henry's overt focus on Islam as the main external threat to the church and some of his numerical theories to calculate how long Islam would endure. Both Burr and Reeves express understandable disappointment at Henry's conservatism, but I think that to any reader who *knew* the Olivian tradition, Henry's implicit message was relatively daring. Henry's focus on Islam, for instance, sounds *prima facie* like a safe externalizing of the Apocalypse's threats as coming from outside the church, but this is in part a code for anyone "with an ear." To look toward the end of the reign of the beast, running from the death of Mohammed *(mortem Machometi)* to the end of Islam *(dissipata secta eius* [fol. 123]) is *implicitly* also to look for the end of the Second Status, and the beginning of the Third. Given that Henry had just been under arrest c. 1330 and then released, might we even be justified in looking for a parallel personal note of relief in the end of this particular beast's reign of terror? That he is expecting a Third Status is evident from his belief in at least one (fol. 82v), and possibly even two new orders (fol. 114), as Burr shows, which will have a brilliant gift of *spiritualis intelligentia* and use it to convert non-Christians — itself a pretty clear picture of Third Status life for those "with an ear" to hear. Moreover, for Henry, just as for Olivi, *Christians* — the laxity of monastics especially, and any corrupt clergy — are part of the bestial persecution that the faithful endure. *Clergy* are, then — even if the modern papacy is not named — implicit in the onslaught of the "infidels," spoken of as followers of "Mohammed" in the section that survives in Laud (fol. 123–123v). So Henry's exegesis, like his mentor Olivi's, does not simply work on the literal level and leaves much room for (quiet) speculation.

What is left of a marginal annotation in the Laud copy, "notate de bestia," suggests that the passage attracted attention and perhaps further annotation in one of the other columns on the missing page. Annotation is where we often find controversial historical identifications (like Kirkestede's unflattering identification of Pope Urban VI shown above in figure 3). Whether these things or the text itself were the motivation for tearing out the leaf in Laud we can only speculate, but we do know that Laud is the only extant manuscript of Henry's works traceable to mid-fourteenth-century Cambridge itself. We also know that the guardian of the friary at Cambridge was ordered to surrender Henry and the other three prisoners to the provincial.[52] With so many friars having recently met their fate in prison or in the flames under John XXII, it is easy to imagine someone in Cambridge taking this kind of precaution. (The passage in question is dated 1333 in Laud [fol. 123], and 1331 in St. Bonaventure University, Holy Name College MS 69 [fol. 95], so Henry was composing the commentary in the immediate aftermath of his arrest.) Given the heavily Franciscan nature of Laud's contents, I would suggest that this particular copy may even have been originally in the Franciscan house itself, before Bale found it at Pembroke College two hundred years later.[53] It is, despite its mutilation, textually the best extant copy, and so may be closer to Henry's original than any others we now have. Written and annotated in a mid-fourteenth-century hand,[54] whoever wrote this manuscript's copy of the *Commentarius* was writing at the very least within recent memory of the arrests — and may also have mutilated it for safety's sake.

Manuscripts Containing Genuine Works by Joachim and Their Owners:
Richard de Kilvington, Dean of St. Paul's, and William Ebchester,
Bishop of Durham

Many other extant Insular Joachite manuscripts bear such "marks of concern." There is not space here to list all of the manuscripts of certain English provenance containing Joachimism, but as I have shown elsewhere, many betray evidence that self-identified owners considered them questionable or dangerous possessions in some way.[55] What seems particularly striking when these manuscripts are examined as a group, and then within the context of the larger group of about sixty manuscripts with Joachite material of some sort, is that only a tiny number of prelates, all in relatively prominent positions — and so relatively untouchable — seem willing to sign themselves as individual owners or patrons of serious *Joachitia*. This includes men such as Richard de Kilvington, dean of St. Paul's; Henry Kirkestede, librarian of Bury St. Edmunds; John of Beverly, lector of Durham College, Oxford; John Erghome, bibliophile York Austin friar; and William Ebchester, bishop of Durham.[56]

Even sanctioned by these august names, however, manuscripts of Joachim's genuine writings have often been marked or mutilated to shore up the impression of orthodoxy by *someone*. Tactics can include the removal of the first (and thus identifying) leaf of Joachim's work, or sometimes the final leaf (presumably containing an explicit), too. As in the Laud manuscript of Henry of Costesy, there seems to be a similar impulse at work in Ebchester's copy of Joachim's *Enchiridion super Apocalypsim* (British Library, MS Harley 3049), and also in a copy of Joachim's *Praephatio super Apocalypsim* (MS Harley 3969), a manuscript with no visible ownership marks, but likely associated with Cambridge.[57] The case of Harley 3969 seems quite deliberate because there is only one part of Joachim's *Praephatio* which, we know from other extant European copies, deals overtly with Joachim's dramatic prophecies for the Third Status, and this is precisely what has been torn out (see figure 6).[58] Here Joachim describes how the capacity for spiritual goodness that was planted in the Status of the Father germinated in the Status of Son and will come to a sweet fruition in the Status of the Holy Spirit.[59] The Old Testament he associates with the Father, the New Testament with the Son, and with the Holy Spirit, the phenomenon of Pentecost and its mysteries (by implication) yet to be fully understood.[60] All this, as well as Joachim's claim to receive his biblical knowledge by the gift of "intellectus spiritualis" (line 8) was on the missing leaf. From what is left of the work, one can still glean Joachim's optimism from this text (for instance, his belief that after double tribulations of the imminent period of the opening of the Sixth Seal, the consolation of a double portion of "manna" will be given) but one has to work much harder to glean it—and none of these famous, familiar, and dangerous ideas are so obviously retailed again in what remains.

In Ebchester's manuscript Joachim's *Enchiridion* is also missing its first leaf,[61] and especially noticeable is an overt assertion of orthodox propriety at the end of the volume, which finishes with added extracts claiming to be from "Joachym super ysaiam," a pseudonymous work, fols. 253v–254. But in fact this is, at best, *Pseudo*-Pseudo-Joachim, that is, someone pretending to be the author of the *Super Esaiam*, writing a little treatise against the heresy of the Waldensians, the Wycliffites, and the Hussites (which makes the twelfth-century Abbot Joachim far-sighted indeed!). The treatise especially condemns their opinions on temporalities and disendowment (the manuscript, of course, was owned by a prior). The false authorship attribution clearly sets "Joachim" among the orthodox. Copied into the manuscript just ahead of this is a rare item by Walter Hunt, a Carmelite, also concerned with orthodoxy and heavily dependent on Netter's *Doctrinale*.[62] Ebchester was professed at Durham Cathedral Priory in 1406 (the same year legislation forbade disendowment prophecies). He commissioned the manuscript much later when he was made prior (1446), but even so, either he or a contemporary at Durham decided to hedge his ownership of a genuine piece by Joachim with a few safeguards.

A different kind of concern with orthodoxy is evident in an earlier collection of Joachite materials owned by Richard de Kilvington, dean of St. Paul's (1353–61). Kilvington's *Liber excerptionum abbatis Joachim* (British Library, MS Royal 8.F.XVI) contains an anthology of genuine and spurious works, and something even rarer—a copy of the Anagni condemnation of Gerard's "Eternal Gospel." An antimendicant propagandist is the last person one would expect to find enjoying Joachim, and exactly what he was doing with such material is a real question. As I will suggest in the next chapter, the condemnation in the wake of the scandal of the "Eternal Gospel,"[63] now over a century ago, was likely tantalizing to him as potential ammunition against contemporary friars. The physical manuscript itself, however, is full of puzzles. Most interesting for our present purposes is that, even though the book deals with issues a hundred years old, Kilvington himself seems to have been nervous that the *Liber* might get loose. His full name appears in a neat early *anglicana formata* hand on the top of every second page (that is, every odd-numbered page)—a highly unusual,

deme et sciuntur et non exprimunt. Q in enī aliquid dicat: sed aliqd
diat. et cogitat qd diat. et qd diat: deum nominas et uas filia
bas formias et totum dinisse putas. Q uis ergo cogitas aut qle-
cum dicas deus. Si enim deum sub hac noīe omnia inspicientel
timorem inspitaris. quis explicant potest quid inspiat deus. I
quō timor sit deus. Q uomo potest timeri quod nō pt uideri.
nec cogitatur ul scīt. et iā ergo quid cogites ul dicas. cum diat
deus. et ergo cum dicas deus. cogitas q omnia ficat. et nō cogitas
qd est yt qui ficat. animus est totum hec qd dicas. et non est hec to
tum ipe et quo dicas. et nī et yp hec dicas. non ut ad ipm accedas.
Si ut ipi approprinquies. magni cui est homī nunc ad ipm uce
si non deuir puenire. dabitur a postea cum uenit quod prefectī
est. et capit uidere homo non p specīlum imaginem. Si sic ad
faciem ueritatem. Nunc a interim totī imago est. que longe a
intate est. et siat qd potest. aī. Sed comiertit. Si non peruenit.
Dicitur namq qp deus ignis est. et manifesta figura est ad deus
ad proprietatem ignis non est. qnī ignis corpus est. deus corpus
non est. Et aut alia natura incorporea que magis deo una
ta dicitur. Et quam ad deum nob sublimus similitudo format
cum dicitur. deus est sps. Sapiencia. et amor. qp anima spec
et angelus spiritus est. et in ipo spu mao. Sapiencia et amor. Et est
nouim quid sit spec. quanti aiam nominat. et p angeli aiam no
uimus. Et cum ergo audim quia deus sit est. cogitamus aiam t an
gelum. et estimamus similitudinem. qt tale aliquid deus est. qt
anima ul angelus. qt sps est. Et nescimus q longe est hec a ui
tate. qd incomphensibile est excellentiae. In tali a collacaone imī
ciuium est aliud corporale. unū uniuersum. alind comphesibi
le. unū semp idem manens. aliud mutabile. Et cui q aliud dia
nō potest hec dī. ne mdi dicitur. qt ad inte ipam utitte nō possu
mus donec figura transferat t iutas manifeste pateat. Quic ergo
manent figurae ut signa ueritatis acupiant qi p utitate. donec
ueniat qd perfectum est in ipa ueritate. propterea hec primū
principiū et cetera omnes querunt studiosius in trino. et qui
ciunt uspicia in qdāuino. perquiruit subtil in theologie t phie
seruino. Et omnes querunt. si non inueniunt. qnī mod iqī
siaonis et ignorantia ueritatis eis obsistunt. unde nō nosī. qt au
plex est ueritatis causarum seu principior inquisitio. a triplex
cogitatio. prima inquisitio est matematica. que contemplatur

Deest unum folium.

signat. Et si eni̅ pferamus breuit̅ que no̅ breui co̅artanda su̅t ser
mone ꝑ sua dignitate dicam: quod ita dom̅s e̅t die pasche. ut si
oc̅lis cerneretur aliquid. uel uirtus eius maria ut postea fue
tim e̅t sentiretur. die uo pentecostes lingue ignee cerneret̅
e̅t. sonus auribꝫ peragetur. uirtus quoꝫ maxima amoris e̅t
sapientie sentiretur. in l ꝑfecto aliud q̅ quod fide et spe teneret
designat. ꝗ̅ ia̅ quid aliud tenuer fides n̅ra qua̅ ut credamus
baptizatos in ꝼpo mortificatos e̅e ꝓ̅ resuscitatos qꝫ iustiae
in forma passionis et resurrectionis diuist̅ datum qꝫ sꝑm sa̅
omnibꝫ catholice baptizatis: et capimus ergo mu̅s sꝑm sc̅m per
manu̅ impositionis eor qui receperu̅t ꝫ aplis in die pasche. in
remissionem peccator in futuro illi et gloriam et felicitate sa̅
uior n̅im plenitudie̅ uirtutem qꝫ sc̅m? At pretiu̅ retu̅
ti opera litterales nobis historie una uice commendat. in u
tim ut crox uel n̅e fidei solido fundamento consistat. Gesta uo
noui testame̅t. futura adhuc erant. q̅ a̅p̅ uenit in mu̅di.
Et q̅ historice nec diu̅ scribi poterant in libri apocalipsis ner
uis su̅t ꝓphias co̅artata. ut discerret uenem̅ etas uolando si
bi cum ꝓrudine escam accipe spiale eu̅ et iam ia̅ uerba histo
rici carne̅ sapientia̅. uel ut mortiam̅ consitur̅e. Sane si futu
rim no̅ solu̅ uerba historica et que carne̅ et terra̅ sapere in
tentur deficie̅t. ut̅m et eni uerba mistica que ꝑ figuras et enigma
ta ꝑrudentibꝫ ingeruntur cessabu̅t. q̅ iam non ꝑ figuras aliqꝫ
si in sꝑu dei n̅ra faciem uidebimus condicionis. si los eidem effe
ti dicente Iohe. Scimus q̅ cu̅ apparuerit siles ei erim̅? q̅ ui in
rebu̅is eum sicut est. uerum si idcirco dicam̅ ut libri apocalip
sis materia̅ utimare possim̅? et que sit intendo opis cho dace̅
tiale est deo postulantibꝫ que petiutur inpende̅dim mo̅ ca̅e
stes credat. Et si eni in loco aliquo co̅ existimetur thesaurus:
mieu̅ refugit forte et castis hinc labori. Fatigari. Si u̅e ergo co̅
sidare̅ est cursum peccator tempor: quibꝫ ueteris testi opera sa
cro su̅t signata uel camine. ut hui quoꝫ etatis serie que tota̅
continet in se noui plenitudie̅ resti. distincte intellige uale
amus. et quale singul apocalipsis pub̅r tempora reputantur ꝑ
p̅ri. primo quide̅ simpliciter ponere. deinde auctore ꝼpo auctori
tatibꝫ et racionibꝫ comprobare. cap. vi. cap̅bꝫ mundi. et de diuersis
  I Olenne est l ecc̅a ser numerodꝫ temporum distinctionibus
    et etates. et quas ser diebꝫ amicti sua opera fecit deus. ꝗ̅a

and unusually thorough, way of marking medieval book ownership (figure 7). This could only be an act of unprecedented caution, because, given the quire structure, if the book were unbound (and the staining of the outer leaves strongly suggests it was), no single loose bifolium would go into circulation without the dean's name on it somewhere. It looks, then, as if even a highly placed fourteenth-century church official could not own a copy of a Joachite text without making provision in case it, or even part of it, went astray.

Moreover, Kilvington, or the editor in charge of making his manuscript or even its exemplar, decided to make at least one massive direct intervention in the text. Kilvington's copy contains the pseudo-Joachite *De oneribus prophetarum*, which, if we look closely, is carefully edited to have the entire section of that work entitled "De statibus" (that is, on the three *status*) suppressed.[64] We saw a parallel phenomenon in Harley 3969, and we have already seen the Wycliffite *Opus* author inveigh against Joachim's "heresy" on this very point, and chroniclers, too. This brings us to a critical question in the history of Joachite influence. For decades scholars have talked about the rarity of Joachite notions of the Third Status in English exegetes who otherwise are often content to draw upon Joachim.[65] The argument for rarity has been used to show that in England radical apocalypticism never occurs. In fact, English writers, editors, and owners often *believed* it was heretical, or that they might be considered unorthodox for using it, and *that* is why it is often suppressed in owner-identified manuscripts of English apocalypticism. Where it does occur in all its glory is usually in anonymous manuscripts, safely cloistered manuscripts (in Case Study 1 we will see an example, likely from the York Austins) or, in a very few cases, named manuscripts owned by unimpeachable authorities. The other place it appears, most frequently in fact, is on the business end of a polemical broadsword—as an attack on the friars, and all who think like them. This is antimendicant anti-Joachimism, and this, as the next chapter will show, is why Kilvington was interested in the manuscript. But even he, that is, even as a *detractor* of Joachimism, was nervous about it.

Moreover, even a Renaissance owner of Kilvington's manuscript felt the need to write in bold letters (now in a classicized Latin) that Joachim was a condemned heretic (fol. 55). (See figure 8.) One can only conclude that these were ideas that had grown more dangerous with time. The association of the institutional church with Babylon, for example, sounded bad in 1255, but by 1357—when, one assumes, Kilvington had acquired the Protocol for the campaign mounted that year at the curia—it would have been a signal of Olivian-

7. London, British Library, MS Royal 8.F.XVI, owned by the dean of St. Paul's, Richard Kilvington, and containing excerpts from works by Joachim and Joachite writers, along with a copy of the Protocol of Anagni condemning Gerard's *Evangelium eternum*. The detail here shows fol. 51r, a leaf from the Protocol, with Kilvington's signature in the top right hand corner, similarly repeated on every bifolium in the manuscript. Reproduced by permission of the British Library.

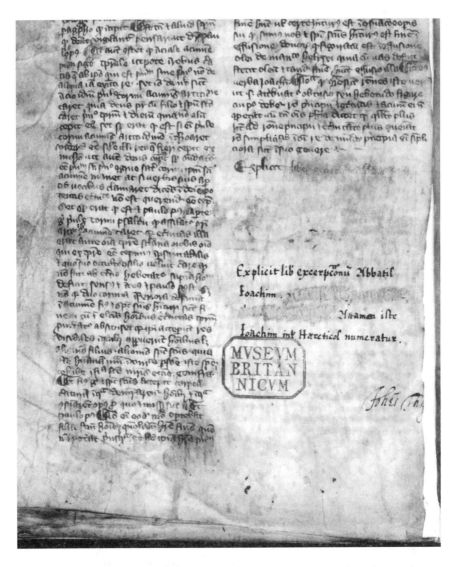

8. London, British Library, MS Royal 8.F.XVI, fol. 54v, showing a note in later classicized
Latin asserting that Joachim is numbered among the heretics ("inter haereticos numeratur").
Reproduced by permission of the British Library.

influenced Franciscan Spiritual thought. It was the kind of thing, that is, for which people were burned. (By the Reformation, of course, even more people had been burned for such sentiments.) We might add that after Kilvington's death the association between the church and Babylon would also occur, for instance, in the writings of Walter Brut and the *Opus* author. So no wonder the Wycliffites were scrambling to condemn Joachim, and the authorities were attempting to confiscate the whole lot by 1389–90,[66] a full generation before Netter's charge of this very Olivian doctrine against Wyclif.

Manuscripts of Peter Olivi in England and Their Readers

A more complete suppression than Joachim's genuine thought endured appears in the case of Olivi. The friars who confiscated his books in England in 1389 did an efficient job of it: two copies of his Matthew *Postilla*, both of English origin survive, but given the scarcity of this text *anywhere*, this is a significant survival. Moreover, there are some scattered attestations, mainly from safehouses like Merton College, Oxford, and Syon Abbey.[67] We have already seen something of the horrors of Continental persecution of the Franciscan Spirituals, the *Beguini/ae,* and others who read Olivi at their peril.[68] Continental inquisitors considered an interest in Olivi as good evidence of heresy.[69] Nor were England and Ireland "insular" in this regard. FitzRalph and Kilvington, for instance (as we will see further in the next chapter), had high-level connections with one of the most notorious of these, Cardinal Guillaume Court,[70] an inquisitor who had tried John of Rupescissa and sent less fortunate Franciscan Spirituals to the flames.

In one of the two extant English copies of Olivi's *Postilla* on Matthew, now Oxford, New College, MS 49 — in fact the copy commissioned by the powerful abbot of St. Albans, John Whethamstede — the flyleaves, as we saw, were cut away, likely to suppress ownership and full attribution, but the name "Petrus Iohannis" survives, and on the final folio (figure 9) the note in a fifteenth-century cursive hand[71] discussed in the Introduction above:

Erat quidam Petrus Iohannis hereticus, unus ex complicibus Ioachimi abbatis heresiarche. Cum ergo non constat cuius Petri Iohannis hoc opus sit, non alienum putavi ab offitio meo imprudentem lectorem admonere. (fol. 159v, col.b)

9. The final leaf
(fol. 159v) of Oxford,
New College, MS 49,
showing the note
added in a cursive hand
at the bottom of the
page warning of
Olivi's and Joachim's
status as heretics.
Reproduced by
permission of New
College, Oxford.

(detail)

There was a heretic named Peter, the son of John, an accomplice of the heresiarch, Abbot Joachim, and as it is uncertain which Peter, son of John, wrote this work, I have thought it my duty to warn the imprudent reader.[72]

This is harsh, officious language indeed, written by someone (apparently at Oxford, and apparently well informed) who did not share the *Opus* author's motives for salvaging Olivi, at least, from the charge of Joachimism. It is no wonder that the other extant English copy of this commentary of Olivi, which comes from Ramsey Abbey (a house which quietly collected other *Joachitia*), is prudently attributed to William of Auvergne, likely because it is a late fourteenth-century manuscript.[73] There was also a third copy, as we know by attestation in a will, in which William Duffield bequeathed it to Merton College for chaining. This puts the only named copies in academic hands.[74]

What would we find in a work that had to be so protected by its readers? In fact, a significant amount of the Olivian doctrine that was censured under John XXII, as we are about to see, and even parallels to the kind of radical Joachimism such as was censured in the (much clumsier) *Evangelium eternum* of Gerard. But we also find a great deal of original, brilliant, and controversial thought on many topics — topics, indeed, that parallel certain ideas found in writers like Porete, Uthred, Langland, and the *Pearl* poet. *Pearl*, for instance, shares with Olivi's Matthew *Postilla* a highly unusual reversal of the standard Vineyard Parable exegesis, a reversal which privileges children ("little ones," a coded metaphor for the new religious orders) as latecomers among the labourers, allowing Olivi to dilate on the theme of "adult" jealousy of divinely chosen "children." Those who were called in childhood, he asserts, are more fervent and more humble (Hii qui in puericia uocati fuerunt . . . feruentiores & humiliores sunt [fol. 122r, mis-foliated 121r]). The parallel with the way the same parable is famously treated at the heart of *Pearl* is tantalizing.

There is hardly an important controversy or censure of the later Middle Ages that is not touched upon or anticipated in the Matthew *Postilla*. When Olivi wrote, for instance, the opinions of Aquinas were still held to be highly dangerous in Franciscan circles and were permitted reading only to the exceptionally intelligent lectors of the order, and only in copies containing William de la Mare's marginal corrections.[75] But Olivi's *Postilla* contains, for instance, his attack on Aquinas (New College 49, fols. 78ra–81va),[76] showing how fiercely Olivi held to the belief of Christ's and his disciples' complete ("perfect") poverty as the real model for Franciscan and Dominican observance. More dangerous is the daring style of Olivi's mysticism, which often, for the modern reader, evokes Porete. This cannot be entirely accidental. The Council of Vienne was examining the two types of heresy in conjunction, and Porete was arrested with a Franciscan Joachite adherent, Guiard de Cressonessart (see Chronology, 1310). Guiard is called a "beguinus" in the trial records, a vague word that can be associated both with Free Spirit heretics and with Olivian *sectatores*. Guiard's testimony raises suspicions of the latter because he boldly claimed to be the "Angel of Philadelphia," the figure from the Apocalypse who signified the sixth period of church history for Olivi and the rejection of the "carnal church" by followers of evangelical poverty. In fact, the only mutilated and annotated page in New College 49 deals with this very subject, as we are about to see. This link between Olivi's radical Franciscan mysticism and Porete (explored further in chapter 7) comes up in relation to his distinguishing of "two churches" and his radical treatment of the unitive phase of mystical experience.

For Olivi the higher faculties of the mind, the intellect and the will, freed from earthly things (by adherence to evangelical poverty) will reach the mountain of contemplation to see the glory of Christ (ad supramundana transmigrarent in montem contemplationis . . . et ibidem *Christum in gloria sue maiestatis adorant et vident*).[77] This is actually a form of beatific vision (although Olivi does not call it that) possible while the soul is still a *viator* in *this* world, and it is thus one of the many daring features of his mysticism. In fact, this makes Olivi more radical than Uthred de Boldon, who was censored in 1368 for a far more cautious view of this sort (discussed in chapter 10). Under Pope John XXII, issues of beatific vision became dangerous, and here we have doubtless another reason John wished Olivi were still alive to prosecute in the 1320s.[78] (The pope, of course, had to content himself with censoring his Apocalypse commentary.)

There is also some physical evidence, showing that even the Benedictine readers of Whethamstede's copy found this mysticism extraordinary. Olivi often ducks into oblique authority attributions when he knows he is risking heterodoxy. He is also very shy of autobiographical reference and, as David Burr has convincingly argued, shields himself by the use of a Pauline third person when he ventures into truly controversial revelatory theology.[79] A significant example appears on the one mutilated page (aside from the flyleaves) of the entire New College 49 Matthew *Postilla*. Olivi has been predicting that a second historical resurrection, concording with the one experienced when the dead came out of their tombs at the time of Christ's crucifixion (Mt. 27:52–53), will occur in the present age after Christ's "life and rule" are again crucified by the leaders of the "heretical church." The implicit reference, of course, is to the persecution of the Spirituals. But, he continues, in a passage that merits the second of two "nota" marks on this page (a rare phenomenon in the manuscript generally): "I have heard it has been revealed by a very holy man . . ." (A viro valde spirituali audivi revelatum esse).[80] What he had "heard" was that the Passion and Resurrection of Christ would be renewed in the angel of the sixth seal (a coded reference to St. Francis or, more generally, the herald of the Third Status), so that his followers would have a teacher and comforter as the disciples had. But though he cautiously insists that he will leave this to divine judgement (divino iudicio [fol. 155, col. B]), still, "learned men," he says, now believe that there will be two Resurrections(!). As Kevin Madigan points out, the 1318 commission to examine Olivi's Apocalypse commentary dismissed this same idea as "a fantastic fiction." In New College 49, the entire margin immediately below where these lines appear is cut away right up to the text line—why, we do not know, but it was one of the few pages in the manuscript to attract medieval annotation on this sensitive topic, some of which was apparently cut away. The controversial "angel of the sixth seal," equivalent in Joachite exegesis to the "angel of Philadelphia" (famously in the Guiard-Porete inquisitional records), may be to blame.

What is especially illuminating about the reception of Olivi in England in this period is that we know of four important, and utterly different, individuals who were reading him: the Wycliffite author of the *Opus* (who, as we will see in chapter 5, borrowed from Olivi extensively but silently); William Butler, regent master of the Franciscans at Oxford, who quotes Olivi knowledgeably, and as an orthodox writer, in his "determination" against translating the Bible into English;[81] Whethamstede, the abbot of St. Albans, who commissions Olivi for the Benedictine college at Oxford; and, finally, Netter, who cites Olivi as a teacher of Wyclif's. The *Opus* author was attracted to just the kinds of passages in Olivi that Netter would imagine, but, unusually for a Wycliffite, he is a little more tolerant of the revelatory dimension as well. Let us take two examples: the first of the kind of thing that the *Opus* author likes and Netter hates; the second, the kind of thing they *both* hate. The first is Olivi's prophecy of the Third Status, when the remnant of the elect contemplatives, living in apostolic poverty, would (re)found the spiritual church (ecclesia spiritualis), just as the disciples once did for the church of the Second Status after Pentecost (fol. 104v).[82] One can see an early Wycliffite responding to this (this is, in fact, why early Wycliffites responded to Langland, because this kind of refounding of the church is exactly what is enacted in *Piers Plowman*—whether or not this has to do with Olivi, the parallel is striking). For Olivi this remnant will have the power to open the hidden (archana) things of scripture, but will be condemned by the scribes and elders of the "carnal church" (ecclesie carnalis [fol. 104v]).[83] This is exactly the kind of passage Netter speaks of in the *Doctrinale*, as we saw, flattening the delicacy of Olivi's handling into literal heresy.

Matthew is the most apocalyptic of the Gospels, and so the *Postilla* is full to bursting with genuine Joachite expectation, such as, again, modern scholars repeatedly assume was unavailable to English thinkers. There is much that any inquisitor of the Franciscan Spirituals (like Netter's source, Guido) would jump on here. But there is much that even a Wycliffite like the *Opus* author would jump on as too close to opinions condemned since Gerard's *Evangelium*: thus Christ's healing the man with the withered hand (Matt. 12:9–13) signified the *conversion* of the carnal Sabbath of the Second Status into the spiritual Sabbath of the Third (fol. 90ra). This is exactly what, as we saw, the Wycliffite *Opus* author condemns as outright heresy in Joachim.[84]

It is precisely this kind of teaching that papal legates and inquisitors were looking for in later Olivian-influenced Joachites like Henry of Costesy and his three companions. As persecution became harsher, Olivi's works were used more selectively (as in Henry's commentary)—not only in England, *but all over Europe*—to weed out the explicitly dangerous Joachite references to the Third Status.[85] Even Wycliffites condemned them. It is time, then, that modern scholars of medieval England stopped interpreting lack of overt reference to the Third Status as ignorance or innocence in Insular writers. As in the rest of Europe, it was caution, only more so.

Benedictines and Universities: Early Lancastrian Clerical Attitudes from Alan of Lynn to Thomas Netter

Who, then, dared to own Joachite manuscripts? And what was a man like John Whethamstede doing openly commissioning a book that neither the Carmelite provincial Netter nor, in many cases, Wycliffites found tolerable? And what was Alan of Lynn doing creating a detailed index to Henry of Costesy's

Apocalypse commentary? To further its study, perhaps, among Cambridge Carmelites? These are the questions we will tackle in the present section, along with a look at the champions of Joachite prophetic propaganda in fourteenth-century England, the York Austins, and their remarkable library.

John Whethamstede was abbot of St. Albans, one of England's most important Benedictine houses, and known mainly to Middle English scholars as the man who attacked Reginald Pecock's heterodoxy, so he was no stranger to inquisitorial questions.[86] Whethamstede commissioned the Olivi manuscript during the same decade that Netter was writing his *Doctrinale* and claiming that Wyclif has been a "sectator" of Olivi. The manuscript bears Whethamstede's "lamb and flag" symbol proudly on the first folio and probably before the excision of the flyleaves bore his name like other manuscripts he donated. It was made for Gloucester College, the Benedictine college of Oxford where he had been *prior studentium*, 1414–17.[87] It is impossible that a man of Whethamstede's learning would have been ignorant of Olivi's reputation. Rather, the commission would seem to represent the kind of open-mindedness that Whethamstede demonstrated on other fronts—at least with respect to what *Benedictines* and their students should be free to read. Was it that he wanted students to be aware of condemned doctrine? Was it that he wanted them to make their own judgements? Was Olivi's brilliant mysticism and exegesis something he thought appropriate to a contemplative order? We do not know for certain. But we do have other evidence to suggest that it was some combination of all three. So, although Whethamstede famously said that the cause of modern heresy was the "possession and reading of books written in our vernacular" (librorum possessio et lectura qui scribuntur in vulgari idiomate), he also, as Anne Hudson has pointed out, commissioned a copy of *Dives and Pauper* for the library at St. Albans. And he did this even though *Dives and Pauper* was considered suspect and was actually confiscated from an unbeneficed chaplain in a Bury St. Edmunds trial at about the same time.[88]

A look at Whethamstede's own commonplace book, Cambridge, MS Gonville and Caius 230/116, gives us some sense of a man who would dare to publicly commission a work by Olivi. Whethamstede was a representative of his order at many of the major church councils (including the councils of Pavia and of Basel, and he knew the proceedings of Constance well); he was a brilliant administrator and patron. His modern biographer sums him up this way: "eminent churchman, diplomat, preacher, letter writer, encyclopedist, munificent builder at St. Albans and Oxford, a magnate, patron and benefactor of the arts."[89] To this I would add, ecclesiastical humanist, especially after studying Gonville and Caius 230, which contains, for instance, extracts from Dante, Marsilius, and other controversial writers on papal power. These writers were not easy to come by in England, and Gregory XI had named Marsilius as one of Wyclif's teachers in error.[90]

This is not the only time we see Benedictine independence at work in the preservation and transmission of thought that challenged official thinking. The majority of the institutions holding manuscripts bearing genuinely Joachimist (that is, work by Joachim, Olivi, or Henry) ideology in England were Benedictine, although Syon Abbey also held works by all three.[91] Henry, the most conservative of the three, appears most often in England. A copy of Henry of Costesy's Apocalypse commentary was given to Evesham in 1392 and is well represented in Benedictine libraries like St. Mary's, York, and Canterbury. But Henry's works also had a more diverse institutional audience than Olivi's or Joachim's, ending up even on the roadways, in a great many friars' tiny, personal *vade mecum* books.

It also turns up in the hands of the Carmelite, Alan of Lynn, who was a mentor to Marjery Kempe. Henry's work had remained in circulation for nearly a hundred years when Alan decided to index it, and practically under the nose of his provincial, Netter.[92] Because he also indexed Bridget (this survives, though unfortunately the index of Henry does not),[93] we can glean a sense of his attitudes. His index or *tabula* of Bridget appears in Oxford, Lincoln College, MS Lat. 69 (s.xv), fols. 208–(234),[94] in a contemporary hand (not impossibly Alan's own). The *tabula* is a real labour of love and shows much more fascination with both apocalyptic thought and activist women visionaries than likely Netter would have approved. This difference of opinion may account in part for Netter's prohibition against Alan's speaking with Margery in 1415, a case we will discuss in chapter 6 below. Since Alan is very likely the "Whyte Frer" who, Margery tells us, "proferyd hir to wryten frely" (*BMK* 6.9), the spectrum of Alan's tastes in the revelatory is instructive.[95] One of the things that might account for Alan's engagement with these two ostensibly dissimilar writers (Henry and Margery) is the issue of alternative salvations.[96] It is in any case jarring to modern distinctions that usually set a Joachite commentator apart from a visionary like Bridget, or indeed a *vernacular* female visionary like Margery. Alan's *tabula* on Bridget's *Revelaciones* has entries for "antichristi" (fol. 209) and for clerical issues, especially those involving corruption (e.g., "cardinales," fol. 210v;

"castigat," fol. 210v, "clerici," fol. 211, and "papa," fol. 228v). The latter contains a long entry on papal *auctoritas*, and on the pope having believed an illusion (fol. 228v). There are also many entries on vision (e.g., "sompnus," fol. 235v) and on visionary *discretio* (e.g., "spiritus," fol. 236, particularly "bonus cognoscitur"). In the absence of his index of Henry, we can say little more, but Alan chose to focus on writers like Bridget, Margery, and Henry at about the same time that the provincial of his order was blaming Olivi for corrupting Wyclif and trying desperately to keep the lid on women teaching publicly.[97] Alan had associations with Cambridge (this may be where he encountered Henry's text), and his case shows brilliantly the fifteenth century's split personality over revelatory theology. Netter would prohibit members of his order from encouraging women as public teachers and, more specifically, prohibit Alan from speaking to Margery, but the prohibition was lifted. Like all such prohibitions against the revelatory (and we will see a significant one in Case Study 3 below), it failed.

To summarize what we have found so far: overt ownership of Joachim at Durham, Bury, York, St. Paul's, and the Oxford Franciscans; overt ownership of Olivi at Merton, Syon, and Gloucester College, Oxford; and ownership, overt or otherwise, of Henry of Cossey at Evesham, York, Syon, Norwich, Cambridge, and Canterbury. Oxford and Cambridge colleges, then, along with some major convents (Benedictine, Bridgettine, Franciscan, and Austin especially) were important centres for the preservation and tolerance of suspect apocalyptic doctrine. Another Oxford manuscript carrying banned material is Oxford, Balliol College 149, owned by Robert Thwaytes, who was master of the college and twice chancellor of the university, which we will study in more detail in chapter 10. The manuscript contains a radical Joachite prophecy (though unlabeled as such) predicting the demise of the papacy, a copy of William of St. Amour's banned *De periculis*, and a fragmentary copy of Uthred de Boldon's defence of his condemned opinions in 1368. Memoranda to the Rising of 1381 and other current events tell us that the manuscript weathered the St. Amour confiscations of 1389.[98] But even Oxford was not inviolate: that was where Whethamstede's copy of Olivi would be marred; nor was Cambridge, where the marred Laud Costesy manuscript and Joachim's *Praephatio* likely were. Universities were perhaps less private than convents. At Oxford, where fellows lived communally in colleges and were apparently under some pressure to share books and notes, freedom is a relative concept. There were complaints about Nicholas Hereford, for instance, that he refused to share his notes and books with other fellows.[99]

Sometimes condemned material travels in Oxford manuscripts under tongue-in-cheek headings. Queens, the college where Hereford and Wyclif taught, held at least part of what is now Oxford, Bodleian Library, Lat. Misc. c. 75, which has material attributed (falsely) to Joachim and material by Arnold of Villanova[100] (a Franciscan Joachite layman at the court of Boniface VIII, condemned and imprisoned at Paris in 1300). In England, Arnold was attacked by the chancellor of Oxford, Henry of Harclay, for being in effect too pro-Jewish, a tendency that Joachite thinkers come by honestly from Joachim himself and which we will have cause to note again among the "intolerable tolerances" discussed in Case Study 1 below. He also attacked Arnold, much as Wyclif, another Oxford man, would later attack Joachim himself, for being among the precise "calculatores" of the End. "Ista opinio est heretica," Harclay said contemptuously.[101] But in the composite manuscript Lat. Misc. c. 75 (part of which perhaps began its life in the Oxford Franciscan house and moved from there to Queens College), works by Arnold and "Joachim" are copied under the running head, both accurate and ironic, of "Apologia de . . . perversitatibus *pseudotheologorum*" (my emphasis).[102] Reasons for such caution abound: Arnold was posthumously condemned once again in part for valuing the Joachite revelations of the *Epistola Cyrilli* more than the scriptures, a text which appears next to Arnold's in the Lat. Misc. c. 75 manuscript. As we are about to see, the York Austins' medieval library catalogue shows a shelf reserved for "Prophecie et Supersticiosa," which may indicate the same sort of cautionary impulse. Both provide insight into how intellectuals saw—or how they *protected* (which is it?)—revelatory theology. Whatever it means, we note that the material itself was copied and held, not discarded.

"Prophecie et Supersticiosa": Franciscan and Austin Owners of Joachite Books and the Period of Avant-garde Disendowment Activism, 1368–80

The persecutions endured by Joachite books have to be studied over against both the traditional Benedictine and scholarly sense of openness and the love affair of the friars' orders—most especially the Franciscan and Austin—with a Joachite sense of mission. This is nowhere better epitomized than in the York Austin catalogue and also in the pro-Franciscan *Continuatio* of the *Eulogium historiarum*. I spoke above of the apparently "purposeful lull" in prosecutions of Joachite or Franciscan ideologies or ideologues that occurred between about

1368 (when the friars engineer the censure of Uthred de Boldon) and 1380 (when Friar Richard Helmyslay was charged with heresy). This was a window of opportunity for the friars' orders to push their agenda for more access to lay revenues of the kinds traditionally enjoyed by the secular and monastic clergy—a window not created by Wycliffism, but rather exploited by it. Renewed war with France in 1369 on one end and the rise of Wycliffite prosecution, at least by 1382, on the other are the benchmarks that set off this period as special. There are several items of material evidence that we can add to the historical evidence to help us understand this, among them the manuscripts of the *Eulogium*, those of Rupescissa, and the library of the York Austins.

The *Eulogium historiarum* and its *Continuatio* (continuation) contain praise of Joachim and also genuine Joachite expectation of positive things to come, especially through the new "spiritual men" or *viri spirituales*, which the chronicler refers to as the "acts" of the future "virorum Apostolicorum." The language is clearly that of Third Status Joachimism, here given full biblical resonance. In a recent brilliant article, Ruth Nissé has shown how "the prophecies in the *Eulogium* all speak to a Joachite ideology of reform," as does its politico-historical sweep and grand narrative toward "universal conversion." This is the same hopeful expectation, again, that past scholars assume to be absent from English sources. The chronicle travels in three manuscripts with copies of John of Rupescissa's *Vade mecum*, in two of which it is actually embedded within it—a textual oddity that betrays a great deal about the Franciscan empathies of the chronicle, and perhaps (though this cannot be proven) of "burying" a suspect book.[103] A similar impulse, again, not provable, may account for the omission of John of Rupescissa's name in the manuscript containing Walsingham's *Chronicle*, British Library, MS Royal 13.A.IX, a manuscript politically censored for safety's sake when Henry IV came to the throne in 1399, and in progress at the time of the Rupescissa confiscations of 1389.[104] In the *Eulogium* Joachim is also remembered as the prophet who correctly predicted the failure of the First Crusade as well as for his comments on the Apocalypse and the "Libros Prophetarum" (usually a reference to the spurious *De oneribus prophetarum*, very popular in England). Franciscan persecutions for the period of 1361–1413 are also recorded in the continuation of the *Eulogium*, which as Jeremy Catto has argued, was written for a Franciscan-sympathetic audience. English Austins, like the Franciscans, were especially interested in prophecies relating to disendowment issues. Both Franciscans and Austins in mid-century England would have admired a sensational account in the *Eulogium* of the humiliation of Uthred de

Boldon and the other representatives of the antimendicant, wealthy "possessioners" orders at the Great Council of 1374, which portrays the Franciscan John Mardisley and the Austin Thomas Ashbourne as triumphant.[105] Their triumph, which we will examine in greater detail in chapter 3, lay in convincing the Black Prince that the church has only spiritual, not financial dominion. The prince was a receptive audience.

The *Eulogium*, which alone (and perhaps a little suspiciously) contains this story, is also extremely interested in accounts of English Franciscans and heresy, prophecy, or sedition. This association becomes increasingly common later, especially by the reign of Henry IV, during which we will see an instance of eight friars hung for their incautious prophetic interpretations of a "Bridlington" prophecy.[106] While it appears to have been dangerous for Franciscans to look too overtly Joachite, especially since the arrest of Henry of Costesy and his companions, it seems to have been slightly safer for Austins. Moreover, Austins were not, as an order, burdened with the draconian papal legislation or inquisitional history of their Franciscan brothers. With the Conventual wing of the order increasingly in the dominant position throughout the mid-fourteenth century, Franciscan houses became places where radical material was held (literally, as the *Opus* author tells us) under lock and key (Appendix B). This may go some way toward explaining why it is that two *Austins* laid disendowment proposals before Parliament in 1371 (playing, of course, to the king's urgent need for money from 1369 onward), and why they figure so prominently as allies of the Franciscans. This, I would suggest, is why we see the Austin friars take on a more proactive role in this period. The power and prestige and isolation of the Benedictine monasteries appear to have made the safest haven for beleaguered Joachite optimism, with the Austin convents running a close second place.

This would appear from the case of Austin friar, John Erghome, with his stunning collection of Joachite and other prophetic texts forming part of those of his convent's library (the York Austins') during and after his lifetime. Indeed, as we will see in Case Study 1 below, the York house was likely also home to a Langland manuscript carrying one of the most dangerous Joachite prophecies extant in England. Erghome has long been known as the author of the commentary he wrote in 1362 on the so-called "Bridlington Prophecies," dedicating it to Humphrey de Bohun, earl of Hereford—political prophecy at its most obscure and audacious.[107] But there is a Joachite dimension to it as well, and a larger connection between the Austin friars and radical prophecy generally—and censorship.

For the Augustinian order, Joachim's prediction of the *viri spirituales* had long had a special resonance. Joachim had seen not one, but *two* forthcoming orders, one order of clergy and one order of monks. The Austins, unlike later Franciscans and Dominicans, traditionally cited a genuine text of Joachim[108] to support their claim to fulfill this much contested role, his famous description in the *Expositio* of an "order of hermits emulating the life of the angels" (ordo heremitarum emulantium vitam angelorum [fol. 175v]). This order will preach and defend the faith until the consummation "in spiritu Helye."[109] As Marjorie Reeves has noted of Erghome himself, the Augustinian bibliographers stress his search for such writings.[110] The extant catalogue of the York Austins gives an impressive list of his own extensive holdings in this kind of prophecy. It is headed with a dual title that leaves it up to the reader to decide which are "prophecie" and which are "supersticiosa":

Prophecie et supersticiosa
361. Ambrosii merlini prophecie
Joachim de seminibus literarum
Joachim de oneribus prophetarum
Joachim de duobus ordinibus
Joachim de successione papali [i.e., *Vaticinia de summis pontificibus*]
versus cuiusdam canonici de actibus anglie [i.e., Bridlington prophecy]
multe prophecie de anglia breves
prophecia Roberti de usecio
oraculum cirilli cum exposicione ioachim
excerpciones prophetie fr. Johannis de rupescissa
prophetia iohannis de basyngneio
prophetia cibelle cum multis aliis
compendium literale petri aureole super apoc.
prophetia canonici. *frebribus* [i.e., Bridlington prophecy][111]

This is a staggering collection, containing some extremely rare items (like the prophecies of Robert of Uzès, almost unknown in England),[112] a great deal of pseudo-Joachite prophecy, and John of Rupescissa.[113] It is also eclectic. These works rub shoulders with prophecies by Methodius, the Sibyl, and Merlin (whom Wyclif felt compelled to associate unflatteringly with Hildegard). This impressive collection rivals Henry of Kirkstede's at Bury and the Oxford Franciscans' and outflanks even collections like Canterbury's and smaller collections of

Joachitia at Benedictine abbeys like Ramsey and Byland.[114] Most interestingly, in the library catalogue the prophecy is shelved with the necromancy books (of which "I augur no good," as its modern cataloguer, M. R. James, memorably remarked). And their being *all together* (in shelf 361) would surely make it easier to control reader access or even quickly remove items from the library should the need arise.

The Bridlington prophecies circulated widely, appearing in manuscripts with Langland, Hildegard, and other visionary works.[115] As Reeves has succinctly put it, the Bridlington prophecies are "really a form of political satire on the politics and personalities [c. 1362], yet they show something of the Joachimist optimism in its expectation of an Age of Glory which is forecast to begin shortly under the Black Prince."[116] This is very similar in tone to the *Eulogium* account of the Great Council which also valorizes the Black Prince, with its glorified roles for the friars arguing against the church's right to temporal lordship (see chapter 3). Joachimism was often politicized on the Continent, and many of the most important works reached England where political prophecy was a national passion. But the force of Reeves's observation has not been fully appreciated, I think. It implies that Erghome created an original, *native* version of the genre, using current English history—that is, he was doing on the political front what Henry of Costesy had done on the exegetical, and what the *Eulogium* continuator would do shortly, as Nissé has shown. That Erghome's was recognized as such at the time is underlined by the fact that the text *circulates* with Joachite material.[117] Both the Bridlington prophecy and commentary are so deliberately enigmatic as to be impenetrable to an unwanted reader, and almost so to a desired one. They joined the ranks of Joachite books under suspicion in collections and libraries across England, and would, by the reign of Henry IV, provoke the death penalty for injudicious friars on one occasion (see chapter 5).

It is against this backdrop that we can now examine the copying of a genuinely dangerous Joachite work containing a Third Status prophecy into a *Piers Plowman* manuscript (the subject of Case Study 1 below). That manuscript was part of a collection owned, scholars believe, by the York Austins, and I offer further evidence for this provenance. They figure repeatedly in this book (being the 1368 accusers of Uthred, too) as some of the boldest and most politically savvy dealers in revelatory prophecy.[118] They were much more savvy than their Dominican colleague, Richard Helmyslay, who was condemned by the papacy for overzealous courting of lay revenues and preaching Joachite ideologies, a story for chapter 3. But first, the wiley York Austins.

CASE STUDY 1 OF DANGEROUS
READING AMONG EARLY *PIERS* AUDIENCES

The York Austins and "The Kingdom of the Holy Spirit"
in Cambridge University Library Dd.i.17

Morton Bloomfield, along with other *Piers* scholars of his generation, sought Joachite "trinitarian" patterns in *Piers Plowman*, but had to do so largely in a vacuum of historical evidence.[1] In an appendix to his *Piers Plowman as a Fourteenth-Century Apocalypse*, called "Joachim of Flora in Fourteenth-Century England," Bloomfield wrote, "The time is not yet ripe to argue the case positively, for much more needs to be known about the intellectual life of fourteenth-century England than is possible at present. Too much important material lies buried in Latin manuscripts not well known or not easily available."[2] The time, as our previous chapter has shown, is now *riper*.[3] Moreover, we have a remarkable example of just such "buried" material, and one that offers new support to Bloomfield's case in a Cambridge *Piers* manuscript, University Library Dd.i.17 (hereafter Dd). Dd contains a Joachite prophecy ensnarled in papal condemnation, but echoing many of the prophetic themes of Langland's poem. The manuscript, which scholars believe was associated with the York Austins, is entirely copied in the hand of the same scribe. It is a large, multi-volume formal anthology of historical and theological works that shows every sign of thoughtful selection and planning.[4] We have already seen much evidence for the spread of Joachite ideas in contemporary English reformist circles which, along with Dd's witness, newly enhances our understanding of the intellectual context in which Langland wrote and his audience read.

As James Simpson observed in his groundbreaking article, "The Constraints of Satire in *Piers Plowman* and *Mum and the Sothsegger*," "[the B text of] *Piers Plowman* stands on the borders of active repression."[5] Investigating some of the ecclesiastical and royal legislation of the period, Simpson suggested that the reticence Langland's narrator sometimes expresses about speaking out or offering interpretations of impolitic allegory is not merely a literary *topos*. Looking at ecclesiastical legislation (in all but one case only Wycliffite-related records), Simpson concluded that passages in the poem *could* be interpreted as suspect if read in relation to some of it. Whether or not any passages *actually* were, of course, we do not know. But certain aspects of the readership of the poem have always given cause for such speculation. The authors that still constitute some of the best-known readers of *Piers Plowman* for modern scholars include John Ball and maybe a coterie of rebel readers, or the clutch of *Plowman* tradition authors, some of whom can be associated with Lollard thought.[6] Recent scholarship has given us an idea of how such "borders of active repression" impacted upon the most famous Langlandiana: Simpson himself illuminated the ways *Mum and the Sothsegger* ran serious risks. *Pierce the Ploughman's Crede* has, we know, Lollard sympathies, even if it is not itself heterodox; and, although *Richard the Redeless* is not as politically dangerous a text as it pretends to be, its author certainly resorted to allegory of the kind usually found in political prophecy for conveying delicate matters.[7]

As Anne Hudson has observed, *Piers* was a poem that historical events made more radical as time went on.[8] But, it has been argued, this (potential for) radicalism has left little trace in the extant manuscripts. John Bowers, for instance, once expressed frustration that he could find only one manuscript, London, Society of Antiquaries, MS 687, to justify espionage into Langland's subversiveness.[9] MS 687 does indeed have a little Lollard content, but not an impressive amount—not enough to turn evidence on the poem as anything like a burnable book. However, it is not in the vernacular literature of the period that one usually finds the most radical commentary on any subject exposed. If we expand our definition of radicalism to take in more than Lollardy and rebellion, we find a good deal more.[10] So, for instance, among the indicators that the poem was seen in connection with radical or suspect thought—and not always Wycliffite—

are some of the minor Latin pieces found in manuscripts with it, material not much studied as yet, some of it even unedited. Anonymous Latin poems, broadsides, and short treatises (like exegetical prophecy) were marvelous vehicles for advancing the unspeakable. The fact that *Piers* spoke to many religious groups with radical ecclesiastical agendas is important—as important as, in the political realm, its associations with readers as different as John Ball, the Appellants, Irish factional politicians, and civil service scribes.[11] It is a sampling of anonymous Latin pieces found together with *Piers Plowman* in three different manuscripts that we will examine here and in the second and third Case Studies. These include revelatory texts transmitting radical or officially suppressed ideas about schism, disendowment, sedition, women's spiritual leadership, and inclusive views on salvation. In fact, seen from this angle, the company *Piers* keeps in certain manuscripts is surprisingly daring.

The unnoticed Joachite Schism prophecy in Dd is quite possibly the most dangerous text found in any *Piers* manuscript. The prophecy itself was cited as part of the evidence leading to Jan Hus's execution for heresy at his trial in Constance. The Joachite text in the Cambridge manuscript represents, to the best of our knowledge, a little explored audience for *Piers*: the York Austin friars, one of the largest purveyors of Joachite prophecies in England as we have just seen in chapter 2. This manuscript gives us a new window on the early reception history of *Piers*—and makes us reexamine whether it was dangerous reading by looking at what it was being read *with*.

A Suspect Joachite Schism Prophecy and Its Inquisitional History

The Cambridge prophecy, which I will call by its incipit "Regnum spiritus sancti" (The Kingdom of the Holy Spirit), is of a kind that many scholars still believe to be rare in England (the supposed rarity of this material had always been a key argument against Bloomfield's thesis). It prophesies, using genuine and full-fledged Joachite exegesis, the coming of the Age of the Spirit. In fact, as we have just seen, this sort of *Joachitia* is not so rare in medieval England, but rather its circulation has been obscure to modern scholarship for the very good reason that reference to Joachim's Third Status was considered suspect by medieval authorities. So, as chapter 2 has just shown, it was often suppressed or anonymously or pseudonymously transmitted, as indeed it is in the Cambridge *Piers* manuscript.

The prophecy is made up of two distinctive types of suspect writing: Jo-achimist exegesis of the coming "Status" of the Holy Spirit and the *Belial*, a dar-ing legal and theological text,[12] written in 1382 as propaganda in support of the schismatic pope Urban VI by Jacobus de Theramo, an Italian canon lawyer and bishop of Florence.[13] The Cambridge prophecy, a blend of material from these two unlikely sources, is cleverly hidden by a false authorship attribution to an im-peccable authority on papal law, John of Legnano (1320–83). Legnano was an in-ternationally known canon lawyer from the University of Bologna; he had writ-ten widely on censorship and excommunication issues, which made him an ideal man to attribute a prophecy to—as other ghost writers of Schism polemic al-ready knew.[14] But in fact, "Regnum" is a very radical text—some of its predic-tions are drawn verbatim from the *Belial*, which had its own censorship history, most conspicuously in the trial of Jan Hus. The reformist leader of the Hussite movement, Hus was charged with citing the *Belial* at the Council of Constance in 1414 prior to his execution, a charge we will examine in more detail below.[15]

Taken all together, the histories of these prophetic traditions indicate that not only was an apocalyptic view of history a deliberate and passionate choice of Langland's, but also that it was not entirely a *safe* choice. In fact, at the pre-cise time Langland was writing, less safe than Wycliffism—as this book shows, even Wycliffite writers usually tried to distance themselves from it, even into the fifteenth century, and wisely, it appears, in view of Hus's incrimination on this score. Moreover, in choosing this material Langland also made an *intellec-tual* choice—and a slightly unusual one, one that had an aura of Continental intrigue and high drama, tainted (long before Hus's execution) by official con-demnation or (depending on one's point of view) ennobled by the innocent deaths of those who had refused to give up their belief in radical church re-form. Reformist apocalypticism of the Schism era (of which Joachimism was by no means the only type) was also associated with entirely orthodox, but sen-sational European prophetic figures (many of them, like Hildegard,[16] Bridget of Sweden, and Catherine of Siena, women) who had famously swayed kings and threatened popes. Its attraction for Langland, then—an advocate of many just causes—was that reformist apocalypticism was a tool of the powerless and an effective one, too. Moreover, because of its revelatory nature, it could and did open up intellectual 'spaces' for new kinds of thought, spaces where a cer-tain freedom of expression and tolerance of doctrinal pluralism (even some-times non-Christian) could flourish. All in all, it must have seemed rather charismatic to Langland—a writer who empathetically portrays, for instance, spiritual suffocation under Christianity's apparently arbitrary intolerances in the breakdown of the A text and elsewhere. Langland's project, then, in borrowing from this genre, looks like a poet's attempt to infuse a tradition of Continental apocalypticism into the vernacular English scene.

We now know a good deal more not only about Joachite manuscripts, but about Langland himself than when Bloomfield wrote. We know that he was almost certainly associated in some capacity with the Westminster world of legal professionals and civil servants, a group whose interests and book ownership patterns showed them to be part of international culture.[17] This is also a culture in which not only John of Legnano, but also Joachimism, and most especially the *Belial* were known.[18] The *Belial* poses as a legal textbook teaching courtroom procedure, but its agenda was much more politically and doctrinally subversive: in effect, it puts on trial the legitimacy of God's method of effecting salvation. The *Belial* is also known in Latin by the more benign title, the *Consolatio Peccatorum* (The Consolation of Sinners), which is part of a fuller title claiming to be nothing less than a compendium on the redemption of the human race (*Compendium perbreve de redemptione generis humani*).[19]

Attribution to Legnano must have given the prophecy serious credibility in England, which was pro-Urban in Schism politics. (Legnano's defence of Urban, published internationally by Urban himself, was so convincing to the English court that it never bothered to mount its own defence on Urban's behalf.)[20] But the choice of Legnano as a name with which to 'launder' a radical prophecy in a *Piers* manuscript is an intriguing one for literary scholars both because of his great reputation at the court of Richard II and because in the "Clerk's Tale" Chaucer ranks Legnano (Lynyan) with Petrarch as the two great luminaries of Italy:

Fraunceys Petrak, the lauriat poete,
Highte this clerk, whos rethorike sweete
Enlumyned at Ytaille of poetrie,
As Lynyan dide of philosophie,
Or lawe, or oother art particuler;
But deeth, that wol nat suffre us dwellen heer,
But as it were a twynklyng of an ye
Hem bothe hath slayn, and alle shul we dye.[21]

As J. McCall points out, Chaucer's tone here has a kind of confidence that suggests that Legnano was as well or better known to his audience than Petrarch was.[22] Chaucer's own diplomatic mission to Milan in 1378 had coincided exactly with the outbreak of the Great Schism, an event which likely altered what it could achieve. This would account for Legnano's topicality, both for Chaucer and his Westminster audience. So finding Legnano's name in a Langland manuscript (given Langland's likely Westminster connections as well) is not entirely surprising.

Langland makes an apparently explicit reference to the Great Schism in lines from the B Prologue (108–11) he would later partially censor, originally written, scholars believe, sometime between 1378 and 1381. These and related lines we will examine below. But a bigger factor than historical allusion in Langland's case were the large "symbolist" systems constructed by reformist apocalyptic writers, which would have been extremely attractive in moments of crisis or doubt, especially as a window on the trans-historical (much as Chaucer used the classical *historia*). What Wyclif, for instance, misunderstood about Joachimism was that it was much more than a pack of predictions about the date of Antichrist's coming; it was a complex, majestic exegetical form, a "system" in William Blake's sense.[23] We know that the majesty of this symbolist system, along with its trajectory, however, was always somewhat uncomfortable to church authorities because it usually imagines a faithful remnant (for Joachim they were the "viri spirituales"—spiritual men) within the church hanging onto purist ideals and fighting not only demons without, but *within*. This is true of all the major thinkers: Hildegard, Joachim, William of St. Amour, Olivi, Rupescissa. And it is certainly true of Langland, vividly imagined in the battle for Unity Holy Church, itself a schism nightmare. When Antichrist makes his attack on Unity, "Proute *prestes* cam with hym—passyng an hundred," armed to the teeth, "And hadden almost Vnite and holynesse adowne" (C.XXII.218, 227). The besieged "Vnite" is by this time populated only with the faithful remnant, who for Langland are the "fools" (a concept he has used earlier in the poem to invoke both St. Paul's fools for Christ and St. Francis's *joculatores Domini*).[24] The allegory is complex. The siege is moral, historical, eschatological, and even ethnic (the priestly attackers come from Ireland [C.XXII.221]), but the outlines are clear. When Antichrist wins over the friars and the religious, the "foles were wel gladere to deye / Then to lyue lengere, sethe leautee was so rebuked" (C.XXII.62–63), and they are gathered into Unity (74–75). When these lines were first written (in B), the most recent "fools" who had died for "leautee" were the Franciscan Spirituals and the current "fools" under serious threat were those who dared to confront a newly schismatic pope. We know from manuscript evidence (to which we can now add Dd itself) that clergy concerned with precisely these matters were owners of *Piers Plowman*. Case Study 3 will examine another such owner, John Wells, who was called upon as proctor of the English Benedictines to try to save Cardinal Adam Easton from Urban's prison, and whose *ex libris* appears in the manuscript, Bodleian Library, Bodley 851, into which the Z text of *Piers Plowman* is bound.[25]

The Dd manuscript, as all modern scholars agree, is a convent production, almost certainly of the York Austin friars.[26] It is an "Olympian" compilation of works concerning salvation history and missions to the non-Christian peoples, the intertwined themes always intimately associated with medieval apocalyptic expectation.[27] Not only does the manuscript contain *Piers*, but under the *Consolatio* title the Dd scribe also copied the full Latin *Belial* itself not far from where he copied the Joachite prophecy that borrows liberally from it (fols. 231ra–261vb). The presence of both shows an unusually knowledgeable compiler, though folio 262, which contained the very end of the *Belial*, therefore presumably its overtly partisan colophon, is gone from the manuscript, a defect supplied only by a sixteenth-century hand. There is also no rubric heading the author's address ("Universis Christi fidelibus . . ."). These things may point to some awareness of the danger of the text. By 1400–10 Jacobus was in official trouble with the papacy and prevented, even as bishop of Florence, from traveling to the Council of Pisa. Jacobus was well known across Europe for this work and in Hussite circles where Joachimism also traveled.[28] The *Belial* was cited in the inquisition records of Jan Hus,[29] a fact that likely prompted the radical bowdlerization of the text when it was translated into German. In its Latin form, however, the full *Belial* exists in dozens upon dozens of manuscripts on the Continent, where it travels in just the kind of company as *Piers* does, that is, with works like *Mandeville's Travels* (also in Dd) and other writings concerned with the peaceful conversion of the non-Christian peoples.[30] It also travels with other works concerned with the "legal" issues surrounding the redemption of humankind with the potential for universal salvation that Christ's Harrowing seems to hold out.

Jacobus's treatment is so staggering because for him these "legal" issues refer to the validity of *God's* judgement, reminiscent of the spirit in which Langland's narrator rails himself into near unorthodoxy at the end of the A text. The *Belial* is constructed as a case involving the devil's claim on the souls that Christ "stole" during the Harrowing of hell and a debate between the Four Daughters of God. This is portrayed as a stunning courtroom drama such as Langland himself might have written if he had chosen to compose in the dialogically "roomier" forum of Latin. Just to give a brief sense of why this work startled its readers, it shows Belial (acting for the Conclave of the Devils in a scene reminiscent of *Paradise Lost*) pointing out that God is ineligible as a judge because of his relationship with the defendant (Christ)![31] Solomon, therefore, is deputed to act for God, thus beginning a series of evolving court battles in which Moses is a lawyer for Christ, an appeal is heard before the Patriarch Joseph, and, eventually, brought to a close by the mediation of David. It is perhaps no wonder that some of the vernacular versions of *Belial* would later find their way onto the Index.[32]

In addition to the daring theological maneuvers that Jacobus makes to get fair legal representation and counsel for the devil's party, the text was also suspect for the radical apocalypticism it espoused. In this context, it is interesting that the *Belial* also travels with the *Ackermann aus Böhmen*, that is, the German work about a peasant-husbandman (Ackermann) that Konrad Burdach thought most like *Piers Plowman* in radical social thought and in chiliasm. (He mentions especially the fight with the devil over the stolen fruit in Langland's Tree of Charity passage, the Harrowing, and the Four Daughters of God.)[33] In German, this much copied legal textbook was propagated by the German chancery, who also, in another interesting parallel with the Westminster transmission of *Piers Plowman*, propagated *Der Ackermann*.[34] These works testify to the vitality of the legal literary tradition in which Langland himself wrote, and the parallels between and among these texts and our little Joachite prophecy that borrows overtly from *Belial* are indeed striking.

Often denounced as blasphemous right down to the nineteenth century, it is from this popular (extant in over 114 manuscripts) and very suspect work that the author of the Cambridge prophecy borrowed large verbatim chunks. Using a detailed exegetical analysis, genuinely Joachite in both the positive role it gives to Old Testament women in salvation history[35] and to the Jewish people generally, the Cambridge prophecy explains how the different faiths arose from the children of Leah and Rachel and their handmaidens. "Regnum" proves, after exhaustive exegesis, that the Age of the Spirit had its beginning in Rachel, "through whom the seed of Abraham is saved."[36] Rachel, it says, represents the Synagogue, whose fruitfulness was not ultimately "barren" (sterilem), but merely delayed, conceiving spiritually by the Holy Spirit and bringing forth both the people of Israel and the people of Judah, that is, both the unfaithful and faithful.[37] What is especially striking here is the timelessness of Rachel's contribution, as present and enduring for this writer as we more usually find in Marian devotion. Mary, we should note, is not ever mentioned in the prophecy, which is a 'de-centering' of conventional ideas of the "church" more radical than even Joachim's own exegesis represents (where Rachel is usually paired with Mary).[38] Through Rachel, the prophecy asserts, all salvation comes and the kingdom of the Holy Spirit itself, described in true Joachite fashion as coming *after* Antichrist.

What is especially interesting about the "Regnum" theme of Rachel and Leah is that another Schism prophecy, also falsely attributed to Legnano, begins, "In illo tempore erunt duo sponsi, unus legitimus et alter adulter" (In that time there will be two spouses, one legitimate, and the other an adulterer) and goes on to prophesy that the adulterer will reign (adulter regnabit).[39] The application to the Schism is obvious, and the Cambridge "Regnum" prophecy (note even the similarity in diction) seems, by comparison, much more subtle and original in giving this theme of the two wives a Joachite exegetical twist.

The "Regnum" prophet tells us that following the abomination of Antichrist against the true vicar of Christ in his church and kingdom, "through the time and times and half a time, which are three and a half years, according to Daniel,"[40] the whole church and kingdom of Christ will be renewed (renouabitur), and the greatest peace would descend upon Jerusalem and throughout the whole world for 1,000 years.[41] But before these marvelous events there will be apocalyptic horrors, and for these the author liberally plagiarizes the *Belial*: the time "from the desolation of the temple of the Jews until the Infernal Power" is complexly calculated by consulting Daniel—I spare you the mathematics— but Antichrist will be vicar of the church against "the true vicar" sometime between the years 1364 and 1409. He will persecute the holy in the worst tribulation ever seen and will command the destruction of the Holy of Holies and the burning of the Old and New Testament (sancta sanctorum destrui ac novum & vetus testamentum concremari).[42] This last section, and the 1409 dating, is taken over entirely from the *Belial*.[43] It suggests a creative reworking both of the Joachite "angelic pope" tradition and the prophecy made infamous by the 1255 condemnation regarding the superceding of the Old and New Testaments by the "Eternal Gospel" in the Age of the Spirit. This, we have seen, was widely regarded by writers as different as the imprisoned *Opus* author and Thomas Netter as the essence of Joachite heresy.

This was a convenient prophecy to present to a pope locked in schism, especially a pope one is hoping to flatter—and this is apparently just what Jacobus did when he wrote the *Belial,* the colophon of which stresses that it was composed in 1382, during the pontificate of "the most holy . . . Lord Urban VI, pope of the *Universal* Church."[44] Whoever created the Cambridge prophecy knew precisely what he was doing, then, in attributing it to Urban's chief apologist, Legnano, and, in fact, he refers directly to Jacobus's *Belial* ("vt dictum est in tractatu Belial nuncupato compositum per [sic] urbanum sextum"). And he was clearly also well versed in genuine Joachite thought—knowledgeable enough (as we saw with his handling of Rachel) to be creative with it. The expectation of a coming Age of the Holy Spirit is a touchstone, perhaps the most reliable of any, for what distinguishes Joachite from non-Joachite apocalyptic thinkers. Elsewhere I have discussed the complexities of this argument, especially as they relate to Langland's own sense of the future, as in the blissful *pacis visio* (C.III.436 ff.) with its end to war, its "o cristene kyng," and universal illumination of Jews and Muslims, who "shal syng *Credo in spiritum sanctum.*"[45] Another such passage is his *ad pristinum statum* prophecy of C.V.168 ff. with its sweeping vision of wealth redistribution for the reform of Holy Church, "clothed newe."[46] My concern here, however, is with the aspects of this expectation on record as having *worried the authorities* and which we do find echoed in *Piers* or, at the very least, in passages that could be mistaken for such an expectation.

By 1400 Jacobus himself was in official trouble, and by 1414 his *Belial* was, too. Among the charges against Hus at the Council of Constance was that he had cited this prophecy as applying to Pope Alexander V.[47] This inquisition record runs: "Likewise, article nine, in which is contained that Joannes Hus said in the vernacular to the people (dixit in vulgari ad populum), "Behold fulfilled is the prophecy which was foretold by Jacobus de Theramo, that in the year of our Lord 1409 will arise one who will persecute the Gospels and the faith of Christ, through these things denoting Lord Alexander, who in his bulls commanded the books of Wyclif to be burned."[48] Here, the burning of the Old and New Testaments (some thirty years after Jacobus first wrote these lines in 1382) is associated with Wycliffism. Indeed, on the Continent, the *Belial* does travel in several manuscripts with Wycliffite material.[49] But the *Belial* portion of the Cambridge prophecy says nothing about Wyclif. It is lifted, as we have just seen, almost verbatim from the original *Belial.* It describes the coming period of Antichrist's reign as pope during which the church will be persecuted through temporal kings for nine years, the blood of the clergy will flow just like water, and there will be great famine and tribulation such as "has not been seen before among the people of the church of Christ," not to mention schism (of course), and the destruction of "the Holy of Holies" and the burning of the Old and New Testament.[50] All this is to occur before the kingdom of the Holy Spirit on earth, though the timing of various events after that is confused, and the prophecy eventually winds down with the Last Judgement in the vale of Jehoshaphat.

Now, there is much here that would interest a reader of Langland's own prophecies, copied in Dd, of course, not many folios away. His are not quite so sensational as this, but they were not that far off: *Piers Plowman* also envisions Antichrist taking over the papal throne (a prophecy certainly *in vulgari ad populum*):

> For Auntecrist and hise al the world shal greue
> And acombre þe, Consience, bote yf Crist the helpe.
> And false profetes fele, flateres and glosares,
> Shal come and be curatours ouer kinges and erles.
> And thenne shal pryde be pope and prince of holy chirche,
> Coueytise and vnkyndenesse cardynales hym to lede.
>   (C.XXI.219–24; B.XIX.217).

There is also the disendowment prophecy of a temporal king "beating" the church (C.V.168) and forebodingly predicted famine and flood (C.VIII.343 ff.), all motifs that occur in *Belial* and in "Regnum." Langland, too, has elaborate schemes of future church history that posit patterns of tribulation and renewal, all easily—whatever his own views—*mistaken* for Joachimism. As we saw in chapter 2, Langland's refounding of the church after Pentecost parallels Olivi's, as does his treatment of the "incurable wound" as a metaphor for evangelical poverty. And his fourfold allegory of the Harrowing of hell scene, which rages against arid clerical intellectualism via the threatening apocalyptic image of the vintage of Jehoshaphat for which Christ thirsts (XX.410), is nearly Joachite in exegetical complexity:[51]

> Y fauht so, me fursteth 3ut, for mannes soule sake.
> *Sicio.*
> May no pyement ne pomade ne preciouse drynkes
> Moiste me to þe fulle ne my furst slokke
> Til þe ventage valle in þe vale of Iosophat,

And I drynke riht rype must, *resureccio mortuorum*.
And thenne shal y come as kynge, with croune and with angeles,
And haue out of helle alle mennes soules.

(C.XX.408–14)

This same combination of apocalyptic exegesis and salvational generosity appears in various Joachite contexts.[52] Of the Schism itself, Langland had much more to say than he felt able to write: his contempt for the college of cardinals is first thinly veiled, "And power presumed in hem a pope to make," and then tantalizingly withheld, "Forthi I can and can nauȝte of courte speke more" (B. Prol.108 and 111)—a kind of toying with would-be censors that he suppressed in the C text (when, as Adam Easton's case in the mid-1380s shows, speaking out on Schism matters was becoming more dangerous—at least for those within Urban's reach!). We see in Langland's C some of the limitations of speaking "in vulgari ad populum"—but also why the Cambridge "Regnum" prophecy and the *Belial*, both couched in the safety of Latin, would be of interest to the compiler of a manuscript containing *Piers Plowman*—or vice versa. There is even a handy finding tab on the first folio of "Regnum" for ease of cross-comparison within the collection (figure 10a).

How aware was the English compiler that he was dealing with a dangerous or at least a potentially dangerous text? And did he, like Hus's inquisitors, see the text (especially the reference to the Old and New Testament being burned) as a Wycliffite motif? Or was the impulse for copying it an interest in Joachite or Continental or Schism prophecy? The question may seem minute, but it is not: it can teach us, first of all, not to jump to conclusions that Wycliffism was the dominant mode of radical reformist thought in the last quarter of the fourteenth century. And it can help us narrow the date of compilation for the long undateable Dd, which has not been dateable more precisely than the last quarter of the fourteenth century or the first quarter of the fifteenth. In answer to the first question, we recall that neither the *Belial* nor the Cambridge prophecy mentions the burning of *Wyclif's* books (Dd reads just "novum, et vetus testamentum concremari," while "libros Wiclifi cremari" occurs only in the Hus inquisition records). Jacobus, we remember, was writing on the Continent in 1382. What was in Jacobus's mind was most likely a memory of the Joachite scandal of the Eternal Gospel in 1254, in which the fanatic Gerard of Borgo San Donnino claimed that the Old and New Testaments would be "superceded" (in some later accounts, as we have seen, this becomes "destroyed") in the imminent Age of the Holy Spirit.[53] Nor did the English scribe of the Cambridge manuscript react to the particular passage on burning books. We know this because he supplied marginal brackets highlighting what *he* thought were the two most important passages, the first (figure 10a) beginning with the description of the coming reign of the Holy Spirit following the reign of Antichrist, the reference to the *Belial* tract and Urban VI, and ending with the description of schism and clerical desolation; the second bracket (figure 10b) highlighting the passage giving the dates 1364 and 1409 and the verbatim quotation from the *Belial*. These marginal brackets strongly suggest Schism concerns and Joachite interests, not Wycliffite ones. His bracket, moreover, stops *before* the mention of the burning of the Old and New Testaments, which is unlikely to have been missed by any reader after this actually begins to happen in England (after 1388) — or at least any reader as preoccupied with Wycliffism as modern scholars assume normative for Ricardian England. A further clue to possible dating is that the copyist either invoked or at the very least retained the name of John of Legnano, who died in 1383 and whose currency value or topicality belongs not so much to the fifteenth century but earlier, to the period of the Schism from its outbreak in 1378 until Urban's death in 1390 and shortly thereafter. Other items in the manuscript that can be dated point to about this period of the 1380s (for their composition, at least, if not their copying).[54] There is no doubt, however, that for this writer, the avant-garde way of thinking about the Schism is Joachite, which makes sense, given its prominence as an *older*, radical "left-wing" reformist ideology. The evidence of "Regnum," then, puts two interesting possibilities before us: either it indicates that the prophecy was *copied* before about 1390 or, if it was copied any later, the scribe did not care a tuppence for current Wycliffite-related events. If by some chance the manuscript was copied *after* Constance (which is at least paleographically possible), he did not bother to update any of his chronicles — even on fol. 93 to make reference to the Rising of 1381. And he was a brave compiler indeed.

Some further evidence for the thesis that the scribe was interested in Joachite, not Wycliffite matters comes from Ian Doyle's evidence that the manuscript was associated with the York convent of the Austin friars (the older view that it came from Glastonbury is problematic).[55] The Joachite materials of the York Austins, in fact, as we saw in chapter 2, are among the most extensive and exciting collection of English *Joachitia* known to us today, thanks largely to John Erghome, active there in the decades between 1360 and 1390. He is, of course, most likely the author of another suspect prophetic work, the commentary on the Bridlington

10 a and b. Fols. 203v and 204 of Cambridge University Library, MS Dd.i.17, showing scribal highlighting brackets in the Pseudo-Legnano "Kingdom of the Holy Spirit" prophecy ("Regnum spiritus sancti"), and on 203v a finding tab so that the prophecy can be easily

located in the manuscript. On 204, the scribe takes no notice of the reference to the burning of the Old and New Testaments, which occurs further down. Reproduced by permission of the Syndics of Cambridge University Library.

prophecies, which can also be found in manuscript with *Piers Plowman* (Bodley 851, with Ramsey associations, another convent known today to have held *Joachitia*, and a manuscript we will examine in Case Study 3).[56] If Dd were made among the York Austins or even simply had a provenance there, this suggests strongly that the scribe was motivated by Joachite interests, for which he had a superb library at his fingertips and colleagues passionate on the subject to consult.

Both Jacobus and the author of the Cambridge "Kingdom of the Holy Spirit" prophecy who plagiarized him are close to Langland in mentality. Along with Walter Brut, that "idiosyncratic" Lollard, all of them strive for a more inclusive approach to salvation history, all are pushing the limits of freedom of discussion—only Langland is pushing them in the vernacular and perhaps, then, it is no surprise that Langland's is the most conservative of the three. But Langland was prompted by an impulse—which suited his inclusivist temperament very well—to import a charismatic and slightly dangerous Continental apocalypticism, well represented by but not limited to Joachimism, into his English poetic project. He was using reformist models of an older stripe, models which after the later 1380s would be, like his own poem, under pressure of appropriation into a Wycliffite agenda (where they underwent a kind of censorship, too). Langland, I will suggest later in the book, resisted that appropriation with everything in him, just as we see evidence that in C he resisted the 1381 rebels' appropriation of what his poem was about.

Both Chaucer and Langland, then, experimented with Continental models and genres—Chaucer, as is well known, with foreign literary and humanist texts, but Langland with reformist apocalypticism most of which was composed abroad at the time.[57] Both did so for similar reasons, I would suggest—to explore possibilities that could not otherwise be explored within a strict sense of Insular orthodoxy. Chaucer, then, was not the only Ricardian author to be seduced by Continental genres in an attempt to explore difficult philosophical problems unhampered by his present historical moment. Just how strict Chaucer's sense of the confinement was may be seen finally by his "Retraction" (if it is what it seems to be) and by the medieval reception of his work (discussed in chapter 9). Langland's literary world was more parochial, but his theology and his sense of orthodoxy seem to have been much more spacious. He, too, however, turned to a trans-historical and trans-cultural genre for room to breathe.

Chapter Three

TWO THIRTEENTH-CENTURY CONDEMNED BOOKS AND THEIR REVIVAL

Amourian Eschatology, Antimendicant Polemic, and
Ricardian Literature, 1358–89

In the second half of the fourteenth century the York Austins, as we have just seen, were at the forefront of the study and transmission of radical prophecy. This project was part of a wider fraternal-led campaign to court the laity with ideas of church reform which was to have, the friars hoped, two happy effects: a redistribution of opportunities for the cure of souls (a lucrative business) and a redistribution of the considerable wealth of the established religious orders. As is well known, this programme did not win friends and influence people among the monastic and secular clergy, and what modern scholarship has studied as the mendicant controversies resulted. Less widely understood is that prophecy, both Joachite and Amourian, was to play a key role in the battle that ensued. This chapter is about three phases of that battle, and two banned books that would prove significant weapons in each.

During these years Richard Kilvington went to the trouble to acquire, as we saw in chapter 2, one of the most officially damning documents against the friars known to history at the time, the exceedingly rare Protocol of Anagni. The Protocol, once again, was the 1255 record of the condemned opinions of Gerard, who, of course, had creatively pressed Joachim of Fiore's trinitarian notions of history into ham-fisted heterodoxy by insisting that he had predicted the demise of the New Testament. In acquiring a copy of the Protocol, Kilvington was, I will argue, fantasizing that he was following in the footsteps of his hero, William of St. Amour, who had used the extremist views of Gerard to gain the papal condemnation of the friars in 1255. These books, both prophetic, played a pivotal role in England in the second half of the fourteenth century as first the antimendicant forces, and then the mendicant forces dominated the agenda. Nothing shows the shift between those two phases more clearly than the tracing of two significant silencings in this period. The first was an Oxford condemnation of an Austin friar known only as John for Joachite-inflected heresy in 1358. The second was the silencing of the Benedictine, Uthred de Boldon, and other high-level representatives of the antimendicant alliance in a Great Council called by the king in 1374. Even by 1368 the antimendicant forces had engineered the condemnation of Uthred's unique revelatory theology,[1] but 1369 gave the fraternal powers the upper hand decisively when renewed war with France brought an urgent need for new government finances. A third silencing signals the final phase, and a reversal of mendicant fortunes, with the trial for heresy of Friar Richard Helmyslay in 1380 for opinions like those for which Friar John was condemned in 1358.

Our two major Ricardian writers wrote across these historical shifts, and these battles were the route by which Chaucer, Langland, and at least one talented Anglo-Irish poet encountered Joachimism, albeit as hostile sources. Gerard's text had by then been made famous by William's widely publicized "eight signs of the End," which, in literary vernacular circles, were famously employed in Jean de Meun's continuation of *Le Roman de la Rose*. In chapter 2 we also saw that there is a history of condemnations, suspicions, and negative press about Joachite thought in England going back as far as 1215, enough to prompt the hiding and mutilation of several texts. This chapter will deal with the two condemned thirteenth-century books as they were known in the mid-fourteenth century, especially in Kilvington's strangely marked copy of the condemnation of Gerard, in various readers of William's book, and *The Romance of the Rose*'s account of both books. It will also deal with Chaucer's sophisticated knowledge of the *Roman*'s antimendicantism and the way Langland's writing straddles this antimendicant-prophetic divide. The 1358 condemnation of Friar John illuminates the climate in which Langland wrote the A text and together with the 1389 confiscations of Joachite and Amourian books exactly bracket the period of Langland's active work as a writer. The 1389 confiscations perhaps intrude themselves directly into the period of Chaucer's creative antimendicantism as well.

Studying Revelatory Theology from Hostile Sources

In þis tyme were condempned be þe Pope Alisaundre too cursed bokes. On seid þat all religious men, þou þei preche þe word of God, if it be soo þat þei be of swech order as begge, þei schal neuyr be saued. The oþir seyde þat þe gospel whech Crist prechid bryngith no man to perfeccion, and þat same gospel schuld be avoided in þe ȝere of oure Lord mcclx, and þat same ȝere schuld beginne þe doctrine of Joachim, whech doctrine þe maker of þe book clepid þe Euyrlastyng Gospell.[2]

This pope [Alexander IV] also condemned two harmful books. One of these maintained that all members of religious Orders who preach the word of God while living wholly on alms could not be saved. . . .[3] The second book contained many lies [multas falsitates] against the teaching of Abbot Joachim, which the Abbot had never written [non scripserat]. For it maintained that the gospel of Christ and the teaching [doctrina] of the New Testament had never led anybody to perfection [neminem ad perfectum duxerat] and that they were to be superseded in the year 1260 [evacuanda erat MCCLX° anno].[4]

The verbal parallels between John Capgrave's fifteenth-century English account and Salimbene de Adam's fuller thirteenth-century account of Pope Alexander IV's two condemnations show that the two chroniclers, separated by an ocean and two hundred years, are nonetheless part of the same international historians' textual network. The two condemned books were the *Evangelium eternum* of Gerard (especially his *Liber introductorius*) and the *De periculis novissimorum temporum* of William of St. Amour. These two condemnations together were to change late medieval ecclesiastical history—and were still being fought out in fourteenth-century England in a variety of cases of censorship, among which FitzRalph's ill-fated campaign, which so impacted Wyclif's,[5] is only the best known. But the tendency in literary studies has often been to see "antimendicantism" (a term that obscures as much as it explains) as a one-dimensional affair based wholly on the jealousy older clerical groups felt about the arrival of the friars, or on lay "anticlericalism," an even vaguer concept.

In fact, a large amount of "antimendicantism" came from within the friars' orders themselves.[6] This, too, we have seen at work in Olivi, Rupescissa, and the tragic persecution of the Spirituals who admired their commitment to uncompromising evangelical poverty. At the heart of this complex struggle lies the work of William of St. Amour, which fed off, or better devoured Gerard's banned work, and turned it inside out. Both, in their different ways, were revelatory theology: Gerard was attempting a republication of Joachim's main works, fronted by his own extremist apocalyptic claims; William's was an eschatological polemic, unexpectedly like what he was attacking in the *Joachitae*. These intertwined condemnations were also to change both ecclesiastical and literary history, the latter because Jean de Meun's continuation of *The Romance of the Rose* devoured both. The impact of all this digestion on Chaucer's *Canterbury Tales* (which shows forensic evidence of more) and even on Langland's *Piers Plowman* will occupy us here, as will a different way of understanding what happened to suspect revelatory theology between the time of FitzRalph and the time of Wyclif.

Gerard's Condemned Book and Kilvington's Copy of the Protocol of Anagni

We saw in chapter 2 that Richard Kilvington owned a copy of excerpts from genuine and pseudonymous Joachite writings, themselves linked to a copy of the very rare Protocol of Anagni, that is, the condemnation of Gerard's book, and that Kilvington was a very nervous owner of this manuscript. Kilvington was, of course, FitzRalph's key supporter, and they appear together regularly (sometimes as "the two Richards") in the antimendicant polemics and broadsides of the day.[7] But why were FitzRalph and Kilvington doing such serious and (for diehard antimendicants) *unpleasant* homework on Joachimism and the scandal of the Eternal Evangel exactly a hundred years after it happened? One reason, surely, is that it was marvelous propaganda against the friars—if anything, a century of ecclesiastical persecution of Spirituals had made it more, not less sensational. The manuscript is professionally and carefully produced, "censured" by its editor in at least one place, as we saw; it is also minutely corrected throughout by the scribe (who must have been comparing it with another exemplar because he is correcting wrongly expanded abbreviations) and signed by the dean himself on every bifolium. We must assume that Kilvington's interests in it were not merely antiquarian, and that he feared that others' interests would not be either—no one packages and protects a book like this unless its power to influence was somehow cause for anxiety. In fact, Franciscans were still being burned in the 1350s for Joachite-related ideas, as Kilvington and FitzRalph knew from their extensive professional associations at the curia and elsewhere.

When I first discovered the special "packaging" of the manuscript, I assumed it had to do only with suspicions of the Joachite texts that *precede* the Protocol: extracts from the *Liber de concordia* and the pseudo-Joachite *De oneribus*. But I now think it is as much the Protocol itself, a riveting, almost exploratory document written before the serious persecutions of the later thirteenth and early fourteenth centuries had fully taken hold.[8] Moreover, the pseudo-Joachite works that also appear in Kilvington's manuscript, although polemically radical exegetical works, are nonetheless stylistically so obscure that few readers (by Kilvington's time) could likely have penetrated them without a gloss identifying the political players of a previous century. The *De oneribus* and other such Joachite works appear in several other manuscripts of English provenance with a reasonable minimum of fuss, although these are usually anonymously transmitted and owned. These, I think, could justly be called *suspect* works, though not *officially condemned* ones.

The Protocol itself, however, records an officially condemned work at length, and relatively unjudgementally in places. Moreover, the text of the Protocol lifts out every thought from Joachim's work that might possibly be construed as radical, and inevitably, in lifting each out of context, they appear more so (a similar, more egregious process can be seen in the treatment of Olivi's and, later, Marguerite Porete's works).[9] It is a long text, running to fifty pages in print, and is unlike most lists of articles under condemnation I know. Most other lists are worded so as to carefully mark each sentence or article as "falsus," "error," "heresis," or some such official term. But the Anagni commissioners are remarkably content to let the material speak for itself.[10] And in 1263, long before anyone was put to death for Franciscan Joachimism, it was safe to do so. And it was also, perhaps, safer not to be too condemnatory, given the long-standing papal penchant for favouring the friars. But by the 1350s the world had changed dramatically. Open the *Protocol* to any page, then, and the reader is greeted with long passages of unmarked "suspect" doctrine. The commission-ers usually only call Joachim's opinions "curiosa" (or some such synonym), and, on stronger points, "inepta."[11] This is very different from the terminology of condemnation that greets most later opinion under inquisition.

The *Protocol* begins with the problem of Gerard's *Introductorius*, that is, his introduction to his so-called *Evangelium eternum* (the body of which was simply, scholars today think, Joachim's *Liber de concordia*, his *Expositio in Apoca-lypsim*, and his *Psalterium decem chordarum*—in other words, Joachim's three major works). The commissioners' method with Gerard's text, they tell us, speak-ing in the first person, was to note and extract (notavimus et extraximus [59]) samples of the ideas that they found erroneous. They did not even try to list all the "errors and fatuous things" (errores et fatuitates) in the book, concluding impatiently that "the whole book" is replete with these and similar things (quia totus liber istis et consimilibus respersus est). They seem to have tired of writing them down (ideo noluimus plura scribere), because they believe these are suffi-cient for the knowing of the book (quia credimus ista sufficere ad cognoscen-dum de libro [62]). Their main objection to Gerard is the way he uses Joachim's notion of a coming Third Status so literally as to suggest that the *Bible itself will be superceded* by what Gerard calls the Eternal Evangel. They say, for instance, "*expressius* in chapter XXV" he compares "the Old Testament to the brightness of the stars [vetus testamentum claritati stellarum], the New Testament to the brightness of the moon [novum testamentum claritati lune], and the *evangelium eternum* or *Spiritus Sancti* to the brightness of the sun [claritati solis]" (60). This infamous motif, of course, we will also meet in William of St. Amour (from whom we will see it quoted by the English Ricardian chronicler, Knighton) and, even more infamously, in *The Romance of the Rose*.

What worried the commissioners more than finding fault with Gerard (which was like shooting fish in a barrel) was the delicate business of sorting out whether and where Joachim had erred. Joachim was a complex and subtle mind, sugges-tive and inductive, never bald. The commission seems to be alternately fasci-nated with and frightened by his thought; as compared to three pages on Ger-ard's *Introductorius*, they spend forty-five on Joachim's works. They go to the trouble of acquiring "*originalia* Joachim de Florensi monasterio"—clearly they knew that much falsely attributed writing was circulating—and reading them thoroughly for suspect doctrine (a massive task). Joachim was, as William of St. Amour grumbled in his appeal to his own condemnation, a darling of the papacy, so there seems to have been a political issue for the commissioners, too.[12]

This accounts, I think, for a great deal of Kilvington's nervousness a full century later about possession of the Protocol. Both the friars and Joachim enjoyed a great deal of papal favour. So the commissioners made the effort, I believe, to quote Joachim at length, perhaps in the hope that it would speak for itself. Their quotations are, again, all set out *without* the usual language of "pestifer," "detestabilis," "diabolicus" used to describe heretics and heretical doctrine.[13] It is difficult to know, then, whether we are seeing prematurity in the thirteenth-century inquisitional system, or a real openness to intellectual freedom in the Protocol, or the restraint of papal politics here—or all three. In any case, I would suggest, there was not enough *visible* condemnation in the document to make a fourteenth-century owner like Kilvington easy.

Nor would it have made, a few decades later, a Wycliffite easy. Gerard's coming Age of the Eternal Gospel prophesied evangelical poverty for the clergy and a real democratization of the clerical office, highlighting a view of salvation history that gave messianic roles to figures of each of the three ages, including the friars in the present one. So, for instance, after citing the passage on the primacy of John, the commissioners continue, though, again, not with much comment, to extract further evidence for the radical Joachite "decentring" of Peter, and even Christ.[14] They also note that a special order will transmit the Eternal Evangel, the order called "nudipedum" (barefoot) (Gerard's plug, of course, for the Franciscans) with equal parts drawn from the laity and the clergy. We can see why Wycliffites, with their championing of poor clerics and lay preaching, would later be zealous to distinguish their own agenda from this extremely radical Joachite one—which was, thanks to William of St. Amour and Jean de Meun, much the best-known form of "Joachimism" in England.

It is these aspects of Joachim's thought, overblown in Gerard, that finally bring out some intolerance in the otherwise cautious commissioners. Alerted by the egregiousness of Gerard's extreme trinitarian history, their first declaration is that the doctrine of the three *status* is fundamental to Joachim's thought. The "decentring" of Christ's role in history made for a more tacit unease on the commission than with Gerard. So, too, did the Joachite vision (as we saw in Olivi) of the lack of need for clerical mediation in the Third Status, where, spiritual knowledge will be conveyed *sine enigmate et sine figuris.*[15] These things eventually provoke an explicit outburst of disapproval, especially the exalting of one order over the whole church, which they call "new and false opinions" and directly invoke Gratian on heresy: "And therefore the definition of . . . Gratian is pertinent, that a heretic is 'one who chooses [for himself] that discipline which he believes to be better.'" The commissioners are also upset by what they take to be Joachim's repeated tendency to elide Babylon with the institution of the Roman church. They devote a whole chapter to "noting those things which make for or tend *ad depressionem et cessationem* not only of the clergy, but of the *vite active ecclesia*" (78). This is put even more strongly at the end of the chapter as: "how this doctrine tends finally to the *subversion* [subversionem] of the clergy . . . the roman church and obedience to it" (82). They end the Protocol with extracts on Joachim's views of the Trinity, aware of the official condemnation of one technical aspect of these at the Lateran Council in 1215. Finally they complain, in a kind of venting tone, "These extracts are from the books of Joachim, which ought to suffice to the knowing of his doctrine . . . in which are contained much that is *curiosa, inutilia et inepta.*" But, we must note, not "heretical."

We now have a much clearer sense of why Kilvington signed every other bifolium of this manuscript in case any part went astray: it is entirely possible that a loose bifolium might not contain much condemnatory editorializing of any sort. The attempt to acquire the Protocol, however, alerts us to the fact that the Insular antimendicant party was at the forefront of European understanding of this, as of much else. One glance at the extensive list of publications by FitzRalph and Kilvington[16] tells us that they were serious academics, trained in scholasticism and, like Wyclif and other intellectuals, prepared to use revelatory theology against itself.

William of St. Amour's Condemned Book and Tactical Eschatology: A Brief Background to the 1256 Condemnation

William's *De periculis novissimorum temporum* is a tactical work, or better, an allegorical one. Pretending to be a long exegetical commentary on 2 Timothy 3:1–8, *De periculis* never names the friars explicitly, but tells of a group of religious hypocrites (habentes speciem quidem pietatis) that will arise in the last days, leading astray the faithful, especially women (captivas ducunt mulierculas).[17] He then gives forty signs for distinguishing true from false apostles (that is, for telling secular pastors from friars), and a further eight signs that the End Times are nigh.[18] These verses from 2 Timothy 3 had in fact been used earlier in history to castigate the Waldensian heretics and the Beghards,[19] and so it was a sensational move to apply them (as William was apparently the first to do) to orthodox orders within the church. To attack the mendicant orders in the 1250s, however, was to take on a powerful and learned set of enemies, at the apex of which sat the papacy itself. William's *De periculis* was to be itself condemned by the papal court, despite the fact that he, ironically like the Joachite sources he was attacking, availed himself of two protective shields: eschatology and exegesis. William called himself merely an "explanator scripturarum," an *explicator* of scripture and prophecy, and like many who combined exegesis and eschatology, he was suspicious of scholasticism, preferring an older, gloss-based mode.[20]

The whole structure of the *De periculis* is eschatological, but at the same time it is constructed as an overt attack on the Joachite apocalypticism currently fashionable among the friars. Attacking the friars as *Joachitae* William was on safe ground: in fact, it earned him the one papal victory he ever enjoyed against his opponents. When William took the case of the seculars against the mendicants to Rome in 1254, he also took with him a copy of thirty-two excerpts from Gerard's *Introductorius*.[21] The effect was instantaneous: the work was condemned, and Innocent IV began to issue bulls curtailing the mendicant's privileges. However, sixteen days after the most important of these bulls (*Etsi animarum*) was issued, Innocent dashed all of William's success by suddenly dying.[22] With the election of Alexander IV, the tables were turned, and eventually William and several other leaders of the seculars (Odo of Douai, Nicholas of Bar-sur-Aube, and Christian of Beauvais) were deprived of their benefices. Worst of all, the *De periculis* was officially condemned in 1256 and William was banished for life from Paris.[23]

What was the nature of William's eschatology? Was it revelatory or merely rhetorical? Most scholars have thought it simply rhetorical, but James Dawson has significantly challenged this,

> Some have been inclined to dismiss this element as a rhetorical device. But the apocalyptic theme was persistent in William's writings . . . which show a recurrent interest in the schemes of historical periodization and a strong belief that the present age is the climactic age of world history.[24]

Whether William honestly believed that the friars were Antichrist we do not know. But some serious aspects of his eschatology are very clear: first, that he shared with Hildegard and even Joachim a sense of the periodization of history that included waves of Antichristian forces, such as the Pharisees, the heretics of the early church, and the present pseudo-apostles (for him, the friars). Second, his eschatology was the traditional pessimistic sort, apparently seriously rattled by the optimism of the new Joachite version. In the *De periculis,* William made the appearance of the "Eternal Evangel" the first sign that the End was at hand (*De periculis,* 27). In William's thought, then, we seem to have a clash between old and new eschatologies. We know, for instance, that he had attacked Bonaventure for his belief that the church would imminently return to the primitive condition of apostolic poverty in the upcoming and final age, an idea Langland later used (and which proves that Langland was not Amourian in all things).[25] The *De periculis* itself seems bent on reasserting the traditional eschatological view that the world was in its final age, that the eighth age would be one of resurrection only.[26] Certainly one must concede, however *ad hoc* or rhetorical or sensational William's eschatology appears (and it is all those things), that he went out of his way to borrow from even Joachim himself where it suited his argument, for instance, when he wants to show that all dates after 1260 are suspect.[27] As Marjorie Reeves has memorably observed, "William preached and wrote furiously against these pernicious mendicants—in a manner that evoked the same sense of crisis as the Joachites he attacked."[28]

In the Footsteps of William: FitzRalph, Kilvington, and the Condemnation of Friar John

Continental Inquisition Comes Calling

William of St. Amour's stand against Gerard's book and at least temporary victory at the papal court was, I believe, an important inspiration for FitzRalph and Kilvington. That they were seeking to recreate this scenario is evident, I would suggest, both in Kilvington's acquisition of the rare Protocol of Anagni and FitzRalph's role in the Oxford condemnation of an Austin friar promoting radical disendowment ideology. Until now the first has gone completely unnoticed, and even the second has never really been understood in its full historical context. Both incidents illuminate the role of prophecy in ecclesiastical polemic and, especially when considered together, give us a clearer view of how much territory older, rival ideologies already held before Wyclif set foot on the weather-beaten shores of ecclesiastical controversy.

In the 1350s FitzRalph, of course, was pressing his internationally notorious case against the friars at Avignon and using official condemnations and suspect literature to fuel the controversy. FitzRalph and Kilvington were ingenious at digging up "dirt" of all kinds to attack the friars, and FitzRalph had by now many international connections to help in the process. But his own position was coming under suspicion, largely thanks to charges of heresy that the friars were making against him as return fire both at the royal court and at the papal court in Avignon. Large amounts of money were being quietly donated to lobby his cause by both secular and monastic orders, although public moral support was less easy to come by.

I would suggest that it may have been through one of FitzRalph's supporters, Guillaume Court, the high-ranking inquisitor who had a few years earlier been in charge of John of Rupescissa's case, that the Protocol was acquired. Court would have had, if anyone did, access to a deep library on Joachimism and its official repression. Court held several English benefices, including the archdeaconry of Wells, and he shared FitzRalph's interests in ecumenical dialogue with the East. Whether or not he is the source of the manuscript itself, his connection with FitzRalph makes a direct link—so far as I know, completely unnoticed by scholarship—between the spearhead of the English antimendicant lobby and a leading figure in the Continental persecution of Franciscan Spirituals.[29] Guillaume Court in 1354 was just fresh from a horrific tour of duty as inquisitor. Kilvington himself owed his very job as dean of St. Paul's to Court's fellow French cardinal on FitzRalph's tribunal, Pierre du Crois, bishop of Auxerre.[30] This is the sort of information that shatters our modern sense of the English church as a parochial and insular world. Other glimpses of the international world they inhabited might include English clergy at Avignon, for instance, gathered on the annual feast of Becket to hear someone like FitzRalph preach the sermon[31] or the list of extant manuscripts of Kilvington's works with their startlingly heavy European transmission.[32]

In fact, Guillaume Court was now a cardinal and appointed by the pope (sympathetically, it appears) to the Avignon tribunal hearing FitzRalph's case. This seasoned inquisitor of Franciscan Spirituals had held a number of English benefices by papal provision and was one of three cardinals on the tribunal from France (all from areas most troubled by Franciscan Spiritual "heresy"), perhaps all chosen by Innocent VI to load the dice in favour of FitzRalph's case against the friars. Court had just presided over the case of two Spiritual Franciscans burned at the papal court in Avignon in 1354, who, as recorded by Knighton for 1355, advocated evangelical poverty and overtly declared John XXII's bulls on the poverty controversies to be heresy. The confession of one them, Giovanni da Castiglione, Knighton quotes at great length (perhaps from a mid-century account now in the Bedfordshire record office).[33] Giovanni's confession summarizes exactly the bulls that Spirituals found offensive:

> I, Giovanni, an unworthy slave of Christ and St Francis, declare and assert Pope John to have been an heretic and enemy of Holy Church, for the heresies that he published and maintained in his four constitutions, the first beginning *Ad conditorem*, the second *Cum inter nonnullos*, the third *Quia quorundam*, and the fourth *Quia uir reprobus*, which are plainly contrary to Holy Scripture and the life of the Apostles. And I, Giovanni, declare . . . that Popes Benedict XII, Clement VI, and Innocent VI, the successors of the aforesaid John, . . . ought to have been stripped of all dignities, and to have received the punishment appointed for all such as they. And I say the like of all such bishops on earth, and all such others, whatsoever . . . estate [status] . . . they be. (*Knighton's Chronicle*, 134–35)

Innocent was likely not amused. He included Giovanni's inquisitor on the tribunal to decide FitzRalph's case against the friars.

Thus it was that when a certain Friar John (Johannes) started teaching radical disendowment at Oxford in 1358, the university, one gathers, was not about to take any chances. They consulted with FitzRalph in Avignon, as we know from surviving correspondence.[34] From other sources we know more about the immediate university context. As George Rigg puts it, summarizing a great deal of internal antimendicant politics, 1358 was "a terrible year for friars" at Oxford.[35]

The three opinions for which John's *determinatio* was condemned were that he was teaching the necessity of disendowing corrupt clerics (male et inordinate viventibus); that tithes belong more justly to the mendicant orders than to rectors of churches; and, most puzzlingly, that he had called the university a "school of heretics" (gymnasium haereticorum).[36] Although modern scholars of Wyclif and FitzRalph have examined John's recantation, it is always treated as an isolated incident. No one has attempted to explain why official condemnation was deemed necessary (after all, propositions not unlike Friar John's had been around at least since the thirteenth century).[37]

Friar John was an Austin, as we now know,[38] the fraternal order, next to the Franciscans, most active in advocating disendowment and most closely allied with them on these campaigns.[39] This is also the order, next to the Franciscans, most noted for collecting Joachite materials, like the rich collection that appears in the library of the York Austins and especially (although by no means exclusively) in John Erghome's library. Erghome was an exact contemporary of Friar John's and would by 1362 produce his highly political commentary on the Bridlington prophecy, a work that Reeves placed in the secularized Joachite political tradition, aimed directly at a powerful lay audience. The Austins, then, were courting laity with prophetic help.

The details of the case against Friar John are fragmentary, but several important things emerge. First, as the university records put it, John had "thoughtlessly" gone about "appealing, complaining to lords and magnates" (improvide appellando, dominis et magnatibus querelando);[40] generally speaking, the more public—that is, the more exposed to the laity—censurable ideas were, the more severely they were punished. But the lay powers could also *prevent* ecclesiastical censorship if they were powerful enough, and we know from an extant letter to FitzRalph that in John's case, his lay support gained him immunity for a limited time (as would Wyclif's two decades later). The letter to Fitz-Ralph from the chancellor and regent masters of the university reached him at the curia while he was in the midst of his suit against the mendicants there. They were appealing to him for help because "we cannot compel him to a public revocation, or to any other punishment, on account of the confidence he has in the magnates of the realm, who, he says, wish to support him in this matter."[41] But then something caused the collapse of this support and paved the way, most unusually, for formal condemnation. We cannot be certain, but his views smell of something that even Wyclif (at least publicly) would refuse to dabble in: Joachimism. The clue, I would suggest, is in the reference to the "gymnasium hereticorum." We do not know for certain why John called the university this, but this is exactly the kind of insult traded in the debates over the heterodoxy of Franciscan Spirituals ever since John XXII's dramatic overturning of much more moderate or even supportive papal bulls. Benedict XII, more moderate than John, had briefly experimented with ways of funding the friars via endowments—whence, perhaps, John's idea about tithes, and not unlike Langland's prophecy some twenty years later that the friars will be endowed by "Constantine" after a king and his magnates put the rich monastic houses to their "penaunce."[42] But this was the 1350s, and radical members of the Franciscan order were under active serious persecution. And it must be significant that FitzRalph and Kilvington were at that very moment as thick as thieves with a major Continental inquisitor who held benefices in England.

The university was in 1358 in the control of the antimendicant party. Given their consultation with FitzRalph, and the internal politics of the university at the time, Friar John could only have felt that Oxford was enslaved to Johannine opinions. Certainly, the Austin was treated more harshly than Uthred, a Benedictine, would be just ten years later for uttering other radical opinions in the schools.[43] Moreover, he had less immunity than Wyclif would enjoy (at least until 1382) for pronouncing on exactly the same subject not many years later.[44] Taken together, what the constellation of his views have in common with parallel Wycliffite opinions later condemned at Blackfriars in 1382 is that the stiffest of these (the only one condemned as *heretical*, rather than merely *erroneous* in 1382) also has the aura of Olivianism or Franciscan Spiritualism, namely, the view that it was against scripture that ecclesiastics might have temporalities.[45] But, significantly, the Blackfriars Council listed the view (exactly equivalent to John's) that the lords temporal could remove possessions from delinquent clergy only as an *error*, not a heresy.[46] This suggests that radical Franciscan views (here, against the owning of temporalities) were most certainly in 1358 considered officially dangerous, and that, if anything, slightly more so than in the period of Wyclif.

While John's case was being heard at Oxford, the campaign of FitzRalph (1357–58) against the friars both at home and in the papal curia was at its height. A further reason for John's counter-charge that the university was a "gymnasium hereticorum" is that ironically FitzRalph was on the brink of official condemnation himself. In 1358 his fraternal opponents charged FitzRalph with heresy, that is, with repeating the heresy of Jean de Pouilly (that confessions made to a licensed friar had to be remade to the parish priest).[47] As Katherine Walsh has written, ever since the early 1350s FitzRalph "had seemed to be committing himself to a dangerous course when, by arguing that the friars' privileges were a violation of the ideals of their founders . . . he was indirectly attacking the popes who approved such violations."[48] The 1358 charge was serious, and "whereas FitzRalph could argue powerfully and convincingly on the poverty issue when his scriptural expertise came to his aid, he was out of his depth in the canonical problem posed by the conflicting interpretations of *Omnis utriusque sexus, Super cathedram,* and *Vas electionis.*"[49]

These were not, however, FitzRalph's only problems. In this period, King Edward III in fact enacted a form of censorship himself. In an interesting parallel with the king's apparent attempt to keep former Oxford chancellor, Lutterell, at home from his mission to accuse Ockham in Avignon,[50] in 1357 Edward acted against FitzRalph and his ally, Kilvington, prohibiting them from preaching in London against the friars, and even from allowing them to leave the country to go to Avignon. Edward issued orders on April 7 to the sheriff of London and all the portkeepers in the southeast instructing them to ensure that no religious leave the country without royal license.[51] John of Ardene, an Austin, was acting as proctor for all the friars; he did make it to Avignon by November. FitzRalph arrived in Avignon by midsummer—apparently via a northern port! Although closing the seaports to both sides may seem evenhanded enough, friars, as their enemies always bitterly noted, were good at cultivating royalty and nobility. And so it seems: meanwhile, and certainly by 1358, Edward was supporting the embassies of Friar William Jordan in favour of the fraternal cause.[52] Jordan, the likely subject of antimendicant satire in *Piers Plowman*, we might note, was the most prominent of the York friars who would drag Uthred de Boldon into censure and condemnation ten years later (as we will see in chapter 10). Secular power, when courted by friars, was a serious matter, as both FitzRalph and his "successor" Uthred found out.

This, then, with censorship charges and condemnations on both sides of the camp, was the situation when FitzRalph was contacted in Avignon about the Oxford faculty case of the Austin, Friar John. Friar John's case ended in condemnation—but the fact that it did is instructive and tells us that England was not the inquisitionally innocent place we tend to assume. Continental inquisition had come to call—and, indeed, had been active in FitzRalph's Ireland already at least since the time of Ledrede (see Chronology, 1324) and in England at least since the Templars (1308).

The condemnation of Friar John was symptomatic of the larger climate of the 1350s and 1360s. But renewed war with France in 1369 and growing antipapalism would soon turn the tables domestically. I have already mentioned the disendowment activities of the Austin and Franciscan friars in the early 1370s (see Chronology, 1371). In 1373 Pope Gregory XI demanded a subsidy for his Italian wars from English clergy, who were already providing a subsidy to King Edward for the French wars.[53] This, in part, set the stage for the humiliation of Uthred and anyone else willing to speak up for the pope's and the possessioners' unpopular causes at the Great Council of 1374. This wry story, which comes to us only from the *Eulogium historiarum*, is worth telling as a way of showing the decisive shift in attitude that the new political circumstances seem to have created.

The *Eulogium* account explains how the pope commanded King Edward to levy a tax to help in his fight *contra sibi rebelles Florentinos*. The archbishop is asked his opinion, which is that the pope is "omnium dominus" and cannot be denied. Clearly an unpopular position to put to a secular lord (Prince Edward is presiding), a colourful battle of wits and flattery ensues as representatives of each order try to get out of a tight corner. Uthred, the Benedictine representative, is virtually alone in supporting the archbishop (the provincial of the Dominicans excuses himself *de ardua quaestione*, and suggests they all sing *Veni Creator Spiritus* in the hope of inspiration!). Uthred bravely cites Peter's "Ecce duo gladii hic" (Behold, here are two swords) to prove that the pope has both temporal and spiritual dominion, but the Franciscan Mardisley trumps him with Christ's response "Mitte gladium tuum in vaginam" (Put your sword back in its sheath). Mardisley then argues brilliantly for exactly what the prince wants to hear, that is, that scripture, the doctors, and other authorities prove that Christ gave Peter spiritual dominion, not earthly dominion. At the end of this discourse, the archbishop grumbles that "Bona consilia fuerunt in Anglia sine Fratribus" (There was good counsel in England without [or before] friars), but when the prince's temper flares (he calls the archbishop an ass), all opposition to the Franciscan position magically melts. And the prince, turning to Uthred, asks scornfully, "Ubi sunt ergo duo gladii?" (Where, therefore, are the two swords?), to which Uthred responds, "Domine jam sum melius provisus quam fui" (Lord, I am now better counseled than I was).[54]

It is hard to imagine a more different scenario from the one in which Friar John was forced to recant before the assembled congregation of St. Mary the Virgin, the university church of Oxford, in 1358, memory of which appears to have lingered on among later reformist thinkers. Wyclif, for instance, was either told of or remembered the recantation, many years later, if the story he tells about a Franciscan having to retract his stand on church endowment is actually the Austin, John.[55] To mistake an Austin for a Franciscan in this context is very understandable, although I would point out that Wyclif's story may refer to another such recantation altogether. The language of the public recantation that Wyclif gives us, with its direct references to issues of poverty, the early church (status ecclesia primitiva), and the question of the church's "imperfection" in holding endowments (propter suam dotacionem) is much more overtly consistent with Franciscan Spiritual than Austin rhetoric. Either way, Wyclif was moved by the friar's having to reverse what he had preached on these topics in a climate clearly much less friendly than that which Wyclif's early disendowment advocacy was later to enjoy.

The resentment the triumphant friars provoked in their clerical brethren as captured in the *Eulogium* story is reflective of the emboldened attitude of friars throughout the 1370s. Just how bold certain friars had become can be gauged by the sensational 1379 preaching campaign of Dominican friar Richard Helmyslay, which ended in his papal condemnation of 1380.[56] The *reportatio* of the case reads as empathetic with the complainant, Matthew de [B]olton,[57] vicar of St. Nicholas's, Newcastle, charging Friar Richard with having spoken "detraccionem, dampnacionem et iniuriam" to the parishioners of St. Nicholas against its vicars and curates, encouraging them to give their goods to the friars. Among the eleven charges against him are some similar to those against Friar John. Helmyslay is charged with preaching to the people *in lingua materna* that they need not give oblations and tithes (decimas) on account of the cupidity (142v) and illiteracy of the parish clergy (143r). He is also alleged even to have preached that the parish clergy are not able to absolve (soluere [143r]). But most arresting among the charges is the claim that the layfolk of St. Nicholas's parish should adhere to the friars as the "true physicians" of their salvation, "*quia erant in ecclesiam dispositi loco quatuor euangelistarum,* qui suis doctrinis totum mundum gubernabant, et sine ipsis animabus non erat salus*" (Oxford, Bodleian Library, MS Bodley 158, fol. 143, my emphasis) (because they were put into the church in the place of the four evangelists, who governed the whole world by their doctrines, and without them there was no salvation of souls). This sounds very like the pseudo-Joachite doctrine of the Eternal Evangel—the idea of *replacing* or filling the place of the Gospels, here nearly Gerardian in scope, with specially ordained *viri spirituales*—just as we have seen it in Kilvington's copy of the Anagni Protocol and in William of St. Amour's *De periculis*. William's famous First Sign of the end, for instance, as quoted by Knighton for 1382, speaks of the zealots who will claim to preach a more perfect Gospel, "quo adueniente, euacuabitur ut dicunt euangelium Cristi" (which when it comes will displace Christ's Gospel).[58]

It is at first a little surprising to hear this doctrine from a Dominican. Dominicans were temperamentally less prone than either Franciscans or Austins to embrace Joachite prophecy. But they did also have a history of claiming the divinely appointed role of Joachim's *viri spirituali*. As Marjorie Reeves writes of the thirteenth century, "it was in the new Orders of Mendicants — Preachers, Minorites, Austin Hermits . . . that Joachim's prophecies of new spiritual men found a genuine response."[59] But while it was enjoyed mainly as a founding myth among Dominicans, there is Continental evidence that renewed interest in Joachite thought had been on the rise in Dominican sources from 1367 onward, when a new pseudo-Joachite prophecy was created to support the order's claim.[60] It is significant, then, that Helmyslay's case documents survive in Bodley 158, in a manuscript booklet written in a single hand that also wrote the *De periculis* (fol. 126 ff.), the pseudo-Hildegardian "Insurgent gentes" (fol. 145), and the Tripoli prophecy alongside it (fol. 146). This context tells us that the *prophetic* dimension of Helmyslay's case was also very much in the compiler's mind. But these are all antimendicant prophecies and William's is anti-Joachite, so it should give us a little pause that this sort of Joachimism is *exactly* what many English clerics, even on both sides of the Wycliffite divide (like the *Opus* author, Capgrave, and Knighton), regarded as the hallmark of Joachite heresy.

Were the charges accurate or a smear? We have seen the antimendicant lobby's alarm at rising Joachimism and also its willingness to use Joachimism's inquisitional history as a weapon against the friars. Certainly Helmyslay is represented to some extent as a strawman, allegedly using the language of Amourian-circle polemic. The *reportatio* documents him as preaching that the friars had a "mission" or were "sent" (missi), usually expressed by Amourian polemicists in language like this:

[D]icimus eos non esse admittendos, quia timemus ne ipsi sint Pseudo-Prophetae, quia cum ipsi non sint Episcopi et Parochiales presbyteri, nec eorum Vicarii, vel ab eis specialiter inuitati, praedicant non missi contra Apostolum . . . [we say that they should not be admitted because we fear that they may be false prophets, because — insofar as they are not bishops or parish priests or their vicars, or specially invited [into the parishes] by them — they preach without mission [non missi], contrary to the teaching of the Apostle].[61]

But before we assume the implied Joachimism was only a smear, there are further mysteries in connection with this case: the papal curia in Rome formally censored Helmyslay in 1380, but later made him a doctor of theology in 1390 (under Boniface IX), and he became lector of the Lincoln house in that same year.[62] Although Helmyslay was forced to recant, swearing bodily on those very Gospels he had allegedly believed the friars to replace ("coram nobis ad sanctam dei euangelia scripturis corporaliter manibus tactis" [f. 144v]) and even imprisoned for a while in Rome, his later rehabilitation suggests that it would be injudicious to regard the *reportatio* as a purely objective document. Some of the charges are surely trumped up by the rival clergy who stood to lose most if the ministry of a lively, well-trained pulpit orator and satirist were allowed to continue. That he was this is suggested by the most comical of the charges, that is Helmyslay's "gloss" (or "glose" in Chaucer's Summoner's sense) on the famous papal canon *Omnis utriusque sexus* as meaning that only a *person* "of both sexes" need confess annually to the parish priest.[63] Sometimes heresy and humour can be difficult to distinguish, but the papacy of Boniface IX apparently saw humour where Urban VI had seen heresy. The seriousness of Helmyslay's treatment in 1380 shows that radical Joachimism was an effective way of getting into prison. But Helmyslay's knowledge of Joachite issues was likely a factor in his rehabilitation in 1390 as doctor of theology, and as a papal chaplain by 1392. This is intelligible because the then pope, Boniface IX, was mobilizing a force of largely Dominican inquisitors to go out and fight heresy, notably against "Beghardis seu Lullardis et Zwestrionibus"—a sweeping agenda to fight the heresy of the Free Spirit, "Lollardy" (both followers of Wyclif and other suspicious European groups), and suspect sister houses of Olivian and other movements, as we will see in chapter 6.[64] Ironically, both Uthred (condemned in 1368) and Helmyslay appear to have been rehabilitated in the 1380s and 1390s, at least in part, as I suggest in chapter 10, by the need to fight heresy. Helmyslay is appointed lector at the Lincoln convent in 1390, in England's most notorious diocese for intellectual Wycliffism—the diocese in which, as we have seen from the *Opus arduum*, the confiscations of Joachite writers were in full force by that year. What we have most certainly by that time, if not already by 1380, is a chilling of the climate that had allowed for disendowment advocacy, often inspired by Joachite fraternal activism, since at least the condemnation of Uthred in 1368 and the renewal of war in 1369.

Friar John, Anti-Joachimism, and the Early Context of Piers Plowman

The condemnation of Friar John happened just a few years before Langland started to write *Piers Plowman* (that is, the A text, likely sometime in the 1360s, certainly after the Treaty of Bretigny in 1360 and the great windstorm of 1362).[65] As early as B, and in a slightly less cautious tone than C, Langland himself had prophesied disendowment of corrupt religious, advocating as Friar John does, that the proceeds would be used, in part, to aid the friars:

And þanne Freres in hir fraytour shul fynden a keye
Of Constantyns cofres [þer þe catel is Inne]
That Gregories godchildren [vngodly] despended
And þanne shal þe Abbot of Abyngdoun and all his issue for euere
Have a knok of kyng, and incurable þe wounde.

$$(\text{B.X.328–32})$$

As we saw in chapter 2, Olivi's exegesis of the beast's "mortal wound" (plaga mortis) of Revelation 13:11 showed that it had been dealt by clerical poverty, which is exactly how Langland uses it here. In C the "Abbot of Abyngdoun" becomes the "abbot of Engelonde" (C.V.176), and there is some distancing of Will's voice from the question of the role of the nobility, but the passages are substantially the same.[66] Later in BC something emerges a little like the second of Friar John's condemned articles, on tithes, although here in relation to the paring down of over-wealthy clergy generally. After invoking the case of the Templars (C.XVII.209), whose wealth, of course, was confiscated by the crown when they came under inquisition in 1308,[67] Langland challenges the laylords once again to disendow lax clergy: "Taketh here londe, ȝe lordes, and lat hem lyue by dymes" (C.XVII.227). "Dymes" are "tithes" and the argument against endowment is that "if possession be poysen and imparfit hem make . . . Hit were charite to deschargen hem for holy churche sake" (29 and 31). At this point, especially by the time of the C text, Wycliffite disendowment cries are raging, and if one were to look for any of the three texts in which Langland might be suppressing such cries, it should certainly be — according our modern sense of the dominance of Wycliffism — in C. But if issues of disendowment are suppressed anywhere, I would suggest that it is, rather, in the *A text*. If we look closely at the passage in A that was the predecessor of the B disendowment passage quoted above, Clergy himself is saying that he believes that "kinghed and kniȝthed" and other magnates are Dowel, Dobet, and Dobest "of hem alle," because of how Christ counseled the community: "Super cathedram Moisi sederunt *principes / Princes* sit upon the seat of Moses" (A.XI.216–19). In fact, this is not exactly what Christ counseled. The quotation is deliberately adapted by the addition of the word "principes" to Matthew 23:2, where it is the *Scribes and Pharisees* who sit on the seat of Moses, and Christ goes on to advise: "so practice and observe whatever they tell you, but not what they do, for they preach, but do not practice."[68] Only Langland's Latin-reading audience would know the biblical context from which the line is cunningly wrenched and retooled. What it shows is that the poet is already in A hinting at the issue of forcible disendowment by secular powers — and that Clergy himself, albeit with studied ambivalence, anticipates it as a necessary evil. But he does not dare say it. (In B the line is transferred, this time with studied *innocence* to the dreamer [B.X.336], where it immediately follows the flamboyant disendowment prophecy quoted above.)

This must make us stop and think about the tensions of the period when A was written (likely still under revision in 1367–70, but perhaps begun any time after 1362). The A text was written under different circumstances, and if we think that questions of ecclesiastical "danger" began for Langland with the condemnations of the Blackfriars Council in 1382, we must think again. A is the only text, as I have said, in which Langland speaks tolerantly of benefice pluralism[69] and the A text is by far the most uncritically "clergial" in attitude, at least on the *surface*. The potential threats of the 1350s and 1360s were plenty serious — and may go some way toward explaining why A is much the most conservative text on reformist issues. And why, as we will see later in this book, A breaks down into a frayed fragment over the raging doctrinal issue of the day, an issue heavily associated with the liberal salvation theology of Joachite-influenced friars and of the 1368 condemnation of Uthred.[70]

Two Condemned Books Revived: The Legacy of Gerard's *Evangelium eternum* and William's *De periculis* in Jean de Meun, Chaucer, and Langland

William of St. Amour as Pauline Prisoner of Conscience: Jean de Meun's Romance of the Rose *and Anti-Joachimism*

Far from being an oddity lost to posterity in the dusty pages of an inquisitional document, in the later Middle Ages the condemnation of Joachite thought contained in the Protocol was widely known, and indeed, popularized, in part because of William of St. Amour's *De periculis*. And, more importantly, it was known even to vernacular readers from its appearance in Jean de Meun's continuation of *The Romance of the Rose*. The character Faus Semblant, whose dialogue Chaucer plundered to create his Pardoner, and to a lesser extent his

Summoner (he was, I will argue, too wary to create his Friar from it), delivers a surprisingly detailed analysis of the heretical points of Gerard's Eternal Gospel. As John Fleming explains:

> While there is no doubt whatever of Jean's heavy debt to Guillaume's *De periculis novissimorum temporum*, . . . it is possible that Jean actually thought of himself as carrying on, in a formal sense, the task begun by Guillaume a generation before him. . . . The *De periculis* in particular enjoyed a very long run as a reformatory tract . . . clandestinely printed after the Reformation. Heresy, according to one cynical definition, is being on the side that loses.[71]

Heresy is indeed being on the side that loses, at least in ecclesiastical terms, but with some help from popular poets and from the staggering freedom of textual transmission before print, a loser could become, in cultural terms, a winner. As Lee Patterson has so lucidly said about the impact of the Amourian material on the *Rose*:

> Where Raison broadened the poem's perspective by invoking the Platonism of Boethius and Cicero, Faus Semblant turns to the chiliasm of William of St.-Amour. He introduces not merely the mendicant controversy, in other words, but the mendicant controversy as seen in an apocalyptic perspective. He opens the poem not merely to its historical context but to history as seen from the prospect of eternity, dwarfing the Lover's petty concerns by comparison.[72]

Jean de Meun protected himself by placing his encomium of William of St. Amour in the mouth of the unlikeliest of admirers of an antimendicant propagandist, Faus Semblant. Faus is himself a friar, and, as Patterson elsewhere explains, a complex speaking voice: "The ironic smile with which the God of Love accepts Faus Semblant's pledge of loyalty is Jean de Meun's perfunctory gesture toward the discontinuity between character and speech implicit in the paradox of the truthful hypocrite."[73] Mixing hypocritical piety and candid self-revelation, Faus nonetheless delivers a historically and exegetically accurate account of the scandal of the Eternal Gospel and William of St. Amour's heroism. The voicing, however, is so complex and paradoxical as to confuse and evade the kind of papal censorship Rutebeuf had recently provoked for antimendicant poetry in 1259.

Several things, for our purposes, are immediately noticeable about Jean's treatment: first, that he has Faus Semblant repeatedly stress the role of the University of Paris in keeping the key of Christendom from heresy, described in Gratianesque terms:[74]

And ne hadde the goode kepyng be
Whilom of the universite
That kepith the key [clef] of Cristendom
.... [missing line in manuscript] [Tout eüst esté tormenté]
Suche ben the stynkyng prophetis.
Nys non of hem that good prophete is,
For they thurgh wikked entenciouns,

. . . .

Broughten a book, with sory grace,
That seide thus, though it were fable:
"This is the gospel perdurable,
That fro the Holy Goost is sent."
Wel were it worth to ben brent!
    (*Riverside Chaucer,* "Romaunt," 7089–104; *Roman,* 11791–806)[75]

I quote the *Rose* from Fragment C of the Middle English version (with periodic insertions from the French original) begun by Chaucer, though perhaps abandoned by him for reasons unknown before he reached this controversial section. Despite Chaucer's well-known plundering of Faus Semblant's monologue for passages of *The Canterbury Tales,* scholars are divided on whether Fragment C of the "Romaunt" translation was completed by a Chaucerian imitator or whether it is "probably" by Chaucer, as Derek Pearsall concludes.[76] Although we cannot solve this crux here, we can note that whoever wrote Fragment C shows some demonstrable sense of constraint when faced with the controversial portion of Faus's discussion of William of St. Amour and the "gospel perdurable" announced in the passage above as from the Holy Ghost. This is, of course, the Eternal Evangel, even the date of which (1255) is accurately rendered into Middle English. Chaucer originally began the *Rose* translation, scholars usually assume, in the earlier period of his career, about the time, perhaps, Langland was writing A. How late he might have been working on it we do not know, but we know he was working on *The Canterbury Tales* in the late 1380s and through the 1390s. Friar Richard Helmyslay was arrested and imprisoned in an internationally known condemnation, as we saw, for preaching that the four orders of the friars were established in the place of the four gospels, and William of St. Amour's writings were being confiscated by 1389. This makes the cautious rendering of the next passage significant. In it, Faus Semblant stresses how widespread among the laity radical Joachite ideas were becoming; any man or woman in all Paris could acquire a copy of this scandalous book in front of Notre Dame, and even copy it:

> There nas no wight in all Parys [A Paris n'ot homme *ne feme*],
> Biforne Oure Lady [Nostre Dame], at parvys
> . . . . [missing line in manuscript] [Qui lors auoir ne le peüst]
> To copy if hym talent tok.
> There myght he se, by great tresoun,
> Full many fals comparisoun:
> *"As moche as,* thurgh his grete myght,
> Be it of hete or of lyght,
> *The sonne sourmounteth [seurmonte] the mone . . .*
> *(I scorne not that I yow telle),*
> *Right so,* withouten ony gile,
> *Sourmounteth this noble evangile*
> *The word of ony evangelist [Ceuls que li. iiii. euangelistre]."*
> (*Riverside Chaucer,* "Romaunt," 7107–21; *Roman,* 11807–21)

Whether consciously or not, the Middle English downplays (though it does not rule out) the possibility of female readership by its choice of the neutral "wight." Chaucer's contemporary Jean Gerson preached that the Joachite Third Status was especially dangerous to women, who too often strive to imitate the Joachite "mental elevation and prophetic spirit," producing teachings that are "suspect." Whether the Middle English writer would have had any sense of this we do not know, but more significant is the contrast between his rendering and the French in line 7121 above, where reference to the four evangelists ("li. iiii. euangelistre) is softened to "ony." This passage from the *Roman* packed a punch; it had made notorious among vernacular readers the sensational doctrine of the "fals comparisoun" (that just as the sun outshines the moon, the Eternal Evangel surpasses any of the Gospels) which we have already seen particularly singled out by the Anagni commissioners in the Protocol. Of course, Jean knew that by poeticizing it he himself was participating in its dissemination to every "wight in all Parys"—male or female, learned or unlearned.[77]

The *Roman* was to make infamous other aspects of Gerard's treatment of Joachim which had also deeply disturbed the Anagni commissioners. For instance, Jean reproduced with painstaking accuracy the exegesis of the passage from the Gospel of John by which Joachim theorized the church's passage from the active life of the Second Status to the contemplative life in the Third Status. The idea, made more sensational by Gerard, was based for Joachim on Christ's words to John, "I want you to wait until I come" (John 21:22). For him this suggested that the primacy of Peter (representing the clerical orders in the Second Status) would in some senses give way in the Third Status to the primacy of John (representing the contemplative orders). As Faus Semblant's clarification of the Joachite viewpoint puts it:

> Thus mych wole oure book signifie,
> That while Petre hath maistrie [ait seignorie],
> May never John shewe well his myght [monstrer sa force].
> Now have I you declared right
> The menyng of the bark and rynde,
> That makith the entenciouns blynde;
> But now at erst I wole bigynne
> To expowne you the pith withynne:
> . . . . [missing line in manuscript] [Par Pierre vueil le pape entendre]
> And [in Peter] *the seculers comprehende*
> That Cristes lawe wole defende . . .
> *And John bitokeneth hem that prechen*
> *That there nys lawe covenable [loy tenable]*
> *But thilke gospel perdurable.*
> That fro the Holy Gost was sent
> To turne folk that ben myswent.
>   (*Riverside Chaucer,* "Romaunt," 7165–82; *Roman,* 11854–70)

Here, the missing line in the Middle English (meaning "By 'Peter' it wishes to signify the pope") falls in a place that obscures the full impact of the fact that it is Peter, or the pope, *and* the secular clergy being superceded. John represents "hem that prechen" (that is, the friars) as saying that there is no suitable law but the Eternal Evangel ("gospel perdurable"). The missing lines in this section, as Alfred David explains convincingly, were originally due to misplacement of leaves in the binding process of some ancestor of the present manuscript G. However, it is important to note that not even Thynne, who normally tries to fill in missing lines, supplied a replacement for this particular one. Whether this represents editorial discomfort among early scribes or not, the passage is a controversial one in the original, and one that Chaucer, despite his passion for Faus Semblant's monologue, never explicitly touched, unless there is a parodic hint of it in the cartwheel scene of the "Summoner's Tale," as we will see below.

Jean de Meun had used Faus Semblant to frame this whole section in a dramatic apocalyptic scenario that pits the forces of Antichrist (the friars) against the faithful remnant who will hold out for Peter:

> Full many another orribilite
> May men in that book se,
> That ben comaunded, douteles,
> Ayens the lawe of Rome expres;
> And all with Antecrist they holden . . .
> And thanne comaunden they to sleen
> Alle tho that with Petre been [de la partie Pierre];
> But they shal nevere have that myght.
>   (*Riverside Chaucer*, "Romaunt," 7187–95; *Roman*, 11875–83)

This passage of Jean's (as we will see at the end of this chapter) may have been one of Langland's models for his final siege of Unity, with its vicious attack of Antichristian clerics upon the beleaguered remnant who follow Piers. (Indeed, there are even apparently tantalizing echoes of Faus Semblant's dialogue elsewhere in Langland, including his C.V *apologia*, although this is not the place to enlarge upon them.)[78]

Such ideas, of course, as *The Romance of the Rose* puts forward are a gross debasement of Joachim's thought, a debasement that began with Gerard's fanaticism and was filtered through the distorted anti-Franciscan polemic of William of St. Amour before finally reaching the vernacular satirist. But what is extraordinary from our point of view is how *recognizable* Jean de Meun's renderings are, satiric though they are, as the condemnations of the Anagni commission, which itself had proceeded with great caution and diplomacy in relation to Joachim, historically, a papal favourite. *The Romance of the Rose* also picked up this point that William (whose polemic, of course, sought to undermine the friars' right to live by begging) was unjustly persecuted and exiled because of papal favouritism. Jean de Meun enshrined it for antimendicant poets and writers of generations to come, having Faus assert that a man may beg to keep himself alive, but for no other reason:

> He may begge, as I telle you heere,
> And ellis nought in no manere,
> As William Seynt Amour wolde preche . . .
> For I wole speke, and telle it thee,
> Al shulde I dye, *and be putt doun,*
> *As was Seynt Poul, in derk prisoun;*
> *Or be exiled in this caas [banis du royaume]*
> *With wrong [A tort], as maister William was,*
> That my moder, Ypocrysie,
> Banysshed for hir gret envye.
>   (*Riverside Chaucer,* "Romaunt," 6761–80; *Roman,* 11482–508,
>   with omissions)

As we saw earlier, William is here equated with St. Paul as a prisoner of conscience, both of whom were wrongly persecuted. Faus, moreover, asserts that he "wole speke, and telle it thee," even though he should die for doing so, or like Paul or William respectively "be putt doun . . . / in derk prisoun / Or be exiled . . . / With wrong." Of course, the irony of having this averred by Faus Semblant, who shamelessly begs for his own living, is not inconsequential. And for Jean, as we have said, it was a protective device that provided a measure of safety in a clerical hierarchy dominated by friends of the friars, and in which a papal ban on antimendicant poetry was already in force, likely aimed at his colleague, Rutebeuf.[79] Another security measure was the allegorical dream vision genre itself. Both these literary techniques are ones from which Chaucer and (likely) Langland borrowed massively, in part from Jean: unreliable speakers, unreliable narrators, allegorical ambiguity, dream-like fluidity, and ironic hyperbole. It gave Jean, in theory, the kind of protection from prosecution that he may have needed. It seems to have given his Ricardian disciples a measure of daring, as the rest of this chapter will indicate. And as we will see in chapter 5, Jean's reference to St. Paul's arrest was itself a watchword for those writing under constraint as well.[80]

Chaucer's Petty Inquisitors and Langland's Siege

Chaucer pilfered Jean's portrait of Faus in order to create not only his Pardoner, but his Summoner, the man who would tell the "Summoner's Tale," the
tale in which Chaucer shows—as scholars have long known—an extraordinarily detailed knowledge of antimendicant polemic. Chaucer, despite his adoration of Jean, I suggest, did not dare use this material (or much of it) for his own
Friar. Friars were tough enemies. They had friends in high places (as both Fitz-
Ralph and, earlier, Ockham's opponent Lutterell found out to their cost). Faus
Semblant himself swaggers about the power of his ilk to drag people before justice or inquisition of any sort, a trait that Chaucer would reassign to the comparative safety of the small-time, perjuring, parish Summoner. Here first is Faus:

> If ther be castel or citee,
> Wherynne that ony bouger [French: *bougre*] be, . . .
> Or elles blamed of ony vice
> Of which men shulden don justice . . .
> Or but he wole do come in haste
> Roo-venysoun, bake in paste . . .
> He shal have a corde a loigne [de corde vne longe],
> With whiche men shal hym bynde and lede,
> To brenne hym for his synful deed . . .
> Or ellis he shal in prisoun dye [a touziors emmurés]
> But if he wole oure frendship bye.
>   (*Riverside Chaucer*, "Romaunt," 7022–55; *Roman*, 11723–58,
>   with omissions)

Jean de Meun's use of the word "bougre" here (that is, "bugger," sodomite,
or heretic)—the word is retained in the Chaucerian (imitator's?) translation
as "bouger"—is a stark reminder of how medieval cultures "queered" dissent
in any form. Indeed, even though the crimes listed are various, this is the trope
that underpins all of them, and the forms of death sentence mentioned here
are also chillingly heresy-related (burning and immuration or confinement for
life). The only defence against the friars, Faus says, whose trademark cords are
now perverted into binding images, is bribery. And it is no wonder—given the
implications of Jean's "bougre"—that Chaucer would downgrade and soften

this collective fraternal self-portrait to create the composite of his officious village bully, the Summoner, and his queer companion, the Pardoner.[81]

It has also has been argued in the past that Chaucer was parodying Gerard's Eternal Evangel in the denouement to the "Summoner's Tale."[82] And it has also been argued that this is impossible. Penn Szittya sums up the scholarship this way:

> The *donum Dei*, Thomas's fire, the speechlessness, the first fruits of Pentecost, and the references to Moses and Elijah all reinforce allusively the Pentecostal pattern within the tale and prepare for the joke to come. But the joke hinges on something external to the tale: a historical connection of the friars and Pentecost. . . . [Previous scholarship has] tried at length to demonstrate a historical connection between the friars and the Holy Ghost, . . . chiefly by reminding us of the thirteenth-century Franciscan Spiritual, Gerard of Borgo San Donnino. . . . *But Gerard had almost no following.*[83] (my emphasis)

All of this is true, but as we now know from chapter 2, not only were Joachite ideas available in England from many sources, but more importantly what Gerard *did* have was articulate enemies who were famous authors: William of St. Amour and Jean de Meun. We know beyond doubt that Chaucer knew Jean, and there is every likelihood that he knew William. Chaucer, moreover, for all that he avoided a straight transfer to fraternal satire of Jean's scathing Faus, was fairly bold in the way he used William of St. Amour's "eight signs," themselves plundered from Franciscan Spiritual sources. John Fleming makes the point that, for instance, most of Hugh of Digne's outward and visible signs of evangelical poverty turn up in negative refraction in the "Summoner's Tale"— Hugh being one of the great Franciscan Joachites forced to retire at the time of the scandal of the Eternal Gospel.[84]

Chaucer's antimendicantism has been well illuminated, and our job is not to rehash it here. It is, rather, to take the measure of his sense of constraint or freedom in relation to using William's eschatological polemic and Jean de Meun's account of scandal and abuse. Chaucer was more courageous, as we will see below, than Knighton, who listed William's prophetic signs, but under the shelter of applying them to Wycliffites. However, Chaucer did not feel, clearly, that he could directly transfer Jean's scathing fraternal satire with its gruesome inquisitional humour directly into satire on an English friar. But what he could do is transfer it to his Summoner (*both* his summoners in fact: to his General Prologue portrait of the Summoner who holds the youth of his diocese in his "daunger" [1.663], extorting from all with the vulgarity of his bullying colleague, the summoner of "The Friar's Tale"—this is Faus *in parvo*). And he could shift William's eschatological signs as well into a fabliau joke centered on the delivery of a gift of "wind," a scatological re-writing of Pentecost, as scholarly consensus now agrees,

> "My lord," quod he, "whan that the weder is fair,
> Withouten wynd or perturbynge of air,
> Lat brynge a cartwheel here into this halle;
> But looke that it have his spokes alle—
> Twelve spokes hath a cartwheel comunly.
> And bring me thanne twelve freres. Woot ye Why?
> For thrittene is a covent, as I gesse."
> (*Riverside Chaucer*, "Summoner's Tale," 2253–64)

But there is also an air of codedness surrounding Chaucer's use of these and other antimendicant motifs; those who knew the exegetical details of the polemic could enjoy the more daring jokes, those who did not would enjoy the broader humour.

Fragment III, which contains the "Summoner's Tale" and the "Friar's Tale," is considered mature work. The fact that William of St. Amour is not reported specifically confiscated in England until 1389 and Henry Crumpe, perhaps by now an ally of the Wycliffites, is prominently charged with antimendicant heresy in 1392 (see Chronology) is important, then. It is also about this time that Scribe D, who copied the important Oxford, Corpus Christi 198 and Bodleian Library, Harley 7334 texts of Chaucer, along with the Ilchester *Piers Plowman* (University of London Library, MS S. L. V.88) early in his career, begins to *soften* antimendicantism in his copies.[85] Scribe D, as I have suggested elsewhere, is an important indicator of what the respectable reading public might think appropriate. He worked for distinguished clients of a London bookshop and is well known for his collaboration on the Gower manuscript, Cambridge, Trinity College R.3.2 (James 59), with Scribe B who copied the Hengwrt and Ellesmere Chaucer (Huntington Library, MS Ellesmere 26 C9 and National Library of Wales, MS Peniarth 392D, respectively). The 1390s, moreover, seem to have produced new sensitivity to ecclesiastical controversy and a change of heart in Chaucer—and not just on antimendicantism. But this is a much larger problem, and one we must reserve for a later chapter[86] and a fuller look at the "Retraction" and what it might mean.

And what of Langland and the thought condemned in the Protocol, made widely known in the *Roman* and trumpeted as heterodox in antimendicant anti-Joachimism generally? We have already noted in passing that the attack by the corrupt clergy among the forces of Antichrist against the faithful remnant who cling to Peter has intriguing echoes in Langland. And, as we have seen, one plausible source for Langland may have been the vivid account given by Faus in *The Romance of the Rose*. In *Piers Plowman* it is friars who finally breach the walls of Unity in the poem's last moments. Moreover, Piers, who is on some levels of the allegory both Peter the disciple and Peter the archetype of all popes, also makes a famous and iconoclastic conversion to the contemplative life (traditionally symbolized by John) in one of the poem's pivotal narratives. I have already mentioned that many earlier scholars of the poem tried to make a direct connection between this conversion and Joachite thought.[87] The famous and difficult Pardon episode (excised in C) has always been tantalizing in this regard, as the centrepiece conversion scene, in which an anglicized Peter rejects the active life:

> And Piers for pure tene pulled it atweyne,
> And seyde . . .
> I shal cessen of my sowyng . . .
> Of preyers and penaunce my plow shal ben herafter.
>
> (B.VII.116–19)

With its dramatic enacting of the destruction of a piece of the creed (the starkest salvational statement in the poem), this mysteriously diminished "Pardon" encapsulates for Langland everything that is too rigid both in official church doctrine and in dogmatic Christian theology. The question of condemned salvational theology in relation to Olivi and Uthred, and Langland's interest in it, we will look at in later chapters.[88] But here it is important to note that Piers takes on a kind of evangelical poverty that Joachim, Olivi, and Rupescissa (not to mention the outlandish Gerard) all wrote of as marking this momentous transition from a Petrine active life to a new age of contemplation.

Whether or not we assume that Langland was consciously influenced by Joachite thought (and the prophetic tenor of much of the poem makes that at least a *respectable* theory, if not yet a definitively demonstrable one),[89] we must now face a new and more concrete reality. Joachimism, in its myriad forms, was both widely known and widely *suspect* in late medieval England. And by the time Langland is writing, it had been given a much higher profile because of the heating up of the antimendicant wars of the 1350s, the salvational disputes of the 1360s (when Uthred was condemned), and the Wycliffite wars of the late 1370s and 1380s. By the time Langland is revising B to make C, Joachite materials are or are about to be under confiscation in certain places, Friar Helmyslay has been famously condemned in 1380, and there is even a *Wycliffite* campaign to discredit Joachimism and to hide any suggestion of its early influence. Langland, perhaps already rattled by the very real and adventitious parallel destruction of documents in 1381, may have thought—or been warned—that the Pardon conversion scene looked inflammatory in more than one regard. What he does not remove, however, making it much more subtle and elusive in C, is Piers's now *quiet* conversion to the contemplative life and a life of patient, evangelical poverty. With the Pardon scene itself gone, the conversion is safer (only reading circles steeped in these issues, and perhaps in Jean de Meun, would pick up the allusion), but in some respects, it is more profound.

To sum up a complex problem briefly, Langland was writing a poem, if seen from the standpoint of contemporary reception, full of potentially Joachite overtones. Early in the poem, he portrays a female figure bedecked as the whore of Babylon (Mede), who overshadows and disadvantages Ecclesia (Holy Church), an Olivi-like *ecclesia carnalis* and *ecclesia spiritualis* pairing. As we have just seen, he threatens the demise of clerical wealth, predicted as a calamity comparable to the fall of the Templars. He is also writing a poem in which an Antichrist takes over as pope, supported by the friars and threatening those who cling to the ideals of Peter. His is also a poem portraying the (re)founding of the church (a major parallel, as we saw, with Olivi), and in which Pentecost's outpouring of the Holy Spirit is allegorically conflated with the various skills of the present-day craft guilds of fourteenth-century England (just the kind of presentism that Joachite texts thrived on), and in which spiritual utopianism abounds. We have also seen that Langland seems pro-Joachite and anti-Amourian on the subject of a coming return *ad pristinum statum*. We have also discussed Piers's overt and decisive shift (more muted in C) away from the active life to the contemplative, supported by voluntary, evangelical poverty. He is also writing a poem in which complex apocalyptic programmes—as complex as any Joachite programme—flower and fail and are reborn persistently.

To take an example, the following passage is very like one in Joachim's *Liber figurarum*[90] much imitated in later Franciscan Joachite writers who also foresaw a period of bliss after the conversion of the non-Christian peoples:

> And such pees among favourite þe peple and a parfit treuthe,
> That Jewes shal wene in her wit and wexen so glade
> That here kyng be ycome fro þe court of heuene,
> That ilk Moises or Messie, þat men ben so trewe . . .
> *Conflabunt gladios suos in uomeres.* . . . They shall beat their swords
>   into ploughshares.
>
> (C.III.452–460a, with omissions)

Like Joachim's vision of the great conversion of the Jews and non-Christians (Iudei et . . . infideles conuertentur) after the greatest Antichrist, Langland sees this period of conversion as following upon "the worste":

> Ac *ar* [that is, *before*] this fortune falle fynde me shal the worste . . .
> And the myddell of þe mone shal make þe Iewes turne
> And Saresines for þat syhte shal syng *Credo in spiritum sanctum.*
>
> (478–80)

The larger passage, as I have shown elsewhere, is laced with arcane symbolism in Langland, which parallels Joachite *archana* minutely.[91]

Even more interesting are significant parallels between Olivi's explication of two parables in his Matthew commentary (whose scarred and valiant transmission history in England we saw in chapter 2) and Langland's use of the same two parables in his new addition to C.V. The parables are the treasure hidden in the field and the pearl of great price (Matt. 13:44–46; fol. 95v).[92] For Olivi they represent the *revival* of the life of evangelical poverty and perfection (renouationem euangelice paupertatis & perfectionis), which, in Olivi's scheme, is a hopeful sign of things to come. This is, in fact, exactly how Langland uses both parables, in a crucial, personal moment of hopeful self-defence in the C.V "autobiographical" passage. Just as he accorded with Olivi on the "incurable wound" exegesis (B.X.332), so again here his narrator is defending his own emphatic claim to be living a life of evangelical poverty and perfection ("parfitnesse"), praying for the souls of those who feed him and living meal to meal just as Christ instructed his disciples to do:

> And so y leue yn London and opelond bothe
> The lomes þat y labore with and lyflode deserue
> Is *pater-noster* and my primer . . .
> This y segge for here soules of suche as me helpeth, . . .
> . . . on this wyse y begge
> Withoute bagge or botel but my wombe one.
>
> (C.V.44–52, with omissions)

But Conscience rebukes him for this way of life: "Ac it semeth no sad parfitnesse in citees to begge" (90), and he responds with a self-justification built largely out of these two parables. The story of the pearl of great price and the wise merchant who sells all he has to purchase it he rewrites into an embryonic personal allegory, ending with the treasure hidden in a field (thesauro abscondito in agro):

> Ac ʒut, I hope, as he þat ofte hath ychaffared
> And ay loste and loste, and at þe laste hym happed
> A bouthte suche a bargayn he was þe bet euere,
> And sette al his los at a leef at the laste ende,
> Such a wynnyng hym warth thorw wordes of grace.
> *Simile est regnum celorum thesauro abscondito in agro.*
>
> (C.V.94–98a)

My point here is not to argue that Langland had Olivi at his elbow as he wrote (although given that he is likely writing before the confiscations, this is not impossible), but that he knew the Franciscan Spiritual exegetical tradition explicitly linking these parables with conversion to a life of evangelical poverty. Scholars have long wrestled with the overtones of Spiritual Franciscanism in this and other passages of the poem, especially of the C text, and here is a revealing parallel with it. It would be natural for someone interested in prophecy of religious reform to have encountered something like this. We know from the way Langland used radical religious prophecy that he imitates Joachite genres, and his empathies with rigorist Franciscan ideals elsewhere, especially in C, are fully documented. With now over sixty Joachite manuscripts still extant from medieval England—and if, as codicologists often estimate, modern survival may often represent as much as one in ten—it seems entirely likely that a man of Langland's empathies would have come across this kind of Franciscan exegesis.[93] If so, I think we must add that Langland made brilliant and complex *literary* capital out of it. His was the kind of mind that could assimilate exegetical beauty like what we find in Olivi's reading of the parables into the very same passage as he appears to be assimilating Faus Semblant's self-revelatory hypocrisy—the C.V. "autobiographical" passage appears to have *both*. The important thing for us to realize is that these two sources—worlds apart to us—were actually very close for medieval readers. Jean de Meun understood the Joachite ideology detailed in Protocol of Anagni perfectly and, via William of St. Amour, conveys that understanding with ruthless clarity.

These are just a few examples, and further to those we saw in the previous chapter, in which Langland is writing a poem that appears to have hauntingly Joachite overtones. Whether or not it *actually* does have them, historical evidence shows beyond a shadow of a doubt that it *could have been read* as suspect on these grounds. Once a text has left its author's hands, reception is everything. And that this idea is not fanciful appears in concrete evidence of manuscript reception showing that some scribes and compilers (like the maker of Cambridge University Library, Dd.i.17) copied *Piers* with exactly this type of literature—literature not only under suspicion, but under condemnation, as we have seen. Although shielded by both visionary and literary decorum and large amounts of ambiguity, the poem's reception marked it and its topics as products of constraint and as vehicles of "archana verba"—or "hidden words," as we will see in chapter 10.

We have talked in this chapter about two phases or climates, and the shift toward greater freedom to experiment with prophetic reformist ideas that occurred between when Langland wrote A and when he wrote B. There was, of course, a second shift in climate, one that would impact on his C text, and on the work of many Ricardian writers. This second shift, bringing about the third "climate" so to speak, occurs early in the 1380s. It has been recognized by literary scholars generally as relating to the Rising of 1381 and the condemnation of Wycliffism at the Blackfriars' Council. But suspicions of Amourian and Joachite eschatology played a role here too, a less recognized facet of this climate change. And as we can tell from some illuminating comments by Knighton, the shift was a decisive one.

In the Footsteps of William Yet Again: Knighton's Scandal of the *Evangelium eternum* and the Wycliffites as the New *Joachitae*

William's attributed works enjoyed a moderate circulation in England,[94] but his banned book, *De periculis*, usually traveled incognito and in manuscripts closely tied to Oxford (three out of four of which also carry other material from censured writers).[95] In fact, William's famous "signs" of the arrival of the "pseudo-prophets" were often reproduced in extract, but the care with which any self-identified writer handled them can be sensed from Knighton's handling. Writing the entry for 1382 and the recent rise of Wycliffism, Knighton reproduces all eight signs and in lengthy verbatim quotation from William. But he does so only under the safe umbrella of an attack on Wycliffism. Even so, however, he conveys a great deal of knowledge of Gerard's condemned book and William's charges, while saying nothing about William's condemnation. Thus, after deploring how the Wycliffites "spread the Evangelist's pearls to be trampled by swine," Knighton continues:

And thus was fulfilled what Guillaume de Saint-Amour had long since predicted, and can fittingly be applied to that people [i.e., Lollards], saying thus: "Some there are who labour to change the Gospel of Christ into another which they claim to be more perfect, . . . and which they call the eternal Gospel [euangelium eternum], or the Gospel of the Holy Spirit [euangelium Spiritus Sancti]." Eternal it might well be called, which now is common and in the vulgar tongue. . . . The aforesaid Guillaume wrote a tract on the coming of such people, which said all that need be said of them.[96]

Knighton here reads the Lollard translations of the Bible as the fulfillment of a latter-day scandal of the Eternal Evangel—we are one full cycle further on from Kilvington's attempt to revive the scandal to help FitzRalph's campaign against the friars, and here it has reared its head once again. Knighton continues with a long verbatim quotation from William, beginning with his assertion that "in the year of our Lord 1255 . . . we are now in the latter age of the world," which we can know by eight signs. What follows are, coincidentally, the details from William that also occur in *The Romance of the Rose* and that go back to the Protocol of Anagni's critique of radical Joachimism. The first, for instance, is the change of Christ's Gospel into the "eternal Gospel" quoted above. The second is that this "eternal Gospel" will be expounded where Holy Scripture is taught (i.e., the university) unless the authority of Peter stops it. The third evokes the handwriting on the wall "in false Babylon" (in Babilone reproba) to explain that the eternal Gospel will be expounded as more perfect, even as the "moon shines less brightly than the sun" (quanto minus lucet luna quam sol), the motif made famous in *The Romance of the Rose*. The fourth is that those who do not accept such "correction" will be chastised and even slain. The fifth is that true holiness will be reproached as feigned. The sixth predicts the arrival of preachers who will seduce the people from the bishops. The seventh promises that those who embrace the Eternal Gospel shall drive out those who embrace Christ's, which we have seen in attacks on Helmyslay's preaching of 1379–80. The eighth sign of the End is that the faithful will recognize the signs that Antichrist is among them.

After copying all these signs, Knighton then says: "Th[e]se things . . . some have applied to the mendicant friars, but which better apply to those new people, the Lollards." Whatever Knighton truly believed about the friars (and it is hard to tell), the things which "some have applied to the mendicant friars . . ." is a stroke of genius and diplomacy. As we saw earlier, Chaucer, whom we think of as so cautious, was in fact much bolder than Knighton on this point, perhaps in part because the conduit by which it reached him was the outspoken *Romance of the Rose*. But the greater significance of this passage is that here we have the kind of evidence that helps us understand Wycliffite skittishness about being associated with the Joachite project—because here they are being *called* the new "Eternal Evangelists"—that is, the new Joachites.

The passage signals that a new phase has arrived. It tells us that the Wycliffites were being labeled as the Joachite pseudo-prophets of William of St. Amour even in a sober chronicle like Knighton's. In his 1382 entry, Knighton seems bent on rehabilitating the friars at the expense of the Wycliffites and driving a real wedge between them. This wedge was much thinner in 1382 than it would be even a year or so later, and miniscule in relation to Wycliffite anti-mendicantism as it would shortly evolve.

CASE STUDY 2 OF DANGEROUS
READING AMONG EARLY *PIERS* AUDIENCES

Anglo-Irish Anti-Joachimism in the Cotton Cleopatra B.II Manuscript and
a New *Piers* Tradition Poem(?)

From what kinds of sources were Joachite and other prophetic texts infiltrating the Wycliffite movement and its literature? A case study of a fragmentary little collection of three poems now in British Library, Cotton Cleopatra
B.II opens up a world of answers to this question and likely even gives us the
identity of one such infiltrator.[1] Peter Pateshull, an Oxford doctor of theology
and apostate Austin friar, was believed by Walsingham to have Wycliffite affinities, at least by the time he left his order in 1387. But his extant work bears no
trace of heterodoxy. Scholars have long known that Pateshull was the author of
an antimendicant treatise drawing heavily on Hildegard of Bingen, but this text
was thought to be lost; extracts from it, however, made by John Bale, have only
recently been rediscovered by Anne Hudson.[2] The text is entitled *Vita fratrum
mendicantium,* and in the extracts found among Bale's notes the author overtly
allies himself with both internal and external critics (or putative critics) of the
mendicant orders, all of whom we have met in the pages of this book: FitzRalph,
Kilvington, Joachim, a certain "canonicus Bridlington," a Dominican called
Robert (quidam frater Jacobinus nomine Robertus [fol. 188]; this would be the

visionary Robert of Uzès), and Hildegard of Bingen.[3] Joachim and Hildegard, of course, lived and died before the friars' orders began, but this did not stop their being recruited to the antimendicant and *intra*mendicant cause. In chapter 2 we saw the Austins in York collecting all the prophetic thinkers named here, even the obscure Robert of Uzès, whose visions, despite his being a Dominican, are very like those Franciscan Joachites launched against their own order. Pateshull must have had access to a similar library in the order, whether York's, Oxford's, or elsewhere.

Though there is no concrete evidence that Pateshull was himself a Wycliffite, he was a reformist thinker who would have agreed with at least two main planks of the Wycliffite platform, at least as it developed after 1382: anti-fraternalism and disendowment. As Anne Hudson has argued, Pateshull may also have authored one of the three poems in the Cotton Cleopatra B.II collection, an early *pro*-Wycliffite broadside in Latin which begins "Heu quanta desolacio." In dealing with figures like Pateshull, it seems important to distinguish between a "pro-Wycliffite" and a "Wycliffite" text—the former I have used to describe a text empathetic to the Wycliffite cause, but not heterodox in any doctrinal way. "Heu," which survives in Cotton and in four other manuscripts, provides an empathetic snapshot of Wycliffism at the time of the Blackfriars Council. Securely datable to 1382, it is also, I will suggest, perhaps the earliest known *Piers Plowman* tradition poem extant today. One reason I find Hudson's attribution interesting is that, seen from the standpoint of the history of apocalypticism, it is clear that the "Heu" poet, whoever he was, seems to be operating in a gray area between Wycliffism and traditional reformist apocalypticism—and likely downplaying the revelatory element to appeal to his Wycliffite audience. If this is Peter Pateshull, whose antimendicant treatise draws upon nearly all the prophetic and polemical writers discussed so far in this book, then we have not only a smoking gun, but a culprit caught red-handed in the act of importing disguised, prophetically derived polemic into a Wycliffite context.

The other two poems in Cotton are antimendicant pieces written down, as Angus McIntosh and M. L. Samuels noted, in a Middle Hiberno-English dialect.[4] "Of thes Frer Mynours" (fol. 65v) and "Preste ne monke" (fol. 63v) are unusually virulent examples of antimendicantism, but they, too, are not Wycliffite in content nor even (like "Heu") overtly in sympathy with the movement. The two poems dealing with apostasy ("Heu" and "Preste") are cancelled with huge Xs in Cotton. "Of thes Frer Mynours," the most obscure of the poems, parodies not only Franciscan Joachite iconography but, in subtle and chilling departure from most Insular antimendicant norms, seems to parody the *burning* of Franciscans, likely Spirituals. These the poet pictures accurately in their characteristic short tunics — something the author has apparently seen. Since there actually were burnings in the Franciscan province of Ireland (Chronology, 1353), not to mention those of laity under the fanatical Franciscan inquisitor Ledrede (1324 and 1328), the Irish dialect of these poems is especially intriguing. "Heu," the Latin broadside with which they are associated in Cotton, also appears in Oxford, Bodleian Library, MS Digby 98, alongside both Irish antimendicant texts and prophecies by Hildegard. And in both the Cotton and Digby manuscripts, "Heu" is associated with poems in which apostasy from a religious order is a trope. Since broadsiding was a historical practice among apostates, this thematic connection between the Cotton and Digby manuscripts is significant in relation to Pateshull's actual history. We begin first with the Hiberno-English poems in Cotton, and we will move on to Pateshull in the next section.

Suspect "Antimendicant Anti-Joachimism" and Cancelled Hiberno-English Poetry

All indications are that the Cotton Cleopatra poems are not just *copied* in a Middle Hiberno-English dialect, but were *composed* in that dialect, both Anglo-Irish in origin and content. They show no signs of having been *translated* into Hiberno-English by the Cotton scribe (signs, for instance, such as are common in the Douce *Piers Plowman*).[5] Moreover, "Of thes" especially treats iconographical issues in a way consistent with earlier iconomachic Anglo-Irish poetry.[6] Anglo-Ireland fostered an intensive culture of antimendicantism, FitzRalph being the most famous but by no means the only son of Anglo-Ireland to prosecute this agenda.[7] The poems, however, have been almost always seen through the lens of Wycliffism by scholars, since they travel in Cotton with the very early pro-Wycliffite broadside, "Heu quanta desolacio." But the two Middle Hiberno-English poems are not themselves Wycliffite in tenor and may stem from the older antimendicant tradition of FitzRalph and Kilvington that continued and ran parallel to Wycliffism, especially in Anglo-Ireland. Two of the three poems ("Preste" and "Heu") are heavily cancelled (as none of the other contents of the manuscript are) with large Xs — large enough to give the suitable *appearance* of cancellation or censorship, but still allow the poetry to be read. As such, it is the perfect form of functional ambiguity or self-protection (see figures 11 and 12). Harder to interpret are the tiny "xs" in the margin beside the most troubling lines in "Of thes Frer Mynors." Such small xs are sometimes corrector's or rubicator's marks in other manuscripts but no corrections are evident here, and the context amidst overtly cancelled poems suggests something possibly like the crosses used to denote erroneous teachings (although incomplete rubrication may also be the cause).[8]

R. H. Robbins suggested that the two Hiberno-English poems, because they accompany "Heu," which was written at the time of the Blackfriars Council of 1382, should also be dated 1382. He was following Thomas Wright's suggestion that all three are by the same author. This remains a theoretical possibility, but there is absolutely nothing certain to base the claim upon. Robbins was influenced by the fact of a poetic convention that "Preste" (lines 159 ff) shares with "Heu" (258), that is, that the speaker claims to have once been a novice of an order who made his escape before profession. But this convention also occurs in the Latin antimendicant poem "Sedens super flumina" and in its inverted (profraternal) form in "O quis dabit." These four poems ("Preste," "Heu," "Sedens," and "O quis") form a grouping of apostasy or "incomplete novitiate" broadsides found largely in the Cotton and Digby manuscripts, with "Heu" appearing in both. We will look at the significance of apostasy broadside collections as a public subgenre of antifraternal writings in the next section, but first, their dating: "Sedens" can be dated to 1357–84 and appears in MS Digby 98 (fol. 194) next to "Heu" (fol. 195). "Quis dabit" alludes to Kilvington as well as FitzRalph, so it is likely earlier in that range. The possibility that the two Hiberno-English poems date from the earlier generation is equally strong,[9] though "Preste" may be later.

The difficult issues in England in the decades just before Wycliffism bursts on the scene were, as we have just seen, disendowment, church dominion, and antimendicantism.[10] Up until the 1370s, radical calls for disendowment of the religious orders in England had always been associated implicitly or explicitly with either Joachites or with the fate of the Templars—both, of course, groups that came under inquisition in the early fourteenth century. The Anglo-Irish poems we are about to consider make use of these older traditions—one invokes the Templars on just this point and the other a vicious iconography of Franciscan Joachite heretics.

Both poems, but especially the first we will discuss, show elements of originality in their antimendicantism such as one does not see in conventional

11. London, British Library, MS Cotton Cleopatra B.II, fol. 63v, showing the cancellation of the first of two poems in Hiberno-English dialect in the manuscript, "Preste ne monke." Reproduced by permission of the British Library.

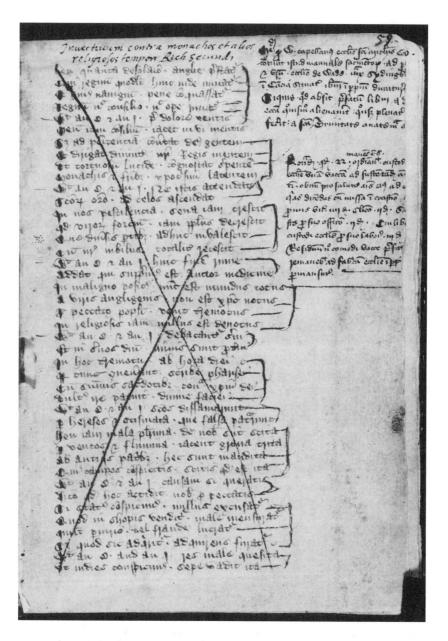

12. London, British Library, MS Cotton Cleopatra B.II, fol. 60r, showing cancellation of the Latin broadside, "Heu quanta desolacio." Reproduced by permission of the British Library.

Wycliffite antimendicantism as it developed after 1382. The poem, "Of thes Frer Myours," tackles in unusual detail the issue of the friars' use of visual iconography, an attack launched with the kind of shocking iconomachia found elsewhere in Anglo-Irish culture and which predates Wycliffism entirely.[11] Take, for example, the poet's objection to Franciscan iconography that typically shows Francis in a state of rapture, receiving the stigmata, usually from the visionary Christ in the form of a six-winged seraph in flight.[12] (See figure 13.) The poet's attack on this solemn Franciscan subject, fully authorized by Bonaventure, is scathing:

> First thai gabben on God, that all men may se,
> When thai hangen him on hegh on a grene tre
> With leves and with blossemes that bright are of ble,
> That was never Goddes Son, by my leuté . . .
> Thai have done him on a croys fer up in the skye,
> And festned on him wyenges, as he shuld flie.
> This fals feyned byleve shal thai soure bye,
> On that lovelych Lord so forto lye.
> With an O and an I one sayd ful still,
> Armachan distroy ham, if it is Goddes will.
>
> (7–18)[13]

Not only is this unusually harsh parody of a widely revered moment, but these stanzas are also lampooning the Franciscan tendency to conflate the "tree" of the cross with the Tree of Life.[14] Though often mistaken for English antimendicantism or Wycliffism, this stanza is Anglo-Irish both in iconographic and political attitudes: note the *tone* of the refrain with its whispered cry to Richard FitzRalph, bishop of Armagh, "*one sayd ful still* [one said very quietly], 'Armachan distroy ham, if it is Goddes will.'"[15] The scene is recognizable as a faintly 'nationalistic' moment because of the quiet desperation of the prayer (very un-Lollard in tone), which is quite characteristic of the Anglo-Irish sense of oppression, especially after the Statutes of Kilkenny in 1361.

Most striking, however, is the poet's awareness of the current inquisitorial practice surrounding persecution of the Spirituals for heresy, and actual executions. So, for instance, the next stanza parodies a Franciscan coming out of the sky in such an impoverished dress that he looks like a keeper of hogs, "There comes one out of the skye in a grey goun, / As it were an hog-hyerd hyand to

13. Beaufort Psalter, London, British Library, MS Royal 2. A.XVIII, fol. 9v, St. Francis receiving the stigmata, a contemporary example of the kind of Franciscan illustration that the poet of "Of thes Frere Mynours" (from Cotton Cleopatra B.II) is parodying. The Psalter was made in London between 1401 and 1415. Reproduced by permission of the British Library.

toun," whereupon the speaker bursts out with an exclamation that they should all be burned: "Ther wantes noght bot a fyre, that thai nere all brent!" (lines 19–24). The reference to burning impoverished-looking friars *in short tunics* as heretics is an unusual one and, at this date, would have to refer to Franciscan Spiritual burnings (which, apparently, this writer would applaud). The Spirituals were always visually distinguished from Conventuals by their short, narrow, patched gowns, or rather, tunics, the wearing of which had been made heretical by the 1317 papal constitution *Quorundam exigit*.[16] The association is further underscored in the next line, which seems at first like a non-sequitur "Thai have mo goddes then we, I say by Mahoun," but which must be a jibe at the Franciscan Spirituals' liberal philosophy of mission to Islam and the non-Christian peoples. After parodying iconography of the pope collecting the blood of Francis in a "dische" (that is, a drinking bowl, line 30), the poet starts in with equal vehemence on their association with Elijah:

> A cart was made al of fyre, as it shuld be;
> A grey frer I sawe ther-inne, that best lyked me.
> Wele I wote thai shal be brent, by my leauté.
>
> (31–33)

A cart, of course, was used to transport condemned criminals, but the iconography being satirized here is of Elijah, whom God took up to heaven in a chariot of fire (2 Kings 2:11). Elijah appeared at the Transfiguration according to Matthew 17 and was expected to play a role in converting the Jews at the End time.[17] John Fleming's account of how these themes influenced Franciscan exegesis and visual art is worth quoting in full:

> Throughout the gospels, the figure of Elijah is associated with the messianic mission of Jesus, since one line of rabbinic teaching held that the coming of the Christ must await the return of Elijah (Matt. 17:10). . . . Elijah is a prefiguration of Christ, Francis a postfiguration. It was accordingly inevitable that Franciscan mysticism should link the *poverello* with the prophet of fire. Among the boldest and most bizarre miracles reported of Francis by Thomas of Celano in the *Vita Prima*, and thence painted on the walls of the upper church at Assisi, is the manifestation of the spirit of Francis as a fiery orb within a chariot of fire. The allusion . . . received a

careful theological development in the pages of Bonaventure. Francis is an alter Elias, the leader of the 'true Israelites', that is, the leader of the 'spiritual men.' In the *Legenda Minor*, he is perhaps even more clearly the leader of the Church—*spiritualis militiae princeps*. These ideas are explicitly Joachite.[18]

All this was known to our Anglo-Irish poet, too. He clearly sees the Franciscan sense of mission not as charismatic, but rather as heretical—its liberalism on salvation issues made it an easy target for such charges. But what is most interesting about this allusion is that within the space of a few short stanzas the poet has managed to target the apocalyptic sense of mission to Moslems and Jews that the Franciscans held dear as well as their most cherished revelatory icons. Immediately noticeable is how knowledgeable he is about Franciscan mysticism, exegesis, Joachite eschatology, missions, burnings of Spirituals, and even relatively obscure visual art motifs. Whoever wrote this intimately knew Franciscan culture in a way that most stock-in-trade antimendicant writing does not. And, most revealing for us, he expected his *audience* to know it.

The other poem in Hiberno-English dialect is not as unique, but it, too, has some features we can connect with the campaign to hereticize the Franciscans put in motion in intellectual circles by FitzRalph's team. "Preste, ne Monke, ne Yit Chanoun" attempts at first a deadpan irony—"No man of religioun / Gyfen hem so to devocioun / As done thes holy frers" (2–3), but then the poet distrusts that mode and moves to outright satire. In it the speaker claims that he was once a novice among the friars, but left before he made his vows (line 159 ff):

> I was a frer ful many a day,
> Therfor the sothe I wate.
> But when I saw that thair lyvyng
> Acordyd not to thair prechyng,
> Of I cast my frer clothing.

The same convention occurs, as mentioned above, in a Latin antimendicant poem likely associated with the circle of FitzRalph and Kilvington, "Sedens super flumina," and in its companion poem.[19] In "Preste," the poet refers to the fall of the Templars and their disendowment in a populist, but legally knowledgeable way (reminiscent of Langland):

Whoso lyves oght many yers
Shall se that it shall fall of frers
As it dyd of the Templers
That wonned here us among.
For thai held no religioun
Bot lyved after lyking;
Thai were distroyed and brought adoun
Thurgh ordynaunce of the kyng.

(125–33)

The best-known part of "Preste," as Dean points out, is the "CAIM" cryptogram, the overused shorthand for the four orders (Carmelites, Austins, Iacobins, and Minorites) found most often in Wycliffite verse. If this is a sign of Wycliffite contact, however, it is the only one in the poem.[20]

Who made the Cotton manuscript and who was its audience? The two poems, of course, have been identified by MacIntosh and Samuels as part of the surviving corpus of writing in Middle Hiberno-English. Based on their association with "Heu quanta desolacio" (discussed in the next section), the copyist of the Cotton manuscript may well have been an Oxford Anglo-Irishman — a sizeable group, among whom antimendicant propaganda figured largely and whose relations with Wycliffism are shadowy and confusing. This group includes men like Crumpe, who is referred to unflatteringly in "Heu," and, later, John Whitehead and Philip Norreys.[21] Crumpe is an especially interesting case: initially an enemy of the Wycliffites, his allegiances become less clear as time goes on. But in Stamford he is condemned for ten conclusions, all antimendicant and one almost certainly anti-Joachite, denying the validity of Pope Innocent III's dream (Chronology, 1392). Moreover, Ireland had had Franciscan-related burnings of heretics within memory of this poem's being written.[22] Whoever the author may be, he deserves our attention because he somehow found the means to challenge, and harshly, devotional iconography (like Francis receiving the stigmata) that gave solace to numberless medieval Christians, Franciscan and otherwise. Here, I would suggest, *is* a "premature Reformation," complete with iconophobia, and of a kind that has largely gone unnoticed because it was largely subsumed into Wycliffism with the latter's appropriation of FitzRalph and his tradition. In Ireland it was likely borne of that peculiar crossbreeding of interclerical and colonial violence that formed FitzRalph and his disciples and clashed with the Joachite element in Insular fraternal cultures.[23]

We get some further and earlier supporting evidence of this Joachite element from the "Kildare Manuscript" (actually created in Waterford c. 1330), British Library, Harley 913. This is the largest extant collection of Anglo-Irish verse and related materials written in Hiberno-English, Hiberno-Norman, and Latin. As we have seen, the period c. 1330 was just a few years after Ledrede's terrible persecution of heretics (or "heretics") in his diocese (see Chronology, 1324, 1328, 1332). Ledrede had been a Continental inquisitor and brought with him the counter-heresy ideologies from the Clementine and Johannine papacies against Free Spiritism, Olivianism, Franciscan Spiritualism, Joachimism, and more. The Harley manuscript contains, for instance, a riddling poem called "Aliz, amo te," almost certainly written about the ordeal of Alice Kyteler and others connected with her, as Deborah Hatfield-Moore has shown.[24] The Harley manuscript also contains an item with explicitly anti-Joachite commentary. The Latin text *Epistola principis regionis gehennalis* and its companion *Responsio Dosithei* are written in the burlesque genre of letters from the devil and replies from the pope. In these letters the devil writes to thank the pope for his help in recruiting souls to his domain. The Harley 913 version of the text, however, is interestingly censored by its editor or scribe, sometimes to soften the clerical satire, especially against the Franciscan order (the order, that is, of the manuscript's maker). But there are also interesting additions, like the one at the end of the devil's closing argument, which suggests that it is appropriate for wandering preachers to exert themselves in the devil's cause because there are many false prophets (quod pseudo prophete multi sunt). The passage continues: "Prophetiam Ioachim cum nigris capis antefissi contra aduentum anticrist(i) menia et regna mundi subuertent" (With their black cloaks, having fixed the prophecy of Joachim in front of them against the coming of the Antichrist, they will overthrow the city walls and the kingdoms of the world).[25] The passage takes up a motif common in antimendicant writings, referring to the phylacteries affixed to the foreheads of the Pharisees, but here, instead of being texts of scripture, the phylacteries are the prophecies of Joachim. This is especially significant in relation to the key charges we have seen now over and over again, that Joachites sought to *substitute* the writings of Joachim for the Gospels in the Third Status—or, as the *Opus* author says, their own new law (lex). What is even more striking, as Hatfield-Moore points out, is that in Continental versions of this text, there usually occurs a long list of Continental heresies, *all* of which, except for Joachimism, have been deleted by the Irish Franciscan maker of Harley. This indicates that he felt that only Joachimism was a threat to Ireland. We have, then, a tradition of anti-Joachite antimendicantism (here from *within* the Franciscan order) in Anglo-Irish literary circles, and doubt-less one that the author of the Cotton poems inherited.

Literature like the Cotton poems may reflect a kind of desperation born of the sudden shift of power away from antimendicant interests in the decade or so following renewal of war with France in 1369. As we have seen in the pre-vious chapter, the war effort made the crown desperate for money, and dis-endowment propositions suddenly looked a good deal less censurable. The poems could have been composed any time between FitzRalph's public at-tacks, about 1356, and 1382, the date of "Heu," the Latin pro-Wycliffite broad-side copied with them in Cotton (discussed in our next section).[26] After 1369, writings and opinions once considered unsuitable were suddenly in demand—and certain enterprising friars were ahead of Wyclif in making capital with them. It is in this context that we saw the Austin friars engaged in ostentatious collecting of Joachite material in the 1360s and 1370s. The important question raised by the Cotton booklet, however, is why would they be married with an Oxford pro-Wycliffite broadside written in 1382 or shortly thereafter? The Wyc-liffites, as we have seen, were desperate for anti-Franciscan Joachite materials to keep their agenda separate from a long-standing heretical one. And these poems do just that.

An Unnoticed Work of the *Piers* Tradition? Cotton Cleopatra B.II's Early Wycliffite Broadside "Heu quanta desolacio" and Apostasy Broadsides in Two Censured Manuscripts

The Cotton booklet's third poem, also cancelled, also in the same hand, is the Latin macaronic "Heu, quanta desolacio" (Alas, how much desolation). It contains what seem to be several previously unnoticed allusions to or borrow-ings from *Piers Plowman*. If so, these would be the earliest, I think, after those of the rebel letters of 1381 (an event, we might add, for which the "Heu" poet shows no empathy).[27] "Heu" is a little-known broadside poem, written for cir-culation in the weeks and months after the Blackfriars Council (or "Earth-quake" Council) of 1382. It reports in partisan detail a series of debates be-tween prominent scholars and Wycliffites, debates that may represent Oxford disputations leading up to the council or debates at the council itself.[28]

The Manuscript Context of "Heu quanta desolacio"

The poem also survives in MS Digby 98, alongside Hildegardian prophecy and other items of clerical controversy, some derived from Anglo-Ireland, in the commonplace book of a scholar and one-time closet Wycliffite, Peter Partriche. What is important about this copy of the poem (which is one of five extant)[29] is that it was added to the manuscript in the *physical* form of a broadside, that is, as an oblong parchment leaf, one of the few such known to survive from street pamphlet wars of the period.[30] The Digby manuscript has been described as a

> notebook of scientific and polemical literature, collected or compiled probably by Mr. Peter Partridge, and perhaps put together about 1408. Later in his career, at the Council of Basel, Partridge defended the orthodox position against his former pupil Peter Payne, who had fled from Oxford about 1413 and joined the Hussites in Prague. In the course of the dispute Payne reminded his opponent of his earlier sympathy with Wyclif. The allegation is born out by several of the items collected by Partridge in this manuscript, including a number of satires against monks and friars; two leaves since removed contained letters of Wyclif.[31]

As I will suggest below, however, some of the items in the manuscript, including our broadside, were copied much earlier than 1408. Whether or not Payne's charge is exaggerated, Digby 98 does testify to just some such private struggle with conscience. A closer examination of the compilation process, for example, shows that probably in the year just before *De heretico comburendo,* Partriche had copied a Hildegard disendowment prophecy on the folio just ahead of two letters by Wyclif, which were later deliberately cut out.[32] Hildegard's disendowment prophecy (one that Wycliffite preacher, William Taylor, would bowdlerize in English translation by 1406)[33] is preceded by a copy of a prohibition issued by Henry IV in 1400 against preaching without a license. This prohibition is followed immediately by a petition of protest from secular clergy against this early form of preaching control, which anticipated on a smaller scale what Arundel's anti-Wycliffite Constitutions would try to establish nearly a decade later. The 1400 prohibition, however, did not stop Partriche from copying the letters by Wyclif, which are beyond doubt (as we can see from the stubs) in Partriche's own hand, but he appears to have felt after 1401 that these were a dangerous luxury.

Partriche, then, was alert to censorship issues, but he was not unwilling to test the limits. He was also catholic in his tastes and tolerant of prophetic texts alongside his Wycliffite ones—tolerance of revelatory thought, as the next two chapters will show, is increasingly perhaps a sign of "soft" rather than "hard" Wycliffism. "Heu" was sewn into the manuscript just a few pages after another Hildegardian piece (an abridged *Pentachronon*)[34] and "Sedens," both in an earlier hand than Partriche's. "Heu" (fol. 195) gives us an idea of what a broadside looked like, that is, a long, narrow, single leaf of parchment, produced with no decoration, only capitulum marks made by the scribe of the text distinguish the stanzas (see figure 14, showing the last stanzas of the poem). The poem is written in three long columns and in a slightly earlier hand not found elsewhere in the manuscript, an *anglicana formata* without some of the secretary features of Partriche's. This hand is paleographically more consistent with a date in the early 1380s—that is, the period when the broadside would actually have been distributed—than twenty-five years later.

One reason why "Heu" and "Sedens" appear together in Digby, I would suggest, is that they both defend apostasy from a corrupt order, and broadsides were used to do just exactly this. In her discussion of Lollard book production, Anne Hudson had pointed out that in official records broadsides (or "bills") were called *schedulae* and were "obviously ephemeral documents." They were used as notices or flyers and contained texts like the "Twelve Conclusions of the Lollards" or the antimendicant complaints posted around London in 1387 by Peter Pateshull at the time of his leaving the Austin order. Broadsides were also nailed to the door of St. Paul's by Hereford and Repingdon in 1382,[35] and "Heu," which mentions both Hereford and Repingdon favourably (see the second stanza in figure 14), was in use at exactly this time. Hudson further notes, "So far as I am aware, no example of a *schedula* survives in its original form," which makes the Digby survival of "Heu" in its original oblong form (clearly not ever intended for insertion in a bound manuscript) exciting. Partriche or an earlier scribe of that quire had apparently salvaged it from use in clandestine circulation and had sewn its top edge vertically into the manuscript right beside the *Pentachronon*, as one can see at the left of figure 14.[36] What is especially interesting about this is that it makes a delightful literary point very real and physical. The narrator of "Heu" claims, of course, that he had been a novice (monachus), but fled before profession (sed nondum professus), scandalized by the corruption he witnessed (258). In fact, there was a long-standing tradition of announcing apostasy by broadside. In 1314, for instance, apostates of the Dominican order "published defamatory writings, and . . . caused the same in public places within the city aforesaid to be read and recited, and . . . left copies of the same in those places fixed upon the walls, that so they might the more widely defame the same order."[37] What is striking about this is that it points to oral recitation (for which the poetic form of "Heu" was especially suited) as well as to this tradition of "broadsiding" in apostate activity. The narrators of "Heu" and a clutch of its companion antimendicant poems ("Sedens" in Digby and "Preste" in Cotton) all make exactly this claim to a form of apostasy.[38] The repetition of "Heu" in Cotton and Digby, alongside these poems, is significant because John Bale attributed "Heu" and "Sedens" to Pateshull himself. The question that arises, then, is whether Pateshull was using these poems for such practical, public purposes? This is a question we will be better able to answer after studying "Heu" itself, but its manuscript context is highly suggestive.

"Heu" itself is followed in Digby by part of a tract against the Dominican friars, a tract against the Jews, and a *determinacio* in Partriche's hand against the friars by John Whitehead, one of the Oxford Anglo-Irish contingent who formed such virulent opponents to the friars as to incur official condemnation.[39] Partriche's anthology, then, is participating in a rich tradition of intra-clerical hate literature, several items of which have Anglo-Irish connections. As Katherine Walsh writes,

> Although it has been pointed out that FitzRalph was not alone in his criticism . . . it is nevertheless a striking feature — unfortunately given little consideration by historians — that in the period between the mid-fourteenth and mid-fifteenth centuries four of the most notable opponents of the friars in England, and indeed in northern Europe, were Oxford-educated Anglo-Irishmen: FitzRalph, the Cistercian Henry Crumpe, the opponent of Lollardy, John Whitehead, who however, shared Wyclif's hostility towards the friars, and the dean of St. Patrick's Cathedral in Dublin, Philip Norreys. This concentration of mendicant opposition among the sons of Anglo-Irish colonists was scarcely pure coincidence and the possibility must be considered that elements peculiar to the nature of Anglo-Irish society in the later middle ages made the friction potentially caused by the friars even more acute.[40]

We might note that among those she lists, FitzRalph, Crumpe, and Norreys were all accused of heresy for their opinions, and the latter two officially condemned.[41]

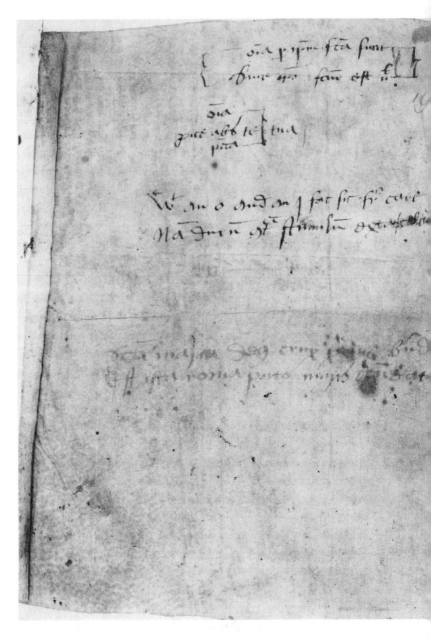

14. The back of the folded broadside leaf (shown fully extended) sewn into Oxford, Bodleian Library, MS Digby 98, fol. 195. The end of the poem (seen here) was written in stanzas down three columns on both sides. In the first stanza of the first column can be seen the passage on Christ's commanding a woman to minister (femine Christus imperavit . . . ipsa ministravit),

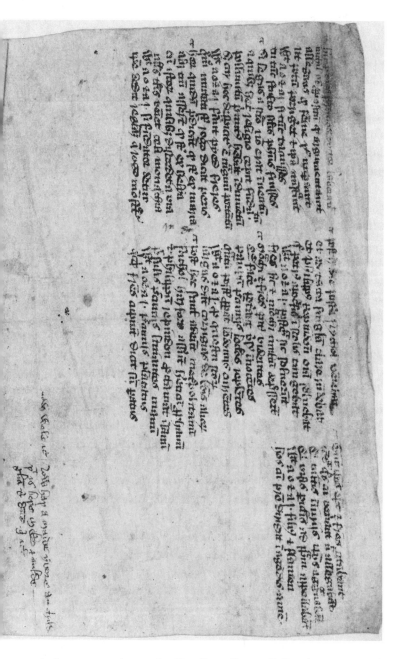

in the next stanza the appeal to Piers ("rogo dicat per(i)s"); judgement is passed on Hereford and Repingdon, named in the last stanza of the middle column. Reproduced by permission of the Bodleian Library, University of Oxford.

Moreover, in 1400 the papal decree, *Vas electionis,* was reissued for Ireland, probably because John Whitehead, an Anglo-Irish cleric from Armagh, was preaching against the validity of friars to hear confessions and other sacraments. So Partriche's collection, even without the help of Wyclif's letters, was pushing the limits of orthodoxy pretty hard, and not always via Wycliffism. The poem "Heu" itself, however, must not have been considered technically heterodox, because it survived the penknife in Partriche's manuscript.[42]

"Heu quanta desolacio" and Piers Plowman, *or Will the Real Peter Please Stand Up?*

Like the Hildegard prophecies copied near it, "Heu" emphasizes the role and the wisdom of the nobility in taking church restoration in hand—a topic we also find, of course, in *Piers Plowman,* which the author appears to know. It also alludes to the prominent Benedictine John Wells, whose name appears in the *ex libris* of Bodleian Library, MS Bodley 851, the manuscript in which the Z text of *Piers* is bound.[43] "Heu" was written during Langland's lifetime, in fact, likely while he is actively creating the C text. It is also written during Wyclif's lifetime. It represents a moment when Wycliffites and their empathizers (these two groups, I would stress, are not necessarily the same) were newly reeling from the first shock of the Blackfriars' condemnation, but when it was still relatively safe to have Wycliffite leanings—still perhaps even fashionably avant garde for reformist thinkers. Tellingly, the articles of condemnation that issued from the council are not taken seriously in the poem; the poet has no real sense of doctrinal danger at all, just reformist indignation and plenty of it.

"Heu" has the kind of meandering structure and sporadic narratorial self-referentialism that grander complaint or estates satire literature like *Piers Plowman* has. It begins by lamenting how much desolation is threatening England,[44] including the plague and the Rising of the peasants, who are unflatteringly described as wild or savagely raving—"debacchantur servi" (serfs rave wildly). The earthquake that struck the Blackfriars Council is evidence of divine wrath; the council itself is described as a gathering of scribes, Pharisees, and high priests "contra Christum Dei," who "have defamed the holy through heresy and schisms" (sanctos diffamarunt, / Per haereses et schismata [254]).[45] From there it wanders with Langlandian catholicity of complaint into a catalogue of estates satire on abuses: fraud in the shops (quod in shopis venditur male mensuratur) and corruption of rectors, prelates, and especially high-living mendicants, who are made to exclaim in Pharisee-like tones "Ecce quanta patimur pro amore Dei" (Behold what we suffer for the love of God!).[46] The passage is very like one in Langland's Feast of Patience scene, one, in fact, also alluding to Oxford mendicant disputes (likely those involving the charges Friar William Jordan laid against Uthred—Jordan, by the way, also appears in Pateshull's *Vita fratrum*).[47] There the learned friar ("this doctour and dyvynour . . . and decretistre of canoen") sits at the high table gluttonizing ("And also a gnedy glotoun with two grete checkes"), Will is heard to grumble:

"Hit is nat thre daies doen, this doctour þat he prechede
At Poules byfore þe peple what penaunce they soffrede,
Alle þat coueyte to come to eny kyne ioye;
And how þat Poul þe apostel, what penaunce he tholede,
For oure lordes loue, as holy lettre telleth:
In fame and *in frigore*, etc."
(C.XV.85–86; 70–74a, citing 2 Cor. 11:27)

Langland is citing Paul's account of the sufferings of true apostles, which is what distinguishes them from the "pseudoapostoli" (vs. 13), by implication, the friars. This whole passage, especially in the B text, deliberately evokes the antimendicant struggles of the late 1350s and 1360s (see chapter 10). One can see this in the slight differences between the passage above and B.XIII.65–67a, where the scourging of the apostle Paul is emphasized both in Latin and English, and where the *dean* of St. Paul's is specified as the key figure in the audience, perhaps with the famous antimendicant dean, Kilvington, in mind?

"It is noȝt foure dayes þat þis freke, before þe deen of Poules,
Preched of penaunces þat Poul þe Apostle suffrede
In fame & frigore and flappes of scourges:
Ter cesus sum & a iudeis quinquies quadragenas & c—
Ac o word þei ouerhuppen at ech type þat þei preche
That Poul in his Pistle to al þe peple tolde:
Periculum est in falsis fratribus"
Holi writ bit men be war—I wol noȝt write it here
In englissh on auenture it sholde be reherced to ofte.
(B.XIII.64–71)

Like the Hiberno-English poem "Of thes" copied with it in Cotton, the "Heu" writer has an unusually sophisticated knowledge of the Franciscans' stormy history of confrontation with the papacy over the issue of poverty—and he expects his audience to have it as well, punning confidently on allusions to one of the key papal bulls, *Exivi de Paradiso*,[48] which confirmed papal ownership of the friars' goods and the ideals of "simple use," which the Franciscans (the poet charges) have deserted (256).[49] This was the last of four bulls overturned by John XXII and a flashpoint for Franciscan Spirituals, some of whom had gone to the flames in protest within living memory (see Chronology, 1354). His complaints against the friars—and this is rare in antimendicant literature—have the ring of, dare one say, realism or historical immediacy, like the stanza providing a practical guide of what to expect if you are a poor man, infirm and seeking sepulchre with the friars: you will be told that the guardian is absent (Gardianus absens est).[50] These features would be consistent with an author possessing knowledge of Franciscan Joachite prophecy and, more concretely, fraternal convent experience. In other words, this could be Pateshull.

The idea of the "Earthquake Council" is never very far from the poet's mind. Take, for example, this stanza:

Tantos *motus* intuens Dominus in mari,
Quosdam viros nobiles fecit magistrari,
Ut fides ecclesiae possit restaurari,
Wyclif et discipulos voluit vocari.

(258)

(Gazing upon so much motion ['motus', a word associated with earthquakes as well as waves] in the sea, the Lord caused certain noble men to govern; in order that the faith of the church could be restored, Wyclif and his disciples he wished to be called.) These are the men, he says, who can guide Peter's ship, but the monks and the friars try to obstruct God's justice, ganging up for this cause like Pilate and Herod (hic amici facti sunt Herodes et Pilatus), and resisting the reforms advocated by both FitzRalph, now crowned (coronavit) in heaven, and Wyclif (259). This brings the poet, and not a moment too soon, to the council itself (or some related Oxford debate). The speakers against the "men of truth" (viri veritatis) are treated as mere caricatures, while Nicholas Hereford and Philip Repingdon, speaking on behalf of the Wycliffite parties, are portrayed as champion debaters, forcing John Wells, for instance, to come to a stand "like

Bayard."[51] A further spokesman for the monks, Goydoun, is dismissed as a literate layman (laicus literatus), a man of great status, dressed up as a monk (sub veste monachatus)—there is no Wycliffite love of the laity here. Goydoun is ridiculed for his baldness and for arguing, with transparent self-interest, that monks should not work, but friars should.[52] The poem has the feel of actual, current reportage in its merciless cataloguing of speakers far less famous, even in their own day, than Wells: "You, Crophorne, the most stupid . . . occupying the schools with frivolous vanities; your sayings are not worth *unum stercus canis*." Unflattering animal imagery abounds, conveying, as here, more insult than information, yet the detailing by name of each academic speaker is revealing.[53]

Whether it describes the council debates or some pre-council debating session at Oxford, this is poetry prompted by an occasion—actual broadside writing. No one would bother to catalogue the minor debaters years after the fact—and, indeed, the poem can be fairly firmly dated to before November 24, 1382, the day that Repingdon recanted, and likely before July 14, if Crophorne is indeed Crumpe.[54] And this precise dating is what makes an apparently direct allusion to *Piers* arising nearly at the end of the poem so intriguing: it comes on the heels of stanzas caricaturing Peter Stokes, who, we know, had been prominently involved along with John Wells in the anti-Wycliffite offensive at Oxford in the months immediately before and after the council. Stokes was a Carmelite, and his laborious argumentation causes the poet to observe how the Carmelites have degenerated since the foundation of the order. He says, "Quomodo mutati sunt *rogo dicat Pers*" (How they have changed, I ask that Pers say) (262, my emphasis). Note that the point of view shifts suddenly back in this line to the narrator's first person voice. George Rigg has suggested that this is an allusion to *Pierce the Ploughman's Crede*, but that poem, at least in the version we *now* have, must post-date 1393 (it mentions the trial of Walter Brut in that year).[55] The only Peter at the council (or council or not, even mentioned in "Heu" for that matter) was Peter Stokes himself, the Carmelite, who would hardly have been represented as uttering the antimendicant comment attributed here to "Pers." Nor, I think, does an ironic reading work well here: since it has no topical antecedent in the earlier lines, if it is irony, its meaning falls flat.[56] It is possible that the reference is to Peter Pateshull, though this seems unlikely if he is actually writing the poem himself, and why switch to *Middle English* if the referent is either Stokes or Pateshull? Also 1382 seems early for Pateshull to be a public authority on antimendicantism—five years before his official departure from his order. It would seem that this must be an allusion to Langland's *Piers*

Plowman. The allusion may be most likely, then, of the type common early in the poem's reception, in which Piers is often conflated with the poet, or, better, consciously made the spokesman of the poem.[57]

Further evidence that the allusion is likely to Langland's poem occurs in the lines immediately before this, in which, ridiculing Stokes's laborious but un- profitable contributions to the debate, the poet uses a Latin quote that also ap- pears in *Piers Plowman*: "With an O and an I, Si tunc tacuisses / Tu nunc stulto similis philosophus fuisses." In B.XI.416a and C.XIII.224a, where the dreamer is being raked over the coals by Imaginatif for the impatient way he interrupted Reason, resulting in the "ejection" from his dream: "Ac for thyn entermetynge her artow forsake: / Philosophus esses, si tacuisses" (You might have been a philosopher, if you had been able to hold your tongue) (C.XIII.223–23a). The quotation was originally adapted from Boethius where it describes the expo- sure of a feigned philosopher when he shows impatience at unjust provocation, but it is not so common in contemporary literature that the coincidence should be ignored, especially coming, as it does, just a few lines before the poet's di- rect reference to "Pers."[58] The ending of the poem, too, which describes an *en masse* exodus to London of the enemies of the Wycliffites (using ill-gotten finances to bribe church officials to condemn Hereford and Repingdon) is a satire devastatingly like Langland's Lady Mede episode.[59] Taken together, these par- allels suggest that "Heu" may be the earliest *Piers* tradition poem extant today, after those in the John Ball letters.

These three poems copied by an Hiberno-English scribe trained to write in mid-century and later cancelled with Xs are ultimately a mystery which Robert Cotton's penchant for dismembering his manuscripts does not help us finally to solve. But the repetition of "Heu" in Cotton and in Digby, alongside other poems ("Preste" in Cotton and "Sedens" in Digby) dealing with apostasy mo- tifs *is* helpful, because Bale attributed "Heu" and "Sedens" to Pateshull, a man who actually left the Austin friars. "Sedens" does indeed have a narrator who has left the friars, after, he says, "I tested" or "tried" (probavi) their novitiate.[60] While no self-respecting literary critic would go looking for transparent auto- biographical circumstances in these poems, the tradition of posting broad- sides at the time of leaving a religious order could certainly explain the pres- ence of such material in Pateshull's papers. Unlike the narrators of these poems, Pateshull was certainly no novice when he left: as Hudson notes, Walsingham recorded that in 1387 Pateshull purchased a papal privilege supposedly releasing him from his vows as an Austin friar, an unusual official "cover" for apostasy, but one that perhaps made him especially sensitive on the point. But, whether there are biographical parallels or not (and recent literary criticism has turned up contemporary cases where historical record and poetic "record" do match, especially in writers like Hoccleve), some of the authorial attributions Bale made are problematic. He also attributed "Quis" to Pateshull, but that poem inverts the motif of the novitiate to show *eagerness* to enter the friars orders— Rigg, in fact, regards "Quis" as a reply to "Sedens." "Quis" also refers to Kilvington as one of two beasts of the Apocalypse, FitzRalph being the other, and Kilvington was less a household name in the 1380s than two or three decades earlier, so a dating for "Quis" a good deal earlier than Pateshull's apostasy seems wise.[61] (As his *Vita fratrum* shows, Pateshull himself had intimate knowledge of the fraternal side of the struggles with FitzRalph during the 1350s.)[62] Bale also listed "Vox in Rama" as Pateshull's, which like "Quis" is written from a positive perspective on religious orders and endowments—certainly not Pateshull's cup of tea.[63] "Vox" sheds interesting light on the confiscations of 1389 noted by the *Opus* author because it blames the books of Ockham ("libros infernales") for promoting reformist ideas of a return to *ecclesia primitiva,* and it uses an argument for historical progression in church development ("Tunc cepit ecclesia et nunc est adulta") most commonly found in monastic defences of clerical ownership. The poem survives in a manuscript we have already met, St. Albans' prior, John Whethamstede's commonplace book (Cambridge, Gonville and Caius 230), and looks very like an attack *on* the friars and/or the Wycliffites supporting disendowment. Even "Heu" itself, which Hudson believes has the best claim for Pateshull's authorship, has a narrator who became disillusioned with the Benedictines, not the friars. Why were all these poems associated by Bale with Pateshull, when they differ widely in ideology?

To answer this, one has to know how much stock to put in Bale's attributions, and second, what the *uses* might be to which a man like Pateshull would have put such literature. To tackle Bale first: the antimendicant, apocalyptic-inspired screed, *Vita fratrum mendicantium,* is further described in one of Bale's lists as "vel eius commentarius in prophetiam Hyldegardis, cum rhythmis facetissimus."[64] Bale, then, understood the *Vita fratrum* to be a commentary on Hildegard's (supposed) prophecies against the friars and, at least the text he knew of it, traveled alongside "most facetious (or witty) poetry," which he also believed to be Pateshull's. In fact, Bale was only partly right on the first count: the *Vita fratrum* cites a great many prophets and polemicists beyond Hildegard— clearly Bale had *not* completely read it. How right he was about attributing the "facetious poetry" then becomes questionable.[65] Bale may have been jumping to conclusions about the authorship of the accompanying poems: an alternative explanation for this particular configuration of anti- and intra-clerical poetry around his name might be that Pateshull was *collecting* apostasy or "incomplete novitiate" broadsides. It would be odd to think of Pateshull as the author of *all* of these, given their varying ideologies. Although, of course, allowing for poetic license, he may simply have enjoyed adopting different polemical personas, but this sounds less and less like the rabble-rousing partisan who would start street riots—what we know of Pateshull's temper does not sound playful in any pluralist sense. In 1387, as Walsingham says, Pateshull incited a London mob, making charges of sodomy, sedition, and murder, especially against the orders, but tensions were diffused with the help of a much admired Austin, Thomas Ashbourne. Pateshull then posted his accusations on the doors of St. Paul's, where they were copied by many knights sympathetic to his views.[66] Here we have scope for practical uses of broadside poetry.

We saw that the Austins along with their cohorts in the Franciscan order were also the two orders from which disendowment activists most often arose in mid-century England. Pateshull is known to have a direct association with at least one of these activists, in fact, the Austin friar, Thomas Ashbourne. Thomas Ashbourne had represented the "winning" side at the Great Council of 1374 against the temporal claims of the church (see chapter 3); he is also believed to be one of the two Austins who presented the disendowment petition before Parliament in 1371. Members of Pateshull's order, then, had been deeply committed to disendowment and voluntary poverty campaigns for decades prior to his apostasy in 1387. It would have been an easy ideological step out of this context and some way toward Wycliffite reformist interests. In Pateshull's case we see first hand the schizophrenic nature of pro-Wycliffite attitudes toward Joachite and other prophetic materials.

The manuscript contexts of "Heu" we have examined, appearing alongside Hildegard in Digby and poetry in Hiberno-English dialect in Cotton, open up the possibility of a broad spectrum audience for Langlandiana. Anglo-Ireland and the Anglo-Irish were an important and early audience for *Piers Plowman*,[67] and the hints of "Heu's" Langlandianism are significant since its date is so early in the period of B transmission and even during C's revision. The "Heu" author, in a strange way, seems to reduce *Piers* itself to a two-page broadside, a mini-estates satire *without* the fictional or revelatory dimension. For him, Langland's poem was likely a repository of antimendicant, moral, and anticlerical satire with a healthy cache of disendowment and other reformist content to choose from—all quite serviceable once it is stripped of its visionary trimmings. This is what he borrows, and it is, in fact, just the way Wycliffites treated any revelatory work from which they chose to borrow, as we are about to see in the next chapter. No wonder "Heu" attracted the same audience as the two Hiberno-English poems that accompany it in the Cotton manuscript: the "Heu" author ignored the visionary, while the author of the iconomachic Hiberno-English poem, more extreme still, had *parodied* it. We have here at least one audience (Oxford Wycliffite sympathizers) and quite possibly two (Anglo-Irish antimendicants) for Langland. Langland's own restraint with iconographic and hagiographic tradition is well known,[68] and likely appealed to both. What we will see, however, is mounting evidence that Langland, in return, was trying to shake off some of this kind of borrowing. The charismatic Franciscan elements he added to the C text, for instance,[69] pull in an opposite direction to the kind of interest we have seen displayed here in the broadside's context in Cotton (and Digby, too, for that matter). But our first task is to better understand the relation of Wycliffism to the revelatory, and that is what is next.

Chapter Four

"EXTRA FIDEM SCRIPTURE"

Attitudes toward Non-Biblical Vision in Great
Schism England and the Vogue for Hildegardiana

"Outside of the faith of scripture" (extra fidem scripture) is how Wyclif described the visionary writings of Hildegard and other contemporary prophetic writers. We saw in the last chapter how pro-Wycliffite polemic, as in "Heu quanta desolacio," tends to strip away the visionary, and perhaps even (as did the compiler of the Cotton booklet) appropriate parody of vision for its project. In this chapter we will learn why such tendencies arose, beginning with Wyclif's own dislike of non-biblical prophecy and vision, and the caveats he raised against them. But this dislike was not itself heterodox: we can locate it in a broader, quite orthodox tradition of scholastic scepticism about vision, going back (at least with respect to our litmus test of Insular Hildegardiana) to the thirteenth century with John Pecham and coming forward in the fifteenth century at least to Reginald Pecock. We have already seen what Wyclif thought of Joachim,[1] but we know even more about what he thought of Hildegard—Hildegard being the figure most widely associated with Joachim in fourteenth-century reception and much more overtly visionary in her style. In this regard Wyclif may serve to some extent as an epitome of the scholastic mind, both orthodox and heterodox. Scholastics tend to stand out as slightly sceptical of vi-

188

sion, especially over against many of their monastic and secular counterparts noticed in the final sections of the chapter.

The Background: Hildegard and the Laundering of Suspect Amourian Eschatology in University Polemics

Scholastically trained thinkers (unlike monastic ones) throughout the thirteenth and fourteenth centuries had a tendency to be sceptical of contemporary revelatory experience or to admit to it only obliquely. There are many reasons why this should have been so, but, in the end, as I will suggest, the revelatory and the scholastic were rivals for the prize of theological illumination, rivals, however, with contempt for each other's methods. This chapter traces the complex relations of these two mentalities in the cool reception of Hildegard among English intellectuals like John Pecham, John Wyclif, and Reginald Pecock. Pecock, whose campaign to promote reason often against revelation echoes Wyclif's realism in certain ways, technically falls later than this study extends, but he deserves at least brief mention for making a challenge in English to Hildegard's orthodoxy. Before we can examine any of these things, however, we need to know a few important things about Hildegard herself.

A veteran polemicist on clerical laxity and schism in her own period and an uncompromising voice of the twelfth-century Gregorian reform tradition, Hildegard was a writer whose radicalism was so unusual that it made her unwelcome for vernacular translation, and made even Wycliffites, despite their dedication to the vernacular, cautious about what they translated. Yet her work was never officially censored and rarely attacked.

This relative paucity of overt attacks on her writing is surprising. She had prophesied, for instance, that Rome would dwindle in status to a mere bishopric, never to recover its authority;[2] that the lay lords would rise up and despoil rich and complacent religious, and do it with justice;[3] that they would be encouraged in this by a future group of pseudo-religious, who, under a guise of austerity and piety, would preach heresy and hatred of the clergy.[4] She had also prophesied, and this even in the early *Scivias,* that the church (Ecclesia) itself would give birth to Antichrist, a birth described in a graphic realization of grammatical gender, as falling "like a great mass of excrement" (uelut magna massa multi stercoris) from her vagina (locum ubi mulier cognoscitur).[5] Extracted thus from their original context amidst the fierce rhetoric of post-Gregorian reformist apocalypticism, these ideas appear even more radical than they would have seemed in Hildegard's own context (where, in certain respects they were more minor themes). But extracted is precisely how they came down to most fourteenth-century readers in England. There, just as elsewhere in Europe, Hildegard's thought was known mainly through a thirteenth-century compilation of extracts, Gebeno of Eberbach's *Speculum temporum futurorum*, or the *Pentachronon*, laboriously and admiringly assembled in 1220, some forty years after Hildegard's death. Gebeno's purpose had been to combat the growing Cathar heresy by supplying prophetic "information" about its rise and by castigating clergy for the corruptions he saw as the root of the problem. He was also concerned to defend Hildegard's reputation as an authority on Antichrist against the prophecies of an interloper of great fame from the south (apparently Joachim of Fiore). To this end he persuaded the nuns of Hildegard's abbey to allow him to do what Hildegard had explicitly forbidden in her epilogue to the *Liber divinorum operum*: abridge her works.[6]

The effect of this radical (in every sense) abridgement of her reformist prophetic ideas on Hildegard's later reputation was incalculable, and it established her instantly as primarily a polemical writer in the eyes of posterity—a writer whose ideas could be readily appropriated for a variety of causes. (Hildegard had also written liturgical songs, biblical exegesis, medical treatises, and visionary mysticism, all voluminous productions, but little represented in Gebeno's anthology.) However, not even the *Pentachronon* was radical enough for some polemicists: several pseudonymous productions, some cleverer than others, were composed, leading even medieval writers to raise concerns about their authenticity.[7] Suspicions emerged as early as the thirteenth century about an allegedly Hildegardian contribution to antimendicant propaganda,[8] modeled on her most famous and widely disseminated piece of prose, her letter to the clergy of Cologne. The letter itself had been written decades before the inception of the mendicant orders (she died in 1179) and contained her prophecy of a coming influential sect of deceptively pious heretics.[9] This prophecy had been taken up as antimendicant propaganda in the second quarter of the thirteenth century, establishing a popular hoax which was still going strong centuries later. The letter was extremely popular in fourteenth-century England and was often excerpted or highlighted in English manuscripts and clumsily imitated more than once.[10] The most famous imitation of the Cologne letter is "Insurgent gentes," a vitriolic attack on the friars likely concocted in the circle of William of St. Amour in mid-thirteenth-century Paris and mothered on Hildegard.[11] None of the many vernacular writers in late fourteenth-century England who cited "Insurgent" seem aware of the hoax, but judicious concerns about its textual authenticity were raised by scholars writing in Latin, and this added to the slight cloud of suspicion and intrigue under which her works traveled.

The opening line of "Insurgent" runs: "Insurgent gentes que comedent peccata populi tenentes ordinem mendicantium" (A group will arise who will eat [or feast upon] the sins of the people, holding to the order of mendicancy). This alludes to Hosea 4:8, in which the Lord had rejected the priesthood of Israel, threatening that they will "eat the sins of my people": "Peccata populi mei comedent . . . (Osee 4:8a)." Masquerading initially as exegesis, "Insurgent" then cleverly predicts the rise and fall of the mendicant orders without ever naming them directly. This is the very tactic used in William's own infamous work, the *De periculis novissimorum temporum*, which proceeds by the same ingenious method as "Insurgent." The two appear together, as we saw, in Bodley 158, which also records the condemnation of radical Joachite opinions held by Helmyslay in 1380. This clutch of texts was being picked up avidly in antimendicant circles in Wyclif's England. For instance, in the *Piers* BC Feast of Patience scene, Langland makes allusion to "Insurgent," ridiculing the greedy friar and his ilk, and issuing a dire warning: "Vos qui peccata hominum comeditis" (You who feast upon the sins of men) (C.XV.51a). The quote continues, "nisi pro eis lacrimas et orationes effuderitis, ea que in deliciis comeditis, in tormentis euometis" (unless you pour out tears and prayers for them, you shall vomit up amid torments the food you now feast on amid pleasures). The "nisi" clause sounds like Langland's own tendency toward compassionate qualifiers, suggesting that here he is composing his own gloss in Latin.

"Insurgent," along with genuine Hildegardian prophecy, was flooding the fourteenth-century reformist market, thanks to readers like the (one time) Austin friar, Peter Pateshull. To understand why Wyclif was concerned about the infiltration of "Hildegard," we need to know something about the flood of new manuscripts he and his contemporaries were facing. About two-thirds of extant manuscripts of Hildegardiana with English provenance and the lion's share of the recorded citation fall between the 1350s and the 1420s, with the reign of Richard II (1377–99) as the high water mark of her popularity. During this time many new copies were made, and old ones dusted off for rereading and annotation.[12] This is also when the longest list of borrowers and users of Hildegardiana crops up: Gower, Wyclif, the author of *Pierce the Ploughman's Crede*, the *Jack Upland* author, Wimbledon, Henry of Kirkstede, Peter Pateshull,

John Blackwell, William Taylor, Peter Partriche, almost certainly Langland (although he does not name her), and a large group of anonymous users of various stripes.[13] Among the writers listed here, the overt Wycliffites, with one exception (Taylor), cite only the pseudonymous "Insurgent"; those using genuine works, most often in the form of excerpts from the *Pentachronon*, usually fall into orthodox categories.[14] One very rough, retrospective guide to her English popularity can be gauged from statistics in Edward Bernard's 1697 *Catalogi librorum manuscriptorum Angliae et Hiberniae*, which lists a total of nineteen manuscripts of Hildegard, compared to only three of Joachim (the prophetic writer most often associated with her on the Continent).[15] Although these statistics fall far short of representing the English transmission of either writer, they do reliably underline one thing we know from other sources: Joachite material frightened librarians more than Hildegardiana did. They also underline the fact that Hildegard's readers were largely erudite males.

Insular compilers and librarians certainly knew the kind of audience Hildegard was reaching, because — and this is telling — they never associate her with other female visionaries in their collections, but rather with male writers such as Joachim of Fiore, Peter John Olivi, John of Rupescissa, William of St. Amour, and Wyclif (all officially censured authors).[16] But despite her gender, the most common attitude toward Hildegard is adulation and piety. Orthodoxy issues haunted all visionary writers, but Hildegard herself, or her literary executors, had virtually succeeded in forestalling them by highlighting her claim to official approval for *Scivias*. That is, until Archbishop John Pecham got suspicious.

Hildegard and the Doctors: Academic Distrust of Revelatory Writing in Pecham, Wyclif, and Pecock

Archbishop Pecham was apparently the earliest English reader to question whether what he was reading was authentic.[17] He was a friar, and Hildegard was, by this time, widely cited by antimendicant propagandists (this, at least, was likely the foundation for the misogyny he invoked against her — a rare case of it in Hildegard reception history).[18] But a university-trained thinker, Pecham was not much given to sympathy with visionary writing of *any* type: in his "Contra Kilwardby," he warned his opponent (a Dominican who had quoted the prophecies of Hildegard and Joachim of Fiore with approbation) against trusting in the prophecies of *both*.[19] His objection was a characteristically scholastic one to the unreliability of revelations, which he denigratingly calls dreams (sompnia). Of course, as a thirteenth-century Franciscan highly placed in church administration, Pecham would have been extremely sensitive to the damage the Joachite condemnations had recently done to his order's credibility, and Hildegardian antimendicantism worried him enough that in his *Tractatus pauperis* he challenged the assertion that her works were approved by St. Bernard and Pope Eugenius. If Bernard did collect and study Hildegard's texts, Pecham snorted, he perhaps (forsan) did so in order to refute them, just as he did the errors of Abelard—rather an intellectually flattering comparison for Hildegard, actually.[20] But for the idea of Eugenius's approval he has no patience: "plane est mendacium," he retorted; the apostolic throne does not confirm such things of its own accord, he continued, and there are many errors still to be found in her writings.[21]

One might be tempted to see this simply as mendicant rancor, but as Grundmann has said about Eugenius's approval of Hildegard, it would have been the first such papal approval of a potentially controversial work, so Pecham's scepticism was perhaps not unreasonable.[22]

Apparently, Pecham had no way of checking the veracity of the papal approval, but he tells us that he checked through Bernard's works in a fruitless effort to find a reference to it. He was also suspicious that what she had prophesied about the friars was actually only negative remarks vaguely directed at certain unspecified religious (Hildegardis, que nonnulla mala dicit de quibusdam religiosis).[23] In fact, he was right. He must be speaking of the Cologne prophecy here: in it Hildegard had projected an ill-defined "erring people" (populus errans) who, feigning pious poverty, would earn the confidence of secular princes, urging them to act against the excesses of ecclesiastical wealth.[24] As a prophetic portrait of the early friars, this was unlikely to convince anyone who was not already convinced, and Pecham denounced it as too vague. But it is hard to be certain that this was the passage he fastened on because in contrast to his scholarly care over Bernard, he was a sloppy reader of writers he did not respect. For instance, although he claimed to have read both Hildegard and Joachim, he equates, or even conflates them, insisting (wrongly) that they both prophesied by "sompnia," a mode which seduces many, and which, he cautions, must be tested carefully, and against the witness of scripture (teste scriptura).[25] But sloppy reading can be valuable for the assumptions it reveals, and Pecham's conflation of the two prophetic thinkers is, like many such errors in reception, an instructive one for us.

At least by the early fourteenth century in England, Hildegardiana was indeed being mistaken for Joachite prophecy: an intriguing instance occurs in a manuscript Wyclif himself may have seen at Queens College, Oxford. In what is today Bodleian Library, Lat. Misc. c. 75, a manuscript once containing Pecham's own *Tractatus pauperis*,[26] is a booklet in an early fourteenth-century hand which contains a copy of the pseudo-Hildegardian "Insurgent," but here attributed to the "venerabilis Abbatis Joachim." This booklet of polemical prophetic texts contains plenty of real Joachite prophecy, including a number of pieces by Arnold of Villanova, whose apocalyptic writings had been condemned by the theologians of Paris in 1300 and later by the chancellor of Oxford, Henry of Harclay, in part for daring to calculate the Second Coming.[27] Arnold suffered imprisonment for his views and his support for the Franciscan Joachites was unflinching. The appearance of "Insurgent" with these other texts is a stark reminder of how easily the fine line between hostile *external* critiques of the mendicants and *internal* critiques of the Franciscan Spirituals could be erased—and why men like Pecham found both so conflatable and infuriating.[28] Lat. Misc. c. 75 bears the chain and staple holes typical of medieval Oxford college bindings and was seen by John Bale (1495–1563) at Queen's College, the college, that was, in the fourteenth century, both Wyclif's and Nicholas Hereford's as well.[29]

This may explain why Wyclif came to doubt, as Pecham had, the authenticity of "Insurgent." He may well have seen it attributed to Joachim either in what is now Lat. Misc. c. 75. or elsewhere, a "prophecy" he certainly knew under Hildegard's name (as did several of his followers). We already know what Wyclif thought of "calculatores" like Joachim and Arnold. But Wyclif's attitudes toward Hildegard are instructive, because they changed over the space of a few years, and, by the end of his life, when he would have liked to have cited a piece attributed to Hildegard as an authority against the friars, what held him back was doubts about the attribution of the texts he had seen. Whether or not the presence of the misattributed "Insurgent" at Queens may be the key to the puzzle (and it need not be), we can trace a trajectory away from hostility and toward tentative acceptance of Hildegard in his writings. In his earliest references to Hildegard—which are in fact not all that early—he, too, sports the contempt of a university man for visionary writing. No one has yet attempted to gather Wyclif's references to Hildegard and chronologize them, so the following list may not be definitive.

The earliest citation I know appears in his *De apostasia* (late 1380), where he equates her prophecies to fictions, insisting rather contemptuously that he will proceed according to scripture, "not according to the prophecies of Hilde-gard, or fables" (non secundum vaticinium Hildegardis vel fabulas).[30] In *De vaticinia seu prophetia* (by late 1382), Wyclif still shows unmistakable irritation with, he says, "my associates" (socii mei) who prophesy "from the sayings of Merlin, Hildegard and similar prophets" (ex dictis Merlini, Hildegardis et vatum similium).[31] What still disturbs him about Hildegard and the others is the extra-biblical status of their revelation (extra fidem scripture), moving him to prophesy by more faithful evidence (fideliori evidencia prophetare). But in the second chapter of *De vaticinia*, he says a little more; this time about Hilde-gard's prophecy that the friars will soon be destroyed (quod ordo Fratrum de-structur in brevi). Here he comes very, very close to echoing Pecham's scepti-cism about her (he may also have read his Pecham in Lat. Misc. c. 75). Pecham's doubt, we remember, was founded on the fact that her prophecies seemed to refer *non-specifically* to corrupt clergy, rather than specifically to the friars. Here Wyclif makes exactly the same point in exactly Pecham's language that Hil-degard is speaking generally against lax clergy (generaliter contra clerum).[32] This, at least, is somewhat less dismissive than the associations with "fabulas" made just a year or so before in *De apostasia*, but Wyclif was soon to really change his tune. In the *Trialogus*, written at the end of 1382 or the beginning of 1383, he suddenly finishes an antimendicant diatribe with an approving appeal to the (now) "*blessed* Hildegard," and the triumphant assertion that she had written her antifraternal prophecy before the friars were introduced (Et idem declarat *beata* Hildegardis, in prophetia sua expressius, *antequam isti fratres fuer-ant introducti*).[33] This is a direct reference to the rubric which usually travels with "Insurgent,"[34] and this identification gives us some real insight into Wyclif's change in attitude.

"Insurgent" is fundamentally a non-prophetic and non-visionary text— it is utterly unrevelatory, written by a polemicist (perhaps even William him-self), not by Hildegard nor by anyone with revelatory pretensions, and so it gets to the point, quickly, biblically, acidly, and with partisan flair. Wyclif ap-parently liked it a lot. He did not like her visionary or prophetic writing gen-erally, and no alert reader of Hildegard would ever mistake "Insurgent" for Hildegard's style or handling of the polemical genre. It would appear, then, that his personal discovery of "Insurgent" sparked the new mood of generosity toward "beata" Hildegard—itself a striking, and quite un-Wycliffian epithet— perhaps prompted by the heating up of the pamphlet wars in the wake of the Blackfriars Council.[35] By the time he wrote the *De fundatione sectarum* (between

August and November 1383) he remarks "how plainly and excellently" (egregie atque plane) Hildegard had foreseen the corruption of the friars, but he now (perhaps rereading with a cooler head, perhaps after discussion with colleagues— who knows?) cautions care, because the authenticity of her writings, he says, could have "deniability" (habere possent colorem negare).[36] He then turns back to biblical sources.

Clearly even Wyclif was under some pressure to read Hildegard and revise his opinion about her—and when one looks at the extent of Ricardian citation and the number of Ricardian manuscripts containing her reformist prophecies, it is not hard to see why. In fact, by now the fad for copying and citing Hildegard's prophecies was well under way—a fad from which even Oxford itself was not immune. The most colourful case, as we saw earlier, is Peter Pateshull, Oxford doctor of theology and apostate Austin friar, whose antifraternalism was so outrageous that in 1387 he started a small riot against the friars in London when he accused his ex-brethren of corruption, sodomy, murder, and treason.[37] He was introducing Hildegardiana and Joachimism into reformist circles, to judge from the excerpts from the *Vita fratrum mendicantium* known to John Bale.[38]

For centuries before Wyclif came along, monastics in England and elsewhere had been quietly fretting over Hildegard's disendowment prophecies in their marginalia, but suddenly during the last decades of the fourteenth century, she has readers and copyists of every ecclesiastical affiliation, and some of none. Even older copies of the *Pentachronon* now gain their new layers of late fourteenth-century annotation or are reincorporated into updated volumes, as readers who knew of her prophecies return to them for guidance amid new ecclesiastical turmoils. Central to Wyclif's early appeal, especially to the secular authorities, was his emphasis on disendowment and its attractiveness to a "financially embarrassed" government, "delighted to be told that confiscating church goods . . . was [in fact] a *duty* to God and neighbour."[39] But though Wyclif's message was politically seductive, Hildegard had beaten him to it, and in precisely the same terms. What Anne Hudson sees as one of the trademarks of Lollard thought on disendowment, namely, that it is the *duty* of the secular powers to take action and reform a church too internally crippled to help itself, is exactly what Hildegard had advocated prophetically some two hundred years before. In her much copied letter to Werner of Kircheim, she prophesied that the princes and the laity would rise up and disendow lax clergy, and she stresses, "in doing this, they will wish to have shown themselves obedient to

God, because they will say that the church is polluted through you."[40] Her most elaborate prophecy to this effect, the *Justicia* prophecy from the *Liber divinorum operum*, begins to be annotated and extracted especially from the mid-fourteenth century onward.[41] In this scathingly witty and cynically realistic satire she had prophesied how the excess wealth of the clergy would have to be forcefully confiscated by a responsible secular leadership of the nobility, despite the whining, special pleading, and shameless threats engineered by the indignant clergy. When all their stratagems (which include excommunication and militarization) fail, they will at last "put aside the inane pride and faith which they have always had in themselves . . . [and] humiliated . . . and howling [ululando], they will cry out and say, 'Because we have cast out the Omnipotent God from the performance of our duties, therefore this confusion has been brought upon us, namely, that we should be oppressed and humiliated by those whom we ought to oppress and humiliate.'"[42]

Her portrait here of the clergy is so cutting that even the Lollard preacher, William Taylor, preaching in 1406, felt the need to soften it for vernacular consumption: he has Hildegard say that the clergy will hand over their goods in "wilful. free. & meek delyueraunce" to the "temperal lordes . . . who sumtyme weren but as erþe in comparison of þe clergie."[43] There is no such romantic nonsense in Hildegard. A veteran of ecclesiastical disputes and herself a member of a powerful noble family, Hildegard would never have imagined the clergy meek in surrender or the lords temporal as dirt ("erþe") in comparison to anyone. Taylor's diluting of her prophecy is, in fact, bowdlerization, such as commonly arises when radical texts are translated into vernaculars by skittish clergy (one thinks here of aspects of the translations of Catherine of Siena or Alphonse of Pecha into Middle English, for instance).[44] It is instructive and ironic, however, to see this in a Lollard preacher, someone speaking for a movement the primary purpose of which was vernacular translation and lay accessibility. It shows that Lollards were nervous about radical visionary sources, and anxious to show themselves part of a sensible mainstream, reflecting a Lollard impetus toward respectability at this time. But the date of the sermon, November 21, 1406, suggests something even more specific: the possibility that Taylor was attempting to dodge a new law against prophecies passed that year, expressly mentioning those preaching or predicting a variety of "seditious" or destabilizing matters, including disendowment of the church.[45] Taylor's mild censorship, though, is unusual and never occurs (to my knowledge) in Latin copies of her works, some of which were coming to the attention of the more powerful laity. To see a Wycliffite bowdlerizing an officially uncondemned visionary opens up, for us, a whole new perspective.

In fact, overt citation from her genuine visions usually falls to the orthodox, and the ostensibly orthodox—the latter being perhaps closet sympathizers of more radical positions, but anxious not to cross the line into heterodoxy. Certainly, Pateshull falls into this category, and so does the university man, Peter Partriche, who had once had Lollard leanings and also collected Hildegard's prophecies into his anthology of radical and satirical texts, now Bodleian Library Digby 98.[46] The conjunction of Langland and Hildegard with what we might call "soft Wycliffism" in Partriche's collection is important. As we saw, the one "hardcore" entry (two letters by Wyclif) in Digby 98 has been physically cut out.[47] Possession of identifiable Lollard texts had become a capital offence by the time Partriche began to receive benefices (from 1419 onward), and he himself may not have been willing to risk so much for a passion of his youth.

Hildegard had a special appeal for closet radicals, and, like Langland, her texts infiltrated the reading circles of some powerful laymen. Perhaps the most intriguing and elusive instance of possible English lay readership is the case of Thomas Woodstock, duke of Gloucester. He was the most materially grasping and politically ruthless of the Appellants, eventually murdered, apparently on Richard's orders, in 1397. This is not the kind of man one would pick out of crowd as a likely reader of Hildegard, and we cannot be absolutely certain he did. Yet among the books which survive from Pleshy (his home seat, collegiated in 1397) is a beautiful copy of the *Pentachronon*, now Cambridge, St. John's College, MS 27. In it, in the informal hand of someone trained to write during the last half of Edward III's reign (someone, that is, who would be Gloucester's exact contemporary), is a note highlighting Hildegard's prophecy that the power of the papacy will decline and will devolve to local officials: "Note that the apostolic authority [dignitas] will diminish and be divided."[48] This idea is, obviously, very close to one of the Lollard conclusions condemned at the Blackfriar Council of 1382: that the papacy should give way to regional jurisdictions.[49] The note comes beside Hildegard's prophecy that

> because neither the princes nor the rest of the people, whether in spiritual orders or secular, will discover any religion in the Apostolic name, the authority of that name will then diminish. They will prefer other teachers and

archbishops under other titles in diverse regions, . . . with the result that only Rome and a few regions adjacent to it will be left under its authority. This will happen partly from the incursions of war and partly through common agreement and consensus of the spiritual and secular people.[50]

Gloucester was likely among those secular lords whose interest in Lollardy (if such it was) was purely pragmatic, galvanized by the prospect of a devolution of church power and property. Whether one of his clerks made the annotation, or (perhaps less likely, though not impossible) he made it, we do not know, but we do know that he himself owned a very large number of Latin books on church and papal history and jurisdiction.[51] We also know that his clerks at Pleshy were closely involved in his political life, most famously, perhaps, on the day he was arrested by Richard II.[52] An enigmatic man whose principles, if any, are hard to know, Woodstock was, on the one hand, the dedicatee of a Lollard dialogue between a friar and a secular clerk and the owner of a complete Wycliffite Bible. However, possession of an English Bible, Wycliffite or otherwise, in a member of an august social class like Woodstock's proves nothing about anyone's orthodoxy.[53] Moreover, we do know that he was never *publicly* associated with the Lollards, not even by chroniclers who did not hesitate to name at least knights belonging to that class.[54] Finally, nothing about his cultural or religious tastes (about which we know a great deal from surviving book inventories) betrays any distinctive Lollard sensibility. The fact, for instance, that he and his wife (a member of the Bohun family, whose patronage of illuminated books was famous) donated one of their daughters, Isabel, to the Minoresses in infancy suggests at least orthodox social habits.[55] But Froissart described Woodstock as "a man of books, devotion, and independent views."[56] What I think we may say with confidence is that the idea of massive ecclesiastical disendowment would have been attractive to him, as to many magnates.

It was not until the mid-fifteenth century that the charge of Hildegardian forgery was made in the vernacular. It took another scholastic reasoner to see it, the ill-fated Reginald Pecock, who translated some key sentences from "Insurgent" in his *Repressor of Over Much Blaming of the Clergy*. The version of it he knew had even appropriated Pope Eugenius's approval to lend authority to the hoax. The opponents of the mendicants, he says, assert that:

The . . . religiose nunne Seint Hildegart, visitid with the spirit of prophecie, wroot manie prophecies which weren examyned and approued in a general counceil holdun at Treuer undir Pope Eugeny the [Thridde], at which conseil Seint Bernard was present, as it is writun in famose cronicles. . . . [S]che spekith that aftir hir daies schulde rise iiij.ordris of beggers . . . 'that thei schulden be flaterers, and enviers, and ypocritis and bacbiters;'. . . . 'that of wijse and trewe men this ordre schal be cursid;'. . . 'that . . . the comoun peplis hertis schulden falle awey fro hem, and her ordre schulde be alto broke'.[57]

Against this he retaliates by attacking the authenticity—and, more unusually, the orthodoxy—of the prophecies circulating under Hildegard's name:

Whether it be trewe or no what [Seinte Hildegard] seide and wroot of . . . the iiij. ordris of beggeris . . . this y dare seie, that among the reuelaciouns and prophecies, whiche been ascriued to hir, is conteyned vntrouthe contrarie to the trewe feith; and for to it proue y durst leie in plegge my lijf, how euer it be that her prophecies and reuelaciouns weren approued. (495)

The suggestion that not all items "whiche been ascriued to hir" are genuine is closely linked for Pecock by 1449 to his suspicion that there were censurable elements in her writing ("contrarie to the trewe feith"). What Pecock had in common with Wyclif especially was an intellectual method powerfully based on the value of "reason"—but in Pecock this was even more stridently articulated, and with conscious opposition to the centrality of scripture which characterizes Wycliffite thought. As several recent studies stress, for Pecock all scriptural interpretation must be subjected to what he called "the doom of pure resoun." In his *Repressor of Over Much Blaming of the Clergy*, Pecock undercuts virtually all the traditional alternatives to "pure resoun" as a theological method: reliance on the church fathers (whom he pronounces as too often "sownyng into the contrarie" of one another) and claims to divine inspiration, even those based on the "meeke[ness] and good wil" of the interpreter (the very cornerstone of the church's method of visionary *probatio*).[58] What Kantik Ghosh has recently called Pecock's "implicit dismissal of the 'spiritual senses' of scriptural interpretation" is of a piece with the stringent way in which his focus on "pure resoun" drove the revelatory to the periphery of his theology. As Paul Strohm summarizes this attachment to reason in his study of Pecock and natural law, "So robust is this sphere in Pecock's view that it leaves only a relative handful of matters—

such as the arcana of the trinity or the mystery of the eucharist—reliant for their acceptance upon revelation or scriptural authority."[59]

Ironically it was not Hildegard's, but his own writings that eventually wound up in the censor's bonfire. As the most substantial survival from the process of examining Pecock, the *Gladius Salomonis* by the Austin John Bury explains, Pecock's privileging of human reason above the Bible was seen by contemporaries as the primary cause of his downfall.[60] He was charged with setting natural law even above the scriptures (which he also saw as full of contradictions only reason could sort), along with the sacraments, the church fathers, and revelation. In a telling move he had deleted the clause about Christ's descent into hell from his version of the Creed—an article of faith arrived at via "the spiritual senses" of exegesis and early revelatory texts like the *Gospel of Nicodemus.*[61] This is an extreme position, obviously, but at its heart lies a deep suspicion of revelatory modes, scholastic in temper.

Attitudes toward Vision in Medieval England and the Health of Intellectual Freedom, 1378–1406

The authorities were slow to move against most forms of prophecy— especially short anonymous prophetic pieces and treatises, unconnected with previously officially censured writers (Olivi's and Rupescissa's works were being locked up at least by 1389). Hildegard's work escaped further bowdlerization except once that I know of, in *The Chastising of God's Children*, a vernacular text aimed, ironically, at women.[62] Parliamentary legislation in 1402 and again in 1406 finally made the dissemination of prophecies illegal, associating them (in 1406) most prominently with disendowment advocacy.[63] The complaint is about false prophecies "diverses fauxes pretenses Prophecies" and various "ceduls & livers" (pamphlets or broadsides and books) that are being published among the people. By 1406, then, as the Lancastrian regime consolidates itself by tarring Richard II with a Lollard brush, the secular authorities (in a self-serving political *volte face*) are finally willing to admit that prophecies of disendowment could be dangerous. Thus, perhaps, we have William Taylor's comparative caution in that year—but by then it was too late. Hildegardiana had already been in use in polemical *vernacular* texts for over two decades (and *Joachitae* since the 1350s), and both types in Latin for centuries.[64] Among episcopal officials in the fifteenth century, only Pecock caught on, and we have seen what became of his campaign against Hildegard.

Perhaps it was the "realist" school of philosophy to which Wyclif gravitated that determined in part his attitude toward revelation. It was not the attitude, apparently, of his colleague (and one-time admirer) Partriche. Nor was it the attitude of a surprising number of Oxford and Cambridge men, in whose personal (indeed, often *private*) manuscripts a large amount of contemporary prophecy and revelatory theology survives.[65] The turmoil of the Schism period, I would suggest, had much to do with this—just as it did at Paris with Gerson and d'Ailly. Among the scholars who chose to bestow their credibility on Hildegard's writings was the Dominican friar, John Blackwell, prior of the Oxford convent 1400–1407. In an astonishing set of annotations this learned friar—clearly desperate for new answers in an age of schism and heresy—glossed a complete copy of the *Pentachronon* to show that she had prophesied the Lollards.[66] The tactic is similar to Knighton's contention that William of St. Amour's "Eternal Evangelists" are not the Joachite-inspired friars, but the Lollards. The layers of annotation in Blackwell's text (now Bodleian Library, MS Digby 32) tell a clear story of how these upheavals changed the reading of Hildegard. The earliest annotator, Hand 1, simply privileged the conventional, perhaps to obscure the impact of Hildegard's radical apocalypticism, by imposing a grid of traditional eschatology upon it in his marginal finding notes. Later hands, however, copying during the Schism age, were far less circumspect and leapt on her prophecies as the key to all current struggles. Among these, Blackwell is the only one to which we can actually attach a name, but the fact that the notes were done by Dominican intellectuals, who were not much known for their tolerance of vision and were well known for their inquisitorial offices, makes this episode an extraordinary indicator of Schism desperation.

In the monastic houses, attitudes toward vision were entirely different. Monastic—that is, cloistered—intellectuals had a much wider tolerance for visions, both in their literature and in quotidian experience.[67] One such is Henry of Kirkestede,[68] the distinguished Benedictine librarian of Bury who archived disendowment threats which he regarded as evidence of apocalyptic imminence, an age-old mendicant menace.[69] In Henry's copy of the *Pentachronon*,[70] he especially highlights with reverence Hildegard's key prophecies of disendowment.[71] During the decades that Kirkestede was copying Corpus Christi 404 (that is, from the early 1350s until his death, which was not likely before 1382), he constantly returned to it for fresh insights and annotation. Reading Hildegard, another Benedictine, must have been slightly comforting to Kirkestede, because she prophesies disendowment as *renewal*, that is, as a return to "the first dawn of justice," a return, as Langland's prophecy also says, *ad pristinum statum ire*.[72] This was the light that illuminated the issue long before Wyclif's party came on the scene. The aging Benedictine librarian was comforted, I would guess, because to Hildegard, this was to be chastisement for *bad* abbeys, so to speak (she tells her own convent, for instance, "*Your* house, my daughters, God will not destroy"), rather than as the sweeping, long-term political measure which, during the 1370s and 1380s in England, began to be mooted.[73]

Hildegard's work, then, was a beacon of visionary hope to some like Kirkestede, an annoyance to Pecham, a safe outlet for suppressed radical frustrations for Partriche, a piece of political pragmatism, perhaps, for Woodstock; a suspect non-biblical mode of "faith" to Wyclif, too potent for Taylor, and revelatory heresy to Pecock. This diversity, testimony itself to the health of intellectual freedom in the period, epitomizes what we are up against when we study vision. Hers could be and was used both against Lollards and in support of them, sometimes sitting cheek-by-jowl with cancelled, or defaced, or otherwise censored material — material with which it had much in common.[74] But her genuine work seems to have passed officially unscathed through its entire extant Insular transmission — unlike many bowdlerized or confiscated visionary reformist writers such as Catherine of Siena, Peter Olivi, and John of Rupescissa, all of whom were actually far less *overtly* associated with Wycliffism than Hildegard. It was mainly the intellectuals who are on record as distrusting her vision.

Why should Hildegard's prophecies have led such a charmed life? First of all, she herself had brilliantly negotiated the shark-infested waters of imperial-papal politics. Second, her writing makes deft use of ambiguity. The result was her deliberately obscure prophetic style, which readers like Pecham and Wyclif hated, and which her original compiler, Gebeno, had gone to such lengths to defend; it would likely have defeated even the most determined censor. As the fifteenth-century abbot, John Trittenheim (Trithemius), wrote in the front of British Library, MS Additional 15,102: "In all her works the blessed Hildegard proceeds very mystically [or symbolically] and obscurely [mistice valde et obscure], whence her writings are scarcely understandable unless by the religious and devout" (fol. 1v)[75] — he recommends prayer as an aid to her readers, but it is possible that ecclesiastical authorities were not disposed to lose sleep over texts which required so much divine support for comprehension.

There are other reasons as well. It lacked (or, in some cases, the centuries had obscured) the historical and polemical specificity which often got prophetic writings purposely made for certain political moments into trouble. And there was not much history of Hildegard-inspired radical *activism* (unless one counts the Amourian appropriation of her good name) such as there was of Franciscan Joachimism. Also crucial was the relative security of the overtly visionary genre. Visionary prophecy was slightly marginalized—it was associated with a maelstrom of difficult validation issues, and with literary ("fictional") enterprises, and certainly with women. These were both its flaws and its strengths.

Chapter Five

VISIONS FROM PRISON

Intellectual Freedom and the Gift of "Intellectus Spiritualis"

At the end of chapter 4 we saw that there were many different attitudes toward vision in the Middle Ages, at least seven, in fact, if one wants to be mathematical about it, in a selective look at the reception of Hildegard alone. Attitudes toward Hildegard's work, we found, included regarding it (1) with credential visionary hope, (2) with annoyance, (3) as a safe outlet for suppressed radical frustrations, (4) with political pragmatism, (5) as a suspect non-biblical mode of "faith," (6) as too potent for vernacular translation, or (7) as revelatory heresy. This chapter explores one of the most powerful of those attitudes—the belief that revelation could protect intellectual freedom, even under inquisition. And we will find this belief where we would least expect to, that is, in two early Wycliffite writers, both trained in university method. More surprising still is that this attitude was recognized and accorded grudging, tacit respect by the authorities holding these writers for heresy. This aspect of medieval spirituality illuminates the little-known historical realm of what we would today call human rights, the rights, particularly, of prisoners of conscience. In a further unexpected twist, it shows how the writings of both Wycliffites reflect a revelatory, charismatic culture originally Franciscan in origin, which, however, Wycliffism had already all but lost by 1389–93.

In a recent article Anne Hudson notes that even though Wyclif drew on an earlier, long-standing reform tradition which Pamela Gradon had called "the reformist *inheritance* of Wyclif and his followers," scholarship since 1980 has often "underplayed that background."[1] And this has occurred, she reminds us, even though "few, if any, of Wyclif's ideas cannot be found in texts that certainly antedate his writings and preaching." Especially underplayed has been the Franciscan aspect of that inheritance, an aspect we will highlight here with respect to Olivi and Rupescissa and the evidence of their impact on two Wycliffites who began writing in 1389 (the *Opus* author) and 1391 (Walter Brut). This impact is all the more important because, "for several years," as Hudson also notes, "the contemporary documentary record deals with a nameless heresy," with labels like "Lollar(d)" or even "*Wycliffiste*" only entering the records between 1387/8 and 1390, and even then only fitfully. What was nameless to the authorities was also a fluid entity to its adherents, as the cases discussed here show. They illuminate the role of revelatory thought in this "nameless heresy" throughout the 1380s and into the very early 1390s. These sources show, ultimately, "a road not taken" in later Wycliffism.[2] And given the incredible popularity of revelatory genres and beliefs in late medieval culture as a whole, they show, perhaps, why the failure to choose that turning may have contributed to the "prematurity" of the Wycliffite reformation.

Spiritual Intellection, Rupescissa as a Prison Writer, and Two Orphans of Early Wycliffism

What will concern us first of all in this chapter is the one credible claim that Latin exegetes were always able to invoke for revelatory support of novel interpretations, the claim to what is biblically called *intellectus spiritualis*, that is, spiritual understanding or intellection.[3] For hundreds of years the gift of spiritual understanding had been a legal refuge of sorts for exegetes in trouble and could be used, in Robert Lerner's inimitable phrase, as "the ecstasy defence."[4] The claim goes back at the very least to Rupert of Deutz, the innovative Benedictine exegete of the Gregorian reform, who, cloistered since childhood, had to fight for academic recognition amidst those who had been free to travel and study with the great masters.[5] His exegesis was novel and often under attack, especially when he privileged his own interpretations over those of the august church fathers, insisting that others (like himself) might also "dig wells with the plowshares of their own genius" (alios fodere puteos proprii vomere ingenii).[6] Even more famous was Joachim of Fiore's claim to *intellectus spiritualis*, likely, in turn, the inspiration for the remarkable, though oblique claims of Olivi.[7] Olivi's formulation, repeated many times in the writers discussed in this chapter, is the insistence that he speaks "not as a prophet foreteller" (non ut vates propheticus), but by "*instinctus interioris spiritus inspiratus.*"[8] For its exponents, the gift is closely related to Augustine's concept of intellectual vision and seems to have been mainly evoked by men. Although some speculative mystics like Hildegard, Porete, and Julian (in fact, three of the four women writers most closely examined in this study) did write intellectual vision, medieval women most often make direct claims to visionary experience conveyed by images (that is, to the second rank of vision in the Augustinian hierarchy). Augustine's third and highest rank, intellectual vision (his metaphor for knowing)—always a paradox in terms—is usually invoked by men and by a long string of apocalyptic writers influenced by Joachim. Its invocation by the late fourteenth century is nearly always, in my experience, a sign that the writer has been reading visionary apocalypticism. The pattern here is that these writers had usually experienced some kind of persecution (this includes Rupert), and that the special gift was a form of legal defence for them in an age that had to respect the *possibility* of revelation, no matter how sceptically.

It was used, surprisingly, given what we have just seen of Wyclif's own anti-visionary stance, by the anonymous author of the *Opus arduum* and Walter Brut. Neither the *Opus* nor Brut's extant affidavits, so far as we know, circulated in England, and this may explain in part why their influence was limited. But they made the claims they did, I will suggest, because both had things to say that were more dangerous (even in the 1390s) and less usual than Wycliffism. So, while fearlessly challenging an episcopal imprisonment for the right to proclaim his Wycliffite theology, the *Opus* author was frightened to reveal that Rupescissa and especially Olivi were among his most serious sources.[9] In making this challenge, he was relying on two important gentlemen's agreements for ecclesiastical tolerance of his ideas: a specific concept of intellectual freedom and openness to speculation within a medieval university community, and in relation to his persecutors (apparently episcopal authorities), his subtle claim to visionary authority (spiritual intellection). His contemporary Walter Brut was making similar, though somewhat less academic claims and in Latin as well. Though a layman, Brut attracted actual academic response from intellectuals who debated his ideas, intellectuals, in fact, who willingly disputed ideas even more radical than his and with speculative abandon.[10]

The *Opus* author was beyond doubt a prison writer, and he speaks overtly of the conditions of his imprisonment and writing. Brut's physical situation is harder to determine,[11] though he was clearly under inquisition. According to Bishop John Trefnant's notary his writings were brought as "diversas papiri cedulas manu propria" (in diverse paper leaflets in his own hand), sometimes "per seipsum" (by himself) and sometimes "per nuncios suos" (by his messengers).[12] Brut was perhaps on bail or most likely, as in Hereford's experience,[13] under the care of trusted lay keepers, because it is clear from the affidavits that he was under some unwelcome form of official surveillance. "Notarios non habeo ne habere possum" (I neither have nor can have notaries) (289) to testify to the authenticity of his writings, he worries, asking Christ to testify for him. Both writers are invaluable witnesses to the process whereby a claim to spiritual intellection could open up safe space for freedom of discussion—and a platform for engaging with one's captors.

To begin with a brief overview, the *Opus* gives us an individual snapshot of early Wycliffite ideas: as Hudson has observed, the author is not at all interested in eucharistic or some of the other "trademark" notions of the movement.[14] His main concerns still overlap largely with those of many orthodox thinkers like Langland, that is, with issues of the abuse of temporalities and church government. The death penalty is not yet in place, though the author worries about cries for it—"hereticum clamant et Lolaldum merito comburendum" (fol. 157v)—and "Lollard" itself is still an unwelcome term of abuse. He uses apocalyptic thought, some of it Continental, to demonstrate that the current pope is Antichrist, "in quo omnia misteria antichristi fuerunt impleta" (fol. 76), and he is greatly preoccupied with the Schism; indeed, obsessively so with the disastrous Flanders crusade Bishop Despenser mounted in 1383 on behalf of Urban VI against his rival pope, Clement. The *Opus* is a work begun late in 1389 and written over the course of a long imprisonment.

Walter Brut also has an extensive knowledge of Continental apocalyptic thought. Ruth Nissé has recently argued for Brut's knowledge of Rupescissa's *Vade mecum* and related materials,[15] and this list, as we will see, can be expanded. Hudson makes the point that Brut never directly cites anything but the Bible, but this citation pattern, I would suggest, is deceptive, because he has thoroughly assimilated popular Joachite and other Continental apocalyptic. These works are used silently, perhaps because he was in enough trouble with the authorities already without the help of Joachimism. Like the author of the Cambridge "Regnum" prophecy, he dares to calculate numerically the coming of Antichrist and harnesses this to an exhaustive demonstration of an argument that the present pope is Antichrist, which he does in pseudo-Joachite style. In order to do this, he has to demolish the popular legendary notions of Antichrist, "quod fabula illa ab errore ymaginancium," which he does by proving that they are unbiblical (a charge Wyclif himself had made) and by extending a degree of respect toward non-Christian peoples which, as we have seen, is a feature of Joachite thought.[16] So, for instance, he assures us that the Jewish people would never be so foolish as to be seduced by a messiah claiming to be from the tribe of Dan—they know, he says, that their messiah will be from the tribe of Judah and will be peaceful, not warlike (quod esset pacificus, non bellicosus). Here he gives an eloquent and moving description based on the Old Testament prophets of the Messiah the Jews expect. In short, for Brut, the Jews are a good deal more intelligent than the multitude of Christians who have fallen for such "fabulae." It should also be said that Brut is very consciously "naturalizing" the imported apocalyptic thinking (which he handles with real surety) to create a new apocalyptic role for the "British," that is, his native Welsh. Like the author of the Cambridge prophecy, and like many who encountered the great Continental female prophets of the Schism period, he gives a striking role to women in the church by his exploration of women's capacities as preachers and in other clerical roles. This is something he assimilated in part from the Continental apocalyptic tradition[17] as much or more as from Wycliffism. In Brut we see writ large what the Cambridge prophecy suggests in parvo—that contact with Continental reformist apocalyptic thought can promote unusual tolerance in how marginalized groups are treated. The question for the authorities, of course, was how much of this freedom of expression was tolerable, and in the end, even many Wycliffite thinkers could not tolerate so much tolerance.[18] Wycliffism, in fact, could be as or more intolerant of alternative perspectives than its persecutors.

The visionary genre was especially attractive to writers who had to mount their case from outside the mainstream. The Great Schism was a period during which visionaries flourished, but the Avignon papacy (1305–78) had already done much to destabilize the hierarchy and to bring the language of visionary protest into purview. It was from the papal prison at Avignon that John of Rupescissa poignantly poured out much of his revelatory reformist thought.[19] The history of John's arrests and virtually unrelieved incarceration between

1344 and at least 1365 is a horrific one.[20] During this time he was shifted between appalling Franciscan prison conditions (which included torture) and relatively mild confinements, the latter especially when he was commanded or allowed to write or when cardinals — such are the contradictions — wanted access to his prophetic insight.[21] Called "the human interest story" of the century by Robert Lerner, Rupescissa was on one occasion commanded to write by the famous inquisitor, Guillaume Court (whom we have seen active in association with FitzRalph and Kilvington), to give a full written statement of his alleged visionary insight. The result, in 1349, was to save his life. Writing with courageous honesty, one of the few things he suppressed was his use of Olivi, whose works had formed the Joachite backbone of his thought. The work he wrote for Court he called *Liber conspectorum secretorum archanorum in visu Dei,* the very title invoking St. Paul's revelation of *archana verba* or secret words confirms the influence of that great model both for prisoners and mystics.[22] Rupescissa's impact in England was, as elsewhere, powerful — indeed, still powerful enough, despite his death c. 1366, to be among our confiscated writers of 1389. He perhaps more than any other writer inspired the *Opus arduum* author to the act of prison writing, and almost certainly Walter Brut, too.[23]

Both Brut and the *Opus* author were writing before 1401 brought *De heretico comburendo* and the death penalty, but medieval imprisonment itself was very often a death penalty. Neither text, then, could be a transcript of unbridled opinion. Each is structured in ways that show the allied acts of self-censorship any writer would commit under such scrutiny. The *Opus* author baits and teases the ecclesiastical authorities holding him, a stylistic technique for registering rebellion against verbal constraint that we also see in calmer literary forms in Langland and in Usk. At the same time, he writes for another, to him, more important audience, early Wycliffite sympathizers in some kind of university-trained coterie.[24] But there is also likely a third audience here, if Anne Hudson is correct in her surmise that the "Lollard knights" William Neville and John Montague may have been involved as jailers at least for a period, and that the imprisoned author himself is Nicholas Hereford.[25] Moreover, if Hudson is also correct in her surmise that the text was composed perhaps in part during incarceration in the Franciscan house at Oxford, we have here the perfect setting for a knowledgeable, but antagonistic audience, suspicious of Continental-style apocalyptic theology.[26]

What I would like to stress is that, wherever he is writing (and it could have been from more than one place during his incarceration of three years or more), he uses various strategies that would not have been necessary had he been writing only for surreptitious release to a sympathetic audience. Especially the audience of academic Wycliffite sympathizers that is the ostensible readership of the text would not be much in need of its implied claims to prophetic status nor, as we saw in chapter 4, would they necessarily be swayed by them. These claims are surely, then, aimed at his captors and critics. So, for instance, the *Opus* author relies heavily on his claim to spiritual intellection and to a special mission; he insists that his reader ought not to imagine that these things he writes proceed voluntarily "from his own head" nor from human invention: "Non debetis vos, quibus his scribo, ymaginari quod hec voluntarie *ex capite meo* aut inventione humana procedunt" (Brno, University Library MS Mk 28, fol. 127r). In fact, this is very close to the wording of the similar claim of John of Rupescissa in a letter from the papal prison in Avignon, which turns up in more than one manuscript of English provenance.[27] Among these, I will cite from a copy in British Library, MS Royal 13. E.IX, which also contains, as V. H. Galbraith argued, a famously self-censured copy of Walsingham's *St. Albans' Chronicle*.[28] In fact, there has been a little softening of Rupescissa's letter in the manuscript, too, especially to downplay the prophetic and certainly to suppress Rupescissa's name.[29] Compare, for example, the deviations from the usual version in the quotation below. In the letter, Rupescissa is responding to the archbishop of Toulouse's 1356 request for his prophetic interpretations, and he retorts:

> ea que dico de futuro non dico *de capite meo*, nec ut propheta, sed *tantum [tamen]*[30] per intelligentiam *scripturarum [prophetarum]*.[31] Quare *ergo [domine]*[32] desideratis querere a me . . . quod est in solius Dei potestate? (Royal 13. E.IX, fol. 94vb, with readings from the usual version supplied in brackets)

> those things I say concerning the future I do not say *from my own head*, but only [nevertheless] through understanding of the Scriptures [Prophets]. Why therefore [lord] do you desire to seek from me . . . what is in God's power alone?

The *Opus* author, too, is driven by a higher, unseen power, as he writes in the passage immediately following his prayer of preparation for martyrdom, "Multa sunt insuper nescio qua occulta disposicione, que alliciunt et provocuant ad onus exsequendum" (fol.127a) (Many things there are which, by I know not what hidden dispensation above, allure and challenge me to follow through with this burden). He then hides his inspirational claim behind a strong identification with John of Patmos himself: just as it is with the prophetic writer, so now with the interpreter (ut qualis fuerat huius prophetie scriptor, talis nunc in plurimis habeatur interpres):

> Ille namque relegatus in insulam, que dicitur Pathmos, hanc sanctam vidit et scripsit prophetiam; ego ergastulo carceris deputatus ac duplici conpede cathenatus, ad ipsius tendo interpretacionem. Ille a Domiciano tyranno, ego ab Anticristo tollero persecucionem. Ille exilium sortitus est propter verbum Dei et testimonium Ihesu Cristi, ego quod tollero pacior propter predicacionem evangelii. Ille librum suum edidit ad correccionem ecclesie Asyane, ego quod scripturus sim intendo ad reformacionem universalis ecclesiae. (fol. 127a)[33]

> He, exiled to an island called Patmos, where he saw and wrote this holy prophecy; I, cut off in the cell of a prisoner, my feet double-bound in shackles, striving to interpret it. He, by the tyrant Domitian, I, by Antichrist, endure persecution. He was cast into exile on account of the word of God and testimony of Jesus Christ; I suffer what I endure on account of the preaching of the Gospel. He shaped his book for the correction of the Church of Asia, what I am about to write I intend for the reformation of the universal Church.

This *tour de force* of rhetorical parallelism lavished on St. John and himself is intended to create a powerful (not to say self-aggrandizing) sense of its author's divine mission, while at the same time, factually at least, pretending to claim no more than an interpreter's role. This is to speak, as Rupescissa had originally put it, "not as a prophet, but nevertheless through *understanding* of the prophets" (nec ut propheta, sed tamen per *intelligentiam* prophetarum).[34] The distinction is important.

It is, in fact, a carefully observed, technical distinction, but one that may at first not be apparent to modern eyes. It is the difference between receiving prophetic *insight* and being a *prophet*. Biblically it was based on the difference between possessing the "spirit of intelligence" or *spiritus intellectus* (Wisdom

7:22) and the "spirit of prophecy" or *spiritus prophetiae* (Rev. 19:10). The lives of both Rupescissa and the *Opus* author may have depended on this distinction. Writing of Rupescissa's nearly twenty-year-long struggle with imprisonment and inquisition, Robert Lerner says, "Had Rupescissa claimed to have been granted the 'spirit of prophecy', a practiced inquisitor . . . would have probably condemned him immediately because such a notion could only have been implanted by an 'unclean spirit'. But having a gift of 'understanding' was plausible, and it was not entirely out of the question that such a gift might have been communicated supernaturally."[35] We should also note that these writers (all male—and that, too, is significant) were consciously choosing the most highly revered type of visionary experience from St. Augustine's tripartite hierarchy. (That hierarchy is, of course, *corporeal*, the most basic and least reliable; *spiritual*, as mediated via images in the mind; and *intellectual*, the highest and most certain form of divine illumination.)[36] When one is writing from prison, and writing, indeed, about the very ideas for which one has been imprisoned, one wants only the best.[37]

Thus it is that we have visionary experience and prophetic intelligence without the overt claim to prophesy—and it was a critical distinction. Both Rupescissa and the *Opus* author try to deny any suggestion that they operate by imaginative or human invention. Fear of the overactive imagination is a critical aspect of visionary testing (*discretio spirituum* or *probatio*), and the accusation of operating *by* the imagination itself, the kiss of death—a cultural assumption we will later recall in relation to Langland's staging of Imaginatif's disapproval of his writing, and even later in relation to Julian. No story demonstrates this more concretely than one told in the Franciscan-empathetic English chronicle, the *Eulogium historiarum*, of eight friars and their spokesman hauled before Henry IV for dabbling in the Bridlington prophecies.[38] They came from the convent of Leicester, led by an old friar and master of theology, who is denounced to the king as "an old man who speaks badly of you, and said [King] Richard will make war against you, and says that this is of the prophets" (senex qui male loquitur de vobis, et dixit quod Ricardus bellabit contra vos, et dicit quod hoc est prophetarum).[39] The master is claimed to have eventually confessed to have interpreted the Bridlington prophecy *juxta imaginationem suam* (according to his own imagination).[40] This was the opposite of responsible spiritual intellection.[41] What is important about this story is the charge that the prophetic interpreter was working *juxta imaginationem suam*, and here it would prove a matter of life and death. The friars were all hung.

Intellectuals like Olivi, the *Opus* author, Brut, and even the flamboyant Rupescissa were smarter; they proceeded, at least overtly, by inspired *exegesis* of biblical texts. Whether the inquisitors were fooled we may very much doubt. The contemporary chronicler Froissart was not. Of Rupescissa he wrote that he "wished to prove all by the Apocalypse, and the proofs with which he armed himself saved him many times from being burnt."[42] The point here is not whether the authorities saw through the strategy—it is that, *couched in these terms, they had to tolerate it.*

The Road Not Taken: Early Wycliffism, Franciscan Joachimism, and the Limits of Tolerance

The *Opus* author is especially forthright about what he expects his captors to tolerate—and he taunts them about it at every chance. He complains that he had been imprisoned so as to prevent him from acting against the interests of his ecclesiastical enemies. But this will backfire, he threatens, as did, ultimately, the incarcerations of Joseph and St. Paul. "Lest Paul evangelize," he writes, "adversaries of the faith imprisoned him. Nevertheless through this he had *greater* occasion and opportunity of instructing the universal [universalem] church through his evangelical epistles. Therefore it is true what the wiseman said, 'There is no prudence, no counsel against the Lord.'"[43] The author's defiance is firmly rooted in the biblical precedents of literary prisoners of conscience like Paul and John, who, along with early Christians like Perpetua and Boethius, provided powerful role models to medieval writers under arrest or confinement.[44] What these famous prisoners all had in common was divinely inspired visionary experience as a means of spiritual triumph over their oppressors, making them attractive to writers who worked under constraint of many sorts, whether from within a prison or not. Perpetua's presence is palpable, for instance, in Christina of Markgate's confinement narratives,[45] and even vernacular literary writers use these famous male role models powerfully in order to *gesture* constraint, especially Langland, John But, Thomas Usk (a self-imagined prison-writer in the *Testament*), the *Mum* author, and, in parody, Chaucer.[46]

The *Opus arduum* is illuminating for the study of Ricardian vision and constraint because its author invokes the rhetorical strategies and visionary models of imprisoned writing in a raw and directly confessional way. Revelation can take unobtrusive forms: a claim to a gift of private understanding (as in Walter

Brut) or oblique self-confessional identification with a biblical visionary like Paul or John or Joseph (as did the *Opus* author). Rita Copeland has observed of Wycliffite prison writers that

> the common ancestors of the witnessings of Wyche and Thorpe as well as of other prison or interrogation narratives by Christian dissenters are the Acts of the Apostles and Paul's prison narratives. All such texts, up through the Protestant Reformation, participate quite consciously in th[is tradition] . . . empathy with the radicalism of the early church is central to the self-definition of later Christian radicalism, which by its nature (and by the very etymology of "radical") looks backward to the purist beginnings of the apostolic church.[47]

Copeland goes on to note that Boethius is the "literary precedent of choice for [prison] writers whose religious orthodoxy is never in question," citing especially Thomas Usk. But that for "religious dissenters, Acts . . . and the Pauline epistles . . . are much the more resonant generic references." All this is broadly true, and I would add that the account of Paul's imprisonment is repeatedly used, not just in Wycliffite texts like those she mentions, but in Langlandian texts (like the But Passus, discussed in chapter 10) and even in parodic form in *The Romance of the Rose* and *House of Fame*. We saw that the *Roman*'s Faus Semblant invokes St. Paul's imprisonment, when proclaiming his willingness to "be putt doun / As was Seynt Poul, in derk prisoun" for the rather dangerous act of speaking out in support of the recently anathematized William of St. Amour.[48] And Chaucer's *House*, as we will see in chapter 9, invokes Paul as part of a parody of Ockhamist ideas on salvation and perhaps a parody of Langland.

The *Opus* author's relationship to the officials in his implied audience is, then, defiant and tests the limits of tolerance. He insists that like St. Paul's, his imprisonment has given him great opportunity to preach through his writing and even to *study* against his captors.[49] This tells us that he was of unusual academic stature and that his captors, however grudgingly, recognized his claim to carry out academic pursuits. If, in fact, as the text claims, he is writing and in prison, he could only have been doing so with the permission of his jailers or, at the very least, their connivance. The *Opus* runs to hundreds of folios in manuscript — therefore the sheer cost and bulk of the parchment alone defies any hypothesis of surreptitious production. More significantly, he makes extensive use of scholarly citation such as only a writer with access to a range of specialized books could have mustered.[50] Anne Hudson, one of the few modern scholars to have written on the text, is understandably bemused by the problem, noting that the extreme ideas the author puts forward could hardly have met with approval from his captors. But since he could not have done this without their help, we must look for some reason for his keepers' apparent tolerance, and even encouragement. One possibility is that he had empathetic keepers (as Nicholas Hereford did at certain points).[51] The second possibility, which does not exclude the first, is that at least part of the time he was writing from the Franciscan convent in Oxford, or from a major episcopal prison, or perhaps even Courtney's own prison with access to the archiepiscopal library.[52] The Franciscan convent at Oxford was known, at least according to the fourteenth-century union catalogue, to have the best *official* collection of genuine Joachite works.[53] When he speaks of such books (specifically Olivi and Rupescissa, and, in a different way, St. Amour and Ockham) being confiscated or held under lock and key *by the friars at Oxford and Salisbury,* there is a specificity here, not only in the geography, but in bibliography, and perhaps firsthand knowledge.[54]

Whether or not, however, we can localize the *Opus* writer's whereabouts on the basis of his hints, we do know that there is Continental precedent for Franciscan prisoners, especially visionaries, to be allowed or encouraged to write.[55] There is also precedent for visionary Spirituals writing from papal or episcopal prisons, as the *Opus* author himself likely knew from reading John of Rupescissa. That something of this nature was afoot emerges if we compare the *Opus* to Brut's affidavits of 1391–93, the only other such extensive piece of original revelatory theology known to have been written *by permission* from under legal surveillance at this time. Writing in a university idiom explicitly at the request of those who had charged him, Brut's lengthy testimony fills over a hundred folios in the bishop of Hereford's register under the year 1391.[56] Brut's writing is full of Continental apocalypticism of a kind very similar to the *Opus* author's, but not found in any significance elsewhere among Wycliffites. What other Wycliffite writers use, and in spades, is *eschatology,* nearly always the pessimistic end-stopped (or End-stopped) kind familiar from traditional sources, but the two writers in question here are *apocalyptic* thinkers. They think in terms of apocalyptic programmes (entire systems of salvation history, chronologies of the future, exegetically calculated). They think in terms of interventions in history and in terms of *reformist* apocalypticism, that is, elaborate plans for divinely instituted reform. The *Opus* author and Brut show a kind of experimentation with vision we do not see elsewhere in adherents of Wyclif and which, in fact, was to have no future in the movement.[57] The key, I think, is that both authors were doing something extremely rare in England (and not at *all* characteristic of Wycliffites): they were composing new revelatory theology in a Continental apocalyptic mode.

England had not seen the composition of much serious or original Latin apocalypticism since the work of Henry of Costesy.[58] The author of the *Opus* knew that it was a dangerous genre as his largely silent treatment of Olivi and Rupescissa shows, the same silent treatment to suppress Olivian material that Rupescissa employed to save his own skin under inquisition.[59] The *Opus* author also mentions another apocalyptic writer, one that (unlike the others) he himself condemns as a dangerous heretic: Joachim of Fiore.[60] This condemnation serves, I believe, two functions: first, to shore up his own orthodoxy by naming the culprit who "ruined" the orthodoxy of the Franciscan tradition with its once laudable ideals of poverty. Second, it is one of many decoy strategies the author uses to deflect attention from what I would argue he is *really* nervous about—his surreptitious importation of Olivian *apocalypse* commentary material into a reformist Wycliffite polemic. The *Opus* has many elements of Olivi's exegesis: an emphasis on the "carnal church," a desire for the end of church temporalities, a juxtaposition of the established church and imperial Rome (e.g., fol. 163rb), and, most telling, he uses the Joachimist term "status" for periodization of salvation history.[61] As Curtis Bostick has indicated, the *Opus* author very cunningly uses pretended citation to the *Glossa ordinaria* to cover for his use of Olivi and other radical interpretations.[62] He persistently uses the word "status," and as Bostick rightly says, the *Glossa* never defines any period as a *status*. Take, for instance, the *Opus* author's interpretation of the opening of the Sixth Seal as the sixth *status* of the church, representing the time of Antichrist "in which we now are" (Ostendendo michi *sextum statum ecclesie*, scilicet temporibus Antichristi in *quo iam sumus* [fol. 155va]).[63] It is an important question, however, and not one addressed by Bostick, whether the author *understood* the presence of Antichrist in what he calls the sixth status in a Joachite or Olivian sense, that is, as tribulation heralding a great period of reform and blessedness. His vision of the reform of what he calls the "universal church," though never elaborated, might indeed suggest such an expectation—because what good would such a reform be at the End of the World? His programme of disendowment, for instance, points in this direction. The Joachite kind of projected optimism for earthly history is virtually non-existent in Wycliffite works and scarce even in the *Opus*. But one could make a case that it is there, between the lines of the text, *implicit* in the reform programme. Bostick, too, points to one renovationist gesture in the text, that is, his interpretation of Revelation 17:8, "Bestia quam vidisti, fuit et non est," which the author sees as referring to the time *after* the destruction of Antichrist, although he says nothing more concrete about this time. Is it, for this author as for Joachites, *within* history and with much positive history still to come?[64] It is very hard to tell, but this could be a glimmer of real Wycliffite Joachimism—a rare sighting, indeed.

Olivi's works had been blacklisted, but it appears that the *Opus* author had access to one of them, though he uses or recalls it silently—which, along with the overt condemnation of Joachim, accounts for why Hudson believes the author innocent of his Joachite inheritance. But he is not.[65] Fascinated with Franciscan Spiritual ideology (and for this author, as for many contemporaries, that includes Ockham), but impatient with Joachim himself, the author has a tough row to hoe. Borrowing from the Spirituals introduces another complexity for him: keeping his agenda distinct from mendicant apologetic—increasingly anathema for Wycliffites after 1382. An excellent demonstration of this appears in his treatment of Christ's poverty. Denial of temporal jurisdiction to Christ had become strongly associated with mendicant apologetic, and Fiona Somerset has made the point that perhaps for this reason the author of the *Opus arduum* inserts a scholastic *quaestio* in his discussion of the issue, declaring that the temporal realm of David does belong to Christ, but denying (ingeniously) that this is transferable to the pope because "papa . . . non sit de semine Dauid"![66] This, like much else in the *Opus*, I would suggest, is a desperate attempt to keep his Wycliffite project distinct from a mendicant one and from a Joachite one. But his insistence that Peter must forsake all temporal things and "follow Christ in naked poverty" (relinquere omnia terrena et Christum sequi in nuda paupertate [fol. 206ra])[67] sounds like it was lifted directly out of one of the popular Joachite texts like *Super Esaiam* or *De oneribus*, both of which use this motif to deny the papacy any hint of transformation, even in the Third Status.[68] The *Opus* here is *terribly hard* to distinguish from this kind of Joachite thought, especially Franciscan Joachimism.

What Olivi and Rupescissa had in common with the *Opus* author and Walter Brut—all four engaged in apocalyptic exegesis—is a claim to a form of spiritual intellection as the basis for their exegesis. The question of spiritual intellection was an extremely delicate one for ecclesiastical authorities, and one, I would contend, the English officials dared not—at least overtly—*dis*respect, however much they suspected it. That they had no intention of allowing such works to be published abroad is clear enough, but that they did not feel it was safe or desirable to *stop* these writers from writing, even voluminously (as both did), is certainly evident. If they were looking to convict these men of Wycliffism, a few pages would have sufficed, a list of answers to the standardized inquisitorial questions on pilgrimage, images, confession, and so forth that make all Wycliffites look so alike to us.[69] But they did not. The case of Brut is really telling here: the text as it survives in Bishop Trefnant's register consists of at least two affidavits, the first (containing two "suppositions") fairly short and heavily apocalyptic, the second, written explicitly at the request of the bishop for more writing, is extremely long (it may have originated as four separate *cedulae* in Brut's hand) and topically diffuse. It is difficult to know exactly why Bishop Trefnant encouraged Brut to use so much parchment to write the second, massively lengthy response, but the clue would have to be found somewhere in his first attempt.[70] There he makes a veiled claim to spiritual insight, proves by elaborate exegetical calculation smacking of Joachimism that Antichrist will appear sometime after 1260,[71] and draws, under cover of exegesis, an Olivian-style comparison between Rome and Babylon.[72]

Trefnant, I would suggest, kept Brut writing for the same reason one of his Continental counterparts would have. First, he thought he was facing something more dangerous, and exotic, than local Wycliffism. We know this because of Brut's unusual ideas and because of the distinguished and large panel of theologians Trefnant brought in to examine a man who was, after all, a layman.[73] In the early 1390s there was renewed papal concern about the problem of "Beguini," and by 1395 "Beghardi seu Lullardi et Zwestriones [sisters]" in France, the Low Countries, and Bohemia, often recognized by their apocalyptic language.[74] Both Joachimism and heresy of the Free Spirit were already playing a large role in Hussite Bohemia.[75] Nor were English officials ignorant of the problem even in the 1380s.[76] By the early fifteenth century, as the chronicler Adam Usk saw it, it was due to the combination of Lollards and *Beguini* (a word, in its Latin *masculine* form, most often used comprehensively to denote the followers of Olivi).[77] Usk wrote to a correspondent in Rome expressing anxiety that an Old Testament disempowerment of the clergy through corruption would subsequently repeat itself in the New Testament period on account of a schism in the priesthood caused by Lollards and *Beguini/ae* (scisma Lollardensibus atque Begwinis operantibus).[78] Other instances of English awareness are plenty. In dealing with Brut, then, Trefnant had bigger fish to fry than local Lollardy, and he knew it. Second—and this has not been enough appreciated—the very nature of early English examination for heresy was to use previous models and recent models obtained from abroad.[79] What late fourteenth-century clergy knew were earlier fourteenth-century precedents, especially for Franciscans and Beguines, and especially from the papal legislation known as the *Clementines*.[80]

Third, however (and this is where issues of respect for vision enter), Trefnant's tolerance of so much more writing suggests an ambivalent attitude on the part of the authorities. Medieval official attitudes toward visionary experience were by no means naïve (we just saw their diversity in the previous chapter), but they were certainly often different from our own, the main difference being that virtually no one questioned the *possibility* of vision. What was questioned was the source (divine or diabolic or just illusory), and *probatio* treatises on how to tell the difference (including prayers for warding off deception in visionary moments) survive in abundance.[81] There is, for instance, a classic one, oddly enough, in *House of Fame*, not the first place any of us would look for such a passage. Drawing on St. John's Revelation and another great visionary, himself associated with Joachimism, Dante, Geoffrey prays:

'O Crist,' thought I, 'that art in blisse,
Fro fantom and illusion
Me save!' and with devocioun
Myn eyen to the heven I caste.
Tho was I war, lo! at the laste
That faste by the sonne, . . .
Me thoughte I saw an egle sore.
                    (*House of Fame*, 492–99)

If lifted out of its comic context, as here, we have a standard prayer for help with "discretion of spirits" (discretio spirituum), a highly serious topic for the medieval church and one on which treatises were now multiplying fast, even in Middle English.[82] Even the highest of Chaucer's contemporary authorities, Pope Urban VI and King Richard II, are on record as having been influenced by, and choosing to deliberately act upon, visions. In fact, prophecies were used in all kinds of official contexts that would surprise us today. The *Opus* author's nemesis, Bishop Despenser, consulted popular Latin political and Joachite prophecies to mount his 1383 crusade on behalf of Urban VI.[83]

And yet it was also during Urban's pontificate that heated controversy over the legitimacy of prophetic visions began to boil over. Walter Brut, in fact, echoes these arguments in one of the maverick opinions he was condemned for—his belief in women's right to preach on the basis of prophetic gifts.[84] More urgently, however, he tactfully lays implicit claim to personal revelatory intellection. And here he is deliberately more oblique:

> All these things have I written to show that he who has the key of David, "Who openeth and no man shutteth, and shutteth and no man openeth," . . . hides secrets of the Scriptures from the wise . . . , and sometimes at his pleasure reveals them to sinners and lay persons and simple souls [laycis ydiotis], that he may have honour and glory in all things. Therefore I have written. . . .[85]

I suspect it was not Brut's Wycliffism (of which he had given ample evidence already), but rather his unusual *apocalypticism*, especially the whiff of Joachimism, that alerted Trefnant to ask for or tolerate so much more writing. This influence goes hand in hand with support for women preachers, an overt supportiveness we do not find solid evidence of in other academic Wycliffite spokesmen.[86] At the time Brut was writing, English authorities still did not know whether or how Wycliffism related to other known heresies or alternative viewpoints, among which one of the most prominent and dangerous was Franciscan apocalypticism.

Brut complains not only of the lack of a notary to help, but also that he is unable to have his writings *notarized*—which suggests to me that he was aware that inquisitorial procedures often recorded condemned articles in a form that the defendant would not recognize.[87] Certainly this had been the case with the condemnation of Uthred de Boldon, whose Ockhamist (and perhaps Olivian) opinions on the possibility of salvation for the unbaptized Brut seems to have known and deliberately reaffirmed:

> God would not be just nor merciful if he would damn anyone because he did not believe in him, unless He had shown him the faith that he ought to believe, and therefore in the case of a little one dying before baptism . . . he [or she] is not damned on this account. *Heresy.*

> Deus non esset iustus nec misericors si dampnaret aliquem quia non credit in eum, nisi ostenderet ei fidem quam deberet credere, et ideo

cum parvulo ante baptismum decedenti . . . , non est propterea damp-
nandus. *Heresis.* (*Registrum Johannis Trefnant,* 362)[88]

And here we have something else that would have arrested Trefnant's attention,
and should arrest ours. The re-emergence, now, in the early 1390s, of radical and
generous ideas on grace, salvation, good works, and the question of God's justice
at the final judgement—views replicating those for which Uthred had been condemned in 1368, and which parallel those that Bradwardine had anathematized as
"Pelagian" in Joachim and Ockham.[89] Most strikingly, whatever their patrimony,
they are certainly *not* Wycliffite. Wycliffites were usually predestinarian—that
is, at the other and more Bradwardinian end of the theological spectrum.[90] Brut
is writing in the early 1390s, more than twenty years after the condemnation of
Uthred's Ockham-inspired generosities. Brut's affidavit is among other little
noticed testimonies of a resurgence of Uthred's ideas in the 1380s (which, as
our final chapter shows, likely affected Langland's C revision and reception). He
is writing only two years after the confiscation of Ockham's and Olivi's books in
1389. Clearly, our picture of the monopoly of Wycliffism on radical thought in
the 1380s and 1390s needs complicating, and seriously. There were multiple heterodox influences at work in Brut's thought (among them Joachite and Uthredian), and the non-Wycliffite ones among them are not simply reflections of an
individual's eccentricity, but rather of whole currents of radical thought going
unnoticed in the period.

An Early "Dialect" of Wycliffism: Representing Voices from Prison

Another thing that needs complicating is our picture of Wycliffism itself.
This emerges most clearly if we examine these two prison writers against a
genre of Wycliffite prison writing we have recently come to understand in
excellent studies of William Thorpe, Richard Wyche, and others.[91] The first
thing we have to account for is the difference in tone. Take, for example, the
question of torture. The *Opus* author mentions being kept in harsh circumstances, especially being bound not only in irons, but perhaps even "ordeal
iron"; "they have given me shackles not only of iron but of steel [or 'ordeal
iron']" (compedes non modo ferreos sed *calibeos* mihi inter ceteros prouiderunt
[fol. 172]). Exactly what this means is unclear, but Hudson argued that it may
have been fictionalized to protect his empathetic keepers.[92] She suggests this

presumably because this was not a common practice in the treatment of Lollards. We can hope for his sake she is right, but it is harder to imagine these shackles, given the general tone of the work itself, as *only* metaphorical. There is a hysterical quality to the *Opus* author's writing that speaks of something else. Introducing the passage quoted above in which he speaks of himself striving to interpret John in shackles, he says, "Because I do not think myself the best, but the worst of sinners, therefore it is frightful to behold that in these most terrible last days I should become the chief commander of the camp [campiductor] against Antichrist."[93] In this long work, written over several months, anxiety is palpable and with it a nearly delusional sense of mission. As we saw above, not only does he seek to interpret John, to imitate John, he goes on, eventually, to *surpass* John. John suffered persecution "under the tyrant Domitian, I," he says, "am persecuted by Antichrist" (Ille a Domiciano tyranno, ego ab Anticristo tollero persecucionem). He wrote for the correction of the church of Asia, "I," he says, write "*ad reformacionem universalis ecclesie.*" One is reminded strongly of Olivian writers under duress, most especially of Rupescissa—but not of Thorpe. The first difference is the grand, if not grandiose, sense of mission (self-appointed saviour through his writings) which may in fact arise from the stresses of what we today call trauma victimization. Manifestations of trauma have recently been traced in the writings of early dissenters under persecution, such as John Calvin.[94] A more modern prisoner, Antonio Gramsci, referred to something very like the *Opus* author's overwrought sense of mission in more literary terms as the "für ewig" (forever) hope in prison writings, the hope, that is, he says, "common, I believe to most prisoners, that one can write something that will last *für ewig.*"[95]

It is, of course, possible that the trauma is plagiarized, that it is wholly "literary." Rupescissa, who was also tortured in prison, was probably the main inspiration both for his specific formulation of spiritual intellection and his remarkable confessionalism. We know from the handling of autobiographical writings elsewhere in the Middle Ages that plagiarism of another person's autobiographical details was an acceptable practice, however bewildering to us, if employed for didactic purposes. But there may be still other, better explanations: we know from the manuscript dissemination of the *Opus* that it likely only ever achieved a Continental audience (all thirteen manuscripts hail from Bohemia, Germany, or elsewhere). It is hard to imagine that the author did not know, at the very least, that Continental audiences would be important to him, and he would certainly know that such audiences might even expect to hear of torture under inquisition. Moreover, if the author is Hereford (a problem we will explore below), it is also all too likely that he did undergo some such abusive experience in the papal prisons (certainly his exact contemporary in Urban's prison, Adam Easton, did). That he might have handily conflated past and present experiences just for good dramatic measure seems possible.

What makes me less likely to opt for fictionalizing here, however, is comparison of these circumstances with the most famous Wycliffite who wrote from an assuredly English prison, William Thorpe. The difference in tone between the two accounts is telling. The *Opus* is, like Thorpe's, a kind of autohagiography, but not in the calm, rarefied hermeneutical tone of Thorpe's, a text likely either smuggled out of a more comfortable prison or even written after Thorpe's escape.[96] Thorpe's almost smug dialectic, a model of unflustered logical deduction under (remembered?) pressure, has been called a "hermeneutic of literalism"— a mode now sometimes thought to exemplify Lollard thinking generally. This tone is far from consistently evident in the *Opus*. William Rankin, recently building on Rita Copeland's analysis of "the Lollard hermeneutic of literalism," highlights the philosophical incompatibility between Thorpe and Arundel that drove Arundel to distraction, memorably "smytyng with his fist fersli vpon a copbord" (87). Rankin's concept of an "incarnational hermeneutic" as "offering a rationale for the overall shape of Wycliffite thought and practice" has plausibility in part because of the important role that realism, reason, and appeal to reason play in the cultural productions of the movement. It would not apply very well, however, either to the *Opus* author or to Brut. It seems important, then—especially when we are confronted with these early writers—to be aware that there are risks in adopting too monolithic a view of "Wycliffite mentality." Working as all of us do with the Lollardy so brilliantly eked out for us by the massive scholarship of Anne Hudson, we have come to assume what is already perhaps too homogenous a Wycliffism. Hudson has done for Wycliffism what Henry Sweet pioneered for Anglo-Saxon: smoothed and regularized a dominant dialect to make learning the language possible for philological novices. But this does not mean that Wycliffites did not speak multiple theological "dialects," and especially the earliest Wycliffites, who clearly had more than one hermeneutic. (The Franciscan Joachite hermeneutic, for instance, is not at all focused on literalism.) What Copeland and Rankin argue about Thorpe is truly illuminating for Thorpe, and for much of what we define as Wycliffite, and perhaps even normative for Thorpe's generation. But the 1380s were different than the 1400s, and especially for those who grew with the cause through the 1370s.

What a writer like Thorpe may have learned from a writer like the *Opus* author (given the primarily Continental circulation of both, perhaps even directly) is a way of drawing the hostile audience into the intended audience. Rankin points to Thorpe's modeling of a hermeneutic that teaches its intended audience to defy traditional hierarchies of meaning and to Thorpe's sly implication of Arundel into the audience, lest perchance "this my writynge come ony tyme bifore the Erchebischop" (25). By invoking the threat of Arundel as actual reader, Thorpe cleverly bolsters his authority with his actual intended audience. As the defiant passage about St. Paul's imprisonment suggests, the *Opus* author had done the same thing, but perhaps in more dire circumstances. The revelatory hysteria of the text seems so very "un-Wycliffite" but is just what we would expect of someone once exposed to Urban's prisons, and to high-level international drama, and to apocalypticism like Rupescissa's. Meanwhile, back in England, three years gave him maximum opportunity for study and writing against his opponents (maximam opportunitatem studenti et scribendi contra eum), as he proudly taunts, confident, apparently, that they were listening.[97]

The Mystery of the *Opus* Author's Identity

The *Opus* author was among the earliest wave of people drawn to Wyclif, and he had his own view of where the movement might go. His use of what was essentially a Franciscan Joachite tradition shows he was formed by the earliest days of Wycliffism (pre-1382) before Wycliffism parted company with the friars. This, then, is a glimpse of Wycliffism fostered in the 1370s, when political changes brought new respectability for radical disendowment campaigns. These campaigns were linked usually to fraternal agitators, either Franciscan or Austin, giving Joachimism a political face in the 1360s and 1370s (as we saw with Erghome). Brut's apocalypticism certainly harks back to that period, and so does (although less politically) the *Opus* author's. Anne Hudson has made a convincing argument that he is Nicholas Hereford, a suggestion to which this study adds, I hope, further evidence.[98] A unique feature, I would stress, of the *Opus* author is his *international* perspective and especially his awareness of the dangers of the Schism-torn papal curia, a world in which even cardinals, as we know from sources like Adam Easton, went in fear of imprisonment for speaking out against Urban.[99] The author, for instance, sees papal election as a hopeless method of resolving the Schism precisely because of the stranglehold that terror exercises upon the cardinals. They all fear, he tells us, that if their candidate loses, they will be held in perpetual imprisonment (carceribus perpetuis mancipantur) at the hands of the victorious party.[100] Moreover, he finds himself *campiductor* of what *he* assumes the Wycliffite movement's campaign to be: to reform the *universal* church.[101] He had a wider sense than most Wycliffites of issues of intellectual freedom in the international church, and of the new role of revelatory theology among clergy in the Schism era. In the list of Continental confiscated authors he gives us, unusually for university-trained men, all (Olivi, Rupescissa, and St. Amour) except Ockham had claimed some form of prophetic or eschatological insight; the first two had written under inquisition; the second two from exile. It seems that the *Opus* author identified deeply and personally with *both* predicaments, and this, along with the suggestion of Continental experience and perspective, can tell us something about who he was. These four writers were powerful *non*-Wycliffite role models for him. Another nearly unique feature of this author is his tendency, I have suggested, to draw more deeply upon the originally Franciscan Spiritual elements buried (inconsistently) in Wyclif's early assumptions. This is rare in any Wycliffite after the very early divisions with the friars gave rise to the movement's invariably shrill antifraternalism, definitively by 1382.[102] The author even manages to put aside some of the anti-charismatic mentality we have seen in Wyclif and other academics, again very unusual, especially by the late 1380s. Nicholas Hereford, we know, after his recantation, chose to end his days in a Carthusian house (in Coventry), an order with a penchant for the mystical or visionary, and in which Continental texts impacted by Franciscan Spiritual radicalism (like Porete's) were in carefully controlled circulation.[103] All these factors point to Hereford's authorship.

The *Opus* author, moreover, constructs a sophisticated confessional or autobiographical voice to frame his controversial opinions.[104] One peculiar aspect of this voice, however, is a preoccupation with martyrdom:

> Because there is nothing in the following things I am about to write against Antichrist and his familiars for which I will not have been prepared to die, if necessary, I trust in the goodness of my God, that whatever dross will remain, will be burned and consumed into the odor of sweet spirit, just as a voluntary holocaust of myself.

Sed quia nichil in sequentibus dicturus sum contra Anticristum et familiam suam, pro quo mori, si oportuerit, non ero paratus, confido in bonitate Dei mei, quod quidquid scorie remanserit, exuret et consumet tanquam voluntarium holocaustum mei ipsius in odorem suavitatis spiritualis.[105]

The style of this passage is very similar to what we find in John of Rupescissa's prison writing.[106] But this same peculiar voice, with its self-preoccupation with suffering, is also present in the Ascension Day sermon by Nicholas Hereford, as Simon Forde has shown. There Hereford says he stands ready "to suffer vexations, and punishments over and above, if necessary" (pati molestias et penas insuper si oportet).[107] At the Blackfriars Council, Hereford also offered to defend one of the most extreme of the censured articles even "under pain of burning" (sub poena incendii).[108] Hereford was later imprisoned by Pope Urban, a harrowing experience from which he only escaped because of an uprising.[109] The psychological effects of this, I have suggested, might well have been similar to those of the contemporary imprisonment of his countryman, Cardinal Easton, which also induced in Easton a sudden conversion to visionary apocalypticism (Bridget of Sweden's). Hereford is, of course, the Oxford Wycliffite whose sermon so tested the university's right to freedom of discussion, despite episcopal condemnation. This means that in the *Opus*, if it is indeed his, he authored a work that directly addressed the topic of confiscation of intellectual property.[110] Such a preoccupation would confirm the profile of Hereford's tendency to isolationism, which first emerged in the Theology Faculty at Oxford when he stopped allowing other scholars and students to see his notes, as Forde points out. If we think about it, this is something a "monophonic" Wycliffite would be less likely to do in the relatively empathetic Oxford environment, but something a man might well want to do if he were reading someone like Olivi (especially) or another officially banned writer.[111] And, moreover, since we know Hereford was protected by "Lollard knights" in the circle of poets Sir John Clanvowe and Geoffrey Chaucer, his identity as the *Opus* author would cast some interesting—if quite unexpected—light on vernacular reading circles of the 1390s.

Nicholas Hereford was likely first protected by Sir John Montague, and most certainly known to have been rescued from harsh prison life and afforded protective custody by Sir William Neville, close associate of Clanvowe and of Chaucer (something we will look at in relation to the "Retraction" later).[112] He is also reported to have spent time in Archbishop Courtney's prisons, according to Knighton, where his welcome would have been far less friendly, but books, if permitted, more plentiful.[113] Where else, aside from the Oxford Franciscan house discussed above, he might have been held in England is less clear, but he was in episcopal trouble in this period, and as Hudson points out, we know little about him between 1387 and his recantation in 1391.[114]

Who, then, wrote the *Opus?* To sum it up: it is written by someone who is confident in relating to the authorities, who knows Continental cases, and who has an international vision of the church. It is also written by someone who sees himself as a plausible "campiductor"—there are not many men who could have answered to this description, for which Nicholas Hereford is a prime candidate. Hereford's characteristic sense of facing suffering (in the 1382 sermon) could easily have spiraled into trauma after his experience of imprisonment under Urban (whom the *Opus* author hates with a personalized fervour). Moreover, the *Opus* is written by someone, as Hudson agrees, who lays little stress on the more radical theological elements of Wycliffism that characterized its heretical profile, but who sees Wycliffism as still having a hope within the established church. The writer sees possibilities for the future, much as Joachites do. This is someone whose Wycliffism might have faded once he saw it marginalized from that larger hope into emphasis on more parochial and eccentric theological positions like eucharistic doctrine. Hereford is an excellent candidate for these qualifications.

Despite the virtually fanatical vehemence of his assertions, Hereford recanted early in the movement, perhaps in 1391, the same year as the second prisoner of conscience Walter Brut was arrested on a broad array of heresy charges, some Wycliffite and some emphatically not. The newly orthodox Hereford was prominent among those brought in to examine Brut, and I think, given the Continental apocalyptic nature of Brut's testimony, we might now see one reason why.

Spiritual Intellection, the Imagination, and Langland's Imaginatif

Spiritual intellection, then, provided the parameters within which a male intellectual writing in Latin and under duress could express novel revelatory opinion—express it, that is, as a matter of *revealed* belief rather than as an exercise in reversible scholastic speculation. This gives us a different insight, I believe, into uses of visionary motifs in texts by learned men (we will later examine how the phenomenon works in texts by women and in vernacular texts by men). For learned men, asserting novel *revealed* conviction was both easier and harder. Women usually claimed direct visionary experience (Augustine's second level) without penalty, indeed, sometimes with international acclaim and approbation if they followed the guidelines for *discretio spirituum* implicitly. (And in the later chapters of this book we will see both Porete and Julian challenging and negotiating these norms.) In an important benchmark of early fifteenth-century culture, the *Speculum devotorum* expresses distrust of affective "imaginings" and prefers instead not just reason, good conscience, and recognized authorities as interpretive guides (as did Wyclif and, later, Pecock), but also, unlike those gentlemen, the revelations of at least three "approved women" (Mechthild of Hackeborn, Bridget, and Catherine).[115]

> Notwythstandynge, I have browgth inne othyr doctorys in diverse placys as to the moral vertuys, *and also sum revelacyonys of approvyd wymmen*, and I have put nothynge too of myne owne wytt but that I hope maye trewly be conseyvyd be opyn resun and goode conscyence, for that I holde the sykyrest. For thowgth there myght have be put to some ymagynacyonys that haply mygth have be delectable to carnal soulys, yytt that that ys doo aftyr conscyence ys sykerest thowgth the medytacyonys mygth have be, be suech ymagynacyonys, haply more confortable to some carnal folke. (no. 1.12, lines 73–80)

What is striking about this position is that, as we saw in chapter 4, it was Wyclif and Pecock who ended up under censure, not the visionaries. The *Speculum*, then, represents flexible orthodox thinking on the visionary and its status. It was this kind of flexibility, I would suggest, that orthodoxy had over Wycliffism. Revelation, even contemporary revelation (even, that is, "extra fidem scripture"), then, is *more trusted than the imagination* in many reading communities of the Schism period.[116] By the turn of the century, after decades of upheaval at the pinnacle of church governance, mystical theology is even being encouraged at the university in Paris and shortly thereafter at Oxford, as we have seen with Whethamstede. We have seen the principle operative in ideological confrontations in prison writing, we will see it shortly in political visions (in the Scrope cult), and we will see it again in Carthusian and Bridgettine circles later in this book. In prisons, in its most careful form, it could save lives, if not secure freedom. Revelation can take the form of visionary narrative, or the unobtrusive form of a claim to a gift of private understanding, or even the oblique self-confessional identification with Paul or John or some other authorized visionary. All three of these options were tactics that Ricardian and early Lancastrian vernacular writers, both male and female, indulged both seriously and playfully as suggested in the following chapters.

Although I believe it changes how we feel about early Wycliffism to see two of its early proponents as so deeply imbued with revelatory apocalypticism, the Wycliffite movement, nonetheless, was to have little tolerance for either prophecy (vaticinia) or poetry (fabulae), including classical humanist varieties. This puts both Langland and Chaucer in an interesting position in relation to Lollard ideas, whether on visionary or poetic writing. And, in fact, it puts the two of them, at least by the end of their careers, in different places from each *other*. By the end of his life, Chaucer appears for some reason slightly closer to the Lollard position, and Langland a little farther away from it. Although unlike most of his colleagues in actually drawing on prophetic writers, even the *Opus* author inveighs against poetry, insisting the "new ministers" (that is, the Wycliffites) preach "non fabulas poetarum aut vane philosophie." This is rather like the voice we hear in Chaucer's "Parson's Prologue" and in his "Retraction." On the other hand, it is also the kind of voice we hear in various *orthodox* critiques of *The Canterbury Tales*, *House of Fame*, and other works by Chaucer. Sorting out in which tone of voice Chaucer invoked this puritanism, both for his Parson and for himself (or at least for the speaker of his "Retraction") is a complex task, unrelated to spiritual intellection, and one we will tackle in chapter 9. But an earlier problem of the same sort that does relate to spiritual intellection crops up in Langland's B text, in his famous dialogue with Imaginatif on the value of poetry.

This is one of the key passages illuminating Ricardian vernacular attitudes to poetry, but was discarded in C. In it, Imaginatif charges Will with the worthlessness of his poetry-making:

And þow medlest þee wiþ makynges and myȝtest go seye þe sauter,
And bidde for hem þat ȝyueþ þee breed, for þer are bokes y[n]owe
To telle men what dowel is . . . .

(B.XII.16–17)

The kind of distrust of the imagination and privileging of the revelatory we have just seen in the *Speculum devotorum* puts a different light on this passage. Like everything else in Langland, Imaginatif is complex, and we will not attempt to exhaust its complexity here.[117] But to summarize recent consensus, the name in its oddly adjectival form suggests a being *given over to* imaginative profusion. And this is just what Langland delivers: visual analogies and similitudes, precariously ungoverned by, though very respectful of, Reason or Clergy. When Imaginatif accuses the dreamer of "meddling with makings," he charges Will with, in effect, misusing his (Imaginatif's own) gifts to create poetry rather than creating prayer. (And presumably this means *meditative* or visual prayer in the sense critiqued by the *Speculum*, given Imaginatif's involvement?) Will's response consists of not one, but two trump cards, both of which I think we can see afresh now: first, he stakes out the one claim to intellectual freedom that could override all others, even episcopal authority, that is the claim to discuss what is necessary to salvation:

> Ac if þer were any wight þat wolde me telle
> What were dowel and dobet and dobest at þe laste
> Wolde I neuere do werk, but wende to holi chirche
> And þere bidde my bedes but whan ich ete or slepe.
>
> (B.XII.24–28)

Second, he makes the implicit claim that *he* knows better than any learned friar what that secret ingredient is and so is duty-bound to write it. Buried deep in the logic of the "Ac if . . . / Wolde I neuere" is the claim that he knows "what were dowel . . ." and will continue to write it. And here is—given the visionary nature of the poem—a buried claim to spiritual intellection. Although he is very polite about it, he has implicitly dismissed Imaginatif's charge that his time would be better spent praying (". . . þer are bokes y[n]owe / To tell men what dowel is . . . / And prechours to preuen what it is of many a peire freres" [17–19]). Will begs to differ.

Langland suppressed this passage in making C for many reasons, but at least in part, I would suggest, because as treatises on *discretio* and vision increasingly became available in the Schism age, his sense of what the implication was of an association between the *imagination* and the act of revelatory writing would have changed. In such treatises, it is at least less desirable than an association between the act of writing and revelation itself. This, in fact, is precisely the conclusion that the Carthusian who translated the *Speculum devotorum* comes to in preferring to trust in, among other things, "sum revelacyonys of approvyd wymmen" over against the "ymagynacyonys" of the *Meditations on the Life of*

Christ tradition—a tradition that Langland mostly shuns in his poetry. Note, again, the link the *Speculum* makes between such "ymagynacyonys" and the "carnal":

> For thowgth there myght have be put to some ymagynacyonys that haply mygth have be delectable to carnal soulys, yytt that that ys doo aftyr conscyence ys sykerest *thowgth the medytacyonys mygth have be, be suech ymagynacyonys, haply more confortable to some carnal folke.*[118]

Second, I would suggest that Langland suppressed it because, read *retrospectively*, he could sound like one of the new-fangled reformers (only recently and fitfully called "lollares" before about 1388).[119] "Stop making and start praying" (to paraphrase Imaginatif) sounds like the kind of advice Chaucer's Parson would give. But Langland's view is rather more nuanced and a great deal less dour. In fact, a few uninteresting vestiges of the B passage survive in the C.V "apologia" and in C.IX, which, most scholars agree, was Langland's attempt to rework it in an utterly new way.[120] This project in C.V and C.IX is one in which he systematically (and sometimes wryly) distinguishes himself from "lollars" of all types.[121] These complex passages have been understood as Langland's attempts to extract himself from trouble in the wake of 1381 (especially its political and perhaps its Wycliffite overtones).[122] I would also suggest that the suppression of the B Imaginatif passage is yet a further piece of evidence that Langland did not want to be tarred with the same brush as the emergent "Lollards," not, however, out of fear of ecclesiastical prosecution so much as out of *discomfort* with certain aspects of their puritanism and anti-revelatory thrust. This seems likely because he takes trouble to add revelatory themes to these new passages. A passionate spiritual romance of poverty and suffering for the Lord is characteristic of Franciscan Spiritual texts, and at least one such passage, on the "lunatic lollars" of C.IX.105–138, Langland famously added to his final revision. This links such sufferers directly to the charism of prophecy and to the Franciscan *joculatores domini* (minstrels of the Lord).[123] This seems to be part of his reclaiming strategy. And it was one of the ways, I would suggest, he wanted to distinguish himself from the new Wycliffite texts, by *explicitly* invoking this sense of Franciscan *charism*. (In this he is perhaps more like the *Opus* author than later Lollards.) Langland, I would suggest, although not himself much given to secularity, came to be repulsed by various aspects of the cultural narrowness of the Wycliffite project as he watched it unfold in the

1380s. His own moves in the "puritanical" direction (for instance, against trivial or obscene entertainment in the C text)[124] seem to me to be a way of reclaiming the middle ground from an audience he could see, daily perhaps, slipping toward the easy literalism or "black and whiteness" of nascent Wycliffism. Langland was trying to regain and keep a spiritually moderate audience.

Langland's poem, moreover, is chock full of *implicit* claims to revealed or higher knowledge. Piers and many others speak their truths from mysterious depths and with mysterious authority. The dreamer himself is a recording visionary (we have just seen the buried claim to spiritual intellection in B.XII). Even more daring, the narrational voice prophesies, often and without warning, especially in its "overvoice" mode.[125] Most daring of all, perhaps, the poem has embedded hints of radical salvational generosity, with visions of the fall of the papacy, juxtapositions of a "carnal" and a "spiritual" church, and calls for the redistribution of wealth in the clergy. In dealing with controversial or dangerous ideas of all kinds then, Langland had two trump cards up his sleeve: the medieval academic ideals of *libere tractare* on what is necessary to salvation, and a widely respected, tacit ecclesiastical tolerance of claims to spiritual intellection. His work was at least potentially dangerous on many scores. And these two cards, I would suggest, were critical to him.

These trump cards also allowed the three women mystics we are about to examine to write. But as they were writing (or, in Porete's case, being translated) during the turn of the century period when legal bans against revelatory writing began to appear, we will look first to some crucial background. The next and last case history of a Langlandian audience involves an important historical event that foregrounded the revelatory in a ban issued by Arundel in 1406, an unnoticed set of constitutions different from the ones we know in relation to Wycliffism.

CASE STUDY 3 OF DANGEROUS READING AMONG EARLY *PIERS* AUDIENCES

Arundel's Other Constitutions and Religious Revelation as
Refuge for Political Protest in *Piers* Manuscript Bodley 851

The story of how Archbishop Arundel came to issue a ban and a set of *constitutiones* on all officially unvalidated visions emanating from the most popular and lucrative cult in fifteenth-century England begins with our third *Piers* audience with a taste for dangerous reading.[1] This is the Benedictine readership of Bodleian Library, Bodley 851, which contains the Z text of *Piers Plowman*. It also contains as a later addition a Latin poem lamenting the execution of Archbishop Scrope ordered by Henry IV in 1405. Bodley 851 is the only version to contain stanzas so critical of the king that they were suppressed when it was copied elsewhere.[2] When the cult of Scrope became a threat, Henry IV had attempted, with the help of Archbishop Arundel, to suppress all such poems and accounts of miracles at the tomb. In the process, they issued a ban on any revelation that did not pass an official test of *probatio*. This attempt to suppress the revelatory is, despite its ostensibly regional focus in the northern half of England, as ambitious in its way as the bans in Arundel's Constitutions against Wycliffism, and equally as hopeless to monitor.

Ironically, the Scrope poem represents an audience on the opposite end of the spectrum from the pro-Wycliffite audience for "Heu quanta desolacio" we saw in Case Study 2 or even (this would be a different spectrum) from the fraternal audience we saw in Case Study 1. Our third audience for *Piers Plowman* takes us into the Lancastrian period and the third generation of Langland's readers, after those who initially (like the York Austins) knew his brand of reformist thought in relation to Joachite-style prophecy and those who (like early Wycliffite sympathizers) came to him for hard reformist critique. The Scrope poem and the Benedictine reading audience it had represent the "possessioner" or pro-endowment forces, who felt equally beleaguered, even after *De heretico comburendo*—a point worth our notice. The Ramsey Benedictines, or more likely their Oxford house, owned the manuscript now containing the unique Z text, and our poem, "Quis meo capiti." The poem describes the execution which sparked a spectacular, long-lasting popular cult of Scrope, one that would outstrip Thomas à Becket's cult itself in comparative donations by early in the fifteenth century. In fact, the legal historian William Stubbs considered the judicial murder of the primate of northern England more significant than the death of Becket, which he thought was "thrown into the shade" by it.[3] Although never officially canonized, Scrope quickly came to be viewed as a latterday Becket, especially in the north where he was regarded as having led a popular insurrection that united northerners of all classes. Behind the support of the York clergy and local gentry "was the recognized principle of ecclesiastical independence, the freedom of the local church and community from the central authority of the crown."[4] This we might think of as quite a different orientation from Langland's, but the high degree of preservation of Langland's poem by ecclesiastical and monastic owners who admired exactly these principles asks us to think again.

The poem appears in its uncensored form only in Bodley 851.[5] "Quis meo capiti"[6] opens with an allusion to Jeremiah 9:1 ("Who will give water to my head and a fountain of tears to my eyes?"), and in the Bodley manuscript has eight more stanzas than the version printed by Thomas Wright, six of which are highly critical of the king (or, as it is more often worded in these stanzas, in an attempt at indirection, *kings* [reges]). Material on Scrope did, in fact, come under official censorship, most especially the accounts of miracles and visions that were experienced by pilgrims to his tomb. By April 1406, the king's council sent instructions ordering the York clergy to abstain from publishing accounts of miracles worked at the tomb and in the field where Scrope was beheaded, but they continued to be published and the command had to be frequently repeated, though to no avail. Moreover, several chronicles of the period record criticism of Henry IV and the judges involved in the case, making the cult a public relations disaster for Henry.

The Bodley manuscript (at least in its earliest form) was originally owned by the Benedictine, John Wells, one of the prominent anti-Wycliffite debaters we have just seen pilloried in "Heu, quanta desolacio."[7] This is a complex manuscript codicologically, with entries and even booklets added at different times. Both the section of the manuscript to which the Scrope poem was added and the section of the manuscript containing the Z text (although not its C continuation) share the same system of decoration and must be regarded as part of the same collection—long before, in fact, the entering of the Scrope piece.[8] Moreover, if A. G. Rigg is correct about the order in which items were added to the manuscript in the fifteenth century, then even the C continuation would have been added before the Scrope poem was copied into some blank leaves.[9]

In contrast to the audiences examined in Case Studies 1 and 2, this text of *Piers* and our poem on Scrope's execution were being read in a fifteenth-century monastic setting in which the greatest fear was of *victimization* by radical policies, not prosecution for them. Anxiety about disendowment was still in 1405 a political reality, and our poem would have been composed just before the 1406 legislation banning disendowment prophecy. Moreover, the death of Archbishop Simon Sudbury at rebel hands was still a relatively recent outrage— recent enough to be piously remembered in 1405. Scrope's heroism while alive, for this Benedictine audience, lay in part with his stand in the 1404 Coventry Parliament, in which he and Thomas Arundel, archbishop of Canterbury, defended clerical privileges in matters of taxation and their possessions against secular confiscation.[10] The irony of Arundel's actions a year or so later to suppress the growing cult of his former ally would not have been lost on this audience either.

In one of the defining moments of the poem, Scrope's death is set in the tradition of the deaths of two earlier archbishops, Becket and Simon Sudbury (during the Rising of 1381):

Ast Thomam militum audax atrocitas,
Symonem plebium furens ferocitas,

Ricardum callide saeva crudelitas,
Obtruncant christos Domini.
(Wright, 116)

————

And [in the case of] Thomas, the bold atrocity of knights,
Simon, the raging ferocity of commoners,
Richard, fierce cruelty cunningly
Cut off God's anointed.

It is fascinating, given what we know about *Piers Plowman* as a hero of the John Ball letters, to find the poem together in the same manuscript with a poem that laments the death of Sudbury at the hands of Ball's rebels. It reminds us that we still privilege political extremism and political correctness in our sense of the reception of Langland.

There were many things that made *Piers Plowman*, however, at home in a monastic library. Among those things in Bodley 851 in particular is the Z redactor's profound understanding of visionary narrative.[11] And, as we saw in Case Study 2, John Wells and the Benedictine contingent at the Blackfriars Council were as antimendicant as Langland or the author of "Heu." Still another factor would be Langland's passionate interest in political history and habit of obliquely invoking dangerous political or seditious points, a passion monastic readers, with their long-standing chronicle traditions, shared—perhaps, as the Scrope poem itself indicates, from a more privileged position of safety.

In order to make sense of the poem we need to know more about Scrope's death and the English tradition of "political canonization."[12] Scrope was archbishop of York (1398–1405), convicted of treason and beheaded outside of York's walls so that "there schuld be no prayer mad" for him, as Capgrave observed. He had originally participated in the political process of dethroning Richard and supporting Henry, and although nominally neutral during the Percy rebellion of 1403, his allegiances were all with northern interests like those of the Percy family. In 1404, as our poet remembers, he strenuously opposed the royal confiscation of the church properties mooted at the Coventry Parliament; by 1405 he was overtly preaching against Henry and had prepared a manifesto of grievances. A small army (apparently including monks) gathered under the archbishop's banner of the Five Wounds of Christ. The rising against royalist forces had been doomed to failure from the start, however. The archbishop was sentenced at Bishopthorpe, his own palace, even though the archbishop of Canterbury argued that no secular court could condemn an archbishop to death, and the lord chief justice, Sir William Gascoigne, refused to pronounce such a sentence. There was no formal trial (which our poem bitterly recalls), and the beheading proceeded with Scrope asking the executioner to inflict five wounds upon him in memory of Christ's, as our poet records in heightened hagiographic language.[13] His body was buried in the new Chapel of St. Stephen in the north aisle of York Minster, referred to, at least by mid-century, as Scrope Chapel (vulgariter vocata Scrop Chapell).[14] Between 1405 and 1408 the numbers of the faithful who came to the chapel as to the shrine of a man they regarded as a martyr to Henry IV's oppression became an embarrassment to the king, especially as Pope Innocent VII had excommunicated Henry.[15]

In December 1405 the archbishop of Canterbury and the chancellor of England wrote indignantly to the York Chapter to reign in the "pretense" of miracles being reported there. Walsingham also attributed the reports of miracles to the "vulgares" gathering as much in the field where Scrope was beheaded (in campo quo decollatus) as at the tomb (quam in loco quo sepultus est). The king's son, John of Lancaster, ordered York sergeants to note the names of pilgrims to the tomb; the city retaliated by dismissing any who did.[16] Barricades of logs and stones had to be erected to stop the crowds. John, duke of Bedford, was scathing in his instructions on erecting the barriers to prevent the "false" crowds arriving there "under colour of devotion" ("les faux foles que y veignont par colour de devocion").[17] But riots ensued, and they eventually had to agree to allow pilgrims to visit the tomb.

Desperate to control the spin (likely as much for Canterbury's sake as for the king's), and yet unable to be seen to deny the possibility of any divine miracle, Arundel's initial letter is a very cunning piece of workmanship. In a mixture of formal prohibition and counsel he appeals, with implicit and devastating rhetorical force, to the only One whose miracles cannot be doubted, that is, the "Great Counselor [magnus consiliarius], our Lord Jesus, marvelous [mirabilis] in all his works." It is His will, however, not to "immediately [statim] manifest to us unworthy ones" knowledge of the Father's secrets.[18] Therefore, we give, he says, "for firm counsel to your discretion [vestrae discrecioni]" that "you by no means [minime] invite or solicit" any of those gathering in honour of the late archbishop, "by word or deed nor by any pretended miracles [opere aut sermone, nec aliqua pretensa miracula]," whether to be made public (propalari) by clergy or laity. Any such event is to be contained, "until it be known whether this thing may originate from God [*donec sciatur an hec res a Deo proveniat*] . . . and will remain lasting [manebit durabile], or whether it proceeds from violent, vain, or superstitious things, by the invention of man [*ex violenta, vana, et supersticiosa hominum invencione procedit*]."

What has not been noticed in this document is the official language of *discretio spirituum* (discretion of spirits) or *probatio* (testing) of visionaries (language we have seen in Augustine, in Rupescissa, in the *Speculum devotorum*, and which we will see especially in the *Epistola solitarii* in chapter 8). Arundel uses this vocabulary very explicitly in this first set of orders and it appears in those that would follow. (I have italicized some of the key words or phrases in the Latin.)[19] This insistence on *probatio* or visionary validation is to be carried out on a massive, officially mandated scale. Each individual pilgrim's revelatory claim will now have to be tried according to the procedures of *discretio* in a move that in telling ways begins to mirror Archbishop Arundel's anti-Wycliffite Constitutions of 1407 and 1409 not many years later. The target here is not Wycliffite heresy, but another problem for orthodoxy, that is, unauthorized revelation (a form of "enthusiasm"), now spreading like wildfire throughout the northern half of the country and attracting pilgrims from all over—Margery Kempe was to be one such pilgrim, in fact (chapter 6). Although spiritual protocol dictated that any revelation had to be given due process, it is clear that the king's advisors and even Arundel (Scrope's one-time ally) had already decided that the miracles were false. In many ways, their starting premise is opposite to the more positive premise of formal canonization proceedings, the situation in which miracles would more normally come under scrutiny. Formal canonization was a strong possibility in this case; donations were being collected, the papacy was in Scrope's camp (Henry IV was personally excommunicated), and lawyers learned in both laws were heavily active in the cult (attracted by the legal issues connected with the execution), as the records indicate.[20] All this was far too dangerous for a king who had recently usurped a throne. The York Minster clergy were ordered to embark on a campaign of *discretio* interrogation larger than any ever undertaken in England.

Suffice it to say, their hearts were not in it. The letter of prohibitions was not to be effective enough. In April 1406 a much less friendly document ("une cedule") arrived, containing a set of five articles (cynk articles) or *constitutiones* written by Arundel and Thomas Langley, the chancellor, and introduced in a covering letter by the king himself, throwing still more impediments in the way of the cult. Specifically forbidden was any form of encouragement or aid to those visiting the tomb, any adoration of the archbishop (other than prayers for his soul), and any financial gain from the tomb (all offerings must be deflected to the tomb of St. William or elsewhere).[21] The prayer injunction especially, of course, like so many other sweeping laws of the period, was hopeless to police. Thus even the famous Bolton Hours flouts the law with its image of a kneeling woman adoring Scrope and holding a speech scroll that reads "Ste ricarde scrope ora pro nobis" (figure 15). Oxford, Bodleian Library, Lat. Liturg. f.2 appears to contain a similar case, where a more generic saint is shown being beheaded, next to a suffrage for Scrope (figure 16).[22] Most importantly, the first 1406 article commands York clergy to abstain from any publishing or making public of miracles "created through Lord Richard" (a quacumque publicacione miraculorum per dominum Ricardum . . . factorum se abstineant).[23]

This is censorship. But it is overtly in line with the way the international church handled cases of *probatio* in claims to revelatory experience, especially those under suspicion. The *possibility* of vision was never to be dismissed out of hand, but the *source* of the vision (whether divine or infernal or merely human invention) was always to be doubted and tested. While no one could be blamed for having visions or even confiding them to a confessor, publicizing or publishing them without ecclesiastical permission was anathema, and indeed, could be grounds for heresy prosecution.[24] Something striking in Arundel's prohibitions is how human invention (anything that *hominum invencione procedit*) is opposed to true revelation—a parallel critique to the one the *Speculum devotorum* author makes of Nicholas Love's project.[25] This is not the last time we will meet it. Revelation was a powerful force in medieval society, and it could be called upon—as we see elsewhere in this book—as the ultimate force. In the case of the Scrope cult, Arundel and the king's party were on the losing side. Offerings mounted and quickly grew to be such a large and significant factor in the Minister's income that much of the new fifteenth-century fabric of the cathedral bears the splendid impression of Scrope's cult to this day. We owe even the great Thornton windows, medieval figural stained glass the size of a tennis court, to this outpouring of wealth and loyalty.[26] An instance of one of the visions may help to convey the spiritual force of the cult. Both Thomas Gascoigne and Clement Maidstone record that the martyred Scrope appeared to an old man, John Sibson, telling him to single-handedly remove the heavy logs barricading the tomb and his sins would be forgiven. The old man miraculously did so, outlifting the strength of three men.[27]

15. The Bolton Hours, York Minster Library, MS 2, fol. 100v, showing an image from the illegal cult of Richard Scrope, archbishop of York, with a woman adoring Scrope and holding a speech scroll that reads "Ste ricarde scrope ora pro nobis." The Bolton Hours, c. 1420–30, belonged to John Bolton, M. P. and lord mayor of York. Reproduced by kind permission of the Dean and Chapter of York Minster.

16. Oxford, Bodleian Library, MS Lat. Liturg. f.2, fol. 146v, showing a saint being beheaded, presumed to be Scrope because of its placement by a suffrage for Archbishop Scrope on the facing page (fol. 147). The manuscript appears to have been adapted for patrons with York connections in the early fifteenth century. Reproduced by permission of the Bodleian Library, University of Oxford.

One can easily see the transparently political nature of attitudes toward these revelations on both sides. In his study of York Minster's Bolton Hours (a manuscript that similarly "canonizes" Scrope), John Osborne remarks that there is a good deal of English precedent for popular "canonization" of those who offered resistance to authority (royal or otherwise) and speaks of this as "a particularly English phenomenon."[28] Among those Osborne (following in part Josiah Russell's research on "political saints") lists are Becket (1118–70), Hugh of Lincoln (1140–1200), Edmund Rich (c. 1175–1240), Thomas Cantilupe (c. 1218–82), archbishops of Canterbury, Stephen Langton (c. 1150–1228) and Robert of Winchelsey (d. 1313), and bishop of Lincoln, Robert Grosseteste (c. 1168–1253). Some of these men were officially saints and others were not, but all were political figures, and it is in this lineage that our "Quis meo capiti" poet places Scrope, at a time, apparently, just after the execution when feelings were running very high. Although even secular political figures could achieve popular "sainthood" in this way sometimes, Becket was the model for all of them.[29] And Becket stands out here, I would suggest, as a compelling reason York Minster supported Scrope's cult: this was York's chance to rival the fame and income of that great tomb in Canterbury Cathedral, which it continued to do on a spectacular scale right throughout the fifteenth century. Certainly in the north, moreover, these constitutions eclipsed Arundel's anti-Wycliffite Constitutions, first issued a year or so later. And important for the entire country was the fact that Henry IV himself was excommunicated because of these events, a sentence only lifted by the pope in 1408. Innocent VII excommunicated all who had participated in the execution, but the bull went unpublished by Arundel. Gregory XII, initially hostile as well, eventually authorized the bishops of Lincoln and Durham to lift the censure and Henry, in atonement, promised to found three monasteries, a task left to his son, Henry V, to fulfill. The Bridgettine foundation of Syon, famously a part of this vow, explains in part the presence of St. Bridget in the Bolton Hours.[30]

Political sainthood, indeed, is precisely what we have in "Quis meo capiti," and it could profitably be added to Osborne's list of sources for political sainthood, especially given the role that Becket plays in it. Our poet is entirely a churchman in his thinking, and it is only clerical figures that interest him. His poem, like its visual analogue in the Bolton Hours, sanctifies Scrope, casting the last hours of his life in the form of a saint's life.[31]

The poem traces the story of the execution, building an oblique case for Henry IV's injustices by beginning with the suggestion of a parallel martyrdom in Richard II. Richard is described as being led to the sword, falling, but rising again in the migration of his soul to joy (Ricardus Angliae primas ad gladium / Ducitur, caeditur, migrans ad gaudium). The poet condemns the sentencing as perverted or preposterous (praeposterus), arrived at without due deliberation (nulla dilatio, / Nulla negotii examinatio)—we have already seen that the trial was to become infamous in legal circles, drawing many lawyers into the Scrope cult. The issue, the execution of a cleric, let alone an archbishop, by secular courts, was a serious one and probably did more to strengthen conservative church interests than any single event during Henry's reign. The poem, as printed by Wright from British Library, MS Cotton Faustina B.IX, emphasizes a series of relatively predictable themes, especially Scrope's nobility in the face of death and his encouragement of his young companion, Thomas Mowbray, earl marshall, to face death with the certainty that he would obtain the heavenly feast (Solatur comitem adolescentulum, . . . Certus obtineat coeli coenaculum [115]). Other hagiographic themes abound: the baptism of blood (Baptismus sanguinis), the precise date of his passion (Dies quo patitur pastor piissimus [116]), and the mournful aftermath. Political elements also intrude: the oppression of Scrope's household and subsequently of the people by unbearable taxes (Post haec extenditur poena in plebibus / Importabilibus exactionibus [117]). There is even an coded reference, as Rigg mentions, to the silencing and suppression of the cult: along with a plea for the reader's willing attentiveness is a more obscure request that the reader "not pollute [polluat] the father [patrem] with the cup of poison."[32] This means, we must assume, by not acceding to Arundel's and the government's demands for suppression of the cult.

But Bodley 851 has two extra stanzas intervening after the third stanza on page 116 of Wright's edition and a further six stanzas which intervene after the first stanza on page 118 of Wright's edition. These give the poem a much harsher sense. The first suppressed cluster deals with the terrible dismemberment— limb from limb (membratim)—of the body of the young Mowbray and his dignity and constancy in the face of death.[33] In this stanza Scrope is referred to as the "Cultor ecclesie" (cultivator or husbandman of the church), an epithet that alternates with "pastor" throughout the poem, suggesting that the original version of the poem contained the stanzas later suppressed (that is, rather than their being a later addition to an established textual tradition). The second cluster of suppressed stanzas is physically more damaged and harder to read, but they criticize Henry (though, again, not by name) much more ferociously for ruling by the rigor of the sword, and, interestingly, they criticize the prelates themselves for inaction and division, literally, for sleeping—"Sub sensu scismatis presules dormunt." Meanwhile "kings" (note the safety of the plural) are void of understanding (Reges disipiunt) and believe themselves justified as plunderers (raptores), likely a reference to Scrope's stand in the Parliament of 1404 against a plan to confiscate clerical temporalities.[34] These stanzas in particular take refuge in classical allusion; one, for instance, deplores the egregious tyranny of one who rules kingdoms with less moderation than even the infamously draconian Theodosius (originator of the Theodosian Law Code)![35] There is no doubt that most copyists of the poem felt safer without these stanzas.

In Bodley 851 we have, then, the presence of material under royal censorship in a manuscript with *Piers Plowman*. The book, associated with the Benedictines of Ramsey Abbey and its Oxford connections, was like Cambridge University Library Dd.i.17 produced in the safety of a convent. Both the Pseudo-Legnano prophecy in Dd and the uncensored Scrope poem doubtless, then, owe their survival to the power and independence of the religious orders—and this makes us wonder to what extent the Benedictines in particular not only fostered, but protected *Piers Plowman* itself during the years of its earliest dissemination. Benedictines are far and away the largest distinct group of identifiable early *Piers* owners[36]—and this may be not only significant for the history of early book production, but also, I would suggest, for the history of freedom of expression in late medieval England. Ironically, of the three instances we have examined here, "Heu quanta desolacio," even with its Wycliffite empathies, is arguably the least dangerous of the texts we have studied. And, significantly, also the only one not overtly protected by revelatory theology.

To conclude, then, revelation in the Scrope case was the one safe mode left to defeated northerners and many others who chafed under Henry's regime,[37] through which they could express political dissent. They did so in droves, seriously threatening not only the stability of the regime, but the economic and spiritual clout of the nation's once primary shrine of Canterbury. As we saw in chapter 4, the government itself legislated against prophecy in 1402 and 1406. This test of spiritual versus political rights would, in the end, do more to strengthen the traditional church *against* Henry—a fact that asks us to rethink some of our assumptions about the early Lancastrian regime. The emphasis on official validation at York Minster, especially from 1406 onward, also sheds a little unexpected light on suspicions of Margery Kempe in York, and why she was hauled before the archbishop there. Bowet, the archbishop who examined her, had suffered the taunt of Henry IV that "nowadays bishops worked no miracles," according to Thomas Gascoigne, but he oversaw the dramatic growth of the cult during Henry V's reign, which is exactly when Kempe was visiting York.[38] It shows us that acute awareness of the need for visionary *probatio* preceded her there by about ten years, and continued as the Scrope cult continued its massive rise to power. But Margery's visit is a topic for our next chapter.

Chapter Six

URBAN DEVOTION AND
FEMALE PREACHING

Constraint and Encouragement in England and Abroad

Margery Kempe and Continental Models for Women Preachers

One of the most extraordinary and downright puzzling things about Margery
Kempe is her penchant for casual, public teaching in a variety of urban settings—
and precisely during the period we are accustomed to think of as full of the danger created by Arundel's 1409 Constitutions. We have just looked at Arundel's
anti-revelatory Constitutions, however, which, while meaning to effect censorship of miraculous revelations, had the rather positive effect of officially promoting *probatio* methods much more common on the Continent as a viable route to
visionary recognition. This chapter will explore Margery Kempe's superb mas-
tery of response to *probatio* in two inquisitorial encounters, first, the archbishop
of York, Henry Bowet's famous challenge to her preaching ministry, and second,
an anonymous York cleric's testing of her for Free Spirit heresy. That both ex-
aminations happened in York cannot have been wholly accidental, given the
heightened state of alert with regard to visionary claimants that obtained there
in the period after Scrope's execution. We have just seen that Henry IV taunted

Bowet that bishops today performed no miracles, which evokes the defensive mood of York's chapterhouse under Henry's reign. But the revelatory always had to be *protected* as well as protected *against* in the medieval church.

Margery visited in 1417, a few years after Henry IV's death in 1413. She was befriended in York, she tells us, by two priests, "Syr Iohn Kendale, and an-oþer preste whech song be þe Bischopys grave" (121.14–15). (John Kendale was also an owner of a copy of *Piers Plowman*, a poem with many links to female readership and writing.[1]) Since Archbishop Bowet was not yet dead, this makes most sense as a reference to Scrope's grave, although we cannot be certain. Here we have a direct link between Kempe and the clergy of York Minster during the most emotional period of the cult, the more so since a third man, Master John Alcorn, a canon of the Minster, also mentored her there. Someone— likely someone in this York Minster group—taught her a careful response to examination, evident in her answer to the test question for Free Spiritism. Here Margery economically parries any hint of *both* that heresy and any implication of allegiance to popular belief in the miracles like those associated with Scrope's tomb. When asked how the commandment "Crescite et multiplicamini" (Increase and multiply) should "ben vndirstondyn," she answers:

> Ser, þes wordys ben *not vndirstondyn only of begetyng of children bodily,* but also be purchasing of vertu, which is frute gostly, as be heryng of þe wordys of God, by good exampyl ʒeuyng, be mekenes & paciens, charite & chastite, & sech oþer, for pacyens is *more worthy þan myraclys wekyng.* (*BMK* 121.3–9)

This question, aimed at teasing out any unorthodox sexual attitudes the respondent might harbour (a marker of Free Spirit thought, as we will see later in this chapter) has *nothing* whatsoever to do with miracles. That Margery would introduce the topic here, however, points to awareness of Arundel's anti-Scrope Constitutions, as does her answer just a few lines later during further clerical examination in the York chapterhouse. When asked, "Woman, what dost þu her?" she replies, "Syr, I come on pilgrimage *to offyr her at Seynt William*" (*BMK* 122.11–13). She has been well schooled: when one comes to York Minster after 1406, the safe answer is to insist that one comes to the shrine of St. *William.* In the ten years or so since Scrope's death, expertise in visionary *discretio* and related inquisitorial matters must have flourished in the Minster, both native and Continental, Latin and vernacular. Margery was, then, part of a network, well informed both at York and elsewhere on visionary *discretio* and the legalities of women's right to teach doctrine.

For a long time we have thought in terms of hagiographical models for *The Book of Margery Kempe*, and in terms of Wycliffite models for the encouragement of women preachers.[2] But I would like to nudge us now in another, or rather, *additional* direction, and suggest that one of the key motivations for Margery's public teaching and mysticism may have come from alternative European models of urban devotion and not necessarily or merely from hagiographical ones (nor likely Wycliffite ones at all). This chapter, then, is about the more daring world of semi-religious[3] women in urban environments abroad, and some possible connections with Margery Kempe's style of ministry.

In his study, *The Church in Late Medieval Norwich*, Norman Tanner remarks that "an important reason for the [city's] lack of interest in Lollardy was that the religion provided by the local Church was sufficiently . . . tolerant towards what might be called the left wing of orthodoxy, as to cater for the tastes of most citizens."[4] Just how tolerant is indicated by his observation that Norwich was "perhaps the only town in England known to have contained communities of lay women closely resembling beguinages."[5] Whether these communities were actually modeled on European beguinages or, as I will suggest, on the sister houses of the *Devotio Moderna* movement, there can be little doubt that the model was Continental, urban, and, for England, somewhat avant-garde. That these houses flourished during Kempe's lifetime is, in itself, interesting, as is the fact that, as Hope Emily Allen points out, the hermits of the Trinity Guild of Lynn "resemble the Continental Beghards (that is, male counterparts to the Beguines) more closely than any other religious in England."[6] These are glimpses of the "urban devout" influenced by European models which apparently did not get a foothold in England much beyond the East Anglian port cities closest to the Continent. But even so, why is this evidence so meager, when the influence of the Low Countries is otherwise widely evident in the economic and material culture, not just of East Anglia (where it is most common), but elsewhere?[7]

The reason surely has something to do with the fact that these groups had come under inquisition at various times on the Continent. In 1398, for instance, a friar-inquisitor working in Utrecht claimed the right to intervene against heretics he characterized as "Lollards, Beghards and Sisters" (in inquisitionibus Lulardorum, Begardorum, et Swestrionum). The friar is likely here invoking the most recent papal decretal against these suspect groups, Boniface IX's *Sedis apostolice prouidentia* of 1395, aimed explicitly at "eisdem Beghardis seu Lullardis et Zwestrionibus."[8] The sister houses of the *Devotio Moderna* suffered repeatedly from unwarranted suspicions of this type. They exemplify influential "left-wing orthodoxy" of the kind especially relevant to late medieval England's only two women mystical writers, whose geographical origins in the port cities of East Anglia cannot be a matter of sheer accident. Just how close Kempe's world in Lynn was has recently been shown by Rosalynn Voaden, who explains that in Kempe's time ships going to the Continent docked right across the street from her parish church, St. Margaret's, in which she prayed daily.[9]

Three particular groups of Continental women encouraged women to teach: first, the Beguines of northern Europe, a name that takes in diverse communities of women of diverse literacies.[10] Of special interest to us are those Beguines who became associated with alternative mysticisms, and some even with the heresy of the Free Spirit.[11] This heresy most certainly reached England in a variety of forms, a fact which illuminates Kempe's examination on one occasion for Free Spirit notions.[12] The second group was the "New Devout" or *Devotio Moderna,* whose numerous sister houses so closely resembled beguine convents that they, too, came under inquisition in the 1390s and sporadically afterward. The New Devout nevertheless managed to stay consistently on the right side of canon law, although they were constantly subject to scrutiny and criticism, including instances of the kind of ostracism in urban streets that Kempe experiences. A third group were the Olivian inspired *Beguini* and *Beguinae*. Some of these, of course, strayed into the supposed heterodoxies famously documented by the inquisitor, Bernard Gui, but many lived a "left-wing orthodoxy" under the guidance of Franciscan Spirituals of Joachite persuasion.[13] They, too, encouraged women preachers and visionaries. Margery's spiritual advisor, Alan of Lynn, was interested in these controversial writings, as we saw in chapter 2, in Bale's record that he had noticed a *tabula* called "In Costasy, super Apocalyps" among Alan's indices at the Carmelite house in Norwich.[14]

The Beguines of the North

The northern Beguines were the earliest of the three groups to arise historically. The freedom from strict enclosure these women enjoyed, freedom to gather in loosely supervised groups and draw upon the multiple resources of an urban clergy, allowed for innovative devotional thought and gave rise to some of the most imaginative medieval mystical theology extant today.[15] In writers like Beatrijs of Nazareth, Hadewijch, Mechthild of Magdeburg, and Marguerite Porete, one can trace a direct line of descent from the *symbolismus* of Hildegardian thought to the more speculative theology that beguine relations with intellectual clergy nurtured.[16] But beguine intellectualism also frightened the medieval church into repressive measures. The first of the famous Clementine decrees against the Beguines, originating at the Council of Vienne in 1312, but promulgated in 1317, says:

There are certain women, commonly called beguines who, although they promise no one obedience and neither renounce property nor live in accordance with an approved rule . . . cling [adhaerent] to certain religious to whom they are drawn by special preference [affectio]. It has been repeatedly and reliably reported to us that some of them, as if possessed with madness, dispute and preach [praedicent] about the Highest Trinity and divine essence and in respect to the articles of faith and the sacraments of the Church spread opinions that are contradictory to the Catholic faith.[17]

These were subjects under disputation (and sometimes condemnation) in learned male circles, which makes this reference to speculative theology among Beguines and their "clinging" to certain religious especially interesting.[18] Although the comments are too general for us to be sure, it sounds as if both Olivian and Free Spirit types of heterodoxies may be alluded to here.

Since much of our information comes from hostile sources, and we know very little about beguine literacy,[19] it is difficult to reconstruct exactly what this speculative theology was like or how widespread it was, but we do know that Marguerite Porete (the condemnation of whose book Robert Lerner calls the "birth certificate of the Free Spirit heresy"[20]) was not the only exponent of it considered heretical. According to the biographer of Ruysbroeck, the Beguine Bloemardinne drew a popular following from among the noble women of Brussels for her erroneous ideas, "writing much on the spirit of freedom," and preaching from a "silver seat which . . . was offered after her death to the duchess of Brabant because of her admiration." He goes on to say, "I can affirm from my personal experience that these writings, though excessively baleful [nefandissima], have such an aspect of truth that no one can perceive in them any seed of heresy *save with the grace and assistance of Him who teaches all truth.*"[21]

This neatly summarizes the conundrum of ecclesiastical officials faced with the task of "discretion of spirits" (that only those spiritually gifted by God could discern whether spiritual insights were divine or diabolical), but never, it seems, had *discretio* been so difficult. It is exactly this charge of "subtlety" that was made against Marguerite Porete,[22] whose condemned book, *The Mirror of Simple Souls,* travels in some manuscripts with the *approbationes* of three clerics.[23] One of these is by the Paris theologian, Godfrey of Fontaines, who had himself written a fascinating defence of what we would today call academic freedom after Bishop Tempier's famous condemnations rocked the University of Paris in 1277.[24] Kent Emery points out that Godfrey's severe "Aristotelianism" makes him an unlikely sympathizer with spiritual teaching like Porete's, but what has to be taken into account, I believe, is his commitment to intellectual speculation. He did recognize "special and privileged illustrations which God gives or can give to private persons."[25] If, as it appears, this eminent university professor also took it upon himself to write a defence of a book by a woman, here is an aspect of urban devotional culture of the type that suggests real intellectual possibilities for women — and apparently real dangers as well. But Porete's horrible fate notwithstanding, she was by no means the only Beguine who had access to university intellectuals. The same is true of southern, Olivian influenced Beguines like Douceline de Digne, whose intellectual approach to symbolism came initially from contact with her brother, Hugh, and the Franciscan scholars in his circle, and would eventually include even John of Parma.[26]

Among the male clergy who delivered sermons in beguine houses were some of the most distinguished scholars of their day.[27] Moreover, we know that Beguines debated with these speakers in a manner that shows alertness to points of logic. There is a report, for instance, of a beguine superior of Cambrai who objected to a preacher's proposition that "the man whose charity goes straight cannot but act . . . above reproach. . . . She asked him 'Where in holy scripture master, have you seen that charity is lame? If it limps . . . it is no longer charity.' The speaker was confused."[28] This remark suggests at least an aural exposure to scholastic logic of a kind that we will see in other beguine contexts shortly. Most interestingly, however, the Beguines, especially the superiors, also preached, and their sermons were on occasion recorded: two fragmentary homilies on the Feast of the Dedication given by a beguine mistress, for instance, survive in the collection of Pierre de Limoges, copied down *de auditu.*[29] These beguine superiors wielded a surprising degree of pastoral power: known as "Marthas," they not only preached but heard a kind of pre-confession. This charge is repeatedly made against them. We find it as late as, for instance, Friar Johannes Nyder's treatise on the estates of religious life in the 1430s, where he writes that some Beguines: "exceed the limits [exorbitant] . . . by confessing minor faults to [their female] superiors on bent knees on certain days . . . with their leader (the Martha) imposing penance and discipline on them, [and] preaching to one another on the Gospel or Epistle, as if on the assigned text [or theme]" (inter se nonnunquam predicant de epistola et euangelio sumpto quasi themate).[30] This, then, is a world in which female preaching was not just imagined, but *done*. And that it could be done even without recourse to visionary authority is especially instructive. One notes here that Porete never directly claimed image-based vision to authorize her writing, although she claimed revelation of the intellectual kind more common in male circles (that is, intellectual vision, in Augustine's sense) or spiritual intellection.[31] The visionary route, of course, was also open to and used by many beguine women, in the tradition traceable back to Hildegard of Bingen, who was known to some Beguines, at least, as a role model.[32] Moreover, the literary satires on Beguines preaching, recently explored by Renate Blumenfeld-Kosinki, are evidence, albeit of the hostile variety, that female preaching and teaching was a common enough experience at least to be mockable in certain quarters.[33]

The Sister Houses of the Devotio Moderna: Breaking Down Ecclesiastical Walls

A form of preaching was also possible in the sister houses of the New Devout, the remarkable movement known as the *Devotio Moderna* that sprang up in the Low Countries and Germany in the late fourteenth century. Striving to avoid the pitfalls of the Beguines, though in many respects sharing the fundamental principles of living that had attracted so many women into beguine convents and beguinages, the New Devout nonetheless came under inquisition in the 1390s, and it was the women's houses that were the initial flashpoint. At this point, the sisters, whose houses were always more numerous than the brothers',[34] were being smeared as "dubious Beguines." Thus, in 1398 one friar inquisitor complained (in the diction of a full-fledged charge of heresy) that the sisters charged their opposers with belonging to the city of Babylon rather than Jerusalem (Quibus tam *pertinaciter* inhaerent, quod omnem oppositum sentientem reputant non de ciuitate Jerusalem sed de Babylone errabundum).[35] Whether the sisters were really using apocalyptic language or whether the inquisitor was using template notions of deviance common to Beguines (especially southern or Olivian Beguines)[36] is questionable. At issue was their unwillingness to live under an approved rule (Non enim uolunt regulam approbatam assumere), but rather in an "in-between state" (status medius)[37] as neither a religious order nor a secular life in the world. At issue also was their right to congregate "in collegio"[38] (and the social tensions and ecclesiastical suspicions this aroused), and, closely related to this last, their right to teach or preach. As Van Engen writes, "Brothers or Sisters lived on ordinary city streets, walked with people to church and to market, maintained relations with family and friends; and yet lived a life apart in religious practice, in dress and in social structure."[39] When disputes arose, it was the civic authorities, not the ecclesiastical ones, who had jurisdiction over their houses. One telling instance records an attempt by the rector of the Deventer house, Egbert (1450–83), to stop male friends and relatives frequenting the sister houses. They, in turn, took the case to the city authorities, who actually found in favour of the friends and relatives until Egbert reminded them that they would be responsible for the souls of these women—at which point the civic authorities relented![40] Set apart by their humble clothing (critics were offended by their wearing a kind of habit), the New Devout were ridiculed in the streets as "Lullardi" (the term, of course, was Dutch in origin, "Lollaert," and throughout Europe referred generically to nearly any suspiciously over-pious person). When we read repeatedly of Margery Kempe being called a "Lollard" by casual passersby, it is important to remember this vaguer sense of the term—not all townsfolk were specialists in Wycliffite doctrine. The term, moreover, apparently had currency in England (in *Piers Plowman*, for instance) independently of Wycliffism.[41] An instance that illustrates this social tension comes from the New Devout *Vita Egberti*. Egbert was walking across town, his eyes cast humbly down, carrying a plate of food to someone. When he failed to respond to the greeting of a female relative, she knocked the plate from his hand and cried, "What sort of a lollard have you become?" (Ut quid lollardus iste ita procedit?).[42] Such anecdotes give some sense of urban tensions as well as devotions and parallel the kinds of social alienation experienced by Margery Kempe on numerous occasions and, in a different vein, set out in the *apologia pro vita sua* of Langland's C text.

Prominent in legal defences of the Devout are the suspicions aroused by their gathering in congregations ("in collegio"). One defence in particular distinguishes three kinds of illegal gatherings, those of conspirators, heretics, and the seditious, absolving the Devout, of course, from association with any of these and drawing upon glosses of the word "conventicula" from the anti-heretical decretal, *Cum ex iniuncto,* and from the anti-beguine decretal, *Sancta Romana,* to show that these are irrelevant.[43] The Clementine anti-beguine legislation heavily preoccupied defenders of the New Devout, who had to argue that it did not apply, since the sisters formed no new religious order and elected no superior.[44] But this took finesse, since, like the beguine houses, the sisters were overseen by a "Martha," who could have, it appears, significant pastoral powers, including, again, the right to hear a (non-sacramental) confession and the right to correct, teach, or even preach in the genre of *admonitiones* or *collationes.*[45] Most significantly, this form of teaching was open to *all.* Even the women, argued one of the Devout's chief apologists, should engage in this form of admonition, because, he said, one need not be a superior or a literate cleric to admonish someone else (Unde patet quod non requiritur quod sit superior uel litteratus qui alium debet ammonere).[46] His source here is a passage from Thomas Aquinas, which in England in the same decade appears (on the losing side) in the heresy trial of Walter Brut.[47] Here it is exciting to see it cited in an orthodox context in defence of women's participation in teaching — a participation which, along with that of lay brothers, was *not* suppressed, although it upset friar-inquisitors mightily. This New Devout practice of *collationes* (the word had come to mean brief discourses on a single theme)[48] was a serious challenge to ecclesiastical authorities. As John Van Engen writes, "exhortations to interested laypeople, clerics and students on feastdays, Sunday afternoons and other suitable occasions, appeared to infringe upon the license to preach properly delegated to priests and friars. Indeed the founder of the movement Geert Groote had died fighting a suspension of his right to preach [in 1383]." The *collatio* was defined by one of the Devout's chief apologists as "charitable admonition and fraternal correction," which, he writes, can take place "in a house or city street, not only in a church" (Item hec ammonicio potest fieri ubique in domo, in platea, et non solum in ecclesia).[49] As such, the *collatio* breaks down the formal walls of churches, and — so to speak — potentially sanctifies the entire urban setting (an impulse seen earlier in beguine exempla as well).[50] Often based on wise "sayings" (*dicta*) or exempla from Devout *vitae,* *collationes* were, thus, a form eminently suitable to women and, judging by the massive popularity of the sister houses, an empowering one.[51]

Margery Kempe's Urban Ministry and Netter's Prohibition

Returning, then, to England, I would like to suggest that at least some of the dynamic that motivated Margery Kempe to teach in urban settings in the *admonitiones* style may have come from alternative European models of devotion and not necessarily just from hagiographical ones. She seems, in fact, very well informed of the distinction between *admonitiones* and formal preaching when she comes before the archbishop of York for examination. As is customary in trials of *discretio spirituum*, the archbishop examines her morality and fixates on her publicity, always the most suspect part of any *probatio* inquiry, especially for women.

> Þan seyd þe Erchebischop to hir, "Þow schalt sweryn þat þu [ne] xalt techyn ne chalengyn þe pepil in my diocyse." Nay, syr, I xal not sweryn," sche seyde, "for I xal spekyn of God & vndirnemyn *(rebuke)* hem þat sweryn gret othys wher-so-euyr I go vn-to þe tyme þat þe Pope & Holy Chirche hath ordeynde þat no man schal be so hardy to spekyn of God, for God al-mythy forbedith not, ser, þat we xal speke of hym. . . . As-swyþe a gret clerke browt forth a boke & leyd Seynt Powyl for hys party ageyns hir þat no woman xulde prechyn. Sche, answeryng þerto, seyde, "I preche not, ser, I come in no pulpytt. | I vse but comownycacyon & good wordys, & þat wil I do whil I leue." (*BMK*, 125.37–126.20, with omission)[52]

Margery shows clearly that she knows her rights: she will continue to deliver *admonitiones* (she uses the verb "vndirnemyn" [rebuke]) and "good wordys," but never from a "pulpytt." The *vitae* of sisters of the New Devout are teeming with such *admonitiones*. That Margery could have come in contact with the New Devout, either in her extensive travels abroad (especially in Germany) or even in Norwich itself, is quite likely. With over ninety sister houses in the Low Countries alone during Margery's lifetime, it seems highly likely that this form of devotion was known to her somehow. And, indeed, as Riehle, Bazire and Colledge, Sargent, and Biggs, among others have mentioned, the literature of the *Devotio Moderna* was already making an impact on the English devotional scene.[53] But much work remains to be done on the impact of the *Devotio Moderna* movement in England. One important piece of evidence we have is the very early translation of Thomas à Kempis's *The Imitation of Christ* into English and testimony to its circulation in Carthusian circles.[54] There is also the fact that it was the founder of the New Devout, Gerhard Grote's own very recent Latin translation of Ruysbroeck's attack on the heresy of the Free Spirit that the author of *The Chastising of God's Children* used.[55] Together with his use of the equally recent *Epistola solitarii* defending Bridget of Sweden, *The Chastising* is important evidence of English awareness of the very latest Continental issues endangering women's orthodoxy.

The flow of literary productions of the *Devotio Moderna* across the Channel brings us back to the question of the identity of the "communities resembling beguinages" in Norwich that Tanner identified. On the basis of their dates, they may more likely be sister houses of the Devout. The earliest reference to one of these is 1427, the latest is 1472, roughly bracketing the period when the Devout were flourishing across the Channel,[56] but when initiative in the beguine movement had subsided and, in fact, come under recent attack.[57] Further evidence is suggested by the fact that some of the earliest documentary descriptions of these houses are worded exactly like descriptions of Devout sister houses in civic records of the Low Countries: "sorores pariter comorantes" (sisters living equally together) or "sorores simul comorantes" (sisters living together at once), although the slightly later records also emphasize the poverty (mulieres paupercule) and the chastity (sorores castitati dedicate) that the sisters shared with other non-professed groups (such as Beguines and recluses).[58] But most significant is that one of the houses was owned by a John Asger, likely either John Asger, "the merchant of Bruges and mayor of Norwich in 1426 who dies in 1436; or his son . . . who was born in Zeeland in the Low Countries, [and] was a citizen of Norwich."[59] Even this brief biography suggests the kind of social class among which we find patrons of the Devout. And it also suggests the kind of East Anglian cross-channel fertilization that we see in Margery's own family. Her son, who lived and married in Germany (an equally important region for the Devout movement), was apparently the first scribe of *The Book* and clearly himself a convert to some unknown form of urban devotional life. This is evident from his sudden change of demeanor and clothing and his encouragement and practical help in the recording of his mother's story—certainly not the kind of task every merchant would undertake, even for his mother.[60] *The Book* is coy on the subject of why Margery impulsively (or not so impulsively?) decided to accompany her daughter-in-law back to "Duchelond," attributing the action to divine command. Perhaps the flourishing *Devotio Moderna* movement is yet another reason why, as scholars have often noticed in other contexts, Margery Kempe was so attracted to "Duche" travel, "Duche" speakers, and "Duche" devotional habits.[61]

We can connect these aspects of Margery's education abroad with that of a very different writer, Thomas Netter. Netter's awareness of international heresy issues came in part from his reading and international connections, but also in part from his travel to church councils abroad, especially the Council of Constance. The latter may account largely for why he moved, at one point, as Carmelite provincial, to issue a general condemnation of the *publicity* given to women of the world claiming spiritual gifts.[62] The assumption has been that Netter's prohibition stemmed wholly from his anti-Lollard activities, but the *Doctrinale* ranges much more widely than this. The attack on feminine publicity appears in his *Doctrinale*, for instance, in relation to a discussion of Proverbs 9:13, about the "mulier stulta et clamosa" (foolish and clamorous woman) who sits in the door of her house or "super sellam" (upon a seat) in the forum or public place (a *seated* speaker in medieval iconography symbolizes authoritative teaching). Netter, following Bede, interprets these women as heretics or false doctors, who have usurped the seat (cathedram) of preachers (id est, doctoribus falsitatis. . . . Quia cathedram sibi praedicationis usurpat).[63] Netter, however, does allow more possibility for preaching to women who are virgins, especially virgins under vow, thereby upholding a strict hierarchy.[64] He also positively mentions the wise teaching of Euchodia, Jerome's friend and correspondent, but he insists that she did not teach *in church* (1.640). One can see instantly that Margery, an uneducated preacher in public places and certainly not a vowed virgin, would look rather suspect. Netter fully supported women recluses and also women who experienced eucharistic miracles, because he writes in his *Doctrinale* of two such women, one likely St. Lydwine (at Schiedam), the other a Norfolk woman, "Joanna Methles [meaning 'foodless'], id est, sine cibo."[65] Netter was absolutely in line with international church opinion on this topic, which accepted women claiming revelatory experience, but abhorred its publicity, at least until formal *probatio* could be carried out by expert theologians.

In the Proem to Margery's *Book* we are told that "a Whyte Frer proferyd hir to wryten frely. . . . And she was warnyd in hyr spyrit that she xuld not wryte so sone" (6.9). This was likely the Carmelite Alan of Lynn, who may have believed Margery to be another Bridget (as we saw in chapter 2). Alan of Lynn was one of the clerks who defended Margery when she was attacked from the pulpit by a Grey Friar (ch. 69), but "þan sum enuyows personys compleynyd to þe Prouincyal of þe White Frerys [i.e., Netter] þat the sayd doctowr was to co*n*uersawnt wyth þe sayd creatur. . . . Than was he monischyd be v*er*tu of obediens þat he xulde no more spekyn wyt*h* her . . . & þat was to hym ful peyn-ful" (168.4–12). The next two chapters record the sadness of both on being parted, and Alan's gift of a "peyr of knyvys," in token that "he wolde standyn with hir in Goddys cawse" as he had in the past (22.170). Alan's willingness to stand—in spirit at least—in opposition to his provincial is in keeping with his passion for Henry of Costesy's veiled Olivian style and Bridget's prophetic in-dignation. The chapters suggest further reasons why revelation could be so threatening to the church, as Christ tells Margery, "Dowtyr, I am mor worthy to thy sowle þan euyr was . . . alle þo [clerics who had helped her]" (169.2–3). Chapter 70 records Margery's revelation that she would speak with Alan again, his severe illness, recovery, and permission to speak with her once more. This is celebrated by a joyous dinner, reported in Langlandian style ("Þer was a dyner of gret joy & gladnes, meche mor gostly þan bodily, for it was sawcyd & sawryd wyt*h* talys of Holy Scriptur" [170.21–3]).

No one has tried to date this intervention or the period of time of the prohibition, but it must have been before 1423, when Alan likely died.[66] Since Margery was mostly abroad between 1413 and 1415 (in the Holy Land and, for a period in the summer of 1417, in Santiago), and since the period of her being suspect for heresy (at Leicester and at York) was the fall of 1417, it would make sense to date Netter's intervention at about this time. It is at this time, while in York (where Arundel had mandated knowledge of *probatio* from December 3, 1405 onward), that she is asked the "test" question for heresy of the Free Spirit. The question was how she would interpret "Crescite & multiplicamini" (Wax and multiply) (Gen. 1:22; 121.2–3) and she gives an answer showing that she had been well schooled on the subject. As we will see at the end of this chap-ter, sporadic trial records show that there was good reason to test for unusual attitudes toward sexuality during Margery's time. Netter was at the Council of Constance (with the English delegation in 1414),[67] where he would have seen major heresy prosecution underway and learned not only of Wycliffite-Hussite connections first hand, but of the heady mix of Free Spiritism, Joachimism, and Beguinism that injected a revelatory or mystical dimension into suspect female doctrines in Bohemia.

We do not know what changed Netter's mind about Margery. One or more of Margery's persistent efforts at *probatio* must have cleared her name, and Net-ter may have realized, as did many during the Schism age, that orthodox revela-tory practices could strengthen the church's hand (Margery's extreme eucharistic devotion being just such as his *Doctrinale* celebrates). H. E. Allen believes that Alan of Lynn may have offered to help Margery early on, that is, before 1414 when Netter became prior provincial. If, as Allen reconstructs Margery's chronology, she had her first revelation in 1409, four years before her visit to the Holy Land late in 1413 (just after her interviews with Repingdon and with Arundel in the summer of that same year, the first historical events of her conversion period), then it would seem likely that Alan made the offer to help Margery write c. 1413 (or a little before). Given his documented fascination with Bridget (whose chapel in Rome Margery reached in 1414), it seems likely that Bridget would have formed a topic of their discussions. What is intriguing about this is that even if Arundel's anti-Wycliffite Constitutions were an inhibiting factor for Margery ("she was warnyd in hyr spyrit that she xuld not wryte so sone"), they were certainly *not* for Alan at the time he offered.[68] This must help us rethink how the learned, at least, understood the Constitutions to work: not as a threat or an obstruction to vernacular writing, but more as a background security measure, available if indications of extremism appeared.

The Chastising of God's Children and the Context for Porete's Mirror in England: Evidence of Insular Awareness of the Free Spirit Heresy in Carthusian Circles and Beyond

How extensive was the infiltration of "left-wing orthodoxy" and suspect doctrines from the Continent? And to what extent were they understood in England? To take the example of the inquisitorial test question for detecting heresy of the Free Spirit, not only, then, did the York cleric who asked it know enough to associate Margery's lifestyle with those of suspect Beguines abroad, but equally significant is that Margery herself knew how to handle the question. This suggests that among the pieces of advice on *discretio* that Margery's various confessors and counselors had taught her was specific advice on acceptable answers for just such an examination. Indeed several bishops' registers record instances of Free Spirit heresy, and there are several other Middle English texts which record explicit concern about it.[69] In fact, a more general awareness of the dangers of both Free Spiritism and revelatory theology first becomes apparent in the last quarter of the fourteenth century. For literary scholars, three influential texts in particular stand out: the Middle English translation of Porete's *Mirror*, the anonymous *The Chastising of God's Children*, and the Middle English translation of material from the Bridgettine canon, including the *Epistola soli-tarii*.[70] Together these texts represent significant infiltrations of the literature of European "left-wing orthodoxy" (and in the case of Porete, heterodoxy) into England—infiltrations that I believe had an impact on some of our most important religious writers, including probably Langland, Julian, and Kempe.[71]

Although English professional readers and ecclesiastical authorities did not always know exactly what they were encountering in Continental imports, recent scholarship has made too much of Insular ignorance on radical subjects.[72] And this is the first in a series of points I would like to make about knowledge of Continental "left-wing" women's religious culture in late medieval England. The author of *Chastising* knew that women in particular needed to be warned about Free Spirit heresy, and he had a surprising knowledge, via Latin translation of Ruysbroeck, of recent thought on these topics from the Low Countries. He also knew that *discretio* issues were important for a female audience and served them up from the latest Continental Bridgettine defences (which, however, he made a good deal less enthusiastic).[73] Moreover, the English translator of Porete's text, known to us only as "M. N.," provides his translation with explanatory glosses that give a strong indication, I will suggest, of awareness of a source like *The Chastising*'s Ruysbroeck chapters. M. N. may also have been made aware (although this is much less certain) of the basic Clementine legislation against Free Spirit thought prior to undertaking his glosses. In fact, there is a surprisingly lengthy list of references to concern about the heresy in various types of Insular sources, discussed below. The peculiar, though not exclusive, association of much of this material with women is the topic that will preoccupy us here and in the next two chapters—a factor, as I will suggest, important for our understanding of both Margery Kempe's and Julian of Norwich's writings.

What exactly did the English authorities know, and when did they know it? As has often been pointed out, Kempe's, Julian's, and Porete's texts traveled exclusively in Carthusian circles in England, and it therefore makes sense to look to these circles for evidence of Insular awareness of Free Spiritism. On the Continent, the authorities had originally singled out Porete's text—rightly or wrongly—as the definitive statement of Free Spirit heresy, so understanding its reception in England is central to our question, a question intimately tied to the *Chastising*'s readership. Of course, medieval English readers did not know that *The Mirror* was by Marguerite Porete or by a condemned woman. But they did or could know many things: first, they knew by internal evidence (the letters of approval and the M. N. glosses) that the text had a history of some kind of controversy; second, that certain manuscripts of both English and Continental provenance contained external evidence of reader suspicion. Third, they knew by the company it keeps in manuscript and the gendered, courtly language of the text itself that it was at the very least a text to be *associated* with women's mysticism. Fourth, they knew that caveats about "Liberty of Spirit" were appropriate in works intended for female contemplatives. Fifth, in the Carthusian circles in which *The Mirror* traveled, descriptions of Free Spirit doctrines were accessible in a variety of sources, most notably in *The Chastising of God's Children* (and its Latinized source, Grote's Ruysbroeck) as well as in the standard decretal sources and guides available to all clergy.[74] Sixth, some would have known of recent instances of heresy trials involving Free Spirit doctrine and recantation.

It is highly unlikely that when M. N. first produced his translation of *The Mirror* he knew all these things. But by the time he produced the second version, his situation had changed. What he knew by then is a complex problem and can only be dealt with by examining each of these six areas in turn, and then looking at his glosses for evidence. This is what will preoccupy us in the following sections of this chapter and the next, which have to be set out in turn before the glosses can be assessed.

It is clear from the manuscript origins and provenance of the English translation of *The Mirror* that it circulated among Carthusians where it is strongly associated with women's mysticism and guidance to the contemplative life for mixed audiences — most importantly in manuscripts like British Library, MS Additional 37790 (also containing the unique complete medieval copy of Julian's *Revelation*) and Oxford, Bodleian Library, MS Bodley 505 (with a copy of *The Chastising*).[75] *The Mirror*'s prominent use of *la courtoise mystique* alone, not to mention its daring insistence on feminine pronouns, would have given it away to a medieval reader as a work appropriate for an audience of female contemplatives.[76] English professional spiritual directors and writers also knew that caveats about "Liberty of Spirit" were appropriate to women readers. We know this in part because of the effort that the *Chastising* author makes in this regard, and in part because of Margery Kempe's questioning. The connection between women and Free Spirit doctrine had been formalized since the Clementine legislation, *Ad nostrum* and *Cum de quibusdam mulieribus*, of which Gordon Leff says: "These two bulls together were a landmark in the history of the Beguines and the

Free Spirit . . . from this time forward the Beguines—and the Beghards—came irrevocably to be treated as the source of the heresy of the Free Spirit."[77] The contents of these bulls were well known and appear in many standard canon law collections available or compiled in England. It has not been sufficiently appreciated that these would have been among the first items consulted by English ecclesiastical officials in the early scramble to understand and diagnose Lollardy in a country with no real history of inquisitional procedures.[78] The Vienne legislation was issued under the rubric of heresy and was exclusively doctrinal, so English officials and controversialists would have reconsulted the Clementine and Johannine legislation not only in the early, confusing days of the rise of Wycliffism[79] but also prior to this in the cases mentioned in chapter 2.[80] This is an important point, and one that has been missed amid recent eagerness to show medieval English ignorance of Continental heresy and its issues— eagerness, that is, to insist upon the "insularity" of Insular spirituality. Medieval churchmen condemned opinions by reference to established heresies: whether of the recent past (as we saw in Grandisson's collecting material on the sentencing of Franciscan Spirituals from abroad when confronted with unknown heresy in his Exeter diocese), or the remote past (as we will see in designations like "Pelagian" in the condemned articles of Ockham). Moreover, certain concerns and events, both at home and abroad, between the death of St. Bridget in 1373 and the Council of Basel (which recondemned *The Mirror* in 1433)[81] played an important role in making the English sensitive to revelatory theology and its controversiality. This and other factors can shed new light on what was at issue, for instance, in the English transmission of Porete's book and its glosses. These are significant pieces of evidence of reception history in their own right and suggest important parallels to Middle English visionary works, most especially Kempe's and Julian's, but also Langland's.

The Chastising, which was certainly conceived for a female audience (likely the nuns of Barking), contains translations of lengthy portions, two chapters in all, of Ruysbroeck's *Die Geestelike Brulocht* against the Free Spirit. The author must have thought it important to have translated at such length and, as his interpolation of allusions to recent events shows, urgent. His handling of Ruysbroeck's *Brulocht*, which is interventionist, but careful, is based on a Latin translation from the heart of the *Devotio Moderna* movement: Gerhard Grote's rendering of the text as *De Ornatu spiritualium nuptiarum* (On the Adornment of Spiritual Espousals). Both Grote's movement and Ruysbroeck's writings are excellent instances of Tanner's "left-wing orthodoxy." (Both had attacked Free Spiritism, and both had incurred charges of unorthodoxy themselves, but never charges that stuck.)[82]

Some scholars have read these passages in *The Chastising* as utterly benighted, a merely muddled attempt to appropriate Ruysbroeck's text to describe the Lollards. Robert Lerner, for instance, wrote, "The clearest indication that there was no Free-Spirit movement in England comes from the English translation of Ruysbroeck's *Adornment* (ca. 1382), which recasts attacks on false mystics to make them apply to followers of Wyclif."[83] This view is untenable,[84] as a careful reading of the syntax of the Middle English bears witness.[85] At the end of the two chapters the *Chastising* author devotes entirely to a description of "freedom of spirit" he explicitly says that these heretics are *more dangerous* than the Lollards, whose tenets against confession, images, and ecclesiastical hierarchy he then describes in very brief and distinctive terms:

> *Many mo* [heretics] I miȝt shew to make ȝou be war of hem, as of sum þat now holden plainli, and nat ȝit opinli, but priueli for drede, aȝens confessions and fastynges, aȝens worshippyng of ymages, and shortli, as men seien, aȝens al states and degrees and þe lawe and þe ordynaunce of hooli chirche. *But al þese I leeue*, because it nediþ nat greteli, for I trowe *heere bien rehersid þo þat bien most in our knowyng to be dred*. (my emphasis)

The syntax makes it clear that Lollards are "some" among the "many more" he *could* name, but that "it nediþ nat greteli" to do so. The ones he has already spoken of are the ones "most in our (present) knowledge to be feared." This passage comes from a paragraph at the end of chapter 12 that has no counterpart in Ruysbroeck's Dutch, and which makes clear that what the writer has been concerned to show is "hou manye perels and disceites fallen and haue falle *to goostli lyuers*" (145.15–16), that is, to contemplatives (for the benefit of the nuns of Barking especially, one assumes). It is also clear that he is conscious that he has emphasized the topic unusually: "Now longe I haue taried ȝou to shew ȝou in general wordis and in special hou sum men walken to ferre out fro oure louyng lord ie*s*u crist, . . . hou sum wiþ her errours bien taken wiþ wikked spirtis, and *hou sum in [disseit][86] after her desire han reuelacions*" (my emphasis). His target concern in this passage is what affects "goostli lyuers," including their "desire" for "reuelacions." This is not a description of Lollardy in any recognizable form, but of Free Spiritism (which he has just finished describing at length via his translation of Ruysbroeck) and of some dangers attached to revelatory theology.[87] Judging by the relative amounts of space he gives each topic (Lollardy gets a mere sentence; Free Spiritism two chapters), in his opinion, his women readers needed to have much more knowledge of the latter than of Lollardy.

We ought to take his judgement seriously.[88] While the rise of Lollardy may have been a factor in his choice of topic, it is evident that it is not at all his primary target.[89] Adding his use of these chapters against the Free Spirit from Ruysbroeck together with his use of chapters from the *Epistola solitarii* (on discerning true and false visions), we see that substantial portions of *The Chastising* are comprised of the latest material from the Continent on dangers of revelatory theology to which women contemplatives are particularly prone. The fact that *discretio* issues are also typical of New Devout thought is helpful here,[90] as is the fact that the *Chastising* author looks to have had access to the kind of material one finds in manuscripts transmitting defences of the Devout.[91]

The author demonstrates a much more lucid understanding of what he is writing about than he has been credited with: the rubric for chapter 11 advertises that some "wenen þat þei haue fredom of spirit, and þat þei bien ooned to god wiþoute any meane, wherfor þei seie þei bien bounde to no lawes of hooli chirche, and þei bien discharged of al maner wirchynges, and of al outward uertues" (ch. 11, 138). Now, this is a very clear understanding of Free Spirit thought, and, as the rubric does not appear in any of the Dutch manuscripts and is in the style of *The Chastising* text, it may be original to it.[92] He initially attacks the quietist element of Free Spirit thought: "What tyme a man haþ in suche ydelnes(s)e kyndeli reste . . ." as a life "ful of goostli errours and al maner wrecchidnesse. What such men bien, and how ȝe shullen knowe hem as bi þer opynyons, I shal shewe ȝou." The word "opinions," which he uses repeatedly in this section (not really justified by the Dutch, see 139.4), suggests that he is aware of language used in the persecution of heresy and is quite consciously adopting it in his English. That he is actually thinking of some quite recent recantation of heresy in England appears from this comment, explicitly amplified from the Dutch (141.20 ff): "Of þese men, whos lyueng and opynyons I haue rehersid, I hope to god þer bien ful fewe, *but sooþ it is, þer han bien suche but late in our daies, and aftir haue bien turned* and com aȝen into þe riȝt wei." In the Dutch, this runs merely as: "Ic hope men dierre menschen niet vele en vendet; maer diet sijn, dat sijn die quaetste ende die scadelijcste die leven, ende si moghen qualic emmermeer bekeren." (I hope that we will not find many of these people; but those who are such are the most evil and the most pernicious [people] alive, and they can henceforth scarcely be converted).[93]

Bazire and Colledge assumed that this interpolation in the Middle English (emphasized above) referred to the abjurations of John Ashton and Philip Repingdon in 1382,[94] and dated the text accordingly. But these were well-known Oxford Wycliffites and their cases were conducted largely with reference to the Blackfriars' articles of condemnation.[95] It is hard to imagine that a man so well informed and educated as the *Chastising* author, a man who could, as we have just seen, accurately characterize the key Wycliffite tenets in a single sentence, would imagine that Ashton and Repingdon confessed to the very different errors he himself calls "fredom of spirit." It seems more likely, then, that the allusion is to some well-publicized abjuration(s) of the 1380s that *did* involve Free Spirit thought. Since surviving records are incomplete, and not all bishops' registers have been thoroughly studied, we are in a poor position to guess at particular instances, but we know of at least one such case: William Ramsbury, tried in 1389 and accused of a remarkable number of Free Spirit tenets (see below).[96] Moreover, as Anne Hudson has shown in relation to Ramsbury's case, there are other instances of Free Spirit convictions in the trial records, including those of John Russell, a Minorite from Stamford, whose Franciscan identity suggests some similar associations with Free Spirit thought such as caused concern on the Continent.[97] Ramsbury's case, however, is very suggestive as the subject of the *Chastising* author's allusion for a variety of reasons, not least of which is that it was well enough known to have been mentioned by Walsingham in his chronicle, and because Ramsbury's penance involved extensive travel to a long list of towns and cities where he had preached, publicly recanting in each. Moreover, the strange mix of Free Spirit and Lollard ideas among Ramsbury's tenets would explain the juxtaposition of the two types of heresy in *The Chastising*, which, however, the *Chastising* author *himself* never conflates.

What is further significant about the text is that the *Chastising* author is tailoring his Ruysbroeck to suppress ideas he thinks inappropriate, apparently, for an audience of female contemplatives. In the passage just quoted, he completely suppresses Ruysbroeck's comment that such heretics "can scarcely be converted" (referring instead to a recent success in reconversion, "aftir haue bien turned"). He also suppresses the comment that: "And sometimes they are possessed by the fiend, and then they are so crafty that one can scarcely vanquish them by reason [Latin text reads: ut difficile possint ratione superari]. But by Holy Scripture and the teaching of Christ and our faith, we can well prove that they are deceived."[98] The suppression here suggests that proving heresy is wrong on the basis of scripture is not part of women's (or laity's) work. (Indeed, the Latin version perhaps underlines the clericalism of the task even more strongly.)[99] We will see a similar pattern of suppression in his treatment of the *Epistola*, and even more so in the free-standing *Epistola* translation created by someone else in the fifteenth century.[100]

Moreover, the *Chastising* author seems, in true late fourteenth-century Insular fashion, more able to tolerate or inadvertently encourage notions of Pelagianism among his audience. Ruysbroeck had described those who "are empty of all works, and [believe] that they are nothing other than an instrument with which God works what He wills. . . . And therefore, they say that they are in a pure passivity without working, and that the works which God performs through them are more noble, and merit more *than another can who performs his works himself* by the grace of God [quae Deus ipsis tanquam suis organis perficiat, praeclariora ac meriti maioris esse *quam cuiuslibet alterius, quae ipsemet in Dei gratia peregerit*]."[101] The *Chastising* author renders this as: "[they] wol bien clepid goddis pacientis. Þese men . . . stonden al ydel as an instrument of god, in a maner of abidynge and suffraunce, til god wil worche in hem . . . þei seien þat alle þe werkis þat god worchiþ bien more noble and *medeful þan any oþer men mowen disserue*" (differences emphasized). This would seem to be an overtly deliberate allusion to "salvation via works" theology (Pelagianism) on the part of the Middle English translator.[102] Nor is this the only place this issue appears.[103] His discomfort with the word "emptiness" is also interesting in terms of a policy of silent censorship — he persistently translates it as "ydelnesse" (e.g., 139.17), and one wonders why, unless it is because the idea of "works" is so central to the Insular psyche, or because the Middle English concept of "self-noughting" had had its own problematic connotations.[104] Here the *Chastising* author seems to operate with the kind of informed caution that J. P. H. Clark has noted in Walter Hilton (in fact, as Sargent has shown, *The Chastising* was ascribed to Hilton in manuscripts connected with Sheen or Syon, so contemporaries, at least, felt the similarities of thought strongly).[105]

The *Chastising* author is also acutely aware of Schism issues, as suggested by his insertion in one place of the word "cardinal," not in his source (and given English attitudes toward the papacy, not a very obvious thing to do). These heretics, he says, give "obedience to no man, neiþer to pope ne to cardinal, to þe bisshop ne to þe parishe preist" (140.21–22). If we imagine this being composed in the heady days of controversy at the *curia* leading up to the canonization of

Bridget (just prior to or after 1391), several of these references begin to make sense. So also does a date during or not long after the date of Ramsbury's abjuration in 1389. Especially interesting is his handling of Ruysbroeck's assertion:

> These people can hardly be recognized except by one who would be enlightened and would have the discernment of spirits and of divine truth [nisi quis illuminatius sit, et spirituum ac divinae veritatis discretionem obtinuerit]. For some of them are subtle [acuti et subtiles] and they can easily make and gloss over their contrariness. And they are so obstinate and have fixed themselves so firmly in self-will that they would rather die than to abandon any point they have seized upon.[106]

In translating this passage, the *Chastising* author (143.16 ff) suppresses the idea of someone who possesses the gift of discernment being able to adequately recognize such errors (again, this appears not to be seen as a woman's job), but reproduces quite exactly the point about such heretics being willing to suffer death for their beliefs.[107] This cannot be an allusion to cases of those who have already suffered the death penalty for Lollardy (passed in 1401), as some readers have assumed, since it is taken over from Ruysbroeck's Dutch ("dat si eer sterven souden eer si eenich poent lieten") via Grote's Latin (cf. *Brulocht*, 561). Furthermore, it seems likely that *The Chastising* (from external evidence) must have been in circulation before 1401.[108] But the passage is immediately followed by the "Now longe I haue taried ȝou . . ." paragraph on heretics quoted above, which is of course not in Ruysbroeck at all. This paragraph was certainly added to mention the Lollards explicitly, as an afterthought or adjunct. No other part of the *Chastising* author's translation is specific to Lollardy, but rather to the heresies he finds of most concern in contemplatives: reliance on revelatory theology, quietism, "self-noughting," extremist notions of union with the divine, and, last, instrumentality (which troubles him, as an Englishman, in relation to unresolved "Pelagianism" and which he censors even in Ruysbroeck).

The *Chastising* author was not alone in his concern: there is a surprising amount of evidence in the Middle English mystical literature of concern about the Free Spirit. As J. P. H. Clark's careful exposition has shown, both Hilton and the *Cloud* author were alert to the potential difficulties, not only of the homegrown "enthusiasm" of Rollean mysticism, but also of foreign imports.[109] Hilton refers quite explicitly to Free Spirit contemplatives ("eciam contemplatiuus qui spiritum libertatis adeptum se putat") and goes on to give a lucid account in this passage (from a letter to a priest) of Free Spirit disregard for the religious forms and rites of the church. Moreover, in the writing of *Scale 2* something, we know not what, aroused Hilton to attempt a "preventative theology" on questions of grace, quietism, pantheism, self-forgetfulness, antinomianism, and enthusiasm. Most especially, he notes with concern the view that one can reach a state of perfection in which one is "maad so freo & so heigh in grace & so brennynde in loue that he schal not synnen" (*Scale 2*, 26).[110] This most certainly suggests familiarity with *Ad nostrum* (whether directly or via a manual) which would be a natural source for a man of Hilton's education and agenda to consult. It also suggests familiarity with Ruysbroeck (whether in Grote's Latin translation or *The Chastising*). He is also concerned to counter the notion that contemplative experience can be unbroken.[111] Taken together, these points parallel the concerns in M. N.'s glosses to *The Mirror* in several respects, the focus of our next chapter. This suggests that in Carthusian circles — especially those geographically situated in the east of England, and thus close to Continental points — conscious efforts were being made to mount at least a preventative campaign. What, one wonders, prompted Hilton's informed campaign in *Scale 2*? Probably the same kind of concern that prompted others in Cambridge and the southeast, like Luis de Fontibus. His *Eight Chapters on Perfection*, which in manuscripts is ascribed to Hilton, makes explicit association of "liberty of spirit" with antinomianism in the Continental mode (this Spanish author was at Cambridge in 1383).[112]

Harder to get at, at least until more unedited bishop's registers are studied, is the Insular evidence of Free Spirit ideas (and practices) on sexual mores. Margery Kempe's response at York to what God's command in Genesis, "Crescite et multiplicamini" (increase and multiply) meant (*BMK*, 28.28–29.3), refers to the increase of virtues — an allegorical exegetical interpretation, surely, that she had been coached to give. This is the one clear instance we have of English mystical literature overlapping with ecclesiastical inquisition on this subject, a brief glimpse at the kind of link between lay female contemplative aspirations and heterodoxy that officials most feared. Sexual freedom is the essence of Free Spirit beliefs in the cases known so far from English bishop's registers. Others suspected of Lollardy must have been asked similar questions because as Anne Hudson has shown, Free Spirit beliefs turn up in the inquisition records of several Lollards, most interestingly, those of William Ramsbury, examined by the bishop of Salisbury in 1389. As Hudson notes, Wycliffism is not mentioned by name in the Ramsbury records, which is intriguing in itself because by 1389 the label was beginning to appear in ecclesiastical records.[113] But this may be because, I would suggest, his foreign heresy loomed larger in the minds of his inquisitors (who were in fact well informed in canon law)[114] as being more exotic and distinctive than the homegrown variety. At least six of the fifteen articles of which Ramsbury is accused can be associated with Free Spirit doctrine: four of these (numbers 9, 10, 13, and 14) deal with teachings on sexual freedom. These are variations on the central Free Spirit tenet condemned in *Ad nostrum*, as issued at the Council of Vienne (Article 7): "That sexual intercourse is not a sin when desired." Article 14 of the Ramsbury case in fact makes explicit reference to the Free Spirit interpretation of "crescite et multiplicamini" in its assertion that it is licit (even for priests) to know women of any status carnally, apparently justified because this is "*multiplicacionem generis humani.*"[115] Article 10 likewise deals with the priority of procreation over marital vows.[116] This is an area of sexual sin that one does not see explicit concern about in texts like *The Chastising*, Hilton, and male writers on mysticism (although *The Mirror* itself is full of subtle sexual imagery), but which recurs in inquisitorial records. One has to wonder whether this is the reason that Chaucer has the Wife of Bath so famously offer her own interpretation of the "increase and multiply" command—which accords much more closely with Free Spirit concerns than with rank and file Lollard ones.[117]

These sexual attitudes would have struck Insular authorities as highly unusual, but even more gripping for them was Ramsbury's account of his performance of a heterodox version of the mass, described in detail in the trial records. These explicitly record his silent contempt of the elevation, even though, it appears, he went through the motions so as not to arouse too many suspicions ("ad Leuacionem nichil dicendo"). The eucharist is a place where Free Spirit and Lollard thought both find themselves at odds with orthodox positions and are sometimes not easily (at least from trial records) distinguished, but the eighth article of *Ad nostrum* is very clear on this point. There the erring belief appears as "That there is no obligation to rise [non debent assurgere] before Christ's body in the elevation of the host, or to show him any other signs of respect [reverentiam exhibere], since this would entail descending from their heights of contemplation [a puritate et altitudina suae contemplationis], and so mean imperfection."[118] Was Ramsbury's mass indeed a "Lollard mass," or was it equally a Free Spirit mass? And might this explain why the trial records *nowhere* refer to Ramsbury as a Wycliffite?

Ramsbury was tried by Waltham, bishop of Salisbury, and his advisers (among whom is listed at least one doctor of civil law). It is significant, surely, that Waltham himself was particularly aware of Continental heresies, which we can deduce from the fact that in the same year *the same bishop* was allegedly confiscating texts by our four condemned Continental writers (Olivi, Rupescissa, Ockham, and William of St. Amour) as recorded in the *Opus arduum*.[119] What is especially interesting about this is that two of these authors share views implicated in Free Spiritism as well: Olivi and Ockham especially.[120] We also know that Waltham was especially interested in both civil and canon law from the remarkable library he assembled, the catalogue of which is extant. This interest he shares with Walter Hilton and with Bishop Trefnant, who prosecuted the maverick Walter Brut.[121] There were other cases of inquisitions of Free Spirit doctrine in England, some of which appear at later dates in the 1430s and 1440s,[122] that are relevant to Margery's questioning. What Hilton, Luis (both associated with Cambridge), and the *Chastising* author have in common are eastern locations, a feature they share with the Norwich and the Ely heretics.[123] Oxford has stolen the limelight as the centre of Lollardy in the minds of modern scholars, and Cambridge as a stronghold of anti-Wycliffism, but Cambridge also deserves a little more attention for its concern with Continental heresy—and geographically it had more reason to be. It was, along with Norwich itself, at the barricades.

Here, perhaps, is the reason Margery was so well schooled in responding to the test question for Free Spiritism. But Carthusian transmission provides us with an even more striking case than Margery's glancing encounter, and that is their dissemination of Porete's *Mirror* itself.

Chapter Seven

THE M. N. GLOSSES TO PORETE'S *MIRROR* AND THE QUESTION OF INSULAR SUSPICION

Having examined the evidence for awareness of heresy of the Free Spirit in England, I would like to turn now to the unusual set of glosses that "M. N." provided for his[1] Middle English translation of Marguerite Porete's *Le Mirouer des simples ames* when he undertook to revise his text in the wake of disconcerted reader response. *The Mirror* Porete herself names within the book as *Le Mirouer des simples ames aneanties qui seulement demourant en vouloir et en desir d'amour.*[2] This gives the work a marvelously complex title, translatable as *The Mirror of Simple Souls Who Are Annihilated and Remain Only in the Will and Desire of Love.*[3] Even the title, then, heralds a mystical treatise of dazzling and audacious (or better, pugnacious) originality. It was for this text that Porete was burned at the stake in Paris in 1310.

The tragic uniqueness of Porete's terrible fate as the only medieval woman known to have been executed for a book she authored should not blind us to the fact that she was writing from a largely orthodox, although specialized tradition of love mysticism. As Romana Guarnieri pointed out, Free Spirit speculative mysticism could trace its roots back to Cistercian sources that drew upon St. Bernard's concept of *gratia et libero arbitrio* and William of St. Thierry's *libertas spiritus* of the contemplative.[4] This is an important point because, as we will see, it explains why *The Mirror* could slip unobtrusively into transmission within orthodox contemplative circles, especially those steeped in Cistercian thought.

Guarnieri also cites an impressive list of other women associated with beguine groups and Cistercian spirituality, some of whom, like Porete, employ an *amour courtoise* mysticism: Beatrijs of Nazareth, Marie d'Oignies, Christina Mirabilis, Ivetta of Huy, Julianna of Mont Cornillon, Mechthild of Magdeburg, and Hadewijch of Antwerp.[5] What drove Porete to the stake—while someone like Mechthild, for instance, working in largely the same tradition and also in a controversial vein was able to retire to the safety of the convent at Helfta and continue writing—is complex.[6] But one important factor is timing: Mechthild lived a generation earlier, before the onset of the Clementine and Johannine papacies, during which both the beguine movement and speculative theological opinion became increasingly dangerous and even male writers as different as Ockham and Olivi came under attack. Nor were these developments in the scholastic world irrelevant to issues of freedom of expression in female mysticism. First, Godfrey of Fontaines, an influential writer on issues of intellectual freedom in the medieval university, provided a letter of approval for Porete's work. This in itself suggests that either she or her supporters had access to theologians in distinguished circles of academia. Second, there is, I would suggest, likely a distinctive strand of Olivian thought in Porete's book, and some historical evidence pointing in that direction at the time of her arrest with Guiard de Cressonessart, as we saw in chapter 2.[7]

Guiard, who had tried to intervene on Porete's behalf, was apparently knowledgeable in radical Apocalypse commentaries, and especially, the inquisitorial record suggests, those associated with the south of France, prime Olivian cult territory. Guiard believed himself to be the angel sent to defend the "Church of Philadelphia" and the life of apostolic poverty he and his followers led, clothed in special habits which from the description sound part Franciscan and part Beghard. This tendency to bring aspects of Apocalypse exegesis to life in a manner similar to radical Olivian sectarianism suggests why, as Verdeyen pointed out, the inquisitor focused closely on probable connections between Porete's "Holy Church the Less" and Guiard's Franciscan Spiritual leanings.[8] This is not the place to explore the question of Olivian influence on Porete, but a few quick examples will at least help to give a sense of the scope of this rich possibility. The parallel is evident most obviously in fundamentals like Porete's daring two churches, so much like Olivi's *ecclesia carnalis* and *ecclesia spiritualis,* inspired by the "active" church in the Joachite Status prefigured by Peter, and the subsequent "spiritual" church in the Status prefigured by John.

Olivi's Matthew *Postilla* has, thanks to the Sermon on the Mount, an outstandingly original description of contemplative and visionary experience—much of it, Olivi obliquely hints, his own.[9] In a fertile mix of Pseudo-Dionysian and Joachite tradition, he associates Peter with the active phase of the church in the Second Status and John with the contemplative Third Status,[10] but also with female contemplatives, Mary Magdalene, and especially Rachel, whose death in childbirth with Benjamin is a symbol of ecstasy in its final stage.[11] His description of contemplation—which for Olivi comes with the freedom that only perfect disregard for all earthly things can bring—in some respects defies translation. For him the final two beatitudes lead the soul towards

> complete abstraction [abstractio] from any thought [ab omni cogitatu] or image impeding [impediente] pure and simple contemplation of God; the last is truly the *summa tranquilitas seu summum silentium* of any activity hindering [impedientium] that sweetest intoxication and most quiet rest [requies] and savour [saporatio], and yet most God-like *transformation of the mind into God [deiformissima transformatio mentis in Deum]* called by the apostle the unity of spirit [*unitas spiritus].*[12]

John XXII had objected to the sensual qualities of Olivi's description of the Third Status because of its mediation-less-ness, and here, too, we see that quality. If Augustine's third level of vision can be sensual, here it is. Such glimpses of writing remind us strongly of Porete's strange combination of transformative or unitive annihilation and love.[13] Reading Olivi himself and then recalling Guiard's striking conjunction of heresy of the Free Spirit with Franciscan Joachimism, we see suddenly why the Council of Vienne was treating both groups at the same time—and why the modern scholarly distinction between "Beguins" (followers of Olivi) and "Beguines" (northern women's movements) tends sometimes to collapse.[14]

Certainly *The Mirror* itself shows that Porete, like Bloemardinne, whom we met in relation to Ruysbroeck's attack on Free Spiritism, had a grasp of at least the basics of scholastic thought.[15] How she came by this we do not know, other than to point to the evidence discussed in the previous chapter, and alluded to with hostility in *Cum de quibisdam mulieribus,* that certain clergy were actively engaged in teaching Beguines theology and disputation. *The Mirror* itself is a dialogue (dialogus), or more often "trialogue" (trialogus), in which, although many minor allegorical characters come and go with dream-visionlike suddenness, most often three characters dominate: Love (Amour) as the teaching voice, Reason (Raison) the "dotede daffe" (as Langland's Holy Church would say [C.I.138]) who needs to be taught, and the Soul (Ame), the narratorial or witnessing voice (in the evangelical sense of that word) to how much Love has done for her. Porete's brilliant and unusual move in casting *Reason* as the bumbling and benighted pupil immediately destabilizes all ordinary readerly assumptions, as logic and traditional learning of any sort repeatedly prove useless in mastering the perspective necessary to an "annihilated soul." In both literary and theological terms it is a revolutionary text, which in England at least anticipates—perhaps even impacted?—possibly two, and maybe even three, very important vernacular writers: Langland, Julian, and the *Pearl* poet. This is too large a problem for the present study to embark upon, but we will return to the question of this possible, distinguished literary audience at the end of this chapter, after we examine what evidence there is that *The Mirror* was regarded as a suspect text, especially in England—and the one Middle English reader who has left concrete evidence of both his fascinations and fears, its translator and glossator, M. N.

Internal and External Evidence

There is no indication that anyone in England, including M. N., knew that *The Mirror* was written by Marguerite Porete, or that it was an officially condemned book, or that its author had paid for it with her life. But even though *The Mirror* traveled largely incognito in England, there is both internal and external evidence that the book aroused suspicion. We do not really know who M. N. was. One theory makes him Michael of Northburgh, bishop of London (1354–61), but what evidence we have of the transmission of the Middle English translation points to the likelihood that he (or a later redactor) was a Carthusian working sometime in the Ricardian or early Lancastrian period.[16] The fact that early in the sixteenth century another Carthusian, Richard Methley, would translate the book into Latin and again provide it with a set of "normalizing" glosses, suggests that both found the text a stimulating challenge to contemplative life, and yet worrying in an unglossed form.[17] Just as clearly the Ricardian or early Lancastrian translation was intended not, like its Insular Latin successor, simply for clerical use.

Exactly what audience M. N.'s Middle English text initially reached is an important question because M. N. explicitly tells us that he has returned to the translation in response to explicitly expressed reader concern. We know that Carthusians did loan manuscripts out for lay use, and for lay female use, too.[18] And *The Mirror* is a book which, even in a transmission entirely innocent of its tragic and horrific history, nonetheless attracted censorship or suspicion or caveats repeatedly. For instance, in a fifteenth-century Bodleian Library copy of the Latin translation (a copy in England at least by 1637), the text is completely and deliberately torn out, the first page alone surviving because a text by Lulle was written on the recto.[19] (See figure 17.) A late fourteenth-century Vatican copy of the Latin *Mirror* is entitled "Incipt liber *speculatissimus*" (!).[20] A 1521 copy of the Latin has a note saying that the writer does not believe the text is approvable for printing (Credo quod non probaretur hic libellus pro typo) because it was inappropriate for the more simple (pro simplicioribus) or because it was "quasi scandalosus."[21] Yet another Vatican copy of the Latin text, c. 1437, survives with thirty articles presented as errors drawn from the book and followed by a refutation of them.[22] The book was also the subject of famous attacks in the fifteenth century, like Gerson's, in which he named the author "Marie of Valenciennes," calling *The Mirror* a book "of incredible subtlety."[23] There is also the re-condemnation at the Council of Basel where it becomes fodder for discrediting a pope.[24] Most intriguing in Insular terms is the sixteenth-century note in the Pembroke copy of Methley's Latin translation pointing to *Ad nostrum*: the note directs the reader explicitly to the section in the *Clementines* on the Beghards, especially the chapter *Ad nostrum* ("De beguardis In clementinis de Religiosis decretalibus. capitulum Ad nostrum" [fol. 40v]), which is right on the mark. (*Ad nostrum* dealt with doctrinal error and was codified with heresy legislation, widely known given its context in the *Clementines*.)[25]

Singly, any one of these responses might be dismissed as lucky hits. Together they are hard to ignore. This was a book under suspicion that, even in *utter anonymity*, recreated new suspicions. Two of the instances cited above (the first and the last) appear in manuscripts of English provenance, and yet in England *The Mirror* also traveled, safeguarded by M. N.'s glosses, with Middle English texts of unimpeachable orthodoxy written by and for women. Among them was the caveat-laden *Chastising* itself and, in the Amherst manuscript, British Library, Additional 37790, Julian's own *Revelation* (Short Text) and the prayers of Bridget—here, as elsewhere, in manuscripts created *after* Arundel's Constitutions. This indicates, first of all, the safety of Carthusian transmission among

17. Oxford, Bodleian Library, MS Laud Lat. 46, fols. 70v (old foliation 66v)–71r (96r), showing stubs of thirty leaves (the old foliation reads "96" in top right hand corner) that once contained a complete Latin text of Margaret Porete's *Mirror of Simple Souls*. The scribe, significantly, gives an alternative title of "Margarita" to the *Mirror*: "Incipit liber qui appellatur speculum animarum simplicium, Alias vocatur Margarita." The text is copied alongside a text by Raymond Lulle, composed about the time Porete composed the *Mirror*. The Lulle text ends on fol. 70r, a circumstance to which we owe the preservation of the first page of the *Mirror* on 70v. The manuscript, which also contains a text by Angela of Foligno, was written in Germany in the fifteenth century, but when it came to England is unknown. It was in Archbishop of Canterbury William Laud's collection by the time it came to the Bodleian in 1637. Reproduced by permission of the Bodleian Library, University of Oxford.

manuscripts containing Hilton's *Scale* and *The Chastising*, texts meant to temper, not inflame. It also points to the plausibility of the shield of revelatory theology, evidence of which we have seen elsewhere in this book. And perhaps most interestingly it also underscores the remarkable lack of impact of Arundel's 1409 Constitutions in the monastic world—and the even more remarkable lack of impact on the "semi-religious" contemplative world and its *lay* outreach.[26] Together, these account for a large amount of English readership.

To turn now to internal evidence of a history of suspicion, there are three letters of approval attached to *The Mirror* in its Middle English and Latin versions. One is by the well-known Paris theologian Godfrey of Fontaines; one by a "Ion of Querayn," "a Franciscan of great name" (frater minor magni nominis [405.9]), and one by a Cistercian (Franco de Villariis), cantor of the abbey of Villiers.[27] So far as we know, these letters were requested as a late and ill-fated attempt on Porete's part to turn the tide running against her. But her choices were informed and intelligent. In choosing a Franciscan and a Cistercian Porete had representatives of the two types of clergy arguably most sympathetic to women's ministry and mysticism (respectively); in choosing a university theologian she had a champion from the one group capable of challenging an episcopally commissioned inquisition with credibility. The Cistercians' long-standing "love affair" with women's mysticism is well attested, and at Villiers itself, it should be pointed out, there had been a fascination with women's mysticism going back to Guibert of Gembloux's adulation of Hildegard.[28] Franco de Villariis's letter uses the formal language of visionary *probatio* and simply says that *The Mirror* "probaret bene per Scripturas" and that all contained in it is truthful. The concern here is simply with a traditional monastic testing of the spirits, as one might expect from a Cistercian. In contrast, the Franciscan's *approbatio* actually uses the language of liberty of spirit ("hem þat ben made free of God"), blending it with language that hints vaguely of Joachite Franciscan Spiritualism. This is most evident in the Middle English version: phrases like "a frere menour of greet name of *liif of perfecioun*" (404.8–9) or "He seide soþeli, þat þis booke *is maad by þe Holli Goost*" (404.14) do not, by themselves, prove Olivian or Joachite tendencies, but they lean intriguingly in that direction.[29] Given that one of the questions examined at the Council of Vienne in 1311, a year after Porete's death, was whether Free Spirit doctrines had infiltrated the Franciscan Spirituals, this letter is even more intriguing. (The council was simultaneously examining Olivi's doctrines.)[30] The third letter, by Godfrey of Fontaines, an eminent university theologian of his day, also represents a group some of whose members did impact upon the beguine movement. Porete was not alone among Beguines in her knowledge of scholastic commonplaces and ideas. The Council of Vienne, as we have seen, was concerned that: "It has been repeatedly and reliably reported to us that some of [these women], as if possessed with madness, dispute and preach about the Highest Trinity and divine essence."[31] Godfrey's *approbatio* of *The Mirror* asserts, however, that he could find nothing amiss in the book (nihil sinistrum de libro dixit [407.25]), but (like the Franciscan, John of Querayn) recommends that not many should see it. His concern is that too many might try to aspire to the life it describes and never be able to attain that goal (aspirando ad istam ad quam forte numquam peruenirent [407.28–29]). In the Middle English translation the passage runs:

> And he blamede it not. . . . But . . . he coun*n*sailide not þat fele schulden se it, and for þis cause: for þei my3ten leue her owen werkynge and folewe þis clepynge, to þe whiche þei schulden neuere come; and so þei my3ten deceyue hemsilf, for it is ymaad of a spirit so strong and so kuttynge, þat þer ben but fewe suche or noone. . . . (Doiron, 250)

The assessment is an astute one, especially the characterization of "the spirit" that created the book as "so forceful and so penetrating" (so strong and so kuttynge).[32] Godfrey's view seems to be that the book is not dangerous to doctrine so much as to *vocation*—that many might founder trying to live up to what they had no capacity to achieve. He represents the intellectual world of theological speculation, and we need to know much more than we do about how this world interacted with non-cloistered religious women.[33] But we do know that Godfrey himself cared about intellectual freedom (at least as it was conceived in the medieval university) and the scholastic right to conduct speculative theology.[34]

The language of *probatio* runs right through Porete's Prologue, both in the letters of approbation and in her concluding assertion: "For þe pees of auditoures was þis *preued*." This statement tells us a great deal: first, that her "implied readers" were hearers—and one of the causes for alarm on the part of the Council of Vienne legislators was doubtless the spectre of semi-religious or lay gatherings at which ideas like this would be heard. (Heard, that is, perhaps by the illiterate and especially among unregulated beguine communities.) Second, it tells us that Porete herself understood the concept: in going to these three clerics for written approval Porete was in essence submitting her work for *probatio*, which, as Colledge suggested years ago in relation to St. Bridget, was a standard ecclesiastical procedure for the testing of revelatory authenticity.[35] What is telling, however—and this is likely why it did not prove effective in protecting her from execution—is that she was seen to be controlling the outcome herself by choosing empathetic authorities.

This, then, is the primary *internal* evidence that would have confronted M. N. that the book had come under suspicion. The significant fact is that the Middle English version of the letters of approbation is the fullest and most informative extant, maintaining, I would suggest, much better than the Latin does, the distinctive styles of the different clerics.[36] This means that M. N.'s French exemplar must have been closer to the original than the exemplar used by the first Latin translator. Romana Guarnieri suggested that a copy of the French text may have reached England as early as 1327, but if so, how many copies were disseminated from it or parallel with it, we do not know.[37] In any case it is impressive that M. N.'s translation contained the letters even though the extant French version does not, and that he obviously translated them with the same painstaking faithfulness he lavished on Porete's own text.

M. N.'s own Prologue to the second version tells us that he is undertaking a revision of his translation because readers have objected to or misunderstood passages in his first version:

> But now I am stired to laboure it aȝen newe, for *bicause I am enfourmed þat some wordis þerof haue be mystake*. Þerfore if God wole, I schal declare þo wordis more openli; for þouȝ loue declair þo poyntes in þe same booke, it is but schortli spoken, and *may be taken oþirwise þan it is iment* of hem þat reden it sodeynli and taken no ferþir hede. Þerfore suche wordis to be twies iopened . . . it schal þe more profite to þe auditoures.[38] But boþe þe firste tyme and now I haue greet drede to do it, for þe boke is of hiȝe diuine maters and of hiȝe goostli felynges, & kernyngli [pithily] and ful mystili it is spoken. (emphasis added)

The crucial word here, "mystake," can mean both misunderstood and ill-received, and so there is an ambiguity—one is tempted to say a *functional ambiguity*—that is, one that M. N. may have intended.[39] The debate about exactly what M. N.'s informants motivated him to do in revision and why ranges from the view put forward by Colledge and Guarnieri (that M. N.'s glosses arose from his having been made aware of the now lost list of condemned propositions from the Paris process[40] against Porete) to the view more recently put forward by Watson (that the "errors" M. N. was seeking to correct were simply textual obscurities). Watson believes, moreover, that M. N. was operating in Insular ignorance of any inquisitional issues that Free Spirit thought raised abroad. As Watson writes:

> Far from testifying to the cosmopolitan nature of English religious writers and readers, and their wide knowledge of the controversies surrounding mystical writing on the continent, the *Mirror* evokes an Insular environment which was still firmly local, even parochial, and to which news of such controversies had never penetrated; one in which the work could be read without any of the aura of fear and suspicion with which Colledge and Guarnieri try to surround it.[41]

I would like to propose a *via media* between these two opposing positions and suggest that if we contextualize M. N.'s glosses in relation to other kinds of editorial decisions he is making, and to both Carthusian manuscript transmission and English censorship history, we are in a better position to see what kinds of concerns *actually* impacted on an English translator of speculative mysticism working in the Ricardian period.

What needs to be said at the outset is that—no matter what M. N. knew or did not know—he added glosses (and also emended) Porete's text *most often* at key points of doctrinal pressure associated with Free Spiritism. This cannot be an accident. Those few glosses that do not pertain to Free Spirit discrepancies with orthodoxy are consistent in addressing other sensitive topics, notably, Insular preoccupations with issues such as "self-noughting" and Pelagianism. The most accessible and standard source of information (or "information") about Free Spiritism in any quarter of late medieval Christendom would have been in the *Clementines*, notably in the Council of Vienne's *Ad nostrum*, or in manuals for clergy citing them.[42] *Ad nostrum*, for which scholars believe Porete's book was likely a partial source, condemns as heretical eight extreme propositions it claims are held by Free Spirit adherents. Six of the propositions are somehow paralleled in passages M. N. found it necessary to gloss:

(1) that a man in this life can attain to such perfection that he is incapable of sinning or surpassing his present degree of grace;

(2) that he no longer needs to fast or pray because he has gained such control over the senses that he can allow them complete freedom;

(3) that he is free from all obedience to the church;

(4) that the free in spirit can obtain full blessedness in this life;

(5) that the need for virtuous actions belongs to the imperfect man only;

(6) that there is no obligation to rise before Christ's body at the elevation of the host, or to show him any other signs of respect, since this would entail descending from the heights of contemplation.[43]

Whether M. N. or someone advising him consulted these directly we do not know. It would have been an easy matter to do so in any decent or even relatively modest English ecclesiastical library. The real question is: did M. N. or one of his "informants" suspect official heresy *enough* to have gone to such a source? Or did his information come from — as I will suggest — a less legally freighted source? We will likely never know for sure, but that he did come to have information that something was worrying is certain. Not only are the positioning and content of the glosses persistently doctrinal in concern (and this is highly unusual in itself among medieval English annotators),[44] there is a level of anxiety in the language of some of the glosses that concern over merely philological obscurities would hardly elicit.

To begin with, there is a kind of defensiveness about the rhetoric of M. N.'s own Prologue, which intervenes between the reader and Porete's Prologue itself.[45] In a bold borrowing from the Psalms (the very metaphor, as we saw in chapter 1, that upset John XXII in Olivi's use of it) for tactile experiencing of the gifts of the Holy Spirit,[46] he urges the reader to "taste and see" (Gustate et uidete) *before* judging the book, because only a soul "touched wiþ grace" will be "ioyeful to heere and to rede of al þing þat perteneþ to þese *hiȝe felinges.*" The present book, then, he deftly suggests, is a manual for spiritual connoisseurs and the divinely inspired:

> Therfore to þese soules þat ben disposed to þese hiȝe felynges, *loue haþ made of him þis boke* in fulfillynge of her desire, and often he leieþ þe note and þe kernel wiþinne þe schell vnbroke. Þis is to seie . . . [p]riueli hid vndir derk spech.

The subtext here is that those who cannot appreciate the difficulty of this text are simply not among those souls capable of "þese hiȝe felynges." As such M. N.'s Prologue reinscribes, in subtler and politer form, the message of the poem that accompanies the French text, although not the translations:

Theologiens ne aultres clers,
Point n'en aurez l'entendement
Tant aiez les engins clers . . .
. . . mettez toutes vos fiances
En celles qui sont donnees
D'Amour, par Foy enluminees. . . .
    (Guarnieri and Verdeyan, 8.7–10, 24–26)

Theologians and other clerks,
You will not have the intellect for [this book],
No matter how brilliant your abilities . . .
. . . [P]lace all your fidelity
In those things which are given
By Love, illuminated by Faith.[47]

M. N.'s claim that the book comes of divine revelation, "loue haþ made of him þis boke," also recasts Porete's own claim that "I, creature ymaad of the maker, *bi me þe maker haþ maad of him þis booke*" (I.249.14) into a slightly less sensational form. This claim, which comes from Porete's introduction to the three letters of approval that do not survive in the French manuscript, echoes chapter 119's claim that "Amour l'a fait escrire par humaine science" (Guarnieri and Verdeyen, 334.23–24). Nonetheless, not only here, but in the glosses, as apologist and interpreter, M. N. asserts that what we are witnessing is revelatory theology at work. What the book records, he insists, are moments of such sublime religious experience as to break down most normative guidelines to faith and doctrine. These rhetorical strategies, and the anxiety he displays in some of the glosses, suggest that he was not relaxed about the book's more extreme doctrinal positions. Nor was he entirely ignorant of the perils: too many of the glosses appear at points almost exactly corresponding to Ruysbroeck's critique of Free Spirit thought as rendered in *The Chastising*.

The *Mirror* was traveling in Carthusian circles, where, we know for certain, awareness of Free Spirit concerns in relation to women's mysticism was going the rounds in the Ricardian period in, first, Grote's Latin translation of Ruysbroeck (hot off the press from *Devotio Moderna* territory where women's activities were currently coming under suspicion), and second, *The Chastising* itself. It seems entirely possible that, although M. N. knew neither when he first did the translation, one or more of his Carthusian colleagues or contacts did and brought this to bear on their reading of the new translation. (As we will see in the next chapter, it was likely contact with *The Chastising* that motivated an even more famous writer than M. N. to some serious revisions: Julian of Norwich probably encountered it between writing her Short and Long Texts, though she may have known *The Mirror* itself early on.) What is especially suggestive about Carthusian transmission is that it gives two routes (aside from the standard decretal manuals)—Grote and *The Chastising*—by which English readers on the contemplative life could come in contact with *Ruysbroeck's own critique of The Mirror.*[48] Any reader of even average alertness who knew either Grote or *The Chastising* would recognize the parallels, but because Ruysbroeck never named his source as *The Mirror* or mentioned Porete or her fate, there would be no cause for full-scale alarm about the new English translation. Instead, there would be concern to minimize the parallels and to be sure that passages would not be *"taken opirwise pan it is iment"*—a wording M. N. uses explicitly in the glosses when doctrinal accuracy is at stake. To achieve this M. N. chose a tried and true method: he set about making revisions to "repoint" the text through minor (and sometimes silent) changes in wording and the addition of annotations discreetly marked off, with every appearance of scholarliness, from the authorial text. The Carthusians, as we can see in relation to the Kempe manuscript, were adept at reining in maverick enthusiasms of future readers through annotation and "benign" censorship (that is, minor deletion and editing).[49] A further historical clue that supports the evidence for this kind of informed English awareness in educated contemplative circles is that M. N.'s glosses, as J. H. P. Clark has shown, are very like Hilton's concerns about "Liberty of Spirit" in the doctrinal issues they target.[50] This suggests that Hilton and M. N. shared the same source: likely Ruysbroeck, whether in Grote's Latin or *The Chastising*'s Middle English.

The Chastising's Translation of Ruysbroeck's *Spiritual Espousals* and the M.N. Glosses

If M. N. had had either Grote's Latin translation of Ruysbroeck or *The Chastising*'s Middle English translation of Grote's Ruysbroeck brought to his attention, what would we expect to see in the glosses? In fact, exactly what we do see. Twelve of M. N.'s fifteen glosses can be closely paralleled in Ruysbroeck, either in Grote's Latin translation or in *The Chastising*'s Middle English version (the latter will be cited here for comparison since sometimes even the wording coincides with M. N.'s). I do not mean to imply that M. N. was following Ruysbroeck in either language slavishly, especially because in some of the glosses he has his own agenda. But on the whole there is too much overlap to be coincidental. Whether the co-existing parallels with *Ad nostrum* came from M. N.'s having been made aware of it or came simply at second hand via Ruysbroeck in either language is less certain, but several of the glosses contain concerns that run parallel to *Ad nostrum* as well. It is the Ruysbroeck connection, however, I wish to highlight here because I think it represents, especially via *The Chastising*, a plausible source of accurate information in M. N.'s milieu.[51] Let us have a look at some of the parallels between the points at which M. N.'s glosses appear and *The Chastising*. In what follows I will cite five sample passages from *The Mirror* which M. N. glosses, then the corresponding discussion in *The Chastising*, and finally M. N.'s attempt to rectify or contain the problem. Parallels with *Ad nostrum* will appear in parentheses for comparison where they arise.

(1) M. N.'s second gloss appears where Reason is shocked because the Soul[52] takes leave of the virtues and says:

Uertues, I take leeue of ȝou for euermore [je prens congé de vous a tousjours]. Now schal myn herte be more fre . . . ȝoure seruyse is to *trauelous*. . . . It is meruaile þat I am ascapid wiþ þe liif. But now I make no forse, siþen it is þus þat I am departed out from ȝoure daungers . . . and þerfore in pees I dwelle. (Doiron, 254.27–255.7; Guarnieri, 524.37–525.4)

The Chastising similarly translating Ruysbroeck had taken up this theme at some length, warning of "fredom of spirit" heretics who "say þat a man nediþ more to *traueile* for to be discharged of uertues þan for to gete hem" (140.18–19).[53] (Cf. article 6 of *Ad nostrum*, "That the need for virtuous actions belongs to the imperfect man only" [Quod se in actibus exercere virtutum est hominis imperfecti].)[54]

M. N. comes to the rescue in this passage with a lengthy gloss explaining that it is to be understood "goostli" (the word that is used by a later Carthusian annotator to "rescue" some of Kempe's more extreme enthusiasms). M. N. saves the day by asserting that when a soul is so spiritually advanced, "Þanne is sche mastresse and lady ouer þe uertues"—which neatly (and deliberately?) sidesteps the real problem.

(2) M. N.'s fourth gloss appears where Porete has Love startle Reason again by saying that such a soul gives to Nature all he asks. Thus she

ne desireþ dispite ne pouert ne tribulacion ne diseese ne masses ne sermons ne fastynge ne orisons, and sche ʒiueþ to nature al þat he askiþ *wiþoute grucchynge of consience* [donne a Nature tout ce qu'il luy fault, sans remors de conscience]. (Doiron, 258.12–15; Guarnieri, 527, 17–19)

The Chastising's rendition of Ruysbroeck had warned that "fredom of spirit" heretics believe "þat þei bien enhaunsid bi perfeccion aboue al obseruances of hooli chirrche" (139.14–15); "Of fastyng þei take noon heede, ne of festis of hooli chirche, ne of þe ordynaunce ne obseruance of hooli chirche . . . for in al þing þei lyuen *wiþout doome of consience*" (141.16–19). (Cf. article 2 of *Ad nostrum*, "That he no longer needs to fast or pray for he has gained such control over the senses that he can allow them complete freedom" [quia tunc sensualitas est ita perfecte . . . quod homo potest libere corpore concedere quidquid placet].)

M. N.'s rescue operation in this case is a complex one. His gloss here takes brilliant refuge in semi-Pelagianism, which in fact—and this an interesting point because it explains some of the English fascination with Porete—made him disposed to fixate on her own extreme stance on instrumentality. So in this gloss he wants to have his cake and eat it too. The soul, he says, after years of fasting and other practices, realizes "þat þe werk of loue is more worþ and drawiþ more to þe unyon in God þan doiþ hir owen werk." Still—and here is the rescue operation—the soul continues "bi usage of good custom" to perform these "outward werkis. But sche doiþ it *wiþoute desire* . . . [because she is] so unyed to loue, þat it is *loue þat doiþ it,* and þus sche suffriþ loue to werke in hir." Having thus transformed Porete's quietism into semi-Pelagianism, M. N. is nonetheless still left with fires to put out. He is overtly anxious about the appearance of outright rejection of church practices and fleshly continence.[55] Taking the strategy that a good offence is the best defence, he accuses any reader who would think such things of being "blynde" and later "fleischli," and once again deflects attention away from the literal to the safe haven of the "goostli": "Perfore . . . þat þese soules ne desiren masses, ne sermons, fastinges ne orisons, it schulde *not be so ytake* that þei shulde leeui it vndoon. *He were to blynde þat wolde take it in þat wise;* but *alle such wordis in þis booke moste be take goostli and diuineli.*" This is strong rhetoric, but it is still not enough and he insists adamantly that the "sche ʒiueþ to nature al his asking" is on no account open to literal interpretation: "*God forbeede þat eny be so fleischli* to þenke þat it schulde mene to ʒiue to nature eny lust þat drawiþ to fleischli synne, for God knowiþ wel it is not so ymened."[56] The tone of such glosses is unarguably defensive and, especially by English annotating standards, emotional.[57] And this in itself bespeaks uneasiness. What he claims to be doing is teaching reading: "alle such wordis in þis booke *moste* be take goostli," but the use of the imperative here is more than hortatory.

(3) M. N.'s seventh gloss appears where Love is saying that "þis nouȝted soule" (262.32) no longer knows how to do good works, nor needs to because "sche haþ ynouz of feiþ wiþouten werke to bileeue [sans oeuvrer de croire]. . . . [And so Love] sauiþ hir bi feiþ wiþouten werke, for feiþ surmounteþ al werke."[58] *The Chastising* similarly translates at length Ruysbroeck's attack on passivity (which the author calls "ydelnesse" of self-appointed "goddis paciencis"), stressing that "hem þenkeþ þat þer ydelnesse and her kyndli reste is so hiȝ of perfeccion and so greete þat þei shuld nat be lette wiþ no maner worchynge."[59] The passage was either corrupt in M. N.'s exemplar, as Sargent suggested, or it distressed M. N. because not only does he suppress (or miss out) key words from the line: "et sans faille aussi elle est assez *excusee et exoniee*, sans oeuvrer,"[60] that is, that the Soul is excused and exonerated merely for believing without good works. But he also adds a saving gloss to say that it is not that these souls stop doing good works "for euermore," rather that they "leuen not ne tristen not to her owen werkis, but al in Goddis goodnesse" (262.4–12). Usually he regards Porete's anti-Pelagianism as a good corrective to the well-known English penchant for "semi-Pelagianism," but this is too much of a good thing, even for M. N.

(4) M. N.'s tenth gloss appears where Love says that the soul will do nothing "aȝens þe parfite pees of hir spirite [contre la parfaicte paix de son esperit]" (Doiron, 279.5; Guarnieri, 545.19). She gives the example of the innocent child who will neither do anything nor allow anything to be done, "for hiȝ or for lowe, but if it plese him." At this point Reason acquiesces meekly, but this disturbed the Latin translator, because he suppressed it.[61] This kind of quietism disturbed Ruysbroeck, too, and in *The Chastising* translation we find:

> Þerfor freeli and boldeli hem þenkeþ þei mowen doo what bodili kynde desiriþ, *for þei bien comen to innocencie*, and subget to no lawe. If her bodili kynde . . . be stired to any lust or likyng so ferforþ þat þe spirit haþ nat his freedom, ne stondiþ nat in reste for þe tyme, þan þei wol fulfille þe wil of þe kynde, þat her ydelnesse *ne reste of þe spirit be nat lette*. (141.10–17)

M. N. rescues the passage ingeniously by putting the best face on Porete's quietism as simply waiting upon the Lord, "So þei stonden for to attende and wait to folewe þe lordis werk" (279.19–20). (We are reminded forcibly of Julian's Lord and Servant parable here, especially in M. N.'s Middle English.) In so doing he completely ignores the fact that the passage is about freedom of spirit in the most literal sense. This is the kind of gloss that provoked Nicholas Watson to comment that M. N. shares astonishingly little of Porete's spirituality, but given indications elsewhere to the contrary, I think we must assume rather that M. N. is deliberately providing a protective coating for those who might find this passage hard to stomach.

(5) M. N.'s fifteenth gloss appears where the annihilated Soul asserts that she cannot sin. Porete's careful qualifier "if my wille wole it not" is easily overlooked. The Soul continues: "For no more þan God may synne þat may not wille it, no more may I synne [je puis ne pecher] if my wille wole it not, such fredom haþ þe su*mm*e of me of his pure bounte bi loue yȝouen me" (Doiron, 329.8–10; Guarnieri, 599.19–21). Similarly, *The Chastising* had described the "fredom of spirit" belief "þat þei mowe no more synne, in as moche as to her owne siȝt þei lyuen wiþouten wil, and þat þei haue god þeir spirit, and þat þei be ooned to god" (141.6–10). (Cf. article 1 of *Ad nostrum*: "That a man in this life can attain to such perfection that he is incapable of sinning. . . .")

M. N.'s response here is to stress that it is the goodness of God that is at work in the Soul *whenever* it is unable to will sin (again, we are reminded forcibly of Julian). As in so many of his glosses, his working assumption is that all these radical claims of Porete's mysticism are true *for the moment* of divine inspiration, but no more—at least this is the strategy by which he reclaims each of them to orthodoxy.

There are other glossed passages that can be paralleled in *The Chastising*, but these are enough, I believe, to give a sense of how closely attuned the glosses are to the Middle English version of Ruysbroeck. Given that *The Chastising* itself was likely authored by a Carthusian, and given that in one manuscript, Bodley 505 (which, like all Middle English *Mirror* manuscripts, is of Carthusian origin), *The Chastising* and *The Mirror* appear together, it seems entirely likely that the worries that prompted M. N.'s informants arose from just this kind of conjunction. The transmission of Grote's Ruysbroeck and also of Hilton within the Carthusian order are further possible points of contact. All three together point to a milieu much more informed than has hitherto been thought, yet not dogmatically or legalistically rigid. And this fits M. N.'s profile nicely.

M.N., Revelatory Theology, and Safe Reading: Carthusian Spirituality and the Toleration of "Left-Wing Orthodoxy"

Did M. N. himself believe that these glosses were convincing? What is most interesting is to note the places where M. N. seems most panicked and, by contrast, the places we would expect him to be panicked but where no gloss appears. There are also passages he silently suppresses or alters; there are the places he silently adds to the dialogue; there are the places where he is bold enough to retain sections the Latin editor does not. By examining some of these we can perhaps come closer to understanding his sympathies and his motivations — and, I think we will find that these may surprise us. What we find at the end of the day is that an orthodoxy/heterodoxy binary is simply not sophisticated enough to understand Middle English reception of this text. I suggest, rather, that issues of tolerance and of "left-wing orthodoxy" will take us much further in understanding just how speculative mysticism could be, even against a backdrop of the rise of Wycliffism.

We have already seen the anxiety apparent in his lengthy fourth gloss on Love's statement that the annihilated soul "ȝiueþ to nature al his asking," in which he charges dissenting readers with being too "blynde" or "fleischli." For a similar sense of panic we can turn to M. N.'s third gloss on Love's startling statement that this Soul does not take heed of shame or honour, poverty or riches, nor even hell or heaven ("This Soule, seiþ loue, ne reckeþ of schame, ne of worship . . ." [256.7]).[62] In *The Mirror* the Soul's radical statement elicits Reason's usual desperate plea for explanation, to which Love responds that only those whom God has given understanding will know, because "no scripture [escripture] techiþ it," no wit can grasp it, nor can any labour attain it. It is, rather, a gift given "of þe riȝt hiȝe, in whom þis creature is lost bi plente of knowynge, and bicome nouȝt in hir vndirstondinge" (10–14).

This is a loaded passage. In M. N.'s Middle English the Old French word "escripture" becomes "scripture," with its specialized sense of "Scripture," and this makes Porete's "no scripture techiþ it" a very powerful claim to revelatory theology and extra-ecclesial authority. Whether prompted by this, or the earlier reference to indifference to heaven or hell, or the final allusion to how the soul has "bicome naught"—or all these things together—the passage launches M. N. into a flutter of anxiety: "*M.* O, þese wordis semen ful straunge to þe rederis . . . [and] also many mo oþir wordis þat ben writen bifore and aftir, *semen fable or errour, or hard to vndirstande.* But for þe loue of God, ȝe reders, demeþ not to soone."

What he is setting out here, and with a good deal of urgency, is the three possible negative reader responses (at least some of which he likely encountered in his experience with his first edition). The charge that something is "fable" is a typical scholastic response to revelatory theology (one could cite here, for instance, Wyclif's use of the word in rejection of Hildegard). The term "error" arises in inquisitorial contexts for opinion that is rejected as wrong although not labeled (more seriously) "heresis." But in the language of academic theology (and M. N.'s Prologue shows his familiarity with this discourse), "error" is also a technical word with a significant meaning—and it appears in lists of suspect articles created in internal enquiries.[63] "[H]ard to vndirstande" refers to the kind of complaint commonly made about revelatory and mystical texts (as Trithemius said of Hildegard)[64] and it is M. N.'s favourite refuge throughout the glosses. It is related to wording like his "mystake," which is the kind of wording used to *politely* point out heterodoxy in the Middle English *Book of Ghostly Grace* by Mechthild of Hackeborn (there it is "mysunderestode").[65] But M. N. goes on to profess certainty that anyone who reads the book over

> *bi good avisement* twies or þries *and be disposed* to þo same felynges, þei schulen vnderstonde it wel ynowȝ. And þouȝ þei be not disposid to þo felynges, ȝitt hem schal þenke at it is al wel yseid. But who so takeþ þe nakid wordis of scriptures and leueþ þe sentence, he may liȝtli erre. *N.* (15–23)

The word "erre" here is crucial—it deftly rounds on the condemning reader and throws the charge of "error" back in his face. It all depends, M. N. asserts, on the reader's being able to read "bi good avisement," being able to be "disposed to þo same felynges," and above all, being able to suspend literalism. This is M. N.'s classic method of containing negative response. Having parried the assault, he can now deflect attention onto more traditional issues of the difficulty of mystical language. M. N. is, thus, a master of functional ambiguity. And he had good reason. He badly wanted the text to be read (at least two or three times!), and he wanted nothing to overshadow a text he had laboured over and held so dearly.

I would argue M. N. was deeply attracted to Porete's spirituality, and that several of the "safeguards" he feels he must mount on behalf of the unsophisticated reader are just that. They are an insurance policy which allows him to submit the text—ostensibly—to the church for correction, as he does in the

Prologue, while maintaining a surprising degree of ambiguity. Like so many Middle English texts of the Ricardian period, this one is produced for an audience of stratified abilities—with the most fascinating meanings *left to be made* by those with the sophistication to do so. I have said elsewhere that we can only envy the readerly agility of the top stratum of Langland's audience. The same is true of Chaucer, the *Pearl* poet, Julian, and, I would suggest, the Middle English *Mirror*. M. N.'s Prologue and glosses are subtle packing devices which, on the whole, belie M. N.'s own real adventurousness with the text.

One of the areas in which he actually shares a degree of radicalism with Porete is in his frustration with "scholars" and his insistence that contemplatives should be superior to them. In Porete herself this is flamboyantly present; in M. N. it is, of course, milder and reminiscent of other Middle English mystics (like Hilton), and also of the kind of tension that Bridget of Sweden's *Revelations* and the entire *discretio spirituum* genre triggered between *antiqui* and *moderni*.[66] These were newly topical at the time M. N. was working. At the opening of chapter 11 Reason says that Love has called the Soul by many names, for the sake of the "actyues," but asks now that she speak "for þe contemplatiues," who always "desiren to encrese in diuine knowledge." So far M. N.'s text follows the French original, but suddenly he departs by (silently) adding this sentence to the dialogue: "Þei ben yuel constreyned, reson, seiþ loue, to þat þat þou seist"— that is, "contemplatives are wrongly constrained, Reason, to do what you say." This must have been a subject on which M. N. felt strongly (as did his contemporary Langland judging from the "Feast of Patience"). Immediately following this M. N. inserts one of his glosses, flagged, as usual, by his initials, which says that contemplatives should have no desire but God's desire, "for as bi riȝt, þe *contemplatyues schuld passe þe state of scolers*, as maistres of diunite ben passid scoles." And here we have, I think, a clue to M. N.'s real interest and agenda in promoting *The Mirror* to a broader audience.

The reception of revelatory theology often divided the *antiqui* from the *moderni*, and M. N.'s reading of *The Mirror* proves to be no exception. As his Prologue demonstrates, M. N. was theologically sophisticated: he handles the genre of the academic prologue well; he is versed in biblical and mystical texts; he is rhetorically trained.[67] But as his additions here indicate, he is impatient with "scholastic" approaches—those, that is, that privilege reasoning over religious experience. This, it seems, speaks to the heart of the Carthusian contemplative project, with its roots in the texts of Bernard, William of St. Thierry, and the Victorines (all writers traceable in Free Spirit thought as well), and its astonishing passion for female mysticism—a passion to which we owe the preservation of many of our most important texts by women, including Julian's Short Text and Margery's *Book*. But this project was being carried out over against other clerical subcultures—this is perhaps best seen in the case of the Bridgettine controversies (going on even as M. N. was writing, and to which we will turn in the next chapter). But in this passage we have a small window on it in the English scene. This accounts perhaps for why M. N. does not "tone down" (indeed, rather, tones up) the passages in the text in which Reason is condemned, even though many are quite radical and made the Latin translator nervous.

The Mirror is, on one level, *a text about the death of Reason;* it is certainly a text in which Reason, of course, is repeatedly humiliated by her incapacity to grasp the spiritual truths of which Love and the Soul speak. Reason, in fact, dies in chapter 87,[68] in a scene both poignant and tongue-in-cheek: Love has announced that the Soul is Lady of the Virtues, Daughter of the Deity, Sister of Wisdom, and the Bride of Love—and Reason, instead of rejoicing in this good fortune, protests (in a mood that reminds the student of Middle English literature of nothing so much as the benighted and begrudging father in *Pearl*): "Ah, God! Says Reason, how dare anyone say this? I dare not listen to it" ("Hay, Dieux, dit Raison, comment ose l'en ce dire? Je ne l'ose escouter" [Guarnieri and Verdeyen, 246.11–12])—a response that encapsulates the whole book's problematizing of reception, audacity, orthodoxy, and transcendence. Reason goes on immediately, like an eighteenth-century romance heroine who has lost her virginity, to die of her own primness: "Truly, Lady Soul, I lose my senses as I listen to you, and my heart falters. There is no life in me" (112) ("Je deffaulx vrayement, dame Ame, en vous oïr: le cueur m'est failly. Je n'ay point de vie" [Guarnieri and Verdeyen, 246.12–13]). Although the last sentence is suppressed in all but one Latin copy, there is not much grief over her death in any of the languages: "Alas! Why did she not die long ago? ejaculates the Soul" ("Helas! pourquoy n'est pieçs, dit ceste Ame, ceste morte!" [Guarnieri and Verdeyen, 248.14–15]).

The death of Reason is not unlike two scenes of similar comedy in *Piers Plowman*: the silencing of Wit (C.XI.1 ff), which Langland makes partly a satire on gender by employing the virago Dame Study, and, second, the dreamer's being cast out of his own vision of Reason (C.XIII.204 ff). He is humiliated, but then "taken higher" by Imaginatif, who proves to be a more important figure than Reason could have been for getting over the barriers to faith. The message here is very similar to Porete's: to advance in the contemplative life, one needs to puncture the "dream" of Reason. In revising for C, a much more contemplative poem than B, Langland downplays Reason's role most often in favour of the faculty of interiority par excellence, Conscience. There are two crucial moments in the poem that signal movement deep into an interiority reminiscent of this kind of move in Porete: first, when Piers tears the Pardon and explicitly moves to contemplative life. This is a rejection of the ecclesiastical, followed later in the text by a rejection of the scholastic in the Feast of Patience. Langland, I would suggest, might even have learned much from *The Mirror* itself. We cannot be certain of course that he knew it, but he appears to have known some other Continental women's mystical texts or related genres, and this one has more resonances deep in his allegorical method than any other.[69] He even adopted the habit of intruding sudden, disembodied, and unintroduced speeches by allegorical characters who appear and then vanish just as suddenly—a classic feature of Porete's method.

What kind of impact could *The Mirror* have had—untranslated, unbowdlerized, and unglossed? It is a question worth asking given the flow of French literature to England's Anglo-Norman reading public. Guarnieri suggests that the text might have reached England, and a lay audience, in its French form as early as 1327. If so, this French copy would have arrived from Porete's home city, Valenciennes, in the entourage of a woman of royal blood, Phillipa of Hainault, consort of Edward III.[70] This association highlights another key strand in *The Mirror*, its use of *amour courtoise* language and idealism.[71] So passionate is Porete's handling of this genre that parts of the text could be extracted out for "secular" reading, and doubtless were, although there is no need to assume that Phillipa's would have been such a use, or that the main thrust of the book—the annihilation of all will other than God's—could not speak to those in courtly life. (Porete herself is concerned for common people as well as "actives" and contemplatives.) What we know of Phillipa is that she spoke French and Dutch fluently, endowed Queen's College, Oxford, and was apparently romantically in love with her husband, in whose service she gave herself with a vigour and selflessness even her countryman Froissart thought unusual.[72] *The Mirror* would not seem out of place in a court circle headed by such a woman. From such a circle it might easily have reached the world of a writer like the *Pearl* poet and the world even of Langland, whose earlier versions are deeply imbued with romance conventions, which he handles with subtlety. But we cannot know.

Of M. N.'s own agendas in promoting this text, and his own remarkable tolerance for some of its more extreme notions, not enough can be said. Certainly his commitment to the wider dissemination and appreciation of the text is profound, and some of his glosses are willing to go relatively far down the "quietist" road in support of this cause. This is apparent because there are places and topics in which we might expect more panic or more protective glossing, but this does not materialize: a particularly telling one is the shocking image Porete uses to describe the mystery of the eucharist. In the fifteenth chapter, Love has been saying that Christians receive the divinity and the humanity of Christ in the sacrament. Whereupon a new allegorical figure, Light of Faith (Lumiere de Foy), suddenly speaks:

> And so we shall tell you, says Light of Faith, to what we can liken this sacrament, the better to understand it. Take this sacrament, put it into a mortar with other substances, and pound it until you can no longer see or perceive the person which you place there. (33)

> Et pource nous vous dirons, dit Lumiere de Foy, comment nous ferons comparaison de ce Sacrament pour mieulx l'entendre.
> Prenez ce Sacrement, mectez le en ung mortier avec aultres choses, et breez ce Sacrement tant que vous n'y puissez point veoir ne point sentir de la Personne que vous y avez mis. (Guarnieri, 62.6–11)

> And we schal seie ʒou hou, seiþ þe liʒt of feiþ, hou þis humanite dwelliþ wiþ hem, as þus by similitude:
> Take þis sacrament and putte it in morter wiþ oþir þinges and bray þis sacrament so þat ʒe may not se ne feele of þe persoone þat ʒee haue put yn. (Doiron, 268.12–15)

Faith and Truth then discuss the fact that the humanity of Christ "does not come and go" ("ne va ne ne vient" [line 17]). None of this perturbs M. N. enough to provoke immediate comment, but it is only when Temptation speaks and says "Then what can this be?" ("et que peut ce donc estre?" [18]) that M. N. inserts a gloss restating exactly what Truth has said, in which he says, "It is þus þat þe manhode neiþer comeþ ne goiþ of Crist Ihesu . . ." (Doiron, 268.23).

What is astonishing about this gloss is that the image of what is done to the sacrament in the mortar does not upset him. Nor did it perturb Richard Methley when, in the early sixteenth century, he turned M. N.'s Middle English text into Latin, and like M. N. he draws attention to the image itself and stresses that it is a "similitude" ("likening" being the more common Middle English concept for "similitude" in the literary sense): "It is noteworthy that this says first, 'how shall we compare.' It follows from this that this neither commands nor counsels that this in fact be done."[73] Fear of Wycliffism just seems not to be a factor of any sort for M. N. (nor for Methley). And this is important for us to realize. In fact, the passage caused a great deal more fuss on the Continent than it did in England: this passage frightened the (Continental) Latin translator so much he suppressed the whole chapter.[74] But here we have M. N. writing in the supposedly Lollard-frenzied Ricardian or very early Lancastrian period that modern scholarship has portrayed for us. How could he have let this stand?

Perhaps it was not as frenzied as we assume, and certainly not in Carthusian circles. The eucharist is one theme in which Free Spirit heterodoxy and Lollardy overlap (as in the trial of Ramsbury), and M. N.'s restating of Porete's opinion (which he himself reads as orthodox) might be read as a preventative measure aimed at both targets. But this seems unlikely, because if we look carefully, he is glossing *Temptation*'s words, not Love's. But like his contemporary colleague, the *Chastising* author, M. N. is remarkably relaxed about eucharistic radicalism. What he is most concerned about seems to be quietism (and related doctrines), "self-noughting," and revelatory theology. These factors taken together suggest that he had no fear that Lollardy would infect his audience (nor did the *Chastising* author). He was certainly concerned, however, that Porete's more extreme annihilationist and passivist ideas—in short, her Free Spirit doctrines—might. His main goal seems to be to teach a style of "safe reading" that will protect the reader's orthodoxy throughout the book. His "revisions" are not unlike Langland's—that is, not systematic, but "working outward from centres of dissatisfaction"[75]—and not unlike professional annotators, whose enthusiasm for glossing usually wanes early in the text.[76] But he behaves most like the Carthusian annotator of the *Book of Margery Kempe* who consistently shapes opinion, reigns in "enthusiasm," deletes or suppresses what he fears might be unorthodox or too suggestive, but equally—and this is important—shares wholeheartedly in the spirit of even Kempe's most controversial passages.[77] I think this comparison between the two annotators is helpful because in it we see both the independence of Carthusian spirituality and its measured caution with texts that would reach a vernacular audience. We can see in these texts the laying of a protective stratum of orthodoxy defence, while those with sophistication are left free to entertain the deeper subtleties.

We turn now to another text, the preservation of which we owe to the Carthusians, and it is one that *reads* at least as if it is deeply imbued with the stamp of *The Mirror*—Julian of Norwich's *Revelation*.

Chapter Eight

FORENSIC VISION AND INTELLECTUAL VISION

Julian's Self-Censorship and Books of
Carthusian Transmission

At the end of the Long Text of Julian's *Revelation*, the scribe added a warning:

> I pray almyty God that this booke come not but to the hands of them that
> will be his faithfull lovers, and to those that will submitt them to the feith
> of Holy Church and obey the holesom understondyng and teching of the
> men that be of vertuous life, sadde age and profound lernyng. For this
> revelation is hey divinitye and hey wisdom; . . . *And beware thu take not on
> thing after thy affection and liking and leve another, for that is the condition
> of an heretique.* But take everything with other. And trewly vnderston-
> den, all is according to Holy Scripture and growndid in the same—and
> that Jhesus our very love, light and truth shall shew to all clen soules that
> with mekenes aske perseverantly this wisdom of hym.[1] (emphasis added)

Most vernacular works of this period do not come with this kind of caveat attached.[2] But both *The Cloud*, another "elite" work of Carthusian transmission,

and M. N.'s translation of Porete's *Mirror* do. This passage is most immediately reminiscent in tone of the *approbationes* provided for Porete's text by the learned men examined in chapter 7. It is also reminiscent of the method of "safe reading" that we saw M. N. teaching in his translation of *The Mirror*—and the functional ambiguity he employed to protect some of Porete's more daring speculative material. We have already seen that Carthusian circles were important "safe spaces" for unusual or even radical revelatory spirituality, and because our only extant medieval copy of Julian of Norwich's Short Text of her *Revelation* appears along with M. N.'s *Mirror* in the Amherst manuscript, we can be certain that both texts were moving in exactly these circles.[3] Since we know the manuscript to have been in the hands of James Grenehalgh, whose monogram appears on fol. 33r, there is most certainly a Carthusian context for reception here, and likely a Carthusian origin as well.[4] Many scholars have already pointed us toward some of the more daring aspects of Julian's work, such as her reworking of the Trinity to accommodate a spirituality of "Jesus as mother," originating in the Cistercian tradition,[5] or her suggestive theology of "universal salvation."[6] This chapter will deal with three further aspects of Julian's daring: (1) the areas in which, at least in *reception*, her text sounds like Porete's *Mirror*; (2) her brilliant negotiation of a woman's right to teach; and (3) her use of a nearly "forensic" visionary descriptive technique to take her readers *beyond* the authority of official church art.[7]

Many, many passages in Julian call to mind the uncompromising theology of love and the unembarrassed attitude toward sin of *The Mirror*. So, for instance, when we hear Julian say, *"for till I am substantially onyd to him,* I may never have full rest" (WJ, Long 5.16–17; G, 5),[8] or when she continues, "Of this nedeth us to have knowinge, that us liketh *to nought all thing that is made for to love and have God* that is unmade . . . for we sekyn here rest in these things that is so littil, wherin is no rest" (WJ, Long, 5.19–23), we feel we are just skirting the safer side of a line, on the *other* side of which is the kind of extreme quietism and annihilationism that drove Porete's brilliant and perilous prose. When M. N. rescues just such a passage in *The Mirror* by ingenious, indeed Miltonic, glossing as simply waiting upon the Lord, "So þei stonden for to attende and wait to folewe þe lordis werk" (279.19–20), one cannot help but think of Julian's brilliant allegory of the Lord and the Servant in her Long Text, as mentioned in the previous chapter. Or when Julian politely puts aside all "means" (menys) between herself and God, "Than saw I sothly that is more worshippe to God . . . that we faithfully pray to himselfe of this goodness and clevyn thereto be his grace, . . . than if we made all the menys that herte can think" (WJ, Long, 6.4–7), there is a hint of Porete's iconoclastic spirituality. Julian's list of politely shelved mediators includes Christ's "holy flesh and . . . blode," his passion, his wounds, his mother, the cross, saints, and all the company of heaven (Long only, 6.10–18). These, she says, "we use for lak of understonding and knowing of love" (26–27). Even if this is not Porete's dismissal of Holy Church the Less (Saincte Eglise la Petite), or the Free Spirit indifference to the eucharist, masses, and other sacraments,[9] it is *at the very least* the kind of radical interiorist impulse that so frightened the church about visionary and mystical experience. John XXII, we remember, reacted to something very similar in Olivi when the pope himself went through Olivi's Apocalypse commentary. Olivi's belief that during the Third Status knowledge of the Incarnate Word would be so profound as to be available by simple spiritual *intelligentia* upset John terribly. So much, in fact, he preached a sermon c. 1325–26 saying that Olivi's predictions of greater human knowledge in the final age would make men "not *viatores* but *comprehensores,* needing no mediator."[10] Direct experience of God, such as only the visionary enjoys, Olivi saw as characterizing the Third Status generally, even through taste and touch (gustativa et palpativa experientia). This last, I suggested in an earlier chapter, was one of the aspects of his thought that attracted Free Spirit devotees, possibly including (or so her arrest with Cressonessart suggests) Porete.[11]

Perhaps the most significant parallel, as Colledge has pointed out, is that Porete and Julian share an unusually positive attitude toward the role of sin in the spiritual life. To quote here the summarizing rubric in the French original of *The Mirror,* "The Soul says here that in Paradise, to her great glory, her sins will be known" (Icy dit L'Ame que en paradis a sa grant gloire seront cogneuz ses pechez). The idea emerges in Julian's Short Text (chapter 17), and in her Long Text, too, in a way that is instantly reminiscent of what Porete's Soul (Ame) says of her sins: in Paradise, they will be to her "very great glory," not to her shame ("Mais, sire, en paradis tous ceulx qui y seront en auront cognoissance, non mye *a ma confusion, mais a ma tres grant gloire*" [Guarnieri and Verdeyen, 118.5–7]). Compare Julian:

Also, god schewed me that syn is na schame, bot wirschippe to ma*nn*, for in this sight my*nn* vnderstandynge was lyfted vp in to heve*nn*; and tha*nn* co*mm* verrayly to my mynde David, Pet*er and* Paule, Thom*a*s of Inde and the Maudelay*nn*, howe thaye er knawe*nn* in the kyrke of erth with

thare synnes to thayre wirshchippe. And it is to tha*m*m no schame that
thay hafe synned — na mare it is in the blysse of heven — for thare the
takenynge of synne is tou*r*ned into wirschippe. (CW, Short, 17.17–24)

Julian's astonishing, perpetual optimism (a stark contrast to the plunging despair this very topic, and these very biblical figures, provoked in Langland's
dreamer at the end of A) is always secure in all things. So, although with in-
finitely more iconoclasm, is Porete's invincible Love (Amour), who says that
whoever always has perfect charity of will (voulenté parfaicte charité) would
never have remorse or qualms of conscience (n'auroit jamais remors ne repren-
ement de conscience [Guarnieri and Verdeyen, 120.12–15]). Elsewhere Porete
writes of the Soul feeling no disquiet for any sins she has committed, which, as
Colledge points out, is not unlike a point of doctrine condemned in Eckhart's
trial, "if a man had committed a thousand mortal sins, and were rightly disposed, he should not wish not to have committed them."[12] Perhaps the idea
originated in a radical dilation on Augustine's "Even our sins are necessary to
the universal perfection which God established," but it seems more than mere
coincidence that both women should make the same dilation.

Although, sadly, it is not possible here in a study of censorship to examine
the whole question of Julian's apparent knowledge of or similarities to Porete,
we can be very clear in this book about a few key things. The previous two
chapters have made us aware that many in the very Carthusian reading circles
in which Julian's Short Text was traveling were alert to a range of possible dangers, including Free Spirit issues. They were also actively trying to balance
such risks against the exciting possibilities this literature opened up for contemplatives. The danger of Free Spiritism, *per se*, I would suggest, did not stand
out for someone like Hilton or the *Cloud* author or M. N., except as part of a
larger concern about irregular speculative theology and its role in mysticism.
Nicholas Watson has recently pointed out that "like the *Cloud* author, Hilton
often associates formal learning and heresy" — and to Watson's list we can
now add M. N. Watson goes on to say that this concern

> justifies Hilton's suspicion of visions, of the devotional imagination, and
> of a bodily understanding of spiritual experiences such as Rolle's cele-
> brated 'fire of love' — even if this phrase is also used with approval, one
> of the several signs of Rolle's underrated influence on Hilton.[13]

The line, then, that writers in and for these reading circles were walking is a fine one. To this group of suspicions we must now add Free Spirit concerns, which certainly related to women, as well as some of the Continental suspicions we have examined. But unlike other revelatory texts (especially visionary ones), speculative mysticism was more usually a man's world. Julian starts in an overtly female visionary mode with her Short Text. But by the time she created her Long Text, she had moved ever more deeply into speculative mysticism. Having already seen some of the suspicions that speculative mysticism fell under, our task is to examine why Julian maneuvered her authorial voice toward intellectual vision and away from female authorship, and what factors of contemporary history may have played a role in the reception of her Short Text. But first we have to look a little further at what role suspicion of revelatory writing and teaching generally, especially for women, may have played in causing Julian to suppress her identity as a female author and teacher.

Julian and Contemporary Controversy over a Woman's Right to Teach

When Julian of Norwich wrote the first version (Short Text) of her *Revelation*, she self-deprecatingly, but directly addressed the topic this way:

> Botte God forbede that ȝe schulde saye or take it so that I am a techere, for I meene nouȝt soo, no I mente nevere so. For I am a woman, leuede [unlearned], febille, and freylle. Botte I wate [know] wele this that I saye: I hafe it of the schewynge of hym that is souerayne techare. Botte sothelye [truly] charyte styrres me to telle ȝowe it, for I wolde God wared knawen and myn evyncrystene [peers] spede—as I wolded be myselfe— of the mare hatynge of synne and lovynge of God. Botte for I am a woman schulde I therfore leve that I schulde nouȝt tell ȝowe the goodenes of God—syne that I sawe in that same tyme that it is his wille that it be knawen? And that schalled ȝe welle see in the same matere that folowes aftyr, if it be welle and trewlye takyn [understood]. (CW, Short, 47.34–48.12)

Setting aside as merely conventional her apology that she is "lewed, feeble and frail," an apology used even by authoritative male writers, we can discern the elements of formal theological argument here. Note the incremental logic of the four "buts"[14] which carefully build the case: first, that her knowledge comes from divine revelation, second, that she is speaking out of charity for her fellow Christians, and (finally, and rhetorically well placed) that it would be absurd if she could not speak of the goodness of God simply because she is a woman. What the passage tells us is that, far from lacking in confidence, she is extremely well informed about the theological arguments supporting female teaching, or even preaching—arguments usually discreetly buried in Latin scholastic discussions and not well advertised to the laity (although in the last two chapters we have seen some routes via which women might learn of them). For instance, Thomas Aquinas, one of the standard and most widely cited authorities on this subject, had given three "proofs" that a woman may use the "*gratia* of discourse" ("de gratia quae consistit in *sermone*").[15] In brief summary, these are:

(1) the verse in Proverbs 4:3–4 implying that Solomon had been taught by his mother ("Vnigenitus fui coram matre mea, et docebat me");

(2) various biblical accounts of women who exercised the gift of prophecy (including Miriam (Exod. 15:20), Deborah (Judges 4:4), Huldah (4 Kings 22:14), the daughters of Phillip (Acts 21:9) and "omnis mulier orans aut prophetans" (1 Cor. 11:5);

(3) the obligation, following 1 Peter 4:10, for those who have a gift of knowledge to use it for the benefit of others ("Unusquisque sicut accepit gratiam in alterutrum administrantes").

These three arguments were very closely followed by his contemporary Henry of Ghent, who added to the third argument that Mary and Martha had evangelized just as the Apostles had.[16]

Julian's justifications draw upon arguments similar to (2) and (3); moreover, her disclaimers suggest that she was aware of arguments similar to those Aquinas makes "*contra*." He stresses that there is a distinction between the private and the public "*sermo*"—and it is the private that befits women (women are allowed to teach in the home, but normally only children and other women). St. Paul, of course, had forbidden women to teach in church or assembly (1 Tim. 2:12 "Docere mulierem non permitto"), and Aquinas gives three reasons for this:

(1) the female sex is subject (qui debet esse subditus), following Genesis 3:16, and teaching belongs to those in authority;

(2) as Ecclesiasticus 9:11 says, a woman speaking can inflame the desires of men (ad libidinem);

(3) women are not sufficiently perfected in wisdom (non sunt in sapientia perfectae).

To these standard arguments, dispassionately put in Aquinas, other theologians added more egregiously misogynist ones, like Humbert of Romans, who cites the folly that ensued from the teaching of the first woman Eve, or Henry of Ghent, who stressed that not only teaching but *learning* is dangerous for women because "owing to the inadequacy of their natural talents [debilitas ingenii], instead of making progress in the mysteries of theology, they regress into heresy."[17] If Julian were aware of these more sensational misogynist assertions, she judiciously ignored them, concentrating instead on her theological right "to tell . . . of the goodness of God," and making a *de facto* claim for the gift of prophetic vision. This would immediately override Aquinas's objection number (3), and neatly outmaneuver his objection (1) by insisting that she teaches her "even-christens"—her peers—a deft reminder of the spiritual equality of men and women.

The strange thing is, however, that by the time she revised this first text to create the longer version of the *Showings,* probably later in the 1390s, likely before 1413, she deleted this passage. We do not know why. Many scholars have suggested that the deletion in the Long Text indicates a new self-confidence. But perhaps also important was the fact that between 1373 (when she tells us she had her first vision) and the 1390s or early 1400s (when she was working at revision), the discussion of a woman's right to teach was becoming more controversial alongside, as we have seen, claims to vision, both, in some quarters, suspect. The rise of Wycliffism, as others have suggested, could be a factor in relation to women as teachers, especially given the Wycliffite sympathy for notions of "a priesthood of all believers" and the well-known trial of Walter Brut in 1391–93.[18] But in Julian's Norwich, Wycliffism was neither the primary temptation nor the primary concern that recent scholarship has tended to assume normative in England.[19] Nor is Lollardy, as we have seen, a real concern of any sort in the Carthusian contemplative circles that were transmitting Julian.

In fact, as we now know, there were concerns other than Lollardy being raised at the time that might have appeared just as or even more relevant to a woman visionary living in England's closest port city to the Continent. We have now had a chance to look at the beguine movement, the *Devotio Moderna* sister houses, and the significant role of women in Joachite exegesis and more concretely in Olivian inspired heterodoxy. The first two, in particular, as we saw in relation to Margery Kempe, present a number of cross-channel connections that need to be considered in relation to women's teaching. Also, and perhaps even more important for England was the Ricardian vogue for Hildegardiana, and the array of attitudes toward vision it fostered (chapter 4); the international scandal of Scrope's 1405 execution and state-imposed anti-revelatory measures enforcing *probatio* of visionary claimants (Case Study 3); and Netter's ban on Carmelite encouragement of women with spiritual gifts—a ban which affected even Julian's acquaintance, Margery Kempe (chapter 7). Moreover, from roughly the death of Bridget of Sweden (in 1373) onward, a parallel fascination with and defensiveness about revelations by women began to emerge.[20] In 1391 Bridget was canonized amidst international controversy—a decision that would be revisited not long afterward amidst further controversy.[21] Unlike Lollardy, Bridgettine, like Hildegardian, writings made extensive use of prophecy or reformist apocalypticism—the one gift which allowed women to preach and teach *publicly*.

Reformist apocalypticism was a genre that had been friendly to female preaching ever since its inception in the twelfth century with the visions of Hildegard of Bingen, and in late medieval England, it was a genre largely spread by friars.[22] And it was a genre that Wycliffite thinkers did not, on the whole, like or trust,[23] so perhaps it is no accident that the one Lollard intellectual known to have *actively* argued for the possibility that women might preach, Walter Brut, is also the one securely identifiable Lollard writer with any extensive knowledge of Continental reformist apocalyptic thought. This tradition provided the most obvious available route to teaching authority for women between the twelfth and fifteenth centuries in a church which otherwise tried its best to exclude them. In addition to those radical or "left-wing" traditions and events affecting women we examined in chapters 4, 6, and 7, and Case Studies 1 and 3, this chapter will look at further historical factors relevant to Julian's time of writing. These are, briefly, the evidence of scholastic debate on women's ministry before and after Brut's trial, the English transmission of the Bridgettine *Epistola*

solitarii, and the negative attitude to female teaching in the *Defensorium* by Norwich's cardinal, Adam Easton.

Walter Brut was the subject of a well-known trial before an unusually large
and impressive team of theologians. Many of them had expertise in international
church matters and civil law. That these men took his arguments for women
preachers and priests seriously is an indication that Brut was not simply perceived
as representing the lunatic fringe.[24] Some of the disputations written in response
to Brut's trial, along with disputations on related subjects, are extant in a collection largely given over to anti-Wycliffite texts, British Library, MS Harley 31.
These disputants handle questions of female ministry in the way that university-
trained theologians dealt with every question, by setting it up as a confrontation of supposedly equal but conflicting assertions. As we have already seen with
Aquinas, this form dictated a more even-handed treatment than a subject might
otherwise get and at the time that Brut was being tried, university theologians
had still relatively rarely been censored for speculations in such discussions.[25]

We have two sources of information about Brut's ideas: the first being the
records of the trial in Bishop Trefnant's register, which contains Brut's own long
and learned testimony to his views, along with official responses and the articles
of condemnation. How much of this material is condensed, we do not know. The
second set of sources occurs in the Harley disputations, where the question is not
concision but attribution. In the writing we know comes from Brut's own pen in
the Trefnant register, we can see how he built his case for women's ability to minister the sacraments by starting with the fact that medieval women (especially
midwives) were allowed to baptize in emergencies. Brut, like other medieval
reformist thinkers (all of whom were fascinated with the early church), may
have been aware of its use of women in the diaconate (references to which had
survived vestigially in canon law until the twelfth century).[26] Good women, he
wrote, along with good laymen, can even consecrate in cases of necessity:

> Since in baptism there is complete remission of sins, women absolve from
> sin those they baptize; hence women have the power of releasing from sin.
> But the powers of 'binding and releasing' are interconnected, so women
> have the power to 'bind and release' which is said to have been granted to
> priests. Therefore women do not seem to be excluded from Christian
> priesthood even though their power is restrained so long as others are
> ordained. . . .[27]

It has been difficult in the past to account for the emergence of Brut's defence of women. We know that issues of salvation (often linked to baptism) were hugely controversial in Brut's day, both inside the academy and outside it.[28] But none of these controversies especially involved women's ministry—and even Wyclif himself, after all, had been emphatic that women could not preach.[29] Moreover, the Harley sources, ostensibly written by orthodox theologians, discuss arguments far more radical than any Brut himself put forward. How, then, to make sense of Brut's initiative? There are, it seems, two strands here: the scholastic debates of the period, recently independently illuminated by Somerset and by Minnis, both building on work by Blamires and Marx. To these we will add just a little more, from a text ten years earlier suggesting that friars were an older source of the debate. The second strand is the impact of prophetic writing, which we saw in relation to Brut himself in chapter 5. This is where we will start.

Brut was extremely learned in the Continental apocalyptic tradition—it was a tradition which also attracted learned laymen abroad (the most famous of whom is Arnold of Villanova, a writer Brut may well have known).[30] The author of the anonymous Harley disputation, *Utrum liceat mulieribus docere*, follows Aquinas's and Henry of Ghent's arguments very closely, and he concedes that, "Although women may not be allowed to teach in public, there are certain cases however where they are . . ."

> First, if it is granted to them as a special favour, as it was to women in the Old as well as the New Testament. . . . The second situation is when it is granted to women as a reproach to men who have become effeminate [effeminati]. It was for this reason that government of the people was granted to women, as appears in Judges 4 concerning Deborah. The third situation is when there is a great number of masses and only a small number of those administering. It was for this reason that it was granted to the women, Mary and Martha, to preach in public and to the four daughters of Phillip to prophesy in public.[31]

We do not know whether it was Brut's trial that prompted this particular disputation or not, but we do know that the reference to the "effeminati" occurs in a second Harley disputation, one much more closely linked to Brut's trial than *Utrum liceat*.[32] Furthermore, we know that in Brut's own handwritten testimony he makes reference to "holy virgins who have constantly preached the word of

God and converted many to the faith, while priests did not dare say a word."[33] These two passages together bring us very close in formulation to the influential views of Hildegard of Bingen, who repeatedly asserted that she lived in an "effeminate age" during which men had lost, through their corruption, the ability to teach. And so, she argued, it fell to women like herself to do so.[34]

Brut's extensive testimony, replete with pseudo-Joachite-style anti-papalism and calculations, indicates that he had encountered more of the Continental reformist apocalyptic tradition—first and foremost the popular Hildegard[35]—than most of his contemporaries, suggesting that it was his apocalypticism, not merely his Wycliffism, that prompted his unusual campaign for women.

Brut's trial, then, insofar as he argued strenuously for women, was not very typically Lollard. It highlighted a Continental campaign for women preachers which Cambridge and Oxford academics took seriously.[36] But there is evidence of even earlier discussion of women's clerical roles, largely in the fraternal orders where it was as old as the thirteenth century.[37] Fraternal support of and interest in preaching holy women is well documented throughout the Middle Ages, and ranges from the view that unmarried women could preach put forward by Franciscan Eustache d'Arras to William Ockham's view that women should on certain occasions take part in general councils of the church, "where the wisdom, goodness or power of a woman is necessary to the discussion of the faith . . . the woman should not be excluded from the general council."[38] Few today would expect this of Ockham, but he shares with Eustache a Franciscan heritage that particularly encouraged medieval women to teach, although members of other fraternal orders were known to do so as well—we have already seen the example of the Carmelite, Alan of Lynn, and Margery Kempe (chapter 6).

In fact, it is possible that this strand of fraternal "feminism" is being parodied in the broadside on the Earthquake Council we studied in Case Study 2. In language very close to that used by Brut and his scholastic disputants, but writing ten years earlier, the poet of "Heu quanta desolacio" parodies another Carmelite, Peter Stokes, trying to speak to an issue in the antimendicant debates (that is, Christ's begging).[39] The doctor, we are told, laboured for many days, producing nothing to the point he was arguing (Hic per dies plurimos doctor laboravit, / Nihil ad propositum quod argumentavit), which was the proposition that Christ commanded a woman that "*she herself minister*, in the manner that she offered him a drink" (Allegans quod foeminae Christus imperavit, / Ut potum porrigeret, *ipsa ministravit* ["Heu," 262]). Even though the mendicancy debates are the ostensible context of the lines, the poet could have used any number of verbs to describe the neutral act of giving someone a drink in the context of begging. "Ministravit" is not a neutral verb. "Ministrare," especially in British Latin sources, is most commonly used in the sense of "officiating" at mass or in church ritual. It is also the verb used most often in relation to the question of women consecrating the eucharist, as in Brut's use of it in that context, e.g., "quare nunc bone mulieres non possunt sacramenta ministrare . . ." (Trefnant, 346). The "ipsa" in the passage is also telling emphasis (preserved in my translation here, even at the cost of clumsiness). What we have as always with this poet (who, as we saw in Case Study 2, may also have been the apostate friar, Peter Pateshull) is a love of wordplay. And since Christ's address to the woman from Samaria in John 4:7 is a famous moment when he welcomes a previously shunned group to partake with him in a new equalitarianism of faith, the allusion becomes especially rich for this learned Oxford audience.

Since we know the poem can be very tightly dated to 1382, and the alleged speaker here, Stokes, is not a Wycliffite — quite the opposite — this little parody is worth our attention, especially because we have so very little concrete evidence other than what appears in relation to Walter Brut's trial a decade later of English academic debate on clerical roles for women. Some of the most interesting scholastic debates, as we are just beginning to understand, took place without reference to Lollardy at all. As Minnis writes in a recent essay, "The scrupulous reporting of the views of Walterus Bryth [Brut] is intriguingly at variance with the latitude which his opponents assume when his name does not set the parameters of their analysis."[40] More evidence comes (to borrow a phrase from Dyan Elliott) from the "reversible" elements of scholastic disputational form (where some astonishing "pro" arguments were at least being debated on this subject), and, more concretely, from the fame of Continental women prophets during the Great Schism.[41]

But scholasticism was not the only forum in England — nor was Lollardy generally — where the issue of women's teaching was being discussed and suppressed at the time Julian was writing. In addition to what we have already seen, there was the ongoing controversy over Bridget's canonization, involving transmission of defences of Bridget in England in the *Epistola* and the *Defensorium* written after Norwich's cardinal Adam Easton's conversion to women's revelation in a papal prison cell,[42] the subjects of the next section.

Julian's Self-Censorship and Intellectual Vision: The Epistola solitarii, Visionary Validation, and Easton's Prison Defence of Bridget

Women's teaching in clerical contexts was also, obviously, a feature of Bridgettine thought, especially in the power-packed defence of Bridget's visionary gifts and leadership skills written by Alphonse of Pecha, the *Epistola solitarii*. Ostensibly intended as a manual on discernment of spirits, the *Epistola* deftly shows how Bridget conformed to every expectation of ecclesiastical *probatio*, and was a heaven-sent prophetess to save and direct the church in a time of crisis (the Avignon papacy). It was twice translated into Middle English (the first time in *The Chastising*), both times tellingly "watered down" for female and for lay consumption. The ways in which it was bowdlerized are significant for us because they can act as a measuring stick for the *kinds* of prejudices that would have confronted someone like Julian (a woman, that is, or even a lay*man*). Indeed, Julian, as other scholars have suggested, may well have known *The Chastising* — Colledge and Walsh cite numerous parallels, especially in the Short Text chapter from which comes the famous passage about teaching as a women quoted above. *The Chastising* provides significant information about visions via the *Epistola*, but it really only renders intact chapter 2 (carefully), and chapter 6 (adaptively) of Alphonse's actual *Epistola*, and therefore it suppresses, as Rosalynn Voaden has suggested, much of the positive tone and content of the original.[43] Suppressed, for example, is Alphonse's chapter 1 in which he states his fear that his treatise will fall among the ignorant, and in which he insists that few today have knowledge of how to judge visions.[44] Also omitted is his insistence that too many condemn visions, *especially women's*,[45] and that, since God often chose the unlearned to convey his messages,[46] it is dangerous to *ignore* visions. Not only are all these major themes of the *Epistola* not translated by the *Chastising* author, in the parts he does render, Bridget's role is dramatically reduced (she is mentioned only once), and the emphasis is upon her exemplary obedience rather than on her role as a visionary leader.[47]

Voaden makes the same point about *The Chastising*'s use of the *Epistola* as Dyan Elliott makes about Gerson's use of it in his *On the Proving of Spirits* (written, in part, to challenge the recent canonization of Bridget). Elliott says that his was a scholastic "reworking of a treatise [originally] *defending* the inspiration of Bridget's revelation" leaving a "shadow text of discarded or disproved tenets."[48] While I believe that the *Chastising* author was not so negative as Gerson, he was (compared to Alphonse's original) conservative and suppressive, ending his rendering with the injunction that "euery man shuld mekeli dreede visions, for perel þat miȝt falle" (182, lines 12–13).

The two chapters he chose to render are, first, chapter 2 of the original *Epistola*, which had outlined the way doctors of the church recommended examining a visionary, stressing that she or he must live under discipline and show "good fruits" (such as obedience, humility, and other virtues).[49] A long list ensues of things that also ought to be examined (Item, examinare debet utrum . . . [II: par. 6]). Among these is the question of whether the visionary is orthodox, virtuous, penitent, patient, of sound intellect, and so forth. Do the visions lend themselves to the salvation of souls or, rather, are they productive of errors against the faith? Do they lead to anything "in errorem catholice fidei" or "monstrum et nouum" (monstrous and new) (II. par. 20), which *The Chastising* renders as "ony errour of hooli chirche, of þe feiþ, or ony wondir or newe þing" (176.12–13). Chapter 6 delineates the seven signs by which one can tell true visions from false ones. In the second sign, for instance, the soul is ravished, feeling heat, and sweetness "or sauour" of God's love (178.18),[50] a sweetness and charity, which the devil could not infuse (faithfully rendered nearly verbatim in *The Chastising*). What is utterly suppressed in *The Chastising*, however, is the impact of this on the visionary, which is lovingly explored by Alphonse in a passage verging on the erotic: the cares of the past go into oblivion, he writes, and the soul exalts, the intellect brightens, the heart is illuminated, desires rejoice (desideria iocundantur). The entire passage builds to a climax which echoes the Song of Songs in the assertion that in vision it is "your beloved" (dilectus tuus) who "visits you" (visitat te).[51] Also in chapter 6, Alphonse makes the crucial point, citing Aquinas in the third sign, that demons can manifest themselves through imaginary but *not* intellectual vision (in illis intellectualibus visis non fallitur anima).[52] This, then, is the most infallible type, but intellectual vision is the kind that is least often associated with women. The distrust of the imagination "per illusionem in imaginatione" throughout this chapter is significant, a phenomenon we have already met in chapter 5. In *The Chastising*, this passage is rendered faithfully as the devil's inability to show "bi goostli liȝt of vndirstondyng aboue kynde, but [only] bi sum oþer *vision imagynatif*, or ellis by sensible speche" (179, lines 13–15). Close study of *The Chastising* might very well make an English woman visionary consider what she is doing. And even more so if she encountered the other translation of the *Epistola*, which I will refer to as the Julius *Epistola* (after the shelfmark of the manuscript) or as the freestanding one to distinguish it from the one in *The Chastising*.

Because *The Chastising* was likely intended initially for the nuns of Barking, it is not as eviscerated as the freestanding Middle English translation, which looks to have anticipated an audience at least in part of laity.[53] Thanks to Rosalynn Voaden's carefully annotated edition and the facing-page edition she has produced with Arne Jönsson's Latin text, we are in a position to see very clearly just how terrified the English translator was of this text.[54] The following central topics, on my reading, are routinely *suppressed* in this vernacular version: (1) the fact that Bridget taught, and the fact that she taught popes, kings, prelates, and people of all ranks; (2) the fact that she had the gift of *discretio* herself, along with Alphonse's emphasis on her experience of intellectual vision; (3) evidence of the example she gave of active ministry for women; (4) the fact that it is a prophet's role to lead the people; (5) the fact that she composed an inspired and approved liturgy. (6) Even elementary Latin is suppressed, along with all references to scholarly sources and authorities, however general, in an effort to laicize the text. (7) Suppressed, too, are all the possible excesses of "enthusiasm," physical experience such as Rollean sweetness, movement within the body, and so forth. This list of seven types of suppressed topics shows the dramatic alteration the translator made in his rendering. This translator shares a nervousness about these kinds of enthusiasms not only with Hilton, but with the later annotator-corrector of *The Book of Margery Kempe*, who explicitly cuts or "spiritualizes" these things—most famously where he inserts the word "gostly" to spiritualize otherwise physical acts.[55] Another feature, however, that the scribe (not the translator) of the Julius *Epistola* shares with the Carthusian corrector of Kempe's book is the insertion of gender-inclusive language at key points.[56] In the *Epistola* text, the scribe suddenly (as Voaden shows) realizes that women are being excluded from intellectual vision and makes an insertion to correct that. After citing "bodily" and "gostly" vision, with examples, the author has just reached Augustine's third type: "Intellectual vision is whan a*man* [sic] <or a*per-sone*> sees the treuþe of ye misteryes of the holy gost scheuyng*e with* the vndirstonding of mynde."[57] It is clear that the translator or copyist of the exemplar assumed that intellectual vision is a *male* mode of experience, and that the Julius scribe (who may even have been a woman) objected to that.

Julian made many revisions, as has often been noted, that strip the Long Text of any reference to its female authorship (indeed, even the name "Julian" is a masculine form for what may have been Julianna). Julian, I think, wanted to be taken seriously as a visionary of intellectual vision, and may have felt her gender was in the way. Certainly the evidence suggests that women "stuck out" as intellectual visionaries. And women, in particular, as we have seen, could provoke suspicions of Free Spirit influence or other kinds of speculative mysticism, increasingly so in the 1390s. This explains why both Hilton and the *Chastising* author addressed these issues explicitly. And scholars have long believed that Julian could have known both, and both texts are datable to the period of her revisions.

We have already looked at the key passage Julian suppressed in the Long Text about women's right to teach. There are other suppressed passages that suggest that she is trying to move away from some of the conventions of overtly female visionary writing and teaching. One is the passage about St. Cecilia, whose association with female preachers like Mary Magdalene and Martha was common in religious art.[58] Moreover, her association with virginity and chaste marriage might suggest a female sensibility—certainly Chaucer thought it a suitable tale for his faceless Second Nun. Another, more political reason for its suppression may have to do with Cardinal Easton's imprisonment under Urban VI in 1385, Easton being from Norwich and having been made cardinal in 1381 with the title of St. Cecilia. This is complex, but several historical and literary passages make it at least plausible.[59] The passage itself appears only in the Short Text,

> For the thirde, I harde a man telle of haly kyrke of the storye of Saynte Cecylle, in the whilke schewynge I vndyrstode that sche hadde thre woundys with a swerde in the nekke, with the whilke sche pynede to the dede. By the styrrynge of this I conseyved a myghty desyre, prayande our lorde god that he wolde grawnte me thre woundys in my lyfe time. . . . (WJ, Short, 1.36 ff)

In the Long Text, this is reduced to: "For the iii, by the grace of God and teachyng of holy church, I conceived a mighty desire to receive iii wounds in my life . . ." (WJ, Long, 2.33–34). The Long Text's tame replacement belies how critical Cecilia's legend is to both the Short and Long Texts because it alone explains the inspiration for Julian's metaphorical request for the "three wounds" which are the very springboard of her revelations themselves.

Why the excision? Colledge and Walsh helpfully point to the significance of Cecilia in literature exactly contemporary with the Short Text, like the *Book to a Mother,* where the saint is listed among those "monye maidens more freel in kinde and lasse strong in bodi" that "schullen arise at þe dai of dome and *condempne such bodiliche stronge men* þat dispisen chastite and Cristes techings" (CW, l.205, my emphasis). The exaltation of the normally "freel" female made capable of rebuking the clergy invokes a long-standing apocalyptic reading as old as Hildegard's reformist visions, reborn with new fervour in the heady 1370s when Bridget of Sweden and other internationally famous women visionaries shamed the papacy into action.[60] This idea of Cecilia appears, though without the apocalypticism, as late as the Longleat sermons, which Watson argues called upon the saint to help face down the conservatism of Arundel's Constitutions: "And take heed of seyn cecyle þat . . . ceside neyþer be day ne by ny3t for to spekin of god & goddys law." And Cecilia was known as a strong woman in other, more famous sources. Following Giffin's work, Lynn Staley recounts the textual evidence that Chaucer himself "gives increased emphasis to Cecilia and her combatitiveness," unlike most versions of St. Cecilia's legend, and unlike his own source texts.[61] This feisty rendition of the legend would have been in circulation by sometime in the 1390s or early 1400s as Chaucer's "Second Nun's Tale," exactly when Julian was composing her Long Text. Aers and Staley sum up the testimony of the English vernacular writings with the comment that "in the 'uses' to which Cecilia was put by Chaucer, Julian of Norwich, the early Wycliffites, Nicholas Love, and the author of the Longleat sermons," we may "have evidence of part of a submerged conversation regarding the boundaries between lay and clerical activities."[62] If so, it seems possible that Julian backed off from re-invoking this legendary figure in the Long Text, currently politicized as an icon of female reformist activism.

To these findings about the "submerged conversation" within English vernacular circles we can now add a little more by way of international ones. There is a strong likelihood that Julian was no longer working on the Short Text by 1388 (see Chronology, 1373). What would have been internationally visible to a Norwich writer at this time? By 1387, her famous Norwich fellow-citizen, Adam Easton, papal proctor for the East Anglican Benedictines, had just been relieved of his brutal prison conditions at the hands of Urban VI.[63] He had been held initially in an old cistern and subject to severe torture along with fellow cardinals accused of conspiring against Urban. All the cardinals except Easton were killed, but high-level English interventions, including a letter from Richard II, helped secure Easton's life and alleviate his physical circumstances by 1387, although not his freedom. Because England was pro-Urban, the politics of this imprisonment were awkward. Chaucer, closely connected with English-Italian diplomacy, and in Italy on a mission at the time the Schism broke, perhaps first wrote his own legend of St. Cecilia to honour Easton's initial appointment as cardinal in 1381, as Giffin suggested, an association that would have been politically charged after 1385.

Immediately after his circumstances were relaxed, Easton, as an act of thanksgiving, wrote a defence of Bridget of Sweden, the *Defensorium sanctae Brigittae*. He wrote, apparently, from prison, but much in the bibliographically luxuriant way that the *Opus* author wrote, given the range of books Easton cites. A prominent opponent of Bridget's canonization, known to us only as a Perugian scholar, had launched charges of heresy against her revealed Rule which Easton had seen (vidi quendam libellum in Perusio compositum per articulos contra regulam suam [Hogg, 232]), as he tells the abbess of Vadstena. Among the charges was one saying that Christ would not dictate a rule through a woman, nor cause it to be published (nec per mulierem eciam fecerat eam publicari [235]). Tellingly, Easton regarded these charges of the Perugian as very hard to answer (libellus fuit valde difficilis ad solvendum [232]), but as a fervent act of posttraumatic thanksgiving, and apparently still in confinement, he wrote the *Defensorium* in support of her canonization.

Just how traumatic his experience had been when he called upon Bridget's intervention can be measured by the style of his letter to the abbess. Even allowing for medieval epistolary rhetoric, it is emotional: the tyranny of his imprisonment was so severe "he had not hoped," he writes in careful gender-inclusive language, "to escape death without a miracle of the saints" (mortem evadere non speravi sine sanctorum miraculo et *sanctarum*" [232]). At the time of the letter, he had written enough of the *Defensorium* at least to send a copy to Alphonse of Pecha, Bridget's last amanuensis and author of the *Epistola solitarii*, which would have been sometime before August 1388 when Alphonse died. The two men, however, could not have been more different in their approaches to defending a woman visionary. The *Defensorium* is (in Roger Ellis's words) "depressingly" conservative and patriarchal on the subject of women's intellectual and preaching capacities, *even for the times*. Most important for us is the way that Easton chose to defend Bridget from the Perugian scholar's charge that women were prohibited from preaching by St. Paul. Easton refers his opponent to the passage from Thomas Aquinas (*Summa theologiae*, Ia, q. 54, art. 1) we examined above, limiting women to the private sphere for any teaching activities, and Easton insists that privately is how Bridget did teach! (Bodleian Library, Hamilton MS 7, fol. 231v; Hogg, 236). Perhaps aware of her private living arrangements with her confessors and amanuenses in Rome (Easton knew Alphonse and Katherine of Sweden, Bridget's daughter), Easton may have stretched a point for all it was worth. But Bridget was *famous* for having publicly swayed popes and other leaders, so his attitude toward both female writing and female publication (in the medieval sense of the word) would hardly give comfort to an aspiring female writer, especially one who understood the Bridgettine legacy or scholastic position on women's teaching the way Julian did.

These factors would have been well known in the clerical circles of the busy port city of Norwich, the home abbey of the imprisoned cardinal of St. Cecilia, and a mere six miles from the town where he was born. In these circles, too, there would have been much discussion of the sobering fact that Bridget's canonization was under controversy right up to 1391. Julian's visionary mode was by now much more intellectual (and we have seen some possible reasons why),[64] much less like St. Bridget's affective piety than a young female visionary of the 1370s might ever have imagined, and much less like the strong Cecilia of legend. Julian surely dropped the passage for some mixture of these reasons.

Julian's Self-Censorship and Forensic Vision: The Politics of Iconography

There are further instances of Julian's deletion of overtly visionary (in Augustine's sense of "imaginative vision") and overtly iconographic passages. Another suppressed passage is her divine commission, which in fact prepares the ground for the passage on a woman's right to teach. Here, Julian is saying "I am not goode but 3if y love god the bett*er*," and she desires that every man who sees and hears her vision with a good will may have the "same profytte" that she was stirred by God to have the first time she saw her vision: "for yt (ys) como*nn and* generale as we ar alle ane, and *I am sekere I sawe it for the profytte of many oder*" (CW, Short, 6.12, 16–18; my emphasis). In the Long Text all but the first line, "I am not goode but 3if y love god the bett*er*," disappears, taking with it, in effect, the declaration of divine commission ("I am sekere . . ."). College and Walsh cite here a significant passage in *The Chastising*, which seems concerned to tone down the pro-revelatory quality of his translation of sections of the *Epistola*: "Alle hooli men and wymmen, which I clepe goddis chosen children, þou₃ þei wirche no myraclis, ne haue no spirit of profecie ne reuelacions ne visions, ₃it her names bien writen in þe booke of lijf" (ed. Bazire and Colledge, 183–84). It is perhaps on account of this kind of sentiment that she finally came to omit her earlier, more overtly visionary declaration of commission, along with her references to teaching as a woman. Instead she adds a heightened passage of *discretio* to the Long Text, another indicator of concern.

Some of her other suppressions tell us more, I believe, about the purpose for which she was willing to sacrifice reference to her gender. Julian, ultimately, had bigger fish to fry. A passage very early in her Short Text gives a careful *apologia* for what might otherwise, she apparently thought, appear impertinent about her wish for a vision of the Crucifixion. Julian is saying that one of the three graces she wished to have by God's gift was that, although she already had "grete felynge" for Christ's Passion, yet she wanted more:

> me thought I wolde haue bene that tyme with Mary Mawdeleyne and with othere that were Crystes loverse, that I myght have sene bodylye the passionn of oure lorde that he sufferede for me, that I myght have sufferede with hym as othere dyd that lovyd hym, *not withstandynge that I leevyd sadlye alle the peynes of Cryste as halye kyrke schewys and techys, and also the payntyngys of crucyfexes that er made by the grace of god aftere the techynge of haly kyrke to the lyknes of Crystes passyonn, als farfurthe as man ys witte maye reche.* Nou₃t with-stondynge alle this trewe be leve I desyrede a *bodylye* syght. . . . (CW, Short, 1.11–19)

Colledge and Walsh were the first to point to a possible relation with Lollard iconophobia (202, note to 14), an idea more recently taken up by Nicholas Watson, as a way of redating Julian's texts.[65] In fact, concern with Lollardy is not likely the thrust of the quotation, because if it were, we would have expected to see it *remain* in the Long Text, where chronologically the issue was much more important than in the time of the Short Text. We have already seen that concern with Lollardy in the city of Norwich itself (unlike the rural area around it) was minimal in Julian's time, that there was little use of vision within the Wycliffite movement, and none at all associated with women. What the passage actually says is that Julian desired a "bodylye sight," not because she did not believe solemnly (sadlye) in the Passion, or *in the paintings of crucifixes* that are made by the grace of God following (aftere) the teaching of holy church, that is (she qualifies) as far as man's wit may reach. She is talking about *belief in* the Passion artwork inspired by approved church doctrine.

What she is referring to here, and this has been little understood by literary scholars, is the fact that church authorities approved, in principle, the artwork displayed in parish churches. We know this because there were occasions when something unapproved was displayed, which then had to be confiscated. The *Annals of London* record for 1306, for example, the case of an unusual cross that had to be removed from the parish of St. Mildred. Described as horrifying (crux horribilis), the canons of St. Paul's brought accusations against the rector, Geoffrey of Wycombe, and the cross had to be secretly removed, despite the numbers of people coming to adore it. It was made by a German artist named Thydemann, and must have been, as Heslop suggests, a *Gabelkreuz*, a type of cross popular in Germany that shows Christ hung on forked branches, as it were.[66] (See figure 18.) We know that it was much more treelike in appearance because Bishop Baldock three times states that the horizontal cross arm was not of the accustomed shape. The word used to describe the arms of the cross is "patibulum," which means "a fork-shaped yoke placed on the necks of criminals." This "Thydemannus de Alemannia" had created "yconiam crucifixi *cum patibulo* sive ligno transversali *veram crucis formam minime pretendente*"! Thydemann is clearly seen in the records as dangerously flouting the iconography of the true cross. As crowds gather, peril to souls is feared (animarum pericula); the artist undergoes inquisition (ad nostram fecimus presenciam evocari et inquisita), and lest worse error persist (ne continuato errore peiora prioribus), Thydemann is forced to swear an oath that he will never again make "yconias similes vel patibula consuetis *deformia*" in the diocese or city of London. The cross itself has to be removed undercover ("quando secretius absque scandalo transferri"). The word "periculum" (danger) occurs three times in the passage. One can easily see, from an artistic standpoint, the attraction of such an image, which underlines the tree typology associated with Passion exegesis. But its unusual shape, coupled with the fact that Christ was, to judge from surviving *Gabelkreuz* examples, portrayed in a state of tortured desiccation (probably, that is, sadly lifelike for victims of crucifixion), meant that the bishop had to act to prevent what was construed as visual heterodoxy. So much for notions of artistic freedom.

This instance tells us a great deal: it tells us that there was *a visual orthodoxy* to be guarded in fourteenth-century England, and that the church was seen to be preserving that orthodoxy, a duty that goes back to the early church belief that the Gospel writer, Luke, had also been a painter and had painted a portrait

18. A Gabelkreuz (forked cross) from the parish church of St. Sixtus, Haltern am See, Westphalia, Germany, an example of c. 1340 made in the Rhine area. Measuring 134 x 103 cm. and made of oak, Christ is depicted as emaciated and in acute pain, an example of the kind of cross reported confiscated and destroyed in London in the early fourteenth century. Image courtesy of website of the parish church of St. Sixtus, Haltern am See, Westphalia, Germany: www.st-sixtus.de/Pfarrgemeinde/Rundgang.

of the Mother of God. (This very painting was even believed in the sixth century to have been sent by Eudocia, the wife of Theodosius II, to Pulcheria, the daughter of the Emperor Arcadius, and a copy of such a painting, according to Bede, reached England in the seventh century.)[67] In the fourteenth century, as Hilmo shows, there was a Europe-wide revival of interest in this subject of Luke's authentic painting, greatly aided by Marian devotion, and it begins entering English vernacular sources at this point. In one case in the fourteenth century this tradition was even used in comments against Lollards (although only once that we know of) by Robert Rypon, sub-prior of Durham and prior of Finchale (after Uthred's time), and patron of Gloucester College, Oxford.[68] But the long history of this connection between Gospel authority and officially approved image-making suggests that we need not turn to the Lollard controversy to explain Julian's use of it.

Rather, I think, Julian's *apologia* about church images in the Short Text springs out of this older tradition we have been describing. If we turn to the best-known medieval practical manual on the arts, *De diuersis artibus* by Theophilus, we learn even more. Theophilus stresses that all creative activity comes from God: "Through the spirit of wisdom, you know that all created things proceed [creata procedere] from God, and without Him nothing is [et sine ipso nihil esse]."[69] Theophilus also wrote of the Lord's filling the creator of the tabernacle with "the spirit of understanding," which is the artist's "intellectus spiritualis." Medieval artists, Michael Camille writes, "were very much aware of the biblical texts that precariously substantiated their practice—a creative context of self-effacement in which, Theophilus tells the novice artist, 'You can do nothing of yourself.'"[70] This is a powerful claim of authority for the church visual artist. And it was a claim backed up, when necessary, by the legal system, and even against the legal system, by claims to revelatory experience. Peter Gunnhouse discusses several such instances, including one in which a dispute between two monastic houses about which one of them owned the true head of John the Baptist as a relic was decided legally by judicial recourse to a painting of the beheading of John the Baptist(!). This is, then, a kind of *forensic* approach to medieval religious art which, I believe, we have not sufficiently appreciated, and which is certainly relevant to Julian, whose visionary descriptions of Christ on the cross are set out with painstaking "scientific" accuracy. There is more yet, however: when challenged by the church, an artist could him- or herself lay claim to visionary experience. Thus, Theophilus tells of an artist who was told to change the way he had depicted something, but the Virgin Mary intervened and said that the artist had represented it correctly. Much depends here on our recovering the medieval sense of the verb "repraesentare," which, as Mary Carruthers has shown going back to the early church, was understood literally to mean the act of "re-presenting"—that is, *presenting once again,* something that had historically occurred or a person who had historically lived.[71]

If we go back now to Julian's passage, we see a number of important qualifiers: she pledges solemn belief in images created both according to the church's teaching "als farfurthe" as human wit can reach *and* created through the "grace" of God—just as Theophilus said. Already we have two criteria not open to empirical scrutiny. What she has asked for then is a "bodylye" showing of the Passion. Julian distinguished three levels of vision, among which "bodylye" is, as for Augustine, the lowest; it is the historical, the temporal.[72] Why would she ask for the lowest, a *bodylye* sight? She wants to see it in the empirical sense of "seeing," as it really, historically happened, as Christ's other lovers saw it. By the time she was working on her revisions, I would suggest, she *had* seen it. Chapter 10 of the Long Text, for example, is a large expansion of the Short Text's Chapter 8's much briefer description of the visual detail of Christ's suffering on the cross. Chapter 10's rubric announces it as the second revelation, which is "of his discolourying . . . of our redemption, and the discolouring of the vernacle. . . ." Here Julian sets out in a now justly famous description the physical state of Christ on the cross, as it changes moment by moment. Part way through this very complex chapter, she suddenly invokes the model of the "vernacle of Rome," in which she makes *Christ himself the artist,* creating his own self-portrait:

> It made me to thinke of the holy vernacle of Rome which he hath portrayed with his owne blissid face whan he was in his herd passion, wilfully going to his deth, and often chongyng of colour. Of the brownehede and blakehede, reulihede [pitifulness] and lenehede [emaciation] of this image, many mervel how it might be, *stondying he portraied it* with his blissid face which is the fairhede [CW: 'fayerest'] of heaven. (WJ, Long, 10.30–35)

Images of Christ do not come in a more authoritative form than this, and Julian's, implicitly, complies with it in minute detail. The whole chapter is hedged round with well-informed *discretio,* and submission to church teaching, some of it directly reminiscent of *The Chastising* in the anxiety it betrays to assure the reader that "sekyng" (which is open to all believers) "is as good as beholdyng" in vision while we are *in via* ("for the tyme that he will suffer the soule to be in travel" [WJ, Long, 10.62–63]). The chapter also contains a strange vision-within-a-vision, in which Julian sees that if a man or a woman "were under the broade watyr" he or she might have "sight of God so, as God is with a man continually, he should be safe . . . *for he will that we levyn that we se him continually*, thowe that us thinkeith that it be but litil" (WJ, Long, 10.18–24), a passage that dexterously skirts a line of Poretian danger in its implication of continual sight of God. None of this appears in the Short Text, and it is, I would suggest, a reworking of the suppressed lines about paintings of crucifixes.

By the time Julian wrote this, I believe that she had seen (in a different sense) the possibility of providing a real, as yet unrevealed witness to supplement existing knowledge, biblical and otherwise, of what actually happened to Christ on the cross. The medieval theology of church art would support the possibility, however slender, that a visionary might be privileged in this way, and for the benefit of the community. Julian was not an artist, but she could paint in words, and that is exactly what she does, with forensic, meticulous detail. Her *Revelation* shows a real knowledge and real sensitivity to the visual arts, as we can see in other passages as well.[73] Her Mary, for example, is the young Mary usually portrayed in representations of the St. Anne Trinity (Long, ch. 4).[74] This was the period when representations that show Mary at a surprisingly childlike age, yet often already holding the Christchild while being taught to read by her mother, St. Anne, were beginning to emerge. (See figure 19.) These images of the "St. Anne Trinity" that begin to appear in the fourteenth century, I would suggest, pushed the iconography of Mary toward absolute youthfulness, well described by Julian's words.

> In this he brought our ladie sainct mari to my vnderstanding. I saw her ghostly in bodily lykenes, a simple mayden and a meek, yong of age, a little waxen aboue a chylde, in the stature as she was when she conceivede. (WJ, Long, 4.24–36)

England was a little slower than the Continent to adopt this grouping, and Julian's awareness of it may suggest East Anglian artistic sophistication often borne out in other instances.

19. An example of the St. Anne Trinity, from the Bedford Hours, London, British Library, MS Additional 18850, fol. 257v, showing a child-like Mary, already having given birth to Christ. The Bedford Hours commemorates the marriage of John of Lancaster, duke of Bedford to Anne of Burgundy in 1423. Reproduced by permission of the British Library.

Lest we find it odd, or even a mark of hubris, that Julian would feel she could do this, we need go no farther than the example of Bridget of Sweden (some prayers of whom also appear in the Amherst manuscript with Julian's Short Text). Julian would have known, by now, the success of Bridget of Sweden's visions in providing widely accepted "supplements" to the Gospels.[75] (We have seen that Bridget was accounted one of the "approved" women, and that other visionaries would later even be censured for differing from her.) But she also knew that Bridget was under fire for reasons of gender, and that not all learned commentators welcomed this intrusion of a vernacular-speaking woman into the canon. Even Cardinal Easton, although he himself rallied to a defence of Bridget after his ordeal in papal prison, did not quite know how to welcome such an intrusion. In the Long Text Julian adds a great deal of formal *discretio*, especially at the exact point that she suppresses her poignant description of teaching as a woman and just before she lists the three types of vision:

> But in althing I leve as holy church. . . . All this was shewid by thre: that is to sey, be bodily sight and by word formyd in my understonding and be gostly sight. But the gostly sight I cannot ne may not shew it as hopinly ne as fuly as I wolde. But I trust in our lord God almightie that he shal . . . make you to take it more gostly and more swetely than I can or may telle it. (WJ, Long, 9.24–28)

Here, then, the *reader* is the partner in vision, and, with God's help, must do what Julian cannot or dares not write. Julian herself, however, chose not to compromise, not on the speculative theology, not on the "quietism," not the revelatory theology itself. Only on her gender. And I believe she thought that was the least of the sacrifices before her.[76]

Chapter Nine

TWO OXFORD PROFESSORS UNDER INQUISITION I

Ockham, Radical Salvation Theology, and the "Creation of Doubt" in Langland and Chaucer

Strands of the theology of William Ockham lurk elusively behind the four-teenth-century mystics, especially Julian and Langland, and perhaps many Ri-cardian writers showing restlessness about conventional salvation doctrine. Pre-eminent among the fourteenth-century nominalists, Ockham's thought opened up the very will of God to new speculation: would the Lord exercise his ab-solute power (potentia dei absoluta), overturning the power he had ordained to himself (potentia dei ordinata) in his recorded promises to humankind (secun-dum leges ordinatas et institutas a deo)?[1] Ockham's theology emphasized God's ability to play this mysterious wild card of his absolute power: might God, ignor-ing his biblical covenants, intervene after all to save the unbaptized? And even the unjust? Or, the more frightening corollary: might he decide to damn the sinless (those *sine omni peccato,* as article 15 of Ockham's Avignon inquisition phrases it)?[2] If, as Langland's narrator cries out in the tortured breakdown of the A text, Christ saved the thief on the cross, a man with no Christian track rec-ord, what might the Lord do beyond human perception?

God's absolute power as presented in Ockham's thought tends to encourage dispensing with the need for intermediaries between God and the soul—at least, this is what the inquisitional articles against his writings on grace and natural merit stress. We turn now to the great contested topic of the fourteenth century, and especially as it was handled by two Oxford writers who came under censure. William Ockham and Uthred de Boldon both contributed importantly to the creation of novel views on salvation and, in highly different ways, to the related beatific vision controversies. Both theologians opened new possibilities for greater inclusiveness in salvation of non-Christians and those traditionally thought to be destined for eternal damnation. Ockham did this largely through radical nominalist propositions on salvation,[3] but, in the political sphere, he also virulently attacked Pope John XXII's position on the beatific vision, throwing his considerable weight behind the international opposition. Uthred made his contribution through, as I will suggest, a unique reading of the theology of beatific vision, a theory he called "visio clara" that opened the possibility of salvation to all non-baptized peoples. By far the most important connection between these two men is their scholastic heritage, and, as modern scholarship has shown, Uthred stands directly in the line of thought for which Ockham is best known and without which he cannot be understood today. There are other, less obvious conjunctions worth noting, however. One is the monastic fascination with theories of salvation history, a tradition that tolerated alternative views including Joachim of Fiore's, and in which Uthred was a leading author and thinker. Another is the Franciscan concept of mission, heavily influenced by Joachimism.[4] The latter, as a Franciscan, Ockham could scarcely have avoided knowing; the liberality of the former he was charged with indulging by no less an opponent than Bradwardine. The monastic tradition and the Benedictine tolerance of the revelatory contributed to making Uthred a famous and original figure in the mid-century Oxford salvation debates, the subject of chapter 10.

The broader history of these debates, and the famous *via moderna* theologians who led them, has been often addressed in scholarship.[5] Our concern here is with their use in a *revelatory* dimension, which for early Ricardian writers loomed large in the very high-profile 1368 condemnation of Uthred, and, more generally, in the unresolved inquisition of Ockham under John XXII and the possibilities opened up by the Ockhamist legacy. I should clarify that I have no hesitation about using the term "Ockhamist" since it is used in a very narrow sense: the only real area of Ockham's thought under discussion here is theological, not epistemological (where the adjective is more problematic).[6] Second, it is used here only in relation to the so-called "Pelagian" theology of salvation that is our main focus. On this most English of tendencies Ockham did have followers and "descendents" in England, where he ranks as the greatest of the nominalist theologians among those called the *moderni* by medieval scholars.[7]

Given the prominence of the Franciscan concept of missions to non-Christians, it is no accident that, although in no way a prophetic thinker, Ockham was connected by his own contemporaries with two suspect Joachite traditions. First, Ockham seems to have been the big fish John XXII was hoping to catch when he had Henry of Costesy arrested (discussed below), and second, one of his most prominent adversaries, Thomas Bradwardine, later to become archbishop of Canterbury, attacked Ockham very specifically with following in Joachim's footsteps. Joachite thought on salvation attracted the attention of the neo-Augustinian Bradwardine, who, writing in fierce reaction to Ockham's salvational generosities, charged Joachim of Fiore himself with Pelagianism in a very well-informed reading.[8] In his *De causa Dei contra Pelagianum*, Bradwardine very carefully reproduces points from Joachim's tract *Dialogi de praescientia Dei et praedestinatione electorum* (the availability of which suggests, yet again, that England was no backwater for Joachite studies). Bradwardine treats Joachim with respect but, in thoroughly English fashion, sees him as a great doctor whose authority was undermined by his censured attack on Peter Lombard's trinitarian views. As Bradwardine saw it, Joachim had later so strenuously tried to avoid the "Arianism" of his attack on Peter Lombard that in the *Dialogi* he fell into "Pelagianism." Joachim's "Pelagianism" had also been imitated and developed by scores of Franciscan missionaries and Joachite-leaning Spiritualists, another reason that Wycliffites (following Bradwardine) would later strive to distance themselves from it. Both Joachimism and Ockhamism were under inquisition at the time Bradwardine began his assault.[9] We do not think of these two traditions (Joachim's and Ockham's) as similar: one prophetic, exegetical, and mystical in orientation, the other purely philosophical and scholastic. Yet the papal court was also to see a connection between them, a complex story involving the heresy-hunting court of John XXII and its disapproval of both.

During this period, many ambitious clerics found denunciations of heresy a good way to recommend themselves to the pope. Jacques Fournier, for instance, the future Pope Benedict XII and immediate successor to John XXII, wrote treatises against the Franciscan Spirituals, Joachim of Fiore, Meister

Eckhart, Ockham, Michael of Cesena, and Olivi, all during John's pontificate, clearly, a smart career move. John Lutterell, about whom we know less, may have recommended himself in exactly this way, both in the case of Ockham and in the beatific vision controversies. Ockham was first called to account for suspect ideas in a Cambridge council (1323), then in the papal court at Avignon, where a commission (headed by his political enemy, former chancellor of Oxford, Lutterell) examined fifty-six allegedly unorthodox articles.[10] The slowness of this inquisition vexed Bradwardine so much that in the 1320s he began working out the views that would eventually fill his *De causa Dei*. Bradwardine, passionate on the subject, felt that in the wake of these new-fangled teachings virtually the whole world was sliding into Pelagian error (Totus etenim paene mundus post Pelagium abiit in errorem).[11] "Simon, dormis?" (Simon, are you asleep? [Mark 14:37]) he asks provocatively.[12]

Bradwardine and, a generation later, Wyclif belonged to the "school" Oberman called Tradition I, that is, those for whom scripture with its interpretation by the fathers and doctors of the church was sufficient. Ockham, on the other hand, and, a generation later, Uthred belonged to the opposing "school" (Oberman's Tradition II), for whom these sources must be supplemented by ecclesiastical traditions, including canon law.[13] Bradwardine, a severe student of Augustinian teachings on predestination and complete human dependence on God's grace, found the "moderns" like Ockham objectionable because they argued for the moral autonomy of human beings *ex puris naturalibus* (that is, acting out of purely natural powers). The *moderni* stressed a human being's capacity "to do what is in him" (facere quod in se est) in order to earn salvation.[14] These Latin phrases are keystones in nominalist terminology and thought.[15] Bradwardine, initially as a confrere of Lutterell's and eventually as archbishop of Canterbury, had real weight to throw behind his denunciation of Ockham's radical questioning of predestinated salvations.[16] Bradwardine, determined to push the pendulum back all the way, insisted that *all* salvations were predetermined.[17]

These, then, were the broad lines of the academic theological debate when Ockham was called to Avignon. His inquisition there is important for fourteenth-century England, not only for his own generation. It was in the next generation, however, that scholars, especially Wyclif, really took up Bradwardine's views and gave them legs. As many literary scholars have shown, these ideas from the schools filtered even into the vernacular writers. Chaucer, who cites Bradwardine by name, exhibits a life-long passion for questions of destiny and free will, on which he was both well informed and expected at least one stratum of his audience to be as well. On these topics, he weighs in as more conservative (Pearsall euphemistically calls him "quietist") than Langland, who, as we will see in the next chapter, leans much more in the Ockhamist-Uthredian direction.[18]

From Beatific Vision to *An princeps:* Ockham *contra papam,* the Inquisition of Ockham, and the Ockhamist Legacy

The pontificate of John XXII, one of the most important chapters in the history of constraint on medieval intellectual freedom, impacted fourteenth-century Edwardian and Ricardian writers more profoundly, because more *formatively,* than did even the latter-day constraints provoked by Wycliffism. In fact, without the writers condemned during this pontificate, it is difficult to imagine Wyclif's thought, or indeed his mentor FitzRalph's, developing at all.[19] This was the pope who resurrected the censorship of Olivi and who oversaw the bloodiest persecution of Franciscan Spirituals. In this he was encouraged initially by a hard-line element among the Conventuals of the order, that is, until the pope's radical attack on even their much watered-down doctrine of Franciscan poverty proved intolerable, causing a revolt under the minister general of the order, Michael of Cesena. This is the pope, then, who re-awoke the antimendicant debate from a fragile peace, both within and without the order, and created the legislation for which many Franciscan Spirituals were persecuted and died.

Prominent among the Michaelist "heretics" (as those who fled Avignon with the minister general were termed) was Ockham, who had been cited to Avignon initially to answer charges concerning his academic philosophical and theological opinions in 1324.[20] These charges had been prepared by his countryman, John Lutterell, perhaps to advance his own career at the papal court and doubtless because of internal Oxford factionalism.[21] Preoccupied with preparing his own defence, Ockham at first took no position on John XXII's sudden overturning of the Conventual position on poverty,[22] but when Michael fled to the court of Ludwig of Bavaria, Ockham joined him. There he launched a series of political writings on papal power, Franciscan poverty, disendowment, and the heresies (as Ockham saw them) of John XXII. Nor were these the only issues. On All Saints Day in 1331 the pope gave the first in a series of three sermons enunciating an unusual opinion of the beatific vision, upon which Ockham and the Munich refugees lost no time in joining with others to charge John XXII with doctrinal heresy again. Ockham's name, then, was famously joined to the *cause célèbre* of the beatific vision controversies, which ended in international scandal, the grudging deathbed recantation of a pope, and the subsequent condemnation of John XXII's opinions by the next pope, Benedict XII.[23] All these events, together with Ockham's disturbing and speculative academic opinions on issues of grace and salvation, were destined to make him one of the most destabilizing figures in the fourteenth-century church.[24]

The flight took place from Avignon, but the impact of all Ockham's actions in his native England was profound and felt for decades to come. We do not know exactly where Ockham stood on the terrifically (in the 1320s and 1330s) dangerous issue of Olivian apocalypticism, but we do know that the papacy had its own suspicions. It was likely in their search to apprehend Ockham that Henry of Costesy and three Franciscan lectors at Cambridge were arrested on charges of heresy in 1329–30. We know this because the papal correspondence regarding the case occurs with letters dealing with Ockham, making a contextual link between his prosecution and that of the very Olivian Henry of Costesy.[25]

We can get a sense of the punch Ockham's political prose packs from his famous 1334 *Letter to the Friars Minor* at Assisi, the kind of Michaelist text copied in Ricardian England in Oxford collections dealing with Wycliffite and Amourian materials:[26]

> So that I may follow in every way the footsteps of the glorious Apostle blessed Paul, I desire to give, as well as I can, an account to you all, Catholic Christians and heretics. . . . [M]ay all Christians know that I stayed in Avignon almost four whole years before I recognized that the one who presided there had fallen into heretical perversity. Because, not wishing to believe too readily that a person placed in so great an office would declare that heresies should be held, I did not care either to read or to possess his heretical constitutions. Presently, however, when some occasion arose, at the command of a superior I read and diligently studied three of his constitutions — or rather, heretical destitutions — namely, *Ad conditorem, Cum inter nonnullos,* and *Quia quorundam.* In these I found a great many things that were heretical, erroneous, silly, ridiculous, fantastic, insane, and defamatory, contrary and likewise plainly adverse to orthodox faith, good morals, natural reason, certain experience, and fraternal charity.[27]

Conciliation was not Ockham's strong point. Even in translation one can see him slinging back the official language of heresy ("heretical perversity," "heretical," "erroneous," "fantastic," "contrary . . . to faith, good morals, etc.").[28] That it was safe to challenge these things only in exile and under the protection of one of the pope's most powerful enemies, Louis of Bavaria, becomes very clear when we see the treatment meted out to those who attacked these bulls head on.[29]

The classic view of Ockham by historians of England is concisely summarized by Peter McNiven,

> His most revolutionary assertion, for which he claimed the best Scriptural authority, was that "the Church" was not the formally-constituted body headed by the ecclesiastical hierarchy, but the whole community of the faithful, comprising all "true believers" from the days of the Apostles to the present. He combined the apparently unambiguous message of the Gospels — that Jesus had counseled submission to the temporal power — with the more peculiarly Spiritual Franciscan doctrine that Jesus and His followers had renounced all worldly possessions. These doctrines enabled Ockham to argue that secular rulers held ultimate jurisdiction over material property held by ecclesiastics, and that the kings of England had the right to tax Church property.[30]

This is broadly true, but his "most revolutionary assertion," I would point out, was not wholly original to him. The idea can be found in Franciscan apocalyptic thinkers like Olivi, whose prominent works, as a fellow Franciscan, Ockham could hardly have escaped knowing. Ockham's mode of intellectualism was scholastic, not apocalyptic or visionary in methodology, but it is impossible that a man as militant as Ockham would remain unaffected by the powerful ideologies of Spiritualism for which members of his order were living and dying throughout his lifetime. It was this, the other "more peculiarly Spiritual Franciscan doctrine," which enabled, as McNiven says, Ockham to argue for confiscation of clerical properties. Whether Ockham *was* a Franciscan Spiritual is an open question: he fled in sympathy with Michael of Cesena, who had persecuted Spirituals mercilessly, but contemporaries and especially the papacy connected Ockham with the Spirituals and hunted him as one.

Ockham's works were to become a rich source of such ideas. His *An princeps*, addressed to King Edward III in England c. 1337, argues that the king ought to be able to draw on clerical finances in time of war. On the same point in his *Octo quaestiones*, he argued that "churches [can] justly be deprived of the honors, rights, liberties, and privileges granted to them if they are not faithful to the laymen who have granted these things. Again, faith should not be kept with a faithless enemy" (7.4).[31] And, as we have just seen in his *Letter to the Friars Minor*, he lambasted John as a heretic in terms that must have struck awe into contemporaries and which make even Wyclif seem moderate at times. Disendowment was always a popular idea with the powerful lay leaders, and the friars were terrifically successful at wooing them. This struck fear into the hearts of the "possessioner" clergy—and long before the rise of Wyclif.[32] It is no accident then that the *Dialogus* Trevisa translated on issues of the papacy and temporal power would be pseudonymously attributed to Ockham.[33] Or that the Latin poem, "Vox in Roma," likely written by a Benedictine, denounces Ockham's books as the source of ideas about disendowment in Oxford. It laments that an alliance of "a few boys now" (pauci modo pueri) want to undo ecclesiastical possessions traditionally established by "popes and emperors" (pape et cesares) (16, lines 2 and 4).[34]

We have already had cause to note struggles between friars and other clergy at Oxford in the second half of the fourteenth century, and the tendency for the friars to form alliances with powerful laity, who were naturally open to ideas of disendowment. Although the king's response was complex, we have seen evidence of Edward's subtle favoritism toward the Dominican William Jordan (later to be Uthred's accuser) over FitzRalph, and the king's attempt to close the seaports to prevent FitzRalph and his opponents from traveling to Avignon. A similar and earlier case appears in relation to Ockham, beginning with Edward II's attempts to prevent John Lutterell from taking abroad his campaign to curtail the teaching freedoms and privileges of the mendicant faction at Oxford. The case is very illuminating on questions of earlier fourteenth-century intellectual freedom, antimendicantism, and the English penchant for dealing with heresy within the secular rather than the ecclesiastical system. In the summer of 1322 the bishop of Lincoln had dismissed Lutterell as chancellor of Oxford because he had imposed draconian restrictions upon teaching and freedom of assembly (conventiculas) within the university. This he had done in an attempt to curb disputes over Dominican privileges there.[35] As Thomas Barton points out, in the *Calendar of the Close Rolls* for that year is a summary of a letter from Edward:

To Master John Luterel. Prohibition of his going beyond the sea, or of the sending thither anything touching the disputes that arose between him, when he was chancellor of the university of Oxford, and the masters and scholars of the university, or of his causing anything concerning the same to be published anywhere, until the king, having had information from both sides, shall order to be done what he shall see fit.[36]

Edward ordered Lutterell to appear before him at court in York, and representatives of the opposing (i.e., university mendicant parties) to do so as well. But Edward had—in canon law—no jurisdiction to resolve disputes of academic freedom, and within a year (by 1323) the provincial chapter in Cambridge was examining suspect portions of Ockham's writings and Lutterell was on his way to Avignon for the same purpose.[37] This is yet another English instance of secular or royal courts attempting to deal with or intervene in cases of heresy, raising the inevitable tensions with ecclesiastical authorities.

Both Ockham's disendowment ideas, then, and to some extent the inquisition of his philosophical ideas are ultimately inseparable from the larger political contexts in which he found himself. His anti-papal writings go hand in hand with Ockham's influential emphasis on the church as the distinct and less tangible entity composed of all believers rather than the visible institution (perhaps with some echo of his fellow Franciscan, Olivi).[38] The institution as such not only could err, but its divinely ordained laws could be overridden at God's desire—or "whim," on a cynical reading. Ockham's perspective also made strict notions of predestination or determinism untenable. Wyclif was to take such ideas entirely in the *opposite* direction. This suggests that the motivations for the 1389 confiscations were not entirely the suppression of Wycliffism, because on just as many points (like salvation or revelation) Ockham, Olivi, Rupescissa, or even William of St. Amour (on elitism of the priesthood) could have been used to *refute* Wyclif.

For Wyclif the church was the invisible number of the elect (and only the elect) at any point in time. The severe predestinarian thought of Archbishop Bradwardine, which was later magnified in Wycliffism, may account for a kind of theological counter-thrust we can trace in the resurgence of Ockhamist and Uthredian thought in the 1380s.[39] It is also relevant to the salvationally liberal writers of the period (including Langland and Julian, both of whom would likely have abhorred Wyclif's position on these points). The kinds of theological ramifications of such a doctrine were enormous, with implications debated in all the major Ricardian writers.[40] In what follows I will look at some of those aspects of Ockhamist thought that were considered suspect and that seem relevant to revelatory theology in Ricardian writers. We will go back to the list of censurable articles compiled by former Oxford chancellor Lutterell to know what originally distressed the authorities, including subsequent church leaders like Bradwardine. Previously unnoticed among these are the kinds of salvation issues — issues that directly questioned *the role of the church* in both salvation history and personal eschatology — that parallel articles of Olivian thought previously condemned. These, in fact, would re-emerge in 1368 in England with the censure of Uthred, and we will see Langland actually and increasingly revising to play down the role of the church in inclusive salvations (especially in C). University thinkers like Chaucer's friend Strode were debating these ideas and working to counter Wyclif's opposite extremism through the 1370s and 1380s (at least until their respective deaths in 1387 and 1384).[41] Strode, for instance, argued strenuously against Wyclif's view of predestination as destroying any hope of salvation among individuals and denying free will. This very concern, I will suggest in chapter 10, brought a revival of interest in liberal ideas in the tradition of Uthred, evident even in the vernacular writers.

Ockham under Inquisition and the Creation of Doubt

One of the most significant contemporary critiques of Ockham's writings was that, as the rector of the University of Paris stressed in his 1340 condemnation, they had engendered in the arts faculty an attitude of doubt. The official condemnation forbids, among other things, anyone to assert, "without distinction," that "Socrates and Plato or God and creatures are nothing [nichil sunt]."[42] This was, more generally, doubt toward "the accepted authorities and towards the correspondence between terms and things."[43] This is certainly *not* the kind of critique one would level at Wyclif, who, if anything, returned theology to new regard for literalism and for the literal level of scripture. All the evidence suggests, and largely for chronological reasons, that Ricardian writers were much more deeply intrigued by Ockhamist thought than by developing Wycliffite thought. Their poetry is riddled with issues of faith and doubt, something we hardly see in the Lollard texts. Turning now to the articles under papal inquisition at the time Ockham fled leaving his case undecided, we find a wide range of topics. The topics Lutterell and his commissioners objected to include: salvation of the non-baptized, the so-called "Pelagian" meritocracy questions, the role of the church in mediation, the question of God's absolute power (*potentia absoluta*), the question of God's unknowability, and the limits of human knowledge. These things, especially when put in the form of extreme propositions for disputation, could be heard as creating deniability—if not fully as modern "atheism," in Jill Mann's sense, most certainly as "creating doubt."[44] There are also articles that object to what we might call Ockham's exercises in "shock value": the theological speculations or better, exercises in speculation, that pose shocking questions, such as whether God can be hated, whether he can act unjustly or act tyrannically.[45]

What is remarkable about Ockham (and important at least for modern literary scholarship) is that his thought was debated relatively unimpeded in Oxford's schools. Even Lutterell's campaign may have had a little more political than doctrinal motivation (and the same is almost certainly true of Friar Jordan's attack against Uthred). But once mounted, they caused real damage for the careers and lives of the accused. We do not know to what extent Ockham's flight from Avignon was prompted by "Michaelist" loyalties and to what extent by academic fears, but we know he fled leaving his academic inquisition unfinished and had to remain in exile for the rest of his life.[46]

Ockham's speculative thinking, of course, emphasized the divine *potentia absoluta* (God's power to do as he pleased) at the expense of his *potentia ordinata* (God's ordinances, as covenanted with man and recorded in scripture).[47] Taken to extremes (and medieval academic speculation did wander into extremes in sometimes probing disputations) this had the effect of unsettling, or calling into question, any aspect of doctrine. And most especially it called into question issues of salvation, the area in which earlier scholars like Godfrey had argued that theologians should *not* bow to episcopal censure or repression. Leff summarizes the risks of Ockhamist theology this way:

> If taken to extremes its effects were far-reaching. Thus it was held that God could mislead; that Christ could be misled; that revelation could falsify; that God could love the mortal sinner more than the man in grace, that God could want a man to hate him; that grace and mortal sin could coexist; that free will was more important than grace, and so on. In this

aspect, it need hardly be said, God in his *potentia absoluta* was a very different God from that of tradition.[48]

Next to Ockham's revolution, even Wycliff's theology often pales into conservatism. Even modern commentators can be scandalized by Ockham.[49] And given that Ockhamist influence was much more pervasive among all our writers than *concrete* evidence of Wycliffism (indeed in Langland the *formative* evidence almost certainly goes the other way: that Langland influenced Wycliffites), it seems important to understand exactly what papal commissioners condemned among these speculations.

Ockham's writings are very technical, and needless to say, this technicality was usually lost on later non-academic reception. He is also extremely difficult to quote,[50] because the terms used in his logic are very technically defined, and the definitions are cumulative. Because this is not a study of Ockham, but rather of his later cultural impact on revelatory writing, I have minimized quotation from Ockham, emphasizing the articles of condemnation launched against him instead. But let us hear an example of such technicality from the man himself, translated by leading modern scholars of Ockham. In his *Predestination, God's Foreknowledge, and Future Contingents,*[51] Question IV, he asks:

> Is there a cause of predestination in the predestinate and cause of reprobation in the reprobate? It is proved that there is no cause . . . since baptized infants are saved although they never earned merit (habuerunt merita). . . .

> ———

> I maintain that there is a cause . . . [f]or this inference is correct: 'He commits the sin of final impenitence; therefore he will be reprobate.' Similarly: 'He will persevere to the end; therefore he will be predestinate.' For just as God is not a punisher before a man is a sinner, so He is not a rewarder before a man is justified by grace.

He then wanders into a dangerous area:

> Nevertheless, I maintain as well that a cause . . . can precede in the reprobate (or predestinate) or in [his] parents. For instance, an infant dying

in original sin is punished with the penalty of damnation (*poena damni*) because of the sin of the parents, but not with the penalty of bodily suffering (*poena sensus*) unless because of his own sins. Similarly, a baptized child can be saved and hence predestinate because of the good works of the parents.[52]

This is the kind of assertion that for many readers—Lutterell chief among them—verged on or trespassed into Pelagianism. Rega Wood has discussed both the charges of Pelagianism (which she defines as the view that "for Ockham the scope of God's power is restricted by the human will") and semi-Pelagianism (which "questions predestination" and "affirms that human free will has occasionally taken some initiative in faith").[53] She concludes, "Ockham's theology is a celebration not only of divine freedom but also of divine mercy and liberality. It would be a poor liberality that allowed no role at all to the sinner in human salvation" (366). This rings true not only of Ockham,[54] but of Langland, and also of Julian. One can see how easily this sort of merit-based thinking might filter into the vernacular, and how awareness that it might be heterodox would also. In fact, the fifteenth-century English translator of Mechthild of Hackeborn's *Book of Ghostly Grace* flags with a caveat lector a statement of hers extrapolating a similar point about parental ability to save a child: "Offe this ensaumple before, *beware*, that es to saye that a childe be the moderes vowe of Cristiante schalle be savede, thowe itt dey before, *for clerkes holdene the contrarye opynyon*. For I trowe the furste wrytere mysunderestode."[55] This is a good example of "trickle down" of academic questions into vernacular theology and nervousness about quasi-Pelagian ideas nearly a hundred years after Ockham.

The articles Lutterell alleged against Ockham contain an accompanying interpretive list of "errores" that define or clarify what is "contra veram et sanam doctrinam" about each individual article extracted from Ockham's works.[56] This interpretive list is very helpful as a tool of reception—one can often see in it how an article of thought meant (surely) as stimulating speculation or as a mental exercise in "what if . . ." is reductively rendered as a bald statement. Yet in Ockham's writings, as in those of other *via moderna* thinkers, formulae such as "non asserendo sed disputando" recur throughout, a distinction entirely flattened by both Lutterell and the six-man commission (which included Lutterell) later appointed by the pope to make a fuller report.[57] This denial of the right to freely discuss (libere tractare) goes right to the heart of issues of intellectual freedom. Especially important is that Lutterell and his commission resurrect the category "Pelagian" to condemn several of the articles, sometimes even, perhaps wryly, condemned as "peius errore Pelagii."[58] So, for instance, the sixteenth article labels as "similiter error Pelagii" (similarly, the error of Pelagius) the idea that just as a man acting purely out of his natural powers can lose merit (toward salvation), so he may also earn merit.[59] So, too, the eighteenth article, which suggests that an act elicited out of charity does not exceed the natural faculties is labeled as "error Pelagii et peius" (error of Pelagius and worse)![60]

These articles and others like them obviously open the way for speculation about the salvation of the righteous non-Christian (a huge topic, as George Russell and others have shown, in Langland and especially in his revision of the C text). Other articles condemned as "Pelagian" might, when decontextualized from academic debate, even suggest the "whimsical" nature of God's salvational choices: e.g., that even supernaturally inspired grace might not merit eternal life, *unless* God chooses to accept it (article 35).[61] These kinds of thoughts, as we will see, dominate both the breakdown of Langland's A text and seem to be parodied in Chaucer's *House of Fame*. This idea of a "whimsical" God is reinforced by other articles which stress that God could act unjustly in making either angels or men reprobate "sine omni peccato" (article 15), or that to hate God could be an "actus rectus" (article 23). Several of the condemned articles appear to destabilize the centrality of love in Christian theology, at times wanting to privilege free will (liberum arbitrium) over it.[62] Langland and Thomas Usk both wrestled mightily with these problems: Langland most originally, and especially in C where he creates the new character *Liberum Arbitrium*; Usk to some extent likely following Langland and to some extent following Chaucer's works on predestination issues (*Troilus, House of Fame,* and *Boece*).[63] Lutterell's commission doubtless chose to put as first on the list of censures the idea that Christ could have [potuit] sinned, just as he [chose to] die, if he had assumed human nature without gifts, grace, and love (article 1). The idea is arresting— and that is certainly what Lutterell wanted.

Some Echoes of "Doubt" Theology in Langland's A Text and Chaucer's *House of Fame*

Did the condemnations and suspicions of Ockhamist and Uthredian thought impact vernacular Ricardian literary visions in any concrete way? Poets write poetry, not theology, and so this is always a difficult call to make. Still, as their works show, Langland and Chaucer were alive to these debates, though they perhaps leaned to slightly different sides of them. Chaucer refers to Bradwardine by name in the "Nun's Priest's Tale," at the moment when Chaunticleer's fate hangs most in the balance (VII.3243). Chaucer's use of destiny, both here and throughout his poetry, is very different from Langland's, his treatment of God and god-like figures entirely different. Chaucer, for example, as scholarship has suggested, seems sometimes to explore Ockhamist issues allegorically, in (for instance) Walter's uncomfortably "god-like" role in the "Clerk's Tale." Also, among radical speculations in Ockhamist theology are questions that deal in God's ability to create illusion, some of which are reminiscent of what Chaucer explores—in a safely pre-Christian setting—in the "Franklin's Tale."[64] We can also see Langland wrestling with, and once in a while even condemning, just this kind of speculation. Take for instance his frustration about speculative mealtime theological disputation in which even the laity now participate:

> Nowe is þe manere at þe mete, when munstrals ben stille,
> The lewed aȝen þe lered þe holy lore to dispute,
> *And tellen of þe trinite how two slowe þe thridde . . .*
> Thus they dreuele at the deyes, the deite to know
> And gnawen god with gorge when here gottes fullen.
> (C.XI.35–41)

Line 37 (emphasized) describes just the kind of speculation that Lutterell and his colleagues objected to in Ockham. In fact, so shocked were some scribes of this passage in Langland's B version that they substituted "a tale ouþer tweye" for the second half of the line (B.X.54).

My interest in what follows, however, is not to try to pin down exactly where Langland or Chaucer stood on what Richard Green has rightly called "covenantal theology." Green, Coleman, and others have given us superb guidelines in this difficult task. My goal is, rather, to illuminate the spots where Langland and Chaucer write revelatory material that might, at least in *reception* if not conception, be mistaken for Ockhamist ideas under academic inquisition for "creating doubt." Whatever the case may be, it is clear that when Chaucer and Langland explore the kind of radical Ockhamist thought that came under inquisition earlier in the fourteenth century, they do so invariably in visionary or allegorical works or in safely classicized moments.

Langland and the Crisis of Doubt

We have seen that the Avignon commissioners objected strongly to elements in Ockham's speculative thought prompting the idea that God could love the mortal sinner more than the man in grace. This is exactly the objection that Langland's narrator raises at the breakdown of the A text, citing several biblical examples of what he believes is precisely this phenomenon of God's choosing to love, and worse, *reward* the sinner. At the opening of the passage, Will is in a state of despair over predestination:

> Ȝet am I neu*er*e þe ner for nouȝt I haue walkid
> To wyte what is dowel witt*er*ly in herte,
> For howso I werche in þis world, [wrong] op*er* ellis,
> I was markid wiþoute m*er*cy, & myn name entrid
> In þe legende of lif longe er I were.
> (A.XI.258–62)

To one believing himself "markid wiþoute m*er*cy," it is an easy leap to envy of those who committed mortal sin but are presumed by learned theologians to be saved. Throughout the list that ensues, Will's assumption that an inscrutable God exercised his *potentia absoluta* to override a system of just desert is palpable. The dreamer begins a long and doctrinally dubious rant (which, tellingly, in C would be much expanded and given over to the enigmatic figure of Will's wild-eyed alter ego, "Recklessness"). In it, he complains that no one did better than Solomon and Aristotle, yet "al holy chirche holden hem in helle" (A.XI.271). The dreamer's comments get more and more outrageous: he complains of the thief on the cross, whose last-minute conversion bought him salvation "son-ner*e*" than St. John the Baptist, Adam, or Isaiah, "that hadde leyn w*it*h Lucifer manye longe ȝeris" (284). Who might do worse, he rails, than Mary Magdalene, or David when he killed Uriah, or Paul in the days when he persecuted Christians? Yet "arn no[ne] . . . sou*er*eynes in hevene / As þise þat wrouȝte wykkidly" (291–92).

Finally, just lines before the text breaks off completely,[65] Langland offers a sensationally altered quotation from Augustine: "Ecce ipsi ydiot[e] rapiunt celum ubi nos sapientes in infernum mergemur" (A.XI.305) (Behold, these ignorant ones [ydiote] seize heaven by force, while we learned ones are plunged [mergemur] into hell). This is adapted from the *Confessiones*, 8.8, which merely has the learned "mired in flesh and blood" rather than "plunged into hell."[66] This audacious idea is never really translated into the Middle English of the text as some of the other quotations in this section are—ironically, only the Latin literate would understand it. The poem nevertheless breaks off with the idea that heaven is granted to the poor, such "as plouȝmen . . . / Souteris, and seweris," who "Percen with a *pater noster* þe paleis of heuene / Wiþoute penaunce, at here partyng, into [þe] heiȝe blisse" (A.XI.310–13).[67] This is the thought with which the A text breathes its last. However, as the very first line of the new B continuation makes clear, even this salvation of the poor and simple, the dreamer feels, is utterly *undeserved* reward. In the corresponding point in B, that is, we find the poor going "Into þe [parfit] blisse of Paradis for hir pure bileue, / *That inparfitly here knewe and ek lyuede*" (B.X.470, my emphasis).

Later in the next chapter we will look at the B continuation for the light it sheds backward on A's demise. As the A text's editor George Kane established, both internal and external textual evidence points to the fact that A is an unfinished text. Among the chief arguments for seeing the text as broken off are the disproportionate length of its *Vita* (which is "sketchily developed") compared to its *Visio,* the fact that the Dreamer falls asleep in A.IX.58 and is not reawakened by the poet (as he is in B's and C's endings); the fact that A.IX's incipit promises to develop *secundum witte and Resoun,* but Reason is never mentioned again (nor is the phrase a scribe's borrowing from B or C). Such textual disruptions point quite strongly to authorial, not scribal disruption.[68] But taking just for the moment the A ending itself, we can be struck by the fact that several of Ockham's statements labeled by Lutterell's commission as erroneous or "Pelagian" also present an inscrutable God—a God, that is, whose qualities and judgements we cannot know nor predict, not even on the basis of the covenantal theology of scripture and the learned. Covenantal theology, of course, deals only in God's ordained (*ordinata*) power, not his absolute power. This, I would suggest, helps us understand the tortuous connection between learning and salvation at the end of A, or more precisely, between learning and despair—the "creating of doubt." In the B continuation this will emerge more clearly as *fear* of and anger about predestination, but at the end of A the emphasis is *unknowability* (the topic, by the way, of Lutterell's fourth article against Ockham) and unpredictability of God's actions. Langland is treading, then, on thin ice, or at least ice that in academic contexts had given way to inquisition. My point here is not to invoke a Lutterell look-alike watching menacingly over Langland's shoulder as he writes vernacular poetry. It is, however, to suggest why Langland was *uncomfortable* for a while with the way A ended (which must have been the case given the dramatic development of BC), and why for a while A (as our extant manuscripts show) does not seem to have gone into much circulation until very late in Langland's productive life. If we stop and think about it, B and C are much more comfortable and comforting on personal salvation. They offer solutions to these issues, but A does not.

Chaucer and the Creation of Doubt

This, I believe, is one of the unlikely elements from Langland's A text that Chaucer plays upon in his teasing satire of the revelatory in *House of Fame*. Indeed, the A text's breakdown into doubt about God's ultimate judgements may be echoed in as unlikely a spot as Chaucer's *House of Fame*, the first work of his in which, as J. A. W. Bennett, George Kane, James Simpson, and Frank Grady have noted, we can hear Langland's voice.[69] In passages like the *House of Fame*'s description of swarming pilgrims, "with scrippes *bret-ful of lesinges*" (2122) or folk running "alle on an *hepe*" (2149), one sees language and images so very like *Piers Plowman* (A. Prol.41 and 50), and not generally typical of Chaucer's style elsewhere. To list the parallels between the two poems is not our task here, but they range from such language to their dreamers' perspectives from "above" to (in relation to A especially) the fragmentary ending of each—Chaucer's perhaps in imitation or even parody of Langland's elusive hunt for a "man of gret auctorite" (*Fame*, 2158). Chaucer and Langland, once thought to inhabit entirely different worlds, are now understood by recent scholarship as sharing a much smaller world: the civil service and writing offices of Westminster, and, smaller still, the *English*-reading literary public of Ricardian London (a relatively tiny group compared to the larger extant evidence of Latin-reading clergy and French-reading nobility).[70] In this context, intertextuality between two contemporary English London poets seems much more likely than earlier generations of scholarship imagined. Whatever the reason, *House*, in fact, seems to explore (among the significant Dantean, Virgilian, and Ovidian threads well established by scholarship),[71] though much more playfully, these same Ockhamist or nominalist notions about the arbitrariness of salvation as may have helped bring the A text to crisis. Fascination with suspect Ockhamist thought and revelatory theology, however, act on Chaucer's entirely different imagination in different ways.

The obliquely Langlandian style of *House* (only one aspect of which I will highlight here) is part of Chaucer's tendency to cite and allude to revelatory writing everywhere in the poem—overtly to John's Apocalypse and, of course, to Dante's *Divine Comedy* and visionary moments in Virgil's *Aeneid*. The humanist side of this equation has long been recognized. As James Simpson puts it, *House* "has been hailed as the first evidence of Chaucer's 'Renaissance' capacities, since it so obviously situates itself in a tradition of vastly ambitious, especially Dantean, vernacular enterprise; makes the first invocation in English poetry; and lays claim to poetic fame."[72] But Dante's humanism is also a Christian one, and in this book we have already noted that there is a surprising moment of serious Christian visionary convention in *House*. We recall that the moment that Geoffrey sees the eagle, if lifted out momentarily from the satire, could be extracted from any sober account of visionary experience:

'O Crist,' thought I, 'that art in blisse,
Fro fantom and illusion
Me save!' and with devocioun
Myn yen to the heven I caste.
Tho was I war, lo! . . .
          (*House*, 492–96)

And we cannot forget how fundamental Macrobian terminology is to the project:

Why that is an *avisioun*,
And this a *revelacioun* . . .
Why this a *fantom*, these *oracles*,
I noot; but who-so of these miracles
The causes knoweth bet than I
Devyne he . . .
          (*House*, 7–14, with omissions)

Moreover, a good deal of revelatory allusion comes as part of Chaucer's brilliant displacement of John's Apocalypse into a semi-classicized visionary world—an elusive Christian humanism which, I would argue, seems to have been a kind of early experiment Chaucer would later abandon. As the eagle takes him to the threshold of the House of Fame, he even uses the ecstatic experience of St. Paul in gentle self-parody, perhaps at the same time mimicking Langland (in B.XI.116). Here is St. Paul in 2 Corinthians 12:1–4:

1. If I must glory (it is not expedient indeed), but I will come to visions and revelations of the Lord.
2. I know a man in Christ: above fourteen years ago (*whether in the body, I know not, or out of body, I know not; God knowth*), such a one caught up to the third heaven.
3. And I know such a man (*whether in the body, or out of the body, I know not; God knowth*),
4. That he was caught up into paradise and heard secret words [*archana verba*] which it is not granted to man to utter. . . .

This passage, with its allusion to "archana verba" and revelatory "out of body" experience spoken by the recently imprisoned St. Paul, was to become, in fact, a way of signaling constraint issues and revelatory license among Ricardian writers (of which we will see more in chapter 10). It also appears where we might least expect it. In Chaucer's *House of Fame*, for instance:

> 'Tho gan I wexen in a were,
> And seyde, "I woot wel I am here;
> But where in body or in gost
> I noot, y-wis; but god, thou wost."
> (*House*, 979–82)

That Chaucer is echoing Paul, and also Dante's own echo of Paul in *Paradiso* 1.4–9, is well known. But the first part of the passage sounds very Langlandian. Compare this passage in *Piers*

> Al for tene of here tyxst tremeblede myn herte
> *And in a wer gan y wex* and with mysulue to despute
> Where y were chose or not chose. . . .
> (B.XI.115–17)

Chaucer was apparently an astute, if whimsical reader of Langland. A "wer" is a state of doubt or complexity (as the editors of both Chaucer and Langland gloss it). More precisely, according to the *Middle English Dictionary*'s sense of the word 3.1, it is "the less morally acceptable of two states," and most interestingly, there are no citations of the phrase "wexen in a were" (Chaucer) or "in a were gan y wex" (Langland), nor any uses exactly like these quite sophisticated ones. It is hard to avoid the conclusion that this is a deliberate echo. In Langland the context is one in which Scripture preaches shockingly about predestination and the autocratic, unpredictable way that the elect will be chosen—the very way, it should be noted, that "fame" is bestowed in *House*. The passage immediately preceding the lines Chaucer appears to have mimicked gives a brief, embryonic allegory of *multi* and *pauci* (the *many* who are invited to the Lord's feast and the *few* who are "priueliche" chosen). They encapsulate what is for Will a horrific view of Christianity, one in which predestination reigns supreme, registered with equal bleakness at the end of A when he believes himself "marked wiþoute mercy." This theme rears its head in conjunction with the apparently arbitrary and inscrutable salvational doctrine that causes despair for the narrator both at the end of A and early in B's continuation. Neither this passage nor its resolution later on in BC suggest that the Bradwardinian predestinarian views that Wyclif inherited were empathetic to Langland. But this passage on predestination which Chaucer imitates appears just at the beginning of the new BC continuation of the *Vita*, where the dreamer is wretched, fearing for his damnation. It is perhaps not coincidental that fear of rejection from "eternal life" (in the form of eternal *fame*) also encapsulates the central theme of Chaucer's (deliberately?) fragmentary work, albeit "reenacted" in humanist form. It is tantalizing to think that Chaucer knew Langland's text so well, but verbal echoes are exactly what he might have recalled.

House is ostensibly a humanist "take off" (literally) on John's Revelation, in part as sifted through a Dantean filter. So, for instance, the narrator invokes thought as the source of his dream: "O Thought, what wrot al that I *mette*" (523), translating Dante's *Inferno* (2.8), "O mente, che scrivesti ciò ch'io *vidi*" (the latter just slightly closer to St. John's recurrent and more dignified "vidi" [I saw]). Geoffrey, the hapless visionary, is literally taken up into the heavens by an eagle, symbol of St. John and the agent of Dante's ascent in the *Purgatorio* (9.19–33). There, in a scene anticipated earlier by Dido's Virgilian lament for the loss of her good name ("O wikke Fame" [349]), Geoffrey witnesses the female figure of Fame (in Latin *fama*—rumour, reputation) presiding over an unpredictable, whimsical "Last Judgement" of aspirants. In this Judgement, expectations are dashed or exceeded with seemingly arbitrary abandon, as Fame presides with absolute power (*potentia absoluta*) over the throngs of her court, and Geoffrey looks on with concern:

"As thryve I," quod she, "ye shal faylle,
Good werkes shal yow noght availle
To have of me good fame as now.
But wite ye what? Y graunte yow,
That ye shal have a shrewed fame . . .
Though ye good loos *have well deserved.*"

. . . .

"Allas," thoughte I, "what aventures
Han these sory creatures!

. . . .

Allas, thus was hir shame yronge,
And *gilteles*, on every tonge."
    (*House*, 1615–55, with omissions, my italics)

The various different judgements meted out by Fame all have only one thing in common: their sheer unpredictability. Merit (as here) is just as useless as demerit (to use the language of one of Lutterell's articles against Ockham)[73] in gaining, or even predicting the outcome of, reputational salvation ("good loos"). While Geoffrey expresses shocked sympathy, both Fame's and his own language play on exactly the kind of language, anglicized in form, we have just seen used in debates about and condemnations of Ockhamist "Pelagianism": "good werkes," "deserved," "gilteles," and so forth.[74] But the stark difference is in their theologies. Geoffrey, our reporter on the scene with the "human interest" perspective, is also the stock "narrator of limited vision" from dream genres. He believes (naively, it appears) that "good loos" can be merited (by being *gilteles*). But Fame sweeps all before her with a *potentia absoluta* frightening in its ruthlessness. In this theology, human judgement is fairer and gentler than divine judgement is, yet totally powerless.

Exactly how shocking a thing this was to write in the later Middle Ages is perhaps indicated by the fact that even the humanist Gavin Douglas felt it important to correct the impression Chaucer left in *House of Fame* of the seemingly arbitrary way that fame is awarded by an inscrutable divinity. Douglas's response in his *Palice of Honour* was to create a counterweight to fame through honour as a concept of enduring social and artistic value.[75] For Chaucer, it appears, however, that *House* was (among other things) a way of exploring the destabilizing implications of Ockhamist philosophy. Whether his parodic treatment suggests rejection of that philosophy or genuinely bemused or else just *amused* experiment we will never really know. But it is as if Chaucer is re-enacting in a pagan setting an Ockhamesque nightmare of the Last Judgement gone mad—a Last Judgement, that is, in which *everything* is decided by divine *potentia absoluta* and nothing by *potentia ordinata* (God's ordained power, as covenanted with humankind). It is also, more locally, as if he is re-enacting the breakdown of Langland's A text in a pagan setting.

How this "Last Judgement" gone mad relates to Ralph Strode's now lost "Fantasma Radulphi" we may never know, but the title implies a disreputable form of vision, likely a satire.[76] One look at Strode's list of academic publications suggests that Chaucer had access to a serious philosopher in his own circle, but apparently one with a sense of humour about visions.[77] Chaucer, of course, cited Bradwardine by name in the "Nun's Priest's Tale," but in a light-hearted satirical tone that virtually masks his own opinion. Derek Pearsall, discussing a passage from Bradwardine's *De causa Dei,* suggests that the archbishop's views in favour of predestination were so absolute and so "ruthless" that they "would provoke and disturb any thinking human being." Bradwardine, Pearsall notes, writes, "All who are to be saved or damned or punished or rewarded in whatever degree, [God] has decided to save or damn or reward or punish in the same precise degree from all eternity."[78] The moment Chaucer invokes Bradwardine is the one in which the narrator calls down a curse upon "that morwe" that Chauntecleer "flaugh fro the bemes," even though, "Thou were ful wel ywarned by thy dremes" of the perils of the day to come. What follows is nearly twenty lines of brilliantly vernacularized technical scholastic discussion of the matter of God's foreknowledge and human free will, a matter on which "in scole [university] is greet altercacioun" (lines 4420–40). The nun's priest confesses, however, that he cannot

"... bulte it to the bren
As kan the hooly doctour Augustyn,
Or Boece, or the Bisshop Bradwardyn."
(4430–32)

I said above that the tone *virtually* masks his opinion, but the company Bradwardine keeps here may not. He is here alongside the heavy-hitters of Chaucer's philosophical and theological discourse, and Chaucer's great favourite, Boethius. Pearsall points out that the Boethian explanation that God's foreknowledge (that is, as merely an "eternal present," and not a form of determinism) was something of a revelation to Chaucer: the "delight with which Chaucer came upon th[is] answer is an informing freedom in all his later poetry."[79] This may very well be true of his private relationship to Boethius, but that "informing freedom" is *in practice* scarce upon the ground in Chaucer's poetry. Scholars have long agreed that both the narrator and even the heroes of the "Knight's Tale" in fact miss exactly this point in Boethius.[80] What *is* common in Chaucer's poetry is pre-determined history of the future: in *The Canterbury Tales*, dreams foretell (as in the "Nun's Priest's Tale") and events concur; the gods foretell (as in the "Knight's Tale") and events concur. Chaucer, then, uses dreams and what they prophesy just as Shakespeare does, as exact, if initially riddling, mirrors of the future. Langland, on the other hand (who rarely cites Boethius),[81] also writes histories of the future that are prophetic, but *never* binding. That is, he uses prophecy and revelation in the Old Testament way, always heavily qualified with "unless" clauses.[82] The Hunger prophecy of C.VIII.344 ff. is wholly typical of Langland: "Hunger hiderwardes hasteth hym faste," followed by dire predictions, which end, however, "*But yf* [unless] god of his goodnesse graunte vs a trewe." In Langland there is always a qualifying clause, and nothing is predictable.

In comparing the two writers, we cannot also help but notice that both in *House of Fame* and in the "Clerk's Tale" Chaucer reserves his most satirical tone, and carefully disguised theological experimentation, for ideas Bradwardine *attacked*, that is, the nominalist or Ockhamist ones. But in *House of Fame* he also — and this is Chaucer's complexity — allows his dreamer to *lament* the harsh and arbitrary determinism he sees and express a different, more "Pelagian" (merit-based) and, I would point out, *Langlandian* view. It is a view, however, that is never allowed to materialize in Chaucer — it is derailed by those who hold the real power (like Lady Fame, or like the bickering gods of the "Knight's Tale," or, as we are about to see, Walter in the "Clerk's Tale"). Chaucer and Langland, I will suggest, seem to have leaned (in Chaucer's case, perhaps gently and certainly with regret) toward different "sides" in the salvation debates. Although we must be careful not to treat either poet as writing theology or as taking sides, there are real differences between the way the two writers handle Ockhamist thought and ideas of determinism. Ockhamism appears to have been a theological way of thinking that struck Chaucer as both exhilarating and mad; determinism, though rather reluctantly, I think, had a ring of sanity to it for him and probably also a ring of classicism.[83] (Or was it just that, like the ancient poets and like the later Shakespeare, it made for better drama?) Nor does revelatory theology seem to be personally resonant for Chaucer, although he could imitate it brilliantly, especially on behalf of his female religious.[84] Those, of course, are just educated guesses, but what is certain is that Chaucer never wrote anything quite like *House* again.

There could be many reasons for this. Scholarly consensus dates *House of Fame* to 1374–80 (with 1379–80 as most likely). Stephen Russell has even suggested that allusions in lines 935–49 refer to the Rising of 1381, which may mean that Chaucer was writing or tinkering as late as that.[85] If we think about what happened immediately following those years—the Rising of 1381 and the shadow it cast over *Piers Plowman*; the condemnations of Wycliffite doctrine at the Blackfriars Council of 1382; the factional struggles at court in the mid-1380s that resulted in the Appellants crisis (a group with which *Piers Plowman* was in part associated and Chaucer was not); Chaucer's temporary "exile" in Kent;[86] the execution (although political) of Usk in 1388, another vernacular writer on issues of destiny;[87] the confiscation of Ockham in 1389—it may well be clear why Chaucer did not write in this voice again. Moreover, the climate of intellectual opinion had changed. Uthred's ideas about salvation were merely condemned as "error" in 1368; Brut's (the same opinion) as "heresy" by 1391–93. By the end of the 1390s Chaucer would write his "Retraction," which, of course, revokes his *House of Fame* along with most else that we love today. For Chaucer, by the mid-1380s, I would suggest, only humanism *utterly* devoid of Christian context and safely distanced in the past remained. The Franklin's attitude toward the classical astrological and magical beliefs of his characters as "swich folye / As in our dayes is nat worth a flye—For hooly chirches feith in oure bileve / Ne suffreth noon illusioun us to greve" (1131–14) is a superb cover for the disjunction he felt he had to advertise.

Chaucer later, and once more obliquely, but now disturbingly, explored the absolute power of God—in that unpredictable, sometimes even shocking Ockhamist sense—in the strained allegory of the "Clerk's Tale." As Elizabeth Kirk writes,

> The crux of the problem [with the allegory] is Walter, whose behaviour is made so repellent that to relate him to God is repugnant. . . . Yet in this difficulty, I would argue, lies the point of the tale. To create a situation in which Walter's actions are compared to those of God is not to suggest a merely ridiculous incongruity but to raise a central and troubling theological problem.[88]

James Simpson, in a more recent reading, writes that "if Walter is a God figure, then God is also pathological, even more so since he already knows the result of his testing."[89] For Simpson this "new emphasis" in Chaucer "incapacitates the allegorical reading." But, I would suggest, it also *enables* some daring theological exploration via incapacitated allegory (which fits an "incapacitated" salvational theology like the one parodied in *House* remarkably well). Insofar as the "Clerk's Tale" is about a capricious, inscrutable God-like lord (and that is not all it is about), it is utterly and *safely* allegorical. Building upon work by Elizabeth Salter, Geoffrey Shepherd, David Steinmetz, Robert Stepsis, and others,[90] Kirk had suggested that Chaucer used Petrarch's story to explore Ockhamist theology and especially the darker side of God's *potentia absoluta*. But even read as deliberately incapacitated allegory, the tale is uncomfortable and has to be further distanced by invoking, while pretending not to invoke, the famous gender satire at the end:

This storie is seyd nat for that wyves sholde
Folwen Grisilde as in humylitee,
For it were inportable, though they wolde. . . .
(IV.1142–44)

The "Clerk's Tale," not a visionary text, nonetheless functions as a darker reworking of the themes of arbitrary power explored in *House of Fame*. It looks to be participating in this exploration because of Chaucer's handling of Petrarch's text.[91] As critical consensus has long established, Chaucer's adjustments to Petrarch serve to deliberately blacken Walter's character, make him more tyrannical and remote and less explicable in any human sense.[92] And still, "Deth" says Griselda to Walter (in Chaucer's version), "may noght make no comparisoun / Unto your love" (IV.666–67). As David Wallace has said, the immediate political context might have given rise to Chaucer's exploration of tyranny, too. Following the death of Anne of Bohemia in 1394, "Richard without Anne has been characterized as a tyrant; the Lombard scenario—the nightmare of Fragment IV—loomed more threateningly than ever during Chaucer's final years. Alone in a milieu of despotic violence, a poet might come to greater understanding of Petrachan sensibility."[93] There is a darkness about the exploration of an arbitrary *potentia*, both ordained and absolute, in the "Clerk's Tale," unlike the playful, parodic turn of *House*. As Geoffrey Shepherd once wrote, "the *via moderna* down which Ockham had beckoned also induced various forms of scepticism: clearly scepticism about the certainty of knowledge and about human competence—Chaucer expresses doubt on both."[94]

Chaucer would explicitly retract his *House of Fame*, but whether his "Clerk's Tale" was also intended for retraction is less clear (though certainly its satirical Envoy was). By the late 1380s and 1390s, there are Lollard attacks on the classics, one, in the *Opus arduum*, perhaps written by someone (Hereford) under the protection of Chaucer's closest friends. By the time Chaucer wrote his "Retraction," he appears to have been boxed in on all sides. Or, at the very least (and I find it hard to believe Chaucer was this cynical), he wanted his public to believe he was. But the strong possibility that the "Clerk's Tale" survived the final cut is as sobering a thought for the legacy of Chaucer as it is for the legacy of the *via moderna* and Ockham himself.

"Non Fabulas Poetarum": Chaucer's "Retraction," Pluralist Puritanisms, and "Lollard Knights"

In chapter 5, we discussed Langland's deletion of the B passage against the making of poetry, a gesture, I will suggest here, virtually opposite to the one Chaucer makes in his "Retraction." Chaucer battled out his own serious ideological questions, whatever they were, carefully and virtually privately, behind a wall of poetic classical displacement, dream vision allegory, parody, and narratorial sophistication. What really troubled him is hard to know, but we have seen that the traditions represented by two of the *Opus* author's confiscated writers mattered in Chaucer's thought and writing, those of William of St. Amour and William Ockham. We have also seen that Chaucer reacted to important revelatory and speculative theology of his day, as his use of St. John, Dante, and Ockhamist thought (possibly via his friend, Ralph Strode) suggests, especially in *House of Fame*. What mattered a great deal more to him was surely the classical and humanist tradition with which he so boldly experimented. But in the end, if we take the "Retraction" at face value, he either utterly succumbed to a very severe view of faith (whether Wycliffite, or simply, like some of his later critics and imitators, narrowly conservative). Or (if not) he must at least have wanted the approval of a reading circle who would *value* such a sacrifice—or (the most cynical reading of all), he wanted the publicity it would bring. We will end this chapter with a look at that circle.

There is a strong likelihood, although we do not know for certain, that Hereford wrote the *Opus*. But we do know that Neville was one of the "Lollard knights"[95] who provided bail for Hereford, and being intimate with Chaucer personally and his circle at court makes a connection plausible. We also know, if the "Retraction" is any guide, that at the end of his life Chaucer caved in to just the kind of anti-humanist agenda the *Opus* author sets out. The *Opus* author asserts that the new (i.e., Wycliffite) ministers of the gospel "do not preach the fictions of the poets or vain philosophy . . . nor by verses or by fine fictions, but rather by the Gospels" (non fabulas poetarum aut vane philosophie . . . non in poematibus et fabulis delectantes . . . sed in evangelicis). This attitude is familiar to us especially from the Parson's Prologue ("Thou getest fable noon ytoold for me, / For Paul . . . / Repreveth hem that . . . tellen fables and swich wrecchednesse" [*Riverside Chaucer* X.31–43]), but also, and most pointedly, from the "Retraction" itself.

> Wherfore I biseke yow meekly . . . that ye preye for me that Crist have mercy on me and foryeve me my giltes; / and namely of my translacions and enditynges of *worldy vanitees,* the which I revoke in my retracciouns: / as is the book of Troilus; the book also of Fame . . . the tales of Caunterbury, thilke that *sownen into synne.* (*Riverside Chaucer,* X.1081 ff., my emphasis)

More pointed yet in the *Opus* is the specificity of the charge that the "perversi" preach "de historia Hectoris, Troye, Achilis aut unius talis pagani"—the *kind* of charge that might have made a writer like Chaucer sensitive.[96] My interest here is not in whether Chaucer ever encountered the *Opus* (although if Hereford was indeed its author, then this denunciation came from someone protected by one of Chaucer's closest friends), but whether or not Wycliffite anti-classicism such as we find in the *Opus* and the latter-day Chaucer had anything to do with each other. The literary attitudes of this close circle of Chaucer must certainly be of interest to us in relation to his "Retraction." Neville, a protector and keeper of Hereford, was a very close friend of Sir John Clanvowe, and both men stood by Chaucer at some of the most important moments of his life.[97] Clanvowe is also the earliest known *identifiable* Lollard author and, as such, an especially important witness. Hudson, however, finds him, understandably, exasperatingly "unhelpful."[98] But as an index of literary attitudes he *is* helpful. He represents the "moral fervour" common to this difficult category, as Strohm says, of "Lollard knights." His literary taste for both moral prose and animal allegory nicely epitomizes Lollard genre choices as they later developed. Clanvowe is best known to scholars of Wycliffism for his lament against the derision of good living men as "lollardi" in his *Two Ways*.[99] But Clanvowe is also the author of the courtly love poem, "The Cuckoo and the Nightingale," which is explicitly framed as a "phantasma" (the same type of vision, in Macrobius' terminology, that appears in the title of the lost piece by Strode).[100] A. C. Spearing has argued convincingly that Clanvowe's poem is one of the most intelligent responses to Chaucer before Skelton. It, too, obliquely registers concern about rising heresy and about the death penalty: "'Ey!' quoth the Cukkow, 'this is a queynt lawe, / That eyther shal I love, or elles be slawe!'" (136–37). This is apparently a stark comment on the enforced "love" of orthodox Christianity and records a moment when the sobering reality of serious persecution was just setting in, written sometime between 1386 and 1391 (when Clanvowe died), that is, just about the time that the *Opus* was written. Although Clanvowe died ten years before *De heretico comburendo* was enacted, as Spearing rightly points out, the poem has none of the innocence of Chaucer's Prologue to *The Legend of Good Women*, whose dreamer had been arraigned for heresy against the religion of love (F Text, 330 ff.; G Text, 256 ff.), suffering only the penance of writing tales of Love's martyrs. Clanvowe's dreamer wishes to have the cuckoo burnt, and even intervenes to stone the cuckoo, an oblique reference to a particularly biblical kind of martyrdom.[101] We catch, then, a glimpse of a sobering reading circle in which jokes now fail, as we see with the loss of the Endlink to the "Man of Law's Tale," and in which genres are quietly being sorted as either sheep or goats, so to speak.[102] Clanvowe and Neville were to perish on crusade to the Holy Land in 1391.

Before we jump to conclusions about Wycliffism as the source of Chaucer's end of life impetus to retract, it is important to point out that Lollards were by no means the only people who disapproved of dabbling in classical texts. Chaucer was shortly to have many "orthodox" imitators, as Ian Johnson has shown, who would seek to rewrite or purge his project of unwelcome paganism. These—some long known to literary scholars, others little known—provide an important benchmark by which we can measure just how daring Chaucer's career-long love affair with the classics actually was. What Johnson calls the "corrective imitation" of Chaucer by fifteenth-century writers (some of it, like Walton's, very soon after his death) has long been known, of course, to literary historians. Perhaps most famous in this regard is Henryson's *Testament of Crisseid*, Lydgate's *Troy Book*, and, much later, Gavin Douglas's *The Palice of Honour* and his *Eneados*.[103] Henryson, of course, appears to have wanted a harsher, or at least clearer, morality than he felt Chaucer doled out to Criseyde. Lydgate, less sensational, but more explicit on the subject, was trying to rescue the story from Chaucer's questionable indulgence in poetic "fables."[104] Indeed, despite its subject matter, the Prologue's tone is not friendly to classical poets, who, in Lydgate's view, alter the truth:

> But it is transformed in her poysy,
> Thorugh *veyn fables*, which of entencioun
> They han contreved by false transumpcion
> To hide trouthe falsely under cloude.[105]

The very poets for whom Chaucer expresses adoration in *Troilus* are then impugned, especially Homer, Ovid, and Virgil, in what must be seen as a direct hit on Chaucer's famous "Go, lytel book. . . ."[106] Douglas's *Eneados*, moreover, although not early, is the earliest translation into English of a classical epic and would at first seem an unpromising place to look for renunciation of the classics along the lines of Chaucer's "Retraction," but this is exactly what we find. As Johnson points out, although his admiration for Virgil's morality is great, it has the same painful complexity as Dante's attitude toward Virgil—a great guide necessarily relegated by his pre-Christian birth to a limbo of the poet's regret. His Book V prologue ends with the poet distancing himself from Virgil by refusing to invoke his deities:[107] "Sal I you call as [since] your namme war [was once] dyvyne? / Na, na, it syffysyt of you *ful smal memorie*." Rather, the poet will "byd nothir [take heed neither] of your turmentis nor your glorie / Bot he quhilk [who] may . . . brynng us tyll hys blyss on hym I cry" (57–61). The "proheymm" ends with a rejection of earthly pleasures as well, close in spirit to Chaucer's "Retraction."

Closer to Chaucer's own time than the great Scottish Chaucerians are Walton's Boethius translation, Metham's *Amoryus and Cleopes*, and Osbern Bokenham's *Legendys of Hooly Wummen*. Metham's *Amoryus* is a romance that explores the pagan in order to Christianize it, borrowing from Chaucer's *Troilus*. Like *Mandeville's Travels*, it is fascinated with the East (Metham claimed to have procured the story from a Greek manuscript). Its hero and heroine, Pyramus and Thisbe, are converted after death and return to life to convert the Persians, grafting hagiographic conventions onto a classical tale in direct defiance of *Troilus* even as it echoes it.[108] Bokenham's *Legendys of Hooly Wummen* is also a corrective imitation, perhaps substituting Christian virgins for Chaucer's seduced and betrayed female pagans.[109] As also with Walton, there is a deep conservatism on gender issues in Bokenham (a topic on which, unlike Walton, Bokenham is just plain rude).[110] Walton is one of the very earliest, even before Lydgate, to undertake implicit moral "revision" of Chaucer—and here, in a place we would not expect it, that is, by rivaling him in translating Boethius. In fact, his translation was much more popular than Chaucer's if we can judge by surviving manuscripts.[111] He, too, but this time in a manner reminiscent of Gerson's contemporary attack on the *Roman,* speaks out against pagan classicism:

> Noght lyketh me to laboure ne to muse
> Upon these olde poesyes derke,
> For Cristes feythe such thynge shulde refuse;
> Witness upon Jerom the holy clerke.
> Hit should not bene a Cristen mannes werke
> Tho fals goddes names to renewe . . .
> Yif he do so to Criste he is untrewe.
>
> (lines 41–47)

Instead of calling upon the three Furies, as Chaucer's narrator does in the *Troilus* (IV.24), Walton prays that "God of his benignite / My spyrite enspire wit his influence" (62–63). That Chaucer was doing something daring in employing this degree of classical realism seems even more likely when we realize that, as Johnson notes, in Trivet's famous commentary on the *Consolation,* the three Furies are interpreted as lust, cupidity, and anger.[112] New evidence for just how conservative Walton was on issues of pagan gods, and also on the role of women, appears in the possibility, recently convincingly advanced by Heather Reid, that Walton was the translator-author of *The Storie of Asneth.*[113] This remarkable translation, written for an aristocratic female patron (probably Elizabeth Berkeley, as Reid shows) departs from the Latin text to insert marked antipagan comments.[114] The *Asneth* manuscript was owned by the wife of John Shirley, whose entrepreneurial lending "bookshop" carried many "utility grade" manuscripts with versified tables of contents written in the same style as Lydgate's Prologue. We may speak confidently of Chaucerian reading circles here, and even though negative in their attitudes toward classicism to some extent, still utterly orthodox, of course, and not long after Chaucer's death. But—and this is where the problem becomes more complex—Walton succeeded Trevisa as translator-in-residence to the Berkeley family and Trevisa's orthodoxy, at least, is shadowy. (As Stephen Shepherd has said, Trevisa's *Dialogue* "invites speculation" about the Lollard sympathies of that productive team, and Hudson speaks of Trevisa's "vernacular Wycliffism.")[115] Although we have no hard evidence linking Walton and Lollard thought, there is a virtually fanatical vehemence about the treatment of idols in the *Asneth* translation that gives pause, not to mention similarities with the Lollard text "Of Wedded Men and Wifis and of Here Children Also," also aimed at a female audience.[116] Other hints of relationships between early Chaucer reception and Lollardy have been documented elsewhere, too, of course.[117] So it is not possible everywhere and always to separate *Lollard* anti-classicism from *conservative* reaction to Chaucer's classicism as thoroughly as one might think.

There is some evidence, however, that tips the balance in favour of Chaucer's sensitivity, at least, to his coterie's Lollard empathies, allowing us to say a few things with certainty and draw in some textual evidence to help us out. All of these writers are responding *to* Chaucer—their conservatism and diversity show, of course, that we cannot and need not look to Lollardy to explain Chaucer's original impulse to retract. But the *Opus* is a witness to anti-poetic classicism dated *prior* to the "Retraction" and may be linked directly with Chaucer's circle—which makes it worth noting.

That Chaucer was sensitive to sensitivities within that circle appears, I believe, much earlier than the "Retraction" was likely written. An early suggestion of the possibility is the treatment of the Man of Law's Introduction and Endlink, both by Chaucer himself, and by scribal editors during his lifetime. In the Endlink, of course, the Host famously insults the Parson, "O Jankin, be ye there? / I smelle a Lollere in the wynd," and the Shipman[?], in lines that appear to have originally been written for a woman, intervenes to stop the Parson from speaking with "he wolde sowen some difficulte, / Or springen cokkel in our clene corn" (II.1172–73 and 1181–82). The textual problems of the Link and of the Man of Law's Introduction are many, and there is much we do not know. But as the *Riverside Chaucer*'s Textual Notes explain in more detail, it looks like what began as a project to put the *Melibee* in the Man of Law's mouth ended in its being shifted to the uncontroversial safety of the inept teller of *Sir Thopas*, Geoffrey—teller of childish fantasies, as Lee Patterson has eloquently argued. Lynn Staley, in a recent discussion, quite rightly draws attention to possible political reasons for that transfer, including David Wallace's view of *Melibee* as a lesson for a king, and thus perhaps a timely one for Richard.[118]

The infamous Endlink disappeared, of course, in Chaucer's revision process — not just shifted, but apparently *suppressed* — and anticipated reception could certainly have played a role here as well. Either he, or a very early scribe, did not want controversial references to Lollardy at all. Or, more likely, Chaucer's sense of what his *intended* audience would tolerate by way of insults to Lollardy changed sometime in the period between 1387–91. This is exactly the period (1386–91) during which the marked shift in tone away from playfulness on the subject of heresy is registered in Clanvowe's "Cuckoo," as we saw in relation to the Prologue to *The Legend of Good Women*. He and other "Lollard knights" were among some of Chaucer's closest friends and most astute coterie readers, and they cared deeply for the genuine reformist impulses of the movement.[119] Harry Bailey's feeble joke might not have appeared so funny to such readers, especially after 1389–90 when Lollards began to incur serious prison terms and, if the *Opus* author is truthful, perhaps sporadically the threat of harsh treatment. Clanvowe's pain at the term "Lollard" is well known, and the *Opus arduum* account, which is more dramatic on every score, has the same sense of personal pain about it.[120] In the context of this more specific sense of the history of Lollard attitudes and sensitivities c. 1390, we can also make more historically specific Paul Strohm's view that "the 1380s and 1390s were a period when a certain amiable state of not-having-decided-yet about the Lollards was still possible, especially amid the urbane circles in which Chaucer moved."[121]

To better pinpoint the moment of loss of that "amiable state," I would suggest that Chaucer may simply have felt, especially by c. 1387–91 (during which Neville had protected Hereford, the *Opus* author [perhaps Hereford] was imprisoned, and certainly after Neville and Clanvowe were lost on crusade), that it was insulting to audience members he cared about — even though one senses more respect than affection for the Parson on Chaucer's own part. One thing we do know for certain is that many manuscripts do not contain it. One explanation is that in some cases scribes or professional readers suppressed the Endlink. The maker of the Ellesmere manuscript (San Marino, California, Huntington Library, MS Ellesmere 26 C 9) in the first decade of the fifteenth century may have suppressed it, as Lee Patterson suggested, as a safeguard "when the alarmed Archbishop Arundel was mobilizing . . . forces of repression against the Lollards."[122] On the other hand, if we remember that the Endlink is *anti*-Lollard comment, it would not really be necessary to suppress it for safety's sake, and since Ellesmere was prepared very likely for a powerful member of the aristocracy, less reason still.[123] Ralph Hanna and other textual scholars explain the missing Endlink as the result of Chaucer's shifting of tales and tellers during later revisions.[124] Part of those revisionary considerations surely would have been one of *intended audience sensitivity* among his intimates during or after 1387–91. This seems further indicated because the link stands in Oxford, Corpus Christi College MS 198, which was one of Scribe D's earliest tasks.[125] That this was allowed to stand suggests that the Loller joke was not offensive at the time of the production of *this* manuscript's archetype—on this point at least, Corpus Christi 198 may reflect Chaucer's earlier wishes, earlier even than the Hengwrt manuscript (Aberystwyth, National Library of Wales, MS Peniarth 392D). The change, then, I would suggest, came during the same period as Clanvowe's "Cuckoo," that is, 1391 or not long before. And the suppression suggests beyond reasonable doubt authorial self-censorship. What it is most important to note, however, is that if Chaucer had been worried about being *mistaken* for a Lollard, he would have most certainly left the remark *in*. He, then, like Langland, is not revising out of fear of inquisition. Nor was he later on, even as late as 1400, when he was writing his "Retraction." Rather, I believe that there is a strong chance that at the end of his life Chaucer no longer found the wager of trans-historical and trans-Christian culture worth the risk. The simpler piety of Clanvowe and Neville (after 1391 mourned in memory) and their confreres might have looked good to an intellectually, emotionally travel-weary soul.[126]

What is most significant, given the evidence we have seen so far, is that neither Chaucer nor Langland seems cowed by ecclesiastical repression of Wycliffite ideas (though some of their later scribes and editors may have been). They were, however, concerned about some things—at least to judge by the caution with which they handle certain specific topics, whether the Man of Law's Endlink and its potential to offend friends, or the "Pelagian" theology in Langland's fragmentary A ending. In previous chapters, we have seen some of these already in the way Chaucer selectively adapted Amourian antimendicantism, which was officially banned, but widely available in *Le Roman de la Rose*. Langland, I have suggested, came to see his poetry, and especially his later revisions, as both a battleground and buffer zone between a clash of cultures. This clash involved an older, partially revelatory-inspired way of thinking about topics like prophecy, church reform, and salvation history, and the newer, Wycliffite perspectives on these issues of perennial concern. We turn now to further evidence of this clash of cultures, the revival of liberal Uthredian salvation theology—and what Langlandian reading circles made of it all.

Chapter Ten

TWO OXFORD PROFESSORS UNDER INQUISITION II

Uthred de Boldon's *Visio Clara*, Langland, and
Liberal Salvation Theology

A Brief Background to Liberal Salvation Theologies:
From *The Gospel of Nicodemus* to Bradwardine
and the "New Pelagians"

Centuries of hope and ingenuity had resulted in a host of alternative solutions, both visionary and theological, to the problem of inclusive or, better, *more* inclusive salvation theology. At least since the early apocryphal *Gospel of Nicodemus*, a source widely known to Ricardian writers, there had been attempts to do just this. There has been a tendency, however, in recent Middle English studies to see the issue of salvational generosity or, at the top end of the spectrum, full "universal salvation" as original to vernacular theology.[1] In fact, the Latin tradition had much to say about these subjects, too. Many theologians and visionaries (often, as Newman notes, women) from the time of Christian antiquity onward had attempted serious theologies of inclusiveness, and some had even suffered persecution for doing so.[2] This chapter will examine the history of these controversies leading to one such landmark case, Uthred de Boldon's, and the evidence for their impact on Langland.

As we saw in chapter 1, Augustine had a habit of raining upon many optimistic theological parades, and here, too, the great rainmaker ruled. Unlike many earlier church fathers (such as Tertullian, Clement, and Origen), Augustine did not believe that Christ descended to hell to preach before his Resurrection. He thereby "dramatically alter[ed] the traditional gloss of I Peter 3:18–20, which states that Christ preached to the 'spirits in prison' . . . that is, those Old Testament righteous who were generally assumed to be suffering in Hell."[3] For historical reasons Augustine was forced to take a hard line on this in order to counter Pelagianism, the view that human nature alone, without benefit of grace, could fulfill divine law and merit salvation.[4] St. Paul had explained that while God's chosen people, the Jews, had rejected Christ, their blindness had allowed the fulfillment of the mission to the Gentiles. But, he prophesied, when that mission was complete, then all Israel would be saved (donec plenitudo gentium intraret, et sic omnis Israel saluus fieret [Rom. 11:25–26]).[5] This crucial passage with its "omnis Israel" strongly implying universal salvation for the Jews has a long exegetical history. It was used as an argument by Bernard and others for allowing the Jews to keep their own faith without persecution, in the belief that it was God's will that they not be converted until the end.[6] In addition to tantalizing promises of inclusiveness in scripture itself, other key early texts like the *Gospel of Nicodemus* held out enigmatic hopes for inclusive salvations by alluding to secret revelation given to two witnesses, Karinus and Leucius, divinely commissioned visionary scribes who were to record the salvations, but remain mute about who had been saved at the Harrowing. Revelation had always been the loophole via which non-standard salvation doctrine could be expressed. Most famous, perhaps, are these passages in the *Gospel of Nicodemus* and St. Paul's account of his having heard "secret words" (archana verba) during his revelatory experience (2 Cor. 12:4). Both of these passages Langland, for instance, plundered for his own veiled gesture of hope for inclusiveness in the Harrowing of Hell scene.[7] Jesus' own promise that the Gospel would be preached in the whole world (in uniuerso orbe) prior to the End (consummatio) was taken throughout the Middle Ages to mean that missions would first have to reach the ends of the earth.[8] Franciscans in particular, partly influenced by a Joachite sense of election, saw themselves as appointed to this task.

In the twelfth century, Joachim of Fiore had offered one of the most vibrant, methodical, and long-lived hopes for inclusion of the non-Christian peoples.

Although like so many of his age Joachim's fears of coming Islamic invasions were apocalyptic, he came to believe that crusading generally was futile and wrong (a point also under strenuous debate in 1380s England). Joachim's ambitious apocalyptic programme projected that the *viri spirituales* would go forth, endowed with a new *spiritualis intelligentia*, just as the Holy Spirit proceeds from the Father and Son.[9] This concept, as we saw in Knighton, looked to Ricardians influenced by William of St. Amour very like the Wycliffite agenda of vernacular mission to the laity, even though nothing could be further from Joachim's position on salvation, as we saw when Bradwardine attacked it, than Wyclif's predestinationism.[10] In Joachite thought, these spiritual men would convert the Gentiles, reunite the schismatic Greeks, and bring the Jews, finally, into the fold. Moreover, this would happen via the outpouring of the Holy Spirit upon the world *after* the greatest Antichrist (post ruinam . . . huius antichristi), bringing justice on earth and abundance of peace (iustitia in terra et habundantia pacis) and causing men to beat their swords into plowshares (Conflabunt autem homines gladios suos in uomeres [Isa. 2:4]),[11] to quote the Oxford manuscript (Corpus Christi 255A) of Joachim's *Liber figurarum*.

In the popular early pseudonymous Joachite literature, these ideas were echoed and developed.[12] We have, for instance, Pseudo-Joachim's *Super Hieremiam* (the text quoted in Wimbledon's sermon) with its anti-crusading stance, and more dramatically yet, its appropriation into the philosophy of Franciscan missions in the thirteenth and fourteenth century. Both Joachite-influenced Englishmen like Roger Bacon and Henry of Costesy and Continental Franciscan Joachites like Olivi and, later, Rupescissa made major contributions to this pervasive concept of mission.[13] Olivi especially had turned the generosity of Joachim's salvational theology into an apocalyptic expectation for inclusion of non-Christians, a doctrine of his specifically condemned by John XXII (chapter 2) and, as we saw in chapter 9, directly attacked by Bradwardine as "Pelagian."

Face to Face with God: Uthred de Boldon, *Clara Visio*, and the Legacy of Beatific Vision Controversies in Edwardian and Ricardian England

During the period when Bradwardine was invoking Joachim as a bad influence on the "new Pelagians," Uthred was a young Benedictine student at Oxford. Twenty years later Uthred was a distinguished professor of theology at Oxford when the Dominican, Friar William Jordan (who had been one of Uthred's chief opponents in the antimendicant controversies) accused him of teaching suspect doctrine. When his academic opinions came under condemnation in 1368 he was the key Benedictine spokesman fighting the friars to protect the rights of the endowed religious orders, or the "possessioner" clergy. At this point it appears that the Oxford friars, instigated largely by the York Austins and Dominicans, ambushed him, perhaps out of revenge for his effective leadership in antimendicant debates.[14] The motivation and timing for Uthred's condemnation remains something of a puzzle, but several strands of what he stood for may have made him an easy victim for the powerful Oxford mendicant lobby. In addition to his antimendicantism, we will explore the following: (1) his incautiously creative use of theological ideas, on some of which Ockham had been examined a few decades earlier; (2) previously unnoticed links between his ideas and those of the beatific vision controversies; and (3) the mildly Joachimist and Olivian slant of some of his opinions, the product of his serious attempt to adapt Franciscan philosophy of poverty to Benedictine apologetic.[15] Uthred's theories have always been treated by modern scholars as slightly eccentric, but he was a highly visible, productive academic at the peak of his career in 1368, and his views, when seen in relation to the larger currents of the day, are quite intelligible. Clearly his polemical enemies played an important role (among whom was a Continental inquisitor), as did so far unnoticed English interest in the beatific vision controversies and Joachimism in the 1350s and 1360s.[16]

Uthred was censured primarily for (what Dom David Knowles called) his humanitarian ideas about the possibilities for salvation of the righteous non-Christian and the unbaptized infant: twenty-eight of his opinions were reluctantly condemned by his fellow Benedictine Archbishop Langham and his commission in 1368 after a series of sensational academic disputes with Friar William Jordan.[17] Uthred was in trouble for his belief in a personal revelatory theology: his key opinion (from which many of the others flowed) was that at the moment of death each soul experienced a *visio clara* (a bright or clear vision) at which point the individual would make a conscious choice between good and evil. Uthred's *clara visio* stems in part from Paul's famous passage to the Corinthians on the power of love ("Though I speak with the tongues of men and angels, and have not love . . ." [1 Cor.13:1 ff.]), most specifically, Paul's description of the time "cum autem venerit quod perfectum est, evacuabitur quod ex parte est . . . *videmus nunc per speculum in enigmate tunc autem facie ad faciem;* nunc cognosco ex parte, tunc autem cognoscam sicut et cognitus sum" (when that which is perfect is come, then that which is in part shall be done away. . . . *For now we see through a glass darkly, but then face to face:* now I know in part, but then shall I know even as also I am known" [13:10, 12]). "Clear vision" is, then, the opposite of this world's "seeing in a glass darkly" and identical with the heavenly gift of seeing face to face. This Pauline passage also furnishes the very language adopted by Pope Benedict XII in his constitution of 1336 settling the beatific vision controversies, which, I will suggest, we can hear echoed in Uthred's doctrines. That it was this great eschatological meeting face to face that Uthred had in mind seems likely, too, from the draconian penalties his theology imposed on any who rejected it. Rejecting the *clara visio,* Uthred believed to be the sin "without remedy or possibility of remission." Not even the passion of Christ, he believed, could supply satisfaction for it (pro illo passio Christi non potest satisfacere, condemned in article 5).[18] His examiners found this problematic.

The implications of Uthred's central thesis were radical, because, if accepted, it would follow that even Muslims, Jews, and other non-Christians (Sarazenos, Judaeos, ac Paganos adultos et discretos), as well as still-born and unbaptized infants (alicui parvulo decendenti), could be saved (articles 11 and 8 respectively).[19] The case is difficult for modern scholarship because many of the condemned articles as they have come down to us are simple, and probably deceptively so. As Uthred complained in his written defence, many appear to have been oversimplified in the inquisitorial record. Take, for instance, article 8: "The sacrament of baptism . . . is not requisite to the eternal salvation of any dying little one [alicui parvulo decedenti]. *Error.*" In his lengthy written response to this article, Uthred qualifies the conclusion substantially, and finally formally rejects it ("nunquam tenui set negaui") in the bald form it is listed in the *cedula* (or list of charges). However, like many writers under inquisition, he simultaneously supplies defences for his view and, in the end, he has his cake and eats it, too. He notes, for example, that there are three kinds of baptism, that is, by *spirit,* water, and blood (quod triplex est baptismus, scilicet *flaminis,* fluminis et sanguinis), but that as much for the infant as for an adult, only baptism by *spirit* is necessary for salvation (set tam in paruulo quam in adulto solus baptismus flaminis necessario requiritur ad salutem [335]). "Flaminis" (by spirit) is an unusual word to choose here for what would normally be baptism by *desire.* It is, in fact, the beginning of a loophole that Uthred is only going to make bigger and bigger.

Doctrinally speaking, Uthred is still on firm ground, and he builds upon this with the argument that the judgement of God is never fallacious (iudicium dei veritati, que nec fallit nec fallitur, semper innititur), while the judgement of the church may be (iudicium autem ecclesie . . . fallere sepe contingit et fallit), mentioning especially cases of excommunication (de sentencia excommunicationis). This, for Uthred, opens all kinds of possibilities, which he does not ever really deny, even in his closing statement that he asserts the opposite (ego contrarium asserens dixi), that the sacrament of baptism *is* required for salvation *according to the judgement and law of our mother church* (ad salutem secundum iudicium et legem ecclesie matris nostre). But by now we know that if this is to be baptism by spirit, it is inevitably invisible, so mother church's role is a moot point anyway. We are left with a *pro forma* statement of orthodoxy made with dazzling qualifications: baptism may be by spirit alone, and the judgement of the church may often still be blind.

What disturbed the authorities most profoundly, I would suggest, was not so much the rather generous impulse toward inclusiveness in his thought, though that was theologically problematic, but more his repeated distinction between the external judgement of the church, which, he pointed out, might err, and the unknowable judgement of God, which could not.[20] There is often an Ockhamist strain in Uthred's thought, as here.[21] In the way the articles are handled one can see the authorities trying to weed that out or flatten many of them to literalism. One can also see them puzzled by some apparently Joachite ideas (given that Uthred had read and published voluminously on ideas of monastic perfection as an analogue to the ideal of Franciscan poverty and had access to huge Benedictine libraries, it is not surprising that he would have picked up some Joachite habits of mind).[22] Uthred's theories were unnerving to the authorities, then, because they put pressure on the distinction between the visible and invisible church in exactly the same way earlier Joachite thought had. Olivi and, most especially, Ockham are writers with whom Uthred had much in common theologically and methodologically. These strains would seem to be some part of the explanation for the condemnation, because, theologically, Uthred had even protected his *clara visio* hypothesis by placing the moment of choice just *before* the soul left the body (the soul being still a *viator*), and therefore technically still in a state of probation, as Knowles points out. Moreover, he had never publicized his ideas beyond the schools as Friar John had in 1358 and as Wyclif would in the next decade. But Uthred's theological ideas were clearly radical for medieval readers: they provoked problems parallel to those of both Ockham's and Olivi's apologetics[23] and were soon circulating in manuscripts with other alternative eschatologies.

Uthred's relations to Olivi have never really been studied, and this is not the place to undertake that complex task. But in addition to the instances below, one unnoticed parallel comes in the way each of them treat *clara visio*. Olivi wrote in his *Postilla* on Matthew that, just as Christ's Passion brought the light of the New Testament, so the tribulations heralding the Third Age and the end of the carnal church will bring the new full understanding of the scriptures—*and* the clear vision of God (*claram visionem Dei*).[24] For both Olivi and Uthred, then, *clara visio* comes *before* death. Knowles had footnoted in passing some much more minor similarities between Uthred's thought and Olivi's, but without knowing of the availability of the Matthew *Postilla* in circulation in fourteenth-century Benedictine academic circles.[25] For both Uthred and Olivi, the *clara visio* is an eschatological moment (for Uthred, private and personal, for Olivi, collective, but for both, ultimately still while the soul is technically a *viator* on earth). Olivi's is much the more daring of the two, but for both of them it is tied to the time of sudden new illumination for non-Christian peoples as well (for Uthred, individually experienced, for Olivi, collectively expressed).[26]

In his written defence, Uthred tried to put straight the damage his opponents had done, and by comparing the condemnations as listed in Langham's register with Uthred's response we get an interesting view of what the commissioners found "too free" about the intellectual freedoms Uthred took, and also how they sometimes rewrote or "flattened" an opinion to make it condemnable. Sometimes they simply condemn an opinion because it "sounds bad" (quia male sonat)[27] such as article 10, the tone and substance of which sounds like recognizable academic irritability in a controversy-wearied field: "Grace, according to how it is usually construed, is rubbish [truffa]."[28] Uthred admits to having said this, but goes on to explain that grace is normally now construed as originating outside of the created being in possession of it, which he thinks is rubbish. The commission did not know what to make of this (doubtless considered it loose high-table talk at Oxford), but thought it "male sonat" (in fact, a technical phrase in inquisitorial language). There are also the Ockhamist touches in his thought: several of his opinions hold out hope for the salvation of the canonically excluded, not because, as he readily admits, the church's law excludes them (with this he does not overtly quarrel), but rather because "a man could not say what God might do out of the range of human vision."[29] This is neo-Ockhamist thought and a radical departure from the heavy-handed Bradwardinianism that had established an equally radical predestinarian view which was to come increasingly into prominence with Wyclif, an academic opponent of Uthred. Some of Uthred's views seem nearly—to use Bradwardine's word and the word used by Ockham's inquisitors—"Pelagian."[30] Two condemned opinions also suggest the kind of literal-mindedness that inquisitors brought to Joachite thought: the condemned opinion is "That the Father is finite in divinity, the Son is finite in divinity, and the Holy Spirit alone is infinite. *Error.*" The opinion sounds much more reasonable and interesting in Uthred's explanation, and much more like the genuine thought of Joachim: that just as the Father is "primum principium in diuinis," so the Holy Spirit is the ultimate end, "Spiritus Sanctus est finis *ultimus* in diuinis." But one can see immediately how the article of condemnation not only flattens any nuance and creates heresy where none is intended, but also misinterprets the Joachite concept.

As we saw, Uthred's was a *personal* alternative eschatology, not a *public* one like the Joachite and Olivian brands, but an alternative and mystical eschatology nonetheless. It is no wonder, then, that Uthred's defence, *Contra querelas fratrum* (beginning: "Periculis in falsis fratribus") appears in manuscripts with other alternative eschatologies (Joachite and Amourian). A case in point is Oxford chancellor Robert Thwaytes's anthology (now Oxford, Balliol College 149), where it appears with both,[31] and also with materials Langland knew in some form.[32] Langland, as we will see below, appears to make allusion to Uthred, William Jordan, William of St. Amour, and Pseudo-Hildegard all in the same passus (the Feast of Patience scene)—all, we should note, except for Hildegard, officially censured writers.[33]

Continental Inquisition Comes to Call Once Again: Beatific Vision, Papal Heresy, and Uthred's Bid for Universal Salvation

Until Geoffrey Dipple's recent study situating Uthred clearly in relation to Continental intraclerical controversies, Uthred's views had been studied mainly by David Knowles, whose own confessional interests obscured aspects of the case's history. For Knowles, Uthred is a *unicum*, a single and singly odd thinker, adrift from (the largely) orthodox thought of England. Knowles dismissed connections with the beatific vision controversies by insisting that "clear vision" is to be distinguished from "beatific vision," a distinction he goes on to make even while admitting that Uthred never made such a distinction nor fully defined *clara visio* in his extant writings. This is problematic, especially since, apparently unknown to Knowles, the adjective *clara* was used to modify the *visio* known as beatific vision in the official theology, sometimes as an equivalent. Knowles seems to want to reserve the term "beatific vision" for the "altogether unique case of the human intelligence of Christ" (314–15, n. 2), categorizing the visionary experience of Moses and St. Paul as "*exceptionally exalted* intellectual visions" (my italics). Knowles believes that it is the second and lower category of "intellectual vision" to which we should consign Uthred's *clara visio*. However, intellectual vision could range from intellectual intuition to the Augustinian paradox of vision (that is, revealed knowledge) without images. It is uncertain that this lower category fully describes what Uthred meant, and given that *clara visio* comes at the moment of death, he seems to mean something more dramatic—something more like St. Paul's description above of both perfect knowing and *seeing* face to face. In support of his view Knowles cites Uthred's explanation of article 7, which, Knowles believes, describes intellectual vision. In fact, in the language of beatific vision theology, no such certainty is to be had. In article 7, in the experience of *clara visio*, adults without the faith of Christ (adultum sine fide christi) may merit salvation "per electionem" because at that moment the adult sees the body of Christian revelation—at which point it is not *believed* (as Christians do), but *seen* and *known* (set non quoad actum credendi, quia ipse haberet actum sciendi, ubi nos [i.e., Christians] habemus iam actum credendi [335]). This is *exactly* Benedict XII's description in his constitution on the beatific vision, *Benedictus Deus*, in which faith itself and all anticipatory virtues are emptied (euacuent) and replaced by seeing and knowing in this "intuitiua et facialis visio."[34] Here is Uthred's *clara visio*. (Here, too, is language very close to Porete's claim to such emptying of the virtues while the soul was *still on earth*—no wonder it caused the fuss it did.) It is to this constitution and the history of the controversies we must turn now.

These controversies arose when John XXII suddenly took an interest in ecumenical dialogue with the Eastern churches, particularly the Greek and the Armenian.[35] In what was probably a gesture aimed at finding common doctrinal ground, and perhaps with a goal of securing some kind of historical new accord during his papacy, John departed from his own earlier conservative position on the vision of God in the afterlife. He delivered a series of three sermons (see Chronology, 1331–32) on whether the souls of the just enjoy perceptual (intuitiva) vision of God *before* the resurrection of the body at the Last Judgement. He concluded, unusually, that they do *not*. The second sermon went further, asserting that before the resurrection of the body even the just have, as yet, no eternal life, no true beatitude, and no beatific vision; and the third sermon, its corollary, asserted that the damned did not yet reside in hell.[36]

The sermons caused an uproar: majority opinion was against John XXII on these doctrines. When a supporter of the pope, Guiral Ot, on his way to England, preached the pope's views in Paris, he created an international incident: the university protested, the king was scandalized, and French theologians met to announce their dissent from John XXII's views. The English reaction is, for us, especially interesting: Lutterell, whom we have met as Ockham's papally appointed examiner, supported the pope's views and was richly rewarded for it. At the opposite end of the spectrum, the unfortunate English Dominican, Thomas of Waleys, preached against the pope's position, called the pope's supporters flatterers, and was tossed into prison, where he languished for a decade. Robert Holcot, in his famous Oxford lectures on the Sapiential books (1333–34), also denounced the pope's position, but was apparently too geographically removed to come into harm's way. The scholarly world was stunned, and protests about Waleys's imprisonment were mounted, but to no avail. The pope urged university faculties everywhere to debate the matter, apparently even the more provincial university of Cambridge.[37]

The pope's views fueled the fire that Ockham and the "Michaelist" exiles in Munich had been fanning in their long-standing assertions that the pope was a heretic. Contemptuously calling John's hypotheses the errors of "Jacques of Cahors," they were joined in their derision by Cardinal Napoleone Orsini, who attempted to convene a council to condemn and depose the pope. Before this could be done, however, John fell ill and on December 3, 1334, he recanted, or mostly. "We confess and believe that souls separated from their bodies and fully purged from guilt . . . see God and the divine essence face to face and clearly, *so far as the state and condition of a separated soul permits.*"[38] The last clause, clearly a way of hedging, gestures toward the compromise that Cardinal Jacques Fournier, soon to become Benedict XII, had arrived at not long after the controversy broke. He suggested that there was a kind of "duplex visio" in which the vision enjoyed after the Last Judgement would be more perfect.[39]

When Fournier did become pope, however, one of his first acts was to put into a papal constitution what he hoped would be a new orthodoxy that was to largely obliterate both John XXII's views and his own compromise. Henceforth, those who die and make satisfaction (that is, are purged) are believed *prior to the resumption of the body* (ante resumptionem suorum corporum) to have seen and see the divine essence. This they do by intuitive or perceptual vision and also *face to face* (viderunt et vident divinam essentiam *visione intuitiva et eciam faciali*). This occurs without mediation, but rather as a "vision of divine essence" seen "nakedly, clearly, and openly" (*nude, clare et aperte*).[40] It is very difficult, at least in the absence of more specific instructions from Uthred himself, to fully distinguish this from his *visio clara*. Moreover, because of this vision, faith and hope (the theological virtues of anticipation) will cease—we are, again, close to the condition of Porete's annihilated soul, but in Porete's theology, again, on the "wrong" side of death, and in Uthred's, by comparison, more orthodox and technically during life.[41] This last point, especially about the cessation of the anticipating virtues like faith, is arresting in relation to Uthred's article 7, as we saw above. I think we have to assume that Uthred was, at the very least, aware of Benedict's constitution and working with the possibilities he felt it held for "enlarging" orthodoxy.

Did Uthred believe that, under his system, *anyone* would in fact be damned? The condemned articles and Uthred's responses make it clear that he did not believe anyone could be damned for original sin alone (article 12, "Quod non est possibile de lege communi aliquem precise pro peccato originali dampnari . . ." of which he says, "Hunc tenui" [337]). The next article makes it clear that it is impossible for anyone to be damned without an actual sin (13, "Impossibile est de lege communi aliquem damnari sine peccato actuali ab ipso commisso," of which he also says, "Hunc tenui" [337]). Moreover, his explanation of the first of these makes clear that the final choice offered by the *visio clara* should, so to speak, take care of the problem.[42] Uthred was too shrewd to overtly argue that no one would be damned, but his theories most decidedly *allow* for the possibility, and even cumulatively build toward it. Moreover, during the earlier beatific vision controversies, it was in fact debated whether, of *necessity*, upon seeing God clearly (clare videns), one would love God (e.g., "Queritur utrum creatura rationalis clare videns deum necessarie diligat ipsum"). This *questio* is attributed in its manuscript, probably accurately, to FitzRalph, Uthred's great mentor.[43]

FitzRalph also wrote on the same question in his *Summa de questionibus Armenorum*, books 12–14 of which are devoted to the beatific vision controversies. Here, as elsewhere, he rejected the kinds of compromises Ot and Fournier had proposed and insisted rather that the blessed enjoy "visio nuda et clara divine essencie."[44] FitzRalph is here wanting to show his full support for the unmitigated theology of beatific vision in Benedict's constitution. Furthermore, in FitzRalph's commentary on the *Sentences*, he is wholly opposed to the opinion that the human will is "utterly free to reject any intellection, even the 'clear vision' of God."[45] FitzRalph believed that it would be against the will's own nature to make such a rejection. Given the impact of FitzRalph on Uthred and the larger scholarly context of Uthred's opinions, it seems that he was implicitly arguing for inclusive salvation and borrowing from the language of beatific vision to do it.

Why, we might ask, were Uthred, FitzRalph, and other Oxford scholars revisiting this fraught subject of forms of beatific vision some thirty years later? This is a puzzle that has to be put together in pieces. First, we know that Benedict's *Benedictus Deus* did not succeed in quelling all discussion.[46] Even the illustration of *Benedictus Deus* in the *Omne bonum*, for instance, suggests this with characteristic sardonic humour: it has a historiated initial showing Pope Benedict promulgating the constitution, amusingly, face to face with scholars, one of whose hands is *still* raised in a disputational gesture! (See figure 20.) The fact that the English Dominican, Thomas of Waleys, remained in prison (first the inquisitor's and then the papal one) for the ten-year period between 1333–43 suggests in and of itself how long the issue simmered.[47] Second, Uthred had been actively writing about some of the issues that turn up on the friars' *cedula* during the period 1354–59, which is when his opponents extracted them from his *Sentences* commentary, disputations, and determinations. This is also about when they turn up in one of his opponent's works.[48] The list was being compiled between 1359–66, at least in part by John Klenkok (or Kleinkoch) and William Jordan, with connections, respectively, to the important Austin and Dominican convents in York. Uthred's complaint that the *cedula* was not drawn up "in scolis nec in locis aptis pro veritate discutienda" was justified: it was drawn up in York, and by political enemies. A national of Germany by birth, Klenkok's participation is especially significant because when he attacked Uthred he was on the verge of a successful international inquisitorial career. Making lists of unorthodox opinions earned him the anger of the citizens of Magdeburg in 1369 (from which he took flight by being let down over the city walls in a basket), but his *Decadicon* formed the substance of Gregory XI's antiheretical *Salvator humani generis* in 1374, and he prosecuted heretics' cases in Prague (Jan Milič, a forerunner of Hus) in the same year, just before his death. His extant writings, as Beryl Smalley discovered, also attack the errors of the Beghards.[49] It is, then, a *Continental* inquisitional procedure that faced both Uthred and Archbishop Langham, and one which had been in the making for some ten years.

Third, we can gauge ongoing English interest in the beatific vision during the 1360s in part with reference to the author of the *Omne bonum*, James le Palmer

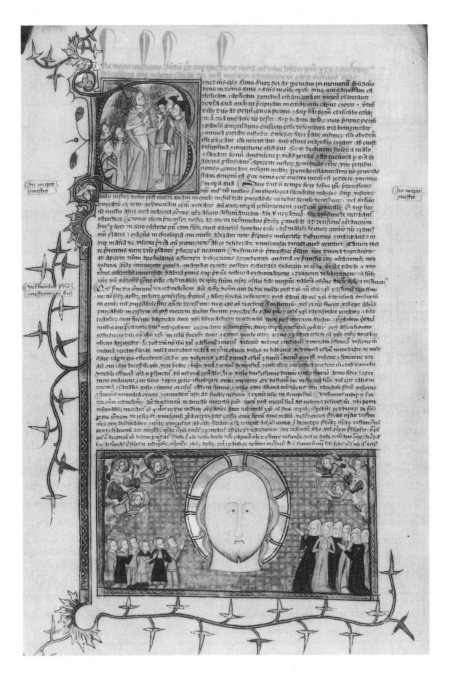

20. London, British Library, MS Royal 6.E.VI, fol. 16v, showing the *Omne bonum*'s text of the constitution of Benedict XII, *Benedictus Deus*, on the beatific vision (1336). The historiated initial depicts the pope promulgating the constitution, even while scholars continue to dispute; the image below shows the beatific vision as seen by the blessed. Reproduced by permission of the British Library.

(another antimendicant propagandist in the line of FitzRalph and Uthred). In addition to the image attached to *Benedictus Deus* mentioned above, the *Omne bonum* contains a startling illustration of the "staring face of God" (figure 21) in the same iconographic tradition as one produced earlier (c. 1325–35) for Roger of Waltham, also in London, at the time of the controversy. James also reproduces for his encyclopedia the text of Benedict's 1336 constitution (from which I have quoted above) where it appears with the other image of the staring face of God (Royal 6. E.VI, fol. 16v, see figure 20). On the previous folio he had included, again, like the earlier one made for Roger, images of St. Benedict and St. Paul, both shown looking up into the face of God. The illustrations are themselves a statement of theological position. They show Benedict and Paul, both still on earth, enjoying *perceived* vision or *visio intuitiva* (that is, what Pope Benedict XII designated as the mode of *seeing* God of the blessed and purified in heaven), rather than as merely intellectual vision.[50]

It seems very likely, then, that Uthred's prominent condemnation in 1368 was of great interest to James, especially since James was, like Uthred, a passionate antimendicantist and admirer of FitzRalph. Moreover James had access to FitzRalph's sermon diaries, among other of his works, and this likely accounts for his extraordinary interest in the beatific vision.[51] FitzRalph's position, one which he dared even to put to John XXII himself, was that the blessed and purified do enjoy the "clear vision" *immediately* after death.[52] Moreover, he argued that the blessed in heaven, having seen God clearly, may be *necessitated to will* what He reveals, unlike mortals.[53] This is very interesting in view of Uthred's implied position — it is a short step from FitzRalph's view here to Uthred's *clara visio* at the moment of death, with its implicit hope that to *see* God is to *love* God. Indeed, Uthred defended his own position with reference to the apocalyptic passage in Isaiah 40:5, as quoted in Luke 3:6, "et videbit omnis caro salutare Dei" (and all flesh shall see the salvation of God).[54] That others held Uthred's views, or something very like them, appears from the phrasing of an argument in an academic collection in Worcester Cathedral MS F.65, containing several pieces relating to Uthred.[55] Here, significantly for us, the anonymous author speaks of Uthred's clear vision *as* a vision of the Divine Essence — that is, beatific vision — in the language Benedict XII had used in his constitution. This then is contemporary, academic evidence that the two were considered virtually the same, at least by someone who likely had better reason to know how the matter was discussed than we do.[56] Uthred, then, although he was unlucky in his enemies, especially the budding Continental inquisitor

21. London, British Library, MS Royal 6.E.VI, fol. 16, also from *Omne bonum*, showing the staring face of God in the visions of St. Benedict and St. Paul, adored by a layman and laywoman below. Reproduced by permission of the British Library.

Klenkok, was far from the eccentric of Knowles's treatment. And inclusive salvation is far from a topic of vernacular theology alone.

Uthred had grown up with the beatific vision controversies, so to speak. He was an arts student at Oxford from 1337–41, and since John XXII had asked all the major universities of Christendom to debate the issue just a few years earlier, it stands to reason that it was a topic of debate during Uthred's student years. As William Courtenay has pointed out, Uthred's case and writings were widely known, and beyond Oxford, which may account for why the condemnation was apparently known to Langland and perhaps other vernacular writers.[57] In "Contra querelas fratrum," Uthred complains about the publicizing everywhere of the *cedula;* he says that the friars have "most falsely fabricated a certain list" (quandam cedulam falsissime fabricatam) that they claim has sayings (dictis) drawn from his scholastic writings.[58] He complains that the *cedula* has been widely disseminated, with the result that his reputation (fama mea) has been gravely denigrated by their malice (malicia).[59]

In canon law, the difference between a heretic and someone who commits error was pertinacity. The opinions of avowed heretics are held "pertinaciter" in legal accounts. Uthred did not insist on his opinions, but relatively soon retired (or was recalled) from Oxford to a much more minor post at a monastic house, Finchale in Northumberland (Uthred was a northerner by birth). We could wish, however, that he had been able to persist as a teacher. His theological notions always err on the side of the hopefulness and dignity of the human species. That is why they make such an interesting test case in the study of intellectual freedom, and the limits of it, in late medieval England. Uthred was allowed to retire from Oxford in dignity. Unlike men and women holding Olivian and Wycliffite opinions in the same century, he was not imprisoned or burned; unlike Ockham, he did not spend his final days excommunicate and exiled. It is slightly comforting to think, at least, not only that some academics were allowed "to err" quietly, but that academics in the period sometimes thought so independently and even lived to be heard.

Uthred's theology leaves open a large loophole for inclusive salvation, and it tries to do so scholastically. As I have suggested, he was probably working with an idea rather like the one in FitzRalph's brief *questio* on whether a soul that sees God must of necessity love God. By theologically providing each human being with that opportunity, Uthred kept the door open—and did not imagine anyone not proceeding through it. His opponent William Jordan tellingly wrote a treatise *contra Utredum,* called *Tractatus de libera electione ante mortem*—that is, on free choice before death,[60] a title which perhaps summarizes his unique theology more attractively than Jordan intended.

The condemnation was the end of Uthred's formal academic career, though by no means the end of his ideas. We saw evidence that Walter Brut, for instance, knew them in the 1390s (chapter 5). How he knew them is an unsolved mystery, but evidence points to a *resurgence* of Uthred's inclusivism in Ricardian England. We know, of course, that his career as spokesman for the English Benedictines and defender of their interests was to continue unabated. We have already seen that Uthred underwent a second experience of humiliation just a few years later at the Great Council of 1374 in a scene recorded for us in the *Eulogium historiarum*. But Uthred did have an active career nonetheless and something of a resurrection at Oxford in the 1380s. He wrote three texts during the 1360s and 1370s defending endowment against the friars, the last of which, *Contra garrulos fratrum dotacionem ecclesie impugnantes,* may have been a response to the proposals that two Austin friars, John Bankyn and likely Thomas Ashbourne, laid before Parliament in 1371.[61] It may also, however, as Hudson has recently argued, have been written in response to Wyclif, as may a second treatise, *De dotacione ecclesie sponse Christi.*[62] During the 1380s in fact Uthred was back in Oxford, partly on business, and partly, it appears, in response to the need for a coalition of the willing in the fight against Wyclif.[63] This is a period of his life still largely unstudied. Both William Courtenay and Anne Hudson have made brief remarks on Uthred's role as an opponent of Wyclif; our picture at the moment, however, is sketchy.[64] British Library, MS Royal 6. D.X contains a complete copy of Uthred's defence alongside scholastic *questiones* against Wyclif. Uthred seems to have issued his *De eucharistie sacramento* after 1384[65] and to have been engaged in anti-Wycliffite concerns pertaining to Oxford throughout this period, so far as we know at least up to 1386. As Hudson mentions, a note in the Durham manuscript beside the opening of one of Uthred's texts: "Contra hostes ecclesie Wicliphisticos pro eius libertate" (fol. 1), shows at the very least the continuing interest of his texts to readers and points to the high profile of their author. Against this backdrop, it is much less surprising that Walter Brut would be reviving Uthredian ideas in the early 1390s (Uthred himself lived until 1397). But we turn now to startling evidence that both Langland and his coterie seem to have been thinking about Uthred's condemned doctrine of *clara visio* during this later period, throughout the 1380s and 1390s.

\

Reclaiming Lost Ground: Langland's Later Revisions and His Turf War with Wycliffism

Langland, whoever he was, composed all three of his texts during Uthred's famous and troubled career. Given the dates of the political references in Langland's A text and its breakdown at the topic of the arbitrariness of God's judgements on the salvation of the unbaptized and the unholy, the possibility of links between the breakdown and the censorship of Uthred in 1368 seems worth considering. Moreover, the condemnation may explain to some extent why Langland likely held the A text back from circulation for so long.[66] In suggesting this I do not mean to imply any one-for-one correspondence between the two events, but rather to point to evidence of a new *climate of constraint* on theological discussion of liberal salvation ideas. It seems likely that Klenkok's Continental inquisitional mode yoked with William Jordan's pugnacious tenacity (he was an "adversarius molestissimus") made a formidable team which took everyone by surprise. FitzRalph and others had created an atmosphere for discourse on salvation issues in the wake of the beatific vision controversy and Uthred was capitalizing upon this when Klenkok and Jordan suddenly chilled the climate. We know the censorship of Uthred was widely publicized, and far beyond the walls of Oxford.[67] Langland would within a few years (probably 1377–79)[68] write the Feast of Patience episode, a part of the B continuation that scholars believe likely targeted Uthred's opponent William Jordan in a brilliant satire on the spiritual emptiness of academic learning (B.XIII/C.XV).[69] In the same scene, Langland has the dreamer cite the Pauline quotation that just happens to form the title of Uthred's treatise of self-defence ("Periculum est in falsis fratribus" [2 Cor. 11:27]). Both of these apparent allusions are retained in C,[70] where later on in the poem another apparent allusion, this time to Uthred's *clara visio*, is added.[71] All of these are so deftly done as to epitomize functional ambiguity and suggest a specific (perhaps coterie) audience for their full appreciation. So, for instance, the one perhaps direct allusion to Jordan's name appears as "Y schal iangle to þis iurdan, with his iuyste wombe" (C.XV.92), in which "iurdan" means "chamber pot" and "iuyste wombe" means "pot-belly." In the same passage there is also an allusion to the opening verse of Pseudo-Hildegard's "Insurgent" (originally written, as we know, by someone in William of St. Amour's circle).[72] We have seen that William of St. Amour's method was to write, ostensibly at least, only "exegesis" rather than polemic and to let the implied allusions to the friars fall obliquely on the ears of readers adept at allegory. In the Feast of Patience, then, Langland is more the student of William than of FitzRalph, and as such he was at the top of the class.

If the Feast of Patience allusion were alone in *Piers,* we would have room to wonder whether chamber pots are just chamber pots. But there is other evidence of the impact of Uthred's *fama* on Langland, and also on his coterie. Russell showed that the C revision was massively preoccupied with the issue of the salvation of righteous non-Christian peoples, which became the test case and the focal point of his larger salvation concerns.[73] Russell linked this to Uthred's condemned opinions, which, though quite intelligible in their context, have been rightly called eclectic, and in fact, are more so than anyone has before realized with their Olivian and Joachite leanings and their indebtedness to the beatific vision controversies. B. X's denial that learning is not valuable if Aristotle and Solomon are not saved because they are unbaptized is importantly altered in C by the *removal of references to baptism* as a guarantee of salvation.[74] This is significant because, as we will see in the section on the John But Passus below, this topic was critical to Langland's followers in the late 1380s and 1390s. Other revisions of C seem to be part of a consistent attempt to play down the necessity of sacramental baptism. The Trajan passage is also strikingly altered in C to emphasize that baptism is not necessary to salvation.[75] And Russell linked this revision campaign to C.XVII.123–24, which is placed in the authoritative mouth of *Liberum Arbitrium*: "For Sarrasynes may be saued so yf they so byleuede, / In the letynge [or in many manuscripts 'lengthynge'] of here lyf to leue on holy churche."[76] The immediate reference to Saracens' "letynge"(which means both "leaving" and "delaying") or even more explicitly "lengthynge" their lives recalls Uthred's *clara visio,* which occurs while the soul is still suspended from death, still technically a *viator.* Langland has left himself the safety net of "to leue on holy churche," but the lines are daring nonetheless and are pointedly missing from one manuscript entirely.

There is other evidence to suggest that the metaphor of leaving, delaying, or lengthening their lives to believe "on holy churche" refers to Uthred's *clara visio.* Langland has orchestrated the lines leading up to this passage in a cunning way, partly perhaps to raise the topic of disputation in the schools. Starting at line 113 we have a detailed critique of doctors of divinity who should be able to "asoile *ad quodlibet,*" now "faille in fylosophye," which could be seen to nicely open the way for the topic of Uthred's condemned opinion. This is followed triumphantly by the potentially dangerous quotation *"sola fides sufficit* [faith alone suffices] to saue with lewede peuple" (line 121) directly introducing the lines about Saracens at the end of their lives. Finally, we read that "Sola fides sufficit" is now necessary because priests are lax (117–21). This last excuse, we might note, is a revelatory reformist trope that goes back at least to the Gregorian Reform and which was used to support all kinds of radicalism. Indeed, from Hildegard onward, it supported even women's claims to critique the church and write revelatory theology. Langland knew the reformist revelatory drill intimately.

Unlike the *sola fides* passage retained from B in C.XVII, a second highly censurable quote is excised from the C text: *"Sola contricio delet peccatum"* (Only contrition deletes sin). In B it comes in as "overvoice" to destabilize (for those who can read Latin) Will's contention that the friars ought to be more concerned with baptism than burying. (The argument is that a baptized man may come to heaven through contrition, "Sola contricio . . ." but a child without baptism cannot be saved [B.XI.81].) How do we read the excision? First of all, not by itself. The modern temptation is to leap on the "Sola contricio" deletion and assume that Langland is trying to avoid getting in trouble as a Lollard. But Anne Hudson has always rightly (in my view) maintained that the complexity of these doctrinal C revisions cannot be boiled down to something so simple. If Langland had had the *slightest* concern that he would be mistaken for a Wycliffite heretic, he would hardly have gone about deleting the whole larger passage that frames the Latin quote, with its ironclad orthodoxy on baptism.[77] But that is exactly what he did. The larger pattern of C revisions is to *discount* baptism, to make heaven, as it were, more inclusive and puts the onus *de libera electione* on the individual. This is a campaign that is more reminiscent of revelatory theology like Mechthild's and Julian's or academic theology like Uthred's but runs counter to Wycliffite predestinarian views.[78]

Now, Langland was no fool about sensitive or even dangerous issues, as the pattern of C revision shows: he can be seen softening his St. Amourian/FitzRalphian line in C.XII.16 by removing verses in which Will advocates burial in one's parish rather than with the friars (B.XI.64–69), a huge flashpoint in the antimendicant controversy. He can be seen softening B's Ockhamist-style pro-disendowment polemic in revisions to B.X.432 ff. He can be seen quietly removing his B.XI.156 insistence that it was not Gregory who saved Trajan ("nou3t þoru3 preiere of a pope"), and his anti-*clergie* diatribe of 160 ff. However, he nowhere says in C that it *was* a pope or *clergie* that saved Trajan and he has Trajan say it was "loue *withoute lele bileue*" that saved him. So we have caution, but not compliance, on all such issues. Langland, unlike Augustine and Dante, never says that Trajan was restored to life and baptized.[79]

What is most clear in C, however, is that what *really* upsets him—even more than it did in the breakdown of A, where it was bothersome enough—is predestination. Constraint, the breakdown of A, the possibility of the salvation of the non-Christian, and (carefully veiled in functional ambiguity) the possible salvation of all peoples, all are themes that had been interwoven not only in Langland's B continuation, but picked up comically in Chaucer's *House of Fame*, as we saw in chapter 9. And in what was likely the preoccupation of their final years, it looks as if these two writers went their separate ways theologically. Langland, that is, went into battle against what he must have viewed as the piracy of Wycliffism and its pernicious doctrine of predestination; Chaucer, as we saw, in a growing sense that questions of determinism of all sorts apparently seemed the most important theology to explore, and perhaps most easily in pre-Christian classical stories.[80]

Archana Verba: Langland's BC Recovery, Uthred, and the Creation of Hope

The revisions outlined in the above paragraphs may suggest that Langland was sensitive to the constraints betrayed by the confiscation campaign c. 1389, especially of St. Amour and Ockham. A closer look at the But Ending, the B revisions, and Uthred's return to Oxford in the 1380s will help to suggest that not only was Langland distressed about predestination issues (as promoted by Bradwardine and later Wyclif), but he and at least his most intimate reading circle felt strongly about all non-generous salvation theologies, and had done since the rupture of A. The growing popularity of the Wycliffite movement was, perhaps, rubbing salt into those wounds. By the time of C, Langland had witnessed both radical political appropriation (in 1381) and likely pro-Wycliffite appropriation of his text (perhaps as early as 1382 in "Heu"). However much he might have empathized with the reformist ideas of this new movement, they were appropriating his protagonist, his reformist polemic, and now, to add insult to injury, they were riding roughshod over decades of carefully constructed poetry aimed at salvational liberality. The C text revisions, together with the But Ending, can be read as a counterattack on what Oberman called Tradition I theologians, especially Bradwardine and Wyclif. In order to do this, I will suggest,

Langland drew upon two sets of tools. First, the Ockham-Uthred strand of Tradition II and, second, the influx of visionary materials during the Great Schism years which had revitalized a revelatory and charismatic approach with its roots in monastic and Franciscan traditions. Some of these we have seen in previous chapters, ranging from Schism Joachite prophecy (at least once copied into a *Piers* manuscript) to Carthusian-transmitted guides on authentic vision, like *The Chastising* or the *Epistola*. Here were weapons big enough to fight back with.

Let us try to reconstruct the history. Langland's B continuation from the point where A left off betrays a great deal about what he appears to have been thinking and how he refound the path forward. As we have seen, the very first line of B that is "added" to A undercuts the value of the simple ploughman's prayer that pierces heaven by stigmatizing the unlearned as those "That inparfitly here knewe and *ek lyuede*" (B.X.471). Langland's mood when he restarted B was perhaps grumpy (these lines disappear in C). The narrator's sense of indignation and hopelessness in both texts, however, rises to a climax when Scripture preaches uncompromising predestination, using the allegory of the Wedding Feast. Here the narrator, desperate that he is not among the predestined, openly challenges the learned who focus solely upon scriptural doctrine (*per modum doctrinae*, as Ockham wrote, to the exclusion of other authorities, that is, *per modum auctoritatis*):[81]

"A saith soth," quod Scripture tho, and skypte an heyh and prechede.
Ac þe matere þat she meuede, *if lewede men hit knewe,*
The lasse, as y leue, louyon þey wolde
The bileue of our lord þat lettred men techeth.

(C.XII.39 ff)

Who is the implied audience of this challenge? It ostensibly makes common cause with the "lewede," but it is not addressed to them. It is an attack on the "bileue" that "lettred men techeth," that is, as preached by *Scripture* — alone. I said earlier that Ockhamist doubt creation also had a corollary: hope creation. Drawing upon the breadth of Tradition II theology, which ranges from scripture to the entire corpus of (often) conflicting church authorities, thinkers like Uthred found elbow room on issues like salvation. This seems to be what Langland stumbled upon as a way out of this unpromising crisis. Caught in his "wer" (the moment that Chaucer may have imitated, as we saw) and disputing with himself whether "y were chose or not chose," the dreamer has a sudden epiphany.

Remembering that Christ welcomes all to come to the waters, for thirst (*sicientes*), for baptism (*ad aquas*), for salvation (bote for bale):

> . . . on Holy Churche y thouhte
> That vnderfeng me at þe fonte for on of godes chosene.
> For Crist clepede vs alle, come yf we wolde,
> Sarrasynes and sismatikes, and so a ded þe Iewes,
> And bad hem souke for synne sauete at his breste
> And drynke bote for bale, brouke hit ho-so myhte:
> *O vos omnes sicientes, venite ad aquas* [O all you that thirst, come to the waters (Is. 55:1)].
>
> (XII.50–56)

The image of saving milk offered to all from Christ's breast was particularly powerful in an age that believed breast milk was processed as blood. The Jesus as mother tradition, as Bynum established, is a long-standing Cistercian tradition, but by the Schism period, it is in circulation in women's mystical texts and even vernacular texts. Moreover, Langland found many of his most profound answers in the literature of the cloister, a rich tradition in both male and female monasticism and, by the fourteenth century, including a rich visionary tradition.[82] This passage is a very important moment — arguably the pivotal point of the entire BC continuation, and the point without which there would simply be no continuation. Its theology is shortly to be even further broadened by Trajan's testimony (C.XII.73 ff.) that he escaped hell without "bileue" or baptism.

The passage feels like a resolution of sorts in another way in that it immediately follows one of Langland's most overt and courageous discussions of how to handle constraint on speaking out. This is the passage in which the hapless dreamer, stranded by his friar-confessor's greed, articulates what James Simpson calls one of the best informed statements on the legalities of moral satire.[83]

> "Y wolde it were no synne," y saide, "to seien þat were treuthe . . .
> *Existimasti inique quod ero tibi similis; arguam te et statuam contra faciem tuam*
> [You have thought wrongly that I should be one like yourself; (but)
> I shall accuse you and lay the charge before you (Ps. 49:21)] . . ."
> "And wherof serueth lawe," quod Leaute, "and no lyf vndertoke
> Falsnesse ne faytreye?"
>
> (C.XII.27–32, with omissions)

It is the powerful moral authority Leaute (Loyalty or Integrity) who bursts in here to urge Will not only to rebuke falseness, but not to hesitate (under just conditions) "to rehercen hit al by retoryk." It is an affirmation both of law and of poetry and must have resonated instantly with members of the "clergial" Westminster reading circles closest to Langland. They would have known without having to check (as we do today) that the quote from Psalm 49 above ("Existimasti . . .") in fact begins "Haec fecisti et *tacui*" (These things you have done and I have been *silent*).[84] It must have been a touchstone for Langland because he also uses it twice in B, once in the corresponding Leaute passage, and in B.X.291, where it is used to encourage the rebuking of bad priests. The problem of silence and constraint was central for him and for his closest circle of readers, and the problem was most often expressed with reference St. Paul's famous utterance during his own revelatory experience that he had heard "secret words" (archana verba).

The Pauline "archana verba" quotation ("I have heard secret words which it is not licet for a man to utter")[85] appears in Langland's BC Harrowing of Hell episode (repeated again in the John But Passus, as we will see shortly).[86] Although not universally accepted, the *Gospel of Nicodemus* was a prime source in much of the literature retelling the Harrowing, including the drama, and as scholars have long believed, known to Langland.[87] In *Nicodemus*, we are given the account of what takes place in hell during the Harrowing by two brothers, Karinus et Leucius, who are divinely commissioned as visionaries and told to write—but only what they are *allowed* to write—of the great moment when the prophets and patriarchs are saved. After the commissioning comes the emotional moment when those who wait in deep darkness see a great light breaking in upon them. What the two brothers are not allowed to write is the *mysteria domini*—especially who was saved and why. And silence is solemnly imposed upon them by the archangel Michael, who makes them mute until the hour when the *diuinitatis mysteria* may be revealed.[88] This explains the prominent position in BC of the Pauline quotation given to Christ, upon whom Langland bestows Paul's "archana verba" in the Harrowing scene.

It first appears in the B Harrowing scene, at the moment Langland has Christ hint at one of the most (especially since 1368) controversial of the poem's suggestions, the possibility of universal salvation:[89]

"For blood may suffre blood both hungry and acale,
Ac blood may noght se blood blede, but hym rewe.
Audivi archana verba que non licet homini loqui.

Ac my rightwisnesse and right shal rulen al helle,
And *mercy al mankynde* bifore me in hevene."
(B. XVIII.396–99, my emphasis)

As scholars like Vitto, Hill, and Watson have noted, it is difficult to see what Paul's words are doing in Christ's speech[90] at this point in the passage if they are not meant to hint at secretive *revelatory* confirmation of a radical position on salvation. Other passages in the poem that suggest at least an unusually generous attitude to salvation are those that share in a largely Franciscan-inspired concept of mission to the non-Christian peoples (like XVII.122 ff.), which was idealistic and humane for its day. We can also point to Scripture's comments at B.X.341 ff., and especially in the Trajan passage (XI.140 ff.), which was very bold (and would get bolder in C). But whether in the Harrowing passage just quoted this is "universal salvation" ("not itself totally heterodox," as Pearsall notes to line 430 of his edition) or simply a radical position somewhat short of that (i.e., *more* inclusive salvation) is a difficult question.[91] In Uthred's teaching, for instance, the mercy of *clara visio* would be extended to all, but would all accept? Uthred implicitly believes they would.

Since doubts about "orthodox" Christian teachings on salvation appear at the point of rupture of the A text, it is impossible to overestimate the importance of this passage in B. But whether this is an unqualified statement of universal salvation is something we need to be a little cautious about. First of all, slightly disturbing to the theory of universal salvation here is the analogy Christ makes just preceding this quotation between himself as judge and a king who unexpectedly arrives at an execution site and pardons a thief (feloun) about to be hung. As the C text, which must be Langland's last word on the subject, puts the passage, if the king "come in þe tyme / Ther a thief tholie sholde deth" then "Lawe wolde he ʒoue hym lyf *and he loked on hym*" (C.XX.423–24). The last half of the line (meaning *if he looked upon him*) suggests a dramatic allusion to God's absolute power (*potentia absoluta*) in the Ockhamist sense, rather unpredictably wielded— and unpredictability hardly assures universality. The arbitrary judgement that was comical in *House of Fame* is terrifying business here. Second, the "yf law wol" clause of line 428 shortly thereafter ("And if lawe wol y loke on hem hit lith in my grace / Where they deye or dey nat") is certainly a conservative qualifying clause.[92] It, too, raises the question of *where* (meaning "if" or "whether") Christ will decide to "loke on hem" and exercise his grace. This is the kind of speculative tone that drew censure down upon Ockham's head, and the charge of creating scepticism. This is one of many possible qualifiers Langland supplied in Christ's long speech and, given that it is both in the vernacular (unlike the Pauline quote) and straightforwardly literal, it sticks out.[93] Still, the complex allegory about the drink of love ("sicio," 408a) that precedes these lines also hints at universal salvation, promising that Christ will "haue out of helle *alle* mennes soules" (414). It is tantalizing to believe that Langland wanted it both ways: an overtly orthodox theology hiding a daringly liberal salvational message — or at least its hope.[94] Langland, however, may have been fundamentally Uthredian in his belief in both God's universal mercy and the primacy of human choice (with FitzRalph's sense that God *seen* is necessarily God *loved* hovering in the background). In any case, Langland, I would suggest, comes by some of his generosity on this point honestly, because he bypasses Augustine's hardline anti-Pelagianism and reaches back to an even earlier source, the *Gospel of Nicodemus*, which also dramatizes Christ's sermon in Hell. And it, too, also relies on silence: indeed, the muteness of its two visionary witnesses to protect a theology of hope with a rhetoric of constraint.[95]

"These Things You Have Done, and I Have Remained Silent": Anti-Wycliffism, But's Attack on Scriptural Fundamentalism, and Langland's Voice in the But Ending

It is the John But Ending, constructed to give closure to the unfinished A text, however, which really affirms use of the Pauline trope to signal constraint in the Langlandian tradition.[96] The But Ending is a notoriously difficult piece of writing, not made any easier by textual corruption. However, carefully read, the But Ending also sheds light on what Langland may have been hiding in his reference to Paul's *archana verba* — or at least what a member of his coterie believed it to be. In the But Ending the quotation appears as part of a complex network of biblical allusions to enforced silence — all on the theology of salvational generosities. The speaker, appropriately, is Scripture:

And Poul precheþ hit often, prestes hit redyn:
Audivi archana verba que non licet homini loqui
"I am not hardy," quod he, "þat I herde with erys
Telle hit . . . to synful wrecches."
("John But" Passus, A.XII.22–24)

This is embedded in a speech that runs for twenty-two lines, using the three biblical injunctions to silence, all in a strangely ambiguous way. The first, "Vidi preuarica[nt]es & tabescebam" (I saw transgressors and was grieved) is sardonically translated into Middle English as "I saw synful . . . þerfore I seyde no þing."[97] He has Scripture next cite St. Paul's "archana verba" passage, "I have heard secret words which it is not licet for a man to utter," again suspiciously and perversely translated as "I am not hardy . . . þat I herde with erys / Telle hit . . . to synful wrecches"—making it further testimony to fear of speaking out. The Pauline quote, like the other Latin quotes in the But Ending, is apparently lifted from elsewhere in the poem, here likely B.XVII or C.XX, where Langland had used it enigmatically in the midst of Christ's broad and hopeful hints about salvation. Third, and perhaps most cynically, Scripture cites Christ's own silence before Pilate (to the question, "Quid est ueritas?"), but:

> God gaf him non answere but gan his tounge holde.
>
> . . . .
>
> And when scripture þe skolde hadde þis [skele] ysheued
> Clergie into a caban crepte anon after
> And drow þe dore after him and bad me go do wel.
> ("John But" Passus, 29–35, with omissions)

These three quotations from Scripture, then, trigger barely suppressed sarcasm as the dreamer observes that they immediately force Clergy to creep "into a caban"[98] and bolt the door. These words are John But's adroit plagiarism of Lady Mede's phraseology from A or B.III (191), used there in a political context to describe the fiasco of the Treaty of Bretigny. The entire But Passus is laced with quite deliberate echoes and cross-allusion to all three versions of Langland's poem—and But must have expected his initial audience to be able to pick up these allusions, too. The implication of these lines, then—for those who know Langland's poetry intimately—is that this is *Clergy*'s great fiasco. But what *is* the fiasco?

The But Ending is a riddle of sorts that needs to be read backward from this moment. What sparks this cynical display of silence and "archana verba" is Clergy's initial unwillingness to teach Will. At the opening of the But Passus Clergy had told Will that he would teach him what he asks if he knew truly what Will would do with the knowledge thereafter. But he fears that Will may simply use it presumptuously to "apose" (question confrontatively, interrogate) in order to injure or aggravate Clergy himself and Theology. The end of the (genuine) A text, of course, breaks off with a belligerent diatribe on the subject of doubt about academic salvation theology, and so it is natural that the But Passus would take its cue from there. However, the But Passus moves the whole issue a giant step further. There, Scripture agrees with Clergy and, in a shocking passage clearly modeled on Scripture's disturbing predestination sermon in Langland's B.XI or C.XII (the one that threw the dreamer into a "wer" of anxiety), she actually urges Clergy not to teach Will anything further unless he has been *absolved* by Wit, *and cristened in a font:*

> Skornfully þ[o] scripture she[t] vp h[ere] browes
> And on clergie crieþ on crist*es* holy name
> That he shewe me hit ne sholde *but ʒif [I schriuen] were*
> Of þe kynde cardinal wit, and *cristned in a font,*
> And seyde so loude *þat shame me thouʒthe,*
> *Þat hit were boþe skaþe and sklaundre to holy cherche.*
>   ("John But" Passus, A.XII.12–17, my emphasis)

This is too much. And here is our fiasco. She says it so loudly, demonstrating such contemptible elitism, that the dreamer is shamed and feels that her doing so is both "harm and slander" (skaþe and sklaundre) to Holy Church. This is a breathtaking glimpse of a standoff between what Oberman would call Tradition I and Tradition II thinkers. (Bradwardine and Wyclif being instances of Tradition I with their reliance on scripture and its inheritance of glosses as the main foundation of Christian theology; Ockham and Uthred being instances of Tradition II, the opposing "school" for whom these sources must be supplemented by and balanced with ecclesiastical traditions, including canon law.)[99] The standoff here also epitomizes the tone and tenor of the end of A with acuity. The narrator feels that Scripture's hardline position, which must necessarily *exclude all those not christened at a font,* is both harm and scandal to Holy Church, which in his view apparently allows for more liberality. Ockham and Uthred would have agreed.

These lines are complex enough to arrest our attention in two other ways: first because they portray a "Scripture" that (or who) at least concedes interior confession (to *kynde cardinal wit*) as sufficient, but is rigid on the necessity of baptism—views arrived at, one assumes, by a literal reading of scripture. This *sounds* like a portrait of early Wycliffism, and But does not seem to agree with it.

The allegory here is of Scripture-as-tyrant, showing what happens when one allows scripture to dominate at the expense of all other ecclesiastical authorities, laws, and revelations (Tradition II). Is this the first English caricature of biblical fundamentalism? Going one step beyond Langland's near parody of Scripture (at C.XII.39 ff.), the second reason these lines should arrest our attention is that they also extrapolate the original A ending to a new, more daring level of confrontation, especially with its charge of *skape and sklaundre to holy cherche.*"[100] The successive use of biblical quotations on silence in this passage must be pointing to a sense that public truth telling is under siege, leaving only "archana verba" as a means of expression. These quotations are complex in themselves because of the slightly odd way they are translated into Middle English. In Langlandian writing, this technique of selective and/or distorted vernacular translation usually signals differing levels of target audience—one level that will appreciate the discrepancy and one that will not. Latin translation in Langland is often, too, a site of contest over constraint. Constraint issues were, in fact, among the primary elements Langlandian imitators imitated (one thinks of texts like *Mum* and *Richard*). The But Passus, however, is probably written by someone closer to Langland than anyone of whom we now know.[101]

Whoever wrote it produced a text showing no particular evidence of Lollard sympathies—indeed, the Tradition II sympathies are the opposite of what Wyclif would have appreciated and come closer to an Ockhamist-Uthredian line of thought. The topic that causes the But author outrage is Scripture's elitism with respect to the unbaptized. And since there cannot have been many unbaptized English men and women in fourteenth-century England, we have to look to two groups, the non-Christian peoples and infants who died prior to baptism, to make sense of the narrator's outrage. These are, in fact, precisely the two groups that Uthred de Boldon championed in the opinions condemned in 1368 (later imitated by Walter Brut c. 1391). However, the But Passus, even though it formally travels with A texts, was not likely written in the immediate aftermath of Uthred's condemnation itself, because, as Anne Middleton and Helen Barr have shown, it contains lines from B and even C, and as I have just shown, it laments the rise of Tradition I theology, likely including Wyclif's. This leads us to two questions: who wrote the Ending, and when was it written?

Whoever wrote the Ending had a powerful sense of an alert Langlandian coterie. This audience appreciates playful allusion to the poem (which it knows intimately) and also legal diction. And it is deeply concerned with freedom of discussion (in academic terms, *libere tractare*). In fact, a closer look at the lan-

guage allows us to be a little more specific about the issue of silence. But's Ending seems to be, at least in part, bitterly alluding to the legal matter of *right* to
silence before ecclesiastical or courtroom questioning.[102] Its pervasive use of
legal diction (e.g., "alegged," "aposed," "defendeth," "answeren") hints rather
graphically at this subtext. The word "aposed," picked up likely from the A ending (A.XI.289), occurs with especial frequency and is used in the *Middle English
Dictionary*'s sense (a) "to confront with a question; to question or examine (esp.
about Scripture, doctrines of the Church, or in court)."

These issues arise naturally out of the end of A, where the dreamer has been
recklessly "aposing" Christian doctrine on salvation in a pugnacious challenge
against the need for clerical learning in any form. The second last Latin quote in
A had been "Dum steteritis ante presides nolite cogitare" (When you stand before authorities, do not take thought for what you will say), which is the promise to Christ's apostles of, in effect, *intellectus spiritualis* or spiritual intellection.

Dum steter[it]is ante [reges &] presides nolite cogitare,
And is as much to mene, to men þat ben lewid,
'Wh[anne] ȝe ben aposid of princes or of prestis of þe lawe,
For to answere hem have ȝe no doute;
For I shal graunte ȝow grace, of god þat ȝe seruen,
Þe help of þe holy gost to answere hem [alle]'.

(A.XI.296–301)

The Ending dilates on this issue of interrogation (being "aposid of princes
or of prestis"), but with a twist: instead of Langland's (and Christ's) promise
of spiritual intellection, we get injunctions to silence before spiritual enemies
(crowned by Christ's own before Pilate). And there are also *archana verba*—
hidden words, tantalizingly referred to as such, but never uttered. There was a
specific audience for this, and whoever wrote it was clearly distressed by—
what he implies to be—a deterioration in tolerance for truth telling, apparently even since Langland first wrote A.XI.

Who is John But? As I have suggested elsewhere,[103] his name itself looks as
suspiciously like a pen name as Langland's own name does (Langland is a very
rare surname and he has never been identified with certainty in historical records). However, a "butt" is, like a "longland," a feature of plowman's lexis: a
"longland" is a long strip of plowland, and a "butt," by contrast, is short strip
at the end of a row. The name "But," then, may simply be coterie code for some

Langlandian who took pity on the "short" (unfinished) version of the poem
and modestly did for it what medieval lawyers were always accused of never
being able to do—"making an end":

> And whan þis werk was wrouȝt, ere wille myȝte aspie
> Deþ delt him a dent and drof him to þe erþe . . .
> And so bad *Iohan but* busily wel ofte
> When he saw þes sawes busyly allegged . . .
> For he medleþ of makyng he made þis ende.
>   ("John But" Passus, A.XII.101–9, with omissions, my emphasis)

This, then, is one argument in favour of a disciple as the author of the But Ending. Another is the pastiche of echoes, borrowings, and jokes about Langland's
text which (as I have also discussed elsewhere) the passage contains. In the passage just quoted, for instance, there is a delightful recycling of Imaginatif's rebuke to Will ("And þow medlest þee wiþ makynges . . ." [B.XII.16], cut from
the C text). Yet another is the extensive use of legal reference in this passage
(39 out of 117 lexical items are legal diction), which places the writer most
likely in Westminster.[104]
    Given that the But Passus contains three quotes on keeping silence (first, in
the face of evil,[105] second, sanctified secrecy,[106] and third, inquisitional silence),[107]
it would be the fashion of our time to immediately assume, and especially given
the likely date of the But Ending in the 1380s,[108] that the complaint is empathetic
with the growing suppression of Wycliffism. However, the author of the But
Passus shows not a shred of sympathy with Wycliffism. Quite the contrary, his
are closer to Uthredian-Ockhamist empathies, as we saw. Further evidence
for this view comes from what may be an overlooked allusion to Uthred's condemned doctrine of *clara visio* in line 96 of the But Ending: "Þou shalt be lauȝth
into lyȝth *with* loking of an eye" (Fever's words to Will as he urges him to "lyue
as þis lyf is ordeyned for the" [90 ff.]). Putting together what we know, then,
of who But was, why he likely chose the pen name he did, and the overwhelm-
ing concern with the silencing of liberal theological speculation on salvational
issues, we have a specific new context for the Ending.
    Given that he is borrowing from the C text, we can piece together when the
But Passus was written. As Anne Middleton's superb essay on the But Ending
has shown, the text was constructed, in places pastiche-style, by someone who
knew and can cite *at least one other version* of the poem. Given the allusion to

C.V. at line 98, for instance, he certainly had access to even Langland's latest text, which is dateable after 1381 and perhaps as late 1388–89 or beyond. Wendy Scase has argued that line 113 of the Passus ("Furst to rekne Richard kyng of þis rewme") is a formulation Richard only assumed after 1388 and more steadily in the 1390s.[109] This accords well with the entirely different evidence offered here, especially if we ask what was it that prompted Langland (in C) and those close to him (perhaps the But author) to return to Uthred's condemned thought of 1368 in the 1380s or 1390s? During this time Langland was creating C, and a disciple was creating the But Ending, possibly (although this is unclear) out of a few fragmentary genuine lines.[110] Whoever he was, he is angry with a current trend in theological thinking on salvation, which he sees (picking up on Langland's hint) as driven by an inhumane new scriptural fundamentalism, and is appropriating Langlandism to express it. By the mid-1380s and early 1390s, there is renewed interest in Uthredian alternatives, at least in the C text; by 1391–93 we know that the eclectic Walter Brut was also using Uthred's ideas on salvation (Wyclif likely turned in his grave!) and coming under scrutiny for this and other heterodoxies.

Could any lines from the But Ending have been originally Langland's own? The crux of the authenticity problem relates to the first thirty-three lines, which, scholars have speculated, may or may not descend from something original to Langland himself. In the form they *now* take, which is also textually corrupt, the attribution is doubtful. The very opening of the lines (1–2) shock the reader with a kind of blunt closure we never see elsewhere in *Piers Plowman*. Lines 6, 7–8, 12, 15, 22a are all lifted in some form from elsewhere in *Piers*. Scripture behaves in this passage the way no other guide figure in the poem does (including herself), when she tells Clergie not even to *teach* Will unless he is baptized. She provokes the dreamer to comment, as we saw, that this is: "boþe skaþe and sklaundre to holy cherche" (17) — a comment so strong that it is hardly paralleled elsewhere in the poem, although it is *just* imaginable. This line begins the matrix of Latin silence quotes, and it is only the sophisticated use of these that gives Middleton pause about completely dismissing the whole thing as spurious.

What we *may* be looking at here (with emphasis on *may*) is a heavily redacted fragment of authentic writing. Middleton's evidence is of the best sort in these matters: the intelligent way the three Latin quotes are handled and gut instinct. It is my sense, too. I would suggest that we can find out a little more by looking at the matrix of *associations* radiating out from the quotations to (or from?) elsewhere in the poem.

To sum up the associations we have very briefly, the *archana verba* no man may utter, implying the forbidden salvation issues of the Harrowing, are used in But's Ending to lead up to Christ's silence under inquisition in response to Pilate's "Quid est ueritas?" Second, But's "Vidi preuarica[nt]es & tabescebam" on silence before the wicked when the speaker is under persecution is in fact an exact analogue to the Psalm quote with which Langland often expressed constraint on freedom of authorship: "Existimasti . . ." (You have thought wrongly that I should be one like yourself; [but] I shall accuse you [Ps. 49:21]), provoking Leaute's famous legal advice.[111] This one begins, "Haec fecisti, et tacui" (These things you have done and I have been silent).[112] It is as if someone has indexed the Latin in Langland's poems (a common scholastic habit) and in more than one version to draw together every reference in the *Latin* quotations to silence and verbal constraint. Is the person who worked associatively to construct this passage a kind of Langlandian Alan of Lynn figure (Alan, we remember, was a passionate, professional creator of indices), or was this person with the intimate knowledge the poet himself?[113]

Whoever created this little matrix of quotations used in the beginning of the But Ending had an intimate sense of how the Latin quotations surrounding freedom of discussion work in the poem in all its versions. That person also had an intimate sense of what caused the breakdown of A—and how the quotations were used in B's recovery. Was this person (originally, that is, before redaction) Langland? We will never know for sure, but what sounds like it *might* be Langland—in an unusually angry mood—is the stark allegory of scriptural fundamentalism as tyrant-shrew and the complex oblique use of biblical Latin quotes. What is beyond doubt is that a writer calling himself John But created the larger But Passus—and he was *not* Langland. He may have redacted into his own composition this little fragment of fifteen to thirty-three lines, perhaps originally the master's own. If he composed the lines 18–33 as well, he had a clerk's knowledge of the Psalms, an encyclopedic knowledge of *Piers Plowman*, and fleetingly his master's touch with free association. The reason I believe that "But" was *at least* very close to Langland himself, indeed, I would call him a disciple or coterie member, is that he has Langland's allegorical habit of mind, but without being able to match or sustain (certainly not ever outside the first thirty-three lines) Langland's skill with language and with embedding biblical quotations. He is a good mimic, however. And what is also beyond doubt is that, composing in the later 1380s or early 1390s, he was concerned with lack of freedom of speech in liberal salvation theology. This could reflect suppression of either Uthredian or Joachite materials (the latter, we know, were by 1389 liable to confiscation; the former re-condemned in the Uthredian article listed from Brut's trial of 1391–93).

Uthred, Left-Wing Orthodoxy, and the Vulnerability of Wycliffism

Uthred returned to Oxford in the 1380s—although we do not know for how long—perhaps, in order to help out generally in the war on Wycliffism (by then even his old enemy, William Jordan, was enlisted on the same side against the common new foe). But more specifically, perhaps, he and others saw that Wycliffism was beginning to be revealed for the rather inhumane and reactionary force it could be, especially on salvation. One of the Achilles' heels of Wycliffism, I believe, was its predestinarian theology, and especially its salvationally brutal view of childhood mortality—in marked contrast to Uthred's. Take the example of the Wycliffite text, "Of Weddid Men and Wifis and of Here Children Also," which gives us a whole different window on Lollardy.[114] The treatise, aimed at the comfortably middle class, blames women generally, and rich women especially, for their attitudes toward the loss of a child: "thes *riche* wifis wepen . . . and crien agenst God . . . and axen God whi He takith rathere here children fro hem than pore mennis."[115] (The emphasis on the "riche" operates rather as it does when Chaucer's Franklin gently mocks Dorigen's lamenting, "As doon thise noble wyves" [line 819].) The text everywhere assumes predestination: even procreation itself is "*to fulfille the noumbre* of men and wymmen that schullen be savyd" (line 96). It goes on, after chastising mothers who weep for their children, to enunciate harshly Wycliffite views on the predestined damnation of dead children:

> See now the woodnesse of this grucchynge! It is great mercy of God to take a child out of this world; for yif it schal be saaf, it is delyverid out of woo into blisse. . . . Yif it schal be dampnyd, yit it is mercy of God . . . lest it lyve lengere, and do more synne. (lines 295–99, pp. 200–1)

These, I would suggest, are among the often overlooked draconian positions that must have contributed toward Wycliffism's lack of broader appeal.

We might note that the "Twelve Conclusions of the Lollards" is against prayer for the dead on the grounds that one might be praying for someone God has predestined to damnation.[116] It is hard to believe that these kinds of attitudes were crowd-pleasers. As Nicholas Orme has shown, parents routinely defied the church itself by burying stillborn children secretly in sacred ground. So harsh Lollard ideas must have helped spark opposition to the movement. And these instances may provide some context for the kind of anger the Langlandian passages show.

Uthred, meanwhile, was back in Oxford between 1383–86, and he must have looked very different to the university community at that juncture.[117] The Blackfriars Council had been a watershed. Uthred was a former prominent academic disputant of Wyclif's and fearless defender of church temporalities and papal dominion. Although by this time he must have been aging, his potential for contribution to the various raging debates must have been highly valued by many at the university. This is especially so since the battle lines between camps were not as neatly drawn as we imagine them to be today. And it must have been in the debating halls that most Oxford academics of all persuasions hoped that these things could yet be worked out — not under inquisition, and certainly not at the stake. Uthred's ideas on salvation, even under the shadow of Langham's condemnation of 1368 (now by comparison politer and officially nameless), must have seemed an attractive "left-wing orthodoxy" to some — and even more so given the draconian ideas of predestination that Wyclif had so successfully peddled.

It would have been an exhilarating, confusing, and nervous time. Many of many different stripes — including our two lone pro-revelatory Wycliffites, Brut and the *Opus* author, were experimenting with Continental apocalypticism. Some were also experimenting with Schism politics, and even stranger things: female preaching, Free Spiritism, inclusivist salvation, and, above all, vision. Three years after Uthred left Oxford (so far as we know) for the last time, our four condemned authors are confiscated, three of whom (Ockham, Olivi, and Rupescissa) had impacted directly on the generous salvations debate. It was likely somewhere against this backdrop that we have the composition of *St. Erkenwald*, which takes up the challenge once again of the righteous pre-Christian, this time in reviving with a touch of Dantean humanism an Antique lawyer of great London civic pride.

There was, then, renewed interest in Uthred's ideas, and in Joachite ideas, too. This can be supported by codicological evidence, sometimes in the same manuscript (as we saw in the evidence of annotation in copies of Uthred's texts mentioned above and Balliol College 149). A revival of interest in Uthred, I would suggest, was part of a new fascination during the Great Schism with revelatory theology that took in strange bedfellows: Joachite thought (with which he was empathetic), Franciscan Spiritualism (with which he shared positions on corporate "poverty" and inclusivist salvation), and Ockhamist speculation. That the authorities were concerned about renewed Joachimism appears after the arrest of Friar Helmyslay in 1380 and his international case, straddling Joachite and antimendicant radicalism—a case that erupted in Uthred's own diocese. Even chroniclers begin noticing Joachim at this time, and even the Blackfriars articles of 1382 contain some eclectic items.[118]

The manuscripts mentioned above, like Balliol College 149, are evidence that Uthred's work was being copied in Ricardian texts at Oxford in the 1380s, and this study has given a number of other examples of revelatory-related texts in circulation in Oxford in the 1380s and 1390s. In fact, from the standpoint of manuscript survival, the university was awash in new copies of reformist apocalypticism and revelatory theology. No wonder Wyclif was grumpy about it and is on record as questioning its orthodoxy. But I would suggest that in the chaos caused by the Schism, which had sent even academics in Continental Europe scrambling to consult prophecies, and the Wycliffite condemnations, the impulse to turn, at least covertly, to revelatory thought, even in an academic environment, was powerful (as in contemporary Paris). We know that no matter how intellectually superior they may have felt, many medieval authorities of all stripes turned to revelation in times of duress. Wycliffites were desperately trying to keep their agenda apart from the revelatory one—and that was not easy given their long-standing Franciscan sympathies. Langland was trying to keep his reformist agenda apart from the Wycliffite one, and trying to regain an alienated audience in the wake of the 1381 Rising. Both he and his closest followers were trying to fight salvational "fundamentalism" with help from both revelatory and speculative theology. Chaucer was finding his own voice after a brief experimentation with Langlandianism and was wrestling quietly with theological and political issues from a safe distance in the pre-Christian past until various sensitivities overwhelmed him, sometime before his death. The evidence shows, however, that neither Langland nor Chaucer regarded Wycliffism as quite as dangerous as we today seem to imagine. Other contested issues loomed as large for them, and older issues with a proven track record for danger were among these. Julian was receptive to texts coming from the Continent, especially via

Carthusian transmission, and to some of the gender issues transmitted with them. In fact, the threat of Lollardy did not even keep Margery Kempe at home, and she, among all our writers, would have been most vulnerable to Arundel's anti-Wycliffite Constitutions. Carthusian and Bridgettine circulation, meanwhile, was opening up a whole new world to certain circles of fifteenth-century laity, and none of the legislation Arundel wrote made much difference to broader manuscript transmission. Rather, I think we need to see a more complex pattern of official suspicions and broad-based tolerances, both before and after Arundel.

Concluding Thoughts

Books under Suspicion has examined the censorship issues that drove major writers of the period to widespread use of visionary genres. In it I have been interested in exploring how a range of both Latin and vernacular authors positioned their work so as to take advantage of the tacit toleration that religious and secular authorities extended to writers of revelatory theology. Revelatory theology, as I have defined it from medieval sources, is novel or sometimes unorthodox thought arrived at via an authorial claim to visionary experience. We have looked at examples like the breakdown of Langland's A text under the strain of Ockhamist, and perhaps Uthredian, salvational theology and, perhaps in response, the experimental humanism of Chaucer poking fun at the whimsicality of such theology in *House of Fame*. We have also looked at some of the condemned and suspect texts that traveled in manuscripts with *Piers Plowman* or which invoked it: the Pseudo-Legnano prophecy that figured at Jan Hus's trial, the poem lamenting Scrope's death, and the Wycliffite street broadside "Heu! quanta desolacio" and its association with Anglo-Irish poetry showing fierce anti-Joachite and anti-visionary polemic. We have also looked at how political refuge could be found in the revelatory, and how hopeless censorship of revelation was in the massive cult inspired by Archbishop Scrope's execution.

In exactly the same period we saw the impact of suspect Continental groups on the missionary activism of Margery Kempe and the failure of Netter's ban on Alan of Lynn's communication with her. The concern about Free Spiritism in England during this period is signaled in a York cleric's testing of Margery, an extensive caveat in *The Chastising of God's Children*, and other texts of Carthusian and Cambridge transmission. The parallels between *The Chastising* and M. N.'s enigmatic glosses on Porete's condemned *Mirror* as it traveled incognito, reveal for us the likeliest source of those glosses. Together with the evidence of how the *Chastising* author adapted Ruysbroeck's *Spiritual Espousals* to arrive at his warning of Free Spiritism, we now have new insight both into how concerned Carthusian reading circles were and—significantly—how *open* they were to protecting freedom of learning in the mystical tradition. This same tradition, it seems, sheltered Julian's passion for intellectual vision and her unique style of forensic vision and the visual arts, even if she did not feel it could fully shelter her true authorial gender. Finally, we have looked at the beatific vision controversy, alternative salvation doctrine, and the response of a member of Langland's early coterie, uncovering what may be an authentic, if heavily redacted, fragment of Langland's writing within it.

Books under Suspicion shows a more pluralist culture than perhaps we have realized, and a more pluralist view of unorthodoxy. This study, which has to be pioneering and cover so much ground at once, has only been able to gesture at much that still lies buried in manuscripts and archives. Although it only examines revelatory-related works, this is the first ever book on non-Wycliffite condemnation and suspicion in fourteenth- and early fifteenth-century England. Attempting to discuss both the intellectual issues and the manuscript evidence, throughout the study I have had to balance this history against the question of its impact on vernacular literary writers. This is a balance, I feel certain, that in our present state of knowledge we cannot yet get quite right. My main concern has been to *begin* to tell a new story—with as much linguistic and literary democracy as possible.

Appendix A:
Arundel's Constitutions of 1407–9
and Vernacular Literature

Long understood as having had some sort of impact on fifteenth-century literary culture, the Constitutions[1] have recently been the subject of a great deal of productive scholarship and debate, especially since Nicholas Watson shifted the terms of the enquiry by memorably calling this legislation "one of the most draconian pieces of censorship in English history" ("Censorship," 826). Even granted, however, that the all-embracing interpretation Watson gives was what the authorities intended, the actual impact of the Constitutions was, historically, relatively minimal. In fact, relatively few book prosecutions (other than some Bibles, the real target, and some readily identifiable Wycliffite texts) occurred under the Constitutions.[2] Even English Bibles, as Christopher de Hamel, Ralph Hanna, and others have now shown, were by no means always suppressed and seem to have remained widely available, particularly to certain classes of society. And, as I have demonstrated throughout this book, censorship in a manuscript culture is especially difficult to enforce, and that the authorities would be so unrealistic about what they could enforce is also no surprise given the failure of other would-be draconian legislation of the period.[3]

How all-embracing was the legislation? Closely examined, it contains a large number of qualifications. The prohibitions that actually affect literary censorship are as follows.[4] Article 1 (in summary) states that all preachers preaching in English have to present themselves to their ordinary for license and that parish priests and *vicarii temporales* "not having perpetuities nor being sent in form aforesaid" (non perpetui, in forma supradicta non missi)—meaning, importantly, those of *unbeneficed* status—should restrict themselves to preaching only those things expressly contained in John Pecham's "Ignorantia sacerdotum."

This restriction, then, does not apply to all preachers and cannot therefore mean that "Here Pecham's minimum necessary for the laity to know if they are to be saved has been redefined as the maximum they may hear, read, or even discuss" (Watson, op. cit., 828). Article 3 commands that preachers preaching chiefly to the clergy shall preach of the sins of the clergy, and those preaching to the laity only of the sins of the laity, though we have little evidence of enforcement. Article 4 restricts preaching on the sacraments to "what already is discussed by the holy mother church, *nor shall bring anything in doubt* that is determined by the church, nor . . . pronounce blasphemous words concerning the same." This is not actually very draconian, and its wording is not unlike what one would find in any earlier canon law manuals (like the *Omne bonum*, as we saw above, written in the 1360s). Article 5 forbids schoolmasters teaching children grammar to "intermingle any thing concerning the catholic faith, . . . [or] sacraments of the church, *contrary to the determinations of the church;* nor shall suffer their scholars to expound the holy Scriptures (*except the text* [nisi in exponando textum], *as hath been used in ancient time*): nor shall permit them to dispute [disputare] . . . concerning the catholic faith or sacraments." This, too, is not as draconian as it has been made to sound: it does not prevent the grammatical teaching or construing of the text of scripture, nor the teaching of any theology that is *not contrary to the determinations of the church.* Moreover, as Nicholas Orme notes, there is no evidence of enforcement in the schools. Article 6 prohibits the reading of any work by Wyclif or others since the time of Wyclif, unless it is first approved by theologians from Oxford, Cambridge, or a board of recognized theologians (the form of which the article spends some time detailing). Interestingly, in this article there is the provision for copying "at a reasonable price" any such book, the original of which is to be kept "in some chest in the university." What is important about this is that the writers of the Constitutions do foresee some dissemination and study even of Wyclif's works, but they want it to be controlled. Article 7, noting that even Jerome confessed to making errors in his translation of scriptures, decrees that no man, hereafter, by his own authority "will translate any text of the scripture into English or any other tongue and disseminate it via book, booklet, or tract" (aliquem textum sacrae scripturae auctoritate sua in linguam Anglicanam, vel aliam *transferat, per viam libri, libelli, aut tractatus*); and that no man read any such translation "now lately set forth in the time of John Wickliff or since," that is, "*until the said translation be allowed by the ordinary of the place.*" The concern here, as in visionary *probatio* cases, is not so much with an utterance as with *publication* of it. The hopeless thing is that this imagines a degree of control over book production that was, as the authorities writing it knew, virtually impossible to patrol. Moreover, no attempt is made, even here, to restrict earlier translations.

To determine whether or not a rigorous or comprehensive interpretation of this last article is "overly fanciful," Hudson consulted a contemporary legal gloss on the text. Following Workman (*John Wyclif*, 2.418), she chose the great canonist Lyndwood's gloss on the Constitutions in his *Provinciale,* who specifically annotated the words "aut tractatus" as including the composition of any treatise using scholarly materials in relation to scripture and translating it into English or another vernacular ("quod de dictis doctorum, vel propriis, aliquem tractatum componat applicando textum sacrae scripturae, et illius sensum transferendo in Anglicum, vel aliud idioma") (Workman's Appendix, 2.418). As Hudson rightly says, Lyndwood's *gloss* extends the scope of the Constitutions vastly. However, there is virtually no evidence that such a comprehensive interpretation as Lyndwood's was *ever* used in practice, especially against *non*-Wycliffite writing in the vernacular. There is, as Hudson mentions, one very late and otherwise anomalous case of a Chaucer text and a few other items coming under suspicion, recorded in the Lincoln register for 1464. Among the books confiscated on that occasion from Wycliffite suspects were a copy of *The Canterbury Tales* and a few standard Middle English devotional works, but the group in question had what the authorities were really after: several biblical translations.[5] It is, as Workman says, largely the possession of Bibles, tragically, that sent people to the flames (for a list see 2.196 n. 3). It is, indeed, *biblical translations* (not interpretations) that contemporaries cite as needing licenses, as in the well-known passage from *Myroure of our Lady*: "For as much as it is forbidden under pain of cursing that no man *should have nor draw any text of holy scripture into English* without license of the bishop diocesan, and in diverse places of your service are such texts of holy scripture; therefore I asked and have license of our bishop to draw such things into English to your ghostly comfort and profit."[6]

The tone of this sounds more like the acceptance of a tightened security measure (the post–September 11, 2001 world comes to mind) than it does intimidation; in fact, as Elizabeth Schirmer has shown, Lollardy was simply not a concern for this author, nor for Syon, which was busy anglicizing some of the most exciting women's theology in Europe.[7] There is no evidence that authors of interpretive works of orthodox intent felt the same constraint. Hudson, with characteristic care, looks at what *might* have happened to the Chaucer text under a strict interpretation of Lyndwood (and had it been the only book under scrutiny—which was not the case). No existing evidence, however, allows for a capacious sense of what "translation" means having been applied. This last is a very important point. In his article "Censorship and Cultural Change," Watson writes, "I accept Hudson's view over that of Deanesly (p. 3, n. 4) particularly because, in medieval texts, 'translatio' routinely refers to acts of interpretation or exegesis or to 'the exposition of meaning in another language'."[8] In fact, *translatio* does indeed have multiple meanings, some of which take in free composition (as Rita Copeland has shown in *Rhetoric, Hermeneutics, and Translation*). But the primary target of the Constitutions was biblical *translation* in the very straightforward and recognizably modern sense that is, in fact, directly addressed in the Prologue to the Wycliffite Bible itself, and even these were not consistently threatened.[9] Indeed, the prosecution records in the years following the Constitutions speak for themselves, as does the abundant evidence of Wycliffite Bibles made after 1409. As Christopher de Hamel has shown, many of those Bibles were lavish and even commercially produced. This puts an entirely different spin on how we read the evidence we have from trial records. Even if, then—to imagine for a moment the most favourable conditions possible for Watson's broader interpretation—Lyndwood's reading were adopted as official and a copy of Lyndwood's gloss to Article 7 was open on the desk of every episcopal official, a massive army of summoners (more literate than Chaucer's) would have to conduct house-to-house searches, with the patience to read through every family's household books. If this were the case (and it was not) we would expect to find a huge drop in vernacular theological production. In fact, the period after Arundel is exactly the period of a massive rise in such books.

What Watson's brilliant study is trying to explain, having noted the traditional English literary view of the fifteenth century as "the drab age" in relation to its glittering Ricardian predecessor, is "the transformation, shortly after 1400, of an impressively innovative tradition of what I shall here be calling 'vernacular theology' into its derivative successor . . . as the result of specific historical forces and acts" (823). What must be taken into account, however, is the influx of brilliant, adventurous Continental works, including those of the *Devotio Moderna* and many women's visionary writings, writings all subjected to exactly that freer, more creative handling of *translatio*—that very sense of translation that Watson invokes in enlarging the scope of the Constitutions. *Translatio* was indeed a creative activity, and works of eye-catching originality were suddenly available, most especially to women, during our supposed "drab age." The range of prologues in *The Idea of the Vernacular*, edited by Wogan-Browne et al. proves this alone. The creativity of Kempe, Julian (who was also writing her Long Text after the Constitutions), the translators of Mechthild, Bridget, Catherine, Thomas à Kempis, the *Speculum devotorum*, and many more therefore must "count" in any calculation of English vernacular theology and its adventurousness.

What I have suggested in this book, however, is that the repression of Lollardy, which was a terrible thing for those in the circle of that distinctive tradition, did encourage for the larger populace a tendency to focus upon what Tanner has called "left-wing orthodoxy"—in which revelatory writing played an important, indeed, even escapist role.

Appendix B:
The 1389 Confiscations of Four
Banned Continental Writers as
Reported in the *Opus arduum*

The passage that records the confiscations of William of St. Amour, Ockham, Olivi, and Rupescissa in the *Opus* is discussed throughout this book. This appendix is simply to clarify textual aspects of it. I have read the passage in a microfilm of Brno, University Library MS Mk 28, fol. 174v, kindly loaned to me by Penn Szittya. Curt Bostick also generously sent me his transcription of the passage for comparison, along with his chapter on the *Opus* prior to the publication of his book, *The Antichrist and the Lollards*. Anne Hudson discusses this passage on page 54 of *Lollards and Their Books* in her superb article, "A Neglected Wycliffite Text." She reads it as saying that Oxford and Salisbury are "the places where the books of Ockham, Rupescissa, Olivi, and William of St. Amour have been *destroyed*" (my emphasis), and again on page 49 she says that "the *bishops* have caused the destruction in Oxford and Salisbury of the works of" these writers. This is a fascinating possibility and may (in time) be supportable by other historical sources; however, the passage is ambiguous, and what exactly was the role of the bishops is not really clear. What is clear is that the *friars* are named as agents ("quia fratres huius negocii procuratores erant" [fol. 174v]) of the prelates who order, first, the destruction of vernacular books, described by the *Opus* author as homilies, gospels, and epistles written in the mother tongue, and, second, that the friars are responsible for keeping the four Latin writers named under lock and key. This seems to be how Bostick and also the Rouses have read the passage as well (see Rouse and Rouse, *Authentic Witnesses*, 412). I am grateful to Anne Hudson for her correspondence with me about this puzzle. It remains to be discovered exactly what the role of the bishops of Oxford and Salisbury was, but what both have in common is unusually superb intellectual resources (see chapter 6 on Bishop Waltham's library) and awareness of international heresy. When the passage occurs, the author is elucidating the verse from the Apocalypse 12:4 that runs (as rubricated in the manuscript) *"et draco stetit ante mulierem que erat paritura, ut cum peperisset filium deuoraret."* For the author the dragon is the devil, the woman *"que erat paritura"* is the church, and the son whom the dragon would devour represents the *veros filios ecclesie* who suffer so many afflictions on account of their doctrine (propter doctrinam suam) (fol. 174v, col. 1). The passage about the four confiscated authors arises predictably enough in relation to the author's exegesis of *"filium deuoraret."* I give the whole passage in the original here to clarify any ambiguity, italicizing the most crucial sections:

Preparet se eciam ad deuorandum filium matris ecclesie, id est fructum per scripturarum studium conceptum destruere; quod iam patet quantum in eo est impletum per generale mandatum prelatorum ad comburendum, destruendum et condempnandum omnes libros, scilicet *omelias ewangeliorum et epistolarum in lingwa materna conscriptos,* suggerendo quasi non liceat nobis Anglicis legem diuinam habere in nostro wlgari, quod tamen omnibus [col. 2] Ebreis, Grecis et Latinis est commune. Et propterea qui sint diaboli in hac causa discipuli speciales facile patet, quia *fratres huius negocii procuratores erant,* capitanei et preduces. Sed quamuis ad hec quantum potuit per se et per suos laborauit diabolus, non tamen profecit, quia non omnes libri tales sunt destructi, sed loco eorum alii iam de nouo conscripti sunt ut in breui, Domino fauente, patebit, ipsis multum forciores. Et propteria subdit *et peperit,* scilicet ecclesia, *filium masculum, quia sicut masculus in vigore prestat femelle,* sic libri tardius conscripti sunt prioribus contra antichristum et fautores suos multum validiores — *cuius oppositum credunt fratres. Ymmo putant se per absconsionem librorum scriptorum contra abusiones suas et aliorum ecclesiasticorum, utpote Wi(lhelmi) de Sancto Amore, cuius libri multis seris et vectibus clauduntur Oxonie et Sarum, necnon per absconsionem librorum Wilhelmi Occam contra papam Romanam, fratis Iohannis de Ripsissa, fratris Petri Iohannis super Apokalipsim, et talium,* se posse subterfugere vindictam Dei contra eos inferendam propter abusiones suas, precipue quia pape Romano fauent in cunctis supersticionibus suis. Cum tamen iram Dei super se eo amplius prouocant quo magis ueritatem contra abusiones omnium ecclesiasticorum diwlgandam abscondunt.

Appendix C:
The Confluence of Terminology for the Beguines, the Olivian "Secta Beguinorum," Franciscan Spirituals, Beghards, and Heresy of the Free Spirit in Official Records and English Sources

Like the word "lollar/e," first used in relation to Beghards in the Hainault area in 1309, the word "beggar" may have emerged in Middle English as an anglicization of a Continental smear term, in this case perhaps "beghard" or "beguine."[1] Both "lollar/e" and "beggar" have a complex history in English reformist texts like *Piers Plowman*, but they are not often studied in relation to the Continental dissent that gave rise to them. When the English chronicler, Adam Usk, writes that he fears modern clerical corruption will once again cripple the clergy on account of the schism caused by Lollards and Beguines (scisma Lollardensibus atque Begwinis operantibus), he shows that English understanding of heresy was not at all insular.[2] The less usual form of "Lollar/d" he uses with the deliberately broader grammatical ending "-ensibus" means that for him it is not necessarily a geographical or sect-specific term. Nor was it always in England.[3] *Beguini* is the word, in its Latin masculine form, often denoting the male followers of Olivi, and *Beguine* (or to classicize it purely for clarity's sake, *Beguinae*) either specifically his female followers or any number of unaligned semi-religious women across (especially) northern Europe.[4] Usk's wording takes in all possibilities. The modern spelling distinction between "Beguine" and "Beguin" which some scholars use to distinguish, respectively, members of women's communities in northern Europe from the Joachite-influenced followers of Olivi (mixed in gender) in the south is an attempt at geographical clarity. The difficulty is that, as David Burr rightly notes, the modern distinction "inevitably injects more clarity into the sources than the sources are themselves willing to grant, particularly when we are dealing with Southern France."[5] The modern distinction breaks down, for instance, when we realize that there were Beguines (that is, northern-style women's communities) in the south, too, initially founded by Douceline de Digne, as her *Vita* tells us explicitly, modeled consciously on those of the north. Yet Douceline and her followers were also passionate Joachites.[6]

Another difficulty for the modern distinction is that the Council of Vienne, famous for its anti-beguine legislation apparently aimed at the substantial women's communities in the north, was *also* investigating the followers of Olivi and the Franciscan Spirituals converting the *beguini seu beguin(a)e* with their charismatic ideals of being "fools for Christ."[7] Burr summarizes Clement's investigations as they culminated at the council (investigations the pope had been making since 1309) by explaining that they were to address *four* issues: "whether the Spirituals had been infected by the heretical sect of the *spiritus libertatis* [that is, heresy of the Free Spirit]; whether the rule and the papal bull *Exiit qui seminat* were being observed properly within the order [that is, the bull forbidding any reopening of the question of Franciscan poverty]; Olivi's orthodoxy; and the persecution in southern France."[8] Given the more famous agenda of Vienne to condemn the widespread women's communities of the north, we have in this single council the confluence of four of the largest dissent headaches for the fourteenth-century church: northern Beguines, Free Spiritism (sometimes also called Beghards), radical Franciscanism, and the *Beguini/e* whom Olivi inspired.

Olivi's *sectatores* were accused of holding his condemned views on poverty, on the coming Age of the Spirit, on the "carnal" nature of the present church (against which John XXII would issue *Gloriosam ecclesiam*), and on marriage (an institution for which Olivi had no fondness).[9] Some were reported to have "termed marriage nothing more than a disguised brothel" (which begins to sound like some of the more extreme Free Spirit cases, not unknown even in England [see chapter 6]). Gui discusses the origin of the *Beguini/e* in southern France and says that their errors began to be detected about 1315. He describes them by saying that they are connected with Franciscan tertiaries, are both male and female, and wear a distinctive brown habit, gathering into communities (domos paupertatis) and on feast days in one house to hear books read in the vernacular; he says, moreover, that they had specific salutations for each other and begged or produced goods in their houses to obtain a living.[10] Some believed that the spiritual powers of the papacy (after Nicholas III) had passed to the Franciscan Spirituals. One group, the Guglielmites, even elected their own pope, a woman.[11] Some expected a reformation of the church to occur in Constantinople. Some believed that priests and other church officials could no longer administer the sacraments. One can easily see the parallels between these views and Wycliffism, and why any associations with them were a threat to the respectability of Wycliffism: *all* such views had been punishable by burning in the fourteenth century by the time Wyclif began his campaign. Moreover, much of the uniqueness that Hudson ascribes to Wycliffite and Hussite movements (including popular inspiration deriving from an academic writer) predated both movements in the Olivian *Beguini/e*.[12] As John Fleming points out, it was not Olivi's very scholarly writings that drew crowds; it was, apparently, his charismatic and humble personality that accounts for his vast impact.[13]

Nicolas Eymeric's *Directorium Inquisitorum* also lumps together the "heresies and errors of the Beghards, Beguini, Fraticelli, or Brothers of Penitence [fratrum de poenitentia]" (299). Pope John XXII had named them as: "fraticelli, seu fratres de paupere vita, aut bizocchi sive beghini."[14] The word is still being used as a smear term at the time the sister houses of the *Devotio Moderna* were on the rise in northern Europe in the late fourteenth and early fifteenth century, when they were repeatedly accused of living the life of "Beguines" (beghinarum). And Boniface IX's *Sedis apostolice prouidentia* of 1395 stigmatized "eisdem Beghardis seu Lullardis et Zwestrionibus [Sisters]."[15] In the midst of such official terminological confusion it is important for scholars of England to remember that usage, even of the term "Lollardi," is not always reliably sect-specific.[16] And so it is that the unusual modes of life adopted by Margery Kempe and, at least in poetry, by Langland's narrator also reflect Europe-wide trends and suspicions of those who live in the *status medius* between the clergy and the laity.[17]

Notes

Notes to A Word about Intellectual Freedom

1. For the excision of the flyleaves and the unusual absence of his name from a book he had donated, see A. G. Watson, *Catalogue of Dated and Dateable Manuscripts*, 141.

2. Transcribed by Douie, "Olivi's Postilla," 68, and see ch. 2 below for full discussion of the manuscript; for analysis of the date of the hand that added the note as consistent with the second quarter of the fifteenth century, that is, during his abbacy, compare plates 415, 426b, and 453 in A. G. Watson, *Catalogue of Dated and Dateable Manuscripts*, and see Kerby-Fulton, "English Joachimism."

3. See n. 8 of the Introduction for the rationale for the 1437 limit.

4. The classic study of Wycliffite history remains Hudson, *Premature Reformation*. Among excellent recent studies of Lollardy and censorship, see N. Watson, "Censorship," 822–64; Justice, *Writing and Rebellion*; Justice, "Inquisition, Speech and Writing," 1–29; Copeland, *Pedagogy*; Somerset, *Clerical Discourse*; and Aers and Staley, *Powers of the Holy*; Simpson, "Constraints of Satire," 11–30; Simpson, *English Literary History*, and Somerset, Havens, and Pitard, *Lollards and Their Influence*. Certain articles in the latter volume have also begun to question the hegemony of Wycliffism; see especially Larsen, "Are All Lollards Lollards?" 59–72. For a very recent collection, see Barr and Hutchinson, *Text and Controversy*.

5. Quoting from a recent summary of my own in "Prophecy and Suspicion." The conclusions condemned at the Blackfriars Council are printed in Netter, *Fasciculi Zizaniorum*, 277–82.

6. Hudson discusses only one instance, and it is a late one (1464), on which see Appendix A below. For the view that the Constitutions of 1409 probably affected the production of vernacular literature, see Pearsall, *Life of Chaucer*, 182, and much more broadly applied, N. Watson, "Censorship."

7. For a recent treatment, see the insightful discussion in Martin, "Wyclif, Lollards, and Historians," 237–50. See the helpful discussion of historiography in Hudson, *Premature Reformation*, 7–60, especially on John Foxe and issues of reliability, 39–40 n. 186, and in relation to Thomas More, n. 188. For a different perspective on broader historiographical issues, see Duffy, *Stripping of the Altars*, esp. 1–8.

8. These issues are discussed from a variety of perspectives in N. Watson, "Censorship"; Aers, *Faith, Ethics, and Church*, and his "John Wyclif: Poverty and the Poor"; and McSheffrey,

Gender and Heresy, who suggests that women's roles in the movement have been overstated. For more recent discussion, see Somerset, "Eciam Mulier," and Kerby-Fulton, "Eciam Lollardi."

9. Hereford was not yet a doctor. See Forde, "Nicholas Hereford's Ascension Day Sermon," 209.

10. "Set, heu . . . quod rex non habet aliquos iusticiarios in regno suo ad hanc iusticiam exequendam. . . . Ideo oportet vos, O fideles Cristiani, manum apponere" (240). For the complete text of the sermon and excellent discussion, see ibid. For the meaning of "luridici" and its relation to Langland's definition of "lollars" as spiritually lame, as well as its international usage, see Chronology, 1382, and the detailed note accompanying the suspension of Henry Crumpe on June 15.

11. Netter, *Fasciculi Zizaniorum*, 296.

12. Courtney's letter forbids the teaching of the twenty-four condemned Wycliffite propositions of the Blackfriars Council. Oxford chancellor William Barton had already delivered a ban in 1381, although only internal to the university and limited to Wyclif's eucharistic doctrine, in an attempt to stop Wyclif from lecturing. Wyclif defied the ban. In the wake of John of Gaunt's intervention shortly thereafter, Wyclif, though still defiant, did retire from Oxford. See Hudson, "Wycliffism in Oxford," 67–84. The twenty-four propositions had been condemned at the Blackfriars Council in London just four days after Hereford's sermon. See Hudson, op. cit., 70; and for the text, see Netter, *Fasciculi Zizaniorum*, 275–82, for the propositions, and 298–99, for Courtney's letter.

13. Netter, *Fasciculi Zizaniorum*, 299; see also Hudson, "Wycliffism in Oxford," 71 n. 23.

14. Rygge had originally chosen Hereford for the sermon and also chose the young Philip Repingdon to give the Corpus Christi Day sermon for the same motives. See Forde, "Nicholas Hereford's Ascension Day Sermon," 209–10.

15. See Thijssen, *Censure*, esp. "Academic Freedom and Teaching Authority." Seen in terms of the continuity of international academic enquiry in this way, Wycliffism seems less phenomenal and monolithic.

16. Hereford's sermon was on May 15, and Rygge finally published the Blackfriars' condemnations on June 15. Rygge told the Blackfriars Council that he feared for his life if he published them, which seems in some part disingenuous given his own earlier recourse to *armatos* (see Netter, *Fasciculi Zizaniorum*, 311, for the final events). See Forde, "Nicholas Hereford's Ascension Day Sermon," 205, and Hudson, "Wycliffism in Oxford," 72–73, on the timing of events.

17. See Chronology, 1382.

18. On Kirkestede, see Forde, "Nicholas Hereford's Ascension Day Sermon," 233–36; Rouse, "Bostonus Buriensis," 471–99; Rouse and Rouse, *Preachers, Florilegia, and Sermons*, 220–22; Kerby-Fulton and Daniel, "English Joachimism, 1300–1500," 324; and the excellent detective work on Kirkestede's hand in Lerner, *Powers of Prophecy*, 93–101. Forde's careful analysis of the manuscript indicates that, given what we know of Kirkestede's interests and marginalia elsewhere, "it seems likely that the John of Tynemouth works [which compose much of the manuscript] and the subsequent miscellany [in which the Hereford sermon appears] were collected by and copied at the instigation of Henry." But Forde assumes that Kirkestede was not alive after 1379 and so proposes a younger monk, John de Gosford, as the "likeminded successor" who added the sermon (op. cit., 234). Lerner has found evidence to indicate that Henry was indeed active in 1382. Either way it is clear that the Bury monks were

continuing to archive all such material. Henry had scoured England for prophecies and other materials on church reform and the future of the clergy, developing the first ever union catalogue, perhaps in part for these materials. E. Randolph Daniel is currently editing Kirkestede's treatise on Antichrist (from his prophetic collection, Cambridge, Corpus Christi College Library MS 404), and I am grateful to him for sharing it with me.

19. Disendowment issues go back in England at least to 1247; see Offler, *Opera Politica*, 1.226. All the historical events are in the Chronology and will be discussed in later chapters. For the events in this sentence, see, respectively, 1308, 1282 (and for the archbishop of Canterbury, John Pecham's position, also the note to 1278), and 1318.

20. For the primary sources and discussion, see Chronology, 1371 and 1374 respectively, and accompanying notes.

21. The faithfulness with which Henry copied and annotated texts of both sorts, even texts with which he was in deep disagreement, is eloquent testimony to the Benedictine ideal of preservation of learning. Indeed, monastic houses, as we will find throughout this book, are one of the primary safe havens for suspect and controversial texts.

22. Thijssen, *Censure*, 90–112; see also Courtenay, "Inquiry and Inquisition," 168–82; Burr, "Olivi and the Limits of Intellectual Freedom," 185–99; Classen, *Studium und Gesellschaft*, 238–41; and Miethke, "Bildungsstand und Freiheitsforderung," 231–40.

23. For the text of Friar John's condemnation, see the note to Chronology, 1358; for Courtney's retort to Rygge in 1382 "universitas est fautrix haeresum," see Netter, *Fasciculi Zizaniorum*, 311.

24. Usk, *Chronicle*, 14–17.

25. As they did for Repingdon's sermon June 5 (Netter, *Fasciculi Zizaniorum*, 306–7).

26. Pressure of all sorts was exerted against the anti-Wycliffite party, e.g., the suspension of Crumpe, see ibid., 311–12, and Chronology, 1382 and note; see also Wendy Scase's more recent "Heu! quanta desolatio," 19–36.

27. Netter, *Fasciculi Zizaniorum*, 300.

28. Classen, *Studium und Gesellschaft*, 255, and see Thijssen, *Censure*, 90–93.

29. Tierney, *Origins of Papal Infallibility*, 39–45, and Thijssen, *Censure*, 94–96; see also Laarhoven, "Magisterium or Magisteria," 75–94.

30. See Swanson, *Universities, Academics and the Great Schism*, and Lytle, "Universities as Religious Authorities," 79–82.

31. "The schism uprooted the traditional methods of validating orthodoxy," as Thijssen puts it (*Censure*, xi). The faculty member in question was John of Monzón; the case generated an important theological discussion on teaching authority in the university, especially as enunciated by Pierre d'Ailly. On a more practical level the university had to decide questions like which pope should receive the *rotuli* containing petitions for benefices. See Bernstein, *Pierre d'Ailly*, esp. 28–30.

32. See Colledge, "*Epistola solitarii*," 19–49, and D. Elliott, "Seeing Double," 26–54; see also Bernstein, *Pierre d'Ailly*.

33. Justice, *Writing and Rebellion*, 5.

34. See the discussion in ch. 1 below of the origin of the early Wycliffite idea that there was to be no pope after Urban.

35. For sources on the Paris condemnations, see Chronology, 1277 note. On the crucial role of revelation in the medieval perspective, see Thijssen, *Censure*, 94, and the discussion of Godfrey of Fontaines below.

36. On the Tempier condemnations and their parallel at Oxford in the visitations of Robert Kilwardby, archbishop of Canterbury, and later his successor, John Pecham, in 1286, see Chronology and the discussion of Pecham below in ch. 4; on John XXII's treatment of academics, especially Olivi and Ockham, see Chronology, 1322 and 1328 respectively, and chs. 1 and 9 below.

37. See Chronology, 1310. This *approbatio* is discussed in ch. 7 below.

38. Godfrey of Fontaines, *Quodlibets*, 402 ff., for question 18; for this discussion, see Thijssen's excellent analysis, *Censure*, 92–93 and 156.

39. Godfrey of Fontaines, *Quodlibets*, *Quodlibet VII*, 404–5.

40. Even where salvation is not at stake, Godfrey recommends (although less strenuously) that a theologian try to have the condemnation overturned, because no one should be prevented from freely discussing truths that will perfect their intellectual faculties (nam homines non possunt libere tractare veritates quibus eorum intellectus non modicum perficeretur [ibid., 404]).

41. Ibid., 402.

42. Bloomfield, *Piers Plowman as Apocalypse*, 227 n. 13, to which should be added the manuscripts referred to below, as well as the abundant evidence in the *Opus arduum*.

43. *Chartularium*, 2.281, cited in Thijssen, *Censure*, 156 n. 12.

44. On Thomas of Waleys, who was imprisoned for disagreeing with John XXII on the beatific vision, see Chronology, 1331–32; for Olivi and Ockham, 1322 and 1328; all three of these figures are discussed in later chapters. See Thijssen, *Censure*, 101–7, on Ockham and teaching authority.

45. Cited from his *Tractatus de corpore Christi*, 209, lines 71–79, by Thijssen, *Censure*, 102.

46. In addition to those academics already mentioned, see Pierre d'Ailly's arguments for the type of judicial authority on the question of heresy that a university faculty rightly holds, discussed in Taber, "Pierre d'Ailly and the Teaching Authority," 168–72.

47. In addition, one could cite the legal battles fought on behalf of the *Devotio Moderna*; see Van Engen, "Devout Communities."

48. See the discussion in Appendix B and the items by Somerset, Hanna, and de Hamel referred to there.

49. D. Elliott, "Seeing Double," 36, and discussed in ch. 8 below.

50. On Paris university chancellor, Jean Gerson's concept of "theologia mystica," see ibid., 33–34; Gerson, *De theologia mystica*, 3.250–92; and Chronology, 1402.

51. See Chronology, 1370, for the case of Nicholas Drayton, apparently one time warden of King's College, wanted on heresy charges, the nature of which, sadly, we do not know.

52. See my "Eciam Lollardi."

Notes to the Introduction

1. Gordimer, "Censorship in South Africa," 166.

2. The passage from *Opus arduum* is fully transcribed in Appendix B and discussed below at the opening of ch. 1. On the *Opus*, see Hudson, *Lollards and Their Books*, 43–66, and Bostick, *Antichrist*, ch. 4; for its author, see ch. 5 below.

3. Anne Hudson remarks on the oddity of the *Opus* list of confiscated authors because three of the four were friars and in general, "Lollard texts are uniformly and shrilly hostile to all the activities of the friars" (*Premature Reformation*, 349). See the extensive discussion below in ch. 1.

4. See Chronology, 1380, and ch. 3 below.

5. "But al þese I leeue, because it nediþ nat greteli, for I trowe *heere bien rehersid þo þat bien most in our knowyng to be dred*" (*Chastising*, 145, my emphasis). For a full discussion, see ch. 7 below.

6. See Chronology, c. 1415–17; Kempe, *The Book*, ed. Meech and Allen, 168.5 (Cap. 69) and 170.7 (Cap. 70) and accompanying notes; and Knowles, *Religious Orders*, 199.

7. Netter's extensive study of the Hussites would have brought him into direct contact with Free Spirit and Joachite materials, both involving women visionaries (see Chronology, 1421–27, and accompanying note). See Lerner, *Heresy of the Free Spirit*, esp. 119–24.

8. Intellectual censorship in the third quarter of the fifteenth century (the period of Pecock's and Fortescue's forced recantations, for instance) is heavily inflected with the political struggles of Yorkist and Lancastrian dynasties, which is one reason this book does not extend into that period.

9. On the question of homogeneity in Wycliffite doctrine, see Hudson, *Lollards and Their Books*, 125–40, and the discussion below in ch. 5, the section "The Road Not Taken."

10. See Chronology, 1338–44 (Bradwardine's *De causa Dei*); R. Adams, "Langland's Theology," esp. 108–9; G. H. Russell, "Salvation of the Heathen," 101–16; Coleman, *Piers Plowman and the Moderni*; and ch. 10 below.

11. See Chronology, 1358 (FitzRalph and de Pouilly), 1385 and 1392 (Crumpe). For the broader issues, see Szittya, *Antifraternal Tradition*; and on the charges of heresy FitzRalph encountered, see Walsh, *Fourteenth-Century Scholar*, 441–45. On the Cistercian, Henry Crumpe, who was also Anglo-Irish like FitzRalph, and in the same category Philip Norreys, dean of St. Patrick's Cathedral, Dublin, whose views against the friars are condemned in 1440, see Walsh, op. cit., 360. Note Walsh's observations on the Anglo-Irish Oxford-trained men who were key contestants against the friars. For a fuller discussion of all these issues, see ch. 3 below.

12. See ch. 3 below, and for more detailed study of these issues, see Bloomfield, *Piers Plowman as Apocalypse*, and Kerby-Fulton, *Reformist Apocalypticism*.

13. For general studies of English contact with Continental mysticism, see Sargent, "Transmission by the English Carthusians," 224–25, and (although only generally) Riehle, *Middle English Mystics*. For an introductory discussion of Langland and women's mysticism, see Kerby-Fulton, "Piers Plowman," 513–38. On Porete's text in England, see ch. 7 below.

14. These are large topics in Chaucer: for preliminary reading on Ockham and bibliography in relation to Chaucer, see Courtenay, *Schools and Scholars*; Coleman, *Piers Plowman and the Moderni*; Rhodes, *Poetry Does Theology*; and the discussion in ch. 9 below. I have chosen to use the word "Ockhamist" in this study recognizing that there is no perfect word to describe the loose confluence of philosophical positions often subsumed under that label, or under its synonym "nominalism." On the difficulties of the word, see Courtenay, op. cit., who rightly points to the fact that "most of Ockham's immediate academic contemporaries rejected one or more aspects of his thought, and that even his most sympathetic supporters . . . show considerable independence of mind" (op. cit., 217). The main issues in this book, however, are salvation-related, and especially those for which Ockham and those of similar

tendencies were labeled "Pelagian"; here we do have something of a tradition, at the very least as identified by Bradwardine and others hostile to these views. On the difficulties of the label "nominalist," see Peck, "Chaucer and Nominalist Questions," 745–60. For Chaucer's antimendicantism, see the seminal studies by Szittya, *Antifraternal Tradition*, and those by Fleming, recently summarized in "Antimendicantism."

15. See chapter 2 below. For one of the more recent discussions of *St. Erkenwald*, see Rhodes, *Poetry Does Theology*, summarizing previous scholarship.

16. That is, in British Library, MS Additional 37790, in which *The Mirror of Simple Souls* appears fols. 137r–225r, and Julian's Short Text on fols. 97r–115r. The manuscript is written in a single hand of the mid-fifteenth century, copying a text of 1413 in the case of Julian's *Revelation*. For a description, see Julian, *Book of Showings*, 1–5; and see ch. 8 below. The manuscript almost certainly belonged to a Carthusian.

17. For English concerns about misguided mysticisms and related issues, see *Chastising*, and John Clark, "Walter Hilton," 61–78; for the controversies surrounding Bridget's canonization, see Colledge, "*Epistola solitarii*," and very recently, Ellis, "Text and Controversy."

18. On Kempe and Free Spirit, see ch. 6 below; on the persistent theme of *probatio* (testing) of Marjorie's revelations, see Voaden, *God's Words*.

19. See Kerby-Fulton, "Medieval Professional Reader and Reception," 7–15; and see especially the article with a complete transcription of the annotations by Parsons, "Red-Ink Annotator."

20. Articulately enunciated in Strohm, *England's Empty Throne*; for the manuscript issues connected with Gower's positioning, see Kerby-Fulton and Justice, "Scribe D," 111–41.

21. After the start of the Hundred Years War England did to some extent become distanced from France in intellectual culture; see Knowles, *Religious Orders*, 24–25. But Chaucer, for example, had many active French literary connections, and, in broader terms, England was by no means isolated from other influences, including Italian and Flemish ones. The necessarily international perspectives of the clergy and religious orders, underlined by shared use of Latin, is an aspect that has been forgotten in recent scholarship.

22. The definition is based in part on Gerson's "theologia mystica" (see Gerson, *De Mystica Theologia*, ch. 30, 77–78, lines 6–45 especially) and awareness of canon law definitions of heresy in which "novel" teachings are consistently anathematized, and on political denunciations of prophecy. Gerson had a key aspect of revelatory theology in mind with his denomination "mystical theology," but "revelatory" attempts to take account of modern English, in which "mystical" has come to mean something more specialized. On Gerson's impact in England, see Gillespie, "Haunted Text," 133.

23. From British Library, MS Royal 6. E.VII, fol. 200a; one of the seven definitions of a heretic, according to London author James le Palmer in his *Omne bonum*, written in the 1360s. The *Omne bonum* is discussed in more detail in the next section.

24. From *Rotuli Parliamentorum*, 3.583.

25. Lerner, "Ecstatic Dissent," 33–57.

26. Reeves, *Influence*, 422.

27. See the discussion below in ch. 2 on John Whethamstede's commission of an Olivi manuscript for the Benedictine college at Oxford, some of his other commissions, and the evidence of his commonplace book. Syon abbey also had two works by Olivi (on which see Bloomfield, *Piers Plowman as Apocalypse*, 227 n. 13, and ch. 2, n. 91 below).

28. As formulated in Stephen Greenblatt's landmark essay, "Invisible Bullets," first published in 1981 and often reprinted. For recent analysis, see Paul Strohm's discussion of Greenblatt's "Fiction and Friction," which Strohm describes as "a classical articulation of New Historicist procedure[;] this essay brilliantly amplifies the premise that we may historicize a text by 'restoring it to its relation of negotiation and exchange with other social discourses'" (Strohm, *Theory and the Premodern Text*, 150, citing from Greenblatt's *Shakespearean Negotiations*, 72). The premise for the various historical approaches in the present book might be well described in another comment of Paul Strohm's: "The emphasis on the contingency of texts, their reliance on a material reality beyond their own bounds, is my rejoinder to those notions of textuality that would view language and text as all there is, as our sole point of access to past events and their understanding" (*Hochon's Arrow*, 7).

29. See Hyland and Sammells, *Writing and Censorship*, especially the fine discussion of Marcuse's concept of "repressive tolerance" and other challenges to "tolerationist" positions, 4–13.

30. For this quote from Marcuse and analysis, see ibid., 5, and Wilkins, *Concilia*, 3.317. For Arundel's attitudes, see also Appendix A; his exemption of any "libri, libelli aut tractatus" written *before* Wyclif in Article 7 suggests that he did not regard literature itself as generically suspect.

31. For a good introduction to theoretical problems in current studies of censorship, see Hyland and Sammells, *Writing and Censorship*. Reception history, as the various approaches in their collection demonstrate in papers from all fields and periods, becomes a crucial aspect of nearly any aspect of censorship study.

32. The adjective is Ralph Hanna's. See the discussion in Appendix A, and its n. 2.

33. In addition to de Hamel, *The Book*, 166–89, see Hyland and Sammells, *Writing and Censorship*, 8–9, especially on the censorship of cheap print runs in the Victorian period.

34. See Case Study 3 for the articles Arundel decreed to control this cult.

35. See Appendix A on the question of what "counts" in the assessment of Arundel's impact on fifteenth-century vernacular theology.

36. This explains in part the odd linkage of prophecy, politics, and disendowment issues in the legislation. See *Eulogium*, 3.480–81, for an index listing of many such episodes relating to the friars; the legislation is discussed below in ch. 4; for the political implications of the legislation, see Strohm, *England's Empty Throne*, 15.

37. See Kerby-Fulton, "Women Readers," 121–34; Kerby-Fulton and Justice, "Scribe D"; Kerby-Fulton, "Professional Readers of Langland," 101–37.

38. See Kerby-Fulton, "Women Readers."

39. I deal with this in my "Langland and the Bibliographic Ego," 65–141.

40. The word used is from *Richard the Redeless* (the passage is discussed in Kerby-Fulton and Justice, "Langlandian Reading Circles"); for a similar injunction asking to keep the work among judicious readers, see the examples of *The Mirror of Simple Souls*, Julian's Long Text, and *The Cloud of Unknowing*, discussed in ch. 8 below.

41. See Goldschmidt, *Medieval Texts*.

42. On patronage and authorial issues across a range of texts, including the *Legend*, see Kerby-Fulton, "Langland and the Bibliographic Ego."

43. Strohm, *Theory and the Premodern Text*, 165, mentioning Gower and Strode in particular. See the discussion below in ch. 9 of Chaucer's interest in issues of predestination and

academic speculation. On Ralph Strode, see Chronology, 1374–80 and note, and Strohm, *Social Chaucer*, 57–59.

44. See, again, my "Langland and the Bibliographic Ego" for Hoccleve, and for the Introduction to the "Man of Law's Tale," especially *Canterbury Tales* Fragment II.77–85, with its implicit jab at Gower; and see ch. 9 below for the Endlink.

45. Kerby-Fulton and Justice, "Langlandian Reading Circles," and "Reformist Intellectual Culture," 149–203. Recent studies are summarized in my "Professional Readers of Langland."

46. See Copeland, *Pedagogy*, for a fine theoretical discussion of this.

47. A. Patterson, *Censorship and Interpretation*, 4.

48. Ibid., 18.

49. See especially the superb essay by Dronke and Mann, "Chaucer and the Medieval Latin Poets," esp. 154–61, for discussions of the *Cosmographia* of Bernard Silvestris, the *De Planctu Naturae*, and *Anticlaudianus* of Alan of Lille.

50. Evident even in, for example, the Prologue of the B text of *Piers Plowman*; Langland excised many of the conventions of this form in the C text Prologue.

51. On the hugely popular "Otherworld" vision form, which sometimes raised theological controversies, see the discussion and lengthy recent bibliography given in the Introduction to Easting, *Revelation of the Monk*, xviii (for bibliography).

52. All forms discussed in this book; for the last especially, see ch. 5.

53. See Kerby-Fulton, "Who Has Written?" 101–16, and Kerby-Fulton, "Langland and the Bibliographic Ego."

54. See especially Brieger et al., *Illuminated Manuscripts*, and Huot, *Romance of the Rose and Its Medieval Readers*; see also the marked differences in literary approach evident in *Piers Plowman* annotation, as discussed in Kerby-Fulton and Despres, *Iconography*, ch. 3.

55. J. S. Russell, *English Dream Vision*. For an introductory study, see Spearing, *Medieval Dream Poetry*, which outlines the basic influences of Macrobius, scriptural and early Christian visions, Boethian elements, and the impact of the important French vision poems, including the *Roman de la Rose*. Another earlier study that has been formative for the field is Piehler, *Visionary Landscape*, focusing on the psychic and participatory dimensions of some of the major visionary works in Middle English. Kerby-Fulton, *Reformist Apocalypticism*, deals with visionary genres in relation to apocalypses in the biblical tradition and the major apocalyptic exegetes of the later Middle Ages. Among very recent studies, see Easting, *Revelation of the Monk*, and Barbara Newman's superb recent book, *God and the Goddesses*.

56. See Augustine, *De Genesi*, and for a translation of the entire passage, see *The Essential Augustine*, 93–97.

57. *Chastising*, 169, lines 12–28, and 170, lines 1–7.

58. Macrobius, in a foundational text for the entire Middle Ages, had identified these three along with two "worthless" types of vision: the *fantasma* and the *insomnium*. The former would seem to be what is implied in the title (all that survives) of a piece by Ralph Strode, dedicatee of Chaucer's *Troilus*. For details see Chronology, 1374 and note.

59. Translated by J. S. Russell, *English Dream Vision*, 66 from *PL* 34, col. 469.

60. Translated by J. S. Russell, *English Dream Vision*, 67, from *PL* 75, col. 827.

61. Quotations from Chaucer are from the *Riverside Chaucer*.

62. From Pecham's "Tractatus Contra Kilwardby," in *Fratris Johannis Pecham*, 122. Kilwardby had quoted the prophecies of Hildegard and Joachim in a letter to novices, say-

ing that the Virgin herself had prayed earnestly for the creation of the order. Pecham responds: "O rarissime, recole scriptum esse, quia 'sompnia extollunt inprudentes' [Ecclus XXXIV.1]. Utinam aliquid alegasses *solidius* in tui sacri ordinis fulcimentum! Sanctorum siquidem revelationes autenticas novimus, apocriphas non curamus." For discussion of Pecham's response and his wariness of revelations, see ch. 4 below.

63. See Synave and Benoit, *Prophecy and Inspiration*, 177.

64. See Kerby-Fulton, "Who Has Written?" and Voaden, *God's Words*. For a very recent discussion in relation to Gerson, see D. Elliott, "Seeing Double." Primary sources, especially those relating to Bridget of Sweden, will be discussed in ch. 8.

65. For these texts, see Gerson, *Oeuvres complètes*, 9.471 ff.; for *De examinatione*, Boland, *Concept of Discretio Spirituum*; for Alphonse's *Epistola solitarii*, see ch. 8 below. On treatises of the same kind by Pierre d'Ailly and Henry of Langenstein, see Smoller, *History, Prophecy, and the Stars*, esp. 93–95, and D. Elliott, *Proving Woman*, 260–62 and 259–60.

66. Van Engen, "Devout Communities."

67. Suppressed, for example, is Alphonse's ch. 1 in which he states his fear that his treatise will fall among the ignorant, insists that few today have knowledge of visions, that too many condemn visions, especially women's, that God often chose the unlearned, and that it is dangerous to ignore visions. (See ch. 8 below.) Walter Brut makes a similar claim, aligning himself, as a layman, with women (see ch. 5 below). In practice laymen had as little right to preach or teach outside the home as laywomen did.

68. For the discussion in this paragraph and the quotes, see Newman, *God and the Goddesses*, 305–8.

69. See Appendix A below.

70. Wilks, "Wyclif and the Great Persecution," and see below for further reasons.

71. Auden, *Collected Poems*, "In Memory of W. B. Yeats," II, line 5. On Langland's *Piers Plowman* and its impact on the Rising of 1381, see Justice, *Writing and Rebellion*; and, on self-censorship issues in relation to it, Kerby-Fulton, "Langland and the Bibliographic Ego."

72. Copeland, "William Thorpe," 201.

73. See Kerby-Fulton, *Reformist Apocalypticism*, 117–21, on Dinzelbacher's distinctions. See Dinzelbacher, *Vision und Vision-literatur*. Newman, *God and the Goddesses*, takes the discussion of Dinzelbacher into other types of visionary writing as well.

74. Staley Johnson, "Trope of the Scribe," 820–38, and see also her *Margery Kempe's Dissenting Fictions*.

75. Copeland, *Pedagogy*; see also her earlier "William Thorpe," 199–222.

76. Newman, *God and the Goddesses*, 25–30.

77. See Daniel Hobbins's fine dissertation, "Beyond the Schools." I would like to thank Dr. Hobbins for kindly providing me with a copy prior to publication.

78. See Hult, "Language and Dismemberment," 104, citing from pp. 73 and 80 respectively of Hicks, *Le Debat sur le 'Roman de la Rose'*; the English translation by Baird and Kane, *La Querelle de la Rose*. See also Gerson, "Contre le *Roman de la Rose*," 7.301–16, and translated in *Jean Gerson: Early Works*, 378–98. The *Roman de la Rose* is cited from Lecoy's edition.

79. Hult, "Language and Dismemberment," 104, citing pp. 74 and 81 respectively.

80. See, for instance, Pantin, *The English Church*; and for a similar list, Knowles, *Religious Orders*, vol. 3.

81. For a detailed listing of the canon law sources (which included Gratian's *Decretum*, the *Decretals* of Gregory IX, the *Liber sectus* of Boniface VIII, the *Clementines* and

the *Extravagantes* of John XXII, William of Pagula's *Summa summarum*, the *Corpus iuris canonici*, and several glosses), see Sandler, *Omne bonum*, 1.47 and 2: Index of Sources. The two massive volumes containing the *Omne bonum* are now British Library, MS Royal 6.E.VI and VII, made sometime between 1359, when James was first appointed to the Exchequer, and 1375, when he died. All the writing in the volumes is in the hand of a single scribe, James himself; there were two illustrators who worked under his direction, and two afterward. James had extraordinary access to, among other sources, antimendicant writings, including William of St. Amour's *De periculis novissimorum temporum* and works by FitzRalph, likely even the sermon diaries (Sandler, op. cit., 1.46). James also, like FitzRalph, was greatly interested in the beatific vision (see ch. 10 below). On James's antimendicantism, see Szittya, *Antifraternal Tradition*.

82. *Omne bonum*, British Library, MS Royal 6.E.VII, fol. 200 (the full article runs to fol. 205). In all transcriptions of Latin, abbreviations are silently expanded (unless otherwise indicated); in all transcriptions of Middle English, expanded abbreviations are italicized.

83. In Douce, it indicates the illustrator's own dissent with Langland's unusual generosity; see Kerby-Fulton and Despres, *Iconography*.

84. See Chronology, 1339-40. This charge is discussed below in ch. 9.

85. For each of these cases, see the Chronology under the date given.

86. The examples given in all the notes to this sentence are only a few samples from obvious cases; for more instances of each, see the Chronology, and for many not recorded here, also Bacher, *Prosecution*. For an example of a bishop who regularly used ritual humiliation, see the cases of Bishop Ledrede (Chronology, 1324, 1328, and 1332), who imposed penances standard in Continental inquisition on repentant heretics, such as fasting, pilgrimage, flogging, badges of infamy, and heavy fines; see Bacher, op. cit., 15.

87. For example, Friar John had to make a public recantation at Oxford in 1358; so, too, Nicholas Trivet in 1315 (although he later made a good career). For the sources of each, see Chronology.

88. Uthred de Boldon's case (1368) and Friar John's (1358). Friar John was forbidden to lecture at Oxford again without express permission.

89. Henry of Costesy is, from all we can tell, a prime example of this. Thus A. G. Little remarks on the disappointing difference between his earlier Psalm commentary and his later (post-arrest) Apocalypse commentary (*Franciscan Papers*, 140-41); Marjorie Reeves has noted the inescapably deliberate self-censorship in his Apocalypse commentary (*Influence*, 86-87).

90. William Outlaw in 1325 and his associate Alice Kyteler had pilgrimages imposed on them as well as fines and the wearing of crosses on their outer garments. See Chronology, 1324, and Bacher, *Prosecution*, 56.

91. In the case of the Cathari (Chronology, 1161-66 and n. 95 below).

92. Used in several cases, but most egregiously by Ledrede in the case of Petronilla of Meath (Chronology, 1324).

93. The punishment is ubiquitous, and the accused often dies in prison: see, for instance, Arnold le Poer (1328) and the Franciscan in the diocese of London, 1336.

94. The Templars, even those unconvicted, were confined to monasteries and perpetual penance (Chronology, 1308 and 1310). The nun, Margery Rye, who denied the eucharist, was to receive severe physical penances and confined perpetually (see Chronology, 1369);

the Dominican convicted of heresy in association with Alice Perrers was confined by his order for the rest of his life (see Chronology, 1376); Reginald Pecock was also confined for life (see Chronology, 1457). Many orders, like the Franciscans, for instance, had their own prisons within major houses.

95. Bishop Grandisson collected materials in preparation for the death penalty in two separate cases (see 1334 and 1355 in Chronology). Vicious cases include: the Cathari of 1166, who were scourged, branded, and driven out half-naked to die of exposure; and a young man and an old woman were immured for life in Oxford in 1222 (see Chronology for both).

96. A writ of *de heretico comburendo* could be issued by the king at any point in English (and post-conquest Irish) history, and in the period before Wycliffism, being relaxed to the secular arm could and did happen in several cases. Canon law did not require the formality of a writ, and local secular authorities were bound to obey a bishop or inquisitor in carrying out death sentences (Bacher, *Prosecution*, 57). An Albigensian (that is, a Cathar) was burned in London in 1210; an apostate deacon degraded and burned in Oxford in 1222 (see Chronology). See Chronology as well for the burnings of Franciscans in England in 1330, as reported by Thomas Burton; and in Ireland the burning of Petronilla of Meath and associates under Bishop Ledrede in 1324; the burning of Adam Duff in Ireland in 1327; and the Bunratty burnings under Bishop Cradock in 1353. These incidents place England and its colony, Ireland, directly in the Continental sphere, especially the early fourteenth-century burnings, which occur during the Clementine and Johannine papacies. The presence of women among the victims (a possibility in Burton's account) makes the configuration especially relevant to the cases of Porete (as Colledge pointed out in *Latin Poems of Ledrede*, xxi; see Chronology, 1324 and note), and to the persecution of Olivian Beguines and Franciscan tertiaries. Not only do the Irish cases bear the marks of friction over English rule at this time, but also of oppression, like Ledrede's, carried out by English (or Anglo-Norman) bishops.

97. See Larsen, "Are All Lollards Lollards?" 60 n. 3, for the view that "the majority of heresy cases" are unrecorded in the registers, a view shared by Hudson and Aston. See, for example, Chronology, 1380, for details of a case in Oxford, Bodleian Library MS Bodley 158, fols. 142v ff., only recently edited, regarding Newcastle Dominican, Richard Helmyslay, in trouble for heresy; and see Chronology, 1431 and 1443 (and the references there to Hudson, *Lollards and Their Books*) for unexamined cases from bishops' registers associated with Free Spirit.

98. See Arnold, "Lollard Trials."

99. See Reeves, *Influence*, Appendix B, for numerous instances of prophecies like "Cum fuerint" (527).

100. On Matthew, see Reeves, *Influence*, 49, 62, 65, 108, 122.

101. Ledrede's career was long and stormy. A draft letter from Edward III to Innocent VI, for instance, that survives among the muniments of York Archbishop John Thoresby, asks for the removal of the notorious *English* heresy-hunting Franciscan, Richard Ledrede, bishop of Ossory. The letter, dated about 1351, makes clear that Ledrede had tried to have himself made inquisitor of heresies in England, and that when that failed he spent years "trumping up charges of heresy and sorcery against the decent, simple, faithful people as a means of extorting money from them" (Raine, *Historical Papers and Letters*, 403–6; Colledge, *Latin Poems of Ledrede*, xxxi). Sorting out the truth of such accusations on either side is a delicate matter, but some things are absolutely clear. First, Ledrede *did* succeed in burning

several people for heresy, among them a woman. And he was able to do so precisely because he came fresh from Avignon at the time Pope John XXII's vendetta against both Beguines and Franciscan Spirituals was underway, when, that is, detecting and exposing heretical conventicles could be a way toward promotion. As Colledge points out, Porete's execution was already a cause célèbre thoughout Europe, and Ledrede may have been in search of more "Poretes" abroad. We note, however, that, if the records are to be trusted, Ledrede did turn up eucharistic heresy (see Chronology, 1328), and that Ireland was widely thought to be a frontier in every sense of the word (see Kerby-Fulton and Despres, *Iconography*). Langland's portrait of the state of the Irish clergy is of anarchy (C.XXII.221 ff.).

102. For example, see FitzRalph's connection with Guillaume Court (Chronology, 1357–58) and note that Ledrede left the papal court just months before October 1317, when John XXII issued his decree, *Cum de quibusdam mulieribus*, a revision of the Council of Vienne anti-beguine legislation (Chronology, 1317; Colledge, *Latin Poems of Ledrede*, xxii).

103. Bacher, *Prosecution*, 57.

104. Arnold, "Lollard Trials," 86–87.

105. Bacher, *Prosecution*, 57.

106. This likely explains how the *Opus arduum* author (who may be Nicholas Hereford) gained access to the books he used while writing from prison. See ch. 5 below.

107. See Peters, *Inquisition*, and Kieckhefer's helpful refining of the distinction between the second and third of these meanings, "Office of Inquisition," 61. For a different perspective, given his particular topic, see Cohen, *Friars and the Jews*, 44 and 77. Other important studies include the still indispensable Lea, *History of the Inquisition*, and Kelly, "Inquisition and the Prosecution of Heresy," 439–51.

108. Arnold, "Lollard Trials," 87.

109. Ibid.

110. See ibid., 88–89, who suggests that Grandisson had access to more than the two sentences of French Franciscan Spirituals.

111. Bacher, *Prosecution*, 48.

112. Both Bacher, *Prosecution*, and Arnold, "Lollard Trials," note examples of this. Some of the sources listed in the Chronology provide further evidence.

113. See Bacher, *Prosecution*, 49–50, and Arnold, "Lollard Trials," who cites more recent studies and makes the point that English usage of standard terminology describing heretics and their associates is uneven before the period of Lollardy, but he also establishes that legal procedures were widely known in England and Ireland via William of Pagula's popular *Summa*. See also, more recently, Larsen, "Are All Lollards Lollards?" 59–72.

114. See the cases of 1236, 1329–30, and 1370 (and accompanying notes in all cases) for example.

115. Translated Coulton, *The Inquisition*, 76, from Eymeric, *Directorium*, 204.

116. Bacher, *Prosecution*, 66–68.

117. Ullman, *Short History of the Papacy*, 254.

118. Bacher, *Prosecution*, whose entire ch. 2 is devoted to these trials.

119. Brentano, *New World*: "Non est torquendus propter famam conseruandam popularum Reatinarum et propter honorem Ciuitatis" (242). See his discussion of the episode, 242–50.

Notes to Chapter 1

1. On the dilemma of revelatory theology, see Newman, "Hildegard of Bingen," 163–75; see also Kerby-Fulton, *Reformist Apocalypticism*, 125 and n. 110; Julian, *Book of Showings*, 1.70; on the censorship of reformist apocalyptic thought, see Reeves, *Influence*, and Burr, *Persecution*.

2. For Wyclif's remark, see ch. 4 below; for instances involving the formation of the biblical canon itself, see Kerby-Fulton, *Reformist Apocalypticism*, especially the cases of the *Pastor Hermas* and the *Muratori Fragment*, 85–96. For twelfth-century concerns, see Van Engen, "Letters and the Public Persona," 375–418.

3. See Bacher, *Prosecution*, and Richardson, "Heresy and Lay Power."

4. The subject of much of the present chapter and the next. For John XXII, see the Chronology, 1323.

5. Discussed in chs. 3 and 4 below; I am here quoting Reeves, *Influence*, 62.

6. The subject of chs. 6–8 below. For English concerns about misguided mysticisms and related issues, see *Chastising*, and John Clark, "Walter Hilton," 61–78.

7. For Uthred, see Chronology, 1368 and note; for Ockham, see 1323 and 1324; for fuller discussions, see chs. 9 and 10 below. Eschatology did not have to be apocalyptic to incur condemnation as the censorship of Uthred de Boldon's theory of the "clara visio" indicates.

8. For a transcription of the whole passage, which is from Brno, University Library MS Mk 28, fol. 174v, and the verses of the Apocalypse the author is elucidating, see Appendix B.

9. We do not yet have direct evidence of what the episcopal role at Oxford and Salisbury was, but a significant piece of information is that the bishop of Salisbury had the case of a heretic whose views were hybrid Lollard–Free Spirit, William Ramsbury, on his hands at that very time (1389), and this may have inspired him to cast a wider net (see below, ch. 7). For recent discussion of Joachite and Olivian influences on Free Spirit Beguines, see Wehrli-Johns, "Mystik und Inquisition."

10. For Rupescissa, see Chronology, 1349 and note; for a recent analysis, see John of Rupescissa, *Liber secretorum eventuum*, 10–87. On the censuring of Olivi, see Chronology, 1282, and Burr, *Persecution*. On William of St. Amour, see Chronology, 1256, and Szittya, *Antifraternal Tradition*, esp. 15–17.

11. On Ockham, see Chronology, 1323 and 1324 and notes for primary sources; the papal commission established in Avignon condemned fifty-one articles on a variety of subjects including grace, free will, vision, and doubt. On this and subsequent clashes with academic authorities, see Leff, *Heresy*, 1.296–397; and Thijssen, *Censure*, 57–72; and chs. 9–10 below. Any number of these points might have worried English church officials in 1389, but one certainty is that they would not have been comfortable with his ideas on disendowment; see his *An princeps* (addressed to Edward III), in Offler, *Opera Politica*, 1.220 ff; and for discussion, Kerby-Fulton, *Reformist Apocalypticism*, 176. On the Pseudo-Ockham *Dialogue* translated by Trevisa, see ch. 5 below.

12. For evidence to the contrary, see Reeves, *Influence*, esp. 46–49, which notes the pioneering work of Morton Bloomfield, as does Kerby-Fulton, *Reformist Apocalypticism*; see also Kerby-Fulton and Daniel, "English Joachimism, 1300–1500," 324, and Kerby-Fulton, "English Joachimism."

13. As Hudson rightly notes, "The *Opus arduum* associates the destruction of books by Peter John Olivi and John of Rupescissa, two Spiritual Franciscans, in Oxford and Salisbury with the persecution of his own Lollard associates, but though this might seem to indicate an affinity with the rigorists of the fraternal movement, the issue is confused by the inclusion of William of St. Amour, that enemy of all friars, amongst the list. In general, however, Lollard texts are uniformly and shrilly hostile to all the activities of the friars" (*Premature Reformation*, 349). Hudson also points to Wyclif's inconsistency even on the Spirituals (see also Workman, *John Wyclif*, 2.97–102).

14. "Istam autem veritatem Christus hic exprimit, ne calculatores se vane solicitent circa precisionem temporis vel instantis, quando hic dies domini inchoabit. Unde circa prenosticacionem hanc vanam abbas Joachym et multi alii sunt decepti" (*Opera minora*, 375, lines 18–22; see also 165–66, and *Opus evangelicum*, 3.102); see Bostick, *Antichrist*, 71, and Leff, *Heresy*, 543, for discussion. On allusions (mainly vague or negative) to Joachim in Wyclif, see my *Reformist Apocalypticism*, 232 n. 6; Workman, *John Wyclif*, 2.99 n. 3; and the discussion at the end of this chapter. Note also Justice's suggestion, *Writing and Rebellion*, 236 n. 135, that a good argument could be made for John of Rupescissa's influence on Wyclif (although Justice does not elaborate on this). Workman had made a similar connection on the basis of a shared fable, which, however, also occurs in other sources, see Chronology, 1371 note.

15. Thomson, *Latin Writings of Wyclif*, 299, notes the invocation of both William of St. Amour and Ockham in Wyclif's *De concordacione fratrum*, 88–106. About allusions to Ockham (pp. 92, 94, 95), Thomson comments (n. 6), "Ockham very seldom appears in Wyclif's writings." The references are general, but Thomson assumes he is referring to Ockham's *Epistola ad fratres minores* of early 1334. Of Wyclif's reference to William (p. 92), Thomson says "it would be of great value to us to ascertain whence he had gathered some of that evidence — especially William of St. Amour, who was little known in England." In fact, William was not little known in England (see the Index of Manuscripts in Szittya, *Antifraternal Tradition*), but the remark is an important measure of how comparatively little use Wyclif made of him. More common in Wyclif (as in this tract) are references to FitzRalph and Grosseteste. Hudson notes that Gregory XI in the 1377 condemnatory bull named Marsilius of Padua and John of Jandun as Wyclif's teachers (neither easy to get in England), and that "later opponents added Berengar of Tours, William of St. Amour, Richard FitzRalph, and William Ockham." This is an important point because it demonstrates how both international and precedent-oriented heresy considerations were; see Hudson, *Selections*, 4. However, to go to the length of confiscating, and perhaps, if Hudson is correct, *destroying all* such books (see Appendix B for the distinction), even though they were in Latin and available only in elite clerical libraries, is another matter entirely.

16. Netter's comments are quoted and discussed in the next chapter.

17. Note Hudson's remark that Wycliffite tradition is "largely innocent of Joachim" (*Premature Reformation*, 264), but I would suggest that antipathy played a large role, too. Walter Brut seems to be the one genuine exception to this.

18. He apparently knew, as Curtis Bostick has shown, Olivi's Apocalypse commentary, but he mined it mostly for exegesis of church history, not for prophetic ideas on contemporary issues, and certainly not for pro-Franciscan ideology (Bostick, *Antichrist*, 84). Anne Hudson has suggested that "even if one may suspect that the *Opus Arduum* is indebted to the Joachite tradition of Apocalypse commentary, its author is apparently unaware of his inheritance" (*Lollards and Their Books*, 49). But whether he was unaware or partly disap-

proving or honestly afraid is a question worth asking, I believe, given his condemnation of Joachim and his anxiety over confiscation of Joachim's two disciples.

19. See ch. 5 below for Joachite borrowings, and ch. 4 for an instance in which William Taylor "censored" a passage from Hildegard before translating it into English.

20. On disendowment issues, see my *Reformist Apocalypticism*, 37–44, 173–77; Justice, *Writing and Rebellion*, 105–6, 236–40; and Scase, *Piers Plowman and Anticlericalism*, 85–88, 109–12.

21. See, for instance, the discussion of Kirkestede below, and for extensive sampling of evidence of anonymous attempts, see Kerby-Fulton and Daniel, "English Joachimism, 1300–1500."

22. Cited in Robson, *Wyclif and the Schools*, 102–3. The date was 1357.

23. Wimbledon's citation linking Hildegard and Joachim of Fiore may come from a chronicle, although full manuscripts of *Scivias* were known in England (see Kerby-Fulton, "Prophecy and Suspicion," n. 21). For the citation, which is from *Scivias*, III, Visio xi, a passage that does *not* appear in Gebeno's *Pentachronon*, see Knight, *Wimbledon's Sermon*, 113–14. A good example of a Continental treatise (which links Hildegard and Joachim) circulating in a fourteenth-century manuscript of English provenance is Oxford, Bodleian Library, MS Bodley 140 (S. C. 1910), containing Nicholas of Strassburg's treatise on Antichrist, in which a late fourteenth-century English hand has noted "hildegardis" and "Joachim" in the margin, fol. 86v. See Hudson, *Premature Reformation*, 424, for a list of manuscripts in which the sermon is associated with Lollard materials. See the end of this chapter for some other examples.

24. See the case of Cambridge, University Library Dd.i.17 in Case Study 1 below.

25. For this genre, see Kerby-Fulton, *Reformist Apocalypticism*.

26. Discussed below in ch. 6. See Burr, *Olivi's Peaceable Kingdom*, 199–200, for Clement V's examination into whether the Spirituals had been infected by *spiritus libertatis* at the same time as the council was examining Olivi's orthodoxy, the poverty issues, and the persecution of *Beguini/e* in the south of France.

27. There has been no systematic study of Free Spiritism, and with large numbers of bishop's registers, documents, and manuscripts still unedited, this study alone cannot rectify the problem.

28. For the possibility, attested in one manuscript note only, that Bernard Silvestrus received a similar approval at nearly the same time, see Silvestris, *Cosmographia*, 2. It remains uncertain whether Hildegard actually received the formal papal approval of her correspondence as later reception universally claims that she did; see Van Engen, "Letters and the Public Persona"; Kerby-Fulton, "Hildegard of Bingen"; and Newman, "Hildegard of Bingen." The origin of the claim is apparently the first letter in the massive collection of her writings known as the Riesencodex (the manuscript prepared late in Hildegard's life, likely under her direction, and used as the base text for the *PL* edition). The letter, now considered inauthentic, is ostensibly from Pope Eugenius to Hildegard; the rubric summarizes its contents in this way: "Auctoritate apostolica concedit ei licentiam proferendi et scribendi quaecumque per Spiritum sanctum cognovisset, eamque ut sine timore revelata sibi conscriberet animat" (*PL*, vol. 197, col. 145 A). The wording is very reminiscent of the wording in her *Vita*: "Ad hec reuerendus pater patrum tam benigne quam et sagaciter assensum prebens litteris salutatoriis beatam uirginem uisitauit, in quibus concessa sub Christi et beati Petri nomine licentia proferendi, quecumque per Spiritum sanctum cognouisset, eam ad scribendum animauit" (*Vita Sanctae Hildegardis*, 9, lines 28–33). John Van Engen (op. cit.) showed that in fact no such

explicit permission appears in any extant letter from either Eugenius or Bernard, any letter, that is, currently accepted as genuine. Independent evidence that Eugenius held her in high regard, however, is available from remarks by John of Salibury and evidence suggests that the approval took the form of a verbal blessing; see Kerby-Fulton, op. cit.

29. Joachim had been encouraged to write by three popes; see Reeves, *Influence*, 28, and the primary sources cited below.

30. An important part of the context here, of course, is "the Reformation of the Twelfth Century" (on which see Constable, *Reformation of the Twelfth Century*), and papacies friendly to reformist initiatives.

31. See "A Word about Visionary Genres" in the Introduction above, and further discussion in ch. 5 below.

32. See Kerby-Fulton, "Prophecy and Suspicion."

33. See n. 28 above.

34. "[C]um nullis litteris nisi tantum psalmis Daviticis esset erudita, per Spiritum sanctum edocta de divinis oraculis et sacramentis sibi revelatis grandia edidit volumina, que ab Eugenio papa mediante sancto Bernardo Clarevallense abbate canonizata et inter sacras scripturas sunt connumerata. Hec per multa temporum curricula doctrine salutaris lampade sanctam ecclesiam illuminavit, epistolis ad diversas personas missis corroboravit et claris miraculis illustravit." The passage appears in the anonymous biography of Gerlach (*Vita s. Gerlaci eremitae*) recorded in the *Acta Sanctorum* (AASS Jan. I, 306–20), and is cited and discussed in Grundmann, "Zur Vita s. Gerlaci," 188–89.

35. Three of the approved authors listed in the *Speculum devotorum* (see Chronology, 1415 and note).

36. The claim, which survives in two manuscripts containing genuine works by Joachim, that Pope Lucius III approved his works is quoted in Grundmann, "Zur Vita s. Gerlaci," 190, and n. 29 (for the manuscripts): "Hoc autem est verissimum, quod illorum <verborum> expositionem papa Lucius pontificali auctoritate canonizavit ac in perpetuum confirmavit, omnibus matribus ecclesiis mitti precepit, ut inter alia vaticinia prophetarum collocentur."

37. Reeves, *Influence*, 4, citing Luke of Cosenza's memoir of Joachim on the subject: "tunc, coram Domino Papa et Consistorio eius, cepit revelare intelligentiam Scripturarum, et utriusque Testamenti concordiam: a quo et licentiam scribendi obtinuit, et scribere coepit" (from the *Acta Sanctorum*, May, vol. VII, Day 29, Joachim Abbas, p. 93). For similar claims to the one above (especially "Hoc autem est verissimum") made in relation to Hildegard in various manuscripts, see Kerby-Fulton, "Hildegard and the Male Reader," 1–18.

38. "[R]ecipientes ab eadem sede vice mea correptionem, et exponentes ei meam circa ipsam devotionem et fidem, et quod ea semper tenere paratus sum que ipsa statuit, nullamque meam opinionem contra eius defendere sanctam fidem . . . ipsa credensque firmiter non posse portas inferi prevalere adversus eam" (trans. McGinn, *Calabrian Abbot*, 29, from *Expositio*, Epistola Prologalis [fol.1v]).

39. McGinn, *Visions of the End*, 26; see also McGinn's "Early Apocalypticism," 2–39, and Reeves, "Development of Apocalyptic Thought," 40–73; see Bischoff, "Early Premonstratensian Eschatology," 41–71, esp. 53–56 on the Augustinian concept of history.

40. See McGinn, "Abbot and the Doctors," 30–47; Daniel, *Bound for the Promised Land* (I am grateful to Prof. Daniel for sharing chapters of his book with me). See also Lerner, "Joachim and the Scholastics" (I am grateful to Prof. Lerner for sharing his typescript version with me).

41. Constable, *Reformation of the Twelfth Century.*

42. See Kerby-Fulton, *Reformist Apocalypticism.*

43. And despite his seeming uncertainty in this same passage. See Augustine, *City of God,* trans. Healey, 2.404–8. All further citations will be from the Healey edition with Latin insertions from *De Civitate Dei, CCSL* 47.

44. The classic study of this is Lerner, "Refreshment of the Saints," 97–144, and see also his "Medieval Return to the Thousand-Year Sabbath," 51–71. For quotations from Hildegard's apocalypticism, see ch. 4; for more detailed study of her periodization, see Kerby-Fulton, *Reformist Apocalypticism,* ch. 1.

45. For Joachim Satan would be loosed at the end of the Second Status. Many of Joachim's works still remain unedited, but see, for instance, the *Enchiridion super Apocalypsim,* 24, lines 549–57: "Duae ergo visiones concludunt statum secundum, duae tertium, quia et id quod continetur in duabus primis in proximo tempore consummandum est, et id quod continetur in duabus sequentibus circa finem cum solvetur Satanas de carcere suo, qui in proximo incarcerandus est ut non seducat amplius gentes usque ad tempus illud, de quo et dicitur: 'Erit tunc tribulatio magna, qualis non fuit ab initio mundi usque modo, neque fiet. Et nisi breviati fuissent dies illi, non fieret salva omnis caro [Matt. 24:21–22],' quamvis et de fine secundi status dictum sit, et de eo plane intelligi possit, quia impetus Spiritus ad diversa dirigitur." For analysis of Joachim's salvation history, see Reeves, *Influence,* 16–27; Reeves and Hirsch-Reich, *Figurae of Joachim,* 1–19, and especially the diagram on p. 9. For a more general, accessible introduction, and translations from selected passages, see McGinn, *Apocalyptic Spirituality,* with passages from, for example, Joachim's *Liber de concordia.*

46. Translated by Daniel, who helpfully preserves the Latin for each term throughout, in McGinn, *Apocalyptic Spirituality,* 124. On Joachim's use of the term "status," see Reeves, *Influence.*

47. For discussion of the meaning of the term, see Lerner, "Medieval Return to the Thousand-Year Sabbath," nn. 2–3.

48. See Kerby-Fulton, "Prophecy and Suspicion."

49. See Lerner's insightful comments in *Powers of Prophecy,* 1 ff., where he quotes George Eliot as saying "Among all forms of mistake, prophecy is the most gratuitous."

50. Bostick, *Antichrist,* 89.

51. The extent to which these ideas stem directly from Joachim himself or were sensationalized by later disciples is a complex problem and will be addressed in more detail below; see also Kerby-Fulton, "English Joachimism."

52. See Markus, *Saeculum, History and Society.*

53. Augustine wrote *City of God* after his own flirtation with Eusebian theology of history was over—Joachimism, by contrast, is deeply Eusebian. See Kerby-Fulton and Daniel, "English Joachimism, 1300–1500," 313–50, esp. 315–16 on Eusebius.

54. See the discussion of *discretio spirituum* treatises in ch. 5 below and Wyclif's negative comments on Hildegard in ch. 4.

55. He even asks "Was not he a persecutor that forbade Christians to be taught the liberal arts?"—it is, of course, an endearing addition to the list of apocalyptic persecutions, but only Augustine would have thought of it.

56. For citation of and commentary on Hildegard's predicted era of peace parallel to the peace before Christ's birth, her *tempus virile,* and the conversion of the Jews in relation to her apocalyptic programme, see my *Reformist Apocalypticism,* 47–48; for contrast with

traditional Augustinian views of the End time, see p. 55. The symbolist method, initially described by modern German scholars as "Deutsche Symbolismus," was in fact international and practiced in leading twelfth-century monastic schools like Chartres, and certainly by Joachim of Fiore. For the Germanic tradition, however, and in relation to Hildegard's thought, see Kerby-Fulton, "Smoke in the Vineyard," 70–98.

57. See ch. 4 below for citations to these texts and my *Reformist Apocalypticism*, 48 and nn. 58–59 for the historical reasons for this. Hildegard watched in disgust as more and more monasteries that came under direct papal control, rather than being overseen by their bishops, deteriorated in discipline.

58. Van Engen, "Letters and the Public Persona."

59. Lerner, *Feast of St. Abraham*. On the exegetical role of women, see Case Study 1 below.

60. McGinn, *Apocalyptic Spirituality*, 101. As for Augustine himself, however, he revered him, and followed in his footsteps wherever he could: he takes up, for instance, Augustine's teaching in *City of God* that the seven ages (tempora) are measured by generations, not years.

61. Discussed in Reeves and Hirsch-Reich, *Figurae of Joachim*, as fig. 9.

62. On Joachim's three status, see above, n. 45.

63. The founder of the southern beguine movement was Douceline de Digne, the sister of the great Joachite scholar and teacher, Hugh of Digne, on whom see below. On Douceline's *Vita*, see Kerby-Fulton, "When Women Preached." Women figured prominently in Joachim's Old Testament exegesis (see Wessley, "Female Imagery," and see Case Study 1 below), and they also played a significant role in Olivi's cult. A woman known as Na (short for "Domina") Prous Boneta was burned at the stake in 1325 for her belief that Olivi embodied the Holy Spirit in the dawning Third Status of Joachim (see Burr, *Persecution*, 88, and for a translation of her confession, Petroff, *Medieval Women's Visionary Literature*, 283–90). For the Lombardy cult of the Guglielmites, whose Joachite convictions even extended to belief in a female pope, see Newman, *From Virile Woman*, and "Agnes of Prague."

64. Reeves, *Influence*, 139; see John 20:4–8; 21:18–21.

65. Reeves, *Influence*, 395–96, "Magnus Petrus apostolorum princeps et totius prelatus ecclesie: sed o quam felix Joannes est. . . . Ille maior in gloria; iste felicior in amore" (*Expositio*, fol. 170v).

66. Discussed in ch. 3 below.

67. Discussed in ch. 5 below.

68. See Reeves and Hirsch-Reich, *Figurae of Joachim*, fig. 9, for discussion.

69. Transcribed by Robson, *Wyclif and the Schools*, 153–54, from Cambridge, Gonville and Caius College Library MS 337/565, fol. 28v.

70. Joachim, *Liber de Concordia*, Book 2, Part 1, ch. 9, trans. Daniel, in McGinn, *Apocalyptic Spirituality*, 130.

71. McGinn, *Apocalyptic Spirituality*, 222.

72. The verse comes from the Book of Jeremiah in which Jeremiah and Baruch are forced into hiding (Jer. 36:19), and Jehoiakim, king of Judah, burns the book (36:23); Jeremiah was then cast into prison for prophesying that Zedekiah (Sedicias) will be delivered up to the king of Babylon. For the association of Zedekiah with Caiaphas, see Reeves, "Abbot Joachim's Disciples," reprinted in West, *Joachim*, 155; in the same article Reeves discusses the manuscript evidence of suppression of visions concerning the condemnation of Joachim in 1215 in the central Joachite works of the thirteenth century.

73. See note to Chronology, 1254.

74. For a clear, brief introduction, see Burr, *Olivi's Peaceable Kingdom*, 14–21. Gerard's project combined his own introduction with Joachim's three major books, the *Liber de concordia*, *Expositio in Apocalypsim*, and *Psalterium decem chordarum*. See Denifle, "Das Evangelium aeternum," 42–149, esp. 68 ff; Dufeil, *Guillaume de Saint-Amour*, 124; and, for the evidence that Gerard did in fact complete his full edition of the *Evangelium eternum*, see Töpfer, "Eine Handschrift des Evangelium aeternum," 156–60.

75. As Burr puts it, "Booksellers were at least peddling an abridged version consisting of [Gerard's] introduction and the *Liber de concordia*, but that is all the Parisian masters seem to have possessed when they swung into action" (*Olivi's Peaceable Kingdom*, 14). For the evidence from *The Romance of the Rose* of the widespread availability of the text, see ch. 3 below.

76. Reeves, *Influence*, 46, mentions that Hugh was a friend of Adam Marsh, the Franciscan scholar and associate of Robert Grosseteste (whom he consulted about Joachim's theology, speaking of him as one who "non immerito creditur divinitus spiritum intellectus . . . assecutus"), see *Monumenta Franciscana*, 146–47. Salimbene (*Chronicle*, 232–33) famously called both Hugh and John of Parma "maximi Iohacite," and then named four friends of Hugh's, including Grosseteste and Adam, thus placing prominent English theologians among the group. For Salimbene's comments on Gerard, see ch. 3 below. Less well known is that Hugh's sister, Douceline de Digne, continued the work in dangerous times. Douceline carried on until her death, a full twenty years later in 1274, founding the southern beguine movement for women, preaching on the Trinity, poverty, and other Franciscan Joachite topics. See Kerby-Fulton, "When Women Preached."

77. Szittya, *Antifraternal Tradition*, 15. This episode is discussed in more detail in ch. 2 below.

78. McGinn, *Apocalypticism in the Western Tradition*, 224. For full discussion of the Protocol of Anagni, see ch. 3 below.

79. A position Langland would parody brilliantly in his learned doctor at the Feast of Patience.

80. For this analysis of the *Liber de Antichristo*, see McGinn, *Apocalypticism in the Western Tradition*, 224–25. The text is edited under the name of Nicholas Oreme in Martene and Durand, *Veterum Scriptorum et Monumentorum*, 9, cc.1273–1446. Both this article and McGinn, "Abbot and the Doctors," 30–47, also deal with Thomas Aquinas's views on Joachim. Aquinas seems to have known the Anagni Protocol, and by c. 1265 arrived at a position against Joachim; see his long *quaestio disputata* of that year, "Utrum possit sciri ab homine quando motus caeli finiatur" (*De potentia*, q. 5, a. 6).

81. See ch. 3 below on William of St. Amour.

82. Compare the quotation from *City of God*, 18.53 (similar to the one from 18.52 quoted above): "In a word, their conjectures are all human, grounded upon no certainty of scripture" (Healey, 228); "Coniecturis quippe utuntur humanis, non ab eis aliquid certum de scripturae canonicae auctoritate profertur" (*Corpus Christianorum*, 652). Even though Aquinas makes some attempt to distinguish Joachim from his looser-lipped disciples, this kind of response was to become standard scholastic fare.

83. "Et similiter videtur esse de dictis Abbatis Joachim, qui per tales conjecturas de futuris aliqua vera praedixit, et in aliquibus deceptus fuit" (Aquinas, *Commentary on the Sentences* [1256], d. 43, q. 1, a. 3, quaestiuncula 4, sol. II, ad 3, quoted in McGinn, "Abbot and the Doctors," n. 46). Aquinas apparently, though cautiously, attributes to Joachim, however, some truths (aliqua vera), because Joachim's prediction of the two coming orders of spiritual

men (viri spirituales) was a halo under which the Dominicans and Franciscans were still sheltering (see McGinn, op. cit., n. 48).

84. Compare Wyclif's "Unde circa prenosticacionem hanc vanam abbas Joachym et multi alii sunt decepti" (*Opera minora*, 375, lines 18–22).

85. Olivi's enormous and extraordinary Apocalypse Commentary remains unpublished, but see Lewis, "Peter Olivi, Author," 135–55, regarding his working edition and the availability of the Latin text at: http://dburr.hist.vt.edu/OliviPage/Olivi_Page.html. On Olivi generally, see especially Burr, *Olivi's Peaceable Kingdom*; also Burr's *Persecution* and his *Olivi and Franciscan Poverty*.

86. Burr, *Persecution*, 74 ff, for the accounts of the sad instances that follow, for the texts of which, see Angelo of Clareno, *Historia septem tribulationum*, 108–336, esp. 300 ff; and for Ubertino da Casale, "Sanctitati Apostolicae," 377–416, esp. 384–87.

87. For a brief summary and select readings, see McGinn, *Visions of the End*, 203–21.

88. See Chronology, 1318.

89. Burr, *Persecution*, 74.

90. Ibid., 87 and n. 45. Women, again, figured here: Olivi's own niece helped her mother to shield escaping Franciscans. See n. 63 and n. 76 above on Douceline de Digne.

91. Burr, *Persecution*, 82.

92. See Chronology, 1323 (November) and note, on *Cum inter nonnullos*.

93. See Chronology, 1305, 1323, and 1318 and notes.

94. See ch. 9 below.

95. Discussed further in ch. 5 below.

96. See Chronology, 1349 for editions, especially the *Vade mecum*, which is a digest of Rupescissa's main ideas. For the comments on Augustine, see Reeves, *Influence*, 227, citing the *Liber secretorum eventuum* from Bignami-Odier, *Etudes*, 125. See the new edition of *Liber secretorum eventuum*, ed. Morerod-Fattebert, with introduction by Robert Lerner. John was indeed a real millenarian—that is, he did believe in a literal millennium of peace—a genuine rarity in the Middle Ages (on which see Lerner's Introduction).

97. The passage was often extracted for copying from the *Vade*; see, for example, British Library, Royal 7.A.IX, fol. 3: "Surget tunc popularis justicia." For the extensive transmission of Rupescissa in England, see the List of Joachite Manuscripts in Kerby-Fulton, "English Joachimism."

98. See ch. 5 below.

99. For accounts (usually translated into French) of Rupescissa's prison sufferings, see Bignami-Odier, *Etudes*, esp. 20–24.

100. *Liber secretorum*, 138, and see ch. 5 below.

101. Ibid., Lerner's Introduction, esp. 68–69.

102. Cited here from Brown, *Appendix ad Fasciculum*. See Chronology, 1344 and note.

103. Kerby-Fulton, "English Joachimism."

104. Burr, *Olivi's Peaceable Kingdom*, 86.

105. Burr, *Persecution*, 87.

106. A good example is British Library, MS Harley 3969, but for others see Kerby-Fulton, "English Joachimism."

107. Trans. McGinn, *Visions of the End*, 209 (see also his brief introduction) from the partial text of Olivi's condemned *Commentary on Revelation* in Döllinger, *Beiträge*, 2.571–72, and compared with Rome, Biblioteca Angelica MS 382, fols. 83va–84ra, for the full passage.

108. Trans. McGinn, *Visions of the End*, 211, from Döllinger, *Beiträge*, 2.569–70, 572–73, and Biblioteca Angelica MS 382, fols. 92vb–93rb. It is easy to see why John XXII took such exception to Olivi's works and to the *Beguini/e* who followed it.

109. See Chronology, 1318, 1322, and 1323 and notes.

110. Delorme, "Constitutiones provinciae," 430.

111. Burr, *Persecution*, 86, for discussion of all these articles; Koch, "Der Prozess," for the text of them.

112. In 1283 Olivi had been condemned for his view that the upcoming tribulations would purge the Franciscan order and make them able to be key players in these missions.

113. See Burr, *Persecution*, 86; and Chronology, 1323, n. 51.

114. See Chronology, 1310, and the trial record edited by Verdeyen, "Le procès d'inquisition"; see also ch. 7 below, on the "beguinus" with Franciscan Spiritual leanings arrested with Porete and described as an adherent. This aspect is also vaguely reminiscent of what alarmed the authorities about devotees of "enthusiasm"; see Parsons, "Red-Ink Annotator."

115. John himself was about to be tangled in theological trouble over his notions of the beatific vision (Burr, *Persecution*, 87), which may account for some of his personal engagement with Olivi. For the sermon, see Pásztor, "Le Polemiche," 365–474. Some of this controversy must underlie Uthred's difficulties in 1368. See below chs. 9–10 for associations with Olivi.

116. Robson makes the same observation about Uthred in *Wyclif and the Schools*, 110.

117. Despite the work of Reeves, Bloomfield, Smalley, and others; see Kerby-Fulton, *Reformist Apocalypticism*; and "English Joachimism."

118. Workman, *John Wyclif*, 2.99, n. 3.

119. *Liber contra Lombardum*, now no longer attributed directly to Joachim himself, but of great interest for understanding early responses to Joachim's battle with Peter Lombard, is found only in Oxford, Balliol College MS 296, fols. 219–49, in a fourteenth-century copy. It was edited by Ottaviano as *Joachimi Abbatis Liber contra Lombardum*. The copy appears to be in a fourteenth-century English hand, and also contains works by Abelard.

120. See Chronology, 1255, and discussion in ch. 3.

121. A complete list appears in my "English Joachimism." See also Kerby-Fulton, *Reformist Apocalypticism*, Index of Manuscripts; and Kerby-Fulton and Daniel, "English Joachimism, 1300–1500."

122. For bibliography on the myth, see Kerby-Fulton, *Reformist Apocalypticism*. For a refreshing change, see Nissé, "Prophetic Nations," 95–115, especially on John of Rupescissa's *Vade mecum* and the *Eulogium historiarum*.

123. For a recent account, see Clopper, "Franciscans, Lollards and Reform," 177–97.

124. Fowler, *Life and Times of Trevisa*, 55, points out that the ambivalence of the Franciscans toward Wyclif, unlike the other orders, especially Dominicans, who turned out in substantial numbers for the Blackfriars Council in 1382, "only two relatively undistinguished members of the Franciscan Convent, Thomas Bernewell and Hugh Karlelle, represented them, and only two others disputed Wyclif's opinions sufficiently for there to be a record of the fact." He goes on to say that the Franciscan William Woodford, Wyclif's colleague at Oxford in lecturing on Lombard's sentences, "did not attend Black Friars, where his presence would certainly have added to the scholarly standing of the council."

125. Workman's list of passages is skewed by his including items not now believed to be by Wyclif, but passages he gives in which Wyclif praises clerical poverty or insists that

Christ had no possessions (a position, of course, made heretical by John XXII) are: *Sermones*, 3.108–9, 152; 4.110; *Civili Domino*, 3.10, 51–54, 60, 100; *Opera Minora*, 158; *Polemical Works*, 2.431, and 1.94 (on Bonaventure's view of poverty); *De officio regis*, 62–63, in which he defends the friars' right to live on charity. Clearly, the bloom was to later go off this rose.

126. See the discussion of John XXII's *Cum inter nonnullos*, Chronology, 1323.

127. See Workman, *John Wyclif*, 2.100, n. 3, for the extensive list. Carter Revard has also kindly pointed out to me these cross-cultural connections. This was, of course, the centre of Olivian persecution.

128. See Arnold, "Lollard Trials," and "Non-Wycliffite Heresy in Late Medieval England" in the Introduction above.

129. Workman, *John Wyclif*, 2.100 n. 3. See also Wilks, "Wyclif and the Great Persecution," 179–204. Wilks's paper is a lively but general overview, suggesting, for instance, that in the 1370s Wyclif was deeply indebted to Ockham, "a leading exponent of the doctrine of apostolic radical Franciscan theory" (183). But Wilks offers no specific evidence of this, and both assertions require careful examining and nuancing (that is, Ockham's relations to radical Franciscanism and Wyclif's debt to him—for a different, more cautious view, see the quotations from Thomson above, n. 15).

130. Wilks, "Wyclif and the Great Persecution," 183.

131. Workman cites Wyclif's *De apostasia*, 69; *De dominio divino*, 94; *De eucharistia*, 278. To Workman's list, however, should be added a reference in Wyclif's *De Trinitate*, 149–50, which refers to Joachim's condemned philosophy of the Trinity at some length. This (very academic and abstract) subject seems to have been the only aspect of Joachim that interested him.

132. *Trialogus*, 453 (in which Wyclif is not citing genuine Joachim, but rather *De semine*); *De ente praedicamentali*, 278; *Opera minora*, 375 (on the prophecies, quoted above). See also Kerby-Fulton, *Reformist Apocalypticism*, esp. 232, 236, 238 on Wyclif and Joachimism.

133. Conclusion 24, see Workman, *John Wyclif*, 2.99.

134. Ibid., 2.100, my emphasis.

135. Ibid., 268 n. 1, citing Wyclif, *Trialogus*, 446; *De blasphemia*, 78.

136. Just before this sentence Olivi explains that the dawning of the Third Status and the temporary ascendancy of the "carnal church" will lead to widespread salvation of the non-Christian peoples: "under pressure from the carnal church, in the Latin west, spiritual men will go to the Greeks, Moslems, and Jews . . . [since] in the time of the apostles the *processus* was principally *quasi dexter* to the pagans, and only secondarily *quasi sinister* to the Jews" (Burr, *Persecution*, 22; Burr is citing from Rome, Biblioteca Angelica MS 382, fols. 73ra–va, and 98rb; on the English manuscripts of Olivi, see ch. 2 below).

137. Burr, *Franciscan Spirituals*, 189.

138. Brown, *Appendix ad Fasciculum*, 502.

139. Burr, *Olivi's Peaceable Kingdom*, 200, citing records of Raymundus de Fronciacho and Bonagratia de Bergamo, *In nomine domini*, in Denifle and Ehrle, *Archiv*, 2:370 ff.

140. Lerner, "Recent Work," 141–57, esp. 149. There are two important English manuscripts among the early ones: Bodleian Library, MS Douce 88, fols. 140r–146v, and the Cambridge, Corpus Christi MS 404, fols. 88r–94v; for a full list, see Lerner, op. cit., 143. There are also several citations to the work in medieval English library catalogues (see Kerby-Fulton, "English Joachimism," and, for instance, the copy owned by the York Austins, men-

tioned below), and the allusion in the Middle English "Last Age of the Church" tract, also mentioned below.

141. Reeves, "Some Popular Prophecies," 119.

142. Hildegard's formulation had none of the historical specificity of this condemned opinion, and it is this sort of specificity (actually daring to apply apocalyptic ideas to current history) which usually provoked ecclesiastical disapproval.

143. Lerner has suggested that Kirkestede's identification may have arisen because Urban provoked the Schism, among other reasons, some more local to Bury (*Powers of Prophecy,* 97–98).

144. Kirkestede also collected prophecies like the Joachite "Columbinus" text, which also predicted the fall of the papacy (see Kerby-Fulton and Daniel, "English Joachimism, 1300–1500"), and several radical items into Cambridge, Corpus Christi 404 (see Lerner, *Powers of Prophecy,* 97–98). As compiler of England's first union catalogue, Kirkestede traced material by Joachim and several other writers who had suffered condemnation.

145. That is, the compiler(s) of Dublin, Trinity College MS 244 (see the description in Abbot, *Catalogue of Trinity College,* 35–36, in which "Last Age" is no. 24 of twenty-six items; for the twenty-sixth item, "A Disputation between a Frier & a secular Priest," see the discussion of Thomas Woodstock, duke of Gloucester, in ch. 4 below). The rest of the contents are largely Wycliffite and related materials (including a Rule of St. Francis) entirely in Middle English. See my *Reformist Apocalypticism,* 184–86, for discussion of "Last Age," and nn. 80 and 85 for modern scholarly misperceptions.

146. These lines begin "Anno millesimo C. ter vicesimo" and end, ominously, "Petro testante perito." Todd comments that the lines "seem to contain an allusion to the Prophetical Doctrines of Peter John, or rather of his Followers. . . . [1325] was one of the Eras fixed by the Beguins for the Revelation of Antichrist, as appears from the *Liber Sententiarum Inquisitionis Tholosanae* . . . [in which a defendant tells inquisitors], 'Credidit et credebat firmiter, tempore quo captus fuit, quod Antichristus esset venturus, et consumpmaturas cursum suum, infra annum quo computabitur incarnacio Domini mccc.xxv'" (Todd, "Last Age," xxxiii).

147. The excerpt is a prophecy concerning Egypt and Damiata very much in the style of the *De oneribus prophetarum,* although in Middle English. It is appended to the "Ego Thomas" prophecy (fol. 1), which on 1v goes beyond the standard ending of the "Ego Thomas" (compare, for example, the Latin version in Bodleian Library MS Ashmole 59), and continues on to fol. 2. See the description of the manuscript in Knight, *Wimbledon's Sermon,* 17–18.

148. The Wycliffite item on the Ten Commandments is added in a different hand on fol. 122 immediately after prophecies envisioning church reform, "Anglia tranmittet" and "Ter tria lustra" (fols. 118–19, old foliation). On "Ter tria" see, most recently, Nissé, "Prophetic Nations," 101 ff.

149. London, British Library, Royal 8. D.XI, fol. 70. The article begins, "Beatus qui exspectat et prevenit vsque ad dies 1335. . . ."

150. See also the Lollard sermon in Cambridge University Library MS Ii.iii.8, fol. 149, which goes on to refer to Joachim and the coming "spiritual men" (see Owst, *Preaching in Medieval England,* 135). Among more vague connections, see Oxford, Bodleian Library, MS Digby 196, which has the Joachite "Columbinus" and "Gallorum levitas" as well as

political items connected with the Rising of 1381 (like "The taxe hath tened us alle"), fol. 20b. Neither these descriptions, nor this list are intended to be exhaustive.

151. See ch. 5, n. 83 below.

152. Discussed in detail in ch. 5 below.

153. See my *Reformist Apocalypticism*, 185.

Notes to Chapter 2

An early version of this chapter was first presented at the 1998 Medieval Academy conference at Stanford in a session in honour of Marjorie Reeves. I would like to express my gratitude to John Fleming, E. Randolph Daniel, and especially the late Marjorie Reeves for their helpful advice and enthusiasm.

1. This history and its manuscript context are discussed in detail in Kerby-Fulton, "English Joachimism."

2. Roger of Wendover, who cites from Joachim's now lost *libellus* accusing Peter Lombard of making the Trinity into a Quaternity. See Reeves, *Influence*, 45, for quotations and discussion. See also Bloomfield and Reeves, "Penetration of Joachimism."

3. "Creditis, o fratres, hec omnia? Credimus. Ergo / Abbatis Joachim dampnamus scripta, Magistri / Petri Lumbardi scriptis contraria" (cited from the transcription of Oxford, Bodleian Library MS Bodley 40 in Bloomfield and Reeves, "Penetration of Joachimism," 784–85).

4. For Bacon's life, see Daniel, *Franciscan Concept of Missions*, 53–66, and for the quotation, 65.

5. Burr, *Persecution*, 22; cited from Rome, Biblioteca Angelica MS 382, fols. 73ra–va. For evidence that Olivi's Apocalypse commentary was in circulation in Ricardian England, see ch. 5 below.

6. See ch. 10 below on Franciscan Joachite liberal salvational theologies.

7. Paris, *Chronica Majora, Additamenta*, 335–39; for discussion, see Reeves, *Influence*, 62–65.

8. Reeves, *Influence*, 60.

9. *John Capgrave's Abbreuiacion*, 109, lines 1–10. His main source is Martinus Polonus, 438–43, in Polonus, *Chronicon*, 22.377–475. Capgrave began composing his chronicle about 1438.

10. See *John Capgrave's Abbreuiacion*, p. lxxvi, for the full list.

11. Pecham did share with his pupil Olivi a view later condemned at the Council of Vienne that the rational soul was not the substantial form of the body (Douie, *Archbishop Pecham*, 39). The poverty issues were to spiral into ever-increasing danger, especially for those who outlived Pecham and Olivi, but Olivi was still able to claim, with justice, that his ideas on poverty followed those of Pecham and Bonaventure. Pecham shared with Olivi and with later moderate Spirituals like Ubertino a concept close to the controversial "poor use" (usus pauper), that is, that friars should restrict themselves to the use of things absolutely essential for their lives and work, the position Ubertino would later defend during

much more dangerous times than Pecham's at the Council of Vienne (Douie, op. cit., 9 and 32). For Pecham's works in transmission with Joachite materials, see the discussion of Oxford, Bodleian Library, MS Lat. Misc. c. 75 later in this chapter.

12. Little, *Franciscan Papers*, 140.

13. Bacher, *Prosecution*, 9. Burton, *Chronicon*, 11–13. Thomas also compiled the Meaux catalogue, see Bell, "Books of Meaux," 25–84; and for the extensive author listing of the library contents, see Bell, *Index of Authors*, 246–47. Presumably, like Kirkstede, Burton's work as a library cataloguer helped him uncover sources his fellow chroniclers might not have known.

14. See Chronology, 1330 and note for full quotation, saying that in 1330 the total in the countries previously listed and also "*in Anglia in quadam sylva*, combusta sunt viri 55 et mulieres 8 eiusdem ordinis et erroris."

15. The phrase is Burr's (*Persecution*, 87, on the role of Olivi's niece and mother). See Appendix C on women in the movement and the reference to Newman's study in *From Virile Woman*.

16. Ledrede, as Colledge has written, may have believed that he had found another Porete (originally arrested with a Franciscan Spiritual–influenced "beguinus") in his prosecution of Alice Kyteler (see Chronology, 1324).

17. For Grandisson's activities, see Chronology, 1334, 1348, and 1355.

18. McDonnell, *Beguines*, 400 n. 92, for a summary of Gui's description of the heretics.

19. See Chronology, 1334 and ch. 9 below.

20. See Chronology, 1337; see Word about Intellectual Freedom, n. 19, on disendowment history in England; see Offler, *Opera Politica*, 1.226.

21. See Chronology, 1336, 1353, and 1358 for examples.

22. In addition to Ledrede's activities, see Chronology for those of Cradock in 1353, also in Ireland.

23. Szittya, *Antifraternal Tradition*, 62; for the letter, see the *Register of Grandisson*, 2.1197–98.

24. Burr, *Persecution*, 35–36.

25. On Waleys, see Chronology, 1331–32.

26. On Bradwardine and Joachim, see ch. 9.

27. See Chronology, 1349 under *Flagellanti* and note.

28. Warnings were also sent to Scotland. The appearance of the Flagellants originally in 1260 had looked inspired by Joachimism because of the apocalyptic importance Joachim and later disciples attached to that date. Marjorie Reeves points out that even though the knowledgeable contemporary chronicler, Salimbene, for instance, associated the movement with Joachimism, it had no discernable relation to Joachite expectation of a Third Status. See Reeves, *Influence*, 54–55; and see Chronology, 1260, 1349, and 1351 and notes.

29. I cite here the Latin from Robert of Avesbury's account of the London group in 1349, which also mentions the hoods with red crosses before and behind "supra caputque singuli habentes singulos capellos cruce rubea ante et retro signatos" (Fredericq, *Corpus*, 121). The misericord, however, is later fourteenth century, and either this detail of the hoods may have been lost by then or the flagellation image may be more generalized.

30. See J. Wood, *Wooden Images*, 132–33, and compare Remnant, *Catalogue of Misericords*, 130, no. 8.

31. Mentioned below in Case Study 2 in relation to the British Library, Cotton Cleopatra B.II manuscript, and discussed in detail in ch. 3.

32. The text is found in Bodleian Library, MS Bodley 158, fol. 142v, where it follows a copy of William of St. Amour's *De periculis* (identified by the rubricator) and immediately precedes a copy of "Insurgent gentes," attributed to Hildegard on fol. 145, and a copy of the Tripoli prophecy. These items form a booklet (Booklet C in Hunt, Madan, and Craster, *Summary Catalogue*, no. 1997), all written in the same hand. This was bound with four other booklets in the fifteenth century, some of which include antimendicant and early anti-Wycliffite writings (the latter, however, are not part of the present booklet).

33. From Knight, *Wimbledon's Sermon*, 113, lines 838–40.

34. This long passage may be found in Netter, *Doctrinale*, 1.412, A.

35. Bostick, *Antichrist*, 63–64 and nn. 59–60 for the full quote from Wyclif's *De Potestate Pape*, 321–22.

36. Netter, *Doctrinale*, 1.581, A, for William of St. Amour and 666, A, for Ockham.

37. See Chronology, 1329–30 and accompanying note for the details in this paragraph.

38. See chs. 9–10 below.

39. Burr, *Olivi's Peaceable Kingdom*, 255. For a review of primary and secondary sources on East Anglia as open to Continental influences, see N. Watson, "Composition," 656–57.

40. Sharpe, *Handlist*, 166, for complete listing of manuscripts. There is a surprisingly small overlap between attestations and survivals, with Bodleian Library, Laud Misc. 85, originally from Pembroke College, Cambridge, being the only certain one. Attestations include Benedictine, Bridgettine, Dominican, secular, and academic locations, ranging from York to Canterbury, and both universities.

41. Ibid., 166.

42. See Reeves, *Influence*, 86–87, who exclaims over his caution in this area, which she believed to be "deliberate." See her note 2 for her massive list of citations to Joachim's *Expositio*. Although not mentioning Henry's arrest and near escape from the clutches of papal inquisition, Reeves notes his tendency to stop short of the dramatic Third Status climax of Joachim's scheme—although he comes as close as he dares.

43. See, for instance, the annotator of the text by Joachim in British Library, Harley 3969, discussed below; and for Henry's exegetical habits, see Burr's discussion in *Olivi's Peaceable Kingdom*, 255 ff. On the English manuscripts of Henry's works, see Kerby-Fulton, "English Joachimism," especially British Library, Harley 7401 and Oxford, Bodleian Rawlinson C.16.

44. Bodleian Library, Laud Misc. 85; see Burr's analysis, *Olivi's Peaceable Kingdom*, 256.

45. See the comments in Reeves, *Influence*, and in Burr, *Olivi's Peaceable Kingdom*, 258–59.

46. See note 52 below. The evidence indicates that two of them were indeed sent on to John XXII's prison at Avignon.

47. Little, *Franciscan Papers*, 141.

48. See the description of Corpus Christi 404 in James, *Descriptive Catalogue*.

49. Three of the five are defective: Lambeth Palace, MS 127, fols. 177r–(199); Bodleian Library, Laud Misc. 85, fols. 67–172; St. Bonaventure, NY, St. Bonaventure University, Holy Name College MS 69, fols. 1r–(116); the authorship is suppressed or absent in three: Laud; British Library, Harley 7401, fols. 1–117; and Bodleian Library, Rawlinson C.16, fols. 133–221. For more detailed codicological analysis, see Kerby-Fulton, "English Joachimism."

50. After fol. 122v, as figure 5 shows; for the discussion, see fols. 120v–123v especially; see St. Bonaventure University, MS 69, fol. 95v–r, for this section.

51. I would like to thank David Burr for his helpful correspondence on Henry. For the specific information in the following paragraph, see Olivi's Peaceable Kingdom, 140–45 and 255–59, for Burr's account. See Burr's account of Henry's treatment of the beast and in relation to two other contemporary Olivian commentators. He does not mention the mutilation of the manuscript.

52. For this particular incident, see Sbaralea, *Bullarium Franciscanum*, 5.819 (March 22, 1330). The pope had sent a letter to Edward III in August 1329 (5.807). See Douie, "Three Treatises," 342.

53. See Coxe, *Catalogi Codicum*, description of Laud Misc. 85, p. 96, for the other contents: works by John Pecham, Robert Grosseteste, and William of Auvergne.

54. The *Commentary* is written in an *anglicana formata* hand in which the height of the two-compartment "a" throughout is too high to be consistent with the later fourteenth century.

55. See Kerby-Fulton, "English Joachimism" for a complete listing.

56. For John of Beverly, see Parkes, "Book Provision," 38. John deposited a Durham book (now Durham Cathedral MS C120) in exchange for the loan of a copy of Joachim's *Expositio*. For a full list of the manuscripts and details of ascription, see Kerby-Fulton, "English Joachimism." Kirkestede, Kilvington, Ebchester, and Erghome are discussed in the present study. Other owners of pseudo-Joachite works include Robert Thwaytes, one time chancellor of Oxford (discussed below in ch. 10) and Bishop Gray of Ely, on whom see Kerby-Fulton, op. cit.

57. In both instances, a medieval table of contents identifies the Joachim as having been there intact. Harley 3969, fols. 216–24, is in a fourteenth-century hand, with later annotation from the second half of the century; see Kerby-Fulton, "English Joachimism." The contents of the manuscript suggest university interests (medicine, history, and classics) and, indeed, exactly match those of a volume M. R. James thought missing when he catalogued Emmanuel College, Cambridge (see *Descriptive Catalogue*, 3.3, 158 and List of MSS Now Missing). In Harley 3049, owned by William Ebchester, the Joachim item is also fragmentary and missing its initial leaf (fols. 137 [135]–140 [138]); on Ebchester, see Emden, *Biographical Register*, 622.

58. The manuscript is collated in the edition by Selge, "Eine Einführung Joachims," 85–131. The folio carrying the opening of the text has been torn out (between fols. 215 and 216) with the result that the text begins defectively at line 28, p. 103 of Selge's edition, thereby omitting the primary discussion of the three *status*, which opens the text. As one can tell from catchwords on fols. 197v, 207v, and 218v, the torn folio, which would have been fol. 216, was never an outer leaf.

59. "Ita enim genus humanum post culpam primi hominis ad sui conditoris notitiam gradatim redire decebat, ut primo quidem certo tempore radicaret in patre, secundo germinaret in filio, tertio in spiritu sancto fructus experiretur dulcedinem, ut videlicet post diuturna tempora ad gaudia celi perductum multipliciter gaudeat" (ibid., 102, lines 16–20).

60. "Sane spiritus sanctus, qui tercia est sancte trinitatis persona, ita miro modo datus est apostolis die pasche, ut tamen sibi adhuc esse dandum sperarent, illa utique ratione misterii, qua dies pentecostes novissime diem sollempnitatis designat" (ibid., 103, lines 25–28).

61. The first leaf of Joachim's piece has been removed (before fol. 135 [old fol. 137]). The pattern of missing leaves here, however, is more complex to interpret; see Kerby-Fulton, "English Joachimism."

62. On Walter Hunt, see Hudson, *Premature Reformation*, 455.

63. Denifle, "Das Evangelium aeternum," 1.99–142. Reeves, *Influence*, 60–61, 91–92. The text of the Protocol is discussed in detail in ch. 3 below.

64. The missing piece would have continued on fol. 39; see Kerby-Fulton, "English Joachimism," for further details, and for comparison with the other manuscripts cited in the modern edition, especially n. 11 to the List of Manuscripts.

65. See Reeves, *Influence*, 81–88.

66. The confiscation of Lollard books began a little earlier, certainly by 1387; see Hudson, *Lollards and Their Books*.

67. For Merton College, see n. 74 below; for Syon, see n. 91 below.

68. Burr, *Persecution*, 82, 87 and n. 45. See Appendix C. Women, again, figured in the counterattack; Olivi's own niece helped her mother shield escaping Franciscans.

69. Ibid., 82.

70. A bishop elevated to cardinal by his uncle, the reformer Pope Benedict XII (1334–42); Walsh, *Fourteenth-Century Scholar*, 427. On Court, see Baluze, *Vitae paparum*, 1.206, 212–13, 2.320–24, 412; Patschovsky, "Strassburger Beginenverfolgungen," 110; and the discussion of Rupescissa, in ch. 5 below.

71. It is difficult to date the hand more precisely, but the "r" and "v" forms are consistent with cursive hands at the time Whethamstede commissioned the manuscript (the text of which is written in a practiced liturgical hand such as one sees in turn of the century manuscripts). For more detailed analysis of the hand, see Word about Intellectual Freedom, n. 2 above, and Kerby-Fulton, "English Joachimism." There are no signs of classicization of the Latin in the annotation (as in, for instance, the note about Joachim's being a heretic that appears later in Kilvington's manuscript [figure 8]). In short, there is no reason to assume a date much later than Whethamstede's initial abbacy 1420–40. This is consistent with Douie's sense of the hand as well.

72. Translated in Douie, "Olivi's Postilla," 68.

73. Cambridge, Corpus Christi College Library MS 321. For a description, see ibid. On Ramsey, see Kerby-Fulton, "English Joachimism."

74. Howlett and Hunt, "Provenance of MS. New College 49," 225–28.

75. See Chronology, 1278 and note; also Douie, "Olivi's Postilla," 70–71

76. I am extremely grateful to Kevin Madigan for sending me his full facsimile printout of the manuscript, from which I cite, unless the quotation has already been transcribed in Douie's superb and detailed article, "Olivi's Postilla."

77. Through Christ's greeting (Post hoc autem Christi occursus et salutare alloquium sequitur . . .) these two superior faculties, "quia illi sunt proprie imago Dei sicut Filius est imago Patris, licet longe dispariter(!) . . . a mundanis ad supramundana transmigrarent in montem contemplationis . . . et ibidem Christum in gloria sue maiestatis adorant et vident" (fol. 158vb; transcribed in Douie, "Olivi's Postilla," 79 n. 60).

78. See the discussion of the beatific vision in ch. 10 below.

79. Burr, "Olivi, Apocalyptic Expectation," 275–77, for this case; see also the discussion of the Pauline mystical experience and Olivi's in ch. 5 below.

80. Oxford, New College 49, fol. 155 col. b, also discussed by Madigan in *Olivi and the Interpretation of Matthew*, 124 and 194. I am grateful to the Bodleian Library staff for their advice.

81. Bloomfield, *Piers Plowman as Apocalypse*, 227–28; Hudson, *Lollards and Their Books*, 81 and 150.

82. Fol. 104v: "Sed in disciplis eius solide confitentibus altitudinem eius fundabitur ecclesia spiritualis; contra quam porte inferni .i. ferre infernales antichristi non preualebunt. Immo habebit summam potestatem aperiendi archana scripturarum & gratiarum & secreta contemplatiui status & claudendi ea indignis."

83. See the quotation in the previous note, especially " . . . summam potestatem aperiendi archana scripturarum," etc. After further describing the glorification of those living the life of Christ, they will nevertheless be "reprobari a scribis & senioribus ecclesie carnalis." See also Appendix C.

84. See above, ch. 1, but also ch. 5, where we see him sipping surreptitiously from Olivi's cup.

85. Douie, "Olivi's Postilla," 91. So, for instance, even St. Bernardino, who lived a long time after the horrors of John XXII, revered Olivi as "an angelic man," but left out all Joachite passages when he cited him.

86. See Scase, *Reginald Pecock*, 109–11.

87. See Howlett and Hunt, "Provenance of MS. New College 49," 225–28.

88. The trial took place in 1430; Whethamstede's commission was sometime between 1420–40. See Hudson, *Premature Reformation*, 418, for details.

89. Howlett, "Studies of Whethamstede."

90 Hudson, *Selections*, 4.

91. For a full listing, see the "Earliest Known Ownership or Provenance" column of the List of Joachite Manuscripts in Kerby-Fulton, "English Joachimism." See Sharpe, *Handlist*, 166. For Syon, see no. 603 (Olivi on Genesis linked with an unidentified Apocalypse commentary which *might* have been his), no. 582 (Joachim's Apocalypse commentary), no. 584 (Henry's), and no. 437 (a *quodlibet* by Olivi) in Gillespie, *Syon Abbey*.

92. Sharpe, *Handlist*, 166.

93. It was one of fifty-six of Alan's works, of which only a handful survive. For the complete listing, see Bale, *Scriptorium Illustrium*, 1.551–53. On Alan's activities, see also John Clark, "Late Fourteenth-Century Cambridge Theology," 13.

94. Not beginning on fol. 197, as Coxe's catalogue records.

95. Citation is to *Book of Margery Kempe* (*BMK*), ed. Meech and Allen.

96. See N. Watson, "Visions of Inclusion" and below chs. 9–10.

97. See ch. 6 for discussion of Margery Kempe's view of the episode.

98. Balliol 149 is discussed below in ch. 10 and in Kerby-Fulton "Langland's Reading." There is some similar evidence for Cambridge, such as John Harryson's commonplace book, now Gonville and Caius 249, which contains John of Rupescissa, the Bridlington prophecies, and an unnoticed fragment of the rare Robert of Uzès (on which see Kerby-Fulton, *Reformist Apocalypticism*, 223); and as we have seen, the Laud Costesy manuscript was kept at Pembroke College.

99. Forde, "Nicholas Hereford's Ascension Day Sermon."

100. On Arnold, see Lerner, "Ecstatic Dissent"; McGinn, *Visions of the End*, ch. 25; and Chronology, 1300.

101. "Utrum Astrologi vel Quicumque Calculatores possint probare Secundum Adventum Christi," cited in Reeves, *Influence*, 316 from Pelster, "Die Questio Henrichs von

Harclay," 59. On Arnold's pro-Jewish tendencies, and his calculations, see Lerner, *Feast of St. Abraham*, 92.

102. The title the rubricator is abbreviating is "Apologia de versuciis atque perversitatibus pseudotheologorum at religiosorum," beginning defectively at fol. 122, and refers to an earnest work of Arnold on how to tell pseudo-prophets from the real thing, but the scope for irony in the running heads is certainly there. For the Lat. Misc. c. 75 manuscript, see Kerby-Fulton, "English Joachimism," Appendix; the *Epistola Cyrilli* begins on fol. 132, where it is even attributed to Arnold. The same texts appeared in British Library, Cotton Vitellius E.II, but were destroyed in the Cotton library fire.

103. The manuscripts are Cambridge, Trinity College 740, and Lincoln's Inn, Hale 73. See *Eulogium*, 3.86 for the quotations here on Joachim, added as a supplement to the reign of Henry II: "praecipue quod suo tempore florebat abbas Joachim in Calabria, qui super Apocalypsim et Libros Prophetarum commenta conscripsit [these are the two works he is best known for in England]. Praedixit etiam Terram Sanctam adeuntibus quod minime proficerent. Tradunt etiam de isto quod quasi prophetice effigiavit mores, actus, et numerum *virorum Apostolicorum qui post venturi forent in ecclesia Dei*" (my emphasis). The John of Rupescissa text is embedded in the two manuscripts (pp. 393–417 in Trinity 740 and fols. 134v–41v in Hale 73) and attached at the front of a third *Eulogium* manuscript at Dublin, Trinity College 497. See Nissé, "Prophetic Nations," 97 and 105 for her quoted remarks. The *Eulogium* also mentions Joachim at 1.387: under 1187: "Hoc anno capta est Sancta Crux in civitate Jerusalem a Saladino soldano Babyloniae. Eo tempore abbas Joachim multa scripsit in Calabria." All three manuscripts are discussed in Kerby-Fulton, "English Joachimism."

104. See J. Taylor et al., *St. Albans Chronicle*, Appendix 1. The editors, however, do not realize that Rupescissa is the author of the letter at fol. 94v.

105. See Catto, "Alleged Great Council," and Chronology, 1374 and note.

106. The chronicle is full of a striking number of incidents of friars and treason, mainly in the Lancastrian period; for a full list, see ibid., 766. The incident involving the Bridlington prophecies is discussed below in ch. 5. See also *Eulogium*, 3.407, on friars of all four orders in the army of Scrope (discussed in Case Study 3 below).

107. See Chronology, 1362, note for sources.

108. Joachim, *Expositio*, from ch. 14.

109. "Et predicabunt fidem quam et defendent usque ad mundi consumptionem in spiritu Helye" (*Expositio*, fols. 175v–176); see Reeves, "Joachimist Expectations," 111–41, for extensive discussion of John Erghome and York Austins' library collection; see p. 115 for echoes of this passage in Augustinian writing.

110. Reeves, *Influence*, 255: "Quaesitis itaque authoribus qui in similibus aperiendis sensibus excelluerunt, nempe Methodio, Joachimo Abbate, Cyrillo Carmelita, Johanne Bridlingtono, Roberto Userio, Johanne Rupescissa, Johanne Barsignacio, Sibillis, aliisque eos dilgenter pervolvit, emedullavitque ac suis studiis adauxit" (citing Ossinger, *Bibliotheca Augustiniana*, 316).

111. For his extensive holdings, see James, *Catalogue of the Augustinian Friars*, 9–14, and esp. no. 361.

112. On Robert, see Kerby-Fulton, *Reformist Apocalypticism*, 96–102. For an analysis of these texts more generally, along with other items in the library, see 24 and 209; and Reeves, *Influence*, 255–56.

113. That Erghome, and likely other members of the convent, knew genuine Joachim is evident from another two items elsewhere in the catalogue, whether his own or the convent's: *Expositio* and the *Liber concordia* (James, *Catalogue of the Augustinian Friars*, 36).

114. See Sharpe et al., *English Benedictine Libraries*, B39 for Glastonbury, B67 for Ramsey, B9 for Battle Abbey, and the extensive listings in the Index for other prophetic texts. The routes by which such material reached England I have discussed elsewhere, but from the twelfth century on, the extensive holdings of the Florensian order in England suggest another route in addition to the Franciscan, Benedictine, and Austin grapevines at work here. For a list of Florensian church properties in England, see Caraffa, *Il Monastero Florense*, 60–64, including locations in the dioceses of Canterbury, Winchester, and Llandaff. See James, *Catalogue of the Augustinian Friars*, 14, for the next remark.

115. With (Pseudo-)Hildegard in British Library, Cotton Domitian IX (appearing at fol. 17r, immediately after the Pseudo-Hildegard); with Langland in Bodley 851, which is discussed below in Case Study 3.

116. Reeves, *Influence*, 256. I have discussed the convent's and Erghome's collections of prophecies, including Hildegard and William of St. Amour, in "Langland's Reading," 137–61.

117. See Kerby-Fulton, "English Joachimism."

118. Courtenay, *Schools and Scholars*, 353, makes this case convincingly. Another accuser, William Jordan was also from York (the Dominican convent).

Notes to Case Study 1

1. The work of Bloomfield, Burdach, Wells, Frank, and other earlier scholars of Langland and Joachimism is summarized in Kerby-Fulton, *Reformist Apocalypticism*.

2. Bloomfield, *Piers Plowman as Apocalypse*, 178.

3. For a summary of new work and the first published list of English manuscripts, see Kerby-Fulton, "English Joachimism."

4. The most recent description of Dd is Benson and Blanchfield, *Manuscripts of Piers: B Version*, 33–37, which also cites bibliography for previous descriptions (33). The manuscript is massive, written throughout by one scribe, and is comprised of three volumes (or more likely two, judging by the continuous quire signatures of the first two) joined together in "a single great book," as Kane and Donaldson (*Piers Plowman: B Version*) put it. This view that it is a single book is not disputed by any modern scholar (see Benson and Blanchfield, op. cit., 33 n. 22).

5. Simpson, "Constraints of Satire," 11–30.

6. In addition to the studies cited below, see Justice, *Writing and Rebellion*; Hudson, "The Legacy of *Piers Plowman*," 251–66; Barr, *Piers Plowman Tradition*; and Cole, "William Langland," 37–58; the succinct bibliography on Langland and Lollardy in Somerset, Havens, and Pitard, *Lollards and Their Influence*, 315; and Somerset, "Expanding the Langlandian Canon," 73–92.

7. For *Mum*, see Simpson, "Constraints of Satire"; for *Richard*, see Kerby-Fulton and Justice, "Langlandian Reading Circles"; for editions of all three poems, and detailed commentary, see Barr, *Piers Plowman Tradition*, and her *Signes and Sothe*. See also chapter 10 of this book, especially on the John But passus and Langland's early imitators.

8. Hudson, *Premature Reformation*, 408.

9. Bowers, *"Piers Plowman* and the Police," 1–50, esp. 28. For a description of Society of Antiquaries 687, see Langland, *Piers Plowman: A Version*, ed. Kane, 11–12. It might be added that the list of ecclesiastical censures at the end of 687 (pp. 552–58) has some strange omissions; compare, for instance, the list in the *Register of Chichele*, 3.257–58.

10. See Middleton, "Audience and Public," 103–23.

11. For some of the topics and recent bibliography on the others, see Kerby-Fulton, "Professional Readers," 101–37; Giancarlo, "Piers Plowman, Parliament," 135–74, along with several other articles in *Yearbook of Langland Studies* 17 (2003) devoted to Langland and Lollardy.

12. I would like to thank Robert Lerner for drawing my attention to the *Belial* tradition and some helpful bibliography.

13. For this, and much of the information about Jacobus below, I am indebted to Ott, *Rechtspraxis*.

14. See McCall, "Writings of John of Legnano," 421–37, 431 for mention of our prophecy, which appears among the spurious items. Other prophecies regarding the Schism were attributed to Legnano (see McGinn, *Visions of the End*, 254 n. 4; and see Rusconi, *Attesa*, 164–67). I am grateful to Robert Lerner for advice on Legnano and this prophecy. There are dozens of manuscripts of his *Commentaria in Clementinas, De interdicto ecclesiastico*, and *De censura ecclesiastica* (on which see McCall, op. cit.). A treatise entitled *De heresiis* was also ascribed to him. See also McCall, "Chaucer and John of Legnano," 486.

15. For the articles of heresy charged against Hus, see Leff, *Heresy*, 2.676–77.

16. Hildegard's contributions had been comments on an earlier schism, of course, which were resurrected during the Great Schism and were a distinct influence on Bridget of Sweden. See Kerby-Fulton, *Reformist Apocalypticism*. Bridget died just before the Schism itself, but was a prophetic presence throughout.

17. See Allmand, *Civil Lawyers*, 155–80; and Kerby-Fulton and Justice, "Scribe D," 217–38.

18. See Kerby-Fulton, "English Joachimism," for evidence of legal manuscripts containing Joachite works.

19. *Compendium perbreve de redemptione generis humani, Consolatio Peccatorum nuncupatum, et apud nonnullos Belial vocitatum*, or sometimes as *Lis Christi et Belial coram judice Salomone* or *Processus Luciferi*. For these and other titles and the translation history into multiple European medieval vernaculars, see Salmon, "Jacobus," 101–15.

20. McCall, "Chaucer and John of Legnano," 487.

21. Cook suggested various historical contacts Chaucer would have had with John of Legnano ("Chauceriana II: Chaucer's 'Linian'," 358–82); see also the note to this passage VI.31–38 in the *Riverside Chaucer*.

22. McCall, "Chaucer and John of Legnano," 484.

23. "I must create a System or be enslaved by another man's," as Blake writes ("Jerusalem," 1.10, line 20, *Poetry and Prose*, ed. Erdman, 676).

24. Langland explicitly evokes both earlier in the poem in his famous description of the "lunatyk lollares," see Pearsall's note to C.IX.105 and 136 (*Piers Plowman: C Text*), and 1 Cor. 4:10 especially. For references to the Schism in *Piers Plowman*, other than those mentioned below, see also C.XVII.243, and XXI.428–29, and likely 443–45.

25. See the discussion of Wells and Bodley 851 in Case Study 3.

26. Hanna, *William Langland* (cited in Benson and Blanchfield, *Manuscripts of Piers: B Version*, 33), following Ian Doyle's suggestion in "Remarks" regarding the coincidence of the contents with the surviving library list of the York Austin Friars, adds "certainly the historical texts of the manuscript suggest origin among the regular clergy."

27. The adjective is Anne Middleton's; see her "Audience and Public," 103–23.

28. Jacobus was restored to favour in 1410 by a bull from John XXIII, but the pope (despite his statement to the contrary) does not seem to have examined the work too closely. The bull refers to the *Belial* as a book called "Somnium Nabugodonosor sive Statuta Danielis," two visions, in fact, that the *Belial* recounts, but which are, for safety's sake, censored from the German. For the bull, and the German censorship, see Salmon, "Jacobus," 108–9. On Joachimism in Hussite circles, see Lerner, *Heresy of the Free Spirit*.

29. For which see Ott, *Rechtspraxis*, 22–25, and the quotations below.

30. For the importance of this motif in *Mandeville's Travels*, see Higgins, *Writing East*.

31. For the Latin text, see Goldast von Haiminsfeld, *Processus Juris Joco-serius*, from which there are also quotations in Ott, *Rechtspraxis*. Salmon ("Jacobus," 105) mentions that comparison with *Paradise Lost* made disapprovingly by earlier critics.

32. The work is variously described: in the 1559 Index it is under "Auctorum incerti nominis libri prohibiti," *B*, "Belial sive de consolatione peccatorum" (the latter being the title under which it appears in Dd); but by 1590 it is also described as "Belial, procurator Luciferi, contra Moysen, procuratorem Jesu Christi" (emphasizing one of the most scandalous aspects of the work). The suppression of Jacobus's name in many manuscripts clearly was effective by the sixteenth century. See *Die Indices librorum prohibitorum*, ed. Reusch, 180 and 467; for commentary, Ott, *Rechtspraxis*, 25; and Salmon, "Jacobus," 103, also for the comments of eighteenth- and nineteenth-century scholars who deemed the work blasphemous.

33. See Burdach, *Der Dichter des Ackermann*, esp. "Eschatologische Züge," 116–39 (which also covers the Taborites), and the fifth chapter, on *Piers Plowman*, the John Ball letters (167 ff.), and the Harrowing-related themes (226 ff.), with comparisons to Hussite, Wycliffite, Joachite, and radical Franciscan materials. See also Kerby-Fulton, *Reformist Apocalypticism*, 240 nn. 107–8, for summarizing quotations from Burdach's argument.

34. Salmon, "Jacobus," 112.

35. As Marjorie Reeves has pointed out, Joachim returns again and again to the fertile women of the Bible because he sees the patterns of history in terms of germination and fructification. Since Rachel, often taken as the contemplative life in relation to Leah as the active life, gave birth to Joseph in the sixth year of her marriage, Joachim took this to mean that the new spiritual *ordo* would begin during the sixth age of history. Joachim also formulated his monastic reforms in the founding of his order at Fiore, with its contemplative emphasis, in terms of the conceptions of Rachel and Mary, as Stephen Wessley has shown. See Reeves and Hirsch-Reich, *Figurae of Joachim*, 167–68 and Wessley, "Female Imagery," 164 and 169.

36. There is no edition of "Regnum spiritus sancti," and no other manuscripts have surfaced as yet; all quotations here come from Dd, fols. 203vb–204rb. (I have only attempted a diplomatic transcription of key passages here, with minimal emendation indicated in brackets.) See also McCall, "Writings of John of Legnano," 431. The prophecy opens "Regnum spiritus sancti distingu(u)ntur in iacob filii Isaac qui duas uxores ex vno patre natas viz. Iyam & aliam rachielem qui jacob ex lya prima sua vxore quatuor filios genuit & cessauit parere. Rachel vero secunda vxor videns qui infecunda est . . ." (203vb).

37. "Post hoc deus respiciet Rachaelem synagogam sterilem & ipsa concipies [sic] spiritualiter de ipso spiritu sancto duos populos infideles & fideles pariet viz. israeliticum populum & populum iudaycum & sic ipse spiritus sanctus totum mundum spiritualiter in semine habrahe saluabit" (203vb).

38. For Joachim's understanding, see Reeves and Hirsch-Reich, *Figurae of Joachim*, 167–68.

39. Cited in Rusconi, *Attesa*, 166; on 164–67 he discusses the prophecies associated with John of Legnano, but does not mention the Cambridge "Regnum" prophecy.

40. "per tempus & tempora & dimidium temporis qui sunt tres anni cum dimidio secundum danielem" (203vb).

41. "tota ecclesia et regnum christi renouabitur . . . & pax maxima erit ierusalem ecclesie & regno christi nec non toti orbi per mille annos" (203vb).

42. "A desolacione templi iudaici vsque ad potestatem infernalem . . . secundum danielem xii.c. erunt anni mille CCti nonaginta que sunt in annis christi millo.ccco.lxiiijo, & durabit vsque ad annos a desolacione templi computando [marginal note: CCCtos] mille xxxv. qui sunt in [quotation from Belial begins here] annis domini millo. CCCCo ix. infra quos ipsa potestas infernalis ponet in christi ecclesia antichristum, qui persequitur ecclesiam christi & eius verum vicarium per temporales reges infra ix annos quibus completis ignaturus [sic] est in ecclesia christi, & quam possidere debet contra verum christi vicarum annis tribus cum dimidio in graui persecucione populi sancti & sacerdotum sanguis effudetur sicut aqua & famis valida erit & tribulacione qualis non fuit ex qua die visus est. In ecclesia christi postea deficiet eius potencia & sine manu conteretur que precipiet sancta sanctorum destrui & [ac- cancelled] nouum & vetus testamentum concremari."

43. *Belial*, in Goldast von Haiminsfeld, *Processus Juris Joco-serius*, 239; and Burdach, *Dichter des Ackermann*, 507: "Anno domini 1409 ipsa potestas infernalis ponet in Christi ecclesiam potestatem Antichristi, qui persequetur ecclesiam Christi et eius verum Vicarium per temporales Reges infra 9 annos; quibus completis regnaturus est in Ecclesia Christi et quam possidere debet contra Christi verum Vicarium annis tribus et dimidio. Ex gravi persecutione populi sancti et sacerdotum sanguis sicut aqua effundetur, et fames valida erit et tanta erit tribulatio qualis non fuit ex qua die visus est populus in Ecclesia Christi. Postea deficiet eius potentia et sine manu conteretur, ac praecipiet Sancta Sanctorum destrui ac Novum et Vetus Testamentum concremari."

44. "Datum Adversae prope neopolim, die penultima mensis Octobris, sextae indictionis, Anno Domini MCCCLXXXII, pontificatus santissimi in Christo patris et domini Urbani et sacrosanctae ac universalis Ecclesiae Papae Sexti anno quinto aetatis meae tricesimo tercio" (cited in Ott, *Rechtspraxis*, 16).

45. In this prophecy, Langland even uses arcane symbolism common to Joachite writings. See Kerby-Fulton, *Reformist Apocalypticism*, 175–76.

46. For the optimistic apocalyptic programmes of both these complex passages, see ibid., 51–52.

47. I would like to thank Robert Lerner for bringing the connection with Hus to my attention.

48. "Item articulus nonus, in quo continetur, quod Joannes Hus dixit in vulgari ad populum: '"Ecce completa est Prophetia, quam praedixerat Jacobus de Theramo, quod anno Domini millesimo quadrigentesimo nono surget unus qui Evangelium Epistolas et Fidem

Christi persequitur," per haec denotando Dominum Alexandrum, qui in suis bullis mandavit libros Wiclefi cremari'" (Ott, *Rechtspraxis*, 21–22; Burdach, *Der Dichter des Ackermann*, 507).

49. At least six extant manuscripts are known to contain both (see the appendix of manuscript descriptions in Ott, *Rechtspraxis*), a fascinating point for medievalists of England because, as we have seen, Wyclif denounced prophecy, thought Joachim a foolish dreamer, and genuinely took a hard scholastic line against visions of all sorts.

50. See Lerner, *Heresy of the Free Spirit*, on the relations between Joachite and Hussite expectation.

51. For the complexity of this passage, which operates on all four levels of exegetical allegory, see Pearsall's notes in *Piers Plowman: C Text*, to lines 402–12.

52. Joachimism and various other kinds of salvational generosity are discussed in chs. 6 and 7.

53. See ch. 1 and Chronology, 1254 and 1255.

54. Another item in the manuscript, the *Chronicon breve rerum Anglicarum*, beginning abruptly without a rubric on 93, was compiled c. 1381 because it does not mention events after that year. See the Dd description in the *Cambridge University Library Catalogue of Manuscripts*, 2.18.

55. For this consensus, see Benson and Blanchfield's entry on Dd's Provenance, *Manuscripts of Piers: B Version*, 33. I would like to thank James Carley for his advice on this as well. Glastonbury also held prophetic materials.

56. For a case in which the death penalty was invoked for citing the Bridlington prophecies during the reign of Henry IV, see below, ch. 5.

57. It is possible that Langland knew Henry of Costesy's Apocalypse commentary since it was widely disseminated, but we have no way of knowing.

Notes to Chapter 3

1. Discussed in ch. 10 below.

2. *John Capgrave's Abbreuiacion*, 123, lines 24–31; compare Martinus Polonus, *Chronicon*, 440, lines 25–32, and Salimbene's account below.

3. After explaining that William of St. Amour wrote the book, Salimbene continues, "But he himself did not remain unpunished, for he was expelled from the University of Paris by both the King of France, St. Louis, and by Pope Alexander IV, without any hope of every returning there 'for ever and ever' (Micah 4.5). . . . 'For there must also be heresies: that they also, who are approved, may be made manifest among you' (I Cor. 11.19)."

4. Salimbene, *Chronicle*, 463–64, with Latin insertions (for the full Latin passage, see Reeves, *Influence*, 66). Salimbene goes on to note Gerard's authorship and his punishment.

5. In addition to the cases discussed here, see 1385 for Wyclif's opponent, Henry Crumpe (who revived some of the errors of Jean de Pouilly), and 1392 for his trial as a relapsed heretic.

6. Even though Salimbene knew Gerard personally, Salimbene adds, "And because he . . . obstinately and shamelessly persevered in his pertinacity and contumacy, the Friars

Minor placed him in chains in prison. Indeed, he allowed himself to die in prison and was buried in a corner of the garden, deprived of Christian burial. May all men know, therefore, that the rigor of justice is preserved in the Order of the Friars Minor" (*Chronicle*, 464).

7. See the Latin broadside poem edited by Rigg, "Quis dabit capiti," which is a lament for the friars who are particulary attacked by "the two Richards," in "Edition of a Commonplace Book"; and see also Szittya, "Sedens," 34.

8. Citations from the Protocol throughout (unless otherwise specified as from Royal 8. F.XVI) are from Luigi Verardi's reprinting of H. Denifle's Latin edition, with Italian translation, in *Il Protocollo*, 59–107.

9. See ch. 7 below.

10. See Koch, "Der Prozess," esp. 264, on the official terminology. Although not mentioned in Koch, some suspect writers like John of Rupescissa were eventually declared not *hereticus*, but *fantasticus*. See ch. 5 below. For a more detailed list, see Koch, "Philosophische und theologische Irrtumslisten," 318–23.

11. Verardi, *Il Protocollo*, 80.

12. Reeves has pointed out that it was left to a provincial council to condemn Joachim, and this was likely political. See Reeves, *Influence*, 60.

13. See Koch, "Der Prozess" above, and Reeves, *Influence*, 66, for the use of these terms against Joachim.

14. Each *status*, Gerard says, has three great men: Abraham, Issac, and Jacob; Zacharias, John the Baptist, and Christ; Joachim, Francis, and (manuscripts differ on this) Dominic (61 n.).

15. See Verardi, *Il Protocollo*, n. 66. Likewise, the commissoners note, he says *expresse* in chapter 21 that the gospel of Christ is *literale* as opposed to *spirituale* in the Eternal Evangel, which he adduces arguments to prove from the Gospel of Matthew (an interesting disregard for consistency!). The Third Status, Gerard says, will belong to the Holy Spirit and will be "sine enigmate et sine figuris" (which, he implies, mar both the present Testaments); this fascinates the commissioners and they cite more such passages, e.g., "then all figures will cease and the truth of the two testaments will appear *sine velamine*" (61).

16. See Sharpe, *Handlist*, 485–86.

17. The Latin quotations are from 2 Tim. 3:5, 6.

18. William of St. Amour, *De periculis*, ed. Brown, 18–41, the edition preferred here because my subject is English reception.

19. Lerner, "Vagabonds and Little Women," 301–6; Dawson, "William of St. Amour," 223–38.

20. In taking on his most formidable intellectual opponent on the mendicant side, Thomas Aquinas, William says he will proceed: "non per disputationem et altercationem philosophicam, aut sophisticam, quae ad nihil vtilis est, nisi ad subuersionem audientium; sed potius per collationem Catholicam, quae sola debet esse inter seruos Christi, iuxta doctrinam Apostoli II Tim. 2, 14 dicentis, *Noli verbis contendere, ad nihil enim vtile est, nisi ad subuertionem audientium*" (William of St. Amour, "Collations," 132).

21. Szittya, *Antifraternal Tradition*, 15.

22. Ibid., 16.

23. See Thijssen, *Censure*, 16–17.

24. Dawson, "William of St. Amour," 234–35 and n. 22.

25. Ibid., 234; Delorme, *Bonaventurae Collationes*, 352–53. For Langland's *ad pristinum statum* prophecy (which is about the reform of the religious orders), see C.V.168–79, and Kerby-Fulton, *Reformist Apocalypticism*.

26. See *De periculis*, esp. ch. 8; and see Leff, *Paris and Oxford*, 261.

27. *De periculis*, 27.

28. Reeves, *Influence*, 62.

29. Grandisson's earlier interest in inquisition of Franciscans is another. See Chronology, 1334, 1348, and 1355 for Grandisson, and see Arnold, "Lollard Trials," who mentions evidence that Grandisson had more access to inquisitorial materials than we had previously thought.

30. Walsh, *Fourteenth-Century Scholar*, 427, on both du Crois and Court.

31. Ibid., 103.

32. See Sharpe, *Handlist*, under "Kilvington."

33. See Chronology, 1354 note, for sources and details.

34. Quoted below, n. 41.

35. See Rigg, *History of Anglo-Latin Literature*, 273.

36. "Quod rex a clericis et viris ecclesiasticis male et inordinate viventibus absque injuria possessiones posset auferre" (*Munimenta Academia*, 1.209); "quod decimae ecclesiarum magis debentur mendicantibus quam rectoribus earumdem" (209); "Item, istam Universitatem vocavit 'gymnasium haereticorum'" (210).

37. See Kerby-Fulton and Justice, "Reformist Intellectual Culture," 149–203.

38. Thanks to the recent work of Catto, "Wyclif and Wyclifism," 183.

39. The Austins and the Franciscans worked together at the Great Council of 1374 (see below). Three years earlier Ashbourne had been one of two Austins advocating disendowment to Parliament. See Chronology, 1371 and 1374.

40. *Munimenta Academia*, 210, from his recantation.

41. "Nec possumus eum compellere ad revocacionem publicam, nec ad aliquam aliam penam propter confidenciam quam habet in magnatibus de regno, quos dicit velle se defendere in hac causa" (cited from Cambridge, Sidney Sussex College, MS 64, fol. 126v, in Aston, "Caim's Castles," 51).

42. "Freres in here fraytour shal fynde þat tyme / Bred withouten beggynge to lyue by euere aftur / And Constantyn shal be here cook and couerour of here churches" (C.V.173–75). See Chronology, 1336 and note, on Benedict XII's reforms; see also Clopper, "Songes of Rechelesnesse," 29.

43. On Uthred, see Chronology, 1368.

44. Given the precedent of Ockham's *An princeps*, and (by now) years of parliamentary tussle over royal rights to clerical wealth in time of war, a serious condemnation of disendowment views has to raise our suspicions.

45. Netter, *Fasciculi Zizaniorum*, p. 279, X.

46. Ibid., p. 280, XVII. This, perhaps, in deference to the powerful faction of John of Gaunt who, despite his embarrassment over Wyclif's recently declared eucharistic ideas, still no doubt cherished the goal of orderly disendowment as feasible and orthodox.

47. Walsh, *Fourteenth-Century Scholar*, 416. This very heresy, in fact, with allusion to Jean de Pouilly, would arise for the university again as late as 1392, in the condemnation of Henry Crumpe, as for the bishop of Meath in 1385. See Chronology and notes.

48. Ibid., 435.

49. Ibid., 420. *Omnis utriusque sexus*, issued at the Fourth Lateran Council (1215), required annual confession to a parish priest. *Super cathedram* had been issued by Boniface VIII (1300) setting out the rights and privileges of the friars in relation to confession and other matters. *Vas electionis* had been issued by John XXII condemning the doctrine of Jean de Pouilly; it had to be reissued in Ireland in 1400 because of the intensity of antimendicant activity there. See Chronology, 1400 and note.

50. See Chronology, 1323 and note, and see *Calendar of Close Rolls*, Edward II, vol. 3, p. 675, discussed in Barton, "Engendering Inquisition," as well.

51. He invoked the Statute of Praemunire in order to do so. See Chronology, 1357, esp. March 31 and April 7 for sources.

52. On support of Jordan, see Chronology, 1358 and note.

53. On pope's demands, see Chronology, 1373.

54. *Eulogium*, 3.337–39.

55. In *De veritate sacrae scripturae* Wyclif writes of "unus Frater Minor, qui gravavit eos ex predicacione paupertatis et status primitive ecclesie, per modum revocacionis confiteretur publice in ecclesia Beate Virginis sanctitatem conversacionis presentis ecclesie sub hac forma: 'non teneo, ecclesiam militantem propter suam dotacionem imperfeccionis gradum incurrere aliqualem aliqualem'" (356). Steven Justice points out the connection in *Writing and Rebellion*, 236 n. 135.

56. This case is quoted here from my transcription of Oxford, Bodleian Library Bodley 158, from which I have recently edited (with Magda Hayton and Kenna Olsen), "Insurgent gentes," its immediate neighbour in the manuscript; see our "Pseudo-Hildegardian Prophecy," 160–93. The documents associated with the 1380 case have only just been edited in 2005 by Spencer, but from the copy in the muniments of Durham, and partially collated with Bodley 158, in "Richard," 13–40. Spencer, however, does not mention the Joachite dimensions of the case nor the connections with William of St. Amour, although she briefly footnotes the other contents of Bodley 158.

57. For Bodley's "Rolton."

58. *Knighton's Chronicle*, 248–49.

59. Reeves, *Influence*, 160.

60. See ibid., 163 ff., on the *Brevis Historia* of 1367.

61. Cited and translated by Szittya, *Antifraternal Tradition*, 22, from the *Historia Universitatis Parisiensis*, 3.287–88, an early list of charges from which William's *De periculis* directly evolved.

62. In addition to the sources cited in the Chronology, 1380, see Emden, *Survey of Dominicans*, 360.

63. See Spencer, "Richard," 21.

64. See Appendix C for this quote.

65. See Kerby-Fulton, "Piers Plowman," on the question of dating the A text (perhaps being revised as late as 1369–70, as Pearsall notes in Langland, *Piers Plowman: C-Text*, 9) and the Chronology, 1367–68 note. There, as here, I follow the traditional dating associating it with the 1360s on the basis of the pattern of historical allusion across all three texts.

66. See Kerby-Fulton and Justice, "Reformist Intellectual Culture."

67. See Chronology, 1308 and note.

68. I would like to thank Noelle King for sharing with me her insights on this passage.

69. There may be autobiographical reasons, too. It is reasonable to speculate that in his younger years Langland may have still hoped for a benefice himself.

70. See ch. 10.

71. Fleming, *Roman de la Rose: A Study*, 164. And later: "Faussemblant does not 'represent the friars'; he represents certain attitudes to which Jean was able to give a local habitation and a name by reference to a peculiar local historical experience. . . . Only in one respect is the *De periculis* on which Jean so heavily leans an ephemeral political tract. It is also an essay in eschatology, an attempt to come to terms with the spiritual implications of the disorders of the 'last days' (II Tim. 3.1)" (166).

72. L. Patterson, "Feminine Rhetoric," 327.

73. L. Patterson, *Chaucer and the Subject of History*, 398.

74. See "A Word about Intellectual Freedom" above.

75. Throughout this section I cite Fragment C of the "Chaucerian" translation of the *Roman* from *Riverside Chaucer*, with occasional insertions from R. Sutherland's facing French edition (*Romaunt and Roman*), checked against Lecoy's edition of the *Roman* where the texts differ. The loss of certain lines arose initially, according to Alfred David, from the misarrangement of four passages in Fragment C (lines 7013–7304) when two leaves were accidentally displaced in binding an ancestor of the present G text. Thynne tried to supply the lost lines, perhaps from other MSS or from the French original and "according to his notion of Chaucerian usage" (*Riverside Chaucer*, Textual Notes, 1198). *Riverside* displaces what the editor believes to be Thynne's lines to the notes and marks the gaps in the text with ellipsis points. The fact that some of these gaps occur right in the middle of the passages spoken by Faus Semblant, especially about William of St. Amour and the scandal of the Eternal Evangel may be purely accident, but nonetheless the Middle English is slightly more conservative than the French in places, as we will note, as is Thynne in at least one instance.

76. See *Riverside Chaucer*, Explanatory Notes to the *Romaunt*, and see Pearsall, *Life of Chaucer*, 82, for the view that Chaucer "probably" wrote the C segment.

77. This was a motif to express intellectual elitism thrown back on its dignity. As Jim Rhodes has mentioned, Ockham is said to have remarked that the topic of free will had attracted so many disputants that "laymen and old women" were poised to challenge theologians in open debate (*Poetry Does Theology*, 26). For the quotations above from Gerson, see Hobbins, "Beyond the Schools," 292–93. Gerson is disapproving of the Joachite writer, Ubertino da Casale: "Rursus per eum nullus extollitur status nisi ille qualem notat se tenuisse conformiter ad feminas aliquas magnae, ut asserit, elevationis et prophetici spiritus, quarum tamen doctrinae sunt suspectae . . ." (he goes on to cite St. Paul against the preaching of women).

78. Compare the conditions under which Faus Semblant says a man may beg (lines 11333–11350) with *Piers Plowman*, the *apologia* at the opening of C.V.

79. See Chronology, 1259 and note.

80. See chs. 5, 9, and 10 on constraint issues in Ricardian poetry.

81. Chaucer's borrowings from the portrait of Faus for his Summoner and especially his Pardoner are well documented in the notes to *Riverside Chaucer*, especially for the "Pardoner's Tale." The two are described side by side in the General Prologue, in portraits, as critical consensus has long established, full of homosexual innuendo.

82. Most fully in Levitan, "Parody of Pentecost," 236–46. See, further, the recent article by G. Olson, "The End of the Summoner's Tale," which reviews all other theories and reaffirms that Chaucer's "certainly seems to be a parody of Pentecost" (216).

83. Szittya, *Antifraternal Tradition*, 236, and see his references on 231 ff to the previous scholarship.

84. Fleming, *Introduction to Franciscan Literature*, 72.

85. On Scribe D, see Kerby-Fulton, "Langland in His Working Clothes," and Kerby-Fulton and Justice, "Scribe D."

86. See ch. 9.

87. They were helped in this endeavor by the enigmatic allusion to the burning of Book, who prophesies his own end (C.XX.264), with its enigmatic, but perhaps only superficial similarity to the Eternal Evangel. For a full discussion of these earlier studies, see Bloomfield, *Piers Plowman as Apocalypse*.

88. Chs. 9 and 10.

89. See Kerby-Fulton, *Reformist Apocalypticism*.

90. *Liber figurarum*, table XIV (Oxford, Corpus Christi College 255A, fols. 4-14), discussed in more detail below in ch. 10.

91. See my *Reformist Apocalypticism*, 171-72, for a reading of the arcane imagery in this passage (not quoted here) and its parallels in Joachite iconography. See also ch. 2, n. 82 above for parallels with Olivi.

92. Fol. 95v of New College 49 where he treats these as two of five parables, which, taken all together, he says "designetur cursum fidei & ecclesie seu noui testamenti. . . . Due ii sequentes .i. de grano sinapsis & de fermento respiciunt eius dilatationem. Tres uero ultime respiciunt finem. *Ita quod due priores respiciunt renouationem euangelice paupertatis & perfectionis:* ultima vero finalem conuersionem mundi." (I have italicized the explanation of two parables pertinent here.) Although also personal, Olivi's larger scheme is apocalyptic: the first two parables represent the growth of the church, the second two the *renovatio* of evangelical poverty, and the last one, the final conversion of the world. There are hints here and elsewhere that Olivi had universalist beliefs.

93. For a listing of these, see Kerby-Fulton, "English Joachimism."

94. See Dufeil, *Guillaume de Saint-Amour*, and Szittya, *Antifraternal Tradition*, and his Index of Manuscripts.

95. Oxford, Balliol College 149; Oxford, Bodley 158; Oxford, Digby 98.

96. *Knighton's Chronicle*, 245-49 for all the extracts and summaries here.

Notes to Case Study 2

1. British Library, Cotton Cleopatra B.II, fols. 60-64, new foliation. In Cotton there are marginal memoranda in the hand of the scribe relating to the loan of a manuscript to a church in Iwade, Kent: "W. Capellanus ecclesie Sancti Michelis Co [cropped] . . . contulit istud manuale Sacramentorum ad pro [cropped] . . . et usum ecclesie De Wade juxta Sidingborne in Cantia." There is no direct evidence of this manuscript's provenance, but there is absolutely no doubt about the Hiberno-English dialect of the two vernacular poems or the distinctive Anglo-Irish style of their satire. An earlier edition of all three, with a full transcription of the legible marginalia quoted above, can be found in *Monumenta Franciscana*, Appendix XI. For the modern edition of the two Hiberno-English poems cited here, see Dean, *Medieval English Political Writings*, 47-54, and discussion of the earlier editions.

See also Robbins, *Historical Poems*, 157–62, and Wright, *Political Poems and Songs*, 1.268–70. An early textual study of one of the poems, "Of thes Frer Mynours," by an early scholar of Hiberno-English poetry is Heuser, "With an O and an I," 283–319; Dean lists other more recent literary studies.

2. On Pateshull, see Walsingham, *Historia Anglicana*, 2.157–59, and for a superb study of the extracts, see the recent article, Hudson, "Peter Pateshull," 167–83. Hudson found the extracts in British Library, Cotton Titus D.X., 188–94v.

3. Accounts of Pateshull by Bale include his *Scriptorum Illustrium*, 1.509–10; his *Index*, 322–23; McCusker, "Books and Manuscripts," 144–65, no. 50; and, as Hudson shows in "Peter Pateshull," in British Library Cotton Titus D.X., 188r–94v. I am indebted to Anne Hudson for informing me of her discovery prior to publication and for her fine article. On Robert of Uzès, see Kerby-Fulton, *Reformist Apocalypticism*.

4. *Linguistic Atlas*, 1.277. I would like to thank Erin Ronsse for her help in double-checking some details in this manuscript.

5. Kerby-Fulton and Despres, *Iconography*, 37–39, and passim on Anglo-Irish culture more generally and ch. 3 for discussion of the annotations and corrections in the Douce manuscript and the dialect of the scribes.

6. It is also worth noting that the booklet is bound together with some other pieces of Irish character, especially the "Walteri de Wyckwane, abbatis de Winchcomb" item, fol. 216, which is Irish in decoration, in a much earlier hand. The manuscript is made up of multiple booklets copied at different times, and some of the compiling work may or may not have been Robert Cotton's.

7. See note 40 below and the quote preceding it.

8. These crosses are especially hard to interpret because they may be corrector's marks, or more likely just simple marks for refrain brackets that were never finished, or they could be crosses indicating disapproval. They appear especially at two of the "O and I" refrain lines: 34–35, which express the hope that the friars will all be burned ("brent") and prosperity to all who help carry out the burning, and at the final couplet 41–42, which charges that for a sixpence the friars will "Sle thi fadere, and jape [seduce] thi modre, and thai wyl thi assoile." For a clear medieval description of marginal crosses used to censure parts of a text, see Olivi's comment on censorship of his own works (Chronology, 1283).

9. On "Sedens" and the Digby manuscript context, see Szittya, "Sedens"; Rigg, *History of Anglo-Latin Literature*, 270–72; and Hudson, "Peter Pateshull," 173–74. Wyclif cited "Sedens" before his death in 1384.

10. See Pantin, *The English Church*, for brief overviews.

11. Kerby-Fulton and Despres, *Iconography*, 37–39. There are some much more limited attacks, usually on the patronage images in Franciscan and Dominican art, for instance, the iconography that places a friar or one of the founders at the foot of the cross, as, for example, in the short poem "De astantibus crucifixo." (See Szittya, *Antifraternal Tradition*, 194; Rigg, "Two Latin Poems," 106–18; and Kerby-Fulton and Despres, op. cit., on "O niger intrusor.") Since such images usually signal wealthy patronage, this kind of envy is quite understandable. This, however, is not the thrust of our Anglo-Irish poem.

12. For other contemporary examples, see Turner, *St. Francis*; for others, see *Francesco d'Assisi: Documenti e Archivi*, esp. 321 (from Matthew of Paris) and 329. For a superb study of Franciscan art and exegesis, see Fleming, *From Bonaventure*. As Fleming writes (13), "Since, as Bonaventure makes clear, the 'seraph' of the Stigmatization was in fact Christ in

angelic form, it is probable that Franciscans believed from the earliest times that the visionary Christ actually printed the wounds with his own hands." Ubertino da Casale has a whole chapter in his fifth book on "Jesus seraph alatus," *Arbor vitae crucifixae Jesu*, V, iv.

13. For both poems I cite Dean, *Medieval English Political Writings*, with parenthetical references to the line numbers.

14. For a superb example, see fol. 345v, reproduced as fig. 37 in Gould, *Psalter and Hours of Yolande*. Note the title of Ubertino da Casale's book, *Arbor vitae crucifixae Jesu*.

15. Internal quotation marks added to clarify the sense. See Kerby-Fulton and Despres, *Iconography*, 37–39, on this passage.

16. Mollat, *Popes at Avignon*, 16. That these issues from John XXII's reign were not old news among the Anglo-Irish in Ricardian Oxford is apparent from Crumpe's condemnations. The tunics would have looked like the short, patched tunic said to have belonged to Francis even now on display in the Church of St. Clare in Assisi.

17. Dean, *Medieval English Political Writings*, 103 nn. 31–33, who also points out that *The Lanterne of Light* uses the motif (91, lines 465–66), but (I would add) only metaphorically: "No man loke aftir Ennok and Hely in persoone, . . . but in spirit."

18. Fleming, *From Bonaventure*, 64–65.

19. On the apostate motif in "Sedens," and in its companion poem, "Quis dabit capiti" (a different poem from the one of that incipit about Scrope discussed later), see Szittya, "Sedens," 34, which also provides an edition and excellent introduction.

20. See Dean, *Medieval English Political Writings*, note to line 110, for a listing of other texts in which the cryptogram occurs.

21. For Henry Crumpe, see Chronology, 1382, 1385, 1392; for Whitehead, 1409; and for Norreys, 1440. For Crumpe in "Heu," see n. 28 below; for writings by Whitehead in Digby 98, see the next section of this case study and n. 39 below.

22. For heretics, see Chronology, 1353.

23. On the colonial issues in relation to antimendicantism, see Walsh, *Fourteenth-Century Scholar*.

24. Alice is the inspiration for "Versus nonnulli de Litteris quibusdam" or "Aliz, amo te" in Harley 913. I am grateful to Deborah Hatfield-Moore for allowing me to cite her unpublished paper, "Seven Hundred Years."

25. Transcribed and translated by Hatfield-Moore, *Paying the Minstrel*, 140. I am grateful to Dr. Hatfield-Moore for permission to cite this passage.

26. The hand that copied all three poems is a form of *anglicana formata* that retains many older, mid-century features (like the two-compartment 'a' that stands higher than the other letters). This, like the contents of the poems, may point toward an older collector of antimendicant thought.

27. "Heu, quanta desolacio," in Wright, *Political Poems and Songs*, 1.253–63.

28. In a very recent essay ("Heu! quanta desolatio," 19–36), Wendy Scase argues the interesting theory that most of the war of words the poem records has Oxford, not Black-friars, as its setting and that the action of the poem moves to London only once it is clear that things cannot be resolved "in scholis." This is quite plausible, although the Blackfriars Council remains the poem's defining occasion, mentioned explicitly near the poem's opening ("In hoc terraemotu ab hora diei / Quia tunc convenerant scribae, Pharisaei" [254]) and later in the text via allusion (discussed below). It is hard to know whether the academic mode of proceeding might equally describe methods of argument at the council. Hudson's

recent study adds to Scase's the information that the participant "Crophorne" (repeated accurately in all four manuscripts) may be Henry Crumpe because, as Hudson points out, the poet is aware that "Crophorne" at present "a nobis sit remotus," likely referring to Crumpe's suspension. If so, Hudson concludes, the poet is writing between June 15 and July 14 of 1382. There was also, one could note, a known Oxford academic named Crophorne, a nominalist and a Dominican (since c. 1340), listed in Emden, *Biographical Register*, under one of the alternative spellings of his name, "Crathorn." But the Crophorne in "Heu" seems to be Irish, as Hudson also observes. This may account for Anglo-Irish interest in copying it.

29. The Digby copy is on fol. 195. Anne Hudson has kindly informed me that there are three further manuscripts of "Heu quanta": Rome, Biblioteca Vaticana Rossiano, Vatican Pal. MS lat. 994, fols. 158–60; Prague, Metropolitan Chapter MS D. 12, fols. 217–22; and Vienna Österreichische Nationalbibliothek MS 3929, fols. 223v–25, where "Heu" appears along with many texts by Wyclif himself; see further Hudson, "From Oxford to Prague," 655–56 and n. 50. Wendy Scase is planning an edition of the poem.

30. Kerby-Fulton, "Prophecy and Suspicion."

31. *Wyclif and His Followers*, 51. On Partriche, see Emden, *Biographical Register*, 2.1430, and very recently, Hanna, "Dr. Peter Partridge." On Payne's role in furthering the tolerance for Wycliffite notions at Oxford up to about 1413, see Hudson, *Premature Reformation*, 99–103. For reasons given below, I would put some of the compilation activity slightly earlier. There are hands other than Partriche's in the manuscript, adding to the complexity of dating.

32. Anne Hudson has very helpfully informed me that the missing items were most likely letters, as indeed, the medieval table of contents says "Epistole multi Johannis Wytcliff." The *Justicia* prophecy is in Partriche's hand, beginning fol. 181r; fols. 182x and 182y are the stubs of the now missing leaves which contained Wyclif's letters. Hildegard's *Justicia* prophecy is immediately preceded by a copy of the preaching prohibition issued by Henry IV. See *Bodleian Library Quarto Catalogues*, IX.53–55: "Litera Regis Henr. IV, vice-comitibus London., quod nullus capellanus regularis vel secularis praedicet *nisi prius ad hoc per diocesanum admittatur*," dated Westminster, 12 May 1400 (fol. 179v) and followed immediately by "Petitio sacerdotum secularium ad Regem contra praedictam literam," on the same folio.

33. See ch. 4 below.

34. Beginning on fol. 186 (not 183, as the *Catalogus* says), followed by the poem "Achab diu studuit" (fol. 194), and then by "Sedens super flumina flevi Babilonis" (also on fol. 194). Both are antimendicant, "Achab" is unprinted, "Sedens" is the Latin poem against the friars with the same macaronic ("With an O and an I") refrain as "Heu" has. One possible reason why Partriche placed "Heu" next to it is because both were written by Pateshull (as Bale thought) or just collected together. See Szittya, "Sedens." Scase, "Heu! quanto desolutio," wants to date "Sedens" later, but does not offer firm evidence for doing so; Hudson dates "Sedens" between 1356 and 1384 ("Peter Pateshull," 173). For a discussion of the "O and I" trope in satirical and complaint poetry, see Dean, *Medieval English Political Writings*, 33.

35. See Wilkins, *Concilia*, 3.165; and for these and other instances, see Hudson, *Lollards and Their Books*, 149 and n. 3, and for references on the posting of the "Twelve Conclusions." On broadsides more generally, see Justice, *Writing and Rebellion*, esp. 29–30.

36. I have not been able to find this hand active elsewhere in the booklet (Hanna agrees; see "Dr. Peter Partridge," 50) which had many contributors. Moreover, if any contributor had initially intended "Heu" for Digby 98 he would hardly have copied it on a long sheet

that did not fit the size or shape of the book. I am grateful to Penn Szittya for first mentioning to me in 1996 that he remembered seeing an odd-shaped leaf, possibly a broadside in Digby 98; on the manuscript, see his article, "Sedens."

37. Letter-Book E, fol. xxv, 18 September 1314, a letter patent from Edward II to the Mayor and Sheriffs of London. (Private communication, May 9, 1996). I am very grateful to Penn Szittya for sending me this reference and for his advice about the broadside.

38. The apostate motif is in "Sedens super flumina" (on fol. 194 of Digby, just beside where "Heu" is sewn into the manuscript) and in the Hiberno-English poem "Of thes" copied with "Heu" in the Cotton manuscript. It also appears in the companion poem to "Sedens," "Quis dabit capiti"; see Szittya, "Sedens," 34.

39. "'Determinacio magistri Joahnnis Whytheed de Hibernia in materia de mendicitate contra fratres' in qua respondet pro Radulpho archiepiscopo Armachano contra fratrem Petrum Russel" (fol. 200 of Digby 98).

40. Walsh, *Fourteenth-Century Scholar*, 360. On the nature of these tensions, see also Kerby-Fulton and Despres, *Iconography*.

41. See Chronology, 1385, 1392 for Crumpe, and 1440, 1448 for Norreys.

42. Oxford scholars were expected to share notes, as we know from complaints against Hereford's secretiveness at Queens. See Forde, "Nicholas Hereford's Ascension Day Sermon."

43. See the discussion of Bodley 851 in Case Study 3 below.

44. "Heu! quanta desolatio Angliae praestatur, / Cujus regnum quodlibet hinc inde minatur" (253). References are by page number to Wright's edition (which is not lineated).

45. "In hoc terraemotu ab hora diei, / Quia tunc convenerant scribae, Pharisaei, / Cum summis sacerdotibus contra Christum Dei" (254).

46. The stanza is about the lavish robes of the mendicants, and ends: "With an O and an I, dicunt Pharisaei, / 'Ecce quanta patimur pro amore Dei'" (256).

47. See Hudson, "Peter Pateshull," 170, explaining that Pateshull narrates Edward III's Dominican confessor's imprisoning (likely in a convent) of Jordan and three other friars, probably in relation to the episode involving FitzRalph's campaign at the curia. See n. 62 below.

48. The bull of Clement V, incorporated into the *Clementines*, the last of four that had begun with Gregory IX's *Quo elongati*, distinguished between ownership (dominium) and simple use (usus facti) of goods, asserting, in keeping with their Rule, that the friars had no right to the former. Next, Innocent IV's bull of 1245 laid down the principle that ownership of goods the friars used was held on their behalf by the Holy See, an interpretation confirmed by Nicholas III in *Exiit qui seminat* and by Clement V in *Exivi de paradiso*. John XXII overturned all of these in his two bulls, *Ad conditorem canonum* (1322) and *Cum inter nonnullos* (1323).

49. Despite the fact that they are to don vile dress, according to their Rule, the poet complains, "Sed ut locum teneant fastis altiorem, / Semetipsos induunt regium colorem. / With an O and an I, exivi de Paradiso, / Absconditur sub modio, papa sit deriso" (256).

50. "Quod si pauper adiens fratres infirmetur, / Et petat ut inter hos sepulturae detur, / Gardianus absens est, statim respondetur, / Et sic satis breviter pauper excludetur" (257).

51. "Nichol [i.e., Hereford] solvens omnia jussit Bayard stare" (260).

52. "Hic dixit quod monachi non debent laborare, / Sed quod fratres validi deberent mendicare" (260).

53. For those present at the council, see the list appended to the proceedings in Netter, *Fasciculi Zizaniorum*.

54. See n. 28 above.

55. The year 1382 is too early for *Crede* (see lines 657–58 and the note in Barr, *Piers Plowman Tradition*), unless some earlier redaction of which no evidence survives were in circulation, which is possible. For discussion of the poem, see Rigg, *History of Anglo-Latin Literature*, 282–83.

56. Scase ("Heu! quanta desolatio," 34) reads the comment as ironic, but Rigg, *History of Anglo-Latin Literature* does not.

57. This seems to me a better way of understanding the phenomenon: see Middleton, "William Langland's 'Kynde Name,'" but see also the use of it in marginalia, like the "prophetia Petri" annotation discussed in Kerby-Fulton and Justice, "Reformist Intellectual Culture."

58. Alford records only one other instance, in Bromyard (see *Piers Plowman: Guide to the Quotations*, for B.XI.416a). It appears in Imaginative's rebuke to Will, after he has been cast out of his dream in which Reason, had Will been patient, would have taught him what "clergie [kan]" (B.XI.414).

59. See 263, especially "Londonias currentes . . . pro quaestu sanctorum, / Largas dant corrigias de bonis aliorum" and the entire next stanza.

60. See Hudson, "Peter Pateshull," 181 n. 53.

61. I have read the poem in Rigg, "Edition of a Fifteenth-Century Commonplace Book," 132–46; I am grateful to Penn Szittya for his extensive help and advice on this poem, on "Sedens," and on antimendicantism generally. On "Quis," see also Hudson, "Peter Pateshull," 170–72, and Rigg, *History of Anglo-Latin Literature*, 272–73.

62. Most interesting is the series of antifraternal (mostly anti-Dominican) anecdotes in the *Vita*, ranging in date from 1347 to 1388, and especially the imprisonment of four Dominicans, including William Jordan, by Edward III's confessor in the mid-1350s, apparently as part of Edward's campaign to keep both FitzRalph and his enemies in England and away from Avignon. Hudson, "Peter Pateshull," 170, and n. 24; cf. *Calendar of Patent Rolls 1354–58*, 298, and ch. 3 above.

63. For "Vox in Rama," which is unedited, see Cambridge, Gonville and Caius 230/116, fols. 112–16; for discussion, see Rigg, *History of Anglo-Latin Literature*, 280–81, and Hudson, "Peter Pateshull," 174–75. Rigg dates the poem 1371–77, but Hudson sees references to the eucharistic controversies in stanza 36. On the "O and I" refrains more generally, see Dean, *Medieval English Political Writings*, 101–2.

64. McCusker, "Books and Manuscripts," no. 50.

65. Hudson, "Peter Pateshull," has studied the incipits given in Bale's *Scriptorium Illustrium* entry on Pateshull, suggesting that Pateshull might be the author of one or more of them, especially "Heu quanta desolacio" itself.

66. For Walsingham's account, see primarily *Historia Anglicana*, 2.157–59, and other sources in nn. 1–3 for the account given by Hudson, "Peter Pateshull."

67. Kerby-Fulton and Despres, *Iconography*.

68. See Langland, *Piers Plowman: C-Text*, ed. Pearsall, notes to the Crucifixion and Harrowing scenes.

69. Discussed below in ch. 5 and ch. 10.

Notes to Chapter 4

1. See "Workman's Shot in the Dark" in ch. 1 above and also Wilks, "Wyclif and the Great Persecution," which, however, offers little by way of concrete citation.

2. Hildegard, *Liber divinorum operum*, c. xxv, p. 446 (*PL* 197, col. 1026D–1027A). I give the *PL* edition references here because they are the only way of negotiating Gebeno's widely disseminated compilation of her prophecies, the *Pentachronon*, still most accessible for English reception in the partial edition *Analecta Sanctae Hildegardis*, ed. Pitra. See also Santos Paz, *La Recepción de Hildegarde*, for an edition of one version of the *Pentachronon*. The passage here, discussed in more detail below, arises after she has predicted the fall of the Holy Roman Empire. See also my *Reformist Apocalypticism*, 48.

3. This idea appears in several prophecies, among the most popular of which is the *Justicia* prophecy in *Liber divinorum* operum, sometimes excerpted from III. V. c.xi, pp. 427–29, "Corona mea schismate errantium mentium obnubilata est . . ." (*PL* 197, col. 1013c), but more often, in Insular manuscripts, excerpted from c. xvi., pp. 433–36, "Justicia enim postquam ad supernum judicem querelam suam . . ." (*PL* 197, col. 1017d) as in Bodleian Library, MS Digby 98, fol. 181r, and MS Hatton 56, fol. 27r. For discussion, see Kerby-Fulton, *Reformist Apocalypticism*, 36–38. This is Hildegard's last and most elaborate disendowment prophecy, and her most flattering portrayal of the role of the lay powers. For other disendowment prophecies (with somewhat more ambivalent portraits of the lay powers), see her well-known prophecy to Werner of Kircheim, "In lecto aegritudinis . . . ," *Epistolarium*, Letter 149R, 335–36 (for discussion, Kerby-Fulton, op. cit., 43); and her prophecy to the clergy of Trier, *Epistolarium*, 91a, Letter 223R, 490–96 (for discussion, Kerby-Fulton, op. cit., 214–15). The famous Cologne letter also contains a brief disendowment prophecy.

4. This notion is central to the prophecy to the clergy of Cologne, *Epistolarium*, 91, Letter XVr, 34–47. For the complex textual history of the Cologne prophecy, see Bund, "Die 'Prophetin'," 171–260, and for discussion, see my Reformist Apocalypticism, 39–41.

5. *Scivias*, III, the opening of Visio 11; for the text and Hildegard's commentary on the passage, see ch. 37, in *Hildegardis Scivias*, 598.

6. *Liber divinorum operum*, ed. Derolez and Dronke, III. V.38, pp. 462–63. *Analecta sanctae Hildegardis*, ed. Pitra, 485; on the rivalry with Joachim, see Bloomfield and Reeves, "Penetration of Joachimism," 772–93.

7. This seems worth stressing since medieval readers have had a rather bad press for laxity about authorship attribution since Goldschmidt's seminal study; see Goldschmidt, *Medieval Texts*.

8. See Kerby-Fulton, "Hildegard and Antimendicant Propaganda," 386–99, for the history of this episode and the texts.

9. See the edition in Bund, "Die 'Prophetin'," or *Epistolarium*, 91, Letter XVr, 34–47; a large excerpt was included in Gebeno's *Pentachronon*, see *Analecta sanctae Hildegardis*, ed. Pitra, 486.

10. One version, appearing in one English and one Irish manuscript, cleverly uses Hildegard's original incipit to give conviction to a forgery: Cambridge, Corpus Christi College 404, fol. 38v, and Dublin, Trinity College 516, fol. 43r; the texts are quite similar, both unedited.

11. For an edition of the main Insular version, see Kerby-Fulton, Hayton, and Olsen, "Pseudo-Hildegardian Prophecy."

12. For more detail, see Kerby-Fulton, "Prophecy and Suspicion," especially the Appendix, listing twenty-four manuscripts, of which sixteen can be firmly associated with the period between the 1350s and the 1420s.

13. On Langland and Hildegard, see Kerby-Fulton, *Reformist Apocalypticism*, 208–10 nn. 52, 59–66, and 68–72. For *Pierce the Ploughman's Crede* and Wimbledon, see Kerby-Fulton, "Hildegard and Antimendicant Propaganda," 389 n. 13; for Gower, "Jack Upland," and several anonymous Wycliffite writers, see Szittya, *Antifraternal Tradition*, 219–21; on Pateshull, Blackwell, Taylor, Partriche, and Wyclif, see below.

14. The list above is not exhaustive. For the *Pentachronon*, see n. 2 above, with references to the *PL*. For textual matters, my *Reformist Apocalypticism*, 28–31; on Gebeno's laudatory attitude toward Hildegard, see my "Hildegard and the Male Reader," 10–13. For the list of English *Pentachronon* manuscripts, see my "Prophecy and Suspicion." Anne Hudson has very kindly informed me of two other Lollard texts that cite *Pentachronon*: the extended sermon contained in British Library, Egerton 2820, and the Cotton Titus D.V tract (for both, see Hudson, *Works of a Lollard Preacher*, esp. 128, line 2635, and 134, line 2808). She mentions further a translated section in the so-called *Lollard Chronicle*, Columbia University Library, Plimpton MS Add. 3, fols. 240–41.

15. I have used the Bodleian Library's copy (Oxford, 1697); the nineteen are distributed, according to Bernard's Index, as follows: three in Irish libraries, five in Cambridge, five in Oxford, six in other libraries ("Publicis quam Privatis Angliae Bibilotecis"), including cathedral libraries.

16. Kerby-Fulton, "Hildegard and the Male Reader" and Kerby-Fulton, "Langland's Reading."

17. In the heading of this section I deliberately echo the title of the illuminating article by McGinn, "Abbot and the Doctors." See Pecham, *Fratris Johannis Pecham*, 76, and see Kerby-Fulton, "Hildegard and the Male Reader" for a fuller discussion of Pecham's views on Hildegard.

18. Kerby-Fulton, "Hildegard and the Male Reader," 15.

19. See Tocco's edition in Pecham, *Fratris Johannis Pecham*, 111 and 122.

20. "Ad quod dicunt quidam Bernardum prophetias Hildegardis collegisse, si verum est huiusmodi prophetie auctoritam non ostendit: collegit enim Bernardus quedam at reprobandum, sicut errores Abelardi, quedam ad experiendum, sicut forsan huiusmodi mulieris verba" (ibid., 76).

21. "Et quod dicunt papam Eugenium ea confirmasse, plane est mendacium, quia sedes apostolica non sole dubia confirmare, maxime cum hec in aliis temeritatis sue scriptitationibus suis noscatur plura erronea reliquisse" (ibid.).

22. Grundmann, *Zur Vitae s. Gerlaci*, 1.187–94, but for more recent scholarship and different findings on the approval, see more discussion above in ch. 1.

23. Little's edition in Pecham, *Fratris Johannis Pecham*, 64.

24. "Sed populus iste, qui hoc faciet, a diabolo seductus et missus pallida facie veniet, et velut in omni sanctitate componet, et maioribus secularibus principibus se coniunget. Quibus et de vobis sic dicet: . . . 'quare eos vobiscum esse patimini . . . ? Isti enim ebrii et luxuriosi sunt, et nisi eos a vobis abiciatis, tota ecclesia destruetur'. . . . *Avaritiam quoque non amat, pecuniam non habet*, . . . Diabolus enim cum hominibus istis est" (cited from Bund, "Die 'Prophetin'," 246, lines 145–51, my emphasis and with omissions indicated).

25. He claims to know "quid scripserit contra aliquos Hildegarde quid Joachim divinaverit, sed probandos scio esse spiritus; quia multos errare fecerunt sompnia et, teste scriptura, visa mendacia plurimos seduxerunt" (Tocco's edition in Pecham, *Fratris Johannis Pecham*, 122).

26. Bodleian Library Lat. Misc. c. 75, also discussed above in ch. 2. Pecham's treatise is listed in the late fourteenth-century table of contents, 55v, but his treatise itself (and a number of other pieces of the manuscript) are now lost. Little, *Fratris Thomae*, xiv–xvii, prints the table of contents (I have dated the hand a little earlier than he has).

27. The booklet is now defective, with running heads in the same fourteenth-century hand (fols. 122 to 131v). Henry's *Quaestio* is "Utrum Astrologi vel Quicumque Calculatores possint probare secundum Adventum Christi" in Pelster, "Die Quaestio Heinrichs von Harclay."

28. The Joachite booklet appears to have been originally made independently, but at about the same date. Although some of the initial treatises in the volume were not apparently bound with it when Bale saw it (see Little, *Fratris Thomae*, xvii), this does not mean that the final (that is, the Franciscan Joachite-oriented) booklet was not, although we cannot be certain. For the evidence about the chain and staple holes on 55v, see Ker, "Chaining from a Staple," 104–7; for the possibility that the manuscript initially (in the early fourteenth century) belonged to the Oxford Franciscan convent, see Parkes, "Books and Aids," 59 and fig. 38. For a fuller discussion of the booklets, see Kerby-Fulton, "English Joachimism," and footnotes to its entry in the List.

29. Nicholas Hereford gave the Ascension Day sermon in 1382 that called for disendowment and is quite possibly author of the *Opus arduum* (see ch. 5 below). On Bale's having seen the manuscript, see Parkes, "Books and Aids," 59.

30. Wyclif, *De Apostasia*, 19. My dating for all these Wycliffite writings follows Thompson's, *Latin Writings of Wyclyf*.

31. "Cum secundum sanctos spectat ad officium doctoris evangelici prophetare et socii mei prophetant ex dictis Merlini, Hildegardis et vatum similium extra fidem scripture de statibus membrorum ecclesie militantis, motus sum eciam sed fideliori evidencia prophetare." This is the opening sentence of *De vaticinia*, 165.

32. "Sed admissa prophecia predicte femine ut verbo Domini, patet quod non probat, cum verba illius prophetisse sunt *generaliter contra clerum* refrigescentem cupidine temporalium et honoris mundani" (ibid., 169, my emphasis). Wyclif is here likely referring to the Cologne letter which his contemporary, the Digby 32 annotator, in fact a friar, glossed in the same way, fol. 55v.

33. Wyclif, *Trialogus*, 338.

34. As, for instance, in Dublin, Trinity College 517, fol. 140v: "Incipit prophecia uel reuelacio beate Hildegaris [sic]. ffloruit beata Hildegaris, cuius est prophecia infrascripta ante incepcionem ordinum mendicancium. . . ." For a longer version, which tries (without success) to give accurate dates for Hildegard and for the inception of the Friars Preachers, see Little and Easterling's transcription, "Insurgent," 60.

35. Wyclif wrote the *Trialogus* in 1383 in a fit of fury at what Aston calls the "miserable volte-face" of the friars in the wake of the Earthquake Council's condemnation of his views. See Aston, "Caim's Castles," 46–81. Steven Justice has suggested to me that, alternatively, Wyclif may have actually enjoyed the new publicity.

36. "Propheta autem Hildegardis prophetavit de ipsis egregie atque plane. Sed quia habere possent colorem negare, dicta sua esse authentica sive fidem . . ." (Wyclif, *De fundatione sectarum*, 67).

37. Hudson, *Premature Reformation*, 66 and note; on Pateshull's riot, and Bale's list of his writings, see Szittya, "Sedens," 33.

38. Discussed in Case Study 2 above.

39. Justice, "Lollardy," 662–89.

40. *Epistolarium* 2, Letter 149R, p. 336: "Et in hoc facto obsequium Deo se exhibuisse uolunt, quia Ecclesiam per uos pollutam esse dicunt."

41. Heavily noticed, for instance, by the mid-century annotator of Bodleian Library, Digby 32 (Hand 2), and by Kirkestede in Cambridge, Corpus Christi College, 404; separate extracts of it appear in Bodleian Library, Digby 98 and Hatton 56.

42. *Liber divinorum operum*, c. xvi, p. 435 (*PL* 197, cols. 1018D–1019A): "Sed cum tandem persenserint quod nec potestate ligandi nec soluendi, nec confirmatione oblationum suarum, nec strepitu armorum, nec blandiciis nec minis ipsis resistere poterunt, diuino iudicio territi inanem superbamque fiduciam, quam prius in semetipsis semper habuerant, deponentes et in se redeuntes coram illis humiliabuntur; at que ululando clamabunt et dicent: Quia omnipotentem Deum in ordine officii nostri abiecimus, idcirco super nos confusio hec inducta est; uidelicet ut ab illis obprimamur et humiliemur, quos obprimere et humiliare debueramus." For discussion, see my *Reformist Apocalypticism*, 38–39.

43. I am grateful to Steven Justice for alerting me to this passage, which is cited here from MS Douce 53, fol. 9v, perhaps pointed for oral delivery. Taylor is translating and paraphrasing the *Pentachronon* extract from *Liber divinorum operum* (which Pitra cites from *PL* 197, col. 1018 ff.). For the edition, see Hudson, *Two Wycliffite Texts*, lines 221 and 244.

44. On Catherine of Siena, see Despres, "Ecstatic Reading"; on Alphonse, see Voaden, "Middle English *Epistola solitarii*," 142–79; the facing Latin edition by Voaden and Jönsson, "Recommended Reading"; and ch. 8 below for detailed citation from the *Epistola*.

45. The statute accuses the Lollards in particular of fomenting the overthrow of the lords temporal and spiritual, and speaks of those who "purposantz de moever les cuers des bones Cristians encountre la suis dite Esglise & les Prelatz & Ministres d'icelle, si b[ie]n en Sermones publikes, come en Conventicles, & lieux secretes appellez Escoles, erronousement & mauveisement ont excitez & moevez publiquement le poeple de v[ost]re Roiaume pur oustier & tollir des ditz Prelatz & Ministres de seinte Esglises lour ditz Possessions temporelx" (*Rotuli Parliamentorum*, 3.583). Prophecies are condemned a few lines later (quoted in n. 63 below).

46. Emden, *Biographical Register*, 2.1430. Partriche was accused in 1432 by Peter Payne of having once converted Payne to Wycliffism, but of having dropped his Lollardy when he was promoted to a prebend. On Payne's role in furthering the tolerance for Wycliffite notions at Oxford, up to about 1413, see Hudson, *Premature Reformation*, 99–103.

47. See Case Study 2 above, especially n. 32.

48. St. John's 27, p. 228 (the manuscript is paginated, not foliated): "Nota dignitas apostolica minuetur et diuidetur." On Gloucester (Thomas Woodstock), see Hudson, *Premature Reformation*, 12; Catto, "Religion and the English Nobility," 45.

49. Netter, *Fasciculi Zizaniorum*, 279, Conclusion ix: "Item quod post urbanum sextum non est aliquis recipiendus in Papam, sed vivendum est, more Graecorum, sub legibus propriis." Discussed in detail in ch. 1.

50. "Sed postquam imperiale sceptrum hoc modo divisum fuerit, nec reparari poterit, tunc etiam infula apostolici honoris dividetur. Quia enim nec principes nec reliqui homines tam spiritalis quam saecularis ordinis in apostolico nomine ullam religionem tunc invenient, dignitatem nominis illius imminuent. Alios quoque magistros et archiepiscopos sub alio

nomine in diversis regionibus sibi praeferent, ita ut etiam apostolicus eo tempore dilatatione honoris pristinae dignitatis attenuatus, Romam et pauca illi adjacentia loca vix etiam tunc sub infula sua obtineat. Haec autem ex parte per bellorum incursionem evenient, ex parte quoque per commune consilium et consensum et spiritalium et saecularium popularum perficientur."

51. For a list of these, see the library inventory done after his death, printed along with the inventory of the books from Pleshy College, in Cavanaugh, "Study of Books Privately Owned," 844–51. Scattergood notes that of his own books, forty-eight were certainly in French, twenty-five in Latin, and only three in English, including his splendid Wycliffite Bible, now British Library, Egerton 617 and 618. See Scattergood, "Literary Culture," 34–35. At least nine of the twenty-five Latin texts deal with church history or jurisdictional matters. Cambridge, St. John's College, MS 27 itself is a copy of Bede's *Ecclesiastical History*, to which the Hildegard was added.

52. *Dictionary of National Biography*, 636, summarizing the various chronicle accounts.

53. De Hamel, *The Book*, "English Wycliffite Bibles;" and Hanna, "English Biblical Texts," 141–55.

54. On the "Lollard knights," see ch. 5 below.

55. The dialogue between a friar and a secular clerk appears in a Wycliffite miscellany, Dublin, Trinity College 244, fols. 212v–219; on Woodstock, see Hudson, *Premature Reformation*, 12. I would like to thank Steven Justice for advice about Woodstock's politics, and Jenny Stratford for advice about his manuscripts. She tells me that, unfortunately, no known instance of his own handwriting has survived. I would also like to thank Lynn Staley for sharing her article on Woodstock with me, which points out his daughter's association with the Minoresses; see "Pearl and the Contingencies," 83–114.

56. Cited in Staley, "Pearl and the Contingencies," 90.

57. Pecock, *Repressor*, 2. 483–84.

58. See the recent discussion of these passages in Ghosh, "Bishop Reginald Pecock," 259. These quotations come from Pecock, *Repressor*, 2.320 and 1.86 respectively. See also Bose's recent "Reginald Pecock's Vernacular Voice," 217–36.

59. For the quotation from Ghosh, "Bishop Reginald Pecock," 259–60. For Paul Strohm, see his *Politique*, 155. Strohm is particularly looking at Pecock's *Donet*.

60. Discussed in Scase, *Reginald Pecock*, 33.

61. *Dictionary of National Biography*, 44, 201a; Hudson, *Premature Reformation*, 442–43. The revelatory theology of the descent in Nicodemus is discussed in ch. 10 below.

62. In ch. 24 of *The Chastising* the author tells an apocryphal anecdote of how Hildegard had her Latin intercessions answered, even though she knew no Latin; see *Chastising*, 72; this undermining of her Latinity is disturbing for a number of reasons. On the difficulty of establishing a later female audience for Hildegard, see my "Hildegard and the Male Reader."

63. *Rotuli Parliamentorum*, 3.583–84. See Chronology, 1402 for details. In 1406 the legislation more overtly addresses the concern that prophecies are being used in both pro-disendowment and pro-Richardian messages, presented to the public "par faux seurementz & signes." It continues, "Et ascuns escrivantz, lisauntz, & publiantz au poeple *diverses fauxes pretenses Prophecies*, & ent monstrantz *ceduls & livers* a mesme le poeple: Et ascuns ycelles pretenses faux Prophecies reportanz, a ycelles autres mensounges adjousteantz fauxement, les diont, & mauveisement les publient auxi entre le poeple, en vraisemblable commocion," etc. (583, my emphasis). For recent discussion of political prophecy, see Strohm, *England's Empty Throne*, and Coote, *Prophecy and Public Affairs*.

64. See the discussion of the "Last Age of the Church" above in ch. 2 for a Joachite text in the vernacular in the 1350s. Langland, Gower, the *Crede* author, Wimbledon, and anonymous vernacular Wycliffite writers were alluding to Hildegardiana, whether genuine or spurious, all well before 1400.

65. See ch. 2 above, especially on Whethamstede, and the discussions of MS Balliol 149 below in ch. 10, and see Kerby-Fulton, "English Joachimism," especially on the Gonville and Caius 230.

66. Emden, *Biographical Register,* 1.196, and see my "Prophecy and Suspicion" and "Hildegard and the Male Reader," 17–18, on Digby 32.

67. For day to day visionary experiences in monastic life, see Holdsworth, "Visions and Visionaries," 141–53, and his "Christina of Markyate," 185–204.

68. I am grateful to E. Randolph Daniel for kindly sharing with me his edition in progress of Henry's treatise on Antichrist from Cambridge, Corpus Christi College MS 404.

69. See Galbraith, "Articles Laid," 579–82. Galbraith suggests that the "preservation [of the disendowment articles] in a Bury cartulary is doubtless due to the abbot of St. Edmund's . . . John of Brinkeley, who was present at the parliament of 1371 . . . [and who] doubtless returned from London with a copy . . . with a view to writing a reply in his official capacity of president of the provincial chapter of the English Benedictines" (580). No such reply survives, however, and so John of Brinkeley's presence at the parliament seems to explain how the document was obtained, but not why it was preserved. Galbraith was not aware of Kirkestede's disendowment prophecy-collecting habits nor of the survival of the Hereford sermon. See above, "A Word about Intellectual Freedom."

70. Lerner is correct (*Powers of Prophecy,* 92 n. 22) in noting that only the first quire of the *Pentachronon* is in Kirkestede's hand, but it should also be noted that the entire text is annotated throughout in his own hand.

71. For instance, beside her "corona mea scismate" prophecy, Henry writes in the margin "temporalia destituunt"; beside the Justicia prophecy, he writes "de laicis contra clericos."

72. C.V.168–79.

73. Cited from "Epilogus ad vitam S. Ruperti," ed. Pitra, *Analecta Sanctae Hildegardis,* 363. For discussion, see Kerby-Fulton, "A Return to 'First Dawn'," 383–407.

74. See the discussion of the MS Cotton Cleopatra poems in Case Study 2 above.

75. On Trithemius generally, see Braun, *Abbot Trithemius.*

Notes to Chapter 5

1. For the quotations in this paragraph, see Hudson, "Langland and Lollardy?" 100–1 and 98.

2. I know of very little evidence suggesting ostensible respect for *contemporary* revelation in the vernacular Wycliffite texts, but there is a hint of it in "Twelve Conclusions of the Lollards," arising in the tenth conclusion on the death penalty ("manslaute") which should not be carried out, the author(s) say, for "temperal cause or spirituel *withouten special reuelaciun*" (Hudson, *Selections,* 28, lines 135–37). Medieval sources record that the text of the "Twelve Conclusions" was affixed to the doors of Westminster Hall during the 1395 Parliament, so it is also relatively early. Its date, its intended audience (populist), and fear of

impending death penalty legislation for heresy may all account for the relatively unusual appeal to revelation.

3. The concept arises in the Book of Wisdom (Liber Sapientiae) 7:22.

4. Lerner, "Ecstatic Dissent," 33–57.

5. Also called Robert of Liège; on Rupert's life, see Van Engen, *Rupert of Deutz*; for brief discussions of Rupert's defensiveness in relation to his writing, see Lerner, "Ecstatic Dissent," and Kerby-Fulton, "Langland and the Bibliographic Ego."

6. Cited in Lerner, "Ecstatic Dissent," 36, from Rupert's *Commentarium in Apocalypsim, PL* 169, col. 827

7. For the record of his deathbed revelation that he had gained all his knowledge by "divine infusion," see Burr, *Persecution*, 5 n. 1, and 73, and see also Lerner, "Ecstatic Dissent," 53–54, and ch. 3 above.

8. De Paris, "Une lettre inédite de Olivi," 416–17; discussed in Lerner, "Ecstatic Dissent," 53 n. 72.

9. On Olivi and the *Opus* author, see Bostick, *Antichrist*, 80, 82, 83, 84 n. 41, 103–4.

10. For these debates and responses, see Somerset, "Eciam Mulier," and Kerby-Fulton, "Eciam Lollardi"; Blamires and Marx, "Woman Not to Preach," 34–49, and see below, ch. 8.

11. See also Hudson, "*Laicus litteratus,*" 222–36.

12. For Brut, see Chronology, 1391–93 and note; *Registrum Johannis Trefnant*, 285.

13. See Chronology, 1387 for Hereford.

14. Hudson, *Lollards and Their Books*, 43–66.

15. Nissé, "Prophetic Nations," 107 ff.

16. *Registrum Johannis Trefnant*, 296–97. For Wyclif's views, see his *De Potestate Pape*, 118, and Bostick, *Antichrist*, 61.

17. See my "When Women Preached."

18. Women visionaries were able to deal in various types of subversive thought because the claim to divine inspiration when handled with *discretio* could bypass the church authorities and traditions. On this subject, see the chapters on Kempe, Porete, and Julian below.

19. On Rupescissa, see Chronology, 1344 and esp. 1349, and accompanying note for editions and background.

20. Quoted and detailed by Bignami-Odier, in the first chapter of her *Etudes*.

21. For the complete history of his arrests, see his *Liber secretorum eventuum*, 29. For the long history of Guillaume Court's work as an inquisitor, see 31–32.

22. On these suppressions and the title, see ibid, 32.

23. See the superb article by Nissé, "Prophetic Nations."

24. See Hudson's comment, "Unlike some of the early Wycliffite texts, it is not apologetic or justificatory," in *Lollards and Their Books*, 61, see also 51–52.

25. This sort of audience seems likely given, for instance, the kind of effort the text expends on the Despenser crusade, as Hudson points out. She also helpfully notes, "The nearest analogy to the *Opus Arduum* is the vernacular standard Lollard sermon-cycle" (ibid., 62).

26. The Franciscan authorities in England, as elsewhere, were expected to police their own order with respect to radical Joachite or Spiritual tendencies. See, for example, Chronology, 1329–30, and the accompanying note, especially referring to Douie's studies of the attitudes of English Franciscans to John XXII; see also the discussion above of Henry of Costesy in ch. 2.

27. See also British Library, Cotton Vespasian E.VII, fol. 122r.

28. See Galbraith, "Thomas Walsingham," 12–28. Galbraith's view has been widely accepted, but see James Clark, "Thomas Walsingham Reconsidered," 833.

29. In Royal 13. E.IX the rubric opens "Erat quidam de ordine minorum qui se asserebat dicere mirabilia quem papa Innocentius incarcerauit postea . . ." (fol. 94vb).

30. E. Brown, who prints the letter on 404–6 of his London 1690 *Appendix ad Fasciculum,* reads "tamen," as does the version from *Prima vita Innocentii VI* printed in *Liber secretorum eventuum,* 40 n. 59. I have chosen to cite the letter from British Library, Royal 13. E.IX, fols. 94v–95r, because the text is of English provenance and has been interestingly adapted. For full bibliography in relation to Rupescissa, see the note accompanying Chronology, 1349.

31. An interesting change; E. Brown, *Appendix ad Fasciculum,* 404, reads "prophetarum," which is more common in Continental manuscripts.

32. Ibid., reads "domine."

33. Transcribed by Bostick, *Antichrist,* 50 n. 6; my own translation.

34. Cited here from *Liber secretorum eventuum,* 40 n. 59, from the edition by Baluze-Mollat, 1.318. Note that the Royal MS quoted above reads "scripturarum."

35. *Liber secretorum eventuum,* 38–39. Ironically, if Rupescissa had been female—and could have been cleared of charges of Olivian Beguinism, I should add—a claim to prophecy might have flown: the same century canonized Bridget of Sweden, Catherine of Siena, and others, who had made overt claims to prophecy. On this problem, see ch. 8.

36. *De Genesi,* c. 12 (*PL* 34, 472–78).

37. See Rita Copeland's helpful categorization in *Pedagogy,* 142–43, of prison writers like Charles d'Orleans or Malory whose works were unrelated to their imprisonment.

38. See *Eulogium,* 3.391, one of a surprising number of incidents relating to friars and treason; see also 3.407, on friars of four orders in the army of Scrope.

39. The Bridlington prophecy, in fact. The friars are described as: "quidam eorum, juvenes et senes, fuerunt parum literati. . . ." The king's comments are recorded as: "Et dixit Rex magistro: 'Isti sunt fatui et idiotae, nec legere sciunt nec intelligunt. Tu deberes sapiens esse, dicis tu quod Rex Ricardus vivit?' Magister respondit: 'Non dico quod vivit, sed dico si vivit ipse est verus Rex Angliae'" (ibid.). From here the dialogue continues with the master showing that he has a good knowledge of the deposition issues. For other discussion of prophecies in relation to the deposition issue, see Strohm, *England's Empty Throne.* On the Bridlington prophecies, see also Rigg, "Bridlington's Prophecy."

40. "Magister confessus est se exposuisse prophetiam quae dicitur ejusdam canonici de Bridlington, juxta imaginationem suam" (*Eulogium,* 3.391).

41. For a study of the medieval concept of "ingenium," see Blamires, "Women and Creative Intelligence."

42. *Liber secretorum eventuum,* 39.

43. "Nisi ea occasione qua se putabaunt michi excludere viam, scilicet me incarcerando, ne unquam agerem aliquid contra eos. Sic quoque putabunt fratres Joseph . . . vendentes eum in Egyptum, quod tamen ad idem obtinendum . . . maximam sibi prebuerat occasionem. Adversarii fidei, ne Paulus evangelisaret, ipsum incarcerabant. Per hoc tamen maiorem occasionem habuit et opportunitatem, universalem ecclesiam per epistolas suas totas evangelicas instruendi. Verum est ergo quod sapiens dicebat: 'quia non est prudentia, non est consilium contra Dominum.' Scripturus eciam erat Iohannes, id est, predicaturus aliis que audierat. Et sic tenetur omnis predicator fidelis in isto tempore Antichristi ex imitatione sua"

(fol. 165r–165v). (The passage is also interesting in that it shows that he equates writing with preaching.) All references to the *Opus arduum* are from Brno, University Library MS Mk 28, in this case cited from Bostick's transcription, *Antichrist*, 108–9 n. 112, but repointed in one instance (I would like to thank Steven Justice for his advice about this and its allusion to Prov. 21:30); transcriptions not marked as from Bostick or Hudson are my own; unattributed translations are my own. Curtis Bostick also generously sent me his chapter on the *Opus* prior to the publication of his book and, in a private communication at that time, confirmed my sense that there is good evidence for Olivian influence in the text. I have added some further evidence of my own (see below). This chapter is also indebted to Hudson, *Lollards and Their Books*, 43–66, and her encouragement.

44. Boethius, of course, is the author of the famous and ubiquitous *Consolation of Philosophy*; Perpetua is known to us only through her prison writings before she was executed in pre-Christian Rome and through a posthumous account of her martyrdom, see Musurillo, "Passio Sanctarum Perpetuae."

45. See Talbot, *Life of Christina of Markyate*, esp. chs. 24–25.

46. See the final two chapters of this book. For Usk, see Strohm, *Hochon's Arrow*, 145–60. The "Appeal" was written under house arrest, but *Testament of Love* only pretends to prison conditions. For *Mum*, see Simpson, "Constraints on Satire."

47. See also the excellent discussion in Copeland, *Pedagogy*, 143, concerning the tendency for Pauline models to appeal to dissident prison writers and Boethian models to non-dissidents.

48. "Romaunt," *Riverside Chaucer*, 6773–6774, discussed in ch. 3 above.

49. The passage is quoted above and in n. 43; for further discussion, see Hudson, *Lollards and Their Books*, 44.

50. He cites authors and titles of a large range of books, more rarely a precise location. See ibid., 48.

51. For Hereford, see Chronology, 1385 and 1387, and notes.

52. One does not know whether it is anachronistic to invoke twentieth-century parallels, but the pages of Amnesty newsletters are full of just such contradictions, that is, of jailers now brutal, now kind; now contemptuous of letters to or from the prisoner, now reverential and afraid to destroy them.

53. See ch. 2, and Kerby-Fulton, "English Joachimism." For Oxford holdings of Olivi, see Douie, "Olivi's Postilla," and the discussion above in ch. 3.

54. The passage is quoted in ch. 1 above, and in Appendix B. Hereford's associations with Oxford are well known, and he is also known to have gone on a preaching mission to Winchester, not far from Salisbury, where at the time the *Opus* was being written Bishop Waltham, one of England's foremost book collectors and scholars of international church law, resided. See the discussion of Waltham in relation to Ramsbury in ch. 7 below.

55. As we saw in the Introduction, in the absence of a physical "office" of inquisition in the Middle Ages, the fraternal convents were most often the locations of inquisitional proceedings and holding places for suspects. More specifically, Conventual Franciscan houses had prisons in which Spirituals were held for interrogation, sometimes in appalling conditions. (See ch. 1.)

56. On Brut's affidavits, see Minnis, "Respondet Walterus Bryth," and Hudson, "*Laicus litteratus.*"

57. Reformation Protestantism once again availed itself of Joachite ideas. See Reeves, "History and Eschatology," 99–123.

58. Henry of Costesy is discussed in ch. 2 above.

59. *Liber secretorum eventuum*, esp. 40, and note Lerner's helpful list of the inquisitorial manuals (Jacque Fournier's and Nicolas Eymeric's) available to Guillaume Court for examining Rupescissa. Eymeric's *Directorium* made reverence for Olivi's writings, especially his *Postilla super Apocalypsim* and other condemned works, a recognizable characteristic of Beguin and radical Franciscan heresy.

60. See Introduction for the quotation.

61. See Appendix B.

62. Bostick, *Antichrist*, 80 and 84–85, esp. nn. 41–42, for convincing examples.

63. Transcribed in ibid.

64. The author writes "Secundum quod autem hec bestia refertur ad Antichristum potuerunt dicere qui erunt post eius destruccionem, 'bestia hec fuit sed non est'" (fol. 193vb, ibid., 87 n. 49).

65. Hudson writes, "even if one may suspect the *Opus Arduum* is indebted to the Joachite tradition of Apocalypse commentary, its author is apparently unaware of his inheritance." But his habit of hiding controversial Olivian-style interpretations under *false* references to the *Glossa ordinaria* ("secundum sententiam sanctorum et Glosse Ordinarie") is most revealing of a conscious agenda, especially his account of what he calls the sixth *status* (discussing Rev. 6:12, the opening of the sixth seal, fol. 155v), which he insists is the present time, the time of Antichrist's arrival (quod semper in sexto signo . . . exprimatur status Antichristi) (see Bostick, *Antichrist*, 84 n. 41 for full transcription of the passage). The author also heavily historicizes his interpretations in Joachite style, but the fact that he says nothing of Francis of Assisi (as Bostick mentions) matters little in assessing Olivian or Joachite Franciscan intertextuality in a Wycliffite context: first, even Olivi himself often makes the controversial references to Francis or Franciscans oblique as we saw in Olivi's Matthew *Postilla* in ch. 2, allusions presumably written mainly for alert and above all *friendly* readers. And Wycliffites had by this time adopted a largely antimendicant stance, so *overt* praise of Franciscanism would have been largely out of place. In addition to paralleling Olivi in assigning each seal to a different *status* of the church (Bostick lists these at length from Warren Lewis's unpublished Ph.D. dissertation, 83 n. 37), he also closely parallels Olivian and Joachite methods of concordance in, for instance, his interpretation of Rev. 6:2 (Bostick, *Antichrist*, 84 n. 38). In addition to the other parallels with Olivi and pseudo-Joachite texts discussed in the present chapter, one could note the *Opus* author's interpretation of Rev. 6:12, the darkening of sun ("Si autem sol hic accipiatur pro [papa] Romano, sicut eciam hic innuit Glossa, qui ceteris eminet prelatis, sicut sol planetis . . ."), which he attributes (falsely) to the *Glossa* (Bostick, *Antichrist*, 85 n. 42), but which, I would add, parallels the interpretation in the pseudo-Joachite *De oneribus*, especially the "Onus Babilonis." This text is often excerpted in English manuscripts, which similarly interpret the darkening as the demise of prelates (see Holder-Egger, "Italienische Prophetien" [1908], 172–73).

66. Discussed in Somerset, *Clerical Discourse*, 62–92.

67. Cited in ibid., 85.

68. *Super Hieremiam*, *Super Esaiam*, and *De oneribus*, the latter two widely copied in England, frequently call for the confiscation of church wealth by reworking of the gospel

scene in which the naked Peter prepares himself to plunge into the water and follow Christ (John 21:7). See *Super Esaiam,* fol. 58v, and *De oneribus,* ed. Holder-Egger, 158.

69. See Hudson, *Lollards and Their Books,* 125–40, for examples of such lists.

70. At the opening of the second affidavit, Brut says only that Trefnant had found his previous affidavit too short and too obscure (*Registrum Johannis Trefnant,* 289). See also the recent treatment in Minnis, "Respondet Walterus Bryth," 231 n. 9 for the possibility of the five *cedulae,* which Minnis divides as 285–89, 289–336, 336–50, 350–57, and 357–58.

71. This is the date quoted in *Super Hieremiam,* from which it was known to Wimbledon (see Chronology, 1388); it is also the date quoted in the ubiquitous Joachite Antichrist jingle, "Cum fuerint," which appears once even in a Wycliffite manuscript as we saw in ch. 2.

72. Brut's use of this is discussed in E. B. Elliott, *Horae Apocalypticae,* 400–3.

73. See Kerby-Fulton, "Eciam Lollardi."

74. For the bulls, see Fredericq, *Corpus,* 2.153–57 and ch. 6 below.

75. See Kaminsky, "The Free Spirit in the Hussite Revolution," 166–86, and for a more political reading, Šmahel, *Die Hussitische Revolution,* 1.690–716.

76. The case of Helmyslay in 1380 and the confiscations of 1389 show official awareness prior to Brut. See also Hudson's note to the "Twelve Conclusions" (1395) in *Selections,* lines 154–62 of Text 3. At least by 1421–27 Netter would present Henry V with his major work on Lollards and Hussites (see Chronology). We have already seen Netter's concern about Olivi in the *Doctrinale.*

77. See Appendix C on general usage and the next note for Usk's wording in which the gender is ambiguous. See also my "Eciam Lollardi."

78. For Adam's apocalyptic sense of Old and New Testament concordances and the ceasing of the "three miracles" of priesthood on account of corruption, see A. Usk, *Chronicle,* for 1402, "Quare sicut ueteris testamenti uenalitate sacerdocium corrumpente tria cessarunt miracula" (160). He later returned to the same theme in a letter to William Swan, "utriusque et templi sequitur confusio in nouo testamento inter Romam et Constanciam ac in sacerdocio subsequens scisma Lollardensibus atque Begwinis operantibus" (lxxvii).

79. See the discussion in the Introduction above, "Non-Wycliffite Heresy in Late Medieval England."

80. For the *Clementines,* see Chronology, 1311–12 note; see also Arnold, "Lollard Trials."

81. See in the Introduction above, the section "A Word about Visionary Genres" on discretion of spirits.

82. In addition to the chapters on Kempe and Julian below, see Kerby-Fulton, "Who Has Written?" 101–16.

83. For Richard, see Sandquist, "Holy Oil," and Strohm, *England's Empty Throne,* 13–15; for Urban, see Colledge, "*Epistola solitarii.*" For Despenser, see Coote, "Crusading Bishop," 45 n. 21 and 47 for prophecies with Joachite affinities.

84. See ch. 8 below, and my "Eciam Lollardi."

85. Foxe's translation, *Acts and Monuments,* 3.141, with my insertions from the Latin.

86. See Somerset, "Eciam Mulier," along with my "Eciam Lollardi."

87. Compare with the discussion of Uthred's condemnation in ch. 10 below. Oddly, the scribe of *The Book of Margery Kempe* opens Book II with a vague reference to a similar concern.

88. Article 15 of the condemnation of Walter Brut; compare Article 8 in the condemnation of Uthred; Knowles, "Censured Opinions," and ch. 10 below.

89. For Uthred's condemnation, see Chronology, 1368.

90. According to Hudson, *Premature Reformation*, 291–92, some of the "more radical" disputed the need for infant baptism, but on the very different grounds that the parents' faith should suffice or on the grounds that baptism might have no effect if the priest or godparents were in mortal sin. These are very different theological positions from Brut's or from Uthred's.

91. In addition to those cited below, see again Copeland, *Pedagogy*, and Somerset, *Clerical Discourse*.

92. Hudson, *Lollards and Their Books*, 61. Hudson does not translate the passage, but "calibeos" (chalybeus) can mean "steel" or "ordeal iron"; a "chalybarium" is a smithy.

93. Bostick, *Antichrist*, 50, no. 6.

94. On Calvin, see S. Jones, *Calvin and Rhetoric*, and her "Calvin's Commentary," 29.

95. Gramsci, *Prison Notebooks*, 1.9–11. The phrase "für ewig" appears three times in a letter of March 19, 1927, in which he writes: "I am haunted by this idea (a common phenomenon among prisoners, I believe): one must produce something 'für ewig' in the sense of a complex notion of Goethe's which I recall, greatly tormented the Italian [poet] Pascoli. In short, I should like, by way of a pre-established plan, to occupy myself intensely and systematically with some subject that would absorb me and provide a center for my inner life" (9). See also Copeland, *Pedagogy*, 159–60, for analysis of the prison as a site of intellectual production.

96. Rankin, "Reading Arundel's Reading." I cite Thorpe's text from Hudson, *Two Wycliffite Texts*, by page number. Most of the extant medieval copies of Thorpe's text are Latin and Continental, though the English version had sixteenth-century currency.

97. "Quamvis antichristi tortores nituntur claudere ora ewangelicorum eos incarcerando, tunc dant eis maximam opportunitatem studendi et scribendi contra eum, cuius oppositum credunt ipsi" (fol. 141), transcribed by Hudson, *Lollards and Their Books*, 44.

98. Ibid.

99. See Chronology, 1381, 1385, and 1387 on Cardinal Adam Easton, whose imprisonment caused his dramatic new adherence to the visionary Bridget of Sweden.

100. The *Opus* author sees the continuing of "divisionis papam Romanum et papam Avinionenem" as strong evidence of the arrival of Antichrist. "Causa iam impellens cardinales ad sic faciendum precipua est timor quia quicumque unius partis vel alterius se parti adverse submisserunt carceribus perpetuis mancipantur" (transcribed Bostick, *Antichrist*, 85 n. 41, from fol. 155va–b, from a long passage on cardinals, the Schism, and the plight of the church in the time of Antichrist).

101. He tells us, in the remarkable confessional passage that we will examine below, that he writes "ad reformacionem universalis ecclesie" (transcribed Bostick, *Antichrist*, 50 n. 6, from fol. 127ra). His claim to be *campiductor* occurs in the same passage: "Quia ergo ego non optimum me sencio, sed maximum peccatorum, temeritatis videtur esse, ut in hoc fine seculi pessimo campiductor fiam precipuus contra Anticristum. Sed quia nichil in sequentibus dicturus sum contra Anticristum et familiam suam, pro quo mori, si oportuerit, non ero paratus, confido in bonitate Dei mei, quod quidquid scorie remanserit, exuret et consumet tanquam voluntarium holocaustum mei ipsius in odorem suavitatis spiritualis."

102. Hudson, *Premature Reformation*, 349, and see esp. n. 193, in which she points out that even early sermons by Wyclif indicate that the friars' failings are virtually impossible to correct.

103. For Hereford's life, see Emden, *Biographical Register*, 2.914–15.

104. On the complex question of fictional versus experienced vision, see "A Word on Visionary Genres" in the Introduction above.

105. Transcribed Bostick, *Antichrist*, 50 n. 6.

106. For example, "J'ignore quant à moi si ma passion est suffisamment accomplie parce que j'ai souffert en ce lieu, ou si je vais encore être conduit, à l'instigation des disciples hérétiques de Mamon, au lieu de ma passion, ou si je serai sacrifié dans le feu pour la pauvreté évangélique, livré en opprobre et en dérision aux réprouvés ou si j'eschapperai à ce sort, si je dois me voir trancher la tête, ou si, après tant d'épreuves, je terminerai me jours en pais sans effusion de sang" (Bignami-Odier, *Etudes*, 23, transcribed and translated from fol. 85v of *Liber ostensor*, Rome, Biblioteca Vaticana Rossiano, no. 753). See Cambridge, Corpus Christi College, MS 138, fol. 183, for an extract from this text in an English manuscript. For other examples of Rupescissa's disarming self-confessional style, see the extracts from the *Vade mecum*, esp. 496 and 497 (where he compares himself to the grudging Jonah after Ninevah was saved!), in Kerby-Fulton, *Reformist Apocalypticism*.

107. Forde, "Nicholas Hereford's Ascension Day Sermon," lines 41–42, discussed 223.

108. The article was the sixth, concerning God obeying the devil (which Hereford insisted God might do not out of necessity, but out of love), whereupon "ad hoc probandum se obtulit sponte sua magister Nicolaus sub poena incendii," quoted in ibid., from *Fasciculi Zizaniorum*, 328. See ch. 10 for the possibility that this was listed as an Ockhamist heterodoxy.

109. See Chronology, 1385 and note.

110. To contextualize these confiscations in relation to other documented book confiscations of Wycliffite writings, see Bostick, *Antichrist*, 98, and Hudson, *Lollards and Their Books*, 53, who mentions especially the case of William Smith and others recorded in Courtney's register (1381–96).

111. It was the Carmelites who made the charge; see Forde, "Nicholas Hereford's Ascension Day Sermon," 223.

112. In additon to Chronology, 1385 and 1387 and notes, see ch. 9 below and Hudson, *Two Wycliffite Texts*, 109–10, note to lines 499–501.

113. For this evidence and the sources, see Emden, *Biographical Register*, 2.914–15, and Hudson, *Two Wycliffite Texts*, 109–10, note to 409–501

114. Hudson, *Lollards and Their Books*, 59, which discusses the inconsistencies in reports.

115. On the *Speculum devotorum*, see Chronology, c. 1415–25 and accompanying note, especially on the author's attitudes toward Bonaventure and Nicholas Love. The author tells his "gostly syster" that "the grounde of the boke folowynge ys the gospel and the doctorys," especially Peter Comester (d. 1179) and Nicholas of Lyra (whose commentaries were written c. 1322–30). He has a very Franciscan sensibility. The author cites Bridget of Sweden in several chapters, Catherine of Siena especially on the Annunciation (ch. 3), and Mechthild of Hackeborn on the Resurrection (ch. 29). The women are clearly used as authorities on the life of Christ who supplement the Gospel accounts. At the time of writing only Bridget had been formally canonized, but formal canonization is not crucial in the Middle Ages for anyone revered to be called a saint (see below Case Study 3 in relation to Scrope). All three women were careful to write in accordance with accepted doctrine of *discretio spirituum*. The *Speculum* seems to regard Elizabeth of Töss as one of the "approved" women; see Gillespie, "Haunted Text," 158–60. Reference to Elizabeth occurs only in chap-

ter 33, which is on the Pentecost and on St. John, both revelatory topics. Elizabeth wrote down the lives of the nuns of Töss in collaboration with Henry Suso, many of which involve visions, thirty-three in total, the same number as there are chapters in the *Speculum*. See Van Engen, "Sisterbooks."

116. Modern readers might more expect to find a position like Walter Hilton's, who distrusts visions, devotional imaginings, and bodily manifestations of spiritual experiences like Rolle's "fire of love." This is not, however, the position we find most in Carthusian materials and marginalia. On Hilton's attitudes, see N. Watson, "Et que est huius ydoli materia?" 95–111. On Carthusian sensibilities, see Parsons, "Red-Ink Annotator."

117. For a recent account of the scholarship and some of the general consensus in this paragraph, see Hanna, "Langland's Imaginatif," 81–94.

118. Wogan-Browne et al., *Idea of the Vernacular*, no. 1.12, lines 73–80.

119. See the fine essay by Hudson, "Langland and Lollardy?"

120. Kerby-Fulton, "Who Has Written?"

121. For a thoughtful new discussion of this problem, reviewing the past scholarship, see Cole, "William Langland," 37–58. I agree wholeheartedly with Cole in his challenge to the current consensus regarding Langland's supposed conservatism in the final version. My reading of Langland's treatment of fraternal culture in relation to Wycliffism is, however, more complex, as the last chapter of this book in particular shows.

122. Kerby-Fulton, "Langland and the Bibliographic Ego."

123. See Langland, *Piers Plowman: C-Text*, Pearsall's note to C.IX.136.

124. For a list of passages, see ibid., Pearsall's note to C. Prol.35.

125. I owe this term to Derek Pearsall.

Notes to Case Study 3

1. The term *constitutiones*, as defined in Latham's *Dictionary of Medieval Latin*, and elsewhere, refers to regulations brought into force by the papacy or episcopate, as are those in Arundel's 1406 *cedula* discussed below.

2. The stanzas are noticed in Rigg, *History of Anglo-Latin Literature*, 294.

3. Stubbs, *Constitutional History of England*, 3.51; Hughes, *Pastors and Visionaries*, 305–6; and McKenna, "Popular Canonization."

4. Hughes, *Pastors and Visionaries*, 310–11.

5. See Rigg, *History of Anglo-Latin Literature*, 294 and n. 167, although with the minor correction that there are actually *eight* stanzas in Bodley 851, which in fact is what Rigg gives in his fuller account in "Medieval Latin Poetic Anthologies II," 387–407, with some further corrections in the introduction to the Bodley 851 in Langland, *Piers Plowman: Working Facsimile*.

6. The poem is edited by Wright, *Political Poems and Songs*, 2.114–18, without lineation, and will be cited here by page number. Wright's edition is based on British Library, Cotton Faustina B.IX only, without knowledge of the Bodley manuscript with its extra stanzas. There is no edition of the censored stanzas, which I cite from Bodley 851 itself, where the poem occupies 74va–76va. Our poem, called by its incipit, "Quis meo capiti," was added to

blank leaves in the fifteenth century. It breaks off at the bottom of 75rb, with a note by the scribe "require in secundo folio post" and ends on fol. 76va. The Bodley manuscript has been badly rubbed and some words from the censored stanzas are partially illegible.

7. Wells died in 1388, long before, obviously, the poem on Scrope was added. There has been a great deal of debate about whether Wells was alive when the Z text of *Piers Plowman* (Part III) was added and that debate does not affect us here. However, the contents of Part I of the manuscript (about which Wells' ownership is not in dispute) sort very well with a taste for Langland, as do the contents of Part II—a blend of ecclesiastical satire and historical texts much like the Scrope poem. See Rigg, "Medieval Latin Poetic Anthologies II," for a complete contents list. Noteworthy items in Part I are Walter Mapes's *De nugis curialium* (of which Bodley is the sole extant copy), a work on the fall of Carthage, an extract from the *Epistola Sathanae* that deals satirically with the Franciscans, and the Scrope poem. Part II contains various religious, antifeminist, historical, and so-called 'anticlerical' satires and includes a copy of the "John of Bridlington" prophecies and of the *Apocalypsis Goliae*. Part III contains only *Piers Plowman*, the C continuation added, in Rigg's view, before the activity of a scribe named Dodsthorp in the mid-fifteenth century.

8. For a technical discussion of the manuscript's gatherings and contents, see Rigg's introduction in *Piers Plowman: Working Facsimile*; Hanna, "Studies in the MSS of *Piers Plowman*," 18; and the review of the *Facsimile* by Kerby-Fulton in *Modern Language Review* 91 (1996): 959–61.

9. Rigg, "Medieval Latin Poetic Anthologies II," 391 and nn. 8–9. The Scrope poem was copied into blank leaves during the fifteenth century by Hand Y in Rigg's description, who ran out of space. A scribe named Dodsthorp added a colophon at the end of our poem, and Rigg believes that Y and Dodsthorp were working at the same time, which he suggests is after 1439 (on the basis of the fact that Dodsthorp's name does not occur in a visitation record of 1439). But there could be other explanations for this sequence of events, and both or either of these scribes may have been not at Ramsey, but at the Benedictine college in Oxford. As Rigg rightly points out, the presence of the *ex libris* suggests that it circulated outside the abbey (see p. 394).

10. On the manifesto written at the parliament, see McNiven, "Betrayal of Richard Scrope," 173–213.

11. See Langland, *Piers Plowman: The Z Version*, 76.

12. For the sources in this paragraph, see McKenna, "Popular Canonization," 611–16; Osborne, "Politics and Popular Piety," 1–21; and for the historical details of his life, Tait, "Ricard le Scrope," 1082–1085, as well as the sources cited below. For the primary accounts cited below of Henry's attempts to suppress the cult, see especially *Fabric Rolls*, 193–96 (for further sources on the decoration of the tomb itself, and individual bequests, see index); Raine, *Historians of the Church of York*, 3.291–92. Chronicle accounts of the miracles themselves and the criticism of Henry IV include *Cronica S. Albani*, 410; *Eulogium*, continuation, vol. 3; A. Usk, *Chronicle*, 99; *Chronicle of John Streche*; *Godstow Chronicle*, 239; Wylie, *History of England*, esp. Appendix T.

13. "Flexis poplitibus post pacis osculum / Offert carnifici columba jugulum; Sic linquit pontifex carnis ergastulum; Fert ictus quinque gladio" (Wright, *Political Poems and Songs*, 116). On the five wounds, see the image in the Bolton Hours, fol. 175v, fig. 3, published in Osborne, "Politics and Popular Piety," and discussed on his p. 9. On Scrope's request for the five blows, see Wylie, *History of England*, 2.240. Friedman, *Northern English Books*, 89, men-

tions the particular observance of this image in the north. For its unnoticed use in the Kempe manuscript made at Mount Grace Priory in Yorkshire, see Parsons, "Red-Ink Annotator."

14. *Testamenta eboracensia*, 2.145–56.

15. Gregory XII lifted this in April 1408. See Osborne, "Politics and Popular Piety," nn. 28–29; French, "Tomb of Archbishop Scrope," 95–102; and McKenna, "Popular Canonization," 608–23.

16. The letter containing the first prohibitions is published in the *Fabric Rolls*, 193–94, from which the quotes below come. The letter is signed: "T. Archiepiscopus Cantuariensis, et Thomas Langley Decanus Ebor., et Angliae Cancellarius." Langley (or Longley) had the misfortune to be both chancellor of England and dean of York Minster at the same time — there can be little doubt that his empathies lay with York, but he had no choice but to act in accordance with the king and sign the letter. Thomas Arundel is the primary signatory and author; he, too, would have had some mixed feelings on Scrope's account (whose execution he had protested), but the cult was a serious threat to the king in the north and fiscally a threat to Canterbury. For Walsingham's remarks, see McKenna, "Popular Canonization," 611 n. 13, and for the sergeants, see *York Memorandum Book*, 1.236–38.

17. The order is sent from "Johan fils au Roy, Constable d'Engleterre," that is, John, duke of Bedford, commanding the complete closing off of the tomb by stronger barriers: "y faces mettre sur la terre entre les pilers et par bonne espace de hors veilles fuystes et grosses piers de bonne hautesse et lacure iffint qils i soyent continuelment pour fare estoppoill a les faux foles que y veignont par colour de devocion" (*Fabric Rolls*, 196). Note that Bedford has a preconceived idea of the validity of the cult ("les *faux* foles que y veignont par *colour de devocion*").

18. *Fabric Rolls*, 194, my translation.

19. Compare these with the language of Alphonse's *Epistola solitarii* (discussed below in ch. 8). At the time Arundel is writing, treatises on *probatio* and *discretio spirituum* are in demand everywhere in Schism Europe, and parts of the *Epistola* itself have just been translated into Middle English, sometime before 1402, in *The Chastising*. See the discussion in ch. 8 below.

20. See especially Hughes, *Pastors and Visionaries*, 307–8.

21. Articles cited from *Fabric Rolls*, 194–95:

Imprimis quod Decanus, Capitulum, singuli canonici et ministri quicumque ecclesiae Ebor. a quacumque publicacione miraculorum per dominum Ricardum nuper Ebor. Archiepiscopum factorum se abstineant.

Item quod nullum ad adorandum prefatum Archiepiscopum invitent quoquomodo vel inducant.

Item quod nullum quominus ad sepulcrum ejusdem accedat causa orationum fiendarum pro anima ejusdem defuncti impediant.

Item quod deputentur magister Johannes Harewod, Thomas Garton, et Robertus Feriby, qui venientibus exponant ut oblaciones quas in ipsius honore facere intendunt non ad sepulcrum, sed ad tumbam Sancti Willelmi, aut alio loco devoto ejusdem Ecclesiae reponant, causam hujus rei exponentes, quod expectabitur determinacio ecclesiae antequam hujusmodi adoracione dependenciae, cerae, vel aliarum rerum, seu aliqua adoracione solemni, honoretur.

Item si quis exposicioni dictorum custodum non obediens ceram aut res alias temeraria voluntate ad sepulcrum suum dimittat, seu oblaciones forsan in auro vel argento, sine mora dicti custodes illud auferant et in alio loco, prout eis videbitur, ad usum Ecclesiae reservent.

22. Fol. 100v. See Osborne, "Politics and Popular Piety," 4, on the lay owners of this manuscript. There is also an image of the recently canonized St. Bridget of Sweden in the Bolton Hours. Bridget is a significant association for the Scrope cult because Henry V was popularly thought to have founded Syon in expiation for his father's sin in executing Scrope. On Bodleian Library, Lat. Liturg. f.2 (figure 16), which also has Bridgettine selections, see Scott, *Later Gothic Manuscripts*, no. 22, vol. 1, p. 92.

23. *Fabric Rolls*, 194–95.

24. For instances of this, and for an introduction to *probatio*, see Kerby-Fulton, "Who Has Written?" 101–16; Voaden, *God's Words*; and D. Elliott, "Seeing Double"; see also ch. 8 below.

25. See ch. 5 and Chronology, 1415–25.

26. Among the monuments are those in the great east window glazed by Thornton, the eight clerestory windows of the choir given as a memorial by the Scropes of Bolton, the east window in the clerestory of the south choir transept given by the Scropes of Masham, and, in many respects, the great lantern tower itself. For a fuller listing, see Hughes, *Pastors and Visionaries*, 309–10, and O'Connor and Haselock, "Stained and Painted Glass," 374.

27. McKenna, "Popular Canonization," 612 n. 14 for sources.

28. Osborne, "Politics and Popular Piety," 7 n. 36, citing J. Russell, "Canonization of Opposition," 279–90.

29. Osborne, "Politics and Popular Piety," 7; J. Russell, "Canonization of Opposition," 280. For a fascinating secular parallel to Scrope, see British Library, MS Royal 12. C.XII, fol. 1, where a poem in praise of "St." Thomas of Lancaster, whose beheading in 1322 by Edward II produced tomb miracles as well, alludes to Becket: "Gaude Thoma, ducum decus, lucerna Lancastriae, / Qui per necem imitaris Thomam Cantriariae" (quoted Osborne, op. cit., 8; for full text and translation, see Wright, *Political Songs*, 268–72). Royal 12. C.XII is copied by the same scribe as British Library, Harley 2253 and is very much in that tradition of political protest. Another example is the *Miracula Simonis Montfortis*, preserved in a late thirteenth-century manuscript, British Library, Cotton Vespasian A.VI, article 10, originally from Evesham Abbey (see Ker, *Medieval Libraries*, 81).

30. See McKenna, "Popular Canonization," 614–15. Maidstone records the pope's words upon receiving news of Scrope's death.

31. A manuscript witness to the cult of Scrope, the Bolton Hours has unusual images and was in the possession of the family of John Bolton, an MP in 1427–28 and York's mayor in 1431. The patron was likely, as Osborne points out, a woman, owing to the presence of St. Sitha (patron saint of housewives). The other unusual "saint" is Scrope. There is a tribute to Scrope in the Bolton Hours, beginning "O gemma lucis et virtutis/ Laus et decus senectutis / Eboraci gloria" and concludes with the usual injunction "Ora pro nobis sancte ricarde" (transcribed by Osborne, "Politics and Popular Piety," from fol. 100v–1; for other tributes, see *Horae Eboracenses*, App. IV, 181–83). There is also an image of Scrope on fol. 202v, showing the saint holding a windmill to symbolize the field of his execution, and his Five Wounds of Christ emblem is on fol. 175r. See Osborne, op. cit., figs. 2 and 3, and for the full manuscript description, see Ker and Piper, *Medieval Manuscripts*, 4.786–91.

32. "Lectorem simplicem supplex expostulo, / Ne patrem polluat veneni poculo; / Benigne audiat quae videt oculo / Factorum Dei nescius" (116).

33. The manuscript is badly rubbed in places and not always legible, so other transcriptions of some readings may be possible than those I have arrived at: "Presuli comiti accessit tercius / Miles ex milibus ad penas socius / Membratim capitur corpus quia tocius / Emissis & viceribus." The second stanza reads "Hi natu nobis modestus in moribus / Arius iusticie constans trepidus / Cultor ecclesie in fide fervidus / Vir verax ex uirtutibus" (fol. 74).

34. Hughes, *Pastors and Visionaries*, 311.

35. "Aut theodosio sit moderacior" (fol. 76v). The first of these stanzas is mainly a list of epithets for Scrope ("Zelus rei publice cultor iusticie"), the second is about the inaction of prelates while kings plunder, the next two are about the appalling corruption of the king's reign (the second of these making allusion to Theodosius), and the final stanza a wry comment on accommodating prelates.

36. For a convenient listing of manuscripts and ownership or provenance where we know it, see the Appendix to Hanna, *William Langland*; see also Kerby-Fulton, "Professional Readers," 101–37.

37. See Strohm, *England's Empty Throne*, on the role of political prophecy in Henry IV's uneasy reign.

38. McKenna, "Popular Canonization," 615 n. 39, for Gascoigne.

Notes to Chapter 6

1. For John Kendale, vicar choral of York Minster by 1409, see Hughes, *Pastors and Visionaries*, and my "Women Readers" on Langland's female readership.

2. Lochrie, *Margery Kempe and the Translations*, esp. 107–14, for discussion of Kempe's teaching and reference to Walter Brut's defence of female preaching; for a recent assessment of the problem, Gertz-Robinson, "Stepping in the Pulpit," 459–82, and Wallace, "Response," 483–91; and more broadly, N. Watson, "Making of *The Book*," and Riddy's response "Text and Self."

3. Kaspar Elm used the word "semi-religious" (*Semireligiosentum*) to describe "a publically recognized middle way," including hermits, penitents, hospitalers, Beguines and others ("*Vita regularis sine regula*," 239–73); see Van Engen, "Devout Communities," 74.

4. Tanner, *Church in Norwich*, 166.

5. Ibid., 64.

6. Kempe, *The Book*, ed. Meech and Allen, 343, 226.23 (hereafter *BMK*).

7. Gibson, *Theater of Devotion*, 22–23.

8. "Secundum predicta potest se regere inquisitor in inquisitionibus Lulardorum, Begardorum, et Swestrionum," quoted from Fredericq, *Corpus* in Van Engen, "Devout Communities," 57 n. 38. For Boniface IX's *Sedis apostolice prouidential* of Jan. 31, 1395: "eisdem Beghardis seu Lullardis et Zwestrionibus" (Fredericq, op. cit., 257).

9. Voaden, "Travels with Margery," 177–95.

10. Lerner follows one scholarly tradition in distinguishing Beguines from Beguins: "The latter term usually designates semi-regular women of northern Europe, mostly cloistered, whereas I use Beguin to denote male and female Franciscan tertiaries, solely of Languedoc and Catalonia, who gained religious guidance from Spiritual Franciscans" (*Heresy and Literacy*, 187). See my Appendix C.

11. However elusive to modern scholarship, the heresy was thought by the Clementine papacy to be largely epitomized in condemned articles gleaned from *The Mirror* of Marguerite Porete; see Lerner, *Heresy of the Free Spirit*, 68–77.

12. *BMK*, 121.1–10; for discussion, see Hudson, *Lollards and Their Books*, 114.

13. A good example of the latter would be Douceline de Digne, on whom see Kerby-Fulton, "When Women Preached," 31–56. See also the discussions in Burr, *Prosecution*, and Lerner, *Heresy and Literacy*.

14. Bale, *Scriptorum Illustrium*, 2.552, gives a long list of works Alan indexed "Hos etaim doctorum indices, seu tabulas, ut uocant, fecit, pro monni materia apud eos inuenienda," including "In Costasy, super Apocalyps." (553), and "In reuelationes Brigittae" (552); the latter survives in Oxford, Lincoln College MS Lat. 69, fols. 197r–234 and was discussed above in ch. 2; see Sharpe, *Handlist*, 33, for extant manuscripts and bibliography. See ch. 2 above as well.

15. For a recent study of the beguine literary culture, see Newman, *From Virile Woman*. On the Beguines generally, see McDonnell, *Beguines*, and Simons, *Cities of Ladies*.

16. On Hildegard's elusive influence, see McDonnell, *Beguines*, and Hemptinne and Góngora, *Voice of Silence*. On beguine relations with the difficult trinitarian theology of Joachimism, see Kerby-Fulton, "When Women Preached," on Douceline de Digne. After the Clementine edicts many beguine houses became Dominican; see Stargardt, "Beguines of Belgium," 277–313.

17. "Cum de quibusdam mulieribus," trans. McDonnell, *Beguines*, 524; see Chronology, 1311–12 note.

18. See Thijssen, *Censure*, and Burr, *Persecution*, for instances in male circles of learning.

19. See Simons, *Cities of Ladies*, 80–85, on issues of literacy and teaching.

20. Lerner, *Heresy of the Free Spirit*, 83.

21. "Expertus enim de testimonium, quod scripta illa nefandissima taliter fuere prima facie veritatis specie supervestita, quod nemo possit erroris deprehendere seminarium, nisi per Illius gratiam et auxilium qui docet omnem veritatem" (trans. McDonnell, *Beguines*, 494, from Fredericq, *Corpus*, 1.186). Both McDonnell (495) and Lerner, *Heresy of the Free Spirit* (192–93) make the point that Ruysbroeck did not attack her until her death, and that even this apparently required courage, given the power and prestige of her followers.

22. For Gerson's attack on Porete's "incredibly subtle book," see Lerner, *Heresy of the Free Spirit*, 165; Lerner remarks "The two [women] could have known each other in Brabant in the early fourteenth century and that one died in the flames while the other lived to teach from a silver chair might have been an accident of birth or circumstance rather than any great difference in doctrine" (192). Parallels of such disparity in heresy dealing with women of mixed social classes can be cited from fourteenth-century Ireland (see the case of Petronilla of Meath, Chronology, 1324) and sixteenth-century England (see Gertz-Robinson, "Stepping into the Pulpit").

23. See the discussion by Kent Emery in his Foreword to Porete, *Mirror*, trans. Colledge et al. (Also see "A Word about Intellectual Freedom" above.)

24. For discussion, see Thijssen, *Censure*.

25. Godfrey was open to the possibility, as Emery points out, of intellectual intervention (*Mirror*, x).

26. See Kerby-Fulton, "When Women Preached."

27. See, for instance, the lengthy list McDonnell, *Beguines,* gives of Dominicans who preached before the Beguines of Paris.

28. Ibid., 344; see also his brief history of official attempts to stop women from preaching, beginning with the Council of Carthage in 398, and ending with Humbert of Romans' infamous attack (343); see also ch. 8 below.

29. Ibid.; de la Marche, *La chaire française,* 33; Bériou, "Right of Women," 138.

30. This is quoted from Van Engen, "Friar Johannes Nyder," 583–615.

31. See Lichtmann, "Marguerite Porete and Meister Eckhart," 71 n. 18, and see ch. 9 below, especially the discussion of the Middle English translation of "Margaret Porete: *Mirror,*" ed. Doiron, 1.249.14.

32. McDonnell, *Beguines,* 320 and passim.

33. Blumenfeld-Kosinki, "Satirical Views," 1–14.

34. Van Engen, "Devout Communities," 54. Deventer itself, the movement's city of origin, had five sister houses while the founders struggled to maintain a single one for men, as Van Engen points out.

35. Ibid., 55; text, Fredericq, *Corpus,* 167–69.

36. The language sounds Olivian. See the third section of the present chapter, and ch. 1 above.

37. Van Engen, "Devout Communities" 55; Fredericq, *Corpus,* 184.

38. Van Engen, "Devout Communities," 10.

39. Ibid., 15.

40. *Vita Egberti,* 171–72.

41. This is a complex subject, even in textual terms in *Piers Plowman.* See my "Langland in His Working Clothes'" on the issue of when it appears in the C text tradition; Middleton, "Acts of Vagrancy"; and also now Cole, "William Langland," 37–58; Hudson, "Langland and Lollardy?" esp. 94–100, and Scase, "Heu! quanta desolatio," 19–36. Hudson concludes importantly that the term "lollar(e)" in Langland's B and C texts is "not sect-specific," and this seems accurate.

42. *Vita Egberti,* 163.

43. Van Engen, "Devout Communities," 59–60, citing Hyma, "Super modo vivendi," 45.

44. Van Engen, "Devout Communities," 55; Fredericq, *Corpus,* 167–69.

45. See Mulchahey, "*First the Bow is Bent,*" 194–96, and esp. 203 on preached *collationes.* Originally, in Benedictine and Cistercian contexts, it had the sense of an informal talk, or a public edificatory reading. Sometime after 1231 the custom of preached collations arises among the Dominicans, with the idea that a *collatio* was a briefer discourse than a *sermo.* The idea of gathering together, and even of light refreshment, comes to be associated with the word as well. What is important for us is to see how much more easily the word could have moved to involve lay "preaching" than "sermo" could. On the genre within the Devout movement, see especially Van Engen, "Virtues, Brothers, and Schools," especially the section "Collations and 'Exempla' for the Brothers and School Boys," 187 ff.

46. Van Engen, "Devout Communities," 84.

47. See Kerby-Fulton, "Eciam Lollardi."

48. Van Engen, "Devout Communities," 82.

49. Ibid., 84.

50. See the introduction to *Chastising*, 81–82, for the exemplum of a Beguine who "visits the sick" in confrontation with a parish priest.

51. "Preaching" on a text from scripture would have been considered too much an appropriation of clerical privilege, as charges against the Beguines (falsely or otherwise) indicate.

52. On Kempe and issues of preaching, see Lochrie, *Margery Kempe and the Translations*; Gertz-Robinson, "Stepping into the Pulpit"; and Wallace, "Response."

53. Riehle, *Middle English Mystics*; *Chastising*, Introduction; Sargent, "Transmission by English Carthusians."

54. See the "Manuscripts" Introduction of the new edition of Thomas à Kempis, *Imitation of Christ*.

55. I am grateful to John Van Engen for his advice on this; see Desoer, "Relationship of the Latin Versions," 129–45.

56. On this time period, see Van Engen, *Devotio Moderna*, Introduction.

57. Van Engen, "Friar Johannes Nyder," 604; see also Lerner, *Heresy of the Free Spirit*, 169–70, on the controversy regarding the beguine life and political exploitation of it by the opponents of the schismatic Pope Eugenius IV, who had defended the Beguines in 1431. Coincidentally, the pope also approved *The Mirror of Simple Souls*, though not knowing that it was by a Beguine.

58. I am grateful to John Van Engen for advice about this. Tanner, *Church in Norwich*, 65, nn. 49–55.

59. Ibid., 65.

60. N. Watson, "Making of *The Book*," 395–434, lays out a convincing case for the son's role as first scribe.

61. See Stargardt, "Beguines of Belgium"; see also Allen's annotations to the prayers at the end of the *BMK*, discussing their Germanic devotional form. Perhaps one of the most striking features of the ministry that the *Devotio Moderna* opened to women (and, of course, lay men) is the emphasis on discernment of spirits, as the manuscript tradition of defences of the Devout emphasizes. See Van Engen, "Devout Communities," 53.

62. See Knowles, *Religious Orders*, 2.199.

63. Netter, *Doctrinale*, 1.628a; see also Allen, *BMK* note to 6.9.

64. "Ecce quam plane dicit Augustinus, virginitatem non esse laudabilem nisi illam Deo consecratam et voto firmatam. Non tamen dicit non laudabilem simpliciter, sed non multum praedicandam, in comparatione virginitatis sub voto, vel virginitatis, monasterialis" (Netter, *Doctrinale*, 1.760–61). I would like to thank Rosalynn Voaden for discussing these passages with me.

65 Netter, *Doctrinale*, 2.c.376; cited by Allen in *BMK* note to 17.10. A similar pun appears in *Piers Plowman* C.IX.297.

66. Sharpe, *Handlist*.

67. Emden, *Biographical Register*, 1344.

68. See *BMK*, 165.5 and note, also 170.7 and introduction, lvii.

69. See Chronology, 1389 (Ramsbury), 1428–31 (Norwich trials), 1443 (Salisbury trial), and see further, Hudson, *Lollards and Their Books*, 114 n. 5, who mentions cases in Chichele's Register, 3.91, 98–100, and a Free Spirit case in Wiltshire of John Russell, Minorite from Stamford. Hudson makes the point that Russell had no Lollard leanings.

70. See ch. 8 below on the *Epistola*.

71. For the *Epistola* in relation to Kempe, see Voaden, *God's Words*, and regarding Langland, see my "Who Has Written?" The others will be mentioned further below.

72. N. Watson, in "Melting into God," speaks slightingly of "what in the 1960's seemed to be a heady line of speculation about the presence of free spirit heretics in medieval England," but for a corrective to this view, with citation from bishops' registers and literary sources, see Hudson, *Lollards and Their Books*, and the instances discussed below.

73. See ch. 8 below.

74. See Arnold, "Lollard Trials," for this point, especially about the amount of information in William of Pagula's popular manual.

75. N. Watson makes the point that "the book seems not to have circulated among the fifteenth-century women readers of Bridget of Sweden, Catherine of Siena, Elizabeth of Hungary and Mechthild of Hackeborn; at least it did not circulate as a *woman's* book, if only because it was assumed to be by a man" ("Melting into God," 26). He cites Riddy on the way these writers helped to define "a specifically female reading community in fifteenth-century England" (n. 19). But these were not the only writers who defined female reading/authorship, and *The Mirror* is associated with not only Julian's work in MS Additional 37790, but also with prayers of St. Bridget and works by Rolle for the female recluse Margaret Heslington. Moreover MS Additional 37790's sister manuscript, Downside Abbey, MS 26542 (so close in "handwriting, rubrication, lay-out and contents, that it is hard to suppose that they are not the products of the same scriptorium" [Julian, *Book of Showings*, 1.2]) contains among other texts suitable for women excerpts from Mechthild of Hackeborn. At the time of the Dissolution, the Downside manuscript was in the possession of two nuns of Dartford (ibid.). Furthermore *The Mirror* is also associated in manuscript transmission with *The Chastising*, a text likely written for the nuns of Barking. Finally, given the association of all three Middle English copies of *The Mirror* (not to mention Methley's Latin text) with the Carthusians, the suggestion of female readership for the book becomes apparent, given the pastoral care initiatives of the order (see Parsons, "Red-Ink Annotator," and the extant books belonging to the various charterhouses listed in Ker, *Medieval Libraries*). It therefore seems important not to overstress the implications of the lack of attribution to Marguerite Porete, lamentable as it is. Porete's book traveled in exactly the company that it would have had it been known to be by a woman. The contrast here with Hildegard's works (see ch. 4 above) is especially instructive. If one compares these manuscripts with, say, the transmission of Hildegard of Bingen's works (which did not travel anonymously and which were read primarily by a male audience), the female orientation, or at the very least, the potential for mixed audience usage, of *The Mirror* becomes clear.

76. See Newman, *From Virile Woman*, on Porete's *Mirror* in the context of the other two great literary Beguines of the period, Hadewijch and Mechthild of Magdeburg in her chapter 5, "*La mystique courtoise*: Thirteenth-Century Beguines and the Art of Love." Newman has an excursus on the *Schwester Katrei* text, which like Porete's was suffused with Free Spirit doctrine and traveled anonymously. Its translator, however, realized that it was by a woman.

77. Leff, *Heresy*, 315.

78. See Introduction above, "Non-Wycliffite Heresy in Late Medieval England."

79. Leff, *Heresy*, 312–14. The Vienne legislation was issued under the rubric of heresy and was exclusively doctrinal, see Lerner, *Heresy of the Free Spirit*, 181.

80. The more so since there was renewed interest in Ricardian England in legislation of John XXII because of the mendicant controversies. (The *Clementines*, that is, the legislation in which the Vienne Council condemnations traveled, were not actually issued until after Clement's death, but rather by John XXII; see Chronology, 1305 and 1317.) The *Clementines* are found in all kinds of collections of canon law, now, e.g., in the *Corpus iuris canonici*, and they were used as sources for English encyclopedic texts like the *Omne bonum* in the 1360s and 1370s. The Council of Vienne itself entered the legislation under the rubric of heresy, so it would be very easy to find, especially for anyone looking for resources on the subject of heresy.

81. This was done in part to blackball the anti-pope, see Lerner, *Heresy of the Free Spirit*, 169.

82. See ibid., 195–99, and his comment about Gerlach Peeter's now lost tract, "De libertate spiritus."

83. Ibid., 195 n. 46. He cites Bazire and Colledge's edition of *Chastising*, 35, 130–45 and 277—that is, the translated portions of Ruysbroeck.

84. Hudson, *Lollards and Their Books*, 113 ff., also provides a good deal of evidence for Free Spiritism in England, including evidence from bishop's registers; see note 69 above listing the dates for these in the Chronology.

85. Moreover, a fourteenth-century English manuscript on the *Sentences* refers to "the errors of the Berengarians in *Ad nostrum*," a comment that Robert Lerner dismisses. But in fact many medieval contemporaries associated Wyclif's ideas on the eucharist with Berengar and so a fourteenth-century scholar's conflation of the two (given Article VIII of *Ad nostrum*) is not at all illogical, even if it is not accurate. See Hudson, *Premature Reformation*, 286–87 n. 47.

86. So in all manuscripts except two; see textual notes to line 3.

87. The author's rather relaxed attitude toward the threat of Lollardy evident here and elsewhere in his attitude toward Bible translation might indicate a date for his work before Arundel's Constitutions. Although, as we have seen from Christopher de Hamel's, Hanna's, and others' research (in Appendix A below), this may not indicate anything. In fact, *The Chastising* was most likely written before 1401 on the basis of an ownership ascription in Bodleian Library, MS Bodley 923, which contains a reference to *The Chastising* on fol. 145r; see *Chastising*, Introduction, "The Manuscripts," 36. And for the possibility of its compilation over an extended time, see A. Sutherland, "*The Chastising*: Neglected Text," 357–58.

88. For a similar reading of the author's attitude to Lollardy, although arrived at for different reasons, see Justice's treatment of the *Chastising* in his "General Words," 377–94.

89. See, too, Hudson, *Lollards and Their Books*, 114.

90. Van Engen quotes a remarkable passage from Gerhart Zerboldt's defence of non-sacramental confession among the Devout, to the effect that what is needed "is not the power of the keys, but a spirit of discernment" ("Devout Communities," 55).

91. Van Engen mentions that two manuscripts of Gerhart's "Circa modum," Cologne, Stadtsarchiv W 342 and Berlin, Staatsbibliothek MS 640 (theol. Qu. 206), contain "a larger set of writings treating suspect groups: works by Johannes Nyder, Gerson's rebuttal of Grabow, Henry of Langenstein on discerning spirits, and the papal decretals employed against the Devout" (ibid., 53).

92. I have compared Bazire and Colledge's Middle English text with the Latin text and Dutch text, and facing English translation of the Dutch, in Ruysbroeck, *De Ornatu Spiri-*

tualium Nuptiarum, tr. Surius, facing *Die Geestelike Brulocht,* ed. Alaerts. Here, compare the Dutch rubrics p. 551; the Latin, "De erroribus male ociosorum, quibus tertio repugnat modo." Grote's own translation, recently edited, does not differ significantly in any of the passages cited in this chapter (see Hofman, *Ornatus,* 198–202); I cite Surius for the convenience of the facing Dutch text. References to *The Chastising* appear in brackets in the text above.

93. *De Ornatu,* tr. Surius, facing *Die Geestelike Brulocht,* ed. Alaerts, 556–57.

94. See their note to *Chastising,* 141.20 ff.

95. Hudson, "Langland and Lollardy?" 97.

96. The Wycliffite heresy is never mentioned in relation to his case, although, interestingly, several of his views are Wycliffite.

97. See Chronology, 1424 and n. 69 above.

98. *De Ornatu,* tr. Surius, facing *Die Geestelike Brulocht,* ed. Alaerts, 556–58.

99. "At tamen scriptis divinis et Christi Iesu sermonibus ac institutionibus bene perspectis, falsos ac eversos eos esse, perspicue potest animadverti" (ibid.).

100. See ch. 8 below.

101. *De Ornatu,* tr. Surius, facing *Die Geestelike Brulocht,* ed. Alaerts, 558–59.

102. Note also different readings in the table of variants, *Chastising,* 142.

103. He similarly obscures Ruysbroeck's very clear distinction between the two groups, again obscuring Pelagian suggestions: "These differ from the previously described group inasmuch as they say they can make progress and gain merit, whereas the others hold that they cannot merit anything more because they are in a state of unity and emptiness" (*De Ornatu,* tr. Surius, facing *Die Geestelike Brulocht,* ed. Alaerts, 560–62, compare *Chastising,* 143.25 ff.).

104. John Clark, "Walter Hilton," 67.

105. Sargent, "Transmission by English Carthusians," 228.

106. *De Ornatu,* tr. Surius, facing *Die Geestelike Brulocht,* ed. Alaerts, 560–61.

107. For a similar fascination, see Knighton's passage on the Franciscan Spirituals martyred in 1354, pp. 136–37 above.

108. See n. 87 above on manuscript ownership.

109. The references in this paragraph are indebted to John Clark's fine "Walter Hilton."

110. Ibid., 65.

111. Ibid., 68, 64, and elsewhere.

112. Ibid., 65.

113. See Hudson, "Langland and Lollardy?"

114. See the discussion of Bishop Waltham below.

115. "Item quod licitum est cuicumque sacerdoti et alij cognoscere carnaliter quascumque mulieres eciam moniales, virgines et vxores et hoc *multiplicacionem generis humani*; et ita fecit dictus Willielmus cognoscendo virgines, vxores et alias mulieres solutas a tempore quo dictas opiniones tenuit" (emphasis added). The articles are cited here from Hudson's appendix to *Lollards and Their Books,* 121.

116. Article 10: "Item quod si quis coniugatus haberet vxorem de qua non posset procreare prolem, quod meritorium ei esset ipsam dimittere et capere aliam de qua posset prolem procreare" (ibid.). See also articles 9 and 13 on the non-necessity of priests and nuns to obey vows of obedience.

117. Ibid., 114 n. 5, on the oddity of the Norwich heretics' irregular sexual ideas, which she associates with Free Spiritism.

118. *Ad nostrum* articles in English I have cited from Leff, *Heresy,* 1.315, with Latin insertions from Fredericq, *Corpus,* 1.168–69.

119. See Appendix B below; Hudson, *Lollards and Their Books,* 120; also present was a doctor of civil law. Note that both Hilton and Trefnant were trained in civil law, which would have given them special insight into international church matters. See Allmand, "Civil Lawyers," 155–80.

120. See Leff, *Heresy,* 1.332, explaining that John XXII's legislation against followers of Olivi in southern France was used against Beguines and Beghards in the north, and 308–13, for parallels with Ockham and Eckhart.

121. On this point, see especially Kerby-Fulton, "Eciam Lollardi."

122. In addition to the Norwich trials (1428–31) and the Salisbury trial (1443), there was another mixed case tried before Bishop Grey in 1457 (see Chronology). The Norwich Lollards were, as a group, particularly given to opinions on sexuality. And Margery Baxter's infamous testimony especially suggests tantalizing parallels with Free Spirit in its starkly sensational treatment of the eucharist.

123. See Emden, *Biographical Register,* 305–6 for Hilton's life and 236 for Luis de Fontibus. Luis was at Cambridge in 1383 and Hilton left Cambridge in 1384.

Notes to Chapter 7

1. Nicholas Watson suggests the possibility that the M. N. glosses could have been composed by a woman. This is certainly possible, I would suggest, especially given the orientation toward women in the Amherst manuscript, British Library, Additional 37790, mentioned in the previous chapter. However, in the absence (as yet) of concrete evidence, I have used the male pronoun.

2. Porete's work is cited here from *Mirror,* trans. Colledge et al., p. 29 and note. The French is cited from Guarnieri, "Il Movimento," where the text runs from pp. 513 to 635, unless otherwise indicated that it is from *Mirouer,* ed. Guarnieri and Verdeyen, from which the Latin is always cited.

3. The modern English title as translated by Don Eric Levine in Petroff, *Medieval Women's Visionary Literature,* 294.

4. Thierry was favourite reading among Free Spirit mystics. See Guarnieri, "Il Movimento," 353–499.

5. Ibid., 358–59, and see Petroff, *Medieval Women's Visionary Literature,* 283.

6. See McGinn, *Meister Eckhart.*

7. Guiard de Cressonessart, a cleric imbued with Franciscan Spiritualism, was arrested as a "defender and supporter" of Porete at the time of her trial. See Kent Emery's Foreword to *Mirror,* trans. Colledge et al., xlii–xliii; and for the documentation of the trial see Verdeyen, "Le procès d'inquisition," 47–94, and the next note.

8. Verdeyen, "Le procès d'inquisition" and Lerner, *Heresy of the Free Spirit,* 77–78, on the habits ("portant tunicam longam et zonam pelliceam"). See also Lerner, "Angel of Philadelphia," for the full Latin texts of the trial.

9. Douie, "Olivi's Postilla," 74–75.

10. Pairing them with Andrew and James respectively.

11. Fols. 36va, 20vb, 29vb, 143rb; Douie, "Olivi's Postilla," 74.

12. My translation with emphasis added, which differs from Douie's; the Latin is transcribed in ibid., 75.

13. Much in this passage would appeal to the love-drenched annihilationism of Porete: "Ac deinde in superexcessum divine speculationis totum suum intellectum suspendere et sublevare. . . . Ac deinde divine fruitioni affectum suum totaliter incorporare, quod est ultimus finis nostre mentis, nostrique desiderii, ac perconsequens et pax eius, ideo non immerito sunt sic ordinate a Christo" (fol. 59ra, transcribed ibid., 75 n. 45)

14. See also McDonnell, *Beguines*, 400 and 434, for some indications of crossover between the northern and southern groups. See also Appendix C and Mens, *Oorsprong en Betekenis*, 295.

15. There is clearly something in the intellectual currents to which both women were exposed that makes for the "subtlety" contemporaries found so worrying. Most importantly for our purposes, although Ruysbroeck's description of Free Spirit mysticism in *The Spiritual Espousals* "is so explicit that it could have been based upon the lost works of Bloemardinne" (Lerner, *Heresy of the Free Spirit*, 192), Romana Guarnieri has noted that this section from the *Espousals* reads like a condensation of Porete's *Mirror* (the theme of bodily desires notwithstanding); see Guarnieri, "Il Movimento," 443–44.

16. The theory, originally Claire Kirchberger's in 1927, is elucidated in Sargent, "*Le Mirouer*," 444–45. Northburgh conceived the idea of founding the London Charterhouse after extended royal service in Paris, Hainault, and The Low Countries (places most associated with Porete and her text). The London Carthusians owned the Cambridge, St. John's College MS 71 copy of M. N.'s *Mirror*, along with copies of *The Chastising*, *The Cloud of Unknowing*, and Hilton (see Ker, *Medieval Libraries*, 122), the perfect setting for M. N.'s work, or that of a later redactor. John Baconthorpe, provincial of the Carmelite order, had been a student at Paris when Porete was burned, and recalled her as "a certain beguine who produced a book against the clergy" (cited in Bale, *Scriptorum Illustrium*, 367: "Beguuina [sic] quaedam, quae libellum quondam adversus clerum ediderat, prope Parisium combusta fuit, cum quodam converso, qui a fide [ut dicunt] apostatasset").

17. Colledge, "Latin *Mirror of Simple Souls*," 177–83.

18. See Parsons, "Red-Ink Annotator," for instance.

19. See Porete, *Mirouer*, ed. Guarnieri and Verdeyan, p. xii, for full description of the manuscript. Written in Germany, but in Laud's collection by 1637, it contains mystical writing by both Porete and Angela of Foligno. The title page of *The Mirror* survived because it was on the verso of the end of a tract by Raymond Lulle—which is itself a sign of alternative tastes.

20. Rome, Biblioteca Vaticana Rossiano, Cod. Chigianus B.IV 41, c. 1398, described in ibid., x.

21. Rome, Biblioteca Vaticana Rossiano, Cod. Chigianus C.IV 85, described ibid., xi.

22. Rome, Biblioteca Vaticana Rossiano, Cod. Vat. Lat. 4953, described ibid., xii; the articles are edited in Guarnieri, "Il Movimento," 650–60.

23. See *Mirror*, trans. Colledge et al., xxxviii.

24. See the previous chapter for the reason behind the re-condemnation.

25. See Chronology, 1317, and see Introduction above.

26. For a parallel argument about the Bridgettines, see Schirmer, "Reading Lessons," and Justice's response, "General Words."

27. The Latin letters are cited by page number and line number from *Mirouer,* ed. Guarnieri and Verdeyen.

28. See Kerby-Fulton, "Hildegard and the Male Reader."

29. The Middle English is cited from Porete, "Margaret Porete: *Mirror,*" ed. Doiron, 243–355, where the letters of approbation are found at the beginning of the text, 249–50.

30. Burr, *Olivi's Peaceable Kingdom,* 201–2.

31. "Cum de quibusdam mulieribus," trans. McDonnell, *Beguines,* 524.

32. Latin reads "ab uno spiritu forti et feruido" (407.30).

33. In addition to the sources cited in the previous chapter, see Emery's Foreword to *Mirror,* trans. Colledge et al.

34. See "A Word about Intellectual Freedom" above.

35. Colledge, "*Epistola solitarii.*"

36. See *Mirror,* trans. Colledge et al., Appendix 1. There is also external evidence in the manuscripts of English provenance that the book aroused suspicions among readers.

37. Guarnieri, "Il Movimento," 434.

38. This suggests an audience of listeners as the primary target of the translation.

39. For the concept of functional ambiguity, see again Patterson, *Censorship and Interpretation.*

40. Colledge and Guarnieri, "Glosses by 'M. N.'," 132. One would not have to postulate, as Colledge does, that M. N and/or those who objected to his translation, had access to the original list of Paris condemnations, now lost. But if they did it would not be the first time in English history: Matthew Paris, for instance, is still the earliest and best source for the condemnations that were issued of the "Eternal Evangel" in Paris in 1256.

41. N. Watson, "Melting into God," 37. Watson feels that Colledge's view privileges his own obsession with the text's heretical status.

42. See Arnold, "Lollard Trials," and the discussion above in the Introduction.

43. All citations in English from *Ad nostrum* come from Leff, *Heresy,* 1.314–15; for the Latin text, see Fredericq, *Corpus,* 1.168–69, no. 172.

44. See Kerby-Fulton and Despres, *Iconography,* ch. 3, on annotation types in Middle English.

45. The Prologue is cited from Dorion's edition.

46. See ch. 1, p. 62, for the quotation from Olivi.

47. *Mirror,* trans. Colledge et al., 9.

48. As Ruysbroeck scholars now believe.

49. See Parsons, "Red-Ink Annotator" and Kerby-Fulton, "Medieval Professional Reader and Reception."

50. John Clark, "Walter Hilton." That Hilton mentioned "liberty of spirit" by name and M. N. did not may be explicable by the simple fact that M. N. had laboured the translation from scratch himself, and who would wish to cast such a shadow over a labour of love? Especially when some preventative glossing would solve the problem.

51. The Council of Vienne investigated Olivi and whether the Franciscan Spirituals had been influenced by Free Spiritism. Both were exceedingly dangerous. If M. N. had known even just the rubrics for the two chapters the *Chastising* author translated from Ruysbroeck, it would have been enough to raise a red flag: "Hou sum oþer men wenen þat þei haue fredom of spirit, *and* þat þei bien ooned to god wiþoute any meane, wherfor þei seie þei bien bounde to no lawes of hooli chirche, and þei bien discharged of al maner wirchynges, *and* of al out-

ward uertues. (Cap*itulum undecimum*)" (138.9–13) and "Hou sum men holden þat to whateu*er* þing þei bien stired, wheþer it accordith to cristis techyng or noon, al comeþ of þe holi goost. (Cap*itulum*) *duodecimum*" (142.11–13). These deal with two distinctive but related groups, both of which Ruysbroeck believed to be Free Spirit (the second one, I would suggest, more influenced by Olivian or Franciscan Spiritual ideas).

52. The idea of this being sung does not appear in the Middle English.

53. They believe that if they "diden any þing wilfulli," even virtuous acts, God would then be "let of his owne werkyng." Therefore "þei maken hem voide of al maner uertues" (140.3–6).

54. See Parsons, "Red-Ink Annotator."

55. Similarly, his thirteenth gloss appears after the Soul says that the practices of the church are simply laborious, and M. N. grasps the opportunity to say this only applies "out of time."

56. Rather, he says, that the Holy Ghost "werkiþ graciousli in þese soules . . . þat þer may no spottes . . . in hem abide" (258.12–259.30).

57. For comparison, see Plummer, "On the Colophons and Marginalia," 11–42.

58. As Michael Sargent has shown, a loss of words in M. N.'s French exemplar has altered the reading here from the original's "elle est assez *excusee et exoniee*, sans oeuvrer. . . ." See Guarnieri, 529.14–19.

59. And later, "þei seien þat alle þe [good] werkis þat god worchiþ [be þayme] bien more noble and medful þan any oþer men mowen disserue" (142.20–22).

60. The emphasized words are present in the French, but not in M. N. (see n. 58 above).

61. Cf. *Ad nostrum*, article 7, that even sexual intercourse is "not a sin when it is desired."

62. The language and philosophy of this passage, one has to remark in passing, are reminiscent of Langland's C text figure of Rechelessnesse — a figure of marked radicalism, perhaps associated with Franciscan Spiritualism.

63. Koch, "Philosophische und theologische Irrtumlisten," 318–19.

64. See ch. 4 above.

65. See Chronology, 1410 and note, and ch. 9 below for full quotation of the passage and discussion.

66. Colledge, "*Epistola solitarii*," 19–49; more recently, Gillespie has argued that the charterhouses were accumulating texts "to guide that process of *probatio* and *discretio* whose nascent technology was known to its *Cloud* corpus"; see "Haunted Text," 135.

67. N. Watson, "Melting into God."

68. Cited here from the translation of College et al.

69. See Kerby-Fulton, "Piers Plowman."

70. Guarnieri, "Il Movimento."

71. Recently beautifully analyzed in Newman, *From Virile Woman*.

72. *Dictionary of National Biography*, 76–77.

73. Trans. Colledge et al., ch. 5, 33 n. 2.

74. Ibid.

75. Pearsall, Introduction to *Piers Plowman: C-Text*.

76. Kerby-Fulton and Despres, *Iconography*, ch. 3, for examples.

77. Parsons, "Red-Ink Annotator," for a transcription of all the glosses, and Kerby-Fulton, "Medieval Professional Reader and Reception."

Notes to Chapter 8

1. Cited from Wogan-Browne et al., *Idea of the Vernacular*, 234, where it is edited from London, British Library, MS Sloane 2499, fol. 57r, and which provides notes and recent bibliography. The Explicit is found in two manuscripts, and "may be scribal but probably originates from Julian's circle. In insisting on a contextualized reading of each part of the book (in a manner that suggests nervousness regarding how some of Julian's ideas will be received), [it] parallels the prologue to *The Cloud of Unknowing*" (Wogan-Browne et al., op. cit., no. 3.4., p. 233). For a political instance of such a caveat, see the one in *Richard the Redeless*, discussed in Kerby-Fulton and Justice, "Langlandian Reading Circles." All other passages from Julian in this chapter are cited from one of three texts, as indicated: *Book of Showings*, ed. Colledge and Walsh; second, *A Revelation of Love*, ed. Glasscoe; and, third, where comparison between the Long and Short Text is helpful, *Writings of Julian of Norwich*, ed. Watson and Jenkins. I am grateful to Nicholas Watson for providing a pre-publication draft of this edition. When the present study was in press production, the new edition emerged with slightly modernized spelling, which is not represented here. In all cases of quotation, I have checked the editions against each other and compared variant manuscript readings. For a clear account of the textual complexities of Julian transmission, see Riddy, "Julian and Self-Textualization."

2. The important exception is *The Cloud of Unknowing* (see previous note), which, as Denis Renevey has put it, describes "moments of mystical union . . . [drawing upon] 'negative' or apophatic, mysticism developed from the works of Pseudo-Dionysius, . . . whose influence in vernacular texts (like Eckhart's *German Sermons* [1320s] or Ruusbroec's Dutch *Spiritual Espousals* [1370s]) was seen by many ecclesiastics as dangerous. The *Cloud* author is anxiously aware of such suspicions and hopes to circumvent them by attempting to restrict his audience and by going on the offensive [against] . . . intellectual superiority" (Wogan-Browne et al., *Idea of the Vernacular*, 230). Importantly, the *Cloud* Prologue anticipates an audience who will access it by ownership, messengers, or borrowing, or who "schal rede it, write it or speke it, or elles here it be red or spokin," and pleads for fully contextualized reading, and above all, for keeping it within a responsible and elite circle. It should not be disseminated by any of these means "to any bot yif it be of soche one or to soche one that hath bi thi supposing in a trewe will and by an hole entent purposed him to be a parfite folower of Criste." It expressly excludes a whole range of false seekers, and even "good men of active lyvyng" (231). For *The Cloud*'s Carthusian transmission, see Hodgson's edition, *Cloud*, manuscript descriptions, esp. pp. xi, xiv–xv, xviii.

3. See the discussion in the previous chapter of the Amherst manuscript, British Library, Additional 37790. See also Cré, "Women in the Charterhouse."

4. *Book of Showings*, ed. Colledge and Walsh, vol. 1, description of MS Additional 37790.

5. Bynum, *Jesus as Mother*.

6. Among the controversial topics developed in the Long Text is the problem of universal salvation, which, as Barbara Newman has shown, was a topic with a long-standing association with women's writings: "Julian's resistance does not stand in splendid isolation: rather, she makes central to her theology a problem that has emerged as at least a subtext in a variety of women's religious writings" (*From Virile Woman*, 130–31).

7. Discussed most recently in Colledge's Introduction to *Mirror*, trans. Colledge et al.

8. I will cite the Watson and Jenkins edition as WJ with chapter and line numbers, the Glascoe edition as G with a page number, and the Colledge and Walsh edition as CW with chapter and line numbers. Long and Short Texts will be designated as Long and Short respectively.

9. *Saincte Eglise la Petite* (and *Saincte Eglise la Grant*) are first distinguished in chapter 19, lines 11–13 of Porete, *Mirouer*, ed. Guarnier and Verdeyen, which may be indebted to Olivi. *The Chastising*'s rendition of Ruysbroeck had warned that "fredom of spirit" heretics believe: "þat þei bien enhaunsid bi perfeccion aboue al obseruances of hooli chirrche" (139.14–15); "Of fastyng þei take noon heede, ne of festis of hooli chirche, ne of þe ordynaunce ne obseruance of hooli chirche . . . for in al þing þei lyuen *wiþout doome of consience*" (141.16–19).

10. See Burr, *Persecution*, 86; and Chronology, 1322.

11. See ch. 7, nn. 7–8 above, on the Franciscan Spiritual Guiard de Cressonessart arrested with Porete and described as an adherent.

12. Article 15 of *In agro dominico*, cited in *Mirror*, trans. Colledge et al., p. 35 n. 3, glossing Porete's "The Soul feels no disquiet for any sins she once committed," ch. 16, p. 35, and quoting Augustine from *Of Free Choice of the Will*.

13. N. Watson, "Et que est huius ydoli materia?" 103.

14. I read this passage more positively than does N. Watson in "Composition," 637–83.

15. Aquinas, *Summa theologiae*, IIa–IIae, q. 177, art. 1 (pp. 128–31) and art. 2 (pp. 132–35); for excellent discussion, see Blamires and Marx, "Woman Not to Preach," 40–41.

16. "(V)nde Maria, et Martha cum Apostolis genera linguarum acceperunt et publice sicut Apostoli docuisse et praedicasse leguntur" (Henry of Ghent, *Summa quaestionum ordinarium*, Book 1, art. 11, q. 2, edited in Blamires and Marx, "Woman Not to Preach," 50–55, here 50, and n. 52 on the development of the legend).

17. Cited in Blamires and Marx, "Woman Not to Preach," from Henry of Ghent, *Summa in tres partes*, Book 1 (193–95), art. 12, q. 1, "Utrum mulier possit esse auditor sacrae scripturae," para 5 (unedited). For Humbert of Romans, see *De eruditione praedicatorum*, 435, cited in Blamires and Marx, op. cit. 41. For the same idea in the church fathers, see John Clark, "Walter Hilton," 161.

18. On which see the exchange of essays, Somerset, "Eciam Mulier," and Kerby-Fulton, "Eciam Lollardi."

19. See Tanner, *Church in Norwich*, 166, and see my "Eciam Lollardi".

20. See my "Eciam Lollardi."

21. See Voaden, *God's Words*, and the studies by Voaden cited below. See also Colledge, "*Epistola solitarii*." For English concerns about misguided mysticisms and related issues, see John Clark, "Walter Hilton," 61–78; and see my "Eciam Lollardi"; for Hildegard of Bingen, see my "Prophecy and Suspicion." For a recent treatment of attacks on Bridget, see Ellis, "Text and Controversy," 303–22.

22. See Kerby-Fulton, *Reformist Apocalypticism*.

23. Kerby-Fulton, "Prophecy and Suspicion."

24. On the panel of theologians, see my "Eciam Lollardi." See Kienzle and Walker, *Women Preachers*, and L. Taylor, *Soldiers of Christ*, 176–78. At any given time throughout the later Middle Ages, there were more women preaching than we today realize, a factor which suggests that the sometimes panicked quality of official and academic attacks on female preaching did not arise in a vacuum.

25. For the Harley 31 sources, see Somerset, "Eciam Mulier." University censorship prior to Lollardy usually only arose when the ideas in question reached the laity or became a public issue of some sort, as we have seen in the 1358 condemnation of Friar John.

26. Raming, *Exclusion of Women*.

27. Trans. Blamires et al., *Women Defamed*, 251, from *Registrum Johannis Trefnant*, 258.

28. See Knowles, "Censured Opinions," and N. Watson, "Visions of Inclusion."

29. Aston, "Lollard Women Preachers?" 441–61. And see now the very recent account in Minnis, "Respondet Walterus Bryth," esp. 229–30 n. 2. For evidence that Langland's readers were interested in the female preachers the poem portrays, see Kerby-Fulton, "Women Readers."

30. Arnold was a Joachite writer who attempted to make many of the kinds of calculations about the coming of Antichrist that Brut makes. Arnold's prophetic writings did circulate in England: see, for example, Oxford, Bodleian Library, MS Lat. Misc. c. 75 (a manuscript at least parts of which were likely available to Wyclif and Nicholas Hereford at Queens College), discussed above in ch. 4.

31. Translated Blamires et al., *Women Defamed*, 254–55. On the complex and as yet imperfectly understood relation of this disputation to the Brut trial, see Somerset, "Eciam Mulier," and Kerby-Fulton, "Eciam Lollardi"; for the Latin text, see Blamires and Marx, "Woman Not to Preach."

32. See Somerset's "Eciam Mulier."

33. "Mulieres, sancte virgines, constanter predicarunt verbum Dei et multos ad fidem converterunt sacerdotibus tunc non audentibus loqui verbum" (*Registrum Johannis Trefnant*, 345, trans. and discussed in Somerset, "Eciam Mulier," and Kerby-Fulton, "Eciam Lollardi").

34. On Hildegard's "*tempus muliebre*" and the 'womanish' weakness of the clergy, see, for instance, her *Prooemium vitae s. Disibodi*, 355, and various other passages, especially in the *Liber divinorum operum* (on which see Kerby-Fulton, *Reformist Apocalypticism*, 46–47, and Newman, *Sister of Wisdom*, "An Effeminate Age," 238–49). I would point out that this was one of Hildegard's best-known concepts in the later Middle Ages, made famous in part by its inclusion in a much-consulted section of Vincent of Beauvais's *Speculum historiale*, 32.107. But it is difficult to know for certain what Brut's source for the concept was. Brut may well have known Henry of Ghent's *Utrum mulier possit esse doctor* in which the "effeminati" argument also appears briefly (Henry of Ghent's *Utrum mulier*, ed. Blamires and Marx, in "Woman Not to Preach," 51 n. 5). Moreover, Wycliffites used the rhetoric of homosexuality as a common smear tactic. But none of these writers extended the argument in the unusual direction Brut did (and Hildegard had), that is, toward urging female ministry on the grounds that "sancte virgines" have constantly done it (and by implication continue to do so), and especially when priests are afraid: "Si beati qui audiunt et custodiunt, magis beati qui predicant et custodiunt verbum Dei, quoniam beacius est magis dare quam accipere" (*Registrum Johannis Trefant*, 345). This suggests to me that Brut's source was the more philogynist Continental apocalyptic tradition, most likely Hildegard.

35. See my "Prophecy and Suspicion."

36. See my "Eciam Lollardi."

37. See my "When Women Preached."

38. See Kerby-Fulton, "Eciam Lollardi" on Eustache, and for the quotation from Ockham, see McGrade, "Political Writings," 319.

39. For the use of this passage from John in the mendicant controversies, see Szittya, *Antifraternal Tradition*, 75. I would like to thank Fiona Somerset for her advice about this passage and questions of women's ministry.

40. Minnis, "Respondet Walterus Bryth," 248.

41. D. Elliott, "Seeing Double."

42. See Chronology 1381 and 1387 and notes.

43. See Voaden, "Rewriting the Letter."

44. I have used the edition by Arne Jönsson, *Alfonso of Jaén*, ch. 1.

45. "Numquid non eciam Maria, soror Aaron, Iudith et Hester spiritu prophecie dotate fuerunt?" (*Epistola*, 1: par. 24). He goes on to mention many more, including Anna, Deborah, and several New Testament females.

46. "Nonne de pastore fecit prophetam et iuuenes ydiotas repleuit spiritu prophecie? Et nonne non doctores sed piscatores et rudes homines elegit in apostolos, qui spiritus sancto repleti sunt?" (*Epistola*, 1.23).

47. For this point see Voaden, "Rewriting the Letter," 176.

48. D. Elliott, "Seeing Double," 36.

49. For a study of these *probatio* questions in the *Epistola*, see Kerby-Fulton, "Who Has Written?"

50. Compare Latin: " . . . dulciter innebriari, & inflammari igne infusionis dulcedinis caritatis" (6: par. 30).

51. "Exhilaratur conscientia, in obliuionem venit praeteritorum dolorum, exultat animus, clarescit intellectus, cor illuminatur, desideria iocundantur. . . . Cui animae ipsemet Hugo sic pulchre respondens, ait Vere ille est dilectus tuus, qui visitat te" (6:34–37). The quote is from Hugh's *Soliloquio de Arra Anime*; see Jönsson, *Alfonso of Jaén*.

52. "Demones, inquit [Aquinas] ea que sciunt hominibus manifestant, non quidem per illuminationem intellectus, sed per aliquam ymaginariam visionem" (citing Aquinas, *Summa theologiae*, IIa–IIae, q. 172, art. 5, reply to obj. 2, "vbi sic dicit . . ." [7.48]). He goes on to quote Augustine, Book 12 of the *Super Genesim ad litteram*, "Illuditur autem anima, & fallitur in corporali visione. . . . In visione autem spirituali, seu ymaginaria, id est, in corporum similitudinibus, que in spiritu videntur fallitur etiam anima, cum ea, que sic videt, ipsa corpora esse arbitratur, &c. Postea hec autem subdit, dicens: At vero in illis intellectualibus visis non fallitur anima, &c." (7.50–52).

53. See Voaden and Jönsson, "Recommended Reading," 149–223.

54. Also helpful is the edition that Voaden provides as an appendix to *God's Words* with its detailed notes.

55. Parsons, "Red-Ink Annotator," e.g., 52.29 or 87.14. At a few of the points he judged as containing too much physical or sexual material, a section in the manuscripts has been crossed through in red (and sometimes a marginal 'd' (for "deleatur"), overlined in red. See Kerby-Fulton, "Medieval Professional Reader and Reception," 8–9.

56. Parsons, "Red-Ink Annotator," 147.

57. Voaden, appendix to *God's Words*.

58. See Rusconi, "Women's Sermons," 173–98.

59. Knowles, *Religious Orders*, 2.57; Ellis, "Text and Controversy," 303–22; Hogg, "Cardinal Easton's Letter," 20–26; and his "Adam Easton's *Defensorium*," 213–40.

60. Kerby-Fulton, *Reformist Apocalypticism*, 68–69, for similar quotations from Hildegard, and 102–12, for Bridget's place in this tradition.

61. See Aers and Staley, *Powers of the Holy*, 205 ff. Chaucer's inclusion of the legend in *The Canterbury Tales*, however, probably came later, given its explicit link with the "Canon's Yeoman's Tale" (199). Aers and Staley's remarks refer in part to the thesis first raised by Giffin, *Studies in Chaucer*, that Chaucer wrote the legend in the early 1380s to celebrate Easton's appointment as Cardinal Priest of St. Cecilia (1381); see Aers and Staley, op. cit., 199 and 208.

62. Aers and Staley, *Powers of the Holy*, "Epilogue," 268, and N. Watson, "Censorship," 855–56, quoting the Wiltshire, Longleat House MS 4, 1r.

63. For all the information and quotations in this paragraph, see Ellis, "Text and Controversy," and Hogg, "Cardinal Easton's Letter," and "Adam Easton's *Defensorium*." Quotations from the letter are cited from Hogg's edition by page number. Hogg quotes the *Defensorium* from Oxford, Bodleian Library, MS Hamilton 7, fol. 229 ff. The original account of Easton's imprisonment comes from Theoderici de Nyem, *De Schismate*, 77–79, 90–95, 103, and 110, and discussed in Hogg, "Adam Easton's *Defensorium*," 225–26. For the most recent bibliography, see Ellis, op. cit.

64. See also Aers and Staley, *Powers of the Holy*, 138. See also N. Watson, "Trinitarian Hermeneutic."

65. N. Watson, "Composition." Hudson, however, gives evidence for *increasing* concern with images after the time of Wyclif, and throughout the early fifteenth century (and beyond). See *Premature Reformation*, 92–94, 165–66, and 301–9.

66. Heslop, "Attitudes to the Visual Arts," 26–32, citing *Registrum Baldock*, 19. The Latin insertions below are my own, cited from Lehmann-Brockhaus, *Lateinische Schriftsquellen*, no. 2984, pp. 231–32, on the 1306 case. The artist was threatened with excommunication; for this sanction more generally and its use against English heretics, see Logan, *Excommunication and the Secular Arm*, 88–69.

67. I am grateful to Peter Gunnhouse for permission to cite his 1994 paper, "Pictorial Narrative as Gospel Truth." In a letter dated April 24, 1994, addressed to Maidie Hilmo, he provided the references used here. I am also grateful to Maidie Hilmo for advice on this subject. The current reference comes from *PG* 86, col. 165A, as excerpted from Theodorus Lector by Nicephorus Calistus Xanthopoulos in the early fourteenth century, when a cult of Mary was spreading across Europe. Bede records that Benedict Biscop brought such an image from Rome to England in the seventh century. The idea of Luke as a painter was popular in the fourteenth century, when Luke starts to be venerated as patron saint of the Painter's Guild. The earliest western representation of Luke as a painter may be the 1368 Gospel book illluminated by John of Troppau, a Bohemian artist (Vienna, Österreichische Nationalbibliothek, MS 1182, fol. 91v; reproduced as Plate XXVI in Egbert, *Medieval Artist at Work*). The idea of Luke's intimacy with the Virgin appears in vernacular English works like Myrc's *Festial* at this point, too: see Owst, *Literature and the Pulpit*, 124. See Hilmo, *Medieval Icons*, on these points.

68. Rypon cites John of Damascus, and claims that Luke painted both Mary and Christ. See Owst, *Literature and the Pulpit*, 140, and Hudson, *Premature Reformation*, 434. Owst is citing British Library, MS Harley 4894, where only fols. 31v–33 are on the topic of images in relation to Lollardy. Hudson suggests that the sermon was one of those in the Harley collection delivered *ad synodum*. On Rypon, see also Hilmo, *Medieval Icons*, and see W. R. Jones, "Lollards and Images," 42.

69. Cited in Hilmo, *Medieval Icons*, from *Theophilus: De Diuersis Artibus*, 4.

70. See also Camille's discussion of why the act of making is avoided in medieval iconography in *Gothic Idol*, 31.

71. Carruthers, *Book of Memory*, and see also Kerby-Fulton and Despres, *Iconography*, for the evidence of this in the work of the Douce artist.

72. For an excellent account of Julian's three types of vision, see N. Watson, "Trinitarian Hermeneutic," 79–100.

73. On Julian's experience of visual art, especially the very sophisticated East Anglian style of her time, see Baker, *Julian of Norwich's Showings*, 40 ff.

74. For good examples, see Sheingorn, "The Wise Mother," 69–80, and plates, including discussion of her number 11, from the Bedford Hours (British Library, MS Additional 18850, fol. 257v), figure 19 here.

75. Ellis, *"Ad Flores Fabricandum,"* 163–86; and see Ellis, "Text and Controversy."

76. For another instance of the erasing of female gender from authorship, see what the Middle English translator of Mechthild of Hackeborn's *Book of Ghostly Grace* does in a passage toward the end in which Gertrude the Great (one of the two authors of this book of Mechthild's visions) writes as one of the editors of the book. In this section Gertrude records her own stunning vision of Mechthild dispensing a eucharistic-like meal of bread and honey. The Middle English translator either assumed that Gertrude was a man (because her self-reference is usually in the third person, "illa persona," which is only grammatically, not referentially feminine in Latin), or suppressed her female identity because of the sensitive nature of the vision. Indeed, it would be difficult, or at the least very inattentive, given the references throughout the book to the convent situation in which both Mechthild and her two biographers are living, to get so far into the book and not know the writer in question was a woman. See Voaden, "The Company She Keeps," 51–70. For the text of Mechthild, *Book of Ghostly Grace*, see the microfiche edition by Halligan, where it is edited from British Library, MS Egerton 2006, fol. 212; for the assumption that it was a grammatical misunderstanding, see Barratt, *Women's Writing*, 50.

Notes to Chapter 9

1. These concepts are central to nominalist thought generally; see Oberman, *Harvest of Medieval Theology*, 473.

2. See Koch, "Neue Aktenstucke II," 302–4, for the complete list of articles, several of which are discussed below.

3. Courtenay, *Schools and Scholars*, 283–91, on Ockham and the Franciscan majority within English theology in the early fourteenth century, especially in relation to beatific vision (283).

4. For the monastic tradition of liberalism (embodied in figures like Peter the Venerable) in relation to the Franciscan one, see Daniel, *Franciscan Concept of Mission*, 8 ff. See also Pantin, *English Church*, 130, on Uthred's treatises; for Joachite connections, see Pantin, "Two Treatises of Uthred," 364–66, and his "Some Medieval English Treatises," 196–97.

5. Courtenay, *Schools and Scholars*, and his "Theology and Theologians," 1–34; Oberman, *Harvest of Medieval Theology*; Thijssen, *Censure*, ch. 3 (for censure of Ockham). Among recent literary studies, see Rhodes, *Poetry Does Theology*, and Minnis, "Looking for a Sign,"

but among the many studies cited below, two superb earlier studies should be mentioned, Green, *Crisis of Truth*, and Coleman, *Piers Plowman and the Moderni*.

6. The issue is very different in epistemology. See Knowles, *Religious Orders*, who makes the same decision to use the term in relation to theology (not epistemology or logic), and see Courtenay, *Schools and Scholars*, 217–18, for a lucid assessment of which principles of Ockham's thought later writers held or did not hold. No one, of course, "accept[ed] all aspects of Ockham's thought" (and the term is not used in this study to indicate that they did); he stresses that it was not so much Ockhamism or nominalism but the "revolutionary innovations in philosophical and theological *methods*" that impacted the period (218). He also points out that nominalism "included rather than stemmed from Ockham," and "lost out to realism after 1350" (ibid). We can see this in the rise to prominence of Wyclif at Oxford.

7. See Coleman, *Piers Plowman and the Moderni*, especially her discussion of Adam Wodeham and Robert Holcot.

8. See Bradwardine, *De Causa Dei*, lib. I, cap. 47, p. 436; discussed in Reeves, *Influence*, 84, and 515 for a listing of the only three extant copies of Joachim's *Dialogi*, all, today, in Italian collections. Reeves points out in relation to Bradwardine that Joachim's thought was "most vulnerable from the angle of scholastic theology" (op. cit., 84).

9. Bradwardine was reflecting a mid-century surge in awareness of Joachimism, prompted in part by John XXII's unusually persecuting papacy. Perhaps most telling is the work of Jacques Fournier, who would be pope after John and who wrote a number of treatises for the pope on current heresy and heretics. These include a treatise on the Italian Franciscan Spirituals (the fraticelli), a refutation of the "errors" of Joachim and of Meister Eckhart, a treatise on Michael of Cesena, Ockham, and—clearly considered aligned with them—Olivi, as well as a treatise on beatific vision issues. At virtually the same time John XXII was engaged in the censure of Olivi, Ockham's case came before him. See Mollat, *Popes at Avignon*, 27–28, and his chapter 3 generally on Jacques Fournier, Benedict XII (1334–42).

10. See Chronology, 1323, 1324, and 1328, and notes for additional sources. And for the articles, see Koch, *Kleine Schriften*, 2.300–8 (274–365 for his full "Neue Aktenstücke zu dem gegen Wilhem Ockham in Avignon Geführten Prozess").

11. *De Causa Dei*, Praefatio 2, cited in Oberman, *Harvest of Medieval Theology*, 372 n. 35.

12. *De Causa Dei*, 3.53.872 E, cited in Oberman, *Harvest of Medieval Theology*, 372 n. 35.

13. Oberman, *Harvest of Medieval Theology*, "The Problem of Extrascriptural Tradition," 371–82; for Uthred and the influence of Ockham, see Knowles, "Censured Opinions," 318.

14. See also Rhodes, *Poetry Does Theology*, 27.

15. See the Glossary of Nominalism in Oberman's Appendix.

16. See Chronology, 1338–44.

17. Knowles, *Religious Orders*, 80, notes that Bradwardine was not initially much read, but that FitzRalph and Wyclif took up his views in important ways.

18. Pearsall, *Life of Chaucer*.

19. Knowles, *Religious Orders*, 81.

20. On the Michaelists, see Leff, *Heresy*, 238–58.

21. Perhaps as preliminary to the six-man papal commission that followed: see Thijssen, *Censure*, 14–15, who summarizes the most recent interpretations by Courtenay and others.

22. See Douie, *Nature and Effect*, who points to his letter to the chapter-general of As-

sisi (quoted below) in which Ockham confesses that he had not taken much interest in the debates prior to the crisis. But as Douie says, "his mind was pre-occupied with his impending trial, and it would have been folly for a man in his precarious position to take any part in the quarrel" (202).

23. In addition to the key primary and secondary sources listed in the Chronology, 1331–32, see also Walsh, *Fourteenth-Century Scholar*, 85–107; Mollat, *Popes at Avignon*, 22–27; and Bynum, *Resurrection of the Body*, 284–91.

24. Another suspect academic, Marsilius of Padua was also cited in 1327 and also fled to Ludwig of Bavaria. See Thijssen, *Censure*, 175. Whethamstede, who commissioned New College 49 manuscript of Olivi, also has extracts in his commonplace book, Cambridge, Gonville and Caius 230, from Marsilius (see above, ch. 2).

25. See Chronology, 1329–30, and ch. 2 above.

26. See, for instance, the anthology written about 1425 by a fellow of Merton College, John Maynsforth, now Oxford, Bodleian Library, MS Bodley 52 (S. C. 1969).

27. *Ockham, A Letter to the Friars Minor*, ed. McGrade and Kilcullen, trans. Kilcullen, from Offler et al., *Opera Politica*. Ockham goes on to discuss these papal bulls in detail, but the central point turns on the pope's assertions that the Franciscan's renunciation of property is meaningless if the papacy must then "own" the very goods that they use on their behalf.

28. See the Introduction above, especially the discussion of the *Omne bonum*, and see cases of Gerard (discussed in ch. 2) and John of Rupescissa (discussed in ch. 5), and Koch, "Der Prozess."

29. See, for example, Chronology, 1354, and ch. 3.

30. McNiven, *Heresy and Politics*, 2.

31. Cited in McGrade, *Political Thought of Ockham*, 87, from Offler, *Opera Politica*, 1.176.

32. Among fearful clergy, Kirkestede (see ch. 2) and Uthred are superb examples.

33. See the discussion of the *Dialogus* in ch. 5 above.

34. See the discussion above in ch. 5, citing Somerset, *Clerical Discourse*, 85–86; for the poem, see Rigg, *History of Anglo-Latin Literature*, 280–90, from whom I quote. Bale attributed the poem to Peter Pateshull (see Szittya, "Sedens" and Hudson, "Peter Pateshull").

35. See Salter, Pantin, and Richardson, eds. *Formularies*, vol. 1, no. 55. In this observation and in the remainder of this paragraph I have benefited greatly from reading Thomas Barton's unpublished paper "Engendering Inquisition."

36. *Calendar of Close Rolls*, 3.675.

37. Scholars disagree about whether Lutterell was Ockham's first accuser, but the evidence points in this direction. See Chronology, 1323 and note.

38. See Leff, *Heresy*, esp. 1.296–307 on Ockham.

39. As Courtenay shows, academic fashion for nominalism had been on the wane and gave way after 1350 to realism.

40. Scholars of Langland and Chaucer have done fine and detailed work on the appearance of *via moderna* (most fundamentally, Ockhamist) notions in their poetry, establishing the importance of this strand of thought in each author beyond doubt. See references to Coleman, Green, and others above, and for helpful comments on the vernacular writers made in a larger historical context, see Courtenay, *Schools and Scholars*.

41. See Wyclif, *Opera minor*, ed. Loserth, for his *Responsiones ad argumenta Radulfi Strode*, the tone of which indicates that relations between the two scholars were respectful. See ch. 5 above on Strode, and see also Strohm, *Social Chaucer*, 58–59, on Strode and

Chaucer's circle. The *Dictionary of National Biography*, 19.57–59, mentions the note in the *Vetus Catalogus* of Merton which calls Strode "Notabilis poeta fuit et versificavit librum elegiacum vocatum Phantasma Radulphi." See also Sharpe, *Handlist*, 452.

42. "Videlicet quod nulli magistri, baccalarii vel scolares in artium facultate legentes Parisius audeant aliquam propositionem famosam illius auctoris cujus librum legunt, dicere simpliciter esse falsam, vel esse falsam de virtute sermonis. . . . Item quod nullus dicat scientiam nullam esse de rebus que non sunt signa. . . . Item quod nullus asserat absque distinctione vel expositione quod Socrates et Plato vel Deus et creatura nichil sunt, quoniam illa verba prima facie male sonant" (*Chartularium*, 2.1042, 506–7; cited in Leff, *Heresy*, 1.296).

43. Leff, *Heresy*, 1.296–97.

44. Mann, "Chaucer and Atheism."

45. See the list of fifty-six articles in Koch's edition in "Neue Aktenstücke," 300–8, from which I cite them below.

46. See Leff, *Heresy*, 1.238–58.

47. See Richard Green's fine discussion of covenantal theology in *Crisis of Truth*.

48. Leff, *Heresy*, 1.298.

49. See, for instance, some of the comments in Knowles, *Religious Orders*, 76–81.

50. Knowles makes exactly the same point (ibid., 79 n. 2).

51. Adams and Kretzmann, *Predestination*, 77, translating from Boehner, *Tractatus de Praedestinatione*. For assessment of the issues raised here, see R. Wood, "Ockham's Repudiation," 350–73.

52. Adams and Kretzmann, *Predestination*.

53. R. Wood, "Ockham's Repudiation," 358–59.

54. Whom R. Wood does not see as Pelagian at all (ibid., 351).

55. Cited from Barratt, *Women Writing*, 59, from British Library, MS Egerton 2006, fol. 194r–v; see Chronology, after 1410. This annotation he attached to an account of one of Mechthild's visions in which an infant, dedicated to God before birth by her mother, dies at the age of two and appears (in a passage similar to *Pearl*) as a "full fayre maydene" in elegant dress, having attained heavenly reward. When Mechthild questions how this can be, the Lord says to her, "Be nowght yonge chyldrene that bene baptized savede thorowe other mens feyth? Ande als a modere, yiffe sche behete a gostleye vowe of Crystiante for a childe, yif itt happe than that the childe dye, yitt schalle the child be saffede be the vowe," to which the translator inserts (within the text, as M. N. does) the comment quoted. What is striking about this is the parallel with M. N.'s method, in which the questionable passage is not suppressed but is annotated (Mechthild's texts were also heavily transmitted by Carthusians in England). This seems to suggest a respect for both the sanctity of the vision and the good sense of the reader.

56. Koch, "Neue Aktenstücke," 2.306: "Hii sunt errores qui sequi videntur ex articulis prescriptis contra veram et sanam doctrinam, sicut apparet in tractatu sequenti."

57. Leff, *Heresy*, 1.305.

58. In what follows the condemned articles are cited from Koch, "Neue Aktenstücke," 2.302–4; the interpretive 'explanation' of why they are condemned from the matching list by Lutterell on 306–8 in italics.

59. "Decimus sextus articulus. Quod sicud homo potest demereri ex puris naturalibus, ita potest mereri. *similiter error Pelagii*." Compare: "Decimus quartus articulus. Quod Deus

potest acceptare actum tanquam ex condigno meritorium vite eterne qui est ex puris naturalibus elicitus, sicud si eliceretur. *error Pelagii.*"

60. "Decimus octavus articulus. Quod actus, qui est a caritate elicitus, non excedit totam facultatem nature. *error Pelagii et peius.*"

61. "Tricesimus quintus articulus. Quod actus elicitus ex forma supernaturali non est meritorius vite eterne, sed solum quia Deus contingenter eum acceptat. *error Pelagii.*"

62. "Vicesimus articulus. Quod meritum dicitur, quia elictur a libero arbitrio, non quia elicitur a caritate. *error Pelagii, et quod non facit caritas opus meritorium, et hoc est peius errore Pelagii.*"

63. See the introduction to Shoaf's edition of Usk's *Testament,* and Kerby-Fulton and Justice, "Langlandian Reading Circles."

64. For illusion in Ockhamism, see Leff, *Heresy,* 1.301. For the "Clerk's Tale," see discussion below.

65. For the alternative view that the A text did not breakdown, see Dunning, *Piers Plowman: An Interpretation,* esp. 129–31 for textual discussion. On the questionable authenticity of the But ending, which follows A.XI, see Langland, *Piers Plowman: A Version,* "The most serious doubts about its authenticity are raised by its poor MS support" (51). Kane goes on to say, and rightly, that the issue of the ending of A is obscured generally by the fact that in manuscripts designated in his edition by the sigla TChH2KWN C endings were added. See also Kane, *Piers Plowman: Evidence,* 21–22, on the reasons for viewing the A text as incomplete. All quotations from A are cited from *Piers Plowman: A Version.*

66. See Pearsall's note to XI.290a, *Piers Plowman: C-Text.*

67. *Eulogium,* 3.394, gives the story of the fool and the learned doctor, both dying, and fool says, "Magister et ego moriemur. . . . Nunc videamus quis coelum citius possidebit." This was in part a Franciscan tradition or orientation and also a reformist revelatory one (a similar story appears in Bridget of Sweden).

68. See Kane, *Piers Plowman: Evidence,* 21–22.

69. For a summary of the cross-echoes or parallels these scholars have noted between *Piers Plowman* and Chaucer's *House,* and bibliography, see Grady, "Chaucer Reading Langland," 3–23, and Hanna, "Emendations," 191. These discussions focus largely on the B text, mine will point additionally to parallels with the A text.

70. On Westminster and on scribes the two authors share, see Kerby-Fulton and Justice, "Langlandian Reading Circles," and "Scribe D"; on the shared early reception, again pointing to Westminster, see Edwards, "Early Reception of Chaucer and Langland," 1–22.

71. For a recent, very lucid account, see Simpson, *English Literary History,* 164–67. Simpson argues especially for Ovidian influence on the poem's genre and its tensions.

72. Ibid., 164.

73. "Decimus sextus articulus. Quod sicud homo potest demereri ex puris naturalibus, ita potest mereri. *similiter error Pelagii.*"

74. Chaucer's Oxford philosopher friend Ralph Strode, to whom with Gower *Troilus* is dedicated, is a plausible source for this kind of discussion; see Sharpe, *Handlist,* 452–53, for a list of Strode's writings and reference to his now lost poem entitled *Phantasma Radulphi* and see n. 41 above.

75. See the further discussion of Douglas below, and Johnson's analysis in Wogan-Browne et al., *Idea of the Vernacular,* 276–79.

76. The *Catalogus Vetus* of Merton, quoted above in note 41. In his treatise on dreams, Macrobius lists the "phantasma" among worthless visions (see above, Introduction).

77. See Sharpe, *Handlist*, 452–53 and note the international circulation of Strode's academic works.

78. Cited in Pearsall, *Life of Chaucer*, 162.

79. Ibid., 163, citing the *Consolation*, V, pr. 4.137–41.

80. See Pearsall himself in *The Canterbury Tales*, 124–25, where he makes clear that there are limitations to Chaucer's Boethian philosophy, partly eschatological.

81. Pearsall makes this point in *Life of Chaucer*.

82. See the discussion of *Piers* C.XI.51a in ch. 4 above.

83. See Eldredge, "Chaucer's *House of Fame* and the *Via Moderna*," 105–19; Peck, "Chaucer and the Nominalist Question"; and for a broader treatment, Delany, *Chaucer's House of Fame*. For a superb general treatment mentioning *House of Fame*, Shepherd, "Religion and Philosophy," 262–89.

84. Vernacular visionary writing was a woman's genre and there were a surprising number of women in Langland's audience; see Kerby-Fulton, "Women Readers."

85. See J. S. Russell, "Is London Burning?"

86. Kerby-Fulton, "Professional Readers."

87. Skeat thought that Usk knew Chaucer's *House*; see Kerby-Fulton and Justice, "Langlandian Reading Circles."

88. Kirk, "Nominalism and the Dynamics of the Clerk's Tale," 113.

89. Simpson, *English Literary History*, 319.

90. Salter, *Knight's Tale and the Clerk's Tale*; Steinmetz, "Late Medieval Nominalism," 38–54; Stepsis, "Potentia Absoluta," 129–46; for Shepherd, see "Religion and Philosophy."

91. See the classic study of this problem in Burke-Severs, *Literary Relationships*, esp. ch. 11, "Chaucer's Originality."

92. For detailed examples of suppressions and additions, see ibid.

93. Wallace, "Italy," 220.

94. Shepherd, "Religion and Philosophy," 276.

95. For recent comments on the Lollard knights in relation to Chaucer, see Strohm, *Theory and the Premodern Text*, 174–75. Strohm very sensibly writes, "Drastically summarizing a complex debate, I find the phrase 'Lollard knights' is unquestionably overspecific and unwarranted, but some aspects of Lollard moral fervour and interest in extrasacramental salvation seem to have found a sympathetic hearing in some court circles." Strohm also reminds us that Knighton describes these knights as having "zelum dei . . . sed non secundum scientiam."

96. Bostick, *Antichrist*, 110 n. 115 (for the whole passage), from 165rb, and 182rb.

97. See Chronology, 1380, 1385 and 1387. In 1385, Hereford is reported as having been sheltered by another of the "Lollard knights," John Montague.

98. Hudson, *Lollards and Their Books*.

99. See Chronology, 1386–91 and note, and see Hudson, "Langland and Lollardy?" 99.

100. For Strode, see Chronology, 1374–80 and note.

101. Spearing, *Medieval Dream Poetry*, 181, and L. Patterson, "Court Politics."

102. See Hudson, *Selections*, notes to "Miracle Plays," 187–88.

103. For the first of these, and Ian Johnson's essays, see Chronology, 1410 and note. For convenient basic information and bibliography on these writers, see Wogan-Browne et al.,

Idea of the Vernacular: Henryson, no. 3.18, Gavin Douglas, no. 3.16. For a recent account and bibliography of the theme of pagan culture in Chaucer, see Fyler, "Pagan Survivals," 350–52, and his references. Peter Brown *(A Companion to Chaucer)* discusses the importance of the work of the classicizing friars (especially Robert Holcot and John Ridewall), as well as astrology and the famous Augustinian injunction on the "despoliation of Egypt" as a reason (and an excuse) for indulgence in the classics.

104. As N. Watson, "Outdoing Chaucer," has argued on the basis of both the political context for the *Book* and the moral tone of Lydgate's Prologue.

105. Wogan-Browne et al., *Idea of the Vernacular*, no. 1.7, lines 135–38.

106. See Chronology, 1410–12 for further details.

107. Wogan-Browne et al., *Idea of the Vernacular*. See Johnson's commentary, no. 3.16, 280 n. 57.

108. Ibid., Johnson, no. 1.8, for Prologue and ending of the tale.

109. Ibid., Johnson, no. 1.11. See also the extensive work of Sheila Delany on Bokenham, especially "Friar as Critic," 63–79.

110. Bokenham affects to be afraid to sign his name to the work for fear of what the Cambridge friars will think of it, urging Thomas Burgh, "of jentylnesse, / Kepyth it as cloos as ye best kan / A lytyl while." And if anyone asks who wrote it, tell them "a frend of yourys that usyth to selle / Good hors at feyrys" (Wogan-Browne et al., *Idea of the Vernacular*, no. 1.11, 211–18).

111. Ibid., Johnson, no. 1.5, 35.

112. See ibid, note to 60–61; and on Chaucer's use of Trivet, see Copeland, *Rhetoric*, 144–50.

113. See Reid, "This was here procreation." I am very grateful to Heather Reid for permission to mention her findings prior to their publication.

114. See the edition by Peck, *Heroic Women*, 1–72.

115. Hudson, *Premature Reformation*, 394–98; Wogan-Browne et al., *Idea of the Vernacular*, Shepard, no. 2.2, introduction to and extract from John Trevisa's *Dialogue between the Lord and the Clerk*, for this discussion and recent bibliography. On Trevisa and Berkeley and also on the translation of the Pseudo-Ockham *Dialogus inter militem et clericem* (Dialogue between a Knight and a Clerk), see Somerset, *Clerical Discourse*, 62–92. The Pseudo-Ockham *Dialogus* argues very strongly against the holding of any secular office by clergy, which it regards as improper encroachment by the church on secular government (see Somerset, op. cit., 81). It is important to note that these ideas, and those of the knight against the pope having temporal jurisdiction, *predate* the rise of Wycliffism by decades, both in English policy and elsewhere (the *Dialogus* was written for Philip the Fair). The attribution to Ockham makes this clear in itself and may indicate in part why Ockham was being confiscated in 1389. Trevisa himself is very concerned about an interchange on whether the pope has temporal jurisdiction (which the clerk argues), inserting metatextual annotation to the effect that Christ did not exercise regal power during his life on earth. (Compare with M. N.'s glosses to Porete and the translator of Mechthild, both seeking to control the doctrinal spin of the text.)

116. The Lollard text, "Of Wedded Men," for instance, emphasizes a rather severe attitude toward procreation and—surprisingly—advocacy of spiritual marriage in a way that parallels the emphasis in *Asneth*. See the next chapter.

117. See Bowers, *Canterbury Tales: Fifteenth-Century Continuations*.

118. Staley, *Languages of Power*, 331–36, and Wallace, *Chaucerian Polity*, 201–2 and 295–98. See *Riverside Chaucer*, Textual Notes, p. 1126 and Explanatory Notes, p. 862 for details, and see L. Patterson, "What man artow?" That Chaucer felt braver poking at ecclesiastical issues than political issues is evident.

119. Strohm, *Theory and the Premodern Text*, 174–75.

120. And Chaucer may also not have wanted trouble from his *un*intended audience. It was every poet's nightmare. Both Thomas Usk and Chaucer had by this time seen what happened to Langland's text in unwanted reading circles, and Usk, of course, was executed for political reasons in 1388.

121. Strohm, *Theory and the Premodern Text*, is discussing the milder "Lollard joke" in the Pardoner's Tale, about how cooks "turnen substance into accident" (538–39). See also Somerset, "Here, There and Everywhere?" 127–40.

122. L. Patterson, *Chaucer and the Subject of History*, 43–44.

123. Hilmo, "Framing the Canterbury Pilgrims."

124. *Riverside Chaucer*, 1126.

125. See my "Langland in His Working Clothes," and Kerby-Fulton and Justice, "Scribe D."

126. In "Christian Ideologies," 80–81, Nicholas Watson discusses what he calls "fourteenth-century puritanism," which he associates with "a severer strand of thinking." This he briefly mentions as devolving from the twelfth-century reformers "partly via the Franciscans" (80). As we have seen in this book, however, the ideas of these reformers traveled on their own steam, too, and even as *anti*-Franciscanism. He mentions also in relation to Chaucer, other sources of this "severity," including Langland, Ralph Strode, and especially the "Lollard knights" of Chaucer's circle, and John of Gaunt (whom Chaucer shared with Wyclif as a patron).

Notes to Chapter 10

1. See especially N. Watson, "Visions of Inclusion," and for a complete recent review of the scholarship and a new approach (which distinguishes universal salvation from conversion-based theologies), see Davis, "'Fullynge' Nature."

2. Vitto, *Virtuous Pagan*; Rhodes, *Poetry Does Theology*; Daniel, "Apocalyptic Conversion," 129–54 and his *Franciscan Concept of Mission*; Gradon, "Trajanus redivivus," 93–114; and Newman, *God and the Goddesses*, quoted above in ch. 8.

3. Vitto, *Virtuous Pagan*, 15 (see 12–14 on Tertullian, Clement, and Origin; 14–17 on Augustine).

4. Augustine resorted to a strained rhetorical argument to defend his position, declaring that this was absurd because there was no need to preach the Gospel now if all could be saved in hell: "aliud sequitur absurdius, ut hic non sit Evangelium praedicandum, quoniam omnes utique morituri sunt, et sine ullo reatu contempti Evangelii venire ad inferos debent, ut eis prodesse possit, cum ibi crediderint: quod sentire, impiae vanitatis est" (*PL* 33 col. 714). For a full study of this problem, see Tch'ang-Tche, *Saint Augustin*, 75–79; for this and further analysis of Augustine's stance, Vitto, *Virtuous Pagan*, 14 and n. 54.

5. In this discussion I am indebted to Daniel, "Apocalyptic Conversion" and *Franciscan Concept of Mission.*

6. Bernard of Clairvaux, writing in 1146, appealed to prophecies of the final salvation of the Jews in condemning the persecution against them initiated by the monk, Rudolph (epistles 263 and 265, *PL* 182.567–68 and 570–71); cited in Daniel, "Apocalyptic Conversion," 137.

7. Discussed in more detail below.

8. "Et praedicabitur hoc euangelium regni in uniuerso orbe, in testimonium omnibus gentibus: et tunc ueniet consummatio" (Matt. 24:14).

9. Reeves, *Influence*, 135–44.

10. *Knighton's Chronicle*, ed. Martin, 248–49, discussed above in ch. 3.

11. See Daniel, "Apocalyptic Conversion," 138–39, and especially Joachim's *Liber figurarum*, table XIV (Oxford, Corpus Christi College 255A, fols. 4–14): "Post ruinam autem huius antichristi erit iustitia in terra et habundantia pacis: et dominabitur dominus a mari usque ad mare, et a flumine usque ad terminos orbis. 'Conflabunt autem homines gladios suos in uomeres et lanceas suas in falces: non leuabit gens contra gentem gladium: nec exercebuntur ultra ad prelium' [Is. 2:4, adapted]. Iudei quoque et multe gentes infideles conuertentur ad dominum, et delectabitur uniuersus populus in pulchritudine pacis: quia contrita erunt capita draconis magni, et draco ipse erit incarceratus in abysso." Daniel (139) makes the further point that in table XXII this is confirmed in *figura* form as two stems representing the *populus Iudaicus* and the *populus gentilis* rise in interlace to form three circles, inscribed successively as the Father, Son, and Holy Spirit. According to Grundmann, *Studien über Joachim*, 119–56, freedom and contemplation are here to be understood as the monastic *libertas* and *contemplatio*. Joachim's *Liber figurarum* has been edited by Tondelli, Reeves, and Hirsch-Reich, *Il libro delle figure.*

12. See ch. 2 above and Kerby-Fulton, "English Joachimism."

13. Peter the Venerable made a pioneering attempt at a rational philosophical approach to inclusiveness, discussed in Daniel, *Franciscan Concept of Mission*, 8 ff. On the censure of Bacon, see Chronology, 1257–68 and 1274–79; on Bacon's fervour for mission to the non-Christians, see Daniel, op. cit, and McGinn, *Visions of the End*, 155–57.

14. See Courtenay, *Schools and Scholars*, 353–54, who has traced the original compilation of the list of accusations against Uthred to the York Austin scholar, John Klenkok, and his *Lectura Oxoniensis*, and therefore to the important Austin convent in York. Klenkok was German, and by 1369 embroiled in persecuting heresy in Magdeburg and Prague, where he was successful and influential with the papacy. He would have been a difficult enemy, and his involvement with Uthred's case is another instance of Continental influence; see Emden, *Biographical Register*, 1057. This list was probably compiled between the years 1359 and 1366—which puts it into the period immediately following FitzRalph's defeat. Courtenay also traces the development of the dispute between Uthred and William Jordan, prior of the Dominicans at York, to at least 1366.

15. See Dipple, "Uthred and the Friars," on Uthred's defence of monastic endowments via analogy to the Franciscan concept of "simple use."

16. On this renewed interest, see Walsh, *Fourteenth-Century Scholar*, 104–7, and 149–51; Sandler, "Face to Face," 224–35; and Gwynn, "Sermon Diary of FitzRalph," 1–57.

17. Langham also likely condemned some of Jordan's opinions; those not listed in Uthred's own defence, as Knowles suggests, are apparently Jordan's own. On the friars

in matters of censorship, see Fowler, *Life and Times of Trevisa*, 55. I cite the articles of condemnation from Knowles, "Censured Opinions," 305–42.

18. For the individual articles cited, see the appendix to Knowles, "Censured Opinions." I am grateful to Aaron Thom for allowing me to cite his unpublished paper, "And if lawe wol . . ." from which I have benefited both on this point and on others in relation to Langland, discussed below.

19. "Sacramentum baptismi non est de lege Dei alicui parvulo decedenti requisitum ad salutem aeternam, si intelligatur universaliter, quod nullum sacramentum, &c. *Error*" (Article 8, Knowles, "Censured Opinions," 336); "Sarazenos, Judaeos, ac Paganos adultos et discretos, qui numquam habuerunt, habent, vel habebunt actum seu habitum fidei christianae, possibile est de communi lege salvari, intelligendo in sensu composito, et de quolibet tali decedente, an salvabitur, est a quolibet catholico dubitandum. *Error*" (ibid., 337).

20. Ibid., 337.

21. One can see that Uthred's opponents objected to some of the more radical Ockhamist or nominalist ideas he uses, especially in their responses recorded in Worcester Cathedral MS F.65, fol. 11v, where the disputant is concerned with issues of God as torturer and natural beatitude.

22. See Pantin, "Two Treatises," and Dipple, "Uthred and the Friars."

23. See Knowles, "Censured Opinions," 322 n. 1, mentioning Olivi. The case for Ockhamism is obvious and treated at length by Knowles.

24. "Semper circa fines est aliqua solemnis clarificatio veritatis. Unde sicut ultimus finis synagoge introduxit claritatem Novi Testamenti et ultimus finis mundi introducit *claram visionem Dei* et finis ecclesie circa Antichristum introducit claram contemplationem fide" (New College 49, fol. 123v., Matt. 21:1–17).

25. Corpus Christi 321 (on which see Douie, "Olivi's Postilla, 67), likely associated with Ramsey (which also sent students and books to Oxford, as we saw in relation to Bodley 851). New College 49 was commissioned for the Benedictine college at Oxford by John Whethamstede in the 1420s. See Howlett and Hunt, "Provenance of MS. New College 49," 225.

26. Uthred was steeped in a monastic tradition of treatises on perfection such as would make Joachimism second nature. He was a young student at the time that controversies over the beatific vision and the Olivian and Franciscan Spiritual censures were raging; these, together with a profoundly Ockhamist outlook, go a long way toward explaining his *clara visio.*

27. Cf. Koch, "Philosophische und theologische Irrtumslisten," for this phraseology, which was standard.

28. See Knowles, *Religious Orders*, on this point and its relation to Ockhamism.

29. Ibid., 319.

30. Ibid, 393.

31. For discussion of the Joachite material in Balliol 149, see Kerby-Fulton and Daniel, "English Joachimism, 1300–1500"; Paris, Bibliothèque Nationale MS 3183 also contains Uthred's works along with eschatological polemics (see Szyitta, *Antifraternal Tradition*, 64, 109); and British Library, Royal 6. D.X contains his "Periculum in falsis fratribus" (*sic*) (fol. 283) along with scholastic anti-Wycliffite materials. On the manuscripts of Uthred's works, see Pantin, "Two Treatises of Uthred," 364–66. The contemporary chronicle which contains the most famous account of Uthred's stance against disendowment, the *Eulogium historiarum,* circulated in its earlier version with John of Rupescissa's writings interpolated

into the middle of at least two of its manuscripts (Lincoln's Inn, MS Hale 73 and Cambridge, Trinity College, MS 740).

32. In addition to the William of St. Amour and the Joachite "Columbinus Prophecy" immediately following the Uthred piece in Balliol 149 are notes, on fol. 65r, on the great windstorm of 1362 ("ventus validus per totam orbem;" here dated 1361) and the decollation of Archbishop Sudbury in the Rising of 1381 (on these see my "Langland's Reading," 249); cf. two Hildegard manuscripts, British Library, Arundel 337, fol. 26v, containing notes on the plague, followed by "Anno domini m°ccc octogesimo ij° fuit tremor in Anglia" and similar notes on the flyleaf of Cambridge University Library Ii. See also n. 118 below on the Bodleian Library, Digby 57 manuscript of *The Chronicle of John Somer*.

33. A look at the relevant extant manuscript collections of the period suggests why Langland and his immediate contemporaries would have made such associations. Much of this material was circulating together in booklets and anthologies made in response to controversies of the moment. (See Kerby-Fulton, "Langland's Reading.") Langland would have been sympathetic to Uthred's eschatology for its implications for the salvation of non-Christians, and Uthred's condemnation may even be related to Langland's withholding of the A text from circulation for some years.

34. I am quoting here from the copy in the manuscript of the *Omne bonum*, Royal 6. E.VI, fol. 16v.

35. For this facet of the argument, see Walsh, *Fourteenth-Century Scholar*, 101 ff., who traces John's initiatives late in his life (i.e., after 1322) to reach out to the Eastern churches and to encourage study of their languages and theology.

36. Mollat, *Popes at Avignon*, 22.

37. Walsh, *Fourteenth-Century Scholar*, 94-95, on Waleys, Holcot, and the evidence that the pope approached Cambridge. On Waleys' inquisitional process, see Chronology, 1331-32.

38. Trans. Mollat, *Popes at Avignon*, 23.

39. Walsh, *Fourteenth-Century Scholar*, 92.

40. "[V]iderunt et vident divinam essentiam *visione intuitiva et eciam faciali*, nulla mediante creatura in ratione obiecti visi se habent, sed divina essentia immediate se nude clare et aperte eis ostendente" (cited in ibid., 106, my emphasis). See also Mollat, *Popes at Avignon*, 27.

41. Bynum, *Resurrection of the Body*, 285.

42. "Hunc tenui et persuasi propter peccatum committendum a quocumque dampnando in electione finali habita clara visione, et adhuc reputo esse verum" (337).

43. Vienna, Österreichische Nationalbibliotek Codex Vindobonensis Palatinus 5076, fol. 65ra, a brief questio which Walsh, *Fourteenth-Century Scholar*, 99, shows to be in all likelihood by FitzRalph, as in the manuscript attribution.

44. Ibid., 151, and n. 74 for the manuscript references.

45. Robson, *Wyclif and the Schools*, 78, citing Oxford, Oriel College MS 15, Questio 8, a. 2, fol. 24, col. a.

46. Bynum, *Resurrection of the Body*, 285.

47. Thijssen, *Censure*, 13-15, and see also Courtenay, *Capacity and Volition*, 152.

48. For these dates and the detective work uncovering them, see Courtenay, *Schools and Scholars*, 353 n. 69. That some of the opinions turn up in Klenkok's *Lectura Oxoniensis* (at Oxford himself between 1359 and 1363) shows that these things were under discussion then.

49. For the *Decadicon*, enumerating the errors of the *Sachsenspiegel*, the events in Magdeburg, and Smalley's information (based on Eichstatt, Staatliche Bibliothek MS 204), see Emden, *Biographical Register*, 1057.

50. Contrary to Knowles' understanding of the distinctions, mentioned above. For the extraordinary frontal images of God in the *Omne bonum*, see figures 20 and 21 in the present book, and Sandler's discussion of her plates 115 and 116, the latter accompanying the constitution of Pope Benedict XII on the beatific vision (see Chronology, 1336). English interest a little closer to the time of the controversies can be seen in Sandler's plate 117 which shows a similar frontal image of God (again, as in 115 from the *Omne bonum*, accompanying visions of St. Benedict and St. Paul), in this instance from Glasgow, University Library MS Hunter 231, p. 85, a miscellany of Roger of Waltham, canon of St. Paul's, London, and likely keeper of the wardrobe of Edward II, c. 1325–35, containing both classical and religious texts. This last is an example of contemporary English manuscripts containing "the staring face of God" made when the controversies surrounding the beatific vision were raging at Avignon (see Thorp, *Glory of the Page*, no. 27). What is important about James le Palmer's interest in the 1360s is that for him it was likely not dated, but relevant, I would suggest, to Uthred's condemnation. For the Visionary Cycle of the *Omne bonum*, see Sandler, "Face to Face," 94–95 and 127–28.

51. For James's access, see Sandler, *Omne bonum*, commentary on plates 114 and 116; for FitzRalph's treatment of the topic in his *Summa de questionibus Armenorum*, see Walsh, *Fourteenth-Century Scholar*, 85–107.

52. Walsh, *Fourteenth-Century Scholar*, 96, citing the manuscript designated as P, fols. 24ra, and 25rb.

53. Ibid.

54. Uthred's use of this is discussed in Knowles, "Censured Opinions," 316.

55. "Solet . . . dici et specialiter per Utredum." Knowles (ibid., 315) dismisses this evidence without saying why.

56. Knowles (ibid., 330) dismisses this evidence for reasons that are unclear.

57. See Courtenay, "Theology and Theologians," 33–34.

58. "Quam dicunt a dictis meis scolasticis verissime reportatam" (Knowles, "Censured Opinions," Appendix A).

59. "cedula . . . iam in diuersis mundi partibus diuulgatur, unde et fama mea penes personas graues ex eorum malicia denigratur" (ibid.).

60. Marcett, *Uthred de Boldon*, 50. (Uthred's name was spelled a variety of ways.)

61. They appear in Durham Cathedral Library, A.IV.33; on the disendowment issues before Wyclif, including these incidents, see Hudson, *Premature Reformation*, 98 and 338.

62. Hudson, "Wyclif and the North," 98–99.

63. Ibid., 100.

64. Courtenay, *Schools and Scholars*, 353–54; Hudson, *Premature Reformation*, 98.

65. Hudson, *Premature Reformation*, 98.

66. On the late circulation of the A texts, see Hanna, *William Langland*, 22–23.

67. Courtenay, "Theology and Theologians," 34. The description of Jordan is cited from Marcett, *Uthred de Boldon*, 52, from Bale's *Scriptorium Illustrium*, 483.

68. In a recent review article, Anne Hudson has argued for a date in the early 1380s.

69. Hanna, *William Langland*, 13.

70. C.XV.76a; and for the pun in William Jordan's name, line 92.

71. G. H. Russell, "Salvation of the Heathen," 101–16.

72. "Vos qui peccata hominum comeditis" at line 51a; see Kerby-Fulton, "Hildegard and Antimendicant Propaganda." See also pp. 181 and 191 here.

73. G. H. Russell ("Some Aspects of the Process," 27–49) lists major revisions, then "To these we may add an example of a revision of the poem which manifests itself at various points over a greater part of its length as a consequence of the rehandling of a theme which is recurrent through the poem: . . . the Salvation of the Heathen, . . . the C-reviser took pains to see [that] a quite different line of thought was developed . . . through the greater part of the poem. This projection of what seems to be a new attitude to one of the notoriously difficult problems confronting medieval Christian thinking . . . [a] strand of thought followed through with care by C-reviser . . . to accommodate the new view."

74. Also an idea found in Olivi, although his views are much more complex; see Burr, *Persecution*, 46–50.

75. Rhodes (*Poetry Does Theology*, 149–52) gives a recent summary (here in relation to his study of *St. Erkenwald*) of previous generous attitudes to salvation of the non-Christian peoples. Following Marcia Colish, he mentions how different periods of the Middle Ages adapted the Trajan story. Early versions stressed the charisma of Pope Gregory, later ones, the mercy of God. John of Salisbury stressed Trajan's virtue as the efficient cause of his own salvation; St. Thomas counted Trajan among a large group of souls who would not finally be damned if they adhered to natural law and practiced the natural theology that would lead to. Rhodes also mentions the view that the author of *St. Erkenwald* knew *Piers Plowman* (150). See also Grady, *"Piers Plowman, St. Erkenwald,"* 61–86, and more recently, his *Representing Righteous Heathens*. Other very recent studies include Benson, *Public Piers Plowman*, 148 ff., and Davis, "'Fullynge' Nature."

76. Russell and Kane, like Pearsall, read the former, Skeat's edition reads the latter. For the variants, see Langland, *Piers Plowman: C Version*, ed. Russell and Kane, note to 124. Both lines are missing from G (Cambridge University Library Dd.iii.13).

77. Hudson, *Premature Reformation*, 291, and her "Langland and Lollardy."

78. See ch. 9, n. 55, above for Mechthild's liberal views on baptism.

79. See Pearsall's note to C.XII.74.

80. We have already seen something of Chaucer's penchant for determinism, on which see Shepherd, "Religion and Philosophy."

81. Quoted from Ockham's *Dialogus* in Oberman, *Harvest of Medieval Theology*, 375.

82. See Kerby-Fulton, "Women Readers," and "Piers Plowman." See also Bynum, *Jesus as Mother*, 132–33.

83. Simpson, "Constraints on Satire."

84. Pearsall points this out in his note to XII.29a.

85. "Audivi archana verba que non licet homini loqui" (A.XII.22a).

86. B.XVIII.395a and C.XX.438a.

87. See, for instance, the *Speculum devotorum* author's distrust of it, "I commytte it to þe dome of þe reder whether he woll admytte it or none," cited from Notre Dame, Indiana, University of Notre Dame MS 67, fol. 91v. See Gillespie, "Haunted Text," 147.

88. *Gospel of Nicodemus*: "Hanc coniurationem audientes Karinus et Leucius contremuerunt corpore et conturbati gemuerunt corde. Et simul respicientes in caelum fecerunt singaculum crucis digitis suis in linguas suas et statim simul locuti sunt dicentes: 'Da nobis singulos tummos cartae et scribamus quod uidimus et audiuimus.' Et sedentes scripserunt

singuli sic dicentes. . . ." What follows (ch. 18) describes when those who waited in darkness saw a great light: "Nos cum essemus cum omnibus patribus nostris positi in profoundo in caligine tenebrarum, subito factus est aureus solis calor purpureaque regalis lux inlustrans super nos. Statim omnis generis humani pater Adam cum omnibus patriarchis et prophetis exultauerunt dicentes . . ." (p. 36). After their narration of the Harrowing episode, however, they conclude in ch. 27, "Haec sunt diuina sacra mysteria quae uidimus et audiuimus, ego Karinus et Leutius, fratres germani. Amplius non sumus permissi enarrare cetera mysteria Domini, sicut contestans Michael archangelus dixit nobis: '. . . Et cum nemine hominum eritis loquentes sed eritis ut muti usque dum ueniet hora ut permittat uobis ipse dominus referre suae diuinitatis mysteria'" (47–48). This solemnly imposed silence adds a great air of mystery to the question of what they saw about salvations — thus the important association between silence and "archana verba."

    89. See N. Watson, "Visions of Inclusion" for this argument.

    90. Watson (ibid., 158) cites an edition of the B text (unidentified) which leaves the "archana verba" quote out of the quotation marks of Christ's speech with some direct consequences for Watson's interpretation. Both Kane and Donaldson's and Pearsall's editions *include* the quote in Christ's speech.

    91. See also Hill, "Universal Salvation," 74, discussing the apocryphal *Visio Pauli* in which St. Paul wins some relief for the damned. The "arcana verba" passage from 2 Cor. 12:4 is the premise for the *Visio Pauli*.

    92. Vitto, *Virtuous Pagan*, 84 and 73.

    93. On this see the fine discussion of Aaron Thom, who points out that line C.XX.430 of the Harrowing scene, "be hit enything abouthe," referring to Christ's sacrifice, may override all other concerns in Christ's speech and relate closely to Article 5 of Uthred's condemnation. I am grateful to Aaron, once again, for permission to cite his "And if lawe wol."

    94. Langland carefully codes parts of the poem for specific audiences, often using the Latin to signal such shifts; Kerby-Fulton, "Langland and the Bibliographic Ego"; Kerby-Fulton and Justice, "Langlandian Reading Circles."

    95. Langland shares with both Julian and Margery Kempe this more open attitude, as Watson has pointed out, unlike Hilton, who, as Thomas Bestul puts it, is "distinctly hard line" on the question of the salvation of non-Christians. See Thomas Bestul's introduction to his edition of Hilton, *Scale of Perfection*, 4.

    96. Printed as Passus 12 of the *A Version* in Kane's edition (see his Introduction), and see also Anne Middleton's superb article, "Making a Good End," 243–66.

    97. See Alford, *Piers Plowman: A Guide to the Quotations*, for A.XII.19a, and the question of how Langland translates "tabescebam."

    98. This is the line that clinches non-authorial status of this portion: Langland never plagiarizes himself like this, but imitators and scribal interpolators do it all the time.

    99. Oberman, *Harvest of Medieval Theology*, "The Problem of Extrascriptural Tradition," 371–82; for Uthred and the influence of Ockham, see Knowles, "Censured Opinions," 318.

    100. Compare the genuine quotation above: "if lewede men knew . . ." which is Langland's oblique way of saying the exact same thing. This new level of confrontation seems *hyper*Langlandian rather than authentic Langland.

    101. Kane, *Piers Plowman: Evidence*.

102. As H. Ansgar Kelly has shown in relation to the Joan of Arc trials, the right to remain silent was a feature of medieval legal proceedings, and "remaining silent before being formally charged was especially important in heresy cases." See Kelly, "The Right to Remain Silent," 993.

103. Kerby-Fulton and Justice, "Langlandian Reading Circles." For concurrance, see Hanna, "Emendations," 186–87, and Matheson's review of Hanna's *William Langland*.

104. That is, thirty-nine items can be found in Alford, *Piers Plowman: Glossary of Legal Diction*.

105. "Vidi preuarica[nt]es & tabescebam" (A.XII.19a).

106. "Audivi archana verba que non licet homini loqui" (A.XII.22a).

107. "Quid est veritas?" (A.XII.28).

108. But knew or borrowed from at least two versions of the poem, one of which was the C text, as Middleton shows in "Making a Good End," and Barr in *Signes and Sothe*, 19–22.

109. Scase, "First to Reckon Richard," 49–66.

110. This is Anne Middleton's astute argument (see "Making a Good End").

111. The first "Vidi" quote of But closely parallels the "Existimasti" quote (B.X.291, B.XI.95, C.XII.29a) and A.XII.19a's "tabescebam."

112. The verse immediately before this is "Sedens *adversus fratrem* tuum loquebaris, et adversus filium matris tuae ponebas *scandalum*" (20).

113. See Alford, "Role of Quotations," 80–90, on Langland's use of a concordance. Another quote used in the B, just lines before A's "Dum steteritis ante Reges . . .", another inquisitional quotation, is *Nemo bonus* (B.X.447, though not recorded in Alford). *Nemo bonus* was to be resituated in the Feast of Patience, the moment when Clergie admits his terrible limitations, provoking Piers' mysterious epiphany.

114. "Of Weddid Men," in Salisbury, *Trials of Joy*. I am grateful to Prof. Salisbury for sending me a copy of her text prior to publication.

115. This gives us a clue to the intended audience, as well as the implied one. The implied audience is meant to share in frustration with the self-centredness of the rich. The intended audience, however, must have included some well-off people — those who "geten grete richessis and heighe statis and beneficis to here children," and some comfortably middle class or gentry, who insist on sending their children into careers in law to the peril of their souls. A treatise aimed at these kinds of households was aimed at substantive people in medieval society.

116. Hudson, *Selections*, 26.

117. Emden, *Biographical Register*.

118. Even the Blackfriars condemnations are more of a hodge-podge than one might expect; the authorities, of course, were not yet absolutely certain what opinions were Wycliffite — they condemn at least one idea, as we have seen, that came from Joachite prophetic circles (in Conclusion IX), and at least one, according to Workman, associated with Nicholas Hereford, but sounding much more Ockhamist than Wycliffite: Conclusion VII, "Item quod Deus debet obedire diabolo." See Netter, *Fasciculi Zizaniorum*, 278 for VII; 279 for IX. For chroniclers, in addition to those mentioned in chapter 2, see especially Catto and Mooney, *The Chronicle of John Somer*, 206, for a list of additions in Bodleian Library, Digby 57, largely of 1380s events, but including Joachim or Fiore (added under 1162 by the Ricardian hand).

Notes to Appendix A

1. For the sources cited here, see Chronology, 1407–9.
2. See de Hamel, *The Book*, and, more recently, Hanna, "English Biblical Texts," 141–54; see also Somerset, "Professionalizing Translation," 145–58; Simpson, *English Literary History*; Orme, *Medieval Children*; Gillespie, "Haunted Text."
3. See Middleton, "Acts of Vagrancy."
4. Cited, with occasional Latin insertions, in the translation made by Foxe, *Acts and Monuments*, 3.242–49.
5. Hudson, *Lollards and Their Books*, 142 n. 5 for the list, and 149.
6. Workman, *John Wyclif*, 2.196, from *Myroure of our Lady*, ed. Blunt.
7. Schirmer, "Reading Lessons at Syon Abbey," and Justice, "General Words."
8. Watson cites Minnis and Scott, *Medieval Literary Theory*, 374, and Deanesly, *Lollard Bible*.
9. Hudson, *Selections*, 67–72.

Notes to Appendix C

1. See Lerner, *Heresy of the Free Spirit*, 40, and Chronology, 1382 and the scholarship listed in the note on Crumpe's suspension. On "lollar/d," see also more recently Scase, "Heu! quanta desolatio," 19–36, and Cole, "William Langland," 37–58; see, too, Cole, "William Langland's Lollardy," 25–54, and for a very recent assessment, Hudson, "Langland and Lollardy?" 93–105.
2. For Adam's apocalyptic sense of Old and New Testament concordances and the ceasing of the "three miracles" of priesthood on account of corruption, see his *Chronicon* for 1402, "Quare sicut ueteris testamenti uenalitate sacerdocium corrumpente tria cessarunt miracula . . ." (160); he later returned to the same theme in a letter to William Swan, "et templi sequitur confusio in nouo testamento inter Romam et Constanciam ac in sacerdocio subsequens scisma Lollardensibus atque Begwinis operantibus" (p. lxxvii).
3. See Hudson, "Langland and Lollardy?" with whose findings I agree (see Kerby-Fulton, "Langland in His Working Clothes").
4. Thus in Bernardus Guidonis, *Practica inquisitionis*, the relevant chapter heading reads "De secta Bequinorum: Sequitur de secto illorum qui Bequini et Bequine vulgariter appellantur." The first sentence makes the connection with Third Order Franciscans and Spirituals: "Bequinorum secta, qui Fratres Pauperes se appellant et dicunt se tenere et profiteri terciam regulam Sancti Francisci, modernis temporibus exsurrexit" (264).
5. Burr, "Olivi, Apocalyptic Expectation," 275 n. 8.
6. See Kerby-Fulton, "When Women Preached" for Douceline's *Vita* and the passages referred to here.
7. Olivi himself had used the verb "imbeguiniri" to describe the process of conversion to his own views; see his letter to the sons of Charles II who had been imprisoned since 1288, "A trustworthy man told me that even your father the King feared that you would be made beguines [timuerat vos imbeguiniri], or to speak more properly, that you would be

made fools [in diuinis infatuari] of in religious matter through my fine words. If he believed that it would happen according to the way the apostle describes when he says, 'We are fools for Christ' (I Cor. 4:10) or 'Whoever wishes to be wise in this world must be foolish in order to be wise' (I Cor. 3:8) . . . then I do not have the wisdom and power to fill you with this supremely wise foolishness" (translated in McGinn, *Apocalyptic Spirituality*, 179, from Ehrle, "Die Spiritualen," 534–40).

8. Burr, *Olivi's Peaceable Kingdom*, 199–200.

9. For all these views, see Burr, *Olivi's Peaceable Kingdom*, 200–3; Burr, *Persecution*, 76–79; and some of the primary sources cited in ch. 2 above, including Olivi's Matthew *Postilla*.

10. For these ideas, see Guidonis, *Practica inquisitionis*, 264–87, and Lee et al., *Western Mediterranean Prophecy*, 49–50, citing from Rome, Biblioteca Apostolica Vaticana, MS Vat. Lat. 606, fols. 26r–27v, for the information below. According to Gui, the *Beguini/e*'s most valued work was Olivi's *Postilla*, available in both Latin and the vernacular.

11. On which see Newman, *From Virile Woman*, ch. 6.

12. See Hudson, *Lollards and Their Books*.

13. Fleming, *Introduction to the Franciscan Literature*, 100.

14. Sbaralea, *Bullarium Franciscanum*, 5.135.

15. For both quotations, and other instances, see Van Engen, "Devout Communities," 65 and 57.

16. As Hudson points out in "Langland and Lollardy?"

17. On the *status medius*, see Van Engen, "Devout Communities," 74.

Works Cited

Primary Works

Angelo of Clareno. *Historia septem tribulationum ordinis minorum*. In *Archiv für Literatur- und Kirchengeschichte*, vol. 2, edited by H. Denifle and F. Ehrle, 108–336. Berlin: Weidmannsche Buchhandlung, 1886. Reprint, Graz: Akademische Druck–U. Verlags Anstalt, 1956.

Annales Monastici. Edited by H. R. Luard. RS 36. Vol. 3. London: Longmans, Green, Reader, and Dyer, 1866.

De antiquis legibus liber. Edited by T. Stapleton. Camden Society 34. London, 1846.

Aquinas, St. Thomas. *Summa theologiae*. Edited by Thomas Gillby et al. 60 vols. London: Blackfriars, 1963.

Augustine. *The City of God*. Vol. 2, translated by John Healey. London: Dents, 1945.

———. *De Civitate Dei*. CCSL 47–48. Edited by Bernhard Dombart and Alphonse Kalb. Turnout: Brepols, 1955.

———. *The Essential Augustine*. Edited by Vernon Bourke. Indianapolis: Hackett, 1964.

———. *De Genesi at litteram*. PL 34, 472–78.

Bale, John. *Index Britanniae Scriptorum*. Edited by R. L. Poole and M. Bateson. Oxford, 1902. Rev. ed. Edited by C. Brett and J. P. Carley. Woodbridge: Brewer, 1990.

———. *Scriptorium Illustrium Maioris Britanniae Catalogus*. Basel, 1557, 1559.

Baluze, Etienne. *Vitae paparum avenionensium*. Edited by G. Mollat. Paris: Letouzey et Ané, 1914–27.

Barr, Helen, ed. *The Piers Plowman Tradition*. London: Everyman's, 1993.

Barratt, A., ed. *Women's Writing in Middle English*. London: Longman, 1992.

Blake, William. *The Poetry and Prose of William Blake*. Edited by David Erdman. New York: Doubleday, 1970.

Boethius. *"De Consolacione Philosophiae," Translated by John Walton, Canon of Oseney*. Edited by Mark Science. EETS, o.s. 170. Oxford: Oxford University Press, 1927.

Bonaventure. *Bonaventurae Collationes in Hexameron et Bonaventuriana quaedam selecta*. Edited by F. Delorme. Quaracchi, 1934.

Bradwardine, Thomas. *De Causa Dei contra Pelagianum*. London, 1618.

Brown, Edward, ed. *Appendix ad Fasciculum rerum expetendarum et fugiendarum by Ortvinus Gratius*. London, 1690.

Burton, Thomas de. *Chronicon Monasterii de Melsa [Meaux]*. Edited by E. A. Bond. RS 43. London, 1866–[68].

Butler, R. ed. *Jacobi Grace Kilkenniensis Annales Hiberniae.* Dublin, 1842.

Calendar of Close Rolls. London: HMSO, 1902–.

Calendar of Entries in the Papal Registers Relating to Great Britain and Ireland: Papal Letters. London: HMSO, 1893–.

Calendar of Entries in the Papal Registers Relating to Great Britain and Ireland: Petitions to the Pope, 1342–1419. Vol. 1. London: HMSO, 1896.

Calendar of Liberate Rolls. Edited by William Henry Stevenson. London: HMSO, 1916–64.

Calendar of Ormond Deeds. Edited by Edmund Curtis. Vol. 2. Irish MSS Commission. Dublin: HMSO, 1932–35.

Calendar of Patent Rolls. London: HMSO, 1901–.

"Calendar of Register of Archbishop Sweteman." Edited by Henry J. Lawler. *Proceedings of the Irish Academy* 29 (1911): 213–310.

Capgrave, John. *John Capgrave's Abbreuiacion of Cronicles.* Edited by Peter J. Lucas. EETS 285. Oxford: Oxford University Press, 1983.

Chartularium Universitatis Parisiensis. Edited by Emile Denifle and Heinrich Chatelain. 4 vols. Paris, 1889–91.

The Chastising of God's Children. Edited by Joyce Bazire and E. Colledge. Oxford: Blackwell, 1957.

Chronicles of Edward I and Edward II, Annales Paulini. Edited by William Stubbs. RS 76. 1882.

Chronicon Angliae. Edited by E. M. Thompson. RS 64. 1874.

Churchill, I. J. *Canterbury Administration: The Administrative Machinery of the Archbishop of Canterbury Illustrated from Original Records.* London, 1933.

"The Cloud of Unknowing" and "The Book of Privy Counsel." Edited by Phyllis Hodgson. EETS, o.s. 218. Oxford: Oxford University Press, 1944.

Colledge, Edmund. *The Latin Poems of Richard Ledrede, O. F. M., Bishop of Ossory, 1317–1360.* Toronto: Pontifical Institute of Medieval Studies, 1974.

Cronica monasterii S. Albani. Edited by Henry Thomas Riley. London: Longman, 1863–76. Reprint, Wiesbaden: Lessing-Drückerei, 1965.

Crow, Martin, and Clair Olson, eds. *Chaucer Life Records.* Oxford: Clarendon, 1966.

Curia Regis Rolls. London: HMSO, 1922–

Dean, James, ed. *Medieval English Political Writings.* Kalamazoo: Medieval Institute Publications, 1996.

Devotio Moderna: Basic Writings. Edited by John Van Engen. New York: Paulist Press, 1988.

Easting, Robert, ed. *The Revelation of the Monk of Eynsham.* EETS, o.s. 318. Oxford: Oxford University Press, 2002.

The English Register of Godstow Nunnery near Oxford, Written about 1450. 3 vols. Edited by Andrew Clark. EETS, o.s. 129–30, 142. London: K. Paul Trench, Trübner, 1905–11.

Etzkorn, Gerard. "Ockham at a Provincial Chapter, 1323: A Prelude to Avignon." *Archivum Franciscanum Historicum* 83 (1990): 557–67.

Eulogium historiarum. 3 vols. Edited by F. S. Haydon. RS 9. London: Longman, 1863.

Eymeric, Nicolas. *Directorium inquisitorum.* Edited by F. Pegna. Venice, 1609.

The Fabric Rolls of York Minster. Publications of the Surtees Society 35. Durham: Andrews, 1859.

Fitzmaurice, E. B., and A. G. Little. *Materials for the History of the Franciscan Province of Ireland, 1230–1450.* Manchester: Manchester University Press, 1920.

Foedera. Edited by T. Rymer. 4 vols. The Hague, 1740.

Foxe, John. *The Acts and Monuments of John Foxe.* Edited by S. R. Cattley and J. Pratt. 8 vols. London, 1853–70.

Francesco d'Assisi: Documenti e Archivi. Edited by Francesco Porzio. Milan: Electa, 1982.

Fredericq, P., ed. *Corpus documentorum inquisitionis haeretica pravitatis Neerlandicae.* Ghent–The Hague: J. Vuylsteke, 1889–1906.

Friedberg, E. *Corpus iuris canonici.* Leipzig, 1879–81.

Gerson, John. "Contre le *Roman de la Rose.*" In *Jean Gerson: Oeuvres complètes,* edited by Palémon Glorieux, 7.301–16. Paris: Desclée, 1960–73.

———. *Ioannis Carlerii de Gerson: De Mystica Theologia.* Edited by A. Combes. Lucani (Lugano): Thesauri Mundi, 1958.

———. *Jean Gerson: Early Works.* Translated Brian Patrick McGuire. New York: Paulist Press, 1988.

———. *De theologia mystica lectiones sex.* In *Jean Gerson: Oeuvres complètes,* edited by Palémon Glorieux. Paris: Desclée, 1960–73.

Gesta Abbatum S. Albani. Edited by H. T. Riley. RS 111. 1867.

Godfrey of Fontaines. *Les Quodlibets V, VI, and VII.* Edited by M. de Wulf and J. Hoffmans. Louvain: Institut Supérieur, 1914.

Goldast von Haiminsfeld, Melchior. *Processus Juris Joco-serius.* Hanau, 1611.

Gospel of Nicodemus. Edited by H. C. Kim. Toronto: Pontifical Institute of Medieval Studies, 1973.

Gramsci, Antonio. *Prison Notebooks.* Vol. 1. Edited by Joseph Buttigieg and translated by Joseph Buttigieg and Antonio Callari. New York: Columbia, 1991.

Guidonis, Bernardus. *Practica inquisitionis heretice pravitatis.* Edited by Canon C. Dovais. Paris: A. Picard, 1886.

Hicks, Eric, ed. and trans. *Le Débat sur le "Roman de la Rose."* Bibilothèque du XVe siècle 43. Paris: Champion, 1977. Reprint, Geneva: Slatkine Reprints, 1996.

Higden, Ranulph. *Polychronicon.* Edited by C. Babington and J. R. Lumby. RS 41. 1865.

Hildegard of Bingen. *Analecta Sanctae Hildegardis.* Edited by Jean-Baptiste Pitra. *Analecta sacra Hildegardis opera,* vol. 8. Monte Cassino, 1882.

———. *Epistolarium.* Edited by L. van Acker. Pars Secunda XCI–CCL. *CCCM* 91a. Turnhout: Brepols, 1991.

———. *Hildegardis Scivias.* Edited by Adelgundis Führkötter and Angela Carlevaris. *CCCM* 43–43a. Turnhout: Brepols, 1978.

———. *Liber divinorum operum.* Edited by Albert Derolez and Peter Dronke. *CCCM* 92. Turnhout, 1996.

———. *Prooemium vitae s. Disibodi.* Edited by Jean-Baptiste Pitra. *Analecta sacra Hildegardis opera,* vol. 8, 352–57. Montecassino, 1882. Reprint, Farnborough: Gregg Prees, 1966.

Hilton, Walter. *The Scale of Perfection.* Edited by Thomas Bestul. Kalamazoo: Western Michigan, 2000.

Historians of the Church of York and Its Archbishops. Edited by James Raine. London: Longman, 1879–94. Reprint, Wiesbaden: Kraus, 1965.

Holder-Egger, O. "Italienische Prophetien des 13. Jahrhunderts." *Neues Archiv* 15 (1890): 143–78; 30 (1905): 322–86; 33 (1908): 96–187.

Horae Eboracenses. Edited by Christopher Wordsworth. Publications of the Surtees Society 132. Durham: Andrew, 1920.

Hudson, Anne. *Selections from English Wycliffite Writings.* Cambridge: Cambridge University Press, 1978.

———. *Two Wycliffite Texts.* EETS, o.s. 301. Oxford: Oxford University Press, 1993.

———, ed. *The Works of a Lollard Preacher.* Oxford: Oxford University Press, 2001.

Humbert of Romans. *De eruditione praedicatorum.* In *Maxima bibliotheca veterum patrum,* vol. 25. Lyons, 1677.

Hyma, A., ed. "Super modo vivendi." *Archief voor de Geschiedenis van het Aartsbisdom Utrecht* 52 (1926): 1–100.

Die Indices librorum prohibitorum des sechzehnten Jahrhunderts, gesammelt. Edited by F. Heinrich Reusch. Tübingen, 1886.

Joachim of Fiore. *Abbot Joachim of Fiore: Liber de Concordia Noui ac Veteris Testamenti.* Edited by E. Randolph Daniel. Philadelphia: American Philosophical Society, 1983.

———. *Enchiridion super Apocalypsim.* Edited by Edward Burger. Toronto: Pontifical Institute of Medieval Studies, 1986.

———. *Expositio in Apocalypsim.* Venice, 1527.

———. [Ps.] *Joachimi Abbatis Liber contra Lombardum.* Edited by C. Ottaviano. Rome, 1934.

———. *Il libro delle figure [Liber figurarum].* Edited by L. Tondelli, M. Reeves, and B. Hirsch-Reich. 2nd ed. Turin, 1953.

John of Rupescissa. *Liber secretorum eventuum.* Edited by Christine Morerod-Fattebert, with introduction by Robert Lerner. Fribourg: Editions universitaires, 1994.

Jönsson, Arne. *Alfonso of Jaén: His Life and Works with Critical Editions of the Epistola Solitarii, the Informaciones and the Epistola Serui Christi.* Lund: Lund University Press, 1989.

Julian of Norwich. *A Book of Showings to the Anchoress Julian of Norwich.* Edited by Edmund Colledge and James Walsh. Toronto: Pontifical Institute of Medieval Studies, 1978.

———. *A Revelation of Love.* Edited by Marion Glasscoe. Exeter: University of Exeter, 1976.

———. *The Writings of Julian of Norwich.* Edited by Nicholas Watson and Jacqueline Jenkins. University Park: Pennsylvania State University Press, 2006.

Kaeppeli, Th. *Le procès contre Thomas Waleys, O.P.* Rome, 1936.

Kempe, Margery. *The Book of Margery Kempe.* Edited by S. B. Meech and H. E. Allen. EETS 212. Oxford: Oxford University Press, 1940.

———. *The Book of Margery Kempe.* Edited by B. A. Windeatt. New York: Longmans, 2000.

Knight, Ione Kemp, ed. *Wimbledon's Sermon.* Pittsburgh: Duquesne University Press, 1967.

Knighton, Henry. *Knighton's Chronicle, 1337–96.* Edited and translated by G. H. Martin. Oxford: Clarendon, 1995.

Laberge, D., ed. *Responsio quam fecit P. Ioannis ad litteram magistrorum.* In "Fr. Petri Ioannis Olivi, O. F. M.: Tria scripta sui ipsius apologetica annorum 1283 et 1285." *Archivum Franciscanum Historicum* 28 (1935–36): 133–55, 374–407.

Langland, William. *Piers Plowman: An Edition of the C-Text.* Edited by Derek Pearsall. Berkeley: University of California Press, 1979.

———. *Piers Plowman: A Working Facsimile of the Z-Text in Bodleian Library, Oxford, MS Bodley 851.* Introduced by Charlotte Brewer and A. G. Rigg. Cambridge: Brewer, 1994.

———. *Piers Plowman: The A Version.* Edited by G. Kane. London: Athlone Press, 1960.

———. *Piers Plowman: The B Version.* Edited by G. Kane and E. T. Donaldson. London, Athlone Press, 1988.

————. *Piers Plowman: The C Version*. Edited by George Russell and George Kane. London and Berkeley: Athlone Press, 1997.

————. *Piers Plowman: The Z Version*. Edited by A. G. Rigg and Charlotte Brewer. Toronto: Pontifical Institute of Medieval Studies, 1983.

Lehmann-Brockhaus, Otto. *Lateinische Schriftsquellen zur Kunst in England, Wales und Schottland, 901–1307*. Vol. 2. Munich: Prestel Verlag, 1956.

Little, A. G. *Franciscan Papers, Lists and Documents*. Manchester: Manchester University Press, 1943.

————, ed. *Fratris Thomae vulgo dicti de Eccleston Tractatus: De Adventu Fratrum Minorum in Angliam*. Manchester: Manchester University Press, 1951.

Lucas, Angela M., ed. *Anglo-Irish Poems of the Middle Ages*. Blackrock, Co. Dublin: Columbia Press, 1995.

Martene, E., and U. Duirand. *Veterum Scriptorium et Monumentorum*. Paris, 1733.

McCusker, H. "Books and Manuscripts Formerly in the Possession of John Bale." *The Library* 16 (1935): 144–65.

Mechthild of Hackeborn. *The Book of Ghostly Grace*. Edited by Theresa Halligan. Toronto: Pontifical Institute of Medieval Studies, 1979.

Memoriale of Walter Coventry. Edited by Williams Stubbs. 2 vols. RS 58. London: HMSO, 1872. Reprint, Wiesbaden: Kraus, 1965.

Monumenta Franciscana. Edited by J. S. Brewer. RS 4. London: Longman, 1858.

Munimenta Academia. Edited by H. Anstey. RS 50. London: Longman, 1863.

Myroure of our Lady. Edited by J. H. Blunt. EETS. London: Trübner, 1873.

Netter, Thomas. *Doctrinale Fide Catholicae contra Wiclevistas et Hussitas*. Edited by B. Blanciotti. Venice: Antonio Bassanesi, 1757–59.

————. *Fasciculi Zizaniorum magistri Johannis Wyclif cum tritico*. Edited by W. W. Shirley. London: Longman et al., 1858. Reprint, Weisbaden: Kraus, 1965.

Nyem, Theoderici de. *De Schismate*. Edited by George Erler. Leipzig, 1890.

Ockham, William. *Tractatus de Praedestinatione et de Praescientia Dei et de Futuris Contingentibus of William Ockham*. Edited by Philotheus Boehner. St. Bonaventure, NY: St. Bonaventure University, 1945.

————. *William Ockham, A Letter to the Friars Minor and Other Writings*. Edited by Arthur McGrade and John Kilcullen and translated by John Kilcullen. Cambridge: Cambridge University Press, 1995.

Offler, H. S., et al. *Guillelmi de Ockham Opera Politica*. 4 vols. Manchester: Manchester University Press, 1940–97.

The Orchard of Syon. Edited by Phyllis Hodgson and Gabriel Liegey. EETS, o.s. 258. Oxford: Oxford University Press, 1966.

Ossinger, J. F. *Bibliotheca Augustiniana*. Ingolstadt, 1768.

Paris, Matthew. *Chronica Majora (1259)*. Edited by H. R. Luard. RS 57, part 5. London, 1872.

Pecham, John. *Registrum Epistolarum Fratris Iohannis Peckham*. Edited by Charles Trice Martin. 3 vols. RS 77. London: Longman, 1882–85.

————. *Fratris Johannis Pecham, Tractatus Tres Paupertate*. Edited by C. L. Kingsford et al. Aberdeen: Typis Academis, 1910.

Peck, Russell. *Heroic Women from the Old Testament in Middle English Verse*. Kalamazoo, MI: TEAMS, 1991.

Pecock, Reginald. *Donet*. Edited by E. Hitchcock. EETS, o.s. 156. London, 1921.

———. *The Repressor of Over Much Blaming of the Clergy.* 2 vols. Edited by Churchill Babington. London: Longman, 1860. Reprint, Wiesbaden: Kraus, 1966.

Polonus, Martinus (Martinus Oppaviensis). *Chronicon pontificum et imperatorum.* Edited by Ludwig Weiland. MGH *Scriptores* 22. Hanover, 1872.

Porete, Margaret. "Margaret Porete: *The Mirror of Simple Souls,* A Middle English Translation." Edited by Marilyn Doiron. *Archivo Italiano per la Storia della Pietà* 5 (1968): 241–355.

———. *Le Mirouer des Simples Ames (Speculum Simplicium Animarum).* Edited by Romana Guarnieri and Paul Verdeyen. *CCCM* 69. Turnhout: Brepols, 1986.

———. *The Mirror of Simple Souls.* Edited and translated by Edmund Colledge et al. Notre Dame, IN: University of Notre Dame Press, 1999.

Raine, J. *Historical Papers and Letters from the Northern Registers.* London: Longman, 1873.

Ralph of Coggeshale. *Chronicon Anglicanum.* Edited by J. Stevenson. RS 66. London, 1875.

Register of Henry Chichele. Edited by E. F. Jacob. Oxford: Oxford University Press, 1945.

Register of John de Grandisson, Bishop of Exeter, 1327–1369. Edited by F. C. Hingeston-Randolph. London: George Bell, 1894–97.

Register of William of Wykeham, Bishop of Winchester, 1366–69. Edited by T. F. Kirby. London: Hampshire Record Society, 1896–99.

Register of William Melton, Archbishop of York. Edited by R. M. T. Hill. York: Canterbury and York Society, 1988.

Registrum epistolarum Johannis Peckham, 1279–1292. Edited by C. Martin. Canterbury and York Society 14. York, 1908.

Registrum Johannis Trefnant. Edited by W.W. Capes. Canterbury and York Society 20. York, 1916.

Registrum Radulphi Baldock. Edited by R. C. Fowler. Canterbury and York Society 7. York, 1911.

Rigg, A. G. "An Edition of a Fifteenth-century Commonplace Book (Trinity College, Cambridge, MS 0.9.38)." PhD diss., Oxford University, 1966.

Riverside Chaucer. Edited by Larry Benson. 3rd ed. New York: Houghton Mifflin, 1987.

Roman de la Rose. Edited by F. Lecoy. 3 vols. Classiques Français du Moyen Age 92, 95, 98. Paris: Champion, 1965–70.

The Romaunt of the Rose and Le Roman de la Rose, a Parallel-Text Edition. Edited by Ronald Sutherland. Berkeley: University of California Press, 1968.

Rotuli Parliamentorum. Edited by J. Strachey. 6 vols. London, 1767–83.

Rutebeuf. *Poèmes concernant L'Université de Paris.* Edited by H. H. Lucas. Manchester: Manchester University Press, 1952.

Ruysbroeck [Ruusbroec], Jan van. *Die Geestelike Brulocht (De ornatu spiritualium nuptiarum).* Edited by J. Alaerts (Dutch and Latin Texts). Translated by L. Surius (Latin) and H. Rolfson (English). *CCCM* 103. Turnhout: Brepols, 1988.

———. *Ioannis Rusbrochii Ornatus spiritualis desponsationis / Gerardo Magno interprete.* Edited by Rijcklof Hofman. Turnhout: Brepols, 2000.

Salimbene. *The Chronicle of Salimbene de Adam.* Translated by J. Baird et al. Binghamton, NY: Medieval and Renaissance Texts, 1986.

Salter, H. E., W. A. Pantin, and H. G. Richardson, eds. *Formularies Which Bear on the History of Oxford, c. 1204–1420.* Oxford: Oxford University Press, 1942.

Sbaralea, J. *Bullarium Franciscanum.* Edited by Conrad Eubel. Rome, 1898.

Scattergood, V. J., ed. *The Works of Sir John Clanvowe.* Cambridge: D. S. Brewer, 1975.

Sede Vacante Register, Worcester, 1301–1435. Edited by J. Willis-Bund. Worcester Historical Society, 1897.

Serjantson, Mary. *Legendys of Hooly Wummen*. EETS, o.s. 206. London, 1938.

Silvestris, Bernard. *Cosmographia*. Edited by Peter Dronke. Leiden: Brill, 1978.

Talbot, C. H., ed. *The Life of Christina of Markyate*. Toronto: Medieval Academy, 1998.

Testamenta eboracensia: A Selection of Wills from the Registry at York. Publications of the Surtees Society 30. Durham: Andrews, 1855.

Theiner, A. ed. *Vetera Monumenta Hibernorum et Scotorum Historiam*. Rome: Typis Vaticana, 1864.

Theoderici de Nyem. *De Schismate*. Edited by George Erler. Leipzig, 1890.

Theophilus: De Diuersis Artibus. Translated by C. R. Dodwell. London: Thomas Nelson and Sons, 1961.

Thomas à Kempis. *The Imitation of Christ*. Edited by J. H. Biggs. EETS 309. Oxford: Clarendon, 1997.

Todd, J., ed. *The Last Age of the Church*. Dublin: University Press, 1840.

Trithemius. *Annales Hirsaugienses*. Edited by Mabillon. St. Gall, 1690.

Ubertino da Casale. *Arbor vitae crucifixae Jesu*. Venice, 1485.

―――. "Sanctitati apostolicae." In *Archiv für Literatur- and Kirchengeschicte des Mittelalters*. Vol. 2. Edited by H. Denifle and F. Ehrle, 377–416. Berlin: Weidmannsche Buchhandlung, 1886. Reprint, Graz: Akademische Druck–U. Verlags Anstalt, 1956.

Usk, Adam. *The Chronicle of Adam Usk*. Edited and translated by C. Given-Wilson. Oxford: Clarendon, 1997.

Usk, Thomas. *The Testament of Love by Thomas Usk*. Edited by R. A. Shoaf. Kalamazoo, MI: TEAMS, 1998.

Verardi, Luigi. *Gioacchino da Fiore, Il Protocollo di Anagni*. Cosenza: Edizioni Orizzonti Meridionali, 1992.

Vita Egberti. Edited by G. Dumbar. *Analecta seu vetera aliquot scripta inedita*. Deventer, 1719.

Vita Sanctae Hildegardis. Edited by Monica Klaes. CCCM 126. Turnhout: Brepols, 1993.

Walsingham, Thomas. *Historia Anglicana*. 2 vols. Edited by H. T. Riley. RS 28. London: Longman, Green, 1863–64.

Walter of Coventry. *Memoriale*. Edited by W. Stubbs. RS 58. London, 1872–73.

Wilkins, David, ed. *Concilia Magnae Britanniae et Hiberniae*. 4 vols. London, 1737.

William of Newburgh. *Historia Rerum Anglicarum*. Edited by R. Howlett. RS 82, part 1. London, 1884.

William of St. Amour. "The 'Collations' of William of St. Amour against S. Thomas." Edited by John V. Fleming. *Recherches de Théologie Ancienne et Médiévale* 32 (1965): 132–38.

―――. *De periculis novissimorum temporum*. In *Magistri Guilielmi de Sancto Amore Opera Omnia*. Constanciae, 1632.

―――. *De periculis novissimorum temporum*. Edited by E. Brown in Appendix to O. Gratius, *Fasciculus rerum expetendarum*. London, 1690.

Wogan-Browne, Jocelyn, et al., eds. *The Idea of the Vernacular: An Anthology of Middle English Literary Theory, 1280–1520*. University Park: Pennsylvania State University Press, 1999.

Wright, Thomas, ed. *Political Poems and Songs*. 2 vols. RS 14. London, 1859.

―――. *The Political Songs of England*. London: Camden Society, 1839.

―――. *Proceedings against Dame Alice Kyteler*. London, 1843.

Wyclif, John. *De Apostasia*. Edited by Michael H. Dziewicki. London: Wyclif Society, 1883.

———. *De Blasphemia.* Edited by Michael H. Dziewicki. London: Wyclif Society, 1893.

———. *De Civili Domino.* Edited by R. L. Poole and J. Loserth. 4 vols. London: Wyclif Society, 1885–1904.

———. *De concordacione fratrum.* In *John Wyclif's Polemical Works in Latin,* vol. 1, edited by R. Buddensieg. London: Wyclif Society, 1883.

———. *De Ente Praedicamentali, Quaestiones XIII Logicae et Philosophiae.* Edited by Rudolf Beer. London: Wyclif Society, 1891.

———. *De Eucharistica Tractatus Maior: Accedit Tractatus de Eucharistica et Poenitentia sive De Confessione.* Edited by J. Loserth. London: Wyclif Society, 1892.

———. *De fundatione sectarum.* In *John Wyclif's Polemical Works in Latin,* edited by Rudolf Buddensieg. London, 1883.

———. *Iohannis Wyclif Tractatus De Apostasia.* Edited by M. H. Dziewicki. London, 1889.

———. *De officio regis.* Edited A. W. Pollard and C. Sayle. London: Wyclif Society, 1887.

———. *Opera minora.* Edited by J. Loserth. London: Wyclif Society, 1913.

———. *Opus evangelicum.* 2 vols. London: Wyclif Society, 1895–96

———. *Sermones.* Edited by J. Loserth. 4 vols. London: Wyclif Society, 1886–89.

———. *Tractatus de civili domino.* Edited by R. L. Poole and J. Loserth. London, 1888.

———. *Tractatus de Trinitate.* Edited by Allen duPont Breck. Denver: Unversity of Colorado Press, 1962.

———. *Trialogus, cum Supplemento Trialogi.* Edited by G. V. Lechler. Oxford, 1869.

———. *De veritate sacrae scripturae.* Edited by R. Buddensieg. London: Wyclif Society, 1905.

York Memorandum Book. Edited by M. Sellers. *Publication of the Surtees Society* 1 (1920): 236–38.

Secondary Works

Abbot, T. K. *Catalogue of the MSS in the Library of Trinity College, Dublin.* Dublin, 1900.

Adams, Marilyn, and Norman Kretzmann. *Predestination, God's Foreknowledge, and Future Contingents.* New York: Appleton, 1969.

Adams, Robert. "Langland's Theology." In Alford, *Companion to Piers Plowman,* 87–116.

Aers, David. *Faith, Ethics and Church.* Cambridge: Brewer, 2001.

———. "John Wyclif: Poverty and the Poor." *Yearbook of Langland Studies* 17 (2003): 55–72.

———. "Julian and the Crisis of Authority." In Aers and Staley, *Powers of the Holy,* 107–78.

Aers, David, and Lynn Staley. *The Powers of the Holy: Religion, Politics and Gender in Late Medieval English Culture.* University Park: Pennsylvania State University Press, 1996.

Alford, John, ed. *A Companion to Piers Plowman.* Berkeley: University of California Press, 1988.

———. *Piers Plowman: A Glossary of Legal Diction.* Cambridge: Brewer, 1988.

———. *Piers Plowman: A Guide to the Quotations.* Binghamton, NY: Medieval and Renaissance Texts, 1992.

———. "The Role of the Quotations in *Piers Plowman.*" *Speculum* 52 (1977): 80–90.

Allmand, C. T. "The Civil Lawyers." In *Profession, Vocation, and Culture in Later Medieval England: Essays Dedicated to the Memory of A. R. Myers,* edited by Cecil H. Clough, 155–80. Liverpool: Liverpool University Press, 1982.

Armstrong, Edward A. *Saint Francis, Nature Mystic: The Derivation and Significance of the Nature Stories in the Franciscan Legends.* Berkeley: University of California Press, 1976.

Arnold, John. "Lollard Trials and Inquisitorial Discourse." In *Fourteenth-Century England*, vol. 2, edited by Chris Given-Wilson, 81–94. Woodbridge: Boydell, 2002.

Aston, Margaret. "'Caim's Castles': Poverty, Politics, and Disendowment." In *Church Politics and Patronage in the Fifteenth Century*, edited by Barry Dobson, 46–81. New York: St. Martin's, 1984.

———. "Lollard Women Preachers?" *Journal of Ecclesiastical History* 31 (1980): 441–61.

Auden, W. H. *The Collected Poems.* Edited by E. Mendelson. New York: Vintage, 1991.

Aylmer, G., and R. Cant, eds. *The History of York Minister.* Oxford: Clarendon, 1977.

Bacher, John Rea. *The Prosecution of Heretics in Mediaeval England.* PhD diss., University of Pennsylvania, 1928. Partially published: Philadelphia, 1942.

Baird, Joseph L., and John R. Kane. *La Querelle de la Rose: Letters and Documents.* North Carolina Studies in the Romance Languages and Literatures 199. Chapel Hill: University of North Carolina Press, 1978.

Baker, Denise Nowakowski. *Julian of Norwich's Showings: From Vision to Book.* Princeton, NJ: Princeton University Press, 1994.

Barr, Helen. *Signes and Sothe: Language in the Piers Plowman Tradition.* Cambridge: Brewer, 1994.

Barr, Helen, and Anne Hutchinson. *Text and Controversy from Wyclif to Bale: Essays in Honour of Anne Hudson.* Turnhout: Brepols, 2005.

Barton, Thomas. "Engendering Inquisition: Ockham's Trial at Avignon Revisited." Unpublished paper.

Bell, David. "The Books of Meaux Abbey." *Analecta Cisterciensia* 40 (1984): 25–84.

———. *An Index of Authors and Works in Cistercian Libraries in Great Britain.* Kalamazoo, MI: Cistercian Publications, 1992.

Benson, C. David. *Public Piers Plowman: Modern Scholarship and Late Medieval English Culture.* University Park: Pennsylvania State University Press, 2004.

Benson, C. David, and Lynne Blanchfield. *The Manuscripts of Piers Plowman: The B Version.* Woodbridge: D. S. Brewer, 1997.

Bériou, Nicole. "The Right of Women to Give Religious Instruction in the Thirteenth Century." In Kienzle and Walker, *Women Preachers*, 134–45.

Bernstein, Allen E. *Pierre d'Ailly and the Blanchard Affair.* Leiden: Brill, 1978.

Bierbaum, M. *Bettelordern und Weltgeistlichkeit an der Universität Paris.* Münster i. W.: Franziskanische Studien, 1920.

Bignami-Odier, Jean. *Etudes sur Jean de Roquetaillade.* Paris: J. Vrin, 1952.

Biller, Peter. "William of Newburgh and the Cathar Mission to England." In *Life and Thought in the Northern Church, c. 1100–c. 1700: Essays in Honour of Claire Cross*, edited by D. Wood, 11–30. Woodbridge: Boydell, 1999.

Bischoff, Guntram G. "Early Premonstatensian Eschatology: The Apocalyptic Myth." In *The Spirituality of Western Christendom*, edited by Jean Leclercq and E. Rozanne Elder, 41–71. Kalamazoo, MI: Cistercian Publications, 1976.

Blamires, Alcuin. "Women and Creative Intelligence in Medieval Thought." In Olson and Kerby Fulton, *Voices in Dialogue*, 213–30.

Blamires, Alcuin, et al., eds. *Women Defamed and Woman Defended: An Anthology of Medieval Texts.* Oxford: Clarendon, 1992.

Blamires, Alcuin, and C.W. Marx. "Woman Not to Preach: A Disputation in B. L. MS Harley 31." *Journal of Medieval Latin* 3 (1993): 34–63.

Bloomfield, Morton. *Piers Plowman as a Fourteenth-Century Apocalypse.* Columbus: Ohio State University Press [1962].

Bloomfield, Morton, and Marjorie Reeves. "The Penetration of Joachimism into Northern Europe." *Speculum* 29 (1954): 772–93.

Blumenfeld-Kosinki, Renate. "Satirical Views of the Beguines in Northern French Literature." In *New Trends in Feminine Spirituality: The Holy Women of Liège and Their Import*, edited by J. Dor et al., 1–14. Turnhout: Brepols, 1998.

Bodleian Library Quarto Catalogues. Vol. 9, *Digby Manuscripts.* 2nd ed. Edited by R.W. Hunt and A. G. Watson. Oxford: Bodleian Library, 1999.

Boland, Paschal. *The Concept of Discretio Spirituum in John Gerson's "De Probatione Spirituum" and "De Distinctione Verarum Visionum a Falsis."* Washington, DC: Catholic University of America Press, 1959.

Bose, Mishtooni. "Reginald Pecock's Vernacular Voice." In Somerset, Havens, and Pitard, *Lollards and Their Influence*, 217–36.

Bostick, Curtis. *The Antichrist and the Lollards.* Leiden: Brill, 1998.

Bowers, John M. *The Canterbury Tales: Fifteenth-Century Continuations and Additions.* Kalamazoo, MI: TEAMS, 1992.

———. "*Piers Plowman* and the Police: Notes toward a History of the Wycliffite Langland." *Yearbook of Langland Studies* 6 (1992):1–50.

Boyle, L. E. "The Oculus Sacerdotis and Some Other Works of William of Pagula." *Transactions of the Royal Historical Society*, 5th ser., 5 (1955): 81–110.

Braun, N. L. *The Abbot Trithemius, 1462–1516: The Renaissance of Monastic Humanism.* Leiden: Brill, 1981.

Brentano, Robert. *A New World in a Small Place: Church and Religion in the Diocese of Rieti, 1188–1378.* Berkeley: University of California Press, 1994.

Brieger, P., et al. *Illuminated Manuscripts of the Divine Comedy.* 3 vols. Princeton, NJ: Princeton University Press, 1969.

Brown, Peter, ed. *A Companion to Chaucer.* Oxford: Blackwell, 2000.

Brownlee, Kevin, and Sylvia Huot, eds. *Rethinking the Romance of the Rose: Text, Image, Reception.* Philadelphia: University of Pennsylvania Press, 1992.

Bund, Konrad. "Die 'Prophetin', ein Dichter und die Niderlassung der Bettelorden in Köln." *Mittellateinisches Jahrbuch* 23 (1988): 171–260.

Burdach, K. *Der Dichter des Ackermann aus Böhmen und seine Zeit.* Vol. 3 of *Vom Mittelalter zur Reformation*, part 2. Berlin: Weidmannsche Buchhandlung, 1926–32.

Burke-Severs, J. *The Literary Relationships of Chaucer's Clerkes Tale.* London: Archon, 1972.

Burnham, Louisa. "So Great a Light, So Great a Smoke: The Heresy and Resistance of the Beguins of Languedoc (1314–30)." PhD diss., Northwestern University, 2000.

Burr, David. *The Franciscan Spirituals: From Protest to Persecution in the Century after Saint Francis.* University Park: Pennsylvania State University Press, 2001.

———. *Olivi and Franciscan Poverty: The Origins of the Usus Pauper Controversy.* Philadelphia: University of Pennsylvania Press, 1989.

————. "Olivi and the Limits of Intellectual Freedom." In *Contemporary Reflections on the Medieval Christian Tradition,* edited by G. H. Shriver, 185–99. Durham, NC: Duke University Press, 1974.

————. "Olivi, Apocalyptic Expectation, and Visionary Experience." *Traditio* 41 (1985): 273–88.

————. *Olivi's Peaceable Kingdom: A Reading of the Apocalypse Commentary.* Philadelphia: University of Pennsylvania Press, 1993.

————. *The Persecution of Peter Olivi.* Philadelphia: University of Pennsylvania Press, 1976.

Bynum, Caroline Walker. *Jesus as Mother: Studies in the Spirituality of the High Middle Ages.* Berkeley: University of California Press, 1982.

————. *The Resurrection of the Body.* New York: Columbia University Press, 1995.

Camille, Michael. *The Gothic Idol: Ideology and Image-Making in Medieval Art.* Cambridge: Cambridge University Press, 1989.

Caraffa, Philippo. *Il Monastero Florense di S. Maria della Gloria Presso Anagni.* Rome: Istituto Grafico Tiberino, 1940.

Carlos, José. *La Recepción de Hildegarde de Bingen en los Siglos XIII y XIV.* Ph.D diss., Universidade de Santiago de Compostela, Spain, 1997.

Carruthers, Mary. *The Book of Memory: A Study of Memory in Medieval Culture.* Cambridge: Cambridge University Press, 1990.

Catto, Jeremy. "An Alleged Great Council of 1374." *English Historical Review* 82 (1967): 764–71.

————. "Religion and the English Nobility in the Later Fourteenth Century." In *History and Imagination: Essays in Honour of H. R. Trevor-Roper,* edited by Hugh Lloyd-Jones, 43–55. New York: Oxford University Press, 1981.

————. "Wyclif and Wyclifism at Oxford." In *History of the University of Oxford,* vol. 2, *Late Medieval Oxford,* edited by J. Catto and R. Evans, 185–261. Oxford: Clarendon, 1992.

Catto, Jeremy, and Linne Mooney, eds. "The Chronicle of John Somer, OFM." In *Chronology, Conquest, and Conflict in Medieval England,* 197–285. Camden Miscellany 34. Cambridge: Cambridge University Press, 1997.

Cavanaugh, Susan Hagen. "A Study of Books Privately Owned in England: 1300–1450." PhD diss., University of Pennsylvania, 1980.

Clark, James. "Thomas Walsingham Reconsidered: Books and Learning at Late-Medieval St. Albans." *Speculum* 77 (2002): 832–60.

Clark, John. "Late Fourteenth-Century Cambridge Theology." In *The Medieval Mystical Tradition in England,* vol. 5, edited by Marion Glasscoe, 1–18. Cambridge: Brewer, 1992.

————. "Walter Hilton and 'Liberty of the Spirit.'" *The Downside Review* 96 (1978): 61–78.

Classen, Peter. "Libertas Scholastica—Scholarenprivilegien—Akademische Freiheit im Mittelalter." In Peter Classen, *Studium und Gesellschaft im Mittelalter,* edited by Johannes Fried. Stuttgart: A. Hiersemann, 1983.

Clopper, Lawrence. "Franciscans, Lollards and Reform." In Somerset, Havens, and Pitard, *Lollards and Their Influence,* 177–97.

————. *"Songes of Rechelesnesse": Langland and the Franciscans.* Ann Arbor: University of Michigan Press, 1997.

Cohen, Jeremy. *The Friars and the Jews: The Evolution of Medieval Anti-Judaism.* Ithaca, NY: Cornell University Press, 1982.

Cole, Andrew. "William Langland and the Invention of Lollardy." In Somerset, Havens, and Pitard, *Lollards and Their Influence*, 37–58.

———. "William Langland's Lollardy." *Yearbook of Langland Studies* 17 (2003): 25–54.

Coleman, Janet. *Piers Plowman and the Moderni*. Rome: Edizioni di Storia e Letteratura, 1981.

Colledge, Edmund. "*Epistola solitarii ad reges*: Alphonse of Pecha as Organizer of Birgittine and Urbanist Propaganda." *Mediaeval Studies* 43 (1956): 19–49.

———. "The Latin *Mirror of Simple Souls*: Margaret Porette's 'Ultimate Accolade'?" In *Langland, the Mystics and the Medieval English Religious Tradition: Essays in Honour of S. S. Hussey*, edited by Helen Phillips, 177–83. Cambridge: Brewer, 1990.

Colledge, Edmund, and Romana Guarnieri. "The Glosses by 'M. N.' and Richard Methley to the *Mirror of Simple Souls*." *Archivio Italiano per la Storia Pietà* 5 (1968): 357–82.

Constable, Giles. *The Reformation of the Twelfth Century*. Cambridge: Cambridge University Press, 1996.

Cook, A. S. "Chauceriana II: Chaucer's 'Linian'." *Romanic Review* 8 (1971): 358–82.

Coote, Lesley. "The Crusading Bishop: Henry Despenser and His Manuscript." In *Prophecy, Apocalypse and the Day of Doom*. Harlaxton Medieval Studies 12. Donington: Shaun Tyas, 2004.

———. *Prophecy and Public Affairs in Late Medieval England*. Woodbridge: Brewer, 2000.

Coote, Leslie, and T. Thorton. "Merlin, Erceldoune, Nixon: A Tradition of Popular Political Prophecies." *New Medieval Literature* 4 (2000): 132–150.

Copeland, Rita. *Pedagogy, Intellectuals and Dissent in the Later Middle Ages: Lollardy and Ideas of Learning*. Cambridge: Cambridge University Press, 2001.

———. *Rhetoric, Hermeneutics, and Translation in the Middle Ages: Academic Traditions and Vernacular Texts*. Cambridge: Cambridge University Press, 1991.

———. "William Thorpe and His Lollard Community: Intellectual Labor and the Representation of Dissent." In *Bodies and Disciplines*, edited by Barbara Hanawalt and David Wallace, 199–222. Minneapolis: University of Minnesota Press, 1996.

Cotter, Francis. *The Friars Minor in Ireland*. Bonaventure, NY: Bonaventure University, Franciscan Institute, 1994.

Coulton, G. *The Inquisition*. 1929. Reprint, Folcroft, PA: Folcroft Library Editions, 1974.

Courtenay, William. *Capacity and Volition: A History of the Distinction of Absolute and Ordained Power*. Bergamo: P. Lubrina, 1990.

———. "Inquiry and Inquisition: Academic Freedom in Medieval Universities." *Church History* 58 (1989): 168–82.

———. *Schools and Scholars in Fourteenth Century England*. Princeton, NJ: Princeton University Press, 1987.

———. "Theology and Theologians from Ockham to Wyclif." In *History of the University of Oxford*, vol. 2, *Late Medieval*, edited by J. Catto and R. Evans, 1–34. Oxford: Clarendon, 1992.

Coxe, H. O. *Catalogi Codicum Manuscriptorum Bibliothecae Bodleianae: Catal. Biblioth. Laudianae*. Oxford, 1858.

Cré, M. "Women in the Charterhouse." In *Writing Religious Women*, edited by D. Renevey and C. Whitehead, 43–62. Toronto: University of Toronto Press, 2000.

Crocco, A. *Gioacchino da Fiore e il Giochimismo*. 2nd ed. Naples: Liguori Editore, 1976.

Daniel, E. Randolph. "Apocalyptic Conversion: The Joachite Alternative to the Crusades." *Traditio* 25 (1969): 129–54.

————. *Bound for the Promised Land*. Forthcoming.

————. *The Franciscan Concept of Mission in the High Middle Ages*. St. Bonaventure, NY: St. Bonaventure University, 1992.

Davis, Rebecca. "'Fullynge" Nature: Spiritual Charity and the Logic of Conversion in *Piers Plowman*." Forthcoming in the 2006 *Yearbook of Langland Studies*.

Dawson, James Doyne. "William of St. Amour and the Apostolic Tradition." *Mediaeval Studies* 40 (1978): 223–38.

Deanesly, M. *The Lollard Bible*. Cambridge: Cambridge University Press, 1920.

De Hemptinne, T., and M. E. Góngora, eds. *The Voice of Silence: Women's Literacy in a Men's Church*. Turnhout: Brepols, 2004.

De la Marche, Lecoy. *La chaire française au moyen âge*. 2nd ed. Paris, 1886.

Delany, Sheila. *Chaucer's* House of Fame: *The Poetics of Sceptical Fideism*. Chicago: University of Chicago Press, 1978.

————. "The Friar as Critic: Bokenham reads Chaucer." In *Mediaevalistas: Reading in the Middle Ages*, edited by Piero Boitani and Anna Torti, 63–79. J. A. W. Bennett Memorial Lectures. Cambridge: Brewer, 1996.

Delorme, F., "Constitutiones provinciae Provinciale saec. XIII–XIV." *Archivum Franciscanum Historicum* 14 (1921): 415–34.

Denifle, Heinrich. "Das Evangelium aeternum und die Commission zu Anagni." *Archiv für Literatur- und Kirchengeschichte des Mittelalters* 1 (1885): 42–149.

Desoer, G. B. "The Relationship of the Latin Versions of Ruysbroeck's *Die Geestelike Brulocht* to *The Chastising of God's Children*." *Mediaeval Studies* 21 (1959): 129–45.

Despres, Denise L. "Ecstatic Reading and Missionary Mystics in the 'Orcherd of Syon'." In Voaden *Prophets Abroad*, 141–61.

Dimmick, Jeremy, James Simpson, and Nicolette Zeeman, eds. *Images, Idolatry and Iconoclasm in Late Medieval England*. Oxford: Clarendon, 2002.

Dinzelbacher, Peter. *Vision und Vision-literatur im Mittelalter*. Stuttgart: Hiersemann, 1981.

Dipple, Geoffrey. "Uthred and the Friars: Apostolic Poverty and Clerical Dominion between FitzRalph and Wyclif." *Traditio* 49 (1994): 235–58.

Döllinger, Johann Joseph Ignaz von. *Beiträge zur Sektengeschichte des Mittelalters*. New York: B. Franklin [1960].

Douie, Decima L. *Archbishop Pecham*. Oxford: Clarendon, 1952.

————. *The Nature and Effect of the Heresy of the Fraticelli*. Manchester: Manchester University Press, 1932.

————. "Olivi's 'Postilla super Matthaeum'." *Franciscan Studies* 35 (1975): 66–92.

————. "Three Treatises on Evangelical Perfection." *Archivum Franciscanum Historicum* 24 (1931): 341–54.

Doyle, Ian. "Remarks on Surviving Manuscripts of *Piers Plowman*." In *Medieval Religious and Ethical Literature in Honour of G. H. Russell*, edited by G. Kratzman and J. Simpson, 35–58. Cambridge: Brewer, 1986.

Dronke, Peter, and Jill Mann. "Chaucer and the Medieval Latin Poets." In *Writers and Their Background: Geoffrey Chaucer*, edited by Derek Brewer, 154–83. Athens: Ohio University Press, 1975.

Dufeil, M.-M. *Guillaume de Saint-Amour et la polémique universitaire parisienne 1250–1259*. Paris: A. and J. Picard, 1972.

Duffy, Eamon. *The Stripping of the Altars: Traditional Religion in England, c. 1400–c. 1580.* New Haven, CT: Yale University Press, 1992. 2nd ed., 2005.

Dunning, T. P. *Piers Plowman: An Interpretation of the A Text.* 2d ed. Revised by T. P. Dolan. Oxford: Clarendon, 1980.

Dupuy, Marc. "The Unwilling Prophet and the New Maccabees: John de Roquetaillade and the Valois in the Fourteenth Century." *Florilegium* 17 (2000): 229–50.

Edwards, A. S. G. "The Early Reception of Chaucer and Langland." *Florilegium* 15 (1998): 1–22.

Egbert, Virginia Wylie. *The Medieval Artist at Work.* Princeton, NJ: Princeton University Press, 1967.

Ehrle, F. "Die Spiritualen, ihr Verhältnis zum Franciscanerorden und zu den Fraticellen." *Archiv für Literatur- und Kirchengeschichte des Mittelalters* 3 (1887): 534–40.

Eldredge, Laurence. "Chaucer's *House of Fame* and the *Via Moderna.*" *Neuphilologische Mitteilungen* 71 (1970): 105–19.

Elliott, Dyan. *Proving Woman: Female Spirituality and Inquisitional Culture in the Later Middle Ages.* Princeton, NJ: Princeton University Press, 2004.

———. "Seeing Double: John Gerson, the Discernment of Spirits and Joan of Arc." *American Historical Review* 107 (2002): 26–64.

Elliott, E. B. *Horae Apocalypticae.* London, 1844.

Ellis, Roger. "*Ad Flores Fabricandum . . . Coronam:* An Investigation into the Uses of the Revelations of Bridget of Sweden in Fifteenth-Century England." *Medium Aevum* 51 (1982): 163–86.

———. "Text and Controversy: In Defence of St. Birgitta of Sweden." In Barr and Hutchinson, *Text and Controversy,* 303–22.

Elm, Kaspar. "*Vita regularis sine regula:* Bedeutung, Rechtsstellung und Selbstverständnis des mittelalterlichen und frühneuzeitlichen Semireligiosentums." In *Häresie und vorzeitige Reformation im Spätmittelalter,* edited by František Šmahel, 239–73. Munich: Oldenbourg, 1998.

Emden, A. B. *Biographical Register of the University of Oxford to A.D. 1500.* Oxford, Clarendon, 1957–59.

———. *A Survey of Dominicans in England, 1268–1538.* Rome: Santa Sabina, 1967.

Fleming, John. "Antimendicantism." In Wallace, *Cambridge History,* 349–75.

———. *From Bonaventure to Bellini.* Princeton, NJ: Princeton University Press, 1982.

———. *An Introduction to the Franciscan Literature of the Middle Ages.* Chicago: Franciscan Herald Press, 1977.

———. *The Roman de la Rose: A Study in Allegory and Iconography.* Princeton, NJ: Princeton University Press, 1969.

Forde, Simon. "Nicholas Hereford's Ascension Day Sermon, 1382." *Mediaeval Studies* 51 (1989): 205–36.

Fowler, David. *Life and Times of John Trevisa, Medieval Scholar.* Seattle: University of Washington Press, 1995.

French, T. W. "The Tomb of Archbishop Scrope in York Minster." *Yorkshire Archaeological Journal* 61 (1989): 95–102.

Friedman, John. *Northern English Books, Owners and Makers in the Late Middle Ages.* Syracuse, NY: Syracuse University Press, 1995.

Fyler, John M. "Pagan Survivals." In P. Brown, *Companion to Chaucer*, 350–52.

Galbraith, V. H. "Articles Laid before the Parliament of 1371." *English Historical Review* 34 (1919): 579–82.

———. "Thomas Walsingham and the *Saint Albans Chronicle*, 1272–1422." *English Historical Review* 47 (1932): 12–30.

Gertz-Robinson, Genelle. "Stepping in the Pulpit: Margery Kempe and Anne Askew as Women Preachers." In Olson and Kerby-Fulton, *Voices in Dialogue*, 459–82.

Ghosh, Kantik. "Bishop Reginald Pecock and the Idea of 'Lollardy.'" In Barr and Hutchinson, *Text and Controversy*, 259–60.

Giancarlo, Matthew. "Piers Plowman, Parliament, and the Public Voice." *Yearbook of Langland Studies* 17 (2003): 135–74.

Gibson, Gail. *The Theater of Devotion: East Anglian Drama and Society in the Late Middle Ages*. Chicago: University of Chicago Press, 1989.

Giffin, M. *Studies in Chaucer and His Audience*. Hull, Quebec: Editions "l'Eclair," 1956.

Gillespie, Vincent. "The Haunted Text: Ghostly Reflections in the *Mirror to Devout People*." In *The Text in the Community: Essays on Medieval Works, Manuscripts, Authors, and Readers*, edited by Jill Man and Maura Nolan, 122–179. Notre Dame, IN: University of Notre Dame Press, 2005.

———, ed. *Syon Abbey*. Corpus of British Medieval Library Catalogues. London: British Library, 2001.

Gleeson, Dermot. "A Fourteenth-Century Clare Heresy Trial." *Irish Ecclesiastical Record*, 5th ser., 89 (1958): 37–42.

Glorieux, P. "Le Chancelier Gerson et la réforme de l'enseignement." In *Melanges offerts a Etienne Gilson*, 285–98. Toronto: Pontifical Institute of Medieval Studies, 1959.

Goldschmidt, E. P. *Medieval Texts and Their First Appearance in Print*. London, 1943.

Gordimer, Nadine. "Censorship in South Africa." In *The Writer and Human Rights*, edited by the Toronto Arts Group for Human Rights, in Aid of Amnesty International, 166–72. New York: Doubleday, 1983.

Gould, Karen. *Psalter and Hours of Yolande of Soissons*. Cambridge, MA: Medieval Academy, 1978.

Gradon, Pamela. "Trajanus redivivus: Another Look at Trajan in *Piers Plowman*." In *Middle English Studies Presented to Norman Davis in Honour of His Seventieth Birthday*, edited by Douglas Gray and E. G. Stanley, 93–114. Oxford: Clarendon, 1983.

Grady, Frank. "Chaucer Reading Langland: The *House of Fame*." *Studies in the Age of Chaucer* 18 (1996): 3–23.

———. "*Piers Plowman, St. Erkenwald*, and the Rule of Exceptional Salvations." *Yearbook of Langland Studies* 6 (1992): 61–86.

———. *Representing Righteous Heathens in Late Medieval England*. New York: Palgrave, 2005.

Green, Richard Firth. *A Crisis of Truth: Literature and Law in Ricardian England*. Philadelphia: University of Pennsylvania Press, 1999.

Greenblatt, Stephen. "Invisible Bullets: Renaissance Authority and Its Subversion." Reprinted in *Political Shakespeare: New Essays in Cultural Materialism*, edited by J. Dollimore and A. Sinfeld, 18–47. 2nd ed. Ithaca, NY: Cornell University Press, 1999.

———. *Shakespearean Negotiations*. Berkeley: University of California Press, 1988.

Grundmann, Herbert. *Studien über Joachim von Floris.* In *Beiträge zur Kulturgeschichte des Mittelalters und der Renaissance* 32, edited by W. Goetz. Leipzig and Berlin, 1927.

———. "Zur Vita s. Gerlaci eremitae." In *Ausgewählte Aufsätze,* vol. 1. Stuttgart: Anton Hiersemann, 1976.

Guarnieri, Romana. "Il Movimento del Libero Spirito." *Archivio Italiano per la Storia della Pietà* 4 (1965): 353–708. Text of Porete, *Le Mirouer,* 513–635.

Gunnhouse, Peter. "Pictorial Narrative as Gospel Truth." Paper given at University of Victoria, 1994.

Gwynn, Aubrey. "The Sermon Diary of Richard FitzRalph, Archbishop of Armagh." *Proceedings of the Royal Irish Academy* 44, sec. C (1937): 1–57.

de Hamel, Christopher. *The Book: A History of the Bible.* London: Phaidon Press, 2001.

Hanna, Ralph, III. "Dr. Peter Partridge and MS Digby 98." In Barr and Hutchinson, *Texts and Controversy,* 41–66.

———. "Emendations to a 1993 'Vita de Ne'erdowel.'" *Yearbook of Langland Studies* 14 (2000): 185–98.

———. "English Biblical Texts before Lollardy and Their Fate." In Somerset, Havens, and Pitard, *Lollards and Their Influence,* 144–55.

———. "Langland's Imaginatif: Images and the Limits of Poetry." In Dimmick, Simpson, and Zeeman, *Images,* 81–94.

———. "Studies in the MSS of *Piers Plowman.*" *Yearbook of Langland Studies* 7 (1993): 1–25.

———. *William Langland.* Aldershot: Variorum, 1993.

Hatfield-Moore, Deborah. "Paying the Minstrel: A Cultural Study of B.L. MS Harley 913." PhD diss., Queen's University, Belfast, 2001.

———. "Seven Hundred Years of Imaginative Reading: B.L., Harley 913." Unpublished paper.

Havens, J. "Shading the Grey Area: Determining Heresy in Middle English Texts." In Barr and Hutchinson, *Text and Controversy,* 337–52.

De Hemptinne, T., and M.E. Góngora, eds. *The Voice of Silence: Women's Literacy in a Men's Church.* Turnhout: Brepols, 2004.

Heslop, T.A. "Attitudes to the Visual Arts." In *The Age of Chivalry: Art in Plantagenet England, 1200–1400,* edited by Jonathan Alexander and Paul Binski, 26–32. London: Royal Academy of the Arts, 1987.

Heuser, Wilhelm. *Die Kildare-Gedichte.* Darmstadt: Wissenschaftliche Buchgesellschaft, 1965.

———. "With an O and an I." *Anglia* 27 (1904): 283–319.

Higgins, Iain. *Writing East: The "Travels" of Sir John Mandeville.* Philadelphia: University of Pennsylvania Press, 1997.

Hill, Thomas D. "Universal Salvation and Its Literary Contexts in *Piers Plowman.*" *Yearbook of Langland Studies* 5 (1991): 65–76.

Hilmo, Maidie. "Framing the Canterbury Pilgrims for the Aristocratic Readers of the Ellesmere Manuscript." In Kerby-Fulton and Hilmo, *Medieval Professional Reader,* 14–72.

———. *Medieval Icons, Images & English Literary Texts: A Study of Illustrated Works from the Ruthwell Cross to the Ellesmere Chaucer.* Aldershot: Ashgate Press, 2003.

Hobbins, Daniel. "Beyond the Schools: New Writings and the Social Imagination of Jean Gerson." PhD diss., University of Notre Dame, 2002.

Hogg, James. "Adam Easton's *Defensorium Sanctae Birgittae*." In *The Medieval Mystical Tradition VI*, 213–40. Cambridge: Brewer, 1999.

———, ed. *Analecta cartusiana*. Vols. 12–13. Salzburg: Universität Salzburg, 1973–74.

———. "Cardinal Easton's Letter to the Abbess and Community of Vadstena." Studies in St. Birgitta and the Brigittine Order. *Analecta Cartusiana* 36, no. 19 (1993): 20–26.

Holdsworth, Christopher. "Christina of Markyate." In *Medieval Women*, edited by D. Baker, 185–204. Oxford: Blackwell, 1978.

———. "Visions and Visionaries in the Middle Ages." *History* 48 (1963): 141–53.

Hollywood, Amy. "Suffering Transformed: Marguerite Porete, Meister Eckhart, and the Problem of Women's Spirituality." In McGinn, *Meister Eckhart*, 87–113.

Howlett, D. R. "Studies in the Works of John Whethamstede." PhD diss., Oxford University, 1975.

Howlett, D. R., and R. W. Hunt. "The Provenance of MS. New College 49." *Bodleian Library Record* 10 (1978–82): 225–28.

Hudson, Anne. "From Oxford to Prague: The Writings of John Wyclif and His English Followers in Bohemia." *Slavonic and East European Review* 75 (1997): 642–57.

———. "*Laicus litteratus*: The Paradox of Lollardy." In *Heresy and Literacy, 1000–1530*, edited by Peter Biller and Anne Hudson, 222–36. Cambridge: Cambridge University Press, 1994.

———. "Langland and Lollardy?" *Yearbook of Langland Studies* 17 (2004): 93–105.

———. "The Legacy of *Piers Plowman*." In Alford, *Companion to Piers Plowman*, 251–66.

———. *Lollards and Their Books*. London: Hambledon, 1985.

———. "Peter Pateshull: One-Time Friar and Poet." In *Interstices: Studies in Middle English and Anglo-Latin Texts in Honour of A. G. Rigg*, edited by Richard Firth Green and Linne Mooney, 167–83. Toronto: University of Toronto Press, 2004.

———. *The Premature Reformation: Wycliffite Texts and Lollard History*. Oxford: Clarendon, 1988.

———. "Wyclif and the North: The Evidence from Durham." In *Life and Thought in the Northern Church: Essays in Honour of Claire Cross*, edited by Diana Wood, 87–103. Cambridge: Brewer, 1999.

———. "Wycliffism in Oxford, 1381–1411." In *Wyclif in His Times*, edited by A. Kenny, 67–84. Oxford: Clarendon, 1986.

Hughes, Jonathan. *Pastors and Visionaries: Religious and Secular Life in Late Medieval Yorkshire*. Woodbridge: Boydell, 1988.

Hult, David. "Language and Dismemberment: Abelard, Origen, and the *Romance of the Rose*." In Brownlee and Huot, *Rethinking the Romance of the Rose*, 101–30.

Hunt, R. W., F. Madan, H. H. E. Craster, et al., eds. *A Summary Catalogue of Western Manuscripts in the Bodleian Library at Oxford*. 7 vols. Oxford: Oxford University Press, 1895–1953.

Huot, Sylvia. *The Romance of the Rose and Its Medieval Readers: Interpretation, Reception, Manuscript Transmission*. Cambridge: Cambridge University Press, 1993.

Hyland, Paul, and Neil Sammells, eds. *Writing and Censorship in Britain*. London: Routledge, 1992.

James, M. R. *Catalogue of the Library of the Augustinian Friars at York, in Fasciculus J. W. Clark dicatus*. Cambridge: Cambridge University Press, 1909.

————. *A Descriptive Catalogue of the Manuscripts in the Library of Corpus Christi College, Cambridge*. Cambridge: Cambridge University Press, 1912.

Jones, Serene. *Calvin and the Rhetoric of Piety*. Philadelphia: Knox Press, 1995.

————. "Calvin's Commentary on the Psalms: Songs to Live and Die By." In *Up with a Shout*, edited by Margot Fassler, 29. New Haven, CT: Yale Institute for Sacred Music, 2001.

Jones, W. R. "Lollards and Images: The Defense of Religious Art in Late Medieval England." *Journal of History of Ideas* 34 (1973): 27–50.

Justice, Steven. "'General Words': Response to Elizabeth Schirmer." In Olson and Kerby-Fulton, *Voices in Dialogue*, 377–94.

————. "Inquisition, Speech and Writing: A Case from Late Medieval Norwich." *Representations* 48 (1994): 1–29.

————. "Lollardy." In Wallace, *Cambridge History*, 662–89.

————. *Writing and Rebellion: England in 1381*. Berkeley: University of California Press, 1994.

Justice, Steven, and Kathryn Kerby-Fulton, ed. *Written Work: Langland, Labour, and Authorship*. Philadelphia: University of Pensylvania Press, 1997.

Kaminsky, Howard. "The Free Spirit in the Hussite Revolution." In *Millennial Dreams in Action: Studies in Revolutionary Religious Movements*, edited by Sylvia L. Thrupp, 166–86. New York: Schocken Books, 1970.

————. *A History of the Hussite Revolution*. Berkeley: University of California Press, 1967.

Kane, George. *Piers Plowman: The Evidence for Authorship*. London: Athlone Press, 1965.

————. "The Text." In Alford, *Companion to Piers Plowman*, 175–200.

Kelly, Henry Ansgar. "Inquisition and the Prosecution of Heresy: Misconceptions and Abuses." *Church History* 58 (1989): 439–51.

————. *Inquisitions and Other Trial Procedures in the Medieval West*. Aldershot, 2001.

————. "The Right to Remain Silent: Before and After Joan of Arc." *Speculum* 68 (1993): 992–1021.

Ker, N. R. "Chaining from a Staple on the Back Cover." *Bodelian Library Record* 3 (1950): 104–7.

————. *Medieval Libraries of Great Britain*. London: Royal Historical Society, 1964.

Ker, N. R., and A. J. Piper. *Medieval Manuscripts in British Libraries*. Vols. 1–5. Oxford: Clarendon, 1992.

Kerby-Fulton, Kathryn. "*Eciam Lollardi*: Some Further Thoughts on Fiona Somerset's *Eciam Mulier*: Women in Lollardy and the Problem of Sources. " In Olson and Kerby-Fulton, *Voices in Dialogue*, 261–78.

————. "English Joachimism and Its Codicological Context: A List of Joachite Manuscripts of English Origin or Provenance before 1600." In *Essays in Memory of Marjorie Reeves*, edited by Julia Wannenmacher. Forthcoming.

————. "Hildegard and the Male Reader: A Study in Insular Reception." In Voaden, *Prophets Abroad*, 1–18.

————. "Hildegard of Bingen." In *Yale Guide to Medieval Holy Women*, edited by Rosalynn Voaden and Alastair Minnis. Forthcoming.

————. "Hildegard of Bingen and Antimendicant Propaganda." *Traditio* 43 (1987): 386–99.

————. "Langland and the Bibliographic Ego." In Justice and Kerby-Fulton, *Written Work*, 65–141.

———. "'Langland in His Working Clothes'?: Scribe D, the C-Draft Passages, and the Nature of Scribal Intervention." In *Middle English Poetry: Texts and Traditions in Honour of Derek Pearsall*, edited by Alastair Minnis, 149–67. Cambridge: University of York Medieval Press, 2001.

———. "Langland's Reading: Some Evidence from MSS of English Provenance Containing Latin Religious Prophecy." In *The Uses of Manuscripts in Literary Studies: Essays in Memory of Judson Boyce Allen*, edited by Charlotte Cook Morse, Penelope Reed Doob, and Marjorie Curry Woods, 137–61. Kalamazoo, MI: Medieval Institute Publications, 1992.

———. "The Medieval Professional Reader and Reception History, 1292–1641." In Kerby-Fulton and Hilmo, *Medieval Professional Reader*, 7–15.

———. "Piers Plowman." In Wallace, *Cambridge History*, 513–38.

———. "Professional Readers of Langland at Home and Abroad." In *Harvard New Directions in Manuscript Studies*, edited by Derek Pearsall, 101–37. Cambridge: Brewer, 2000.

———. "Prophecy and Suspicion: Closet Radicalism, Reformist Politics, and the Vogue for Hildegardiana in Ricardian England." *Speculum* 75 (2000): 318–41.

———. *Reformist Apocalypticism and Piers Plowman*. Cambridge: Cambridge University Press, 1990.

———. "A Return to 'The First Dawn of Justice': Hildegard's Visions of Clerical Reform and the Eremitical Life." *American Benedictine Review* 40 (1989): 383–407.

———. Review of *Piers Plowman: A Working Facsimile of the Z-Text*. *Modern Language Review* 91 (1996): 959–61.

———. "Smoke in the Vineyard: Hildegard of Bingen as Prophet and Reformer." In *Voice of the Living Light: Hildegard of Bingen and Her World*, edited by Barbara Newman, 70–98. Berkeley: University of California Press, 1998.

———. "When Women Preached: An Introduction to Female Homiletic, Sacramental, and Liturgical Roles in the Later Middle Ages." In Olson and Kerby-Fulton, *Voices in Dialogue*, 31–55.

———. "'Who Has Written This Book?' Visionary Autobiography in Langland's C Text." In *The Medieval Mystical Tradition in England*, edited by Marion Glasscoe, 101–16. Papers read at the Exeter Symposium V. Cambridge: D. S. Brewer, 1992.

———. "The Women Readers in Langland's Earliest Audience: Some Codicological Evidence." In *Learning and Literacy in Medieval England and Abroad*, edited by Sarah Rees-Jones, 121–34. Turnhout: Brepols, 2002.

Kerby-Fulton, Kathryn, and E. Randolph Daniel. "English Joachimism, 1300–1500: The Columbinus Prophecy." In *Il profetismo gioachimita tra Quattrocento e Cinquecento*, Atti del III Congresso Internazionale di Studi Gioachimiti, S. Giovanni in Fiore, 17–21 September 1989, edited by Gian Luca Potestà, 313–50. Fiore: Centro Internazionale di Studi Gioachimiti, 1990.

Kerby-Fulton, Kathryn, and Denise Despres. *Iconography and the Professional Reader: The Politics of Book Production in the Douce Piers Plowman*. Minneapolis: University of Minnesota Press, 1999.

Kerby-Fulton, Kathryn, Magda Hayton, and Kenna Olsen. "The Pseudo-Hildegardian Prophecy and Antimendicant Propaganda in Late Medieval England: An Edition of the Most Popular Insular Text of 'Insurgent gentes.'" In *Proceedings of the Harlaxton Conference on England and France in the Fifteenth Centuries*, edited by Nigel Morgan, 160–93. Oxford: Blackwell, 2004.

Kerby-Fulton, Kathryn, and Maidie Hilmo. *The Medieval Professional Reader at Work: Evidence from the Manuscripts of Chaucer, Langland, Kempe and Gower.* Victoria: English Literary Studies, 2001.

———. *The Medieval Reader.* Special issue of *Studies in Medieval and Renaissance History* 1, 3d ser. New York: AMS Press, 2002.

Kerby-Fulton, Kathryn, and Steven Justice. "Langlandian Reading Circles, and the Civil Service in London and Dublin, 1380–1427." *New Medieval Literature* 1 (1997): 60–83.

———. "Reformist Intellectual Culture in the English and Irish Civil Service: The *Modus tenendi parliamentum* and Its Literary Relations." *Traditio* 53 (1998): 149–203.

———. "Scribe D and the Marketing of Ricardian Literature." In Kerby-Fulton and Hilmo, *Medieval Professional Reader,* 111–41.

Kieckhefer, Richard. "The Office of Inquisition and Medieval Heresy: The Transition from Personal to Institutional Jurisdiction." *Journal of Ecclesiastical History* 46 (1995): 36–61.

Kienzle, Beverly, and Pamela Walker, eds. *Women Preachers and Prophets through Two Millennia of Christianity.* Berkeley: University of California Press, 1998.

Kirk, Elizabeth. "Nominalism and the Dynamics of the Clerk's Tale: Homo Viator as Woman." In *Chaucer's Religious Tales,* edited by C. David Benson and Elizabeth Robertson, 1–120. Cambridge: Brewer, 1990.

Knowles, David. "Censured Opinions of Uthred of Boldon." *Proceedings of the British Academy* 37 (1951): 305–42.

———. *The Religious Orders in England.* Vol. 2: *The End of the Middle Ages.* Cambridge: Cambridge University Press, 1950–59. Reprint, 1979.

Koch, Josef. "Neue Aktenstücke zu dem gegen Wilhelm Ockham in Avignon Geführten Prozess." In *Kleine Schriften,* edited by J. Koch, vol. 2, 275–300. Rome: Edizioni di Storia e Letteratura, 1973.

———. "Philosophische und theologische Irrtumslisten von 1270–1329: Ein Beitrag zur Entwickelung der theologischen Zensuren." In *Melanges Mandonnet,* edited by P. Mandonnet, vol. 2, 305–30. Paris: Librarie Philosophique J. Vrin, 1930.

———. "Der Prozess gegen die Postille Olivis zur Apokalypse." *Recherches de Théologie Ancienne et Médiévale* 5 (1933). Collected in Koch, *Kleine Schriften,* vol. 2, 259–74. Rome: Edizioni di Storia e Letteratura.

Laarhoven, Jan van. "Magisterium or Magisteria: A Historical Note to a Theological Note." *Jaarboek Thomas Instituut te Utrecht* (1990): 75–94.

Larsen, A. "Are All Lollards Lollards?" In Somerset, Havens, and Pitard, *Lollards and Their Influence,* 59–72.

Lea, H. C. *A History of the Inquisition of the Middle Ages.* 3 vols. New York, 1988.

Lee, Harold, et al. *Western Mediterranean Prophecy.* Toronto: Pontifical Institute of Medieval Studies, 1989.

Leff, Gordon. *Heresy in the Later Middle Ages.* 2 vols. Manchester: Manchester University Press, 1967.

———. *Paris and Oxford Universities in the Thirteenth and Fourteenth Centuries.* New York: John Wiley and Sons, 1968.

Lerner, Robert. "An 'Angel of Philadelphia' in the Reign of Phillip the Fair: The Case of Guiard of Cressonessart." In *Order and Innovation in the Middle Ages: Essays in Honour of Joseph R. Strayer,* edited by William Jordan et al., 343–64. Princeton, NJ: Princeton University Press, 1976.

———. "Ecstatic Dissent." *Speculum* 67 (1992): 33–57.

———. *The Feast of St. Abraham: Medieval Millenarians and the Jews*. Philadelphia: University of Pennsylvania Press, 2001.

———. *Heresy and Literacy, 1000–1530*. Cambridge: Cambridge University Press, 1994.

———. *Heresy of the Free Spirit*. Berkeley: University of California Press, 1972. Reprint, Notre Dame, IN: University of Notre Dame Press, 1991.

———. "Joachim and the Scholastics." In *Gioacchino de Fiore tra Bernardo di Clairvaux e Innocenzo III*, edited by Roberto Rusconi, 251–64. Rome: Viella, 2001.

———. "The Medieval Return to the Thousand-Year Sabbath." In *The Apocalypse in the Middle Ages*, edited by R. K. Emmerson and Bernard McGinn, 51–71. Ithaca, NY: Cornell University Press, 1992.

———. *Powers of Prophecy: The Cedar of Lebanon Vision*. Berkeley: University of California Press, 1983.

———. "Recent Work on the Origins of the 'Genus nequam' Prophecies." *Florensia* 7 (1993): 141–57.

———. "Refreshment of the Saints: The Time after Antichrist as a Station for Earthly Progress in Medieval Thought." *Traditio* 32 (1976): 97–144.

———. "Vagabonds and Little Women: The Medieval Netherlandish Dramatic Fragment 'De Truwanten'." *Modern Philology* 65 (1968): 301–6.

Levitan, Alan. "The Parody of Pentecost in Chaucer's 'Summoner's Tale'." *University of Toronto Quarterly* 40 (1971): 236–46.

Lewis, Warren. "Peter Olivi, Author of the *Lectura Super Apocalypsim*: Was He Heretical?" In *Pierre de Jean Olivi (1248–1298): Pensée Scholastique, Dissidence Spirituelle et Société*, 135–55. Paris: Librarie Philosphique J. Vrin, 1999.

Lichtmann, Maria. "Marguerite Porete and Meister Eckhart." In McGinn, *Meister Eckhart*, 65–86.

Little, A. G. *The Grey Friars in Oxford*. Oxford Historical Society 20. Oxford: Clarendon, 1892.

Little, A. G., and R. C. Easterling. "Insurgent Gentes." In *The Franciscans and Dominicans of Exeter*, 60–61. Exeter, 1927.

Lochrie, Karma. *Margery Kempe and the Translations of the Flesh*. Philadelphia: University of Pennsylvania Press, 1991.

Logan, F. D. *Excommunication and the Secular Arm in Medieval England*. Toronto: Pontifical Institute of Medieval Studies, 1968.

Lunghi, E. *The Basilica of St. Francis in Assisi*. Florence: Scala, 1996.

Lytle, Guy Fitch. "Universities as Religious Authorities in the Later Middle Ages and Reformation." In *Reform and Authority in the Medieval and Reformation Church*, edited by Guy Fitch Lytle, 79–82. Washington, DC: Catholic University of America Press, 1981.

MacFarlane, K. B. *Lancastrian Kings and Lollard Knights*. Oxford: Oxford University Press, 1972.

Madigan, Kevin. *Olivi and the Interpretation of Matthew in the High Middle Ages*. Notre Dame, IN: University of Notre Dame Press, 2003.

Maitland, Frederic William. *Roman Canon Law in the Church of England*. New York: Burt Franklin, 1898. Reprint, 1968.

Mann, Jill. "Chaucer and Atheism." *Studies in the Age of Chaucer* 17 (1995): 5–19.

Marcett, Mildred. *Uhtred de Boldon, Friar William Jordan and Piers Plowman*. New York, 1938.

Markus, R. A. *Saeculum, History and Society in the Theology of St. Augustine.* Cambridge: Cambridge University Press, 1988.

Martin, Geoffrey. "Wyclif, Lollards, and Historians, 1384–1984." In Somerset, Havens, and Pitard, *Lollards and Their Influence*, 237–50.

Matheson, Lester. Review of Hanna, *William Langland. Yearbook of Langland Studies* 8 (1994): 192–94.

Maycock, A. L. *The Inquisition from the Establishment to the Great Schism.* New York: Harper, 1927.

McCall, J. "Chaucer and John of Legnano." *Speculum* 40 (1965): 484–89.

————. "The Writings of John of Legnano with a List of Manuscripts." *Traditio* 23 (1967): 421–37.

McDonnell, Ernest W. *The Beguines and Beghards in Medieval Culture.* New Brunswick: Rutgers University Press, 1954.

McEntire, Sandra J., ed. *Julian of Norwich: A Book of Essays.* New York: Garland, 1998.

McGinn, Bernard. "The Abbott and the Doctors: Scholastic Reactions to the Radical Eschatology of Joachim of Fiore." *Church History* 40 (1971): 30–47. Reprinted in West, *Joachim of Fiore*, 453–71.

————. *Apocalypticism in the Western Tradition.* Aldershot: Ashgate, 1994.

————, ed. *Apocalyptic Spirituality.* New York: Paulist Press, 1979.

————. *The Calabrian Abbot.* New York: MacMillan, 1985.

————. "Early Apocalypticism: The Ongoing Debate." In *The Apocalypse in English Renaissance Thought and Literature*, edited by C. A. Patrides and Joseph Wittreich, 2–39. Ithaca, NY: Cornell University Press, 1984.

————. *The Flowering of Mysticism: Men and Women in the New Mysticism, 1200–1350.* Vol. 3. New York: Crossroads, 1988.

————, ed. *Meister Eckhart and the Beguine Mystics.* New York: Continuum, 1998.

————. *Visions of the End: Apocalyptic Traditions in the Middle Ages.* New York: Columbia University Press, 1979. 2nd ed., 1998.

McGrade, Arthur. *The Political Thought of William Ockham.* Cambridge: Cambridge University Press, 1974.

————. "The Political Writings." In *The Cambridge Companion to Ockham*, edited by Paul Vincent Spade, 308–20. Cambridge: Cambridge University Press, 1999.

McIntosh, Angus, et al. *A Linguistic Atlas of Late Mediaeval English.* Vol. 1. Aberdeen: Aberdeen University Press, 1986.

McIntosh, Angus, and M. L. Samuels. "Prolegomena to a Study of Medieval Anglo-Irish." *Medium Aevum* 37 (1968): 1–11.

McKenna, W. "Popular Canonization as Political Propaganda: The Cult of Archbishop Scrope." *Speculum* 45 (1970): 608–23.

McNiven, Peter. "The Betrayal of Richard Scrope." *Bulletin of the John Rylands Library* 54 (1971–72): 173–213.

————. *Heresy and Politics in the Reign of Henry IV.* Woodbridge: Boydell, 1987.

McSheffrey, Shannon. *Gender and Heresy: Women and Men in Lollard Communities.* Philadelphia: University of Pennsylvania Press, 1995.

Mens, A. *Oorsprong en Betekenis van de Nederlandse Begijnen-en Begardenbeweging.* Leuven: University Press, 1947.

Middleton, Anne. "Acts of Vagrancy." In Justice and Kerby-Fulton, *Written Work*, 209–317.

———. "The Audience and Public of *Piers Plowman*." In *Middle English Alliterative Poetry and Its Literary Background*, edited by David Lawton, 103–23. Cambridge: Brewer, 1982.

———. "Making a Good End: John But as a Reader of *Piers Plowman*." In *Medieval English Studies Presented to George Kane*, edited by D. Kennedy et al., 243–66. Wolfeboro, NH: D. S. Brewer, 1988.

———. "William Langland's 'Kynde Name': Authorial Signature and Social Identity in Late Fourteenth-Century England." In *Literary Practice and Social Change in Britain, 1380–1530*, edited by Lee Patterson, 15–82. Berkeley: University of California Press, 1990.

Miethke, Jürgen. "Bildungsstand und Freiheitsforderung (12. bis 14. Jarhundert)." In *Die Abendländische Freiheit vom 10. ʒum 14. Jarhundert*, edited by Johannes Fried, 231–40. Munich: Sigmaringen, 1991.

Minnis, A. J. "Looking for a Sign: The Quest for Nominalism in Chaucer and Langland." In *Essays on Ricardian Literature in Honour of J. A. Burrow*, edited by A. J. Minnis et al. Oxford: Clarendon, 1997.

———. Respondet Walterus Bryth': Walter Brut in Debate on Women Priests." In Barr and Hutchinson, *Text and Controversy*, 229–50.

Minnis, A. J., and A. B. Scott, eds. *Medieval Literary Theory and Criticism, c. 1100–c. 1375*. Oxford: Oxford University Press, 1988.

Mollat, Guillaume. *Bernard Gui, Manuel de L'inquisiteur*. Paris, 1926.

———. *The Popes at Avignon, 1305–1378*. 9th ed. London: Nelson, 1963.

Mulchahey, Michèle M. *"First the Bow Is Bent in Study": Dominican Education before 1350*. Toronto: Pontifical Institute of Medieval Study, 1998.

Musurillo, Herbert, trans. "Passio Sanctarum Perpetuae et Felicitas." In *The Acts of the Christian Martyrs*. Oxford: Clarendon, 1972. Reprinted in Petroff, *Medieval Women's Visionary Literature*, 70–77.

Newman, Barbara. "Agnes of Prague and Guglielma of Milan." In *Yale Guide to Medieval Holy Women*, edited by Rosalynn Voaden and Alastair Minnis. Forthcoming.

———. *From Virile Woman to Woman Christ*. Philadelphia: University of Pennsylvania Press, 1995.

———. *God and the Goddesses: Vision, Poetry and Belief in the Middle Ages*. Philadelphia: University of Pennsylvania Press, 2003.

———. "Hildegard of Bingen: Visions and Validation." *Church History* 54 (1985): 163–75.

———. *Sister of Wisdom: St. Hildegard's Theology of the Feminine*. Berkeley: University of California Press 1987.

———. "What Did It Mean to Say 'I Saw'? The Clash between Theory and Practice in Medieval Visionary Culture." *Speculum* 80 (2005): 1–43.

Nissé, Ruth. "Prophetic Nations." *New Medieval Literatures* 4 (2001): 95–115.

Oberman, Heiko. *The Harvest of Medieval Theology*. Grand Rapids: Eerdmans, 1967. 3rd ed. Grand Rapids: Labyrinth Press, 1983.

O'Connor, David, and Jeremy Haselock. "The Stained and Painted Glass of York Minster." In Aylmer and Cant, *History of York Minster*, 313–94.

Olson, Glending. "The End of the Summoner's Tale and the Uses of Pentecost." *Studies in the Age of Chaucer* 21 (1999): 209–45.

Olson, Linda, and Kathryn Kerby-Fulton, eds. *Voices in Dialogue: Reading Women in the Middle Ages*. Notre Dame, IN: University of Notre Dame Press, 2005.

Orme, Nicholas. *English Schools in the Middle Ages.* London: Methuen, 1973.

―――. "Going to School in the Middle Ages." Lecture delivered at University of Victoria, February 6, 2005.

―――. *Medieval Children.* New Haven, CT: Yale University Press, 2001.

Osborne, John. "Politics and Popular Piety: Images of 'St' Richard Scrope in the Bolton Hours." *Florilegium* 17 (2000): 1–21.

Ott, Norbert. *Rechtspraxis und Heilsgeschichte ʒu Uberlieferung, Ikonographie und Gebrauchssituation des deutschen Belial.* Munich: Artemis Verlag, 1983.

Owst, G. R. *Literature and the Pulpit in Medieval England.* Oxford: Blackwell, 1961.

―――. *Preaching in Medieval England.* Cambridge: Cambridge University Press, 1926.

Pantin, W. A. *The English Church in the Fourteenth Century.* Reprint, Toronto: Medieval Academy, 1980.

―――. "The *Defensorium* of Adam of Easton." *English Historical Review* 51 (1936): 675–80.

―――. "Some Medieval English Treatises on the Origins of Monasticism." *Medieval Studies Presented to Rose Graham*, edited by Veronica Ruffer and A. J. Taylor, 189–215. Oxford: Oxford University Press, 1950.

―――. "Two Treatises of Uthred of Boldon on the Monastic Life." *Studies in Medieval History Presented to F. M. Powicke*, 363–85. Oxford: Clarendon 1948.

de Paris, P. Gratien. "Une lettre inédite de Pierre de Jean Olivi." *Etudes franciscaines* 29 (1913): 414–22.

Parkes, M. B. "Book Provision and Libraries at the Medieval University of Oxford." *University of Rochester Library Bulletin* 40 (1987–8): 36–45.

―――. "Books and Aids to Scholarship of the Oxford Friars." In *Manuscripts at Oxford: R. W. Hunt Memorial Exhibition*, edited by A. C. de la Mare and B. C. Barker-Benfield, 57–62. Oxford: Bodleian Library, 1980.

Parsons, Kelly. "The Red-Ink Annotator of the *Book of Margery Kempe*." In Kerby-Fulton and Hilmo, *Medieval Professional Reader*, 143–216.

Pásztor, Edith. "Le Polemiche sulla 'Lectura super Apocalypsim' di Pietro di Giovanni Olivi fino alla sua condanna." *Bullettino dell'Istituto Storico Italiano per il Medio Evo e Archivio Muratoriano* 70 (1958): 365–474.

Patschovsky, Alexander. "Strassburger Beginenverfolgungen im 14. Jahrhundert." *Deutsches Archiv* 30 (1974): 56–198.

Patterson, Annabel. *Censorship and Interpretation: The Conditions of Writing and Reading in Early Modern England.* Madison: University of Wisconsin Press, 1984.

Patterson, Lee. *Chaucer and the Subject of History.* Madison: University of Wisconsin Press, 1991.

―――. "Court Politics and the Invention of Literature: The Case of Sir John Clanvowe." In *Culture and History, 1350–1600*, edited by David Aers, 7–42. Harvester: Wheatsheaf Press, 1992.

―――. "Feminine Rhetoric and the Politics of Subjectivity: La Vieille and the Wife of Bath." In Brownlee and Huot, *Rethinking the Romance of the Rose*, 324–40.

―――. *Negotiating the Past: The Historical Understanding of Medieval Literature.* Madison: University of Wisconsin, 1987.

____. "'What man artow?': Authorial Self-Definition in the *Tale of Sir Thopas* and the *Tale of Melibee*." *Studies in the Age of Chaucer* 11 (1989): 117–75.

Pearsall, Derek. *The Canterbury Tales.* London: Unwinn, 1985.

————. *The Life of Geoffrey Chaucer: A Critical Biography.* Oxford: Blackwell, 1992.

Peck, Russell. "Chaucer and the Nominalist Questions." *Speculum* 53 (1978): 745–60.

Pelster, F. "Die Quaestio Heinrichs von Harclay über die Zweite Ankunft Christi." *Archivio Italiano per la Storia della Pietà* 1 (1951): 51–82.

————. "Das Ur-Correctorium Willelms de la Mare." *Gregorianum* 28 (1947): 220–35.

Peters, Edward. *Inquisition.* New York: Free Press, 1988.

Petroff, Elizabeth. *Medieval Women's Visionary Literature.* New York: Oxford University Press, 1986.

Piehler, Paul. *The Visionary Landscape: A Study in Medieval Allegory.* London: Edward Arnold, 1971.

Plummer, Charles. "On the Colophons and Marginalia of Irish Scribes." *Proceedings of the British Academy* 12 (1926): 11–42.

Raine, J. *Historians of the Church of York.* London, 1886.

Raming, Ida. *The Exclusion of Women from the Priesthood.* Metuchen, NJ: Scarecrow Press, 1976.

Rankin, William. "Reading Arundel's Reading: Hermeneutical Conflict and the Craft of Representation in Thorpe's Testimony." Paper given at Annual Medieval Congress, Western Michigan University, 2002.

Reeves, Marjorie. "The Abbot Joachim's Disciples and the Cistercian Order." *Sophia* 19 (1951): 355–71. Reprinted in West, *Joachim of Fiore,* 151–67.

————. "The Development of Apocalyptic Thought: Medieval Attitudes." In *The Apocalypse in English Renaissance Thought and Literature,* edited by C. A. Patrides and Joseph Wittreich, 40–73. Ithaca, NY: Cornell University Press, 1984.

————. "History and Eschatology: Medieval and Early Protestant Thought in Some English and Scottish Writings." *Medievalia et Humanistica* 4 (1973): 99–123.

————. *Influence of Prophecy in the Later Middle Ages: A Study in Joachimism.* Oxford, 1969. Reprint, Notre Dame, IN: University of Notre Dame Press, 1993.

————. "Joachimist Expectations in the Order of the Augustinian Hermits." *Recherches de Théologie Ancienne et Médiévale* 25 (1958): 111–41.

————. "Some Popular Prophecies from the Fourteenth to the Seventeenth Centuries." In *Popular Belief and Practice,* vol. 8 of *Studies in Church History,* edited by G. J. Cuming and D. Baker, 107–34. Cambridge: Cambridge University Press, 1972.

Reeves, Marjorie, and Beatrice Hirsch-Reich. *The Figurae of Joachim of Fiore.* Oxford: Clarendon, 1972.

Reid, Heather. "'This was here procreation': The Storie of Asneth and Spiritual Marriage in the Middle Ages." Masters thesis, University of Victoria, 2003.

Remnant, G. L., ed. *The Catalogue of Misericords in Great Britain.* Oxford: Clarendon, 1969.

Rhodes, Jim. *Poetry Does Theology: Chaucer, Grosseteste, and the Pearl-poet.* Notre Dame, IN: University of Notre Dame Press, 2002.

Richardson, H. G. "Heresy and the Lay Power under Richard II." *English Historical Review* 51 (1936): 1–25.

Riddy, Felicity. "Julian of Norwich and Self-Textualization." In *Editing Women,* edited by Ann Hutchinson, 101–24. Cardiff: University of Wales, 1998.

Riehle, Wolfgang. *The Middle English Mystics.* Translated by Bernard Standring. London: Routledge, 1981.

Rigg, A. G. "Bridlington's Prophecy: A New Look." *Speculum* 63 (1988): 596–613.

———. *A History of Anglo-Latin Literature, 1066–1422.* Cambridge: Cambridge University Press, 1992.

———. "Medieval Latin Poetic Anthologies II." *Mediaeval Studies* 40 (1978): 387–407.

———. "Two Latin Poems against the Friars." *Mediaeval Studies* 30 (1968): 106–18.

Robbins, R. H. *Historical Poems of the XIVth and XVth Centuries.* New York: Columbia University Press, 1959.

Robson, J. A. *Wyclif and the Oxford Schools.* Cambridge: Cambridge University Press, 1961.

Rouse, Mary A., and Richard H. Rouse. *Authentic Witnesses: Approaches to Medieval Texts and Manuscripts.* Notre Dame, IN: University of Notre Dame Press, 1991.

Rouse, R. H. "Bostonus Buriensis and the Author of the *Catalogus scriptorum ecclesiae.*" *Speculum* 71 (1996): 471–99.

Rouse, R. H., and M. A. Rouse. *Preachers, Florilegia and Sermons.* Toronto: Pontifical Institute of Medieval Studies, 1979.

Rusconi, Roberto. *Attesa della fine: Crisi della società, profezia, ed Apocalisse in Italia al tempo del grande scisma d'Occidente, 1378–1417.* Rome: Istituto Storico Italiano per il Medio Evo, 1979.

———. "Women's Sermons at the End of the Middle Ages." In Kienzle and Walker, *Woman Preachers,* 173–98.

Russell, G. H. "The Salvation of the Heathen: The Exploration of a Theme in *Piers Plowman.*" *Journal of the Wartburg and Courtauld Institutes* 29 (1966): 101–16.

———. "Some Aspects of the Process of Revision in *Piers Plowman.*" In *Piers Plowman Critical Approaches,* edited by S. S. Hussey, 27–49. London: Methuen, 1969.

Russell, J. "The Canonization of Opposition to the King in Angevin England." In *Haskins Anniversary Essays in Medieval History,* edited by C. H. Taylor, 279–90. Boston: Houghton Mifflin, 1929.

Russell, J. Stephen. *The English Dream Vision: Anatomy of a Form.* Columbus: Ohio State University, 1988.

———. "Is London Burning? A Chaucerian Allusion to the Rising of 1381." *Chaucer Review* 30 (1995): 107–9.

Salisbury, Eve, ed. *The Trials of Joy and Marriage.* Kalamazoo, MI: Medieval Institute, 2002.

Salmon, P. B. "Jacobus de Theramo and *Belial.*" *London Mediaeval Studies* 2 (1951): 101–15.

Salter, H. E. *The Knight's Tale and the Clerk's Tale.* London: Arnold, 1962.

Sandler, Lucy Freeman. "Face to Face with God: A Pictorial Image of the Beatific Vision." In *England in the Fourteenth Century,* edited by W. M. Ormrod, 224–35. Woodbridge: Boydell, 1986.

———. *Omne bonum: A Fourteenth-Century Encyclopedia of Universal Knowledge.* London: Harvey Miller, 1996.

Sanquist, T. A. "The Holy Oil of St. Thomas of Canterbury." In *Essays in Medieval History Presented to Bertie Wilkinson,* edited by T. A. Sandquist and M. R. Powicke, 330–44. Toronto: University of Toronto Press, 1969.

Santos Paz, José Carlos. *La Recepción de Hildegarde de Bingen en los Siglos XIII y XIV.* PhD diss., Universidade de Santiago de Compostela, Spain, 1997.

Sargent, Michael G. "The Annihilation of Marguerite Porete." *Viator* 28 (1997): 253–79.

———. "*Le Mirouer des simples ames* and the English Mystical Tradition." In *Abendländische Mystik im Mittelalter,* edited by Kurt Ruh, 443–65. Stuttgart: Metzlersche Verlagsbuchhandlung, 1986.

————. "The Transmission by the English Carthusians of Some Late Medieval Spiritual Writings." *Journal of Ecclesiastical History* 27 (1976): 225–40.

Scase, Wendy. "'First to Reckon Richard': John But's *Piers Plowman*." *Yearbook of Langland Studies* 11 (1997): 49–66.

————. "'Heu! quanta desolatio Angliae praestatur': A Wycliffite Libel and the Naming of Heretics, Oxford 1382." In Somerset, Havens, and Pitard, *Lollards and Their Influence*, 19–36.

————. *Piers Plowman and the New Anticlericalism*. Cambridge: Cambridge University Press, 1989.

————. *Reginald Pecock*. Aldershot: Variorum, 1996.

Scattergood, V. J. "Literary Culture at the Court of Richard II." In *English Court Culture in the Later Middle Ages*, edited by V. J. Scattergood and J. Sherbourne, 30–42. New York: St. Martin's Press, 1981.

Schirmer, Elizabeth. "Reading Lessons at Syon Abbey: The *Myroure of Oure Ladye* and the Mandates of Vernacular Theology." In Olson and Kerby-Fulton, *Voices in Dialogue*, 345–76.

Scott, Kathleen. *Later Gothic Manuscripts, 1390–1490*. 2 vols. London: Harvey Miller, 1996.

Selge, Kurt-Victor. "Eine Einführung Joachims von Fiore in die Johannesapokalpse." *Deutsches Archiv* 46 (1990): 85–131.

Sharpe, Richard. *A Handlist of the Latin Writers of Great Britain and Ireland before 1540*. Turnhout: Brepols, 2001.

Sharpe, Richard, et al. *English Benedictine Libraries: The Shorter Catalogues*. London: British Library, 1996.

Sheingorn, Pamela. "'The Wise Mother': The Image of St. Anne Teaching the Virgin Mary." *Gesta* 32, no. 1 (1993): 69–80.

Shepherd, Geoffrey. "Religion and Philosophy in Chaucer." In *Writers and Their Background: Geoffrey Chaucer*, edited by Derek Brewer, 262–89. Athens: Ohio University Press, 1975.

Simons, Walter. *Cities of Ladies: Beguine Communities in the Medieval Low Countries, 1200–1565*. Philadelphia: University of Pennsylvania Press, 2001.

Simpson, James. "The Constraints of Satire in *Piers Plowman* and *Mum and the Sothsegger*." In *Langland, the Mystics and the Medieval English Religious Tradition*, edited by Helen Phillips, 11–30. Cambridge: D. S. Brewer, 1985.

————. *English Literary History, 1350 and 1547: Reform and Cultural Revolution*. Oxford: Oxford University Press, 2002.

Smahel, Frantisek. *Die Hussitische Revolution*. Vol. 1. Hannover: Hahnsche Buchhandlung, 2002.

Smalley, B. "Thomas Waleys, O.P." *Archivum Franciscanum Historicum* 24 (1954): 50–57.

Smoller, Laura A. *History, Prophecy, and the Stars: The Christian Astrology of Pierre d'Ailly, 1350–1420*. Princeton, NJ: Princeton University Press, 1994.

Somerset, Fiona. *Clerical Discourse and Lay Audience in Late Medieval England*. Cambridge: Cambridge University Press, 1998.

————. "*Eciam Mulier*: Women in Lollardy and the Problem of Sources." In Olson and Kerby-Fulton, *Voices in Dialogue*, 245–60.

————. "Expanding the Langlandian Canon: Radical Latin and the Stylistics of Reform." *Yearbook of Langland Studies* 17 (2003): 73–92.

———. "Here, There and Everywhere? Wycliffite Conceptions of the Eucharist and Chaucer's 'Other' Lollard Joke." In Somerset, Havens, and Pitard, *Lollards and Their Influence*, 127–40.

———. "Professionalizing Translation at the Turn of the Fifteenth Century: Ullerston's *Determinacio*, Arundel's *Constitutions*." In *The Vulgar Tongue*, edited by F. Somerset and N. Watson, 145–58. University Park: Pennsylvania State University Press, 2003.

Somerset, Fiona, Jill C. Havens, and Derrick G. Pitard, eds. *Lollards and Their Influence in Late Medieval England*. Woodbridge: Boydell, 2003.

Spearing, A. C. *Medieval Dream Poetry*. Cambridge: Cambridge University Press, 1976.

Spencer, H. L. "Richard 'of Both Sexes'." In Barr and Hutchinson, *Text and Controversy*, 13–40.

Staley, Lynn [Johnson]. *Languages of Power in the Age of Richard II*. University Park: Pennsylvania State Press, 2005.

———. *Margery Kempe's Dissenting Fictions*. University Park: Pennsylvania State University Press.

———. "Pearl and the Contingencies of Love and Piety." In *Medieval Literature and Historical Inquiry: Essays in Honour of Derek Pearsall*, edited by David Aers, 83–114. Cambridge: Brewer, 2000.

———. "The Trope of the Scribe in the Works of Julian and Margery Kempe." *Speculum* 66 (1991): 820–38.

Stargardt, Ute. "The Beguines of Belgium, the Dominican Nuns of Germany, and Margery Kempe." In *The Popular Literature of Medieval England*, edited by Thomas J. Heffernan, 277–313. Knoxville: University of Tennessee Press, 1985.

Steinmetz, David. "Late Medieval Nominalism and the Clerk's Tale." *Chaucer Review* 12 (1977): 38–54.

Stepsis, Robert. "*Potentia Absoluta* and the Clerk's Tale." *Chaucer Review* 10 (1975–76): 129–46.

Strohm, Paul. *England's Empty Throne: Usurpation and the Language of Legitimation, 1399–1422*. New Haven, CT: Yale University Press, 1998.

———. *Hochon's Arrow: The Social Imagination of Fourteenth-Century Texts*. Princeton, NJ: Princeton University Press, 1992.

———. *Politique: Languages of Statecraft between Chaucer and Shakespeare*. Notre Dame, IN: University of Notre Dame Press, 2005.

———. *Social Chaucer*. Cambridge, MA: Harvard University Press, 1989.

———. *Theory and the Premodern Text*. Minneapolis: University of Minnesota Press, 2000.

A Summary Catalogue of Western Manuscripts in the Bodleian Library at Oxford. Oxford: Oxford University Press, 1922–.

Sutherland, Annie. "*The Chastising of God's Children*: A Neglected Text." In Barr and Hutchinson, *Text and Controversy*, 353–74.

Swanson, R. N. *Universities, Academics and the Great Schism*. Cambridge: Cambridge University Press, 1979.

Synave, Paul, and P. Benoit. *Prophecy and Inspiration: A Commentary on the Summa Theologica II–II, Questions 171–178*. New York: Desclée, 1961.

Szittya, Penn. *The Antifraternal Tradition in Medieval Literature*. Princeton, NJ: Princeton University Press, 1986.

———. "Sedens super flumina: A Fourteenth-Century Poem against the Friars." *Mediaeval Studies* 41 (1979): 30–43.

Taber, Douglas. "Pierre d'Ailly and the Teaching Authority of the Theologian." *Church History* 59 (1990): 168–72.

Tait, James. "Ricard le Scrope." In the *Dictionary of National Biography*, 1082–85. Oxford: Oxford University Press, 1921–22.

Tanner, Norman. *The Church in Late Medieval Norwich, 1370–1532*. Toronto: Pontifical Institute of Medieval Studies, 1984.

Taylor, John, et al., eds. *The St. Albans Chronicle*. Oxford: Clarendon, 2003.

Taylor, Larissa. *Soldiers of Christ: Preaching in Late Medieval and Reformation France*. Oxford: Oxford University Press, 1992.

Tch'ang-Tche, J. Wang. *Saint Augustin et les vertus des paiens*. Paris: Gabriel Beauchesne, 1938.

Thijssen, J. M. M. H. *Censure and Heresy at the University of Paris, 1200–1400*. Philadelphia: University of Pennsylvania Press, 1998.

Thom, Aaron. "'And if lawe wol . . .' (*Piers Plowman*, C.XX.428)." Unpublished paper.

Thomson, Williell R. *The Latin Writings of John Wyclif: An Annotated Catalogue*. Toronto: Pontifical Institute of Medieval Studies, 1983.

Thorp, Nigel. *The Glory of the Page*. London: Harvey Miller, 1987.

Tierney, Brian. *Origins of Papal Infallibility, 1150–1350*. Lieden: Brill 1972. Reprint, 1988.

Töpfer, Bernard. "Eine Handschrift des *Evangelium aeternum* des Gerardino von Borgo San Donnino." *Zeitschrift für Geschichtswissenschaft* 7 (1960): 156–60.

Trapp, D. "Augustinian Theology of the Fourteenth Century." *Augustiniana* 6 (1956): 201–39.

Turner, D. H. *St. Francis, Nature Mystic*. Berkeley: Edward Armstrong, 1976.

Ullman, Walter. *A Short History of the Papacy in the Middle Ages*. London: Methuen, 1972.

Van Engen, John. "Devout Communities and Inquisitorial Orders: The Legal Defense of the New Devout." In *Kirchenreform von unten: Gerhart Zerbolt von Zutphen und die Brüder vom Gemeinsamen Leben*, edited by Nikolaus Staubach, 44–101. Frankfurt: Lang, 2004.

———. "Friar Johannes Nyder on Laypeople Living as Religious in the World." In *Vita Religiosa im Mittelalter: Festschrift fur Kaspar Elm zum 70. Geburtstag*, edited by Franz Felten and Nikolas Jaspert, 583–615. Berlin: Duncker & Humboldt, 1999.

———. "Letters and the Public Persona of Hildegard." In *Hildegard von Bingen in ihrem historischen Umfeld*, edited by Alfred Haverkamp, 375–418. Mainz: Trierer Historische Forschungen, 2000.

———. *Rupert of Deutz*. Berkeley: University of California Press, 1983.

———. "The Sisterbooks." In *Yale Guide to Medieval Holy Women*, edited by Rosalynn Voaden and Alastair Minnis. Forthcoming.

———. "The Virtues, the Brothers, and the Schools: A Text from the Brothers of the Common Life." *Revue Bénédictine* 98 (1988).

Verdeyen, Paul. "Le procès d'inquisition contre Marguerite Porete et Guiard de Cressonessart (1309–10)." *Revue d'histoire ecclésiastique* 81 (1986).

Victoria History of the County of Huntingdon. Edited by W. Page and G. Proby. London: St. Catherine, 1926.

Vitto, Cindy. *The Virtuous Pagan in Medieval Literature*. Philadelphia: American Philosophical Society, 1989.

Voaden, Rosalynn. "The Company She Keeps: Mechtild of Hackeborn in Late Medieval Devotional Compilations." In Voaden, *Prophets Abroad*, 51–70.

—————. *God's Words, Women's Voices: The Discernment of Spirits in the Writing of Late-Medieval Women Visionaries.* Woodbridge: York Medieval Press and Boydell and Brewer, 1999.

—————. "The Middle English *Epistola solitarii ad reges*: An Edition of the Text in B. L. MS Cotton Julius F.ii." *Analecta Carthusiana* 35, no. 19 (1993): 142–79.

—————, ed. *Prophets Abroad: The Reception of Continental Holy Women in Late Medieval England.* Cambridge: Brewer, 1996.

—————. "Rewriting the Letter: Variations in the Middle English Translation of the *Epistola solitarii ad reges* of Alfonso of Jaén." In *The Translation of the Works of St. Brigitta of Sweden into the Medieval European Venaculars,* edited by Bridget Morris and V. O'Mara, 170–185. Turnhout: Brepols, 2000.

—————. "Travels with Margery: Pilgrimage in Context." In *Eastward Bound: Travels and Travellers, 1050–1550,* edited by Rosamund Allen, 177–95. Manchester: Manchester University Press, 2004.

Voaden, Rosalynn, and Arne Jönsson. "Recommended Reading: Defining the Medieval Visionary. A Facing Page Comparison of the Middle English and Latin Text of the *Epistola solitarii ad reges.*" In Kerby-Fulton and Hilmo, *Medieval Reader*, 149–223.

Wailes, Stephen. *Medieval Allegories of Jesus' Parables.* Berkeley: University of California Press, 1987.

Wallace, David. *Cambridge History of Medieval English Literature.* Cambridge: Cambridge University Press, 1999.

—————. *Chaucerian Polity: Absolutist Lineages and Associational Forms in England and Italy.* Stanford, CA: Stanford University Press, 1997.

—————. "Italy." In P. Brown, *Companion to Chaucer*, 218–34.

—————. "Response to Genelle Gertz-Robinson: 'Stepping into the Pulpit?'" In Olson and Kerby-Fulton, *Voices in Dialogue*, 483–91.

Walsh, Katherine. *A Fourteenth-Century Scholar and Primate: Richard FitzRalph in Oxford, Avignon and Armagh.* Oxford: Clarendon, 1981.

Watson, A. G. *Catalogue of Dated and Dateable Manuscripts, c. 435–1600 in Oxford Libraries.* 2 vols. Oxford: Calendon, 1984.

Watson, Nicholas. "Censorship and Cultural Change in Late Medieval England: Vernacular Theology, the Oxford Translation Debate, and Arundel's Constitutions of 1409." *Speculum* 70 (1995): 822–64.

—————. "Christian Ideologies." In P. Brown, *Companion to Chaucer*, 62–81.

—————. "The Composition of Julian of Norwich's *Revelation of Love.*" *Speculum* 68 (1993): 637–83.

—————. "Et que est huius ydoli materia? Tuipse: Idols and Images in Walter Hilton." In Dimmick, Simpson, and Zeeman, *Images*, 95–111.

—————. "The Making of *The Book of Margery Kempe.*" In Olson and Kerby-Fulton, *Voices in Dialogue*, 395–434.

—————. "Melting into God the English Way: Deification in the Middle English Version of Marguerite Porete's *Mirouer des Simples Ames Anienties.*" In Voaden, *Prophets Abroad*, 19–50.

―――. "Outdoing Chaucer: Lydgate's *Troy Book* and Henryson's *Testament of Cresseid* as Competitive Imitiations of *Troilus and Criseyde*." In *Shifts and Transpositions in Medieval Narrative*, edited by Karen Pratt, 89–108. Cambridge: Brewer, 1994.

―――. *Richard Rolle and the Invention of Authority*. Cambridge: Cambridge University Press, 1991.

―――. "The Trinitarian Hermeneutic in Julian of Norwich's *Revelation of Love*." In *The Medieval Mystical Tradition in England: Exeter Symposium V*, edited by Marion Glasscoe, 79–100. Cambridge: Cambridge University Press, 1992. Reprinted in *Julian of Norwich: A Book of Essays*, edited by Sandra J. McEntire. New York: Garland, 1998.

―――. "Visions of Inclusion: Universal Salvation and Vernacular Theology in Pre-Reformation England." *Journal of Medieval and Early Modern Studies* 27 (1997): 145–87.

Wehrli-Johns, Martina. "Mystik und Inquisition: Die Dominikaner und die sogennante des Freien Geistes." In *Deutsche Mystik im abendländischen Zusammenhang*, edited by Walter Haug and W. Schneider-Lastin, 223–52. Tübingen: Max Niemeyer Verlag, 2000.

Wessley, Stephen. "Female Imagery: A Clue to the Role of Joachim's Order of Fiore." In *Women of the Medieval World: Essays in Honour of John H. Mundy*, edited by Julius Kirshner and Suzanne Wemple, 161–78. Oxford: Oxford University Press, 1985.

West, Delno. *Joachim of Fiore in Christian Thought: Essays on the Influence of the Calabrian Prophet*. 2 vols. New York: Burt Franklin, 1975.

Whitfield, D.W. "A Bedford Fragment and the Burning of Two Fraticelli at Avignon in 1354." *Publications of the Bedfordshire Historical Society* 38 (1958): 1–11.

Wilks, Michael. "Wyclif and the Great Persecution." In *Wyclif: Political Ideas and Practice, Papers by Michael Wilks*, edited by Anne Hudson, 179–204. Oxford: Oxbow, 2000.

Wood, J. *Wooden Images: Misericords and Medieval England*. Photographs by Charles A. Curry. London: Associated University Presses, 1999.

Wood, Rega. "Ockham's Repudiation of Pelagianism." In *The Cambridge Companion to Ockham*, edited by Paul Vincent Spade, 350–73. Cambridge: Cambridge University Press, 1999.

Workman, H.B. *John Wyclif*. Oxford, 1926.

Wyclif and His Followers. Exhibition catalogue. Oxford: Bodleian Library, 1984.

Wylie, J.H. *History of England under Henry IV*. 4 vols. London: Longman, 1884–98.

Index of Manuscripts

Index of Historical Persons, Places, and Subjects

Kathryn Kerby-Fulton

is Notre Dame Professor of English at the University of Notre Dame.
She is the author and editor of a number of books, including most recently
Voices in Dialogue: Reading Women in the Middle Ages
(Notre Dame Press, 2005), co-edited with Linda Olson.